The Fire That Consumes

The Fire That Consumes

A Biblical and Historical Study
of Final Punishment

EDWARD WILLIAM FUDGE

Providential Press
Post Office Box 218026
Houston, Texas 77218
U.S.A.

This work
is humbly and worshipfully dedicated
as the offering of an unworthy servant
to God's Son, my Savior,
the LORD JESUS CHRIST,
who alone is able to deliver us
from
the Wrath to Come.

Foreword

While the subject of this study by Mr. Fudge is one on which there is no unanimity among evangelical Christians, it is at the same time one on which they have often engaged in fierce polemic with one another.

If there is no unanimity here among people who are agreed in accepting the Bible as their rule of faith, it may be inferred that the biblical evidence is not unambiguous. In such a situation polemic should have no place. What is called for, rather, is the fellowship of patient Bible study. It is the fruit of such study that Mr. Fudge presents here.

All immortality except God's is derived. The Father, who has life in Himself, has shared with the Son this privilege of having life in Himself. All others receive life in the Son. This is true in a measure even of natural life. "In Him was life, and the life was the light of mankind." But it is of spiritual and eternal life that we are now thinking.

Nor are biblical writers alone in insisting that God only has inherent immortality. Plato in the *Timaeus* points out that, if there is a morally good creator of the world, then all souls apart from himself exist by his will, even if his will decrees their immortality. It is a truism that Plato's teaching has profoundly influenced Christian anthropology. But the main difference between Plato's teaching and the biblical doctrine lies here: whereas Plato predicates immortality (albeit *derived* immortality) of the soul, when the New Testament writers speak of immortality in relation to human beings they predicate it of the *body*—of the body revived or transformed in the resurrection age.

Christian theologians chiefly disagree over the destiny in the Age to Come of those who live and die without God. The New Testament answer to this question is much less explicit than is frequently supposed. Paul is reported in Acts as declaring before Felix that he looked for "a resurrection of both the just and the unjust." But the only resurrection on which he enlarges in his letters is the resurrection of believers, viewed as their participation in the resurrection of Christ. "If we believe that Jesus died and rose again" provides a far more secure basis for the Christian hope than any theory of the innate immortality of the soul, but it throws little light on the destiny of unbelievers.

It gives me pleasure to commend Mr. Fudge's exposition of this subject. All that he has to say is worthy of careful consideration, but there is special value in those chapters where he examines the testimony of successive sections of the Holy Scriptures.

I suppose that, as the terms are defined in this work, I would be regarded as neither a traditionalist nor a conditionalist. My own understanding of the issues under discussion would be very much in line with that of C. S. Lewis. Lewis did not systematize his thoughts on the subject (and I have not done so either); Mr. Fudge would no doubt ask (and rightly so) if our exegetical foundation is secure.

"It is a fearful thing," we are assured by the writer to the Hebrews, "to fall into the hands of the living God." True—and yet into whose hands could anyone more confidently fall? King David knew how fearful a thing it was; but when it came to the crunch, he made the right choice: "Let us fall into the hand of the Lord, for His mercy is great." Christians have the assurance, both for themselves and for others, that the God and Father of our Lord Jesus Christ will never do anything unjust or unmerciful: He cannot deny Himself.

F. F. BRUCE

Contents

Acknowledgments

Special thanks are due Mr. Robert D. Brinsmead, Dr. Jack D. Zwemer and Mr. Norman Jarnes of Verdict Publications for generous encouragement and untiring support of the research represented here. Thanks are also due Mr. Paul Jackson, former assistant at Concordia Seminary Library, St. Louis, and Dr. Robert Bertram of Christ Seminary—Seminex for bibliographical material on Luther; to Dr. Joseph Hall of Covenant Seminary Library for bibliographical material on Calvin; to Mr. Charles Prince of San Antonio, Texas, for bibliographical suggestions, and to Mr. Randall Trainer for a very helpful book he sent me from an expedition to the Harvard University Bookstore. The personnel of the Divinity division of the Joint University Library at Vanderbilt University, Nashville, have also been hospitable, and I am glad to thank them here. Dr. William L. Lane of Western Kentucky University has been a most charitable friend in sharing bibliographical suggestions and methodological advice, especially concerning the intertestamental material, and I am in his debt for that.

Years ago Professor Homer Hailey taught me to love the Old Testament prophets and to tremble before the majesty of the God for whom they still speak. In this day, when basic reverence is so rare, that lesson cannot be overstressed. I also acknowledge his insistence that we let Scripture interpret Scripture, especially when attempting to understand the illustrations and symbols of prophecy. Surely no method rests on a more solid basis.

Throughout this project I have been enriched by the close and loving fellowship of the brothers and sisters at the Elm Street Church in Athens, Alabama. Mr. Mark Whitt in particular has been both Aaron and Hur to me for hundreds of days. Without such prayers the burden of the work would surely have crushed me many times. Numerous friends in many places have spontaneously shared with me financially these past few years in times of special need known only to God. To Him—and them—I now give thanks publicly. Mary Alice, Oak Hill Chapel, Flagstaff friends, John and Linda, Tom, Kerry and Kara, Bill, and all the others—you also had a part in this work.

Melanie and Jeremy are too young to really understand what was happening all those nights their Daddy couldn't play or tell them another story. Their contribution, though constrained, has been very important. And no earthly assistance could approach that of my godly, sensible and sacrificial wife, Sara Faye, who has been as free with her criticisms as with her careful praise. I owe her very much.

Finally, I express my deepest gratitude to Professor F. F. Bruce for contributing the foreword to this volume and for his gracious personal encouragement and friendship of which that gesture is only a part.

Unless otherwise stated, all biblical quotations following are from the New International Version, copyright 1973 by the New York Bible Society International, copyright 1978 by the New York International Bible Society, and published by The Zondervan Corporation, Grand Rapids, Michigan.

Preface

Like the householder's treasures, the conclusions stated in this book included ideas which to me were both old and new. The fact that final punishment will indeed be *final*—irreversible and without restoration or remedy forever—came as no surprise. The Bible clearly warns of destruction and punishment which are *eternal*, even as it speaks of everlasting life. What took my breath more than once was the fact that Scripture so consistently and emphatically teaches the *nature* of that everlasting punishment to be utter extinction into oblivion forever. It was disappointing to realize the extent to which traditionalist authors have passed by the other side of biblical passages unfavorable to their position. The historical development of the common understanding has its own surprises as well, as does the literature of its earliest explicit advocates, who often reasoned from the most unbiblical presuppositions.

This study has elicited a spectrum of emotions in the author—despair and relief, anxiety and peace, incredulity and final surrender. The position presented must stand or fall on the evidence, and that evidence is not personal desire, human philosophy or ecclesiastical tradition but the living and abiding, infallible Word of God.

From early childhood I have learned and believed that the Bible taught the unending conscious torment of sinners in hell, although in recent years I have thought of that pain more in spiritual terms than physical and have come to hope that my youthful estimates of hell's population were greatly exaggerated. I grew up with the suspicion that anyone who questioned that view was little removed from a modernist who also doubted the resurrection of Jesus. I had no desire to change my mind or any inclination that I would ever do so.

The thought of hell never particularly troubled my mind, although like every sober Christian, I recoiled from the actual thoughts of anyone suffering forever. I have never been gifted as an evangelist and have consequently had very little experience with the "offense" which several friends tell me the common doctrine of hell seems frequently to present to unbelievers. (Along that line, we must be careful not to succumb to a kind of reverse reaction which prevents our considering with an open mind an idea that in the end might happen to be of some practical benefit in evangelism or which might give to *godly* minds any measure of relief.)

Some time after I finished graduate work at Abilene Christian University in Abilene, Texas, I asked a favorite former professor to suggest some biblical topic that might lend itself to profitable ongoing research. Perhaps he mentioned more than one; I do not now remember. What did stick in my mind is that he suggested the topic of final punishment. "I find it interesting," he said, "that the particular word *gehenna* is used only in the Gospels for the end of the wicked. You might like to look into the language the rest of the New Testament writers use."

A year or so later I was invited to speak on the subject of final punishment in a small forum at St. Louis (Missouri) Christian College, which made an effort to bring together varying views and to allow public questions and discussion of their respective merits. My thoughts were simple and consisted largely of a brief presentation of a dozen New Testament passages which contrast the final ends of the saved and the lost. The most radical thing I suggested was that the Age to Come will be qualitatively different from the Present Age and that we must therefore leave room for some surprises when we try to understand language drawn from our space-time experience here and now. Professor Russell E. Boatman, a brother from the host school, also spoke, presenting his own personal, admittedly-minority, *conditionalist* views. He is still the only man I have ever heard present such views in person. At that time I had never read such views either.

Someone encouraged me to submit my little paper for consideration to *Christianity Today*. I sent a rough draft first to Professor F. F. Bruce, who has been a beloved and highly-respected mentor, and also to Dr. W. Ward Gasque, a scholar I respected especially for his objectivity and thoroughness and who served at the time on the editorial committee of *Christianity Today*. Both made some suggestions; the manuscript was submitted, accepted and subsequently published.

Among those who read the published article was an Australian avocado farmer named Robert D. Brinsmead. A former Seventh-day Adventist, Brinsmead had separated from that denomination over the issue of justification by faith, a theme he now stressed in his theological journal, *Verdict* (formerly *Present Truth*). In the summers of 1978-1979 he approached me concerning the possibility of a research contract with Verdict Publications on the history of the doctrine of final punishment. I must have tried his patience almost to the limit with repeated questions concerning hidden motives, secret agendas or predetermined conclusions. He and his Verdict associates always responded with the gracious insistence that I follow every possible lead and leave no stone unturned in seeking whatever truth thorough research might bring to light. Verdict backed this verbal insistence with action, making no demands of any kind while sparing neither effort nor expense in assisting the unhampered research. No research person could have asked for less interference or for more genuine help.

My desire has been to be biblical, reverent and fair. The only truth on the subject is contained in the Old and New Testament Scriptures. All else must be measured by that standard. When the Bible talks about God's wrath and the end of sinners (which it does quite often in both Testaments), it speaks in awesome tones which should bring us to our knees in fear and trembling. There is no place here for frivolity or jesting. I pray that this book will reflect the sense of seriousness which the subject demands.

This book is written to be read—and argued with! I have no ax to grind and no cause to champion; I have tried to follow the ordinary methods of sound, biblical exegesis. Competent scholars and serious students are cordially invited to enter into dialogue. Check the statements made here. Weigh the evidence. Examine the arguments. Measure this work by every proper standard. All that matters is that we seek God's truth for His glory and the salvation of sinners!

Throughout this study the "traditionalist" view signifies the understanding that hell will involve the unending conscious torment (whether spiritual or physical or both) of the wicked who have been made deathless (immortal). The term "conditionalist" is used for the view that the wicked will suffer conscious punishment precisely measured by divine justice but that they finally will perish in hell so as to become totally extinct forever. Although some authors on both sides intentionally use loaded terms to describe the two positions, these words are chosen in the hope of avoiding any unfair connotations.

Early in the study I was greatly encouraged by the remarks of John W. Wenham in the fine Inter-Varsity publication, *The Goodness of God*. The conditionalist arguments have never been squarely met, Wenham said there; this subject has not been discussed in the open by the best minds and methods of mainstream evangelical scholarship. While disclaiming any place in such august company, this book is nevertheless presented as one opening contribution toward the study for which Wenham there called. I have learned from so very, very many. May the gracious and sovereign God use me, in even a small way, to bless just a few.

1

Where We Are Starting From

Why Talk about Final Punishment?

Hell is not a popular subject, though one hears the word almost daily. It is sobering for a Christian to walk into his place of employment and hear, as I did not long ago, the final exclamations of two different conversations. "Hell . . . ," one person was saying. "Lord have mercy" crossed its path on the wind. Someone else remarked, "It sounds like judgment day around here." We should tremble at the lack of respect for God and His holiness which surrounds us on every side. May God have mercy indeed!

Sometimes "religious" climates fare little better. I was entering the library at Vanderbilt Divinity School during this research when I met an inquisitive theological coed. "What are you studying?" she asked. "The history of the doctrine of hell," I said. She looked at me with an uncertain expression. "That's interesting," she finally said. "What on earth for?"[1] Harry Buis tells the difficulty he had locating material for his book on final punishment.[2] Of the books he finally found, some

---

1. Donald G. Bloesch opens the chapter on heaven and hell in his *Essentials of Evangelical Theology* with the declaration: "If anything has disappeared from modern thought, it is the belief in a supernatural heaven and hell" (Donald G. Bloesch, *Essentials of Evangelical Theology*, 2:211).

2. Harry Buis, *The Doctrine of Eternal Punishment*, p. x. Buis commends himself by a fair and kind presentation. His book is perhaps the modern classic presentation of the orthodox view of hell.

had been used only once or twice in years. Few people want to study the subject any more. The liberals do not believe in such things, and the conservatives are satisfied that they already have the answers. That leaves few people who are concerned to learn more.

Hell is a very depressing subject. "In over seventy years," a recent writer began, "I have met only two men that I can remember as having pleasure in talking about hell."[3] Any who have a right to discuss the subject wish they did not have to. "Today I must confess that there still lingers an averseness on my part to declare that there is no hope" for the unrepentant after death, says Lehman Strauss.[4] Hell is "the ultimate horror of God's universe,"[5] the "dark side of the far hereafter."[6] But the Bible talks about an inescapable day of judgment for every human being (Acts 17:31; Heb. 9:27), followed by an irreversible and unending retribution for those who have finally rejected God's mercy (Matt. 25:46). So—sooner or later—must the person who takes the Bible seriously.

As painful as it may be, there are good reasons for thinking on this fearful subject. For while such an exercise "is not a direct ministration of grace," it can still be used of God to awaken sinners "to a more piercing sight, and to a more keen sensation of their own guilt and danger; it possesses their spirits with a more lively sense of their misery; it fills them with a holy dread of divine punishment, and excites the powerful passion of fear to make them fly from the wrath to come, and betake themselves to the grace of God revealed in the gospel."[7]

---

3. L. A. King, "Hell, the Painful Refuge," *Eternity*, January 1979, p. 28. King elaborates on Dante's view of hell as a "painful refuge" where sinners are spared the ultimate distress of God's holy presence at close range. He suggests that the fire is symbolic, and his article is a defense of hell in a day of general skepticism and indifference. In spite of his good intentions, however, I have found no passage in either the Old or New Testament which remotely suggests that hell is in any way a sign of divine benevolence toward those who go there.

4. Lehman Strauss, *Life after Death: What the Bible Really Teaches*, p. 48.

5. John W. Wenham, *The Goodness of God*, p. 27. Chapter 2 (pp. 27-41) deals with hell and is intended to "discourage those who hold traditional orthodoxy from surrendering it lightly, while encouraging the serious consideration of the case for conditional immortality" (p. 41). Wenham continues the same high standards of balance, clarity and thoroughness for which Inter-Varsity Press has become known.

6. This is the title for the chapter on hell in Gerald C. Studer's *After Death, What?* The author pastors a Mennonite church in Lansdale, Pennsylvania, and here calls for caution and restudy concerning the subject of final punishment.

7. Isaac Watts, *The World to Come*, p. 298. In keeping with the style of his day, Watts' book has a much longer title, the rest being: *Or Discourses on the Joys or Sorrows of Departed Souls at Death, and the Glory or Terror of the Resurrection; to Which Is Affixed an Essay towards*

This doctrine is "an integral and vital element of our Christian faith," Roger Nicole reminds us. And this "darkest subject on the pages of Scripture" often provides the necessary background for an understanding of "the true gravity of sin, of the magnitude of the human soul, of the depth of Christ's redeeming work, of the power of divine grace which plucks man out of the abyss like firebrands, of the urgency of the Gospel call, and of the supreme importance of the ministry of preaching and of missions."[8]

Hell, along with death, the last judgment and heaven, make up the quartet of subjects traditionally treated under the heading of "eschatology" or "Last Things." The doctrine of final punishment is not only important within itself, but in the same way that eschatology is important in general. And eschatology

> is an indispensable dimension of Christian thought and action. Without it the church becomes static, ineffective, and usually heretical. For eschatology contributes a compelling dynamic to Christian action and obedience. It also sets boundaries and gives direction to Christian thinking about God, salvation, and obedient action in the world. When the basic eschatological perspective of Scripture is minimized or lost, Christian thought becomes heretical and Christian social action merely secular.[9]

Perhaps the greatest reason for talking about hell is also the simplest and most obvious. Jesus our Savior spoke of it—more than once and in the most serious tones. Whenever He speaks, we will do well to listen. We also will do well to be careful *how* we hear. It is very easy for men to hear Jesus against such background noise that they confuse what He is saying with sounds of their own surround-

---

the Proof of a Separate State of Souls after Death: Wherein, after Some Proof of the Happiness of Heaven and a Preparation for It, There Follows, a Rational and Scriptural Account of the Punishments in Hell, and a Proof of Their Eternal Duration, with a Plain Answer to All the Most Plausible Objections. In later years Watts wrote *The Ruine and Recovery of Mankind* . . . , in which he suggested that the second death might mean the death of soul as well as body, and that infants who died unbaptized might be annihilated in hell rather than suffer endlessly. Watts thus provides useful quotations for advocates of eternal torment and of conditional immortality.

8. Roger Nicole, "The Punishment of the Wicked," *Christianity Today*, 9 June 1958, p. 15. This article interprets biblical figures in a traditional manner and gives a short critique of the alternative views of universalism and annihilationism from the point of view of Reformed orthodoxy. Those who have known or heard this gentle Christian theologian appreciate even better the compassion and pathos with which he must write these words.

9. David E. Holwerda, "Eschatology and History: A Look at Calvin's Eschatological Vision," *Exploring the Heritage of John Calvin*, p. 139.

ings. We must not only listen to Christ *reverently*—we must also listen *carefully*.

Our Point of View

What one says about final punishment depends largely on where he stands in relation to other things. Is he a theist, an atheist or an agnostic? If a theist, is he a Christian? If he professes to be a Christian, is he liberal, evangelical or fundamentalist? Is he open to learn on this biblical subject, or does he suppose that the answers are already clear and settled? If he is open to study, what will be his determining authority? Is he committed most of all to a particular Confession, to what he thinks "the church has always taught," to philosophy and reason, or to the words of the Bible itself? If he professes the last, does he reason from a specific truth—such as God's love, wrath or justice—or from an overall gathering and inductive weighing of passages on the subject from both the Old and New Testaments? What will be the final criteria when these various standards do not point the same direction—at times they might not. Is he willing to confess an element of mystery where he cannot find full answers—or does he then bend and stretch some scriptures to cover the gap left in others? The matter of authority is not a simple one, even to the reader with good intentions.

I am a theist, a Christian and an evangelical, persuaded that Scripture is the very Word of God written. For that reason I believe it is without error in anything it teaches[10] and that it is the only unquestionable, binding source of doctrine on this or any subject. This is a negative statement since it eliminates anything else as an unquestionable or binding source of doctrine. It is also a positive statement since it requires that we *use* Scripture as a final authority and not simply *praise* it for that purpose.

Such a high view of Scripture does not take away from a healthy respect for the common opinion of the universal church through the centuries. If someone begins to suspect that he alone has discovered a

---

10. As an active member of the Evangelical Theological Society, I sign an annual affirmation stating that the Bible in its entirety, and the Bible alone, is the Word of God written and that it is inerrant in the original autographs. This conviction may best be seen by one's *use* of Scripture rather than by his arguments *concerning* it. The matter is mentioned here to *remove* a potential issue from the discussion, not to *introduce* an additional controversy into it.

certain truth, he has good reason to doubt its validity. The chances are good that "if it's true it isn't new, and if it's new it isn't true." No uninspired speaker or writer knows anything definitive about final punishment that has not come from the Word of God. At the same time, the church's greatest theologians and most devout believers have always realized that God can continually cause new light to break forth from the Word that has been there all the time. One of the greatest compliments that can be paid the church is that it is *always* reforming, with the guidance of the Holy Spirit and under the authority of the Word.

These are not mere words. They are the standards by which this book is to be critically measured. Not a day has passed during this research and writing without my earnest prayers for divine leading and wisdom. A number of special friends have also supported this work in regular prayer. After reading thousands of pages by uninspired and often conflicting authors, it is very comforting to remember that all they say has absolutely no bearing on what the truth finally is. The best any of them can do is repeat and explain what Scripture says. Any child of God can ask assistance in weighing the message of uninspired authors while beseeching a spirit of wisdom and revelation in the knowledge of the things God has said (Eph. 1:17, 18; James 1:5-7). This not only *comforts*; it creates a sense of *humility* and of *responsibility* (James 3:1). We must open Scripture prayerfully and then handle it with care. We must then listen to it without objection or argument. It is the Word of the living God.

2

Where We Are Going (for Final Answers)

Standards That May Detract

It is very easy to say that the Bible is our final authority, especially when we are comfortably viewing a difficult issue from some distance. It is far more difficult to remember that pledge when we find ourselves deep in study, grappling with texts which seem to conflict or at least to point in different directions. Then the tendency is to look for a way out, to grab some passing straw in an effort to escape the whirlpool from which we see no ready exit. It is easy to deceive ourselves under such circumstances. We need to be very sure, therefore, what we are excluding when we say that the Bible is our final authority.

Desires. It is often very easy to read into Scripture what we *wish* it said. The nineteenth-century Anglican archbishop, Richard Whately of Dublin, warns us not to mistake our own desires for the Bible's teaching.

In judging of the sense of Scripture, we should be careful to guard against the error of suffering our wishes to bias the mind. If indeed we had to devise a religion for ourselves, we might indulge our wishes as to what is desirable, or our conjectures, as to what seems to us in itself probable, or our judgment, as to what may seem advisable. But when we have before us "Scripture-revelations" on any subject, it is for us to endeavour to make out what it is that Scriptures teaches, and what it does not teach.[1]

Easy Answers. The desire for *easy answers* can also mislead our minds during difficult Bible study. Edward White, author of the conditionalist classic, *Life in Christ*, reminds us of this danger.

> Perhaps we never ought to be more suspicious of our arguments than when they are derived from the presumed advantages of the projected conclusion. There can be no doubt that the desire for a neat and simple argument in support of a truth may dispose even able men to offer some little violence to evidence which points in the direction of complexity. What we consider neatness and simplicity is not always a characteristic of Divine working, or Divine teaching. A passion for simplicity of statement has often blinded men to facts which indicated more complexity than might at first have been supposed.[2]

Someone has observed that truth is always true even if it is not plain, while error is often more plain than it is true. We may desire clarity in understanding—and God may well give it—but neat answers must be the sweet juice in the fruit of scriptural accuracy, not the fruit itself.

Evangelicals who profess great fidelity to Scripture have not always been careful to respect its form and manner of speaking. "Evangelical zeal for literal interpretation has too often resulted in running roughshod over those literary forms for which literal interpretation is inappropriate." The problem is compounded because "some Biblical genres, such as Hebrew poetry, wisdom literature and apocalyptic,

---

1. Richard Whately, *A View of the Scripture Revelations concerning a Future State*, pp. 185-186. Archbishop Whately is one of many Anglican clergy who have held to the conditionalist position concerning final punishment. Of the four major Protestant streams since the Reformation, the Anglican has been the most open to conditionalism, followed by the Anabaptist and Lutheran, with the Calvinist tradition holding most tenaciously to the doctrine of unending *conscious torment.*

2. Edward White, *Life in Christ: A Study of the Scripture Doctrine on the Nature of Man, the Object of the Divine Incarnation, and the Conditions of Human Immortality*, p. 293. A Congregationalist minister, White lost his pulpit when he adopted the conditionalist position, thereafter filling an independent pulpit in London. His book is a conditionalist classic which emphasizes the positive aspect that life is to be had only through Jesus Christ rather than the negative aspect which contradicts the doctrine of unending conscious torment. White believed that man's soul survives bodily death in an intermediate state. His conditionalist contemporary, Henry Constable, believed that body and soul both die in the first death. Both men affirm a resurrection of good and bad, a universal judgment, and the entire destruction of body and soul in the case of those who suffer the second death. These two men demonstrate that one's view of hell does not require a certain view of temporal death or the intermediate state.

are strange to western readers." To avoid mishandling Scripture, "the interpreter must deal thoroughly and honestly with the text. He must faithfully follow the principles for grammatical-historical exegesis in order to carefully and painstakingly ascertain the meaning of the passage in its original setting."[3]

So long as we stay in our own meetinghouses and talk only to ourselves, we might gloss over difficult passages without being called into question. But such behavior might also set us up to be exploited later by devious peddlers of pernicious teaching who roam the land in search of disciples. A contemporary Mennonite pastor pounds home the warning.

> Many Christians, perhaps most of us, are simply content to follow the party line. If this leaves some biblical data unaccounted for, we protect ourselves either by saying that not all of us can be theologians or we take comfort in the fact that "this is the way we have been taught!" The cults have a way of sleuthing out what they hold to be inconsistencies in the historic Christian doctrines and needling us with questions and counterviews. We may respond by drawing our doctrinal coat about us even tighter, hoping they will go away, or we may examine the Scripture again and discover that we have drawn conclusions that resolve what the Scripture leaves ambiguous.[4]

Private Interpretation. We also need to avoid the danger of thinking we have discovered new truth never known or taught before. The great Reformers rejected ecclesiastical tradition as of equal authority to Scripture, and so must we. But they never intended that every man should invent his own original interpretation of the Bible. Nor did they intend to enslave the church's corporate interpretation to "the free-lance opinion of any one individual."[5] Robert E. Webber addresses this abuse of a good principle when he exhorts:

---

3. J. Julius Scott, "Some Problems in Hermeneutics for Contemporary Evangelicals," *Journal of the Evangelical Theological Society* 22, no. 1 (March 1979): 74-75. Scott's suggestions are most appropriate to the study we are undertaking here.

4. Gerald C. Studer, *After Death, What?* p. 111. Studer concludes that the exact nature of final punishment must remain a fearful unknown but that we should preach its terror and know that God's ways are both holy and just.

5. This expression is Jon E. Braun's in his *Whatever Happened to Hell?* p. 48. His book is popular in slant and polemical in tone. A bishop in the newly-formed Evangelical Orthodox Church (formerly New Covenant Apostolic Order), Braun has a number of good things to say as a preacher. However, devotion to tradition—an integral part of his church's stance and reason for being—frequently overshadows his exegetical and historical accuracy.

Evangelicals should come to grips with the fact that the Bible belongs to the church. It is the living church that receives, guards, passes on, and interprets Scripture. Consequently, the modern individualistic approach to interpretation of Scripture should give way to the authority of what the church has always believed, taught, and passed down in history.[6]

Webber was one of a group of evangelical leaders who met in May, 1977 for a period of self-analysis, resulting in a document called "The Chicago Call: An Appeal to Evangelicals."[7] In the section, "A Call to Biblical Fidelity," the group said:

> "We deplore our tendency toward individualistic interpretation of Scripture. . . . Therefore we affirm that the Bible is to be interpreted in keeping with the best insights of historical and literary study, under the guidance of the Holy Spirit, with respect for the historic understanding of the church. We affirm that the Scriptures, as the infallible Word of God, are the basis of authority in the church."[8]

To a church often dominated by mass-media pastors, magazine editors, parachurch organizations and free-lance interpreters, these words carry timely wisdom, and we ought to give them careful attention. Even true prophets are subject to the discerning judgment of other spiritual men (1 Cor. 14:29; 1 Thess. 5:20, 21), and many false prophets are in the world (1 John 4:1).

Church Tradition. But this coin has another side. We must not use these legitimate warnings as excuses for laziness or as opportunities to avoid personal responsibility by merely accepting "what the church has always said." Webber is aware of this hazard, too, and he balances his first warning with another.

---

6. Robert E. Webber, *Common Roots: A Call to Evangelical Maturity*, p. 128. Webber was chairman of The Chicago Call, which met in 1977, and co-editor of *The Orthodox Evangelicals*, which describes that meeting and its implications.

7. The text of "The Chicago Call" is included in Webber's *Common Roots*, quoted here and below.

8. Webber, *Common Roots*, pp. 252-253. The text continues with a reminder of the fallibility of all human creeds and Confessions: "We affirm the abiding value of the great ecumenical creeds and the Reformation confessions. Since such statements are historically and culturally conditioned, however, the church today needs to express its faith afresh, without defecting from the truths apprehended in the past" (p. 253).

Because we live on this side of theological formulation, we have the advantage of the cumulative thought of almost two thousand years. However, if we are to succeed in grasping truth as the early church did, we may have to regard our two thousand years of cumulative theology, and especially our current "position," as a disadvantage. In a manner of reflective analysis and self-criticism we may have to suspend our theological presuppositions, denominational teachings, and personal bias in order to stand with the earliest Christians who stood on the other side of theological debate and formulation.[9]

These words, too, are easy to say but difficult to practice.

The shapers of Protestant "orthodoxy" faced the same challenges and temptations that we do now. They were very alert to Rome's false claims of authority, and in many points they weeded out that particular crop of traditional tares. Yet while they refused to make exegesis the servant of councils and popes, they *"were in danger of leading it into bondage to the confessional standards of the Church."* As a result, exegesis *"became the hand-maid of dogmatics, and degenerated into a mere search for proof-texts."*[10] One who explores the labyrinth of literature concerning final punishment quickly agrees with this criticism of Reformed theologian, Louis Berkhof. Over and over, traditionalist writers begin their argument with accepted dogma rather than with the text of Scripture, cite confessional standards with too much authority, and replace actual exegesis with an accumulation of proof-texts left unexplained.[11]

This weakness has particularly plagued Protestantism's treatment of the Last Things. Because the Reformers and their descendants frequently worked amidst the heat of controversy, where quick answers were at a premium, it was easy for them to limit their doctrine of "perspicuity" (that Scripture can be clearly understood) to certain subjects. If Scripture did *not* clearly teach what the Reformation

---

9. Ibid., p. 117.

10. Louis Berkhof, *Principles of Biblical Interpretation*, pp. 28ff, quoted by Ernest F. Kevan, "The Principles of Interpretation," *Revelation and the Bible: Contemporary Evangelical Thought*, p. 291.

11. Traditionalist authors tend to use the proof-text method in presenting their position while simply ignoring the passages presented by conditionalists. New Testament terms such as "unquenchable fire," "smoke ascending for ever and ever," and "the worm that does not die" are borrowed from the prophetic literature of the Old Testament. Legitimate exegesis requires that the meaning of these expressions in the New Testament at least *begin* with their meaning in the Old Testament and be enlarged only with justification from the text itself. Advocates of the traditional doctrine have not done this so far.

church was holding, it was easy to simply say, "This is what our theology holds." In this way the height of doctrine "was gradually identified with the basic dogmatic outlook of the particular theologian. The Confessional view became the interpreter of Scripture."[12]

Many modern voices may be heard within the most hallowed halls of Protestant and evangelical orthodoxy, honestly confessing that the Reformation never did build a doctrine of the Last Things with Scripture as the foundation and storehouse of building blocks. Luther and Calvin both rejected the Roman Catholic doctrine of purgatory—not because they made a thorough study of scriptural eschatology and found it missing, but because purgatory clearly contradicted the doctrine of justification which they had discovered in the Bible. Their problem was not a low view of Scripture but a failure to use their high view to full advantage. James P. Martin gives specific examples for his charge that "in spite of the high doctrine of the authority, perspicuity and inspiration of Scripture, tradition, rather than Scripture, was the real starting point in the eschatology of Orthodoxy" and that "the treatment of the Last Things did not represent a new start in an exegetical way."[13]

The Bible was used as a source for proof-texts concerning eschatology, Martin says, but there was "no attempt at a historical understanding of these texts."[14] He is more understanding of the Reformers themselves, for they were busy men who had to battle on many fronts. The fault lies heavier, he says, on those who came after them—the real shapers of Protestant orthodoxy.

> Both Luther and Calvin neglected the special content of eschatology. It is a reproach against Orthodoxy that it did not supply this lack by a renewed investigation of . . . Holy Scripture. Orthodoxy supplied the lack of content by taking over the general medieval tradition with its spiritualizing and individualistic tendencies. This tradition was altered only here and there in accordance with Protestant ideas. The dogmatic system reigned supreme to the detriment of a biblical eschatology, and consequently, to the whole of theology. Orthodoxy is an example of the truth that a high doctrine of Scripture is no guarantee of its actual or proper use.[15]

---

12. James P. Martin, *The Last Judgment in Protestant Theology from Orthodoxy to Ritschl*, p. 2.

13. Ibid., p. 3.

14. Ibid.

15. Ibid., pp. 4-5.

Although Wenham flashes several yellow lights to any who would lightly abandon traditional positions, he boldly states that "a long tradition of belief within the Christian church is not decisive. Errors creep in," he notes, "and they die hard, especially when they have been elevated to the status of orthodoxy. At the first whiff of supposed heresy the godly are liable to shut their ears and rush upon the well-meaning offender."[16] This is all the sadder if Edward Beecher is correct in saying that "the whole energy of the Church, in the highest state of holiness and communion with God, has never been brought to bear upon this subject, so as to result in a thorough and reliable investigation of the whole great question." Rather than such detailed and in-depth study, Beecher charges the great organized churches of Protestantism with "a fixedness and immobility which is not the result of any antecedent profound investigation, but simply of unreasoning inertia and uninquiring tradition."[17] It does not please us to say it, but this testimony is verified in much of the literature concerning final punishment.

The Challenge before Us

All these warnings and criticisms have come from Protestants, and many of them come from men whose fidelity to Scripture cannot be questioned. Self-analysis followed by honest criticism is itself a sign of healthy life. There are also hopeful signs in our generation of progress that will lay these criticisms to rest. A. M. Hunter acknowledges this return to Scripture and applauds its progress. "Our time has witnessed a revival of interest in the whole subject of New Testament eschatology . . . and it is becoming clear that the time is ripe for a radical rethinking, by our systematic theologians, of the whole Christian doctrine of the Last Things."[18]

Now, as perhaps never before, evangelicals have a perfect opportunity to demonstrate that their high view of Scripture is also practical. Today, more than ever, they are less likely to agree with one who prefaces his study of last things with the remark that the "*safest,*

---

16. John W. Wenham, *The Goodness of God*, p. 39.
17. Edward Beecher, *History of Opinions on the Scriptural Doctrine of Retribution*, p. 311.
18. Archibald M. Hunter, *The Gospel According to St. Paul*, p. 111.

most *sure* way to learn the truth of God is to discover what the overwhelming consensus of the church has been with respect to what God
says in the Scriptures on the subject over the nearly two thousand
years of history."[19] After all, the Reformation is expressly founded
"on the fact that all Europe had erred on the most important doctrine
of Christianity for more than a thousand years, during the darkness
of the middle ages, even on the central doctrine of our justification."[20]

It is a basic rule of interpretation, accepted by all scholars, "that
the interpreter must seek to penetrate into the conceptual forms and
patterns" of the biblical text and times. To do this, the modern interpreter "must be highly critical of himself and the theoretical and
methodological notions he brings with him from his own cultural en-
vironments."[21] Pagan Greek thought patterns entered the Christian
stream early in its history and have flowed along almost unnoticed
for many centuries. But today's culture is not the culture of the Middle Ages or even of the Reformation. Revolutions within science
itself today are encouraging Bible students to reject many of these
alien viewpoints about time and universe. As a result, according to
T. F. Torrance, "we are emancipated in a remarkable way from the
tyranny of dualist modes of thought which have throughout the
history of biblical interpretation done such damage."[22]

This does not speak of the so-called "modern" views of unbelieving
scholars who reject the supernatural in the name of science. It speaks
of the work of evangelical men and women who are determined to
fight their way upstream, past every influx of pollution, to the pure
source of their doctrine. Their progress is seen in the fact that

> Theological work in the last twenty or thirty years, following in the
> footsteps of the reformers, has brought about a thoroughgoing re-
> orientation of evangelical teaching as a whole in the direction of
> eschatology.
>   Connected with this is a new effort to reach a correct understanding
> of the last things themselves. Here attention must be concentrated on
> those aspects of eschatology which were neglected by the reformers,

---

19. Braun, *Whatever Happened to Hell?* p. 43.
20. White, *Life in Christ*, p. 68.
21. T. F. Torrance, *Space, Time and Resurrection*, p. 41.
22. Ibid., p. 44.

and its true Biblical content clarified i.e. within the limits which Holy Scripture itself prescribes for the insights of faith.[23]

One does not despise the universal convictions of the church through the centuries when he seeks to go back to the roots. He is simply attempting to purify the stream by standing with the earliest Christians, as Webber put it, "on the other side of theological debate and formulation." His work poses no threat to the Christian community so long as it builds on the solid rock of divine revelation. Instead, "the work of individual theologians contributes greatly to the general understanding of the tradition of faith and life to which scripture, creed, and liturgy are standing witnesses." If the theologian's freedom is sometimes "in tension with the mind of the community," it "may frequently be the role and duty of official authority to keep legitimate options open." These are not the words of some free-lance interpreter but part of the official report of a joint commission of Anglican and Roman Catholic theologians who dealt with the specific subject of "authority in the church."[24] They are quoted here, not as authoritative within themselves, but simply to show that those who most strongly champion the value of church tradition also leave room for individual Bible students to help the church beyond its present understanding of biblical truth.

E. G. Selwyn compares the work of such individual theologians to lights in the port. Definitions of doctrine which have come down to us from the past are "not ends in themselves but means, not final statements of the truth but statements which admit of supersession by others (if such there be) which do fuller justice to the Gospel." The expressions of doctrine which previous theologians have passed on "are like the lights which guide a ship as it approaches a port at night. They do not illuminate the whole scene, but chart the course for the

---

23. Heinrich Quistorp, *Calvin's Doctrine of the Last Things*, p. 194.

24. E. J. Yarnold and Henry Chadwick, *Truth and Authority: A Commentary on the Agreed Statement of the Anglican-Roman Catholic International Commission "Authority in the Church," Venice 1976*, p. 15. The commentary later affirms, "Even when a doctrinal definition is regarded by the Christian community as part of its permanent teaching, this does not exclude subsequent restatement," but notes that "restatement always builds upon, and does not contradict, the truth intended by the original definition" (p. 50). None of the ecumenical creeds specifically defines the nature of hell as unending conscious torment, though such explicit statements do date to pre-Nicene times. The creeds do affirm in various ways that hell introduces a fixed state of divine retribution which cannot be resisted or overcome by the sinner and from which there is no return or remedy forever. That thesis we wholeheartedly affirm as well and will defend throughout this work as the unequivocal teaching of Scripture.

seafarer. There may be circumstances which require that the lights should be added to or shifted or made of better manufacture; though this will be done only after careful preparation and warning, lest ill befall."[25]

Clark Pinnock uses the same figure as he calls for "a theology for the future." To be truly valid, he says, an evangelical theology must run the risk of displeasing both "the conservatives who are content to rehearse thoughtlessly the slogans of the past" and "the radicals who seek liberation from biblical norms in order to shape a system to suit their own taste." Because theology is a creative activity, it "cannot rest content with mere reiteration of earlier insights." Former theologians did not exhaust the treasures of God's Word, and a theology "which seeks only to restate the system of some honored theological forerunner is less than fully biblical." Those who appreciate Calvin and Luther honor them best "by going directly to Scripture where they began, rather than by slavishly imitating their systems." When theology is reduced to "repetition and imitation," it becomes "stagnant and sterile." Past formulations and definitions have value, but their value is secondary, as lights or roadmaps which chart our course. "But there comes a time when our own faith in response to the Word of God must express itself with conviction. It is now time for evangelical thinkers to forsake the unimaginative mimicry of 'textbook theology' and forge an expression of biblical faith which will have the power to grip our generation."[26]

And so we come—full circle—back where we began, to the authoritative, Christ-centered, Spirit-quickened Word of God. Good men holding various views on final punishment have set this standard before. Their differences reflect the extent to which they fell short of their own noble goals. But that is no excuse for us not to try—or to lower their standard.

We fully agree with orthodox theologian, Charles Hodge, when he says, "If we believe the Bible to be the Word of God, all we have to do is to ascertain what it teaches on this subject, and humbly submit."[27] We are surely incompetent to be judges of God. "Imagine a

---

25. E. G. Selwyn, "Image, Fact and Faith," *New Testament Studies* 1, no. 4 (May 1955): 247.

26. Clark H. Pinnock, "Prospects for Systematic Theology," *Toward a Theology for the Future*, pp. 93-94. Pinnock is typical of an increasing number of evangelical scholars who, while respectful of theologians and Reformers of the past, are committed to imitating their godly zeal and devotion to Scripture even when that requires contradicting their opinions.

27. Charles Hodge, *Systematic Theology*, 3:870.

company of criminals passing judgment on the equity and goodness of the law which had condemned them!"[28] Wenham is surely correct when he says, "For a Christian one simple sentence of revelation must in the end outweigh the weightiest conclusions of man-made philosophy."[29] Of this we may be sure:

> Only God knows the facts, and if His revelation of them is rightly interpreted, no tradition (even an Evangelical tradition) has a good claim to be heard against it. . . . Evangelicals, who criticize the Roman Church for putting tradition on a level with the Bible, must be very careful that we ourselves do not unwittingly fall into the same snare. . . . The question is simply, *What do His words mean?* . . . No Protestant should object to being asked to re-examine any traditional belief in the light of the Word of God, searching the Scriptures to see whether these things be so.[30]

---

28. Arthur W. Pink, *Eternal Punishment*, p. 4.

29. Wenham, *The Goodness of God*, p. 29.

30. Harold E. Guillebaud, *The Righteous Judge: A Study of the Biblical Doctrine of Everlasting Punishment*, pp. 46-47, 49. Guillebaud was the late Anglican archdeacon in Ruanda. He was invited by the Inter-Varsity Fellowship in Britain to write a book on the moral difficulties of the Bible. The last question he was to cover was everlasting punishment. When he came to that point, he could not deal with the subject to his own satisfaction, and that chapter was omitted from the book. He then began an intensive study of the subject, during which his original convictions changed, resulting in this conditionalist book.

3

"Aiōnios"—How Long Is "Forever"?

Through the centuries, the discussion about final punishment has usually been accompanied by controversy concerning the Greek adjective *aiōnios*. Does this word describe time in unending duration ("everlasting"), some unknown quality of the Age to Come ("eternal"), both of these, or neither of them? Do these usual translations represent its sense, or should we coin some new adjective such as "aionic" or "aionian"?

Jesus Himself spoke in a single sentence of "eternal" life and "eternal" punishment (Matt. 25:46). Since Augustine, many theologians have looked at that verse and insisted that the punishment must last as long as the life. The few scholars who have not said that have had to defend their interpretations before the great majority who have. In this chapter we will survey some of the approaches that have been made in trying to understand the meaning of *aiōnios* (and its noun parent *aiōn*) in the New Testament.

Some advocates of the orthodox view of hell have insisted that these words signify *only* endless time. W. G. T. Shedd denies any sense of quality. "The truth is," he flatly states, "that *aiōn* is a term that denotes time *only*, and never denotes the nature and quality of an object."[1] A recent popular writer practically turns purple at the suggestion that *aiōnios* denotes a quality. He calls this idea "wishful

---

1. William G. T. Shedd, *The Doctrine of Endless Punishment*, p. 87.

thinking," "nonsense" and a "biblical word game" that "denies the truth of God" and "has no basis in fact."[2]

Some objectors to the traditional doctrine have been equally as extreme in their response. F. G. Maurice said the word was purely *qualitative*, having nothing to do with time. He said it spoke only of things that are spiritual, essential, beyond present categories of thought.[3] W. H. Dyson looks at *aiōnios* in the New Testament and says "it is clear that 'eternal' and 'everlasting' are not interchangeable."[4] He wishes there were some other English word to use in their place. Frederic W. Farrar claimed that it was already "so ably proved by so many writers that there is *no authority whatever for rendering it 'everlasting'*" that there was no further point in even talking about it![5] We clearly will not settle the matter by merely quoting claims.

Derivation of the Word

Even the derivation of *aiōnios* is disputed. One writer traces our English word "eternal" through the Latin *aeternus* to *aeviternus* to *aevum*, which he says matches the Greek word *aei* that gives *aiōnios*. "Thus the basic sense in both Greek and Latin is of everlasting existence," and the word clearly means "always."[6] Another author insists that "an appeal to the ancients, like that of Aristotle, can never sustain the assertion that eternity is the original sense of *aiōn*," that

2. Jon E. Braun, *Whatever Happened to Hell?* p. 162. Like many other traditionalist writers, Braun seems essentially unaware of the conditionalist position. Although he makes a passing use of the term, he equates it with "annihilationism" and mistakenly limits it to the view that the wicked will never be raised (p. 49). His charge that conditionalists "were those who wanted to be universalists but just couldn't bring themselves to justify it" (p. 49) is as uncharitable as it is inaccurate, and is the kind of exaggeration that has brought needless opposition to the orthodox position. His assumption that no one in 2000 years has suggested the transliteration "aionic" or "aionion" instead of "eternal" (p. 97) overlooks even Shedd's use of the term. The statement that the "Greek used in the New Testament does not have a single adverb with the meaning the same as the English word *forever*" (p. 159) ignores the Greek adverb *pantote*, which means "always" and is so cited by Charles F. Baker in reaching the same view of hell as Braun. See Charles F. Baker, *A Dispensational Theology*, p. 651; see also F. F. Bruce, *Answers to Questions*, p. 202.

3. Don Cupitt, "The Language of Eschatology: F. D. Maurice's Treatment of Heaven and Hell," *Anglican Theological Review* 54, no. 4 (October 1972): 305-317.

4. W. H. Dyson, "Eternal Punishment," *A Dictionary of Christ and the Gospels*, 1:540.

5. Frederic W. Farrar, *Eternal Hope*, p. 197.

6. Cupitt, "Language of Eschatology," p. 314.

this sense was unknown to the Greeks for many centuries and came into use only in the later ages of the language.[7]

Nonbiblical sources from early Christian times offer little help. Moulton and Milligan cite papyri inscriptions from the first and second centuries A.D. There *aiōn* is used for the "life" of a person as well as the life wished for a Caesar, or in centuries B.C. for a Pharaoh. They give no evidence outside the New Testament for a qualitative meaning of *aiōnios*, saying that in their sources "it never loses the sense of *perpetuus*." The word's roots are too deep to dig for, they say, and they conclude that in general the word "depicts that of which the horizon is not in view, whether the horizon be at an infinite distance . . . or whether it lies no farther than the span of a Caesar's life."[8]

We should probably conclude that both "eternal" and *aiōnios* have roots signifying time in both English (and its Latin ancestor) and in Greek. But some are ready then to remind us that in biblical interpretation the important thing is not secular etymology so much as sacred usage. How the Bible uses a word is far more crucial for understanding a passage of Scripture than all the historians of any language. This objection also has merit, and we must now ask how Scripture uses *aiōn* and *aiōnios*.

"Everlasting" Things That Last Forever . . . and Some That Don't

Nicole observes that 51 times in the New Testament, *aiōnios* applies to the "eternal felicity" of the redeemed, and there "it is conceded by all that no limitation of time applies."[9] On the other hand, Pétavel insists that at least 70 times in the Bible, this word qualifies "objects of a temporary and limited nature," so that it signifies only "an indeterminate duration of which the maximum is fixed by the intrinsic nature of the persons or things."[10] The word means "forever," but within the limits of the possibility inherent in the person or thing

---

7. Edward Beecher, *History of Opinions on the Scriptural Doctrine of Retribution*, p. 140.

8. James Hope Moulton and George Milligan, *The Vocabulary of the Greek Testament Illustrated from the Papyri and Other Non-Literary Sources*, p. 16.

9. Roger Nicole, "The Punishment of the Wicked," *Christianity Today*, 9 June 1958, p. 14.

10. Emmanuel Pétavel, *The Problem of Immortality*, p. 574.

itself. When God is said to be "eternal," that is truly "forever." When
the mountains are said to be "everlasting," that means that they last
ever so long—so long as they can last.

Pétavel points out that Scripture frequently uses *aiōn, aiōnios* and
their Hebrew counterparts (*olam* in various forms) of things which
have come to an end. The sprinkling of blood at the Passover was an
"everlasting" ordinance (Exod. 12:24). So were the Aaronic
priesthood (Exod. 29:9; 40:15; Lev. 3:17), Caleb's inheritance (Josh.
14:9), Solomon's temple (1 Kings 8:12, 13), the period of a slave's life
(Deut. 15:17), Gehazi's leprosy (2 Kings 5:27)—and practically every
other ordinance, rite or institution of the Old Testament system.
These things did not last "forever" as we think of time extended
without limitation. They did last beyond the vision of those who first
heard them called "everlasting," and no time limit was then set at all.
According to this view, held by Pétavel, Froom and others, this is the
meaning of *aiōnios* or "eternal" in the Bible. It speaks of unlimited
time within the limits determined by the thing it modifies. Yet
Beecher—a critic of the orthodox doctrine of hell—denies that this is
a proper definition, noting that the Mosaic ordinances and the possession of Palestine "might have lasted to the end of the world, but
did not."[11]

The Quality of Another Aeon

While it is unquestionably true that the Bible uses *aiōnios* to describe the Trinity, as also the redemption, salvation and final bliss of
the redeemed, it is clear that the New Testament sometimes uses the

---

11. Beecher, *History of Opinions*, p. 149. Beecher argues at length for the meaning "age-long"
or "dispensation." He insists that the New Testament meaning of *aiōnios* is formed off this root
by the authors of the Septuagint and so passes into New Testament use (pp. 140-147). To the
extent that this is correct—and there is no question that the New Testament vocabulary contains much fruit born from the union of the Hebrew Old Testament with the Greek language in
the Septuagint—*aiōnios* in the New Testament is loosed from classical meanings discovered
through strict etymology.

Origen used the Hebrew *olam* to argue that *aiōnios* is not everlasting but a very long time,
according to Harry A. Wolfson, "Immortality and Resurrection in the Philosophy of the
Church Fathers," *Immortality and Resurrection*, p. 65. Geerhardus Vos, on the other hand,
argues from the same Hebrew word for the sense of perpetuity and unendingness in his book,
The Pauline Eschatology, pp. 288-289.

"Everlasting" equals ten generations in Deuteronomy 23:3, 6. Salmond discounts all references to temporary things which are called "everlasting" in the Old Testament by saying that
"for the moment the imagination of the speaker or writer gives to the things the quality of the
eternal" (Steward D. F. Salmond, *The Christian Doctrine of Immortality*, p. 654).

word in a qualitative sense. This seems to reflect one common Jewish attitude about history and the Last Things. In this view time is divided into two ages—the Present Age and the Age to Come (Matt. 12:32; Luke 20:34, 35). Jesus speaks of the cares of this age (Matt. 13:22; Mark 4:19), the sons of this age (Luke 16:8) and the end of this age (Matt. 13:39, 40; 24:3; 28:20). Paul also speaks of this age with its debaters (1 Cor. 1:20), wisdom and rulers (1 Cor. 2:6, 8; 3:18), course of life (Eph. 2:2), world rulers (Eph. 6:12, Received Text) and the rich (1 Tim. 6:17). Over against this age he also contrasts the Age to Come (Eph. 1:21).

The Present Age is under Satan's dominion (2 Cor. 4:4), and Christ gave Himself for our sins to rescue us from it (Gal. 1:4). The Age to Come is of another order which may be called "eternal" (aiōnios). To be guilty of an "eternal" sin (Mark 3:29) is to be guilty of one which will not be forgiven even in the Age to Come (Matt. 12:32). That the Age to Come is eternal in quality is seen in the fact that the life of the Age to Come (eternal life) is possible even in the Present Age through faith in Jesus.[12] Where John talks of "eternal life," the other Gospels generally speak of the "kingdom," though these expressions are used interchangeably in the Synoptics (Matt. 19:16, 17, 23; Mark 9:45, 47) and in John (John 3:3, 5, 15, 16). To inherit the kingdom is to enter into eternal life (Matt. 25:34, 46).

Based on this Jewish eschatological usage, aiōnios sometimes suggests "quality of being, almost meaning 'divine' rather than enduring."[13] It describes things which are bound to the kingdom of God, so that it is "almost the equivalent of 'Messianic'."[14] The adjective "eternal" is applied to things "resulting from the final intervention of God, when He will establish the new world."[15] It "takes us

---

12. This is true especially in the writings of John. The adjective aiōnios occurs 17 times in the fourth Gospel and six times in 1 John, always with the noun "life." It indicates "a life that is different in quality from the life which characterizes the present age" (William Hendriksen, *The Gospel According to John*, p. 141), although it also carries a quantitative connotation. For more bibliography see J. W. Roberts, "Some Observations on the Meaning of 'Eternal Life' in the Gospel of John," *Restoration Quarterly* 7, no. 4 (Fourth Quarter, 1963): 186-193.

13. David Hill, *Greek Words and Hebrew Meanings: Studies in the Semantics of Soteriological Terms* (Cambridge: Society for New Testament Studies Monograph Series, no. 5, 1967), pp. 163-201, summarized by D. E. H. Whiteley, "Liberal Christianity in the New Testament," *Modern Churchman* 13, no. 1 (October 1969): 25.

14. Dyson, "Eternal Punishment," p. 540.

15. J. Burnier, "Judgment in the New Testament," *A Companion to the Bible*, ed. J. J. von Allmen (New York: Oxford University Press, 1958), p. 213. While both Gerald C. Studer (*After Death, What?* p. 127) and LeRoy Edwin Froom (*The Conditionalist Faith of Our*

into a sphere of being" where we view things "in their relation to some eternal aspect of the Divine nature."[16] The word speaks of "being of which time is not a measure."[17]

Given this definition, "eternal" punishment or "eternal" fire are fire and punishment which "partake of the nature of the *aiōn*," which are "peculiar to the realm and the nature of God."[18] The real point is the "character of the punishment." It is "that of the order of the Age to Come as contrasted with any earthly penalties."[19] When the New Testament speaks of "eternal" life, in this view, the adjective *aiōnios* refers to "the quality more than to the length of life."[20]

This does not detract from the endlessness of the bliss, for Scripture explicitly states that nothing can ever separate God's people from His love—even things to come (Rom. 8:38, 39). They will "always" be with the Lord (*pantote*, literally "every-then," 1 Thess. 4:17). God will glorify them and give them a body that cannot die (1 Cor. 15:53, 54). The endless joy of the saved does not finally depend on the meaning of *aiōnios*, for even if that word spoke *only* of a quality, Scripture says sufficient to assure believers of everlasting happiness. To say that *aiōnios* has a qualitative meaning is not a "linguistic smokescreen"[21] but represents the sober thinking of a cross section of scholars, including several who hold the traditional view of hell.[22] Nor does it satisfy everyone!

Shedd concedes that Scripture speaks of two ages or *aiōns* and that the adjective *aiōnios* is related to this concept. But he points out that while the Present Age will end, the Age to Come will never end. Both

---

Fathers, 2:949) quote Burnier on this point, it is interesting that Froom stops shorter than Studer, who continues the quotation as follows: "Moreover, every attempt to determine exactly what awaits men beyond judgment comes up against the undefined nature of a concept which was elaborated not to satisfy our curiosity, but to cause us to fear the God who offers us His pardon and eternal life in the fellowship of His Son." Froom would profit from this warning against oversimplification of eternal matters since his Seventh-day Adventist position leaves very little to the imagination. In Froom's defense, however, he quotes Burnier only to show broad support for what is sometimes thought to be a peculiar sectarian view.

16. Archibald Bisset, "Eternal Fire," *A Dictionary of Christ and the Gospels*, 1:537.

17. B. F. Westcott, quoted by Dyson, "Eternal Punishment," p. 540.

18. Joseph Arthur Baird, *The Justice of God in the Teaching of Jesus*, p. 233.

19. Alan Richardson, *An Introduction to the Theology of the New Testament*, p. 74.

20. Donald G. Bloesch, *Essentials of Evangelical Theology*, 2:229.

21. As charged by Jon Zens, "Do the Flames Ever Stop in Hell?" *Free Grace Broadcaster*, March-April 1978, p. 2.

22. In addition to Westcott and Bloesch, cited above, see Harry Buis, *The Doctrine of Eternal Punishment*, pp. 49-50.

ages are described by the Greek *aiōn* and the Hebrew *olam*. Things in both ages are described by *aiōnios*. The crucial question, according to Shedd, is *"in which of the two aeons, the limited or the endless, the thing exists to which the epithet is applied. . . . If anything belongs solely to the present age, or aeon, it is aeonian in the limited signification; if it belongs to the future age, or aeon, it is aeonian in the unlimited signification."*[23]

H. A. A. Kennedy agrees with Shedd. Although in many passages *aiōnios* loses its time-quality to become "virtually equivalent to 'transcendent, perfect,'" Kennedy argues that "the age of God's dominion is necessarily final. If St. Paul does not describe it as 'eternal,' in so many words, it is because the conception is self-evident to his readers."[24]

Just as traditionalist Buis concedes a qualitative sense for *aiōnios*, but insists that it retains a quantitative meaning as well, so conditionalist Guillebaud says that "though 'eternal' is *more* than endless, the idea of permanence is an essential part of it."[25] He cites several passages which contrast the temporary with the permanent (Luke 16:9; 2 Cor. 4:17–5:4) to support this conclusion. The evidence urges us to stand on this solid ground. Shedd and Braun are wrong to deny any qualitative sense. Maurice and Farrar are wrong to say there is no other sense. Buis and Guillebaud differ on the nature of final punishment, but both men concede ground on this point and meet in the middle. We applaud their humility and their objectivity, and join them there.

Having said that "eternal" describes both quality *and* quantity, character *and* duration, what precisely does it describe in the case of final punishment? Traditionalists and conditionalists may strike hands in agreement concerning the word, but they immediately draw swords when they begin to apply it to hell. The wicked go into *eter-*

---

23. Shedd, *The Doctrine of Endless Punishment*, pp. 84-85. Geerhardus Vos, on the other hand, sees no relation between the adjective *aiōnios* and the "formal eschatological distinction" between the two ages (Geerhardus Vos, *The Pauline Eschatology*, p. 289).

24. H. A. A. Kennedy, *St. Paul's Conceptions of the Last Things*, p. 318.

25. Harold E. Guillebaud, *The Righteous Judge: A Study of the Biblical Doctrine of Everlasting Punishment*, p. 7. Another approach to the qualitative sense of *aiōnios* which I have not seen suggested or followed anywhere concerns the qualitative nature of *all* adjectives, formed as they are on nouns. This is particularly relevant in the present case, where the Hebrew construct state often serves in the absence of adjectives and, in the Septuagint and New Testament, sometimes becomes attributive genitives and sometimes Greek adjectives. On the phenomenon see Maximilian Zerwick, *Biblical Greek*, p. 14, #40.

nal punishment. Does that refer to the *act* of retribution or to its *ef-fect*? Which is "eternal"—the punish*ing* or the punish*ment*? As so often happens in exploring this cavernous topic, we finally kindle a light in one dark room, only to discover that it leads into a still deeper cave. We now move into that one.

"Eternal" with Words of Action

Of the 70 usages of the adjective "eternal" (*aiōnios*) in the New Testament, six times the word qualifies nouns signifying acts or processes, as distinct from persons or things. These cases call for special consideration. They are "eternal salvation" (Heb. 5:9), "eternal redemption" (Heb. 9:12), "eternal judgment" (Heb. 6:2), "eternal sin" (Mark 3:29), "eternal punishment" (Matt. 25:46) and "eternal destruction" (2 Thess. 1:9). Three occur in Hebrews; all six have to do with final judgment and its outcome.

Here we see again the *other-age* quality of the "eternal." There is something transcendent, eschatological, divine about this judgment, this sin, this punishment and destruction, this redemption and salvation. They are not merely human, *this-age* matters, but are of an entirely different nature. On the other hand, something about this judgment, sin, punishment, destruction, redemption and salvation will have no end. If in one sense these things are *timeless*, they are in another sense without temporal limits. They belong to that Age to Come which is not bound by time and which will never end.[26]

"Eternal Judgment" (Heb. 6:2). Among the "elementary teachings" which make up the "foundation" of Christian teaching are "the resurrection of the dead and *eternal judgment*." This is literally the resurrection "of the dead *ones*" (plural, *nekrōn*), seemingly both good and bad,[27] and it is linked to that judgment which is of the Age

---

26. We here bypass a larger issue concerning the philosophical and theological nature of "time" and "eternity." On this see Oscar Cullmann, *Christ and Time* (London: SCM Press, 1967), pp. 37-68; James Barr, *Biblical Words for Time* (London: SCM Press, 1962; 2nd ed., 1969), pp. 135-158.

27. It has frequently been stated that, as a general rule, when the New Testament speaks of the resurrection *of* the dead (*tōn nekrōn*), it has in view a general resurrection comprising both good and evil. When it speaks of a resurrection *from* the dead (*ek nekrōn*), it usually has in view a resurrection of the righteous unto life. Joachim Jeremias makes a contrary distinction in one important passage, however, in his " 'Flesh and Blood Cannot Inherit the Kingdom of God' (I Cor. xv. 50)," *New Testament Studies* 2 (February 1956): 155.

to Come, not merely a judgment made by man or God in the here and now. That is its *quality*, but what of its *duration*? How is the last judgment "eternal" in the sense of *everlasting*?

The act of judging will certainly not last forever. But we notice that the text speaks of judg*ment* (*krimatos*) and not judg*ing*. There will be an act or process of judging, and then it will be over. But the judging results in a judgment—and that will never end. The action itself is one thing; its outcome, its issue, its result, is something else. "Eternal" here speaks of the *result* of the action, not the action itself. Once the judging is over, the judgment will remain—the eternal, everlasting issue of the once-for-all process of judgment.

"Eternal Redemption" (Heb. 9:12). Christ has entered upon His high-priestly service through the greater tabernacle that is not hand-made or a part of this creation. "He did not enter by means of the blood of goats and calves; but He entered the Most Holy Place once for all by His own blood, having obtained *eternal redemption*." It is clear that "eternal" here also has a qualitative aspect. These matters are of that order which is not a part of this creation (v. 11). They pertain to the "eternal Spirit" (v. 14), not the flesh. They belong to the new covenant and the "eternal inheritance" (v. 15). By faith these "eternal" things are already operative and even visible (Heb. 11), though they are of an order different from the space-time creation of which we are presently a part.

This redemption is also "eternal" in the sense of *everlasting*. Not that the act or process of redeeming continues without end—Christ has accomplished that *once for all!* Our author specifically makes the point that Christ did not have to suffer "many times since the creation." Rather, "He has appeared once for all at the end of the ages to do away with sin by the sacrifice of Himself" (Heb. 9:25, 26). But this once-for-all act of redeem*ing*, which is finished, will never be repeated and can never be duplicated, issues in a redemp*tion* which will never pass away.[28] "Eternal" speaks here again of the *result* of the action, not the act itself. Once the redeeming has taken place, the redemption remains. And that "eternal" result of the once-for-all action will never pass away.

---

28. This is all the more striking here since "redemption" is in a form (*lutrōsis*) which, if anything, points to the process involved.

"Eternal Salvation" (Heb. 5:9). Through reverent submission and perfect obedience, Jesus became "the source of *eternal salvation* for all who obey Him." This salvation partakes of the eternal *quality* of the new order—that order in which Jesus may be a priest like Melchizedek (v. 10). It is already a reality (Heb. 4:15, 16), for it partially intersects the present order even while it transcends it. But this salvation is also "eternal" in that it will have no end. Jesus is not forever *saving* His people; He did that once for all, as we have already seen. This salva*tion* is eternal because it is the everlasting result which issues from the once-for-all process or act of sav*ing*. The result remains even after the act has ended.

The expression "eternal salvation" here may come from Isaiah 45:17. There God promised that "Israel will be saved by the Lord with an everlasting salvation." It is clear from the following words that God has in mind the result He will accomplish rather than the act He will perform. "You will never be put to shame or disgraced, to ages everlasting." Once the saving has taken place, the salvation remains. And that "eternal" outcome of God's finished action will never pass away.

"Eternal Sin" (Mark 3:29). In a controversy with some teachers of the law, Jesus said: "Whoever blasphemes against the Holy Spirit will never be forgiven; he is guilty of an *eternal sin*." Mark's next statement tells us what this "eternal sin" was. "He said this because they were saying, 'He has an evil spirit'" (Mark 3:30). This sin of attributing to the demonic the Holy Spirit's power manifested in Jesus had a quality other sins did not. It was "eternal" in that sense because it resisted and contradicted the power of the Age to Come. It stood in opposition to the inbreaking kingdom of God, as Luke points out in the parallel passage (Luke 11:20). Nor will it be forgiven, even in the Age to Come, which for Matthew is equivalent to saying it is an "eternal sin" (Matt. 12:32). The *act* of sinning does not continue forever; it was committed on that occasion in Jesus' ministry and may possibly never be repeated in exactly the same way. Men are punished in hell for sins committed during *this Present Age,* not for evil done following the last day (Rom. 2:6-16). This "eternal" sin was committed once. But its result remains for eternity.

"Eternal Destruction" (2 Thess. 1:9). When Jesus comes, He will punish His enemies who have refused to know God and to obey

His gospel. "They will be punished with *everlasting destruction* and shut out from the presence of the Lord and from the majesty of His power."[29]

This destruction clearly partakes of the Age to Come. It belongs to those eschatological realities which are now unseen and mysterious to our Present Age. In that sense it is "eternal" in quality. In keeping with what we have seen already, we suggest that the destruction is also everlasting and unending.

The New International Version uses two verbs to describe what will happen to the wicked on that day. "They will be punished" (with everlasting destruction), and they will be "shut out" from the Lord's presence and power. The second verb is not in the Greek but is supplied by the New International Version's translators to express what they think it means. We will discuss that more later. For now it is important to see that whatever happens will happen "on the day He comes" (v. 10). It will not be happening forever, but when He has brought about their destruc*tion*, its results will never end.

In keeping with the rest of the teaching of both Old and New Testaments, to be examined in following chapters, we here suggest that this "eternal destruction" will be the extinction of those so sentenced. This retribution will be preceded by penal suffering exactly suited to each degree of guilt by a holy and just God, but that penal suffering *within itself* is not the ultimate retribution or punishment. There will be an act of destroy*ing*, resulting in a destruc*tion* that will never end or be reversed. The act of destroying includes penal pains, but they will end. The result of destruction will never be reversed and will never have an end.

"Eternal Punishment" (Matt. 25:46). Jesus concludes His Parable of the Sheep and Goats with the statement that the wicked "will go away to *eternal punishment*, but the righteous to eternal life." Both the life and the punishment partake of the quality of the Age to Come. We have some experience here and now of *life* and of *punishment*. But we cannot know now what the *eternal* life will be—in its fullness—nor can we know now what the *eternal* punishment will

---

29. There is no reason at all why the New International Version should here follow the King James Version in translating *aiōnios* as "everlasting" instead of "eternal" (as in the Revised Standard Version, New English Bible, New American Standard Version and others). It is particularly strange since the New International Version has "eternal" punishment in Matthew 25:46.

be—in its actual horror. There is more to either than a timeless extension of what we can now experience. We are acquainted to some extent with the nouns; the adjective tells us they will then be of a quality we do not yet comprehend. There is clearly a qualitative aspect to
"eternal" punishment.

At the same time, the life and the punishment of this passage are
never to end. They are "eternal" in the sense of *everlasting*. But we
need to note, as in the five cases above, that "punishment" is an act
or process. In each case so far, and indisputably in the first four, the
act or process happens in a fixed period of time but is followed by a
result that lasts forever. In keeping with that scriptural usage, we
suggest that the "punishment" here includes whatever penal suffering
God justly issues to each person but consists primarily of the total
abolition and extinction of the person forever. The punish*ing* continues until the process is completed, and then it stops. But the
punish*men+* which results will remain forever.[30]

Conclusion. This is a powerful argument which conditionalists
have pressed with vigor.[31] In all the literature covered by this study,
no traditionalist writer has dealt with it at all except perhaps to assert
that it is false without giving any reasoning or evidence—and that
but rarely. Like most of the conditionalist arguments, this one has
simply been ignored. If the traditional understanding of hell is to
stand, a cogent and persuasive answer must be forthcoming. Since all
we want to know is God's truth as revealed in Scripture, no one need
be threatened on either side of the discussion. This is a challenge
which calls for careful exegesis and prayerful study within a commitment to the final authority of the Word of God.

---

30. Some have objected that such absolute destruction by extinction would not be sufficient
"punishment" or that it would not suit the description "eternal." We will consider both objections later, noting here only that these points are conceded by Augustine and by Jonathan Edwards.

31. Pétavel, *The Problem of Immortality*, pp. 194-195; LeRoy Edwin Froom, *Conditionalist
Faith*, 1:288-291. Guillebaud says: "We do not claim to have proved that this interpretation is
certainly right, but to have shown that it is legitimate and possible, and cannot (so far as the
texts containing the word 'eternal' are concerned) be called a forcing of Scripture to suit a
theory" (Guillebaud, *The Righteous Judge*, p. 11).

A Summary Concerning *"Eternal"*/Aiōnios

We have seen that the adjective *aiōnios* distinctly carries a qualitative sense. It suggests something that partakes of the transcendent realm of divine activity. It indicates a relationship to the kingdom of God, to the Age to Come, to the eschatological realities which in Jesus have begun already to manifest themselves in the Present Age.[32] It speaks of a particular truth which cannot now be fully known. It reminds us that while the nouns it modifies may be familiar, they are somehow set apart from our present experiences. There is more than meets the eye, a depth we do not fathom, a distance between *this* and *that*. The traditionalist writers who deny any qualitative sense in *aiōnios* have overreacted. Their zeal for one truth has blinded them unnecessarily to another truth. Unless we coin a more appropriate word such as "aionion" or "aionic," this aspect of *aiōnios* is best represented by the word "eternal."

We have also seen that the adjective *aiōnios* has a temporal aspect, indicating something that will never end. God Himself has no limitation, including the limits of time. The Age to Come partakes of that limitlessness. So do the works of God which Scripture calls "eternal." Those nontraditionalist writers who deny any temporal sense in *aiōnios* have also overreacted. They have not needed to deny the unendingness of the "eternal" in order to hold to its *otherness*. Both are true. Many writers holding both positions have happily admitted as much. This unending aspect of *aiōnios* is best represented by the word "everlasting" until someone finds a word more appropriate.

Finally, we have seen that when the word *aiōnios* modifies words which name acts or processes as distinct from persons or things, the adjective usually describes the issue or result of the action rather than the action itself. This is indisputably true in four of the six New Testament occurrences. There is eternal salvation but not an eternal act of saving. There is eternal redemption but not an eternal process of redeeming. The eternal sin was committed at a point in history,

---

32. The Holy Spirit's descent upon the Christian church at Pentecost is also related to this. The Spirit not only guarantees to believers fullness of life in the age to come (Rom. 8:16-23; 2 Cor. 5:4, 5; Eph. 1:13, 14; 2:7); He is also the mediating source by which God demonstrates the power of that age among His people even now (1 Cor. 14:24, 25; Eph. 3:16, 20; Heb. 6:5). There is an *already* to this *not yet*, though there is so much more to come!

but its results continue into the coming age which lasts forever. Scripture pictures eternal judgment as taking place "on a day," but its outcome will have no end. In the light of this usage, we suggest that Scripture expects the same understanding when it speaks of "eternal destruction" and "eternal punishment." Both are acts. There will be an actual destroying, an actual punishing. Both the destroying and the punishing will issue in a result. That resultant *punishment* of *destruction* will never end.

At times it seems this trail of research itself may have no end. For just as we find a ledge strong and wide enough for all parties in the controversy to stand, someone inevitably seems to see another cracked door. In this case it has to do with man himself. Regardless of what one may think about the word "eternal," certain traditionalist writers have raised another question. Can man—who is immortal—ever be completely destroyed? Does not the immortality of the soul require that he continue to exist forever? And does that not require the doctrine of conscious torment that will never end? Let us move on.

4

"If a Man Lives Again, Can He Die?" (The Question of Immortality)

While the linguists and exegetes hammer out a definition of "eternity," popular preachers and men in the pew are often talking about a different subject. Their attention is focused on a man himself, and particularly on that unseen "part" commonly called his "soul." Physical death cannot touch this element of man's being, it is believed, because it possesses immortality. At the last judgment, it is often said, God will sentence the wicked, then banish their never-dying souls to conscious torment throughout the age which never ends. "You have an immortal soul," the revivalist message often puts it, "and it will spend eternity in either heaven or hell."

Theologians also fall back at times on the doctrine of man's immortality as a basis for interpreting Scripture's teaching about the wicked's end. *"If man is admitted to be immortal,"* writes Pusey, "and punishment is not to be endless, there is no other conclusion but that he should be restored."[1] Shedd notes that "Scripture speaks of but two aeons, which cover and include the whole existence of man, and his whole duration. *If, therefore, he is an immortal being,"* he reasons, "one of these must be endless."[2] Hodge ties the two statements together and completes the traditional argument as it is often

---

1. Edward Bouverie Pusey, *What Is of Faith as to Everlasting Punishment? In Reply to Dr. Farrar's Challenge in His "Eternal Hope," 1879,* p. 27. Italics supplied.

2. W. G. T. Shedd, *The Doctrine of Endless Punishment,* p. 86. Italics supplied.

made. "If the Bible says that the sufferings of the lost are to be everlasting, they are to endure forever, *unless it can be shown either that the soul is not immortal* or that the Scriptures elsewhere teach that those sufferings are to come to an end."[3]

Shedd is bolder than most in his expression, but he clearly presents this common understanding of man's innate immortality. He even awes himself as he states what he believes.

> But irrepressible and universal as it is, the doctrine of man's immortality is an astonishing one, and difficult to entertain. For it means that every frail finite man is to be as long-enduring as the infinite and eternal God; that there will no more be an end to the existence of the man who died today than there will be of the Deity who made him. God is denominated 'The Ancient of Days.' But every immortal spirit that ever dwelt in a human body will also be an 'ancient of days.' . . . Yes, man *must* exist. He has no option. Necessity is laid upon him. He cannot extinguish himself. He cannot cease to be.[4]

If someone inquires why this does not fly into the face of Scripture's statement that God alone possesses immortality (1 Tim. 6:16), proponents answer that man's immortality concerns only his soul, which survives bodily death. Writes Henry Barclay Swete:

> God is immortal in the sense that He cannot die. . . . God "only hath immortality" such as this. Man is immortal in the sense that there is in him that which does not die. His body dies, but his soul survives. It lives on after it has left the body. His identity is not lost when he dies; his true self, the ultimate being and personality of the man, remains as it was before death. . . . Not all of him dies; there is a part of him, and by far the more essential . . . [5]

These theologians frankly admit that the expression "immortal soul" is not in the Bible but confidently state that Scripture *assumes* the immortality of every soul. A popular writer says, for example: "The Word of God assumes the eternal existence of every soul regardless of its destiny. Every man's soul is immortal and can never be annihilated."[6] He later notes, "'They that are Christ's' tells us who

---

3. Charles Hodge, *Systematic Theology*, 3:876. Italics supplied.
4. Shedd, *The Doctrine of Endless Punishment*, p. 490.
5. Henry Barclay Swete, *The Life of the World to Come*, p. 3.
6. Lehman Strauss, *Life After Death: What the Bible Really Teaches*, p. 14.

shall become immortal," and "'At His coming' . . . tells us when we shall become immortal,"[7] but still says that "As a matter of fact the soul never lost its immortality."[8]

Since Calvin (whom we shall consider later in detail), Reformed writers in particular have viewed man's immortality as a consequence of his formation in God's image and his quickening by God's breath of life.[9] Buis is careful not to claim too much but says that while "this cannot be considered absolute proof of the natural immortality of man, it certainly points in that direction."[10]

Although advocates often present this view with a quiver in their voice and with a less certain tone than usual, they seem constrained to keep up their insistence. They see the supernaturalist view up against the anti-supernaturalist. The anti-supernaturalist says that man's death is his end—period. These orthodox thinkers know that that is not his end, but how do they distinguish themselves from their unbelieving opponents? The answer has often been to insist that a part of man does not die. Besides his body, every man has a soul, the argument goes. That part of him is immortal and escapes the death to which the body succumbs.

Uneasiness within Orthodox Ranks

The feeling has persisted, however, that something here does not fit.[11] While some orthodox writers have continued to affirm the im-

---

7. Ibid., p. 17.

8. Ibid., p. 16.

9. Calvin's corner of the Reformation has carried the heaviest end of the immortality log the past 400 years. The mortalist position has been widely held among Lutherans, Baptists and particularly Anglicans throughout Protestant history. Fundamentalism seems to have inherited the immortalist position almost genetically through its "Old Princeton" Calvinist ancestry, and the doctrine has since settled in with the unquestioned authority of a venerated relative.

10. Harry Buis, *The Doctrine of Eternal Punishment*, p. 8.

11. Archibald Alexander Hodge (*Outlines of Theology*, pp. 549-552), William G. T. Shedd (*Dogmatic Theology* [Grand Rapids: Zondervan Publishing House, n.d.], 2:612) and Louis Berkhof (*Systematic Theology* [Grand Rapids: William B. Eerdmans Publishing Co., 1953], p. 672) all defend immortality as a biblical doctrine. Herman Bavinck calls it a "mixed article" demonstrated better by reason than by revelation (Herman Bavinck, *Gereformeerde Dogmatick*, 4th ed., 4:567; 3rd ed., 4:648). G. C. Berkouwer comments that "Scripture is never concerned with an independent interest in immortality as such, let alone with the immortality of a part of man which defies and survives death under all circumstances, and on which we can reflect quite apart from man's relation to the living God" (G. C. Berkouwer, *Man: The Image of God* [Grand Rapids: William B. Eerdmans Publishing Co., 1962], p. 276). These references and others are given by Anthony A. Hoekema, *The Bible and the Future*, p. 89.

mortality of the soul—though often with a look over the shoulder —many others have charged that the doctrine has serious deficiencies. These critics have charged that the doctrine of inherent immortality is pagan in origin and crept into Christian thinking through Platonic philosophy. The Bible places hope for life after death in a *bodily resurrection*, they say, not in an "immortal soul." They point to the passages which speak of immortality, and point out that they attribute it to man's future glorified body, not to his present soul, that it is God's gift for the saved, not the inherent birthright of every person born into the world.

"The dream that death is an emancipation of the spiritual essence from a body that imprisons and clogs it, and is in itself the entrance on a freer, larger life, belongs to the schools, not to Christianity," writes James Orr.[12] Salmond calls attention to the fact that Paul, who gives more "of a seeming psychology" than any other New Testament writer, "never contemplates a simple immortality of soul; he never argues for man's survival merely on the ground that there is a mind or spirit in him. He proceeds upon the Old Testament view of man." That view, Salmond continues, "is essentially different from the Hellenic idea which ruled the scholastic theology, and has exercised a deep and unfortunate influence on modern systems of doctrine."[13] Westcott notes that "on principles of reason there seems to be no ground whatever for supposing that the soul as separate from the body is personal." Such a statement goes against popular language and belief, he admits, which "are so strong in the assertion of the personal immortality of the soul . . . that it is very difficult for us to realise the true state of the problem."[14]

Dispensationalist J. N. Darby expressed his conviction that the idea of the immortality of the soul "is not in general a *gospel* topic; that it comes, on the contrary, from the Platonists; and that it was just when the coming of Christ was denied in the Church, or at least

---

12. James Orr, *The Resurrection of Jesus*, p. 282.

13. Steward D. F. Salmond, *The Christian Doctrine of Immortality*, p. 573. Salmond was ahead of his time in noting the tension between the biblical and philosophical attitudes regarding man. Although he comes out in the end against the annihilation of the wicked, he considers the possibility and makes some objections.

14. Brooke Foss Westcott, *The Gospel of the Resurrection: Thoughts on Its Relation to Reason and History*, pp. 146-147. In a footnote Westcott exempts from his comments here quoted the intermediate state of the soul between death and resurrection.

began to be lost sight of, that the doctrine of the immortality of the soul came in to replace that of the resurrection."[15]

Beasley-Murray followed through on the stroke Darby initiated. Philosophical arguments in favor of man's survival of death "usually proceed without reference" to Jesus' resurrection, he observes, and therefore "cannot strictly be termed Christian." In the end they are therefore "irrelevant, for the Resurrection is itself a sufficient revelation both of the fact and the nature of immortality." The kind of liberal preaching which dissolves Jesus' resurrection into an example of every man's immortality is unworthy of the gospel, Beasley-Murray declares, and such an argument "bears little relation to the New Testament."[16]

Such statements could be mutiplied for pages on end—and are, in the second volume of a recent work by LeRoy Edwin Froom.[17] It is not enough today to say that the Bible *assumes* the immortality of the soul even though it does not teach it. John W. Wenham throws down the gauntlet. That "so important a truth should not be explicitly taught is strange. The onus of proof is on those who say it is assumed."[18]

It has generally been thought that the immortality of the soul was a necessary tool for Christian theology. Today, however, the doctrine is increasingly regarded as a post-apostolic innovation—not only unnecessary but positively harmful to proper biblical interpretation and

---

15. J. N. Darby, "Hopes of the Church," *Works, Prophetic* (London: Geo. Morrish, 1866), 1:463, quoted by Emmanuel Pétavel, *The Problem of Immortality*, p. 111. This statement was weakened in a later edition of Darby's book, though the gist remained.

16. G. R. Beasley-Murray, *Christ Is Alive!* p. 153.

17. LeRoy Edwin Froom, *The Conditionalist Faith of Our Fathers*, 2:247-1048. These pages trace the conditionalist witness from 1800 to the present. Froom's massive two-volume work was published after most of the traditionalist books on final punishment so far and has not yet received critical attention by such writers. In spite of an obviously polemical tone and a tendency to overgeneralize at the expense of disagreeable evidence, Froom's encyclopedic presentation is most impressive and must be objectively considered in any thorough discussion of this subject in the future.

Froom cites many sources which carry little weight among evangelicals, and he tends at least to give the impression of extravagance in evaluating his material. In spite of these weaknesses (in which he is certainly not alone, perhaps including this writer!), Froom convincingly establishes his claim of legitimacy for the minority conditionalist position in Christian understanding through the centuries. By constantly ascribing Platonism to immortalists (overlooking important distinctions), he detracts somewhat from the primary thesis, which he firmly establishes. It would be unfair of critics to simply note these subsidiary errors and offhandedly pass by the great mass of Froom's material.

18. John W. Wenham, *The Goodness of God*, p. 35, note 4.

understanding.[19] Critics further charge that the traditional view of immortal souls is without support either from Scripture[20] or from human wisdom.[21]

The relation between the doctrine of the soul's immortality and the doctrine of final punishment is real, though it is deceptively clear. If every soul lives forever, the traditional view of hell as unending *conscious torment* seems to follow. This presupposition has wielded tremendous influence on biblical interpretation in intertestamental Judaism and through most of the Christian centuries. One of Froom's main theses is that "innate Immortal-Soulism" is the villain behind the traditionalist view of hell. Like the persistent officer of *Les Miserables*, he ferrets out the offender, then dogs his heels through nearly 2500 years and practically as many pages.[22]

Yet further reading suggests that much of Froom's energy might be misspent. For orthodox writers through the centuries—from the apologists of the second and third centuries after Christ, to Augustine, to Calvin, to Reformed theologians today—have usually been

---

19. D. W. Gundry writes that "although St. Paul mentions Judaism in *Galatians* as a schoolmaster to bring us to Christ, within the apostolic period itself Hellenistic philosophy soon appears as another schoolmaster. Nor, indeed, did it prove any exception to the failing of schoolmasters at large—that of becoming an intellectual tyrant whose domination of the pupil lingers on long after the pupil has left school" (D. W. Gundry, "The Ghost in the Machine and the Body of the Resurrection," *Scottish Journal of Theology* 18, no. 2 [June 1965]: 164).

The popular view of man's immortal soul has replaced the resurrection as ground of comfort in actual practice, according to several writers. See James J. Heller, "The Resurrection of Man," *Theology Today* 15, no. 2 (July 1958): 217-218; Hans Hofmann, "Immortality or Life," *Theology Today* 15, no. 2 (July 1958): 231; Gundry, "Ghost in the Machine," p. 169; Joseph Blenkinsopp, "Theological Synthesis and Hermeneutical Conclusions," *Immortality and Resurrection*, p. 119; Helmut Thielicke, *Death and Life*, pp. 197-199. Herhold looks at the modern rash of testimonies about "after-death experiences" and comments: "One does not need Easter if the spirit or soul is immortal. But it is precisely because 'when you're dead, you're dead' that the resurrection is such incredibly good news" (Robert M. Herhold, "Kübler-Ross and Life after Death," *Christian Century*, 14 April 1976, p. 364).

20. Oscar Cullmann, *Immortality of the Soul or Resurrection of the Dead? The Witness of the New Testament*, pp. 19-39; Murray Harris, "Resurrection and Immortality: Eight Theses," *Themelios* 1, no. 2 (Spring 1976): 50-55.

21. A Lutheran philosopher critiques the arguments of Plato (pp. 113-118), Aquinas (pp. 119-126) and Kant (pp. 126-132) for immortality and finds them all wanting (Bruce R. Reichenbach, *Is Man the Phoenix?*).

22. If Froom attributes Augustine's dualistic view of man to Plato, so his critics might trace Aquinas' monistic view to Aristotle. Both Greek philosophy and medieval scholasticism encompassed much. It is a form of "grandstanding" to ignore the philosophical precedents of one's own position while charging one's opponent with philosophical presuppositions. For a critique of the monistic view of man from a philosophical standpoint, see Reichenbach, *Is Man the Phoenix?* pp. 28-29.

careful to *qualify* their claim that man is immortal.[23] His immortality, they say, means that something about him survives physical death and ensures a life beyond the grave. They emphasize that he is not immortal in the same way God is. For man's immortality was a gift from his Creator—and that same Creator is at perfect liberty to require it back again! Man is immortal or "deathless," they say, in the sense that physical death will not be his final end. But that does not mean he is inherently indestructible.

Just as Christian advocates of general immortality have qualified their view by saying that *God* can annihilate the soul, so Christian "mortalists" have recognized that God can grant deathlessness and incorruptibility to any person He wishes. In the view of the first, the final annihilation of the wicked is possible—if God so wills. In the view of the second, the eternal preservation of the wicked is possible —if God so wishes. The crucial question does not really concern man's natural mortality or immortality, therefore, for both sides concede the ultimate point to the greater sovereignty of God. The issue really becomes a matter of exegesis. Since God is *able* to preserve or to destroy His human creature, what does Scripture *indicate* that He *will* do to those He finally expels to hell?

Misunderstanding and overstatement have also frequently clouded the historical picture. As a matter of fact, the immortality of the soul has *not* been the universal faith of the church. It has always been questioned by some of her faithful children, as Froom clearly documents and other conditionalists have shown. It was championed, however, by the Roman Catholic tradition and, later, by the Calvinist. Today the doctrine is under attack in both those houses as well[24] —not in the name of science or philosophy but, as the direct result of intensified work in biblical theology, in the name of purifying the stream of tradition from pollutants which for nearly two millennia

---

23. One theologian who identified himself as a "convinced evolutionist" recently argued that man's immortality is not a "borrowed existence" but a "bestowed existence," affirming that "something bestowed is bestowed forever" (Pére S. Dockx, "Man's Eschatological Condition," *Scottish Journal of Theology* 27, no. 1 [February 1974]: 26).

Origen is also an exception to this general rule. He proposed the eternality of souls, including their pre-existence, and reasoned to the ultimate restoration of all men. This view was condemned under Pope Vigilius in 543 according to M. E. Williams, "Immortality of Human Soul," *New Catholic Encyclopedia*, 12:468-469.

24. See Calvinist sources in notes 11, 32, 43-44 among others. Roman Catholic critics of natural immortality include the following: André-Marie Dubarle, "Belief in Immortality in the Old Testament and Judaism," *Immortality and Resurrection*, pp. 37-38; S. B. Marrow and M. E. Williams, in articles under "Soul" and "Immortality," *New Catholic Encyclopedia*.

have slushed into its waters from philosophical factories which line its shore. Furthermore, a great portion of the Protestant world has roots in another view of man which does not insist on his native immortality at all. That includes the Lutheran, Anglican and Anabaptist traditions, which all either sprang from or have from earliest times included the outlook known as "Christian mortalism."[25]

The Biblical View of Man

The Western church—along with the larger culture—bears the unmistakable stamp of the philosophies of ancient Greece and Rome. Biblical scholars continue to identify these alien traces in the theological current and attempt to distinguish them from what is authentic and pure. The nature of man has become a kind of focal point in that enterprise.

Measured by the systematic and analytical standards of Greek philosophy, the Bible meets us here with what one writer has called a "resounding silence."[26] What it does say is often presented as the exact antithesis to "the Greek view," and writers regularly talk of "the Hebrew view" as if the term had a clear and single meaning.[27] Careful scholars have criticized such oversimplifications.[28] They remind us of

---

25. The term belongs to Norman T. Burns, *Christian Mortalism from Tyndale to Milton,* and is the generic description for "the belief that according to divine revelation the soul does not exist as an independent, conscious substance after the death of the body" (p. 13). Burns points out a general confusion of two incompatible types of mortalism by many authors, and he distinguishes between them. "Annihilationists" deny a resurrection of the body, while "soul sleepers" believe in a resurrection which will include the personal soul as well as body (p. 13). The latter ground is further divided between those who hold that man's whole being dies together and those who say he has a personal soul which does not die but sleeps until the resurrection (pp. 13-14).

This same confusion is evident in much traditionalist literature concerning final punishment when Jehovah's Witnesses (who deny that the wicked will be raised) are put in the same basket with Seventh-day Adventists (and others who affirm a resurrection of just and unjust with the ultimate annihilation of the wicked).

26. Milton McC. Gatch, *Death: Meaning and Mortality in Christian Thought and Contemporary Culture,* p. 35.

27. H. Wheeler Robinson, for example, comments concerning the view of certain church fathers: 'This doctrine of resurrection, a common article of the Church's faith, shews the Hebrew parentage of the anthropology of the Church, just as the conception of immortality is largely due to Greek influences" (H. Wheeler Robinson, *The Christian Doctrine of Man,* p. 170).

28. Notably James Barr, *Old and New in Interpretation* (London: SCM Press, 1966), p. 39. Acknowledging this criticism, George Eldon Ladd "deliberately" speaks of "the Greek view" in spite of Barr's objection. He justifies this designation for Platonic dualism in terms of its later

the rich diversity of thought found among "the Greeks" as well as "the Hebrews," particularly at the beginning of the Christian era.[29]

Many evangelical scholars, too, now suggest that traditional orthodoxy has passed lightly over the textual evidence about man. They charge that the church has often drawn conclusions in haste and has frequently overgeneralized in stating them. They point out that while man is made in God's image (Gen. 1:27), immortality is no more an essential quality of God than omnipotence or omniscience, yet no one has considered these to be inherent in the creature man. They note that even if the image of God included immortality, that might have been lost with the fall, for Adam "begat a son in *his own* likeness, after *his* image" (Gen. 5:3).

The tree of life represented immortality in fellowship with God; but sin brought death, and man was cast out of the garden. So far as man becoming a "living soul," they note that the identical Hebrew words are translated "living creature" in the same context (Gen. 2:19; 9:12) and are applied to brute animals. Furthermore, the man who *became* a living soul was told that if he disobeyed God, he would surely die.

---

influence on Christian theology. For an excellent discussion of the Platonic attitude over against the biblical (if not always "Hebrew" or "Jewish") outlook, see George Eldon Ladd, *The Pattern of New Testament Truth,* especially the chapter entitled "The Background of the Pattern."

29. "It is indefensible to assert that Christianity owes its doctrine of resurrection to Jewish thought but its concept of immortality to Greek philosophy," says Murray Harris. He cites the variety of thought found in Jewish literature between the Testaments, some of which we will consider later in detail (Harris, "Resurrection and Immortality," p. 52).

We recognize the diversity of Jewish thought concerning man and his destiny, and acknowledge the validity of the objection that "the Hebrew view" is often grossly oversimplified and unfairly singularized. At the same time, one *might* speak of "the Hebrew view" and mean only "the *biblical* view" given by revelation of God. Insofar as "the Hebrew view" includes elements borrowed from Greek philosophy which are alien to the canonical Scriptures, it is to that extent distinguishable from "the Hebrew view" as here defined. Judaic literature of the intertestamental period and thereafter often reflects "the Greek view" even if the hands which composed it coursed with Hebrew blood!

Nevertheless, it is easy to overstate conclusions and oversimplify the material. Traditionalist writers have frequently done this in assuming that Jesus endorsed by His relative silence the Pharisees' belief in the immortality of the soul. Jewish thought of Jesus' time is then represented as having only two strains—outright Platonic dualism (held by the Pharisees) and utter materialism (held by the Sadducees). Since the Gospels record Jesus' rejection of the Sadducees' doctrine, it is assumed that He agreed with the Pharisees instead. Such reasoning overlooks the rich diversity of Jewish thought now illustrated in the sources. It also proves more than orthodox theologians would wish to affirm! Josephus may indicate a Pharisaic belief in transmigration of souls, and Pusey says that "there would have been no reason to think him wrong. The question of the disciples, 'Did this man sin or his parents, that he was born blind?' implies some such belief (as S. Cyril of Alexandria also thinks)" (Pusey, *What Is of Faith?* p. 69).

Jesus' quotation of the declaration, "I am the God of Abraham, the God of Isaac, and the God of Jacob" (Matt. 22:32), has often been used in support of man's immortality. Staunch conservatives have noted, however, that Jesus uses the quotation to prove, not immortality, but the resurrection![30] The Lukan parallel (Luke 20:37, 38) says that "to Him all are alive," but both the context and the argument point to the resurrection of those who belong to God, not the immortality of every person.[31] When the Bible speaks of the "salvation of the soul" and equivalent expressions (e.g., Mark 8:35ff; Heb. 10:39, KJV; 1 Pet. 1:9), it is simply quoting such passages as Psalms 16:9-11, 49:15 and 73:24, in which the psalmist expresses his hope for abiding fellowship with God, who will not let His own perish. 'The 'soul' . . . does not stand in dualistic contrast to the body, but signifies man himself whom God seeks and saves for life eternal."[32] The *soul*, for New Testament writers as well as Old, generally stands for "the natural life of man . . . in his limitedness and humanity over against the divine possibilities and realities."[33]

Man in the Old Testament. Man is described as a "soul" (Hebrew: *nephesh*; Greek: *psychē*) something over 150 times in the Old Testament and about 16 times in the New. The Old Testament displays *nephesh* in such a rainbow of shades that English translators have rendered it 45 different ways![34] God forms Adam of dust, breathes into him "breath of life," and he *becomes* a "living soul." We use the same kind of language when we say that a man or animal *is* a conscious being and also *has* conscious being.[35]

The Old Testament applies the same terms to both man and the

---

30. Orr, *The Resurrection of Jesus*, p. 283.

31. Harold E. Guillebaud, *The Righteous Judge: A Study of the Biblical Doctrine of Everlasting Punishment*, p. 3.

32. Karel Hanhart, *The Intermediate State in the New Testament*, pp. 238-239.

33. Herman Ridderbos, *Paul: An Outline of His Theology*, p. 120. See also pp. 549-550.

34. Basil F. C. Atkinson, *Life and Immortality: An Examination of the Nature and Meaning of Life and Death as They Are Revealed in the Scriptures*, p. 3. Atkinson was an Under-Librarian at the University Library (Cambridge) from 1925 to 1960 and was renowned in evangelical circles as leader of devotional Bible readings. This book, though small, makes an exhaustive study of the biblical usages of words involved in four topics. The topics are the heads of Atkinson's chapters: 'The Nature of Man," "Rest and Darkness," "Resurrection and Glory" and 'The Doom of the Lost." Atkinson probes deeply and thoroughly, and reaches conditionalist conclusions.

35. Ibid., p. 2.

animals. This is true of *nephesh*/soul-life (Gen. 9:5), *ruach*/spirit-breath (Gen. 6:17) and *neshamah*/spirit (Gen. 7:22). "Soul" is the most comprehensive term for man in his wholeness, and its meanings range from "neck," "life," "self" and "person" to what seems the opposite of life, "corpse" (Num. 19:31).[36]

'The soul is not only the upholder of certain states; it is the full soul-substance with special qualities and powers."[37] It "is man himself viewed as a living creature."[38] Wolff breaks down the Old Testament view of man in his wholeness according to its primary terms. *Soul* speaks of "needy man," *flesh* is "man in his infirmity," *spirit* points to "man as he is empowered," and *heart* signifies "reasonable man."[39] Nikolainen summarized the Old Testament's wholistic anthropology like this:

> Man is an indivisible whole. Seen from different points of view, he is by turns body, flesh and blood, soul, spirit, and heart. Each of these portrays a specific human characteristic, but they are not parts into which man may be divided. Body is man as a concrete being; "flesh and blood" is man as a creature distinguished from the Creator; soul is the living human individual; spirit is man as having his source in God; heart is man as a whole in action. What is distinctively human is in every respect derived from God. Man is in every cell the work of God (body), he is in all circumstances the property of God (soul), he is absolutely dependent on God (spirit), and in all his activity he is either obedient to God or disobedient (heart). The God-relationship is not merely the life of the "highest part" of man. The whole man "from top to bottom" exists only by relation to God.[40]

---

36. Heller, 'The Resurrection of Man," pp. 220-221. The Authorized Version has man become a 'living soul" in Genesis 2:7 but translates the exact same Hebrew phrase 'living creature" in verse 14, where it is applied to the animals. Norman Snaith calls this "most reprehensible" and says "it is a grave reflection on the Revisers that they retained this misleading difference in translation. . . . The Hebrew phrase should be translated exactly the same way in both cases. To do otherwise is to mislead all those who do not read Hebrew. There is no excuse and no proper defense. The tendency to read 'immortal soul' into the Hebrew *nephesh* and translate accordingly is very ancient, and can be seen in the Septuagint rendering of Leviticus 24:18, where the Greek translators omitted the word" (Norman Snaith, "Justice and Immortality," *Scottish Journal of Theology* 17, no. 3 [September 1964]: 312-313).

37. Johannes Pedersen, *Israel: Its Life and Culture*, 1-2:152.

38. Ladd, *New Testament Truth*, p. 37.

39. Hans Walter Wolff, *Anthropology of the Old Testament*, Table of Contents.

40. T. A. Kantonen (*The Christian Hope* [1954], pp. 30ff) so summarizes Aimo Nikolainen's 1941 Finnish-language study, *Man in the Light of the Gospel*. Quoted here from Heller, 'The Resurrection of Man," p. 222.

All these details lead to a single conclusion.

> When *death* occurs, then it is the soul that is deprived of life. Death cannot strike the body or any other part of the soul without striking the entirety of the soul. . . . It is deliberately said both that the soul dies (Judg. 16,30; Num. 23,10 et al.), that it is destroyed or consumed (Ez. 22,25.27), and that it is extinguished (Job 11,20).[41]

This is the consistent witness of the Old Testament.

Man in the New Testament. The New Testament does not take a different view of the matter. Paul uses "soul" (*psyche*) only 13 times, usually with reference to the natural life of man. The adjectival form of this word designates the unspiritual or carnal man as opposed to the spiritual man (1 Cor. 2:14ff), or the natural body of the present life in contrast to the spiritual body of the life to come (1 Cor. 15:44).

Every expression of hope after death, of vindication beyond the present life, or of communion with God beyond the grave is, for biblical writers throughout, grounded on the faithfulness of the living God, who has shown Himself so true in life and will certainly not forsake His own people in death. David expects to "dwell in the house of the Lord forever" for the very same reason he anticipates "goodness and love all the days" of his earthly life (Ps. 23:6). That reason is the fidelity he has always seen in God, who keeps covenant, not any death-proof substance he discovers in his own self. Like Jesus (Luke 23:46), Stephen (Acts 7:59) and Paul (2 Tim. 1:12), the Christian believer's hope is in the faithfulness of his Creator (1 Pet. 4:19), who is able to raise the dead (Rom. 4:17; 1 Pet. 1:21).

Reichenbach probes into man's nature in *Is Man the Phoenix?* He finds Adam's race, like Mr. Kurtz in Conrad's *Heart of Darkness*, to be made of dirt. He concludes that "the doctrine that man as a person does not die . . . is apparently contrary to the teachings of Scrip-

---

41. Pedersen, *Israel*, p. 179. Froom quotes part of Pedersen's statement here as evidence that in the Old Testament view "the soul dies." Yet one wonders if Froom is reading Pedersen with Greek eyes himself. Pedersen says earlier: 'This does not mean that *nephesh* means life or soul interchangeably; still less does it mean, as has been maintained, that *nephesh* does not mean soul at all, but only life. . . . But the fact is that soul as well as life with the Israelites means something else than it usually does with us" (p. 152). Pedersen seems to say that, given the Hebrews' wholistic view of man, it was natural that they should speak of "the soul" dying; he is not taking sides on whether or not "the soul" (in a dualistic or Platonic sense) either can or does "die."

ture. . . . There is no hint that the only thing spoken about is the destruction of the physical organism, and that the real person, the soul, does not die but lives on."[42] Donald Bloesch underscores this conclusion. "There is no inherent immortality of the soul. The person who dies, even the one who dies in Christ, undergoes the death of both body and soul."[43]

Anthony Hoekema says that "we cannot point to any inherent quality in man or in any aspect of man which makes him indestructible."[44] F. F. Bruce warns that "our traditional thinking about the 'never-dying soul,' which owes so much to our Graeco-Roman heritage, makes it difficult for us to appreciate Paul's point of view."[45] Helmut Thielicke tells us that Paul speaks of no "immortal substance which would victoriously break through our mortal fate." Our hope is altogether in God, he continues. And "God has given us the hope that on the other side of the great fissure he continues to be Lord and does not allow his history to be ruptured, that he is for us a God of life and resurrection, that he remains the Creator *ex nihilo* — and his initial installment of this hope is the Spirit (2 Cor. 5:5)."[46]

Murray Harris offers eight theses concerning resurrection and immortality. He concludes: "Man is not immortal because he possesses

---

42. Reichenbach, *Is Man the Phoenix?* p. 54.

43. Donald G. Bloesch, *Essentials of Evangelical Theology,* 2:188.

44. Hoekema, *The Bible and the Future,* p. 90.

45. F. F. Bruce, "Paul on Immortality," *Scottish Journal of Theology* 24, no. 4 (November 1971): 469. The quotation appears also in F. F. Bruce, *Paul: Apostle of the Heart Set Free,* p. 311.

46. Thielicke, *Death and Life,* p. 133. Thielicke puts anthropology and soteriology under the same microscope, compares them side by side, then contrasts Luther's strain with the Roman Catholic strain. Luther saw man in need of God's constant creative gift of life—and of imputed righteousness by grace through faith. Rome pictured man as having immortality in his own soul—and receiving an infused righteousness and grace in himself. Thielicke comments: "Just as no creature on the level of death and life has any inherent qualitative immortality, so also on the level of sin and justification no man has inherent qualitative righteousness" (p. 107). Later he writes that "both righteousness and *zōē* [life] remain exclusively at God's disposal and that I participate in them only to the degree that fellowship with God in Christ is vouchsafed to me . . . for no intrinsic reason at all" (p. 197).

Here, he says, "the reformers' biblical understanding of justification reaches, as it were, its high point. Just as I stand with empty hands before God and remain standing, just as I can only beseech God nevertheless to accept me, in just this fashion do I move into my death with empty hands and without any death-proof substance in my soul, but only with my gaze focused on God's hand and with the petition on my lips, 'Hand that will last, hold thou me fast!' . . . I remain in fellowship with him who is Alpha and Omega, and with this knowledge I walk into the night of death, truly the darkest night; yet I know who awaits me in the morning" (pp. 198-199). Calvin's predisposition toward the immortality of the soul prevented him from making this connection between man's nature and his salvation.

or is a soul. He becomes immortal because God transforms him by raising him from the dead." Platonic thought made immortality "an inalienable attribute of the soul," he goes on. "But the Bible contains no definition of the soul's constitution that implies its indestructibility."[47]

The late apologist and theologian, Edward John Carnell, cut through the humanist's optimism, the scholastic's tradition and the philosopher's wisdom to focus on man before God—man as *creature*, man as *sinner*. He stood on the solid rock of biblical faith, surrounded by the best of orthodoxy's heritage, when he concluded:

> Instead of teaching that man is of such infinitely incontestable value, that God, to be worthy of His name, must preserve him immortally, the Christian follows Paul's judgment that there is none righteous, no not one (Romans 3:10). Man, then, deserves *death*, not life. The Christian cannot appeal to the rationality of the universe, for all rationality is from God. He cannot claim an independent rule of goodness and justice to assure him of life, for all goodness and justice flow from God. In short, the Christian knows that man, a vile, wretched, filthy sinner, will receive immortal life solely and only by God's grace; man neither deserves immortality nor is worthy of it. Unless He that made man sovereignly elects to give him salvation and life, by grace and not by works, man is absolutely without hope. Man came into this world naked and it is certain that he will depart in exactly the same manner; and He Who gave life in the first place can also recall it either to damnation, blessedness, or annihilation.[48]

---

47. Harris, "Resurrection and Immortality," p. 53.
48. Edward John Carnell, *An Introduction to Christian Apologetics*, pp. 344-345.

5

"The Soul Is Immortal, But . . . " (The Philosophers versus the Fathers)

Many Christian writers through the centuries have spoken of man's "immortal soul." In the last chapter we remarked in passing that such theologians generally have not meant that the soul is "immortal" in an absolute sense. There was a time, they say, when it did not exist. They further acknowledge that a time could come when it will cease to exist—unless God sustains it of His own will. This chapter will take a closer look at that distinction—and its implications regarding eternal punishment.

The immortality of the soul was a principal doctrine of the Greek philosopher, Plato, who was born about the time the last Old Testament book was being written.[1] In Plato's thinking, the soul (or *psychē*) was self-moving and indivisible or "simple." Ungenerated and eternal, it existed before the body it inhabited, and it would survive the body as well. To be apart from the body was the soul's nat-

---

1. See any standard sourcebook of philosophy. Reformed author, Anthony A. Hoekema, recently wrote: "It should first be noted that the idea of the immortality of the soul (namely, that after the body dies the soul or immaterial aspect of man continues to exist) is not a concept peculiar to Christianity. . . . The concept of the immortality of the soul was developed in the mystery religions of ancient Greece, and was given philosophical expression in the writings of Plato (427-347 B.C.)" (Anthony A. Hoekema, *The Bible and the Future*, p. 86).

ural and proper state; to be imprisoned in a body was its punishment for faults committed during a previous incarnation.[2]

Plato came to these conclusions by several roads. One line of argument explained his peculiar theory of knowledge. All education, he said, is actually *reminiscence*. When men think they are learning, the soul is really *recalling* something it has known from a previous existence. If this is true, the soul must have its own life independent of its successive bodies. Plato gave this "likely account" of affairs, modestly acknowledging that "the greatness of the subject and the weakness of man" prohibited certainty.[3] His teaching about the soul was given to illustrate his other principles. He did not intend to be taken literally but taught that "about the other world or worlds we can speak for the most part only in figure or allegory."[4] But Plato's successors—like those of many another great thinker—literalized and systematized what he had said. Along the way, they somehow lost all the "disarming tentativeness"[5] of Plato's original dialogues.

Many Christian writers of the second and third centuries wanted to show their pagan neighbors the reasonableness of the biblical faith. They did it the same way the Jewish apologist, Philo of Alexandria,[6] had done long before. They wrapped their understanding of Scripture in the robes of philosophy, choosing from the vocabulary of worldly wisdom the words which sparkled and adorned it best. Paul had often warned against contemporary philosophy (1 Cor. 1:19–

---

2. I. C. Brady, "Soul, Human, Immortality of," *New Catholic Encyclopedia*, 13:464. The argument, made by Gregory of Nyssa and others (Brady, "Soul, Human, Immortality of," p. 465), that the soul is immortal because it is a simple and not composite substance and therefore cannot suffer disintegration comes from later Platonists and not the master himself, according to Leonard Hodgson. Hodgson also says that Plato did not originate the later idea that the body was evil or the source of evil (Leonard Hodgson, "Life after Death: The Philosophers Plato and Kant," *Expository Times*, January 1965, p. 108).

3. Brady quotes these words from the *Phaedo* (107A) (Brady, "Soul, Human, Immortality of," p. 464).

4. E. G. Selwyn, "Image, Fact and Faith," *New Testament Studies* 1, no. 4 (May 1955): 238; Milton McC. Gatch, *Death: Meaning and Mortality in Christian Thought and Contemporary Culture*, p. 32.

5. Gatch, *Death*, p. 32.

6. In response to objections from some who minimized Philo's influence on the church fathers, Harry A. Wolfson refers to evidence in his book, *The Philosophy of the Church Fathers*. He then adds: "Whether even without Philo the Fathers of the Church would have attempted to harmonize Scripture and philosophy is a plausible assumption. Whether the result of their harmonization would have been the same as it is now is a matter of conjecture. But it happens that Philo came before them and it also happens that all kinds of evidence show the influence of Philo upon them" (Harry A. Wolfson, "Notes on Patristic Philosophy," *Harvard Theological Review* 57, no. 2 [April 1964]: 124).

2:5; Col. 2:1-10), but these apologists, zealous for their new-found faith, set out to battle the pagan thinkers on their own turf.

They freely borrowed the Platonic conception of the soul, the chief characteristic being its separability from the body.[7] When these Christian defenders argued for the resurrection and last judgment, they often used the pagan doctrine of immortality to show that these things were not "logically absurd."[8]

Over and over, however, the Christian writers distinguished their concept of the soul's "immortality" from that held by some contemporary Platonist philosophers. The soul is not *inherently* immortal, insisted the fathers. It had a *beginning*—from God. And though it survives the death of the body, its *future* existence also depends entirely on God's will.[9] Even Origen[10] and Augustine,[11] who did sometimes speak of the soul's *natural* immortality, made this distinction clear. Others, like Justin Martyr and his pupil Tatian,[12] viewed the pagan doctrine of immortality as a challenge to the resurrection and fought against it openly.[13]

---

7. Harry A. Wolfson, "Immortality and Resurrection in the Philosophy of the Church Fathers," *Immortality and Resurrection*, p. 79.

8. Ibid., pp. 90-91; Brady, "Soul, Human, Immortality of," p. 464.

9. See Wolfson's "Immortality and Resurrection" for detailed quotations and references in support of this thesis. Included are Justin Martyr (*Dialogue with Trypho* 5), Irenaeus (*Against Heresies* 2. 34. 4), Tatian (*Oration to the Greeks* 13), Theophilus (*Ad Autol.* 2. 27; 2. 24) as well as the undisputed conditionalists, Arnobius and Lactantius (Wolfson, "Immortality and Resurrection," p. 57).

10. Robert L. Wilken, "The Immortality of the Soul and Christian Hope," *Dialog* 15, no. 2 (Spring 1976): 114. A debate continues whether or not Origen was consistent in this position. Wolfson says he was ("Notes on Patristic Philosophy," pp. 125ff) in response to critics of the opposing view. Consistent or not, both sides seem agreed that Origen conceded God the right to destroy the soul. His remark that the soul cannot have "essential" (*substantialis*) corruption means, according to Wolfson, "that the soul, having been created by God as partaking of his own nature, will not be destroyed by God; it does not mean that God could not destroy it, if he so willed" (Wolfson, "Immortality and Resurrection," pp. 59-60).

11. Wolfson, "Immortality and Resurrection," p. 60. Froom makes Augustine a thoroughgoing Platonist and says that in Augustine "Immortal-Soulism reached the high-water mark of post-Nicene times" (LeRoy Edwin Froom, *The Conditionalist Faith of Our Fathers*, 1:1073).

12. Jaroslav Pelikan, *The Shape of Death: Life, Death, and Immortality in the Early Fathers*, pp. 14, 21-22.

13. Although popular books often cite Arnobius as a father of the conditionalist position on hell, he actually said very little on final punishment. His primary thrust was directed against the Platonic world-view as such, especially its anthropology. We will discuss his writing about hell in a following chapter.

The Neo-Platonism which formed the backdrop for the fathers of the fourth and fifth centuries was itself in a state of flux. Its fundamental problem was to "locate the soul metaphysically by defining its relation on the one hand to the visible world which it inhabits, and, on the other hand, to the intelligible world, the intellectual substance, with which it is

Sometimes these ancient writers gave theological reasons for man's immortality. Ignatius saw it as the abolition of the punishment of sin, Irenaeus as the restoration of human destiny, Tertullian as the vindication of God's justice.[14]

Participants in the discussion about final punishment have often waged fierce debate regarding the precise sense the fathers attached to the immortality of the soul. Froom and other conditionalists dogmatically insist that the earliest fathers all rejected innate immortality. Pusey argues just as passionately against Farrar that they espoused it.[15] Robert L. Wilken, a Lutheran professor at the University of Notre Dame and outsider to this discussion, probably sizes up the situation correctly. "The fathers," he says, "modified the notion of the immortality of the soul as it was understood within the Greek philosophical tradition. Yet, in its main lines, they adopted the idea adapting it where necessary to the requirements of Christian faith and they gave it a prominent place in Christian piety."[16]

In later chapters we will look closely at what church fathers and theologians through the centuries actually said about final punish-

---

naturally affiliated" (R. A. Norris, *Manhood and Christ: A Study in the Christology of Theodore of Mopsuestia*, p. 13). Norris warns against the tendency to equate every dualistic statement of the fathers with "Platonism," showing that Platonism of the period included both dualistic and monistic elements which were never fully reconciled (pp. 14-16). At the same time, he stresses that "Christian theology of the fourth and fifth centuries owed to Middle Platonic and Neo-Platonic thought much of the conceptual structure in terms of which it interpreted the Church's gospel." He also notes that "the presuppositions of this philosophical outlook" became, "whether in a disguised or an explicit fashion, part of the framework of Christian theological discussion" (p. 18).

Gatch observes that a contemporary issue within Platonism of the time was the question whether or not the soul was created (Gatch, *Death*, p. 195). The inconsistency which even a created "immortal soul" posed for the biblical view of man was felt by the fathers, says Norris, who adds that "no patristic thinker of this period is willing to pursue the logic of the philosophical tradition which he had inherited to its normal conclusion" (Norris, *Manhood and Christ*, pp. 18-19).

14. This summary comes from Marjorie Suchocki, "The Question of Immortality," *Journal of Religion* 57, no. 3 (July 1977): 294, who offers process theology as a fitting modernization of the biblical and patristic hope. We appreciate her capsuled insight into these three writers but disagree completely with her primary point.

The statements above from Norris, Wolfson and Gatch represent a refinement in patristic studies, since even H. Wheeler Robinson overlooks the distinction they make between the fathers and the philosophers (H. Wheeler Robinson, *The Christian Doctrine of Man*, pp. 169-170). Froom also would profit from these works for the same reason.

15. Froom, *Conditionalist Faith*, 1:757-927; Edward Bouverie Pusey, *What Is of Faith as to Everlasting Punishment? In Reply to Dr. Farrar's Challenge in His "Eternal Hope," 1879*, pp. 172-177.

16. Wilken, "Immortality of the Soul," p. 114.

ment. We will also examine why they said what they did—so far as they state the basis of their conclusions. Because of his influence on later Christian orthodoxy, Augustine gets a special look in an appendix at the end. The same is true of John Calvin.

Here we simply observe that the church fathers, without important exception, stressed that man's immortality is *derived*, not *inherent*, and that the future continuance of his "immortal soul" rests entirely in the hands of God, who made him. So far as the end of the wicked is concerned, *that* is the important consideration.

Immortality and the Reformation: A (Theological) Tug of (Sectarian) War

Whenever one attempts to describe the thinking of people who lived in a distant time, he faces a special danger. Unless he exercises great care, one easily yields to the temptation to smooth over the rough spots of diversity in his data, painting a more uniform picture which tends toward his own point of view. As one reads the literature concerning final punishment, he frequently finds such "polished" accounts of thought in various periods. The thought of every major time-slot is disputed—from Old Testament teaching, intertestamental, the first century, the apostolic fathers, the formative Latin authors and the Reformers. At the same time, if one can keep his head and dodge the whizzing bullets as he walks through these embattled fields, he will also hear some harmonious notes.

The immortality of the soul was a matter of great interest during the sixteenth and seventeenth centuries. The fortunes of this doctrine among the reforming churches make a fascinating tale. We will be aware of the danger of oversimplifying the material as we relate the high points of that story now.

Luther. Luther said little about man's supposed natural immortality or about his "soul" as a separable part of his being. He wrote on many occasions of death as a "sleep." Between death and resurrection, Luther pictured the deceased as having no consciousness of anything—although this sleep was sweet and peaceful for the righteous. In the resurrection, believers would hear Christ's gentle voice calling them and arise. Their period of death would then seem only a moment, as when one falls asleep at night and "instantly" wakes to find the morning.[17]

In keeping with this view of man—totally dependent on God for his existence day by day—Luther rejected the philosophical doctrine of the soul's innate immortality. In one vehement outburst against Roman traditions, following a public burning of his books, Luther classed the immortality of the soul among the "monstrous fables that form part of the Roman dunghill of decretals."[18]

Tyndale. When Sir Thomas More attacked Luther's teaching of "soul-sleeping," William Tyndale came to the Reformer's defense in England. "The true faith," Tyndale wrote, "putteth the resurrection, which we be warned to look for every hour. The heathen philosophers, denying that, did put that the souls did ever live. And the pope joineth the spiritual doctrine of Christ and the fleshly doctrine of philosophers together; things so contrary that they cannot agree,

---

17. Luther's statements about soul-sleeping include the following: "We should learn to view our death [as] . . . a fine, sweet and brief sleep, which brings us release from . . . all the misfortunes of this life, and we shall be secure and without care, rest sweetly and gently for a brief moment, as on a sofa, until the time when he shall call and awaken us together with all his dear children to his eternal glory and joy" (*A Compend of Luther's Theology*, p. 242). "We Christians . . . should train and accustom ourselves in faith to despise death and regard it as a deep, strong, sweet, sleep; to consider the coffin as nothing other than a soft couch of ease or rest" (*Works of Martin Luther*, 6:287-288). One of Luther's most tender statements is worded in very personal terms: "For just as one who falls asleep and reaches morning unexpectedly when he awakes, without knowing what has happened to him, so we shall suddenly rise on the last day without knowing how we have come into death and through death. . . . We shall sleep until He comes and knocks on the little grave and says, Doctor Martin, get up! Then I shall rise in a moment and be happy with Him forever" (quoted by T. A. Kantonen, *The Christian Hope*, p. 37). All the above quotations are documented by Froom, *Conditionalist Faith*, 2:74-77; similar ones are given in Norman T. Burns, *Christian Mortalism from Tyndale to Milton*, pp. 28-32.

Without noting any of these statements, Donald G. Bloesch quotes Luther's commentary on Genesis that "the soul does *not* sleep but is awake and enjoys the vision of angels and of God, and has converse with them" (Donald G. Bloesch, *Essentials of Evangelical Theology*, 2:205, note 32).

18. On June 15, 1520, Pope Leo X issued the bull entitled *Exsurge Domine*, condemning 41 theses from Luther's writings as "heretical or scandalous or false, or offensive to pious ears, or dangerous to simple minds, or subversive of catholic truth." The document was published in Germany that September, and Luther was given 60 days to recant under threat of excommunication. When Aleander and Eck, prominent Catholic adversaries, ceremoniously burned Luther's offending works, the Reformer replied in kind. He burned the papal bull outside the gates of Wittenberg on December 10, 1520 and issued four works (two in Latin, two in German) defending his condemned propositions. This quotation is taken from the Latin reply of November 29, 1520, entitled "Assertion of All Articles Wrongly Condemned in the Roman Bull." The actual Latin said: " . . . *omnia illa infinita portenta in romano sterquilinio Decretorum*," as quoted by Emmanuel Pétavel, *The Problem of Immortality*, p. 255. The historical account and a translation of one of the German responses are found in Martin Luther, *Luther's Works*, vol. 32, *Career of the Reformer, II*.

no more than the Spirit and the flesh do in a Christian man. And because the fleshly-minded pope consenteth unto heathen doctrine, therefore he corrupteth the scripture to stablish it."[19]

Although the moderate reforms of the English church left much of the Roman doctrine untouched, including the immortality of the soul, Christian mortalism was preached to the people of Protestant England from the earliest times. Although established churchmen denounced this teaching, they "rarely examined the concept on its theological merits and only occasionally and superficially considered the scriptural arguments on which it was based."[20]

Anabaptists. The term "Anabaptist" is a very general description which is applied to a wide diversity of Reformation Christians who rejected the state churches of Luther and Calvin. Modern Baptists are among their descendants, as are the various Mennonites, some of the Brethren churches and still other smaller groups. The designation "Anabaptists" was given by their opponents and meant "rebaptizers," based on the practice of establishing churches of believers who were baptized (often but not always by immersion) upon a profession of faith. They differed from the Lutherans and Calvinists also in their attitude toward the state (taxes and war) and the relationship the church should have to both government and society in general.

It is not surprising that these Anabaptists should be more open to new ideas—and to question the established doctrines of those around them. They stressed the authority of the Word of God apart from creeds and confessions of faith. They also championed the right of each individual to study the Scriptures himself, relying on the Holy Spirit alone for guidance in understanding.

Whatever the benefits or abuses attached to these views, they nevertheless encouraged a willingness to question the established ideas. One of the inherited views they questioned was the immortality of the soul. Along with this, many Anabaptists held conditionalist views about final punishment. These minority ideas were perpetuated in England in the seventeenth century by many of the General (Arminian) Baptists. Yet while "the soul-sleeping view was reasonably common in sectarian circles during the first century of the English Reformation, it remained a decidedly minority view which most

---

19. Quoted by Burns, *Christian Mortalism*, p. 101; Froom, *Conditionalist Faith*, 2:94.
20. Burns, *Christian Mortalism*, p. 99.

churchmen . . . did not examine on its own merits."[21]

Calvin. The Anabaptists met perhaps their most furious opponent in John Calvin, who was especially vehement in his denunciation of the "Anabaptist" doctrine of "soul-sleeping." Calvin felt this called the hope of eternal life into question, and he attacked soul-sleeping with special passion in his first theological book, *Psychopannychia*.[22] Quistorp almost understates the case in saying that this essay "is distinguished by the special acrimony of his polemic against the Anabaptists."[23] Calvin outlined this work in 1534 and published it in 1542. Because of the influence of Calvin's position in the Protestant church, and because his *Psychopannychia* reveals so much of his mind on the matter, a separate review of the work is included at the end of this book.

Although Calvin and Luther differed on the soul's state after death, Calvin's intense zeal outweighed Luther's depth of commitment. It is the distinct contribution of Norman T. Burns that he has detailed the way Luther's opinion was conceded, in the interests of Reformed unity, to the hated Anabaptists. As a result, Calvin's view took the match by default to become first the dominant and then the orthodox doctrine of most established Protestant churches everywhere.[24] The doctrine of Christian mortalism, held by Luther in Germany and Tyndale in England, finally was rejected out of hand because of its association in the popular mind with the despised Anabaptists. Burns writes:

> When the Lutheran reformers failed to give vigorous support to psychopannychism, soul sleeping lost what small chance it might have had to be considered a debatable doctrine, a thing indifferent. Once it was identified solely with the Anabaptists, there was no hope for a hearing before respectable Protestants. . . . Unchallenged by the doctrine of a Reformation church of comparable stature, the view of the churches of Geneva and Zurich (and of Rome) on the nature of the soul had to prevail in England.[25]

---

21. Ibid., p. 192.

22. The title comes from a Greek word meaning "to be awake [or watchful] the whole night through," which represented Calvin's position against those who taught "soul-sleeping."

23. Heinrich Quistorp, *Calvin's Doctrine of the Last Things*, p. 55.

24. Burns, *Christian Mortalism*, pp. 31-33.

25. Ibid., pp. 32-33.

Heinrich Bullinger, the gifted pastor of Zurich and a man of enormous influence, linked Calvin's view with the later orthodoxy. Because of his friendship with British exiles during Mary's Catholic reign, his translated works carried much weight in England. Through the enormous influence of the Second Helvetic Confession of 1566 (which Schaff says Bullinger wrote almost single-handedly), Calvin's view was widely adopted as the authoritative standard for Reformed churches throughout the world.[26]

Calvin's "Conditional" Immortality. Calvin held that the soul received immortality from the stamp of God's image, although he agreed with the earlier apologists that the soul had a beginning. He often denigrated the body, calling it "a prison,"[27] a "rotting carcase" and even "wretched dung." Quistorp sharply criticizes Calvin's dualistic view of man as philosophical and unbiblical,[28] and Gatch says Calvin "betrays a greater concern with immortality than with the resurrection."[29] James P. Martin shares Gatch's opinion.[30] But Holwerda comes to Calvin's defense. Over and over he responds to the charge that Calvin's view of immortality overshadowed or negated the biblical hope. Holwerda does not deny that Calvin was powerfully influenced by the philosophical doctrine of the immortality of the soul. Rather, he cites passages in which Calvin rests *ultimate* hope for life and blessedness on Christ, the second advent and the resurrection to come. Whatever Calvin's roots, Holwerda insists that the fruit of his hope carried the aroma of Christ and the flavor of eschatology.[31]

For all his influence on popular piety and religious expression, however, another aspect of Calvin's doctrine of immortality matters more to our study. That is the fact that Calvin, like the fathers of the earlier centuries, expressly and repeatedly stated that the soul depends on God for its existence and that God can put it out of existence if He so desires.

---

26. Ibid., p. 25.

27. John Calvin *Institutes* 3. 9. 4.

28. Quistorp, *Calvin's Doctrine*, pp. 60, 73. He cites many such statements from Calvin.

29. Gatch, *Death*, p. 120.

30. James P. Martin, *The Last Judgment in Protestant Theology from Orthodoxy to Ritschl*, pp. 16-17.

31. David E. Holwerda, "Eschatology and History: A Look at Calvin's Eschatological Vision," *Exploring the Heritage of John Calvin*, pp. 116, 120-121, 134.

In his commentary on Psalm 103:15ff, Calvin said: "Although the soul after it has departed from the prison of the body remains alive, yet its so doing does not arise from any inherent power of its own. Were God to withdraw His grace, the soul would be nothing more than a puff or a blast, even as the body is dust; and thus there would doubtless be found in the whole man nothing but mere vanity."[32] In a sermon on 1 Timothy 1:17-19, he urged: "It behoves us to understand that our souls are not immortal of their own power, nor is the life in them enclosed in themselves, as though it had its roots there. Where is there life then? In God."[33] The soul's immortality, he said in another sermon, is *"not natural.* For whatsoever had a beginning may have an end, and may come to decay, and even perish utterly."[34]

Calvin scholars call attention to this point in the Reformer's understanding. T. F. Torrance notes that Calvin taught that the "soul survives the death of the body only at the mercy of God, and has no durability in itself."[35] He cites commentaries, sermons and other works in which Calvin stresses that the soul is as much a *creature* as the body and that both depend for their being "entirely on the grace of God."[36] According to Torrance, Calvin's view means that if God were to withdraw for even an instant the presence of His Spirit, "we would drop into the nothingness from which we are called into being." So far as Calvin is concerned, Torrance says that is "just as true of the soul of man as of his body."[37]

Quistorp, a recognized authority on Calvin's thought, quotes a sermon in which Calvin says that "everything which has a beginning can also have an end, can perish," while speaking of man's immortal soul.[38] And even Holwerda, who defends Calvin against some of Quistorp's charges, agrees fully on this point.[39]

---

32. Quoted in T. F. Torrance, *Calvin's Doctrine of Man*, p. 27.
33. Ibid.
34. Ibid., note 5. From a sermon on 1 Timothy 6:15, 16.
35. Ibid., pp. 26-27.
36. Ibid., p. 26.
37. Ibid., p. 29.
38. Quistorp, *Calvin's Doctrine*, p. 70.
39. Holwerda, "Eschatology and History," p. 114.

Summary and Conclusion

In the matter of the soul's immortality, advocates of the traditional orthodoxy have had to deflect attacks from both right and left. Church fathers of the first five centuries faced Platonic and Neo-Platonic adversaries who denied the Christian resurrection but affirmed the inalienable immortality of the soul. The philosophers themselves disagreed on some of the fine points. In this setting the apologists reasoned for the bodily resurrection of all men, both good and evil. The common doctrine of the soul's immortality was a convenient tool in handy reach.

These Christian writers were men of their age—and (with exceptions) they accepted the common Platonic view of man's soul as a component separable from his body and unhurt by physical death. In this they agreed with their opponents, but on the eternity of the soul fathers and philosophers parted company. To the soul's *immortality* (survival of the death of the body) the Platonists generally added also its *eternality*. There the fathers stood firm. "No," they said. "Although the soul enters and leaves the body, and even survives its death, it is not eternal. It had its beginning by the creation of God, and God—if He pleases—can also make it extinct. Only God possesses *that* kind of 'immortality.'"

With rare and disputed exceptions, this is the common witness of theologians who affirmed the soul's immortality—from the days of the earliest Greek apologists until and including John Calvin and his descendants today. "Immortality" has not meant "eternality." Christian writers have used the concept as an illustration for their apologetics and as a weapon against anti-supernaturalists who denied the resurrection. Only by a kind of reflex action have they used it as a basis for argument concerning final punishment. Then, like some hidden footlight, the doctrine has tinted exegesis, its own scriptural legitimacy frequently a matter of doubt. Ironically, the writer with the most *biblical* defense of the soul's immortality was probably Origen—who likely bought into the *Platonic* system further than any Christian theologian before him or since.

On the other side, traditional advocates of the immortal soul have faced biblical theologians who charged them with denying God's unique immortality. The apologists of the fourth and fifth centuries felt this inconsistency, and later theologians have not resolved it either. Whenever this objection is raised, Christian advocates of the immortal soul paint the doctrine in faint pastels. It is part of their baggage—stamped with the initials of the church—yet it keeps getting in the way, and no one quite remembers what it really contains.

Faced with this predicament of a two-pronged attack, compounded by a secondary doctrine that only gradually joined the troops, traditional orthodoxy has resorted to a holding action. It has rushed first to one front and then to the other, attempting to keep its own forces intact while repelling the particular adversary of the moment. Today the traditional dualistic dogma of soul-immortality is under increasing suspicion as an interloper. More and more, orthodox writers are concluding that the church will not suffer by its expulsion but, rather, that it would eliminate an unnecessary inconsistency from orthodoxy's position.

Crisscrossing all of this flows the stream of Christian mortalism. Freshly issuing from springs opened by Luther and Tyndale, and fed by tributaries of recent biblical theology, this understanding introduces itself as the sparkling pure water of pristine Christianity. Today, more than ever, orthodox evangelical scholars are taking its claims seriously and are giving it a careful look.

In *either* case—among mortalists or immortalists—there is no reason why anthropology should govern eschatology. The true Christian position about final punishment must finally stand only on a thorough exegesis of the Word of God. Into this sanctuary pagan philosophical presuppositions dare not come. That the history of Christian doctrine permits their dismissal we have seen in this chapter and the last. For, while orthodox theologians have often spoken with the thick accent of Plato's philosophy, they finally have rested all hope on God alone. The immortal soul survives physical death, they say, but it cannot resist the power of God. If God wishes, He can reduce even the immortal soul to nothing.[40]

---

40. Vincent Taylor laments the modern turn from the traditional doctrine of the soul's immortality, calling it "a dark night through which the world is passing" and "a valley of humiliation through which we have to travel with a quagmire on the one side and hobgoblins of the pit on the other." He speaks not so much of the claim to a biblical monism, however, as a secular rejection of hope for life after death (Vincent Taylor, "Life After Death: The Modern Situation," *Expository Times* 76, no. 3 [December 1964]: 77).

Modern philosophical alternatives to the traditional view of immortality of the soul are discussed in John Hick, *Death and Eternal Life*, and Paul Badham, *Christian Beliefs about Life after Death*. On the claim of process theologians to combine the biblical view with modern philosophy, see Tyron Inbody, "Process Theology and Personal Survival," *Iliff Review* 31, no. 2 (Spring 1974): 31-42; Suchocki, "The Question of Immortality," pp. 288-306. This view might satisfy the demands of modern philosophy, but it falls far short of the personal and corporate hope which New Testament writers expect to be actualized in the new cosmos at the return of Jesus Christ!

6

Old Testament "Sheol"—Do the Godly Go to "Hell"?

Harry Buis, a responsible and respected author of the traditionalist view, begins his book practically with the warning that the Old Testament "contains little information about the eschatological future of the individual, and almost all of this is concerned with the future of the godly rather than that of the ungodly."[1] He also cautions against the common tendency to read "back into the Old Testament concepts which were not held until much later in the history of doctrine." But, he notes, a high view of inspiration does call for us to read the Old Testament in the brighter light of the New.[2]

Buis' verdict about the scarcity of Old Testament material does not stand alone. An article on the subject in *Expository Times* concludes that "even in the few Old Testament apocalyptic writings . . . the future state of righteous and wicked . . . is described only in the most general terms."[3] A contemporary evangelical author says that Old Testament references to life after death are "few and rather obscure."[4] The *New Catholic Encyclopedia* states that "the mode of survival after death is extremely confused in its inception, but gains greater clarity with the approach to NT times."[5] Recent conservative

---

1. Harry Buis, *The Doctrine of Eternal Punishment*, pp. 1-2.

2. Ibid., p. 2.

3. S. H. Hooke, "Life after Death: The Extra-Canonical Literature," *Expository Times*, June 1965, p. 273.

4. Gerald C. Studer, *After Death, What?* p. 19.

5. S. B. Marrow, "Soul, Human, Immortality Of," *New Catholic Encyclopedia*, 13:467.

Protestant dictionaries support this view as well.[6]

Conditionalists have discovered more fertile fields in the Old Testament. Like the spies returning from the valley of Eshcol, these writers sometimes come home with a cluster of texts greater than one man can carry.[7] One begins to wonder if traditionalist authors might have gone in search of a particular fruit and, not finding that, returned empty-handed to report that the land was barren. At the same time, closer investigation of the conditionalists' texts sometimes suggests an overenthusiastic picking on their part.

Man's Life in the Old Testament

If we rightly interpret the Old Testament view of man, we must begin where it begins—with the story of creation. Genesis 1-2 comes straight to the point. Once man did not exist. God made him from the elements of the earth—just as He did the animals. Into both man and beast God breathed "breath of life," and they all became "living souls."[8] It is impossible to view Old Testament man correctly apart from this framework of his place in God's creation.[9] Because of man's origin, he exists in a double relationship—vertically with God, and horizontally with the rest of creation.

Because man had no existence until God formed him and gave him life, he should view his life each moment as God's immediate gift of grace. Without God's constant provision of life, man has no claim on his own existence. Man bears God's image so that he can know God in a personal way, but he is still God's *creature*. He does not live or

---

6. H. Bietenhard, "Hades/Hell," *The New International Dictionary of New Testament Theology*, 2:206-207.

7. Emmanuel Pétavel, *The Problem of Immortality*, pp. 88ff; Edward White, *Life in Christ . . .* , pp. 387-390; Basil F. C. Atkinson, *Life and Immortality: An Examination of the Nature and Meaning of Life and Death as They Are Revealed in the Scriptures*, throughout; LeRoy Edwin Froom, *The Conditionalist Faith of Our Fathers*, 1:29-180.

8. The New International Version recognizes this and correctly translates *nephesh* in Genesis 2:7 as "living *being*." See also Hans Walter Wolff, *Anthropology of the Old Testament*; George Eldon Ladd, *The Pattern of New Testament Truth*, especially the chapter entitled "The Background of the Pattern." See also special issues of *Verdict* on "Man," parts 1-3 (August, September, December 1978).

9. Thomas E. Ridenhour surveys Old Testament scholars, H. H. Rowley, Hans Walter Wolff, Gerhard von Rad, Robert Martin-Achard and O. A. Piper, and finds agreement that the Old Testament views human life relationally in respect to God and to His covenant people (Thomas E. Ridenhour, "Immortality and Resurrection in the Old Testament," *Dialog* 15 [Spring 1976]: 104-109).

exist independent of God, although he is capable of lusting after that position. Every attempt to be his own god is doomed to failure because of what man *is*. He is dust—scooped from the earth.

When God takes back man's breath of life, man returns to the clay from which he was taken. Plato would agree with Longfellow's *Psalm of Life* that the soul is above all this. But the Old Testament supports Bryant's *Thanatopsis* instead. It tells man that when he dies,

> earth, that nourished thee, shall claim thy growth, to be resolved to earth again. And, lost each human trace, surrendering up thine individual being shalt thou go to mix . . . with the elements.

Man can rejoice in a hope beyond death—but only in God. Adam's very name also means dust.

Man is also one with the rest of God's creation. He is composed of the same elements found in the rocks and rivers and trees. He participates with them in the cycle of life. Even the sun and moon are active partners in human life on God's earth. Man must not despise his "physicalness," therefore, or disregard the rest of creation around him. He is not constitutionally superior to these things so that he can look on them with disdain.[10]

Because man is a part of God's good creation, the Old Testament invites him to enjoy "a healthy materialism, a reverence for the dignity of the body which is human life in the concrete." He can rejoice in "the healthy eroticism of the Song of Songs" and look forward under God to the "comfortable bourgeois condition" of sitting under his own vine or fig tree undisturbed.[11]

The key phrase even here is "under God." God is the giver and sustainer of life. The Old Testament shows us that "life is manifested in God's entering into covenant with his people. . . . The righteous can have life only by holding onto the God of salvation who is the God of life. Life is understood as a gift."[12]

Traditionalists are absolutely correct when they point out that

---

10. On man's place in creation and the effect of the biblical pattern on philosophical categories of metaphysics, epistemology and ethics, see the excellent popular book by Francis A. Schaeffer, *He Is There and He Is Not Silent* (Wheaton, Ill.: Tyndale House Publishers, 1972), pp. 1-88.

11. Bruce Vawter, "Intimations of Immortality and the Old Testament," *Journal of Biblical Literature* 91, no. 2 (June 1972): 170-171.

12. Ridenhour, "Immortality and Resurrection," p. 104.

"life" means far more than bare "existence." Thielicke describes the God-related quality of true life in the Old Testament for us.

> Wherever God is, there is life. Where God is not, there is death (Ps. 104:29-30; Job 34:15). . . . Whoever does not have this contact with the breath of God, whoever lives in protest against him or in internal detachment from him, is already dead regardless of how much vitality he might have externally (Eph. 2:5; Rom. 5:21; 7:10; 1 John 3:14-15). His life is disconnected from its actual source of power, though still rolling along "in neutral" according to the law of inertia.[13]

Man's Death Apart from God

The opposite of this is also true. The most notable characteristic of the dead in the Old Testament is that they are cut off from God. Death means lack of relationship with God.[14] Here man differs from the animals, who share his earthly origin and gift of life. Thielicke paints a vivid picture of man's uniqueness among God's creatures. Only man is aware of being related to God, of his sinfulness, and of his mortality.

> The flowers and the grass, the whales and the mountains know nothing of being thus related to God. Only man knows this. Only he with his solitary awareness of death protrudes above the creaturely realm and thus has a different form of perishability, as though his were raised to a higher power. He alone must pose the question of the meaning of God's action that comes to expression in his death. . . . Because he is compelled to pose the question, it becomes evident that man's returning to dust is qualitatively different from the simple physical returning to dust of a simply physical being. . . . He sees clearly a decision being made against him here with which he must come to terms.[15]

The first man tasted this death-fear when he ate the forbidden fruit, then heard God approaching in the Garden. Adam must have supposed that God was coming even then to inflict the promised penalty of death. But an eternal purpose had outweighed the historical event. Already grace was abounding more than sin. Man had indeed forfeited his right to exist, but God willed to bring many sons to

---

13. Helmut Thielicke, *Death and Life*, pp. 106-107.

14. Wolff, *Anthropology of the Old Testament*, p. 107.

15. Thielicke, *Death and Life*, p. 138.

glory! "The existence of our race then is a boon beyond the limits of law."[16]

But Cain soon murdered his brother, and before long the entire first family is dead. What becomes of man then? The Old Testament does not agree with Socrates' optimism, which he shared with his disciples while waiting for his own death.[17] Man is not an eternal soul trapped in a crude body. He came from the earth, and to it he returns. The Old Testament speaks of his state after death under the picture of Sheol.

Sheol in the Old Testament

A few traditionalist writers have argued that, to the Israelites, Sheol signified the place of unending future retribution. Shedd calls it "a fearful punitive evil, mentioned by the sacred writers to deter men from sin."[18] He says the Old Testament threatens Sheol "as the penalty of sin, to the wicked, but never to the righteous,"[19] and that it has "the same meaning as the modern Hell."[20] Braun repeats Shedd's views, equating Sheol with the modern conception of hell—the extent of his findings concerning future punishment in the Old Testament.[21]

These claims simply do not stand up under the light of biblical usage. The liberal *The Interpreter's Dictionary of the Bible* flatly states: "Nowhere in the OT is the abode of the dead regarded as a place of punishment or torment."[22] The conservative *Baker's Dictionary of Theology* says that "Sheol is uniformly depicted in the OT as the eternal, amoral abode of both righteous and unrighteous

---

16. White, *Life in Christ*, pp. 116, 119.

17. See Oscar Cullmann, *Immortality of the Soul or Resurrection of the Dead?* pp. 19-27.

18. William G. T. Shedd, *The Doctrine of Endless Punishment*, p. 21.

19. Ibid., p. 24.

20. Ibid., p. 23.

21. Jon E. Braun, *Whatever Happened to Hell?* pp. 130-142. Braun concedes that *sheol* sometimes means the physical grave, but he also insists it is used for a place of punishment for the wicked. Buis strengthens his argument by his honest concessions at times (see notes 1, 24-25); Braun hurts his argument by a bombastic tone in the absence of evidence. Here he writes, "I have seen pompous claims by some that . . . Sheol is the expectation of the wicked and the righteous alike" (p. 133). Specific data supporting his view would be far more convincing.

22. Theodore H. Gaster, "Abode of the Dead," *The Interpreter's Dictionary of the Bible*, 1:788.

alike."[23] Buis corrected Shedd in calling Sheol the "place of shadowy existence where the good and the evil continued to exist together after death"[24] and "where good and evil alike share a similar dreary fate."[25] He quotes "the fine conservative scholar," Oehler, that "In no part of the Old Testament is a *difference in the lot* of those in the realm of death distinctly spoken of."[26]

Anyone with a concordance can verify these statements for himself. Faithful Jacob expected to go "down to Sheol" when he died (Gen. 37:35; 42:38; 44:29, 31). Righteous Job longed to hide in Sheol until God's anger passed him by (Job 14:13). David, the man after God's heart, viewed Sheol as his resting place, though he trusted God to redeem him from its grasp (Ps. 49:15). Even Jesus Christ, the Holy One of God, went to Sheol (Greek: *hadēs*) upon His death (Ps. 16:10; Acts 2:24-31). There is simply no basis for making Sheol an exclusive place of punishment for the wicked.[27]

Etymology and Translation. According to Gaster, the word "Sheol" does not appear in any non-Hebrew Semitic literature yet discovered, other than as a loan-word from the Hebrew.[28] (That situation is subject to sudden change, based on overnight discoveries in biblical archaeology). The etymology is uncertain. Most modern scholars seem to think it comes from a root meaning "ask" or "inquire." Older writers sometimes suggested a root meaning "to bury one's self." The idea of something *hidden* appears in synonyms of several languages. The German *Holle* comes from *Hohle*, a cavern (kin to "hole" in English). The Greek *hadēs* literally means the "unseen" realm. The English word "hell" comes from the Anglo-Saxon *helan*, which meant "to cover" or "to hide."[29]

The Old Testament uses the word *sheol* 65 or 66 times. The King James translators followed their own conception of things and made

---

23. Robert B. Laurin, "Sheol," *Baker's Dictionary of Theology*, p. 484.

24. Buis, *The Doctrine of Eternal Punishment*, p. 3.

25. Ibid., p. 12.

26. Ibid., p. 5.

27. The argument, made by Shedd and repeated by Braun, that Sheol equals modern "hell" because it is never threatened to the righteous vanishes into thin air upon a moment's thought. God does not *threaten* the righteous but the wicked! We have seen passages of Scripture which show that the righteous go down into Sheol, however, as well as the wicked. For a thorough study of the term see Atkinson, *Life and Immortality*, pp. 42-53.

28. Gaster, "Abode of the Dead," p. 787.

29. Pétavel, *The Problem of Immortality*, p. 91, note 1.

it either "hell" (31 times), "the grave" (31 times) or "the pit" (three times). The American Standard Version did not try to translate but left it "Sheol." The New International Version usually translates *sheol* by "grave," though at least once "the realm of death" (Deut. 32:22). This supports conditionalist author, Froom, who distinguishes *sheol* from the material grave but suggests "gravedom" as a suitable translation.[30]

Sheol's Inhabitants. Even if the noun itself is limited to the Hebrew language, the picture it conveys is not. The common understanding of at least a particular region is seen in the Gilgamesh Epic. The dead hero, Enkidu, returns to tell his friend of the wretched state of those in Erkallu, the Land of No Return.

> "Looking at me, he leads me to the House of Darkness,
> . . . To the house which none leave who have entered it,
> On the road from which there is no way back,
> To the house wherein the dwellers are bereft of light,
> Where dust is their fare and clay their food.
> They are clothed like birds, with wings for garments,
> And see no light, residing in darkness."[31]

Job also describes "gravedom" as "the place of no return . . . the land of gloom and deep shadow, . . . the land of deepest night, of deep shadow and disorder, where even the light is like darkness" (Job 10:21, 22). David calls it "the place of darkness" and "the land of oblivion" (Ps. 88:12). It is "the land of dust, forgetfulness, and forgottenness, silence, monotony, loneliness, and sleep." [32]

Although individuals are sometimes pictured as carrying on conversations in Sheol or engaging in other such lifelike pursuits (Isa. 14:9-18), they are not whole persons but mere Shades, personified for

---

30. Froom, *Conditionalist Faith*, 1:160-165.

31. James B. Pritchard, ed., *Ancient Near Eastern Texts Relating to the Old Testament*, p. 87. S. H. Hooke gives a slightly different translation in "Life after Death: Israel and the After-Life," *Expository Times*, May 1965, p. 236. On Egyptian ideas of the afterlife see S. G. F. Brandon, "Life after Death: The After-Life in Ancient Egyptian Faith and Practice," *Expository Times*, April 1965, pp. 217-220. On the relation between Israelite and pagan attitudes regarding this subject and their different use of some common language, see John Barclay Burns, "The Mythology of Death in the Old Testament," *Scottish Journal of Theology*, no. 3 (August 1973): 327-340.

32. Burns, "Mythology of Death," p. 332. *The Jewish Encyclopedia* says: "Sheol is a horrible, dreary, dark, disorderly land" (*The Jewish Encyclopedia*, vol. 11, col. 283).

dramatic purposes.[33] The state of the deceased cannot be called "life" in any meaningful sense. It is "such a pale and pitiful reflexion of human existence that it has no longer any reality, and is only a metaphorical expression of non-being."[34]

This is mythological language for the most part, borrowed from its pagan time and place—much like our kind of language, by the way, when we speak of the sun "rising" and "setting" or use the names January or Saturday (originally honoring Roman gods), or Wednesday, Thursday or Friday (originally honoring pagan gods of Europe). We should not suppose, however, that the Hebrews took the language literally or used it with its original pagan meaning. In a well-reasoned article on the subject, John B. Burns shows how the Old Testament "demythologized" such language and uses it only for effect, contrast or literary purposes.[35]

Because the Old Testament defines man's life by his relationship to God, Sheol is evil. It removes man from his place on earth, where he lived and rejoiced in God's fellowship and praised Him for His goodness (Isa. 38:11, 18, 19). Yet Sheol is not beyond God's sight or reach or power (Job 26:6; Amos 9:2). Righteous men and women repeatedly express confidence that God will restore them from Sheol to enjoy life in His fellowship once more (1 Sam. 2:6; Ps. 16:9-11; 68:20). They have experienced God's joy and faithfulness already on the earth. The joy they have tasted makes them want to live with Him forever;[36] the faithfulness they have seen gives them confidence that they will.[37] The patriarchs died in hope, according to Hebrews 11, but their hope was in the power and love of God, not in a philosophical dogma or any death-proof part of man.

---

33. They are the *rephaim* (Job 26:5; Ps. 88:10; Prov. 2:18; 9:18; 21:16; Isa. 14:9; 26:19). "For the member of the community of Israel, the dead were beyond his interest for they had ceased to live and praise Yahweh" (Burns, "Mythology of Death," p. 339).

34. Robert Martin-Achard, *From Death to Life: A Study of the Development of the Doctrine of the Resurrection in the Old Testament*, p. 17.

35. Burns, "Mythology of Death," pp. 327-340, esp. p. 339.

36. "A man must have great interests, a devouring, hungry sense of life, must have essayed tasks far beyond his powers, have known moments so intense in their heartbreaking loveliness, must have glimpsed meanings so suggestive and alluring that it will take more time than his allotted span on earth to follow through and complete, before he desires a life beyond" (W. B. J. Martin, "Life after Death: The Poets—Victorian and Modern," *Expository Times*, February 1965, p. 141).

37. Throughout the Old and New Testaments God's faithfulness is the ground of His people's hope. Since the resurrection and ascension of Jesus Christ, believers have had historical verification that God is faithful and that He will not forsake them even in death.

No, Abraham died; died and was buried; a stranger and sojourner in the country promised him; and he died in the faith that the promise would still be his. The same applies to Isaac, Jacob and Joseph, and to all the rest of the Old Testament saints. Their 'happy end' was, like Jacob's, made happy because of their knowledge alike of God's ultimate purpose, and of His grace and power over their ashes (Gen. 26:3; 49:29; 50:25; Exod. 13:19; Joshua 24:32). Nothing else and nothing less will explain the quality or intensity of the Old Testament hope and expectation (John 8:56).[38]

Job's poignant expression of hope surely touches deeply anyone who reads it:

"If a man dies, will he live again?
　　All the days of my hard service
　　I will wait for my renewal to come.
You will call and I will answer You;
　　You will long for the creature Your hands have made."
　　　　　—Job 14:14, 15.

Summary

The Old Testament's concept of Sheol belongs to its larger view of man before God. This perspective, framed in light of the creation, determines the Hebrews' attitude toward both life and death—and hope beyond that. Sheol is the common fate of all mortals. It is not a place of punishment.

The wicked have no reason to expect to leave Sheol in most of the Old Testament. The righteous, however, do, for they know and trust the living God! Nothing is hid from His eyes, and no power can withstand His deliverance. His people lie down in peace, fully expecting to live again. That hope is stated explicitly a few times, but it pervades the entire Old Testament.

So far as the destiny of the wicked is concerned, Sheol is not a final word. The Old Testament does say much about the end of the wicked, however. We will consider that positive teaching now.

---

38. Norman A. Logan, "The Old Testament and a Future Life," *Scottish Journal of Theology* 6, no. 2 (June 1953): 170.

7

The End of the Wicked in the Old Testament

The Bible is not cast in the mold of philosophy or of mysticism, but of history. It deals with God's people and God's world within history as God enacts His saving plan, which He purposed even before creation. The Old Testament ends with an unresolved chord—Jesus Christ must come to finish the harmony before we can really know God's song. It is not surprising that Old Testament teaching often leaves us hanging also, waiting for God's revelation in Jesus Christ to tie the loose ends.

The earlier Scriptures foreshadow, hint, suggest, outline, prefigure, illustrate and promise. The New Testament Scriptures fill in the details, flesh out the bones, tint the coloring, fine tune the picture and complete the canonical revelation. We are still in the dark concerning life and immortality until Jesus brings them to light in the gospel (2 Tim. 1:10). It is no less true that God's wrath also is hidden until it is revealed in the gospel (Rom. 1:15-18). Someone has said that the Old Testament is the New Testament *concealed*, while the New is the Old *revealed*. The comparison has much merit.

At the same time, the Old Testament is preserved for our instruction and example (Rom. 15:4; 1 Cor. 10:11-13). Alongside the New, it is profitable for every teaching situation (2 Tim. 3:15-17). On the

matter of final punishment the Old Testament Scriptures have usually been the victim of gross neglect. Traditionalist writers have most
often passed them aside as offering nothing of value on the subject, at
best containing vague hints in two or three passages. Conditionalist
writers have made a number of arguments from the Old Testament,
but largely in a summary form.

A modern example of the conditionalist approach is Froom. He
says the Old Testament uses 50 different Hebrew verbs to describe
the final fate of the wicked and notes that they all signify different
aspects of *destruction*.[1] Such verbs are buttressed, he says, by
figurative or proverbial expressions which also speak "everywhere
and always" of "the *decomposition*, of the *breaking up of the
organism* and *final cessation of the existence of being—never* that of
immortal life in endless suffering."[2] By combining both lists into one,
Froom presents an alphabetical list of some 70 English expressions
which the Old Testament uses to describe the wicked's end. The list is
most impressive in its cumulative impact—particularly in view of the
resounding silence which meets it in traditionalist works.[3] Yet one
could wish for more.

Several of Froom's 70 examples seem less applicable to the subject,
and a few appear to be completely out of place. Some simply call on
God to judge the wicked or give the righteous victory over their
enemies, with no apparent reference to Last Things (Ps. 55:23; 60:12;
94:23; 104:35; 139:19). Others praise God for deliverance over the
wicked (Ps. 118:12; 119:119; Isa. 43:17). One simply states temporal
blessings given or withheld by God (Prov. 13:9). Another prescribes

---

1. LeRoy Edwin Froom, *The Conditionalist Faith of Our Fathers*, 1:106.

2. Ibid., p. 107. For example, the wicked will be *as*: a vessel broken to pieces, ashes trodden
underfoot, smoke that vanishes, chaff carried away by the wind, tow that is burned, thorns
and stubble in fire, vine branches pruned off, wax that melts, fat of sacrifices, a dream that
vanishes, etc.

Pétavel speaks of the "multitude of proverbial expressions, a long succession of images
which sometimes seem to exclude each other, but which always, by association of ideas, and
like fractions reduced to a common denominator, are found to be in accord when used to
describe the end of the existence of evil and of obstinate evildoers. Everywhere we find the notion of a final cessation of being, of a return to a state of unconsciousness, never that of a
perpetual life in suffering" (Emmanuel Pétavel, *The Problem of Immortality*, pp. 88-89).

3. Froom, *Conditionalist Faith*, 1:108-110. Conditionalist writers have produced material here
which traditionalist authors usually overlook or completely ignore. Froom's list of such terms
is quite impressive and has sent the present writer to the text in search of more information. His
contribution to the study is gratefully acknowledged. It is hoped that this chapter will take the
investigation even further, considering these passages in context and with regard to literary
genre and purpose.

the ultimate penalty of excision under the Law of Moses[4] (Exod. 22:20). Closely akin are three passages which speak of sin's original death penalty, itself the subject of much debate (Gen. 3:19; Ezek. 18:4, 20). Two others appear to speak only of God's power to sustain life—a relevant point to the discussion but one needing more explanation than here given (Ps. 75:3; Isa. 40:24). When one reads in context the passages Froom cites, many of them do seem relevant to final punishment. Conditionalists such as Froom have done us a service in calling attention to these texts, and for that we are in their debt. It is no reflection on that contribution for us to inquire further with regard to particular contexts, special purpose and relative bearing on our subject.

For the present study we will examine a number of relevant Old Testament passages under three headings. First are several texts which state *moral principles of the divine government*. From these passages we may learn general truths which shed light on the wicked's end—at least by implication. We do not want to make too much of such statements, but neither do we wish to make too little. Second are a selection of texts which concern *specific divine judgments within history*. Some involve Israel; some involve pagan nations or cities. They add further light on God's punishment of sin. Perhaps most important, they provide concrete definitions for much of the prophetic symbolism with which the Bible describes divine judgment against sin. The examples we give are only a sample of many more. But they will illustrate the point intended and can stimulate the student to further study of the others. Finally we look at a number of Old Testament statements concerning the wicked's end which appear in contexts that are clearly either *Messianic* or *eschatological*.[5] These have special value since they look beyond circumstances of ancient history to the grand revelation of God's *salvation* and the final manifestation of His *wrath*—the two aspects commonly involved in divine judgment.

---

4. This is not irrelevant to the subject but needs to be viewed in theological perspective. That perspective comes at Calvary, where God's *wrath* as well as His *justice* (righteousness) is revealed. We will look at that subject in more detail in a separate chapter.

5. I. Howard Marshall calls "eschatology" a "slippery word" because of its frequent careless use in at least nine different senses. He suggests avoiding the term so far as possible and urges that it be used, when necessary, with care and precision (I. Howard Marshall, "Slippery Words: Eschatology," *Expository Times*, June 1978, pp. 264-269).

I. Passages Containing Moral Principles of Divine Judgment

GENERAL REFERENCES IN THE POETIC BOOKS. Instead of offering comfort in Job's hour of need, his visitors instead accuse him on the basis of the popular orthodoxy. The wicked are punished; the righteous flourish. It is as simple as that, they say, describing in graphic detail the fate they expect will overtake the wicked. So speak Bildad (Job 18:5-21), Zophar (Job 20:4-29), Eliphaz (Job 22:15-20) and Elihu (Job 34:10-28). Through it all, Job asserts his innocence. He is living proof (if barely) that their orthodoxy is mistaken, he says. For he sees wicked men who thrive while he is perishing with clean hands.

We cannot derive a doctrine of final punishment from the statements of Job's miserable comforters. They reflect an uninspired orthodoxy, to whatever extent it should prove correct; and the hero, Job, objects throughout to their arguments. However, Job raises a point we do well to consider. Given the moral government of God over men, why can the wicked die rich and the righteous languish away in misery? Even Job's own final restoration does not erase this troubling issue.

In the Psalms and Proverbs we find David and Solomon using much the same language as that of Job's companions—but this time with apparent divine sanction. According to numerous psalms, the wicked will go down to death and Sheol, their memory will perish, and they will be as if they had never existed. On the other hand, God will rescue the righteous from death and they will enjoy Him forever (Ps. 9; 21:4-10; 36:9-12; 49:8-20; 52:5-9; 59; 73; 92). Proverbs offers the same hope. The wicked will pass away, be overthrown, be cut off from the land, be no more, their lamp put out. The godly will endure and their house will stand, for they have an everlasting foundation (Prov. 2:21, 22; 10:25; 12:7; 24:15-20).

Someone might wish to argue that these texts all refer only to the present life. Nothing in the contexts or in the explicit language demands otherwise. If one had no information other than these passages in Job, Psalms and Proverbs, he might well suppose that the wicked will all perish in death, from which they will have no redeemer, but that God will redeem the righteous from death and they will inherit the earth forever. These poetic books do not specifically threaten a resurrection of the wicked, a final judgment after death, or any ultimate punishment beyond temporal death itself.

Yet beneath the surface and between the lines, one suspects that there is more to the story than this. For Job's problem also rises in Psalms and Proverbs. *Where* do we see all this happening to the wicked? They often prosper in life—and the righteous die. Is that all there is to God's justice? Do the wicked escape so easily? Because of this apparent injustice, such passages as these may fairly be said to suggest a final reckoning and judgment of the wicked beyond temporal death. But they give absolutely no information concerning such events, nor do they even explicitly require it. It is an implication drawn from the moral principles of divine government which are revealed. Six psalms in particular strongly point in this direction.

Psalm 11:1-7. Even now God rules from His heavenly throne, observing and examining both righteous and wicked (vv. 4, 5). Evildoers on earth sometimes destroy the very foundation of moral society, and the godly know nothing they can do (v. 3). Then they may know that God is on the throne and that His day of reckoning will surely come. The godless may hide in the shadows and ambush the righteous—now (v. 2); now they may tantalize and mock those who trust in God (v. 1). But then God will reverse the roles and even the score. "On the wicked He will rain fiery coals and burning sulfur (brimstone, AV); a scorching wind will be their lot" (v. 6). Then "upright men will see His face" (v. 7).

This world does not reward virtue or punish evil, but a day of divine reckoning will surely come. This psalm pictures the wicked's fate in terms taken from the punishment of Sodom, when "the Lord rained down burning sulfur" (Gen. 19:24) and "overthrew" city, people and vegetation (Gen. 19:25). He "destroyed" the wicked in a "catastrophe" so thorough that the next day Abraham could see nothing but "dense smoke rising from the land, like smoke from a furnace" (Gen. 19:28, 29).

Psalm 34:8-22. This psalm praises God, who delivers His people from their troubles. According to the heading, David wrote the psalm after he escaped from the Philistine king, Abimelech (Achish in 1 Sam. 21:10-15). Peter uses this psalm to encourage suffering Christians, quoting from verse 8 (1 Pet. 2:3) and also verses 12-16a (1 Pet. 3:10-12).

The psalm contrasts the fates of those who trust God and those who do not. The one who fears God and takes refuge in Him will find Him good (v. 8). Such a one will lack for nothing good (vv. 9, 10).

God will be close to him in need (v. 18), see his plight and hear his cries (vv. 15, 17), and save or deliver him from trouble (vv. 17, 19). The psalm tells how to have a long and good life (vv. 12-14) and promises that in the end God will redeem His servants so that none of them will be condemned (v. 22).

In contrast to this, God turns His face against the evil (v. 16), who finally are slain by their own wickedness (v. 21). At the last, God will condemn them (v. 21) and cut off their memory from the earth (v. 16).

These contrasts catch our attention and speak to our minds and hearts. Whether a man is good or evil, *God* is the One he finally will face. The righteous may expect to be delivered and vindicated because God is their mighty savior. The wicked must know that their adversary and judge will be God, not man.

But as often as not, men do not reach these destinies in earthly life. The righteous sometimes die in unjust suffering and shame; the wicked sometimes die in prosperity and peace. The psalm therefore looks beyond the present life for its infallible fulfillment. In that sense, at least, it speaks of blessing and punishment in the world to come. Whether we see it now or not, the psalm promises a day when the righteous *will* shine (v. 5) but the wicked will *be no more* (v. 16). This is God's word on the matter, and He will bring it to pass.

Psalm 37:1-40. This psalm describes the security of those who trust in God and the insecurity of the wicked. David observes: "I have seen a wicked and ruthless man flourishing like a green tree in its native soil, but he soon passed away and was no more; though I looked for him, he could not be found" (vv. 35, 36). This is the way with the wicked, he says, as he boldly extends his observation to wicked men in general.

Job's objection comes to our mind: where do we see this happening to the wicked? The answer must be that we do not yet see their end. This is made more certain by Jesus' use of the promise from verse 11 that "the meek will inherit the earth" (Matt. 5:5), which in the Beatitudes is synonymous with the kingdom of God. The meek do not inherit the land—now. But like the writer of Hebrews, Jesus and David speak of the pilgrim's future homeland (Heb. 11:8-16) in the world to come (Heb. 2:5). They look, with Peter, for the new heaven and earth, the home of righteousness (2 Pet. 3:13).

In this light the couplet in verse 10 to the expression Jesus quotes becomes more significant. "A little while, and the wicked will be no more; though you look for them, they will not be found." This is said not once but repeatedly throughout the psalm. David assures the godly that the wicked

- will soon wither like the grass and die away like green plants (v. 2);

- will be no more so they cannot be found (v. 10);

- will be laughed at by the Lord, for their day is coming (v. 13);

- will be pierced by their own swords, and their bows broken (v. 15);

- will be broken in power (v. 17);

- will perish like the beauty of the fields and vanish like smoke (v. 20);

- will be cut off (vv. 22, 28, 34, 38);

- will be destroyed (v. 38).

In this psalm David defines *die* and *destroy* by a variety of figures from nature. The wicked will be *like* grass that withers or smoke that vanishes when they "die" and are "destroyed." These are not mere hollow hopes of Job's shallow and uninspired friends. They are the solemn promises of David as he speaks by the Holy Spirit (Matt. 22:43; Acts 2:30). Those who trust in God might not see it happen now. But they are to wait patiently for the Lord's time, confident that He will bring His word to pass (vv. 7, 34). This psalm is surely instructive concerning the final fate of those who mock at God.

Psalm 50. This psalm of Asaph extols God, who judges both the righteous and the wicked. God comes in fire and tempest to judge His people (vv. 3-6). "Call upon Me in the day of trouble," He invites the godly; "I will deliver you, and you will honor Me" (v. 15). But to the wicked God says: "What right have you to recite My laws or take My covenant on your lips?" (v. 16). "Consider this," He says to those who forget God, "or I will tear you to pieces, with none to rescue" (v. 22).

The picture is the usual one. God comes in fire storm for judgment. It is symbolic, and its words are chosen for impact rather than literal description. But they teach *something*, and what they teach is conveyed to the emotions by the threat, "I will tear you to pieces, with none to rescue."

Psalm 58. Imprecatory psalms have long disturbed Christian readers. How can the godly man call for vengeance on his enemies? Should he not, rather, ask God to forgive them? It is important for us to understand that David's enemies are also God's enemies (which finally is why they are David's) and that David is turning all vengeance over to God. In this context we observe what David expected to happen when God took vengeance.

We must not read back into the Old Testament what is not there. Rather, we must listen to each passage for its own message, however shadowy or vague that message might be. Here is what David regards as God's just punishment in this psalm:

- their teeth will be broken in their mouths (v. 6);

- they will vanish like water that flows away (v. 7);

- they will melt like a slug as it moves along (v. 8);

- they will not see the sun, like a stillborn child (v. 8);

- their blood will bathe the feet of the righteous (v. 10).

The ultimate result will be God's honor. Men will then exclaim: "Surely the righteous still are rewarded; surely there is a God who judges the earth" (v. 11).

Psalm 69:22-28. New Testament writers frequently quote this imprecatory psalm. They apply its words to Jesus (v. 9/John 2:17 and Rom. 15:3; v. 21/John 19:28-30) on the one hand, and to Judas (v. 25/Acts 1:20) and unbelieving Israel (vv. 22, 23/Rom. 11:9, 10) on the other. Here is the desperate cry of a righteous man, outnumbered and overpowered by wicked enemies, calling on God for vindication (justification) and deliverance (salvation).

He longs to see God's wrath poured out on the wicked (v. 24), their place deserted and their tents empty (v. 25). He is sure they will have no part in God's salvation (v. 27) but rather will be blotted out of the book of life (v. 28). God will finally hear the righteous (vv. 32, 33); they and their children will inherit Zion (vv. 34-36).

In this psalm the end of the wicked is that they cannot be found! Their place is empty—they are not listed among the living. They are victims of the righteous wrath of God. The righteous, meanwhile, enjoy God's salvation. The language is figurative, the style is poetic, but the meaning is clear and the message is true. We must make room in our understanding for the imagery of this psalm.

Psalm 145. David praises God for His goodness in this psalm, which is general in tone and universal in scope. It is not limited to a particular occasion or person or incident. God's gracious kingdom is forever (vv. 8-13). He also rules in justice, which gives the godly hope.

"The Lord is righteous in all His ways. . . . The Lord watches over all who love Him, but all the wicked He will destroy" (vv. 17, 20). This is a general statement, but it informs us so far as it goes, and it is in complete harmony with the language of the rest of Scripture.

(Verse 21 in the New American Standard Version pictures a time when "all flesh will bless His holy name forever and ever." Though Scripture elsewhere expresses the same expectation of every creature in the universe praising God in a perfect and unanimous song, other translations do not support it here. The New International Version gives the imperative, "*Let* every creature praise His holy name for ever and ever," as do the Authorized Version and the Revised Standard Version.)

Summary. Throughout the Old Testament, God teaches us about the end of the wicked in various ways. The books of poetry—Job, Psalms and Proverbs—reflect on the meaning and value of life under the sun. What will be the difference between godly and ungodly in the end? How does it "pay" to serve God? Why do the righteous sometimes die in poverty while the wicked lay down in fame and prosperity?

To answer these questions, the poetic books take us behind the scenes. There they point to the sovereign God on His throne. And they tell us that this God who already rules will also one day judge. They reassure us again and again that He will vindicate all who trust in Him. They tell us in many ways that the godless will come to nothing. They will perish, will disappear, will not be found. Their place will be empty and they will be no more. Their bows will be broken, their own spears will slay them. The godly will wipe their feet in the wicked man's blood. The wicked man's name will not be found in the register of the living. Those who trusted in God will re-joice in His salvation. They will endure forever. They and their children will inhabit Zion. They will be vindicated when they see God and dwell with Him. They will inherit the earth.

These things do not happen now. We look for their fulfillment, therefore, in the world to come. Jesus and the New Testament writers quote from these psalms and apply their words to the coming age. They tell men and women of faith today that the same moral principles of divine government rule behind the scenes. They give us, also, the hope expressed by Job and David and Solomon.

The language of poetry is frequently figurative. Figures are not to be taken literally. (God's people will not turn on a faucet of wicked men's blood to bathe their feet.) A figure does, however, correspond to the truth it illustrates. Without some true correspondence, it misleads and deceives. Without being literal, therefore, we may learn from these passages of Scripture. They say nothing of conscious un-ending torment. None of them hints at a fire which tortures but does not kill. They do not envision the presence of the wicked forever—even in a distant place. Rather, they picture a time and a world where the wicked will not be. There the meek will rejoice in God's presence forever. Every living creature will praise God, who has shown Him-self to be a righteous judge.

Someone might wish to find the traditionalist picture elsewhere. That is a permissible pursuit. But as we leave these passages of Scrip-ture, we must remember two things: (1) They do tell us something, and we must include them as we form a total biblical picture. (2) The picture they describe is the one we have just stated.

II. Passages Describing Specific Divine Judgments in Space-Time History

When God told the Israelites how to live in covenant community before Him, He laid down His rules in two forms. He gave specific *commandments* ("do not murder," "honor father and mother"), and

He gave *case laws* ("in the case of an ox which gores a man, do such-and-such"). One might think of theory and practice. God stated the absolute principles, but He illustrated their application in specific, concrete situations. The Old Testament teaches similarly in the matter of the end of the wicked.

We have seen a number of passages from the poetic book of Job, Psalms and Proverbs which state moral principles of divine judgment. Such statements are scattered through the other books as well. But God has not stopped with stating His principles. He has also illustrated how these principles work out in specific, concrete situations. We can learn from the principles and promises of the Psalms. But we can also learn by observing God's acts of judgment, watching and listening as He came in power and might, with fire and smoke and tempest and storm, to punish the sins of cities and nations and empires. In this section we will behold the severity of God. It causes us to bow before Him in reverence. These examples also serve to teach us something about the great day of His wrath which is yet to come.

Genesis 6-9. In the last chapter we considered the Old Testament's view of man in relation to God, his Creator, and observed how that perspective determined the way it looks at man's life and death. In a sense, the Great Flood closes the story which creation began.[6] This cataclysmic[7] judgment brought an end to one world and ushered in a new (Gen. 6-9; 2 Pet. 2:5; 3:4-6). So important is this story to the rest of the Bible that it becomes a standard model for later crises and judgments. Later writers point to its unexpectedness (Matt. 24:38, 39; Luke 17:26, 27), its victims (2 Pet. 2:5, 9), those it saved from the world's wickedness (1 Pet. 3:20-22; 2 Pet. 2:5, 9), Noah's faith (Ezek. 14:14, 20; Heb. 11:7), as well as God's patience preceding the judgment (1 Pet. 3:20; 2 Pet. 3:4-6) and the certainty of His covenant which followed it (Isa. 54:9). Jesus (Matt. 24:38, 39;

---

6. Gary V. Smith applies the method of structural analysis to Genesis 1-11 and finds the Flood story occupying a prominent theological position. His article is "Structure and Purpose in Genesis 1-11," *Journal of the Evangelical Theological Society* 20, no. 4 (December 1977): 307-320.

7. The Greek Old Testament (the Septuagint, abbreviated LXX) and the Greek New Testament both use the word *kataklysmos* for the "Flood." The verb form *kataklyzō* ("to overwhelm with water") appears in 2 Peter 3:6.

Luke 17:26, 27) and Peter (2 Pet. 2:5, 9; 3:3-7) both use it to illustrate elements of their teaching about Last Things.

Because of man's total depravity ("every inclination of the thoughts of his heart was only evil all the time," Gen. 6:5), God decided to "wipe mankind . . . from the face of the earth" (Gen. 6:7). A few verses later God tells Noah His plan "to put an end to all people" (v. 13), "to destroy both them and the earth" (v. 13), "to destroy all life under the heavens, every creature that has the breath of life in it. Everything on earth will perish" (v. 17). Seven days before the Flood, God again tells Noah, "I will wipe from the face of the earth every living creature I have made" (Gen. 7:4). Only life in the ark would survive.

The event itself is as severe as the threats. When the Flood came,

> Every living thing that moved on the earth perished—birds, livestock, wild animals, all the creatures that swarm over the earth, and all mankind. Everything on dry land that had the breath of life in its nostrils died. Every living thing on the face of the earth was wiped out; men and animals and the creatures that move along the ground and the birds of the air were wiped from the earth. Only Noah was left, and those with him in the ark.—Gen. 7:21-23.

After Noah and his family leave the ark, God promises that He will never again "destroy all living creatures" as He had done (Gen. 8:21). Never again will "all life be cut off" by such waters; never again will there be a flood "to destroy the earth" (Gen. 9:11). God formalizes His promise in a covenant with Noah and his sons, and seals the covenant with the sign of the rainbow. Whenever man sees the rainbow in the clouds, he can remember God's promise. He can also know that God remembers His covenant and will be faithful to it (Gen. 9:8-17).

Here there is no doubt about the meaning of "perish," "destroy" or "die." At times the words may be poetic or metaphorical or figurative. In this actual historical example of the end of the world, those terms were clearly literal. They meant being "wiped out," being "wiped off the face of the earth." In this specific event evildoers met the precise end we saw described time and time again throughout the Psalms and Proverbs.[8]

---

8. Not their *final* end, in view of the resurrection and judgment to come, but one typical of it according to New Testament writers.

In light of the way Jesus and Peter use this event to describe the earth's final destruction by fire, we need to consider these things carefully and with much thought. God could have inspired hundreds of pages of philosophical discussion about the exact meaning of "destroy" and "perish" and whether they signified "annihilation" or merely "making inactive." Instead, He points back to what He has already done once, and He warns that it is an example of what the wicked may expect again. We will not press the point beyond that, but surely we can say no less.

Genesis 19:24-29. The destruction of metropolitan Sodom and Gomorrah with their suburbs ranks alongside the Flood as a historical demonstration of divine judgment. Its people's name becomes a synonym for wickedness,[9] its chief survivor a model of one receiving God's mercy (2 Pet. 2:7-9).

Following Abraham's unsuccessful attempt to save the city through intercession (Gen. 18:16-33) and the inhabitants' shameful attack on their two angelic visitors (Gen. 19:1-11), Lot is warned to gather his family and flee for their lives (Gen. 19:12-17). He requests asylum in the nearby village of Zoar, which the angels grant (Gen. 19:18-23).

> Then the Lord rained down burning sulfur on Sodom and Gomorrah—from the Lord out of the heavens. Thus He overthrew those cities and the entire plain, including all those living in the cities—and also the vegetation in the land. But Lot's wife looked back and she became a pillar of salt.
>
> Early the next morning Abraham got up and returned to the place where he had stood before the Lord. He looked down toward Sodom and Gomorrah, toward all the land of the plain, and he saw dense smoke rising from the land, like smoke from a furnace.
>
> So when God destroyed the cities of the plain, He remembered Abraham, and He brought Lot out of the catastrophe that overthrew the cities where Lot had lived. —Gen. 19:24-29.

Biblical writers find this story instructive in many details. Isaiah is impressed by the total destruction of the entire wicked population —not one escaped! (Isa. 1:9). Paul quotes Isaiah's words with the same purpose (Rom. 9:29).

---

9. Deut. 32:32; Isa. 1:10; 3:9; Jer. 23:14; Ezek. 16:46-56; Rev. 11:8. Yet Jesus says judgment will be more tolerable for Sodom and Gomorrah than for the cities which rejected His personal ministry and miracles (Matt. 10:15; 11:23, 24; Luke 10:12).

The suddenness with which the judgment came receives even the attention of Jesus. When God comes against the wicked, the righteous had better drop everything and run! (Luke 17:26-33.) The godly survivors are themselves like sticks snatched from the fire (Amos 4:11; Jude 23). Even the agent of destruction becomes a biblical symbol for divine punishment. This is the origin of "fire and brimstone" in the Bible, with brimstone (sulfur) to suffocate by its fumes, and fire to consume completely.[10]

In keeping with other passages on the wicked's fate, Sodom's destruction also resulted in a barren and empty land void of human inhabitant. Moses later stresses this point (Deut. 29:23), as do Jeremiah (Jer. 49:18) and Zephaniah (Zeph. 2:9).

Even more significant, this desolation was to be *perpetual*. Centuries later God foretells Babylon's punishment of everlasting ruin, and Sodom is the example He gives (Isa. 13:19-22; Jer. 50:40). This is apparently in Jude's mind also when he says Sodom serves "as an example of those who suffer the punishment of *eternal fire*" (Jude 7). The actual burning of Sodom was notably quick—in that regard even merciful (Lam. 4:6). God's wrath struck, "burning them to ashes," and made them "an example of what is going to happen to the ungodly" (2 Pet. 2:6). But we have already seen how the New Testament applies the adjective "eternal" to the *results* of a process, and that fits all the evidence here as well.[11] The fire fell from heaven and burned the wicked to ashes, resulting in a total desolation that would never be reversed![12]

---

10. Brimstone ("sulfur" in the New International Version) is part of the divine retribution against apostates in Israel (Deut. 29:23; Job 18:15; Ps. 11:6), against Assyria (Isa. 30:33), Edom (Isa. 34:9), Gog (Ezek. 38:22), idolaters (Rev. 14:10), the beast and false prophet (Rev. 19:20), Satan (Rev. 20:10) and sinners in general (Rev. 21:8). Pétavel speaks of its suffocating vapor, which he includes as an agent of destruction (Pétavel, *The Problem of Immortality*, p. 193). The final outcome of "fire and brimstone" in the prototypal historical judgment of Sodom was the complete extermination of every sinner and the unequivocal desolation of their land. When the "fire and brimstone" had passed, nothing but smoke was left.

11. See chapter 3, under " 'Eternal' with Words of Action."

12. Constable drives home the conditionalist argument. "In the days of Abraham, four rich and populous cities flourished in the plain of Jordan. On a sudden, fire descended from heaven, and, after a period of terror, regrets, and pain, the inhabitants were deprived of life. They and their works were burnt up; and this ruined, lifeless, hopeless, condition has remained to the present time. The smell of the fire is still over the land,' says Tertullian. The whole transaction conveys the idea of conscious pain for a time, followed by ruin and death for ever. This is, according to Scripture, to 'suffer the vengeance of eternal fire' " (Henry Constable, *Duration and Nature of Future Punishment*, p. 141).

The next day after Sodom's destruction, Abraham went out to view the site below. All that remained was a dense smoke rising from what a day earlier had been a bustling city. Now all was quiet, the smoke a grim reminder of the severity of divine justice. This picture, too, becomes part of the prophetic vocabulary of God's judgment and the fate awaiting the wicked (Isa. 34:10; Rev. 14:11; 19:3).

In a multitude of places, biblical writers from Deuteronomy to Revelation point to Sodom as an example of God's impending judgment. We must not ignore this host of witnesses as we hear the biblical case on this subject. Furthermore, we should hear *what* they say about this example and note carefully *how* they use it. Biblical examples may sometimes illustrate *more* than other writers of Scripture explicitly state, but they certainly teach no *less*. All we ask here is that Sodom's destruction be given the same place and significance in our own thinking that it receives from Moses, Isaiah, Jeremiah and Zephaniah, Peter, John and Jesus.

Deuteronomy 29:18-29. Near the end of his life Moses leads Israel in a renewal of the covenant made at Sinai. In solemn assembly before the Lord (vv. 10-15) he warns them to avoid idols and keep their hearts for Jehovah (vv. 16-18). Anyone who enters the covenant hypocritically, thinking he can avoid God's punishment, will bring total disaster on himself and the people.

> The Lord will never be willing to forgive him; His wrath and zeal will burn against that man. All the curses written in this book will fall upon him, and the Lord will blot out his name from under heaven. The Lord will single him out from all the tribes of Israel for disaster, according to all the curses of the covenant written in this Book of the Law.—vv. 20, 21.

Here is the Old Testament counterpart to the gospel's unforgivable sin—"The Lord will never be willing to forgive him." This man is comparable to the unbeliever on whom Jesus says God's wrath abides (John 3:36). The situation also closely parallels the crisis described in Hebrews 12:15, where believers are also warned about the "bitter root" that may grow up to their great harm (v. 18).

Moses pictures the outcome of God's continuing, unforgiving wrath against the land, comparing it to a previous divine judgment.

> The whole land will be a burning waste of salt and sulfur—nothing planted, nothing sprouting, no vegetation growing on it. It will be like

the destruction of Sodom and Gomorrah, Admah and Zeboiim, which the Lord overthrew in fierce anger. All the nations will ask: "Why has the Lord done this to this land? Why this fierce, burning anger?" And the answer will be: "It is because this people abandoned the covenant of the Lord, the God of their fathers."—vv. 23-25.

God portrays in down-to-earth terms the terrible effects of His covenant wrath. We might also relate this passage—and the picture it shows—to the strokes which fell on Jesus at Calvary. There the One who was always faithful to God's covenant became this man under the covenant's curse.[13] In both Testaments God's salvation springs totally from sovereign mercy. In both cases He establishes it in a covenant with His people. This covenant contains stipulations and blessings, but it also threatens despisers with the direst of curses. In this Old Testament paradigm the curse of the broken covenant is unmitigated disaster—a destruction and extermination from off the land—leaving only the grim reminder of a desolate and fruitless earth (cf. Heb. 6:4-8). The execution of this penalty surely includes great terror, anguish and pain. But when the divine wrath has swept past, no sound is heard in its wake. The silence following the judgment is unbroken.

Isaiah 1:27-31. Isaiah opens his book with an oracle against rebellious Judah and Jerusalem. God has already chastened His people through the Assyrians (Isa. 1:7-9), but they have not repented (vv. 4-6). He will continue to punish, but the punishment will be a purgative, leaving a purified remnant faithful to God. "I will turn My hand against you; I will thoroughly purge away your dross and remove your impurities. . . . Afterward you will be called The City of Righteousness, The Faithful City" (vv. 25, 26). Those who receive correction will be blessed; those who stiffen against God will face a punishment even more severe.

---

13. Hebrews 3:2, 6. According to a growing number of scholars, the expression "the faith of Christ" (Gal. 2:16, 20 et al.) may well refer to Christ's own faith(fulness) to God as a man under the covenant. Although Jesus kept faith with God by perfect obedience to the covenant stipulations and thereby earned the covenant blessings, He willingly "became a curse for us" (Gal. 3:13). To charge the imputed curse of the cross to Jesus' own merit is the blasphemy of 1 Corinthians 12:3, and it fails to recognize that the smitten One receives the stripes due to others (Isa. 53:4, 5). That this One seemingly accursed by God should be the Messiah was the gospel's scandal to unconverted Saul of Tarsus.

Isaiah contrasts these two facts in the vivid symbolism common to the prophets:

> Zion will be redeemed with justice, her penitent ones with righteousness. But rebels and sinners will both be broken together, and those who forsake the Lord will perish. . . . You will be like an oak with fading leaves, like a garden without water. The mighty man will become tinder and his work a spark; both will burn together, with no one to quench the fire.—vv. 27, 28, 30, 31.

The picture is one of total desolation. Like Sodom and Gomorrah, Judah will be left without survivor or remnant (Isa. 1:9). God hammers home this point by figurative language: the people will *burn like tinder* with no one to *quench* the fire. Because the fire will not be quenched or extinguished, it will destroy completely. The result can be compared to an oak with fading leaves or a garden with no water. Destruction, emptiness, ruin will remain alone. The wicked will be no more.

This passage threatens a specific historical judgment of God against Jerusalem. But it is instructive in our study because it helps acquaint us with the prophetic symbolism, the vocabulary by which God often announces divine judgment. In this case we know the outcome—total desolation with no survivors. It is interesting that God describes that outcome in terms of a burning fire which is not quenched and which therefore destroys completely.

Isaiah 5:24, 25. God's woes and judgment-warnings to Jerusalem continue. The land will be emptied, and its inhabitants will go into captivity (vv. 9, 13). Mockers may rise and tempt God now, but their day will come (vv. 19-21). The prophet pictures their fate in these words:

> Therefore, as tongues of fire lick up straw and as dry grass sinks down in the flames, so their roots will decay and their flowers blow away like dust. . . . Therefore the Lord's anger burns against His people; His hand is raised and He strikes them down. The mountains shake, and the dead bodies are like refuse in the streets. Yet for all this, His anger is not turned away, His hand is still upraised.—vv. 24, 25.

Again God shows us an empty land. Only corpses line the streets. The wicked are as helpless against God's judgment as straw and dry grass are against fire. Nothing of them is left—"their roots decay and their flowers blow away like dust."

This is typical prophetic language for a divine judgment. The passage threatens a specific historical event enacted against a particular people through the means of an invading army. But it is instructive for us to see how fire is part of the prophetic vocabulary used to describe such judgments.

We should not interpret this language literally. Isaiah's hearers did not puzzle over the inconsistency of corpses in the streets on the one hand and destruction by fire on the other. Such prophetic language strikes like a series of thunderbolts or like bolts of lightning. God is not previewing the *Jerusalem Evening News*; He is painting an abstract landscape. He is not informing the mind or satisfying the curiosity; He is arresting the attention and enlivening the conscience.

One writer compares such prophetic language to Picasso's abstract painting, *Guernica*. Here the artist shows the terrible tragedy that befell a particular Basque town on April 28, 1937. His work is not a photograph but an impressionistic painting. By "de-calendarizing" the scene, Picasso universalizes it. It is still specific, but it has become far more. Now it is also a symbol of the ravages and trauma of war throughout history.[14]

Obadiah 15-21. The one-chapter book of Obadiah is "what the Sovereign Lord says about Edom" (v. 1). Throughout the vision God contrasts the fates of Edom (Esau) and Jacob, of Mount Teman and Mount Zion. In a larger sense Edom and Jacob stand here for those who trust in God and those who do not. In this light we may find the passage instructive on our subject as well.

God will punish Edom for her pride (vv. 3, 4), indifference to injustice (vv. 8-11) and betrayal of a brother (vv. 12-14). Divine judgment will be manifested on "the day of the Lord," a day which is near not only for Edom but for all nations (v. 15). When God does judge, the wicked nations

> will drink and drink and be as if they had never been. —v. 16.

> The house of Jacob will be a fire and the house of Joseph a flame; the house of Esau will be stubble, and they will set it on fire and consume it. There will be no survivors from the house of Esau. The Lord has spoken. —v. 18.

---

14. The illustration is Vernard Eller's in his *The Most Revealing Book of the Bible: Making Sense Out of Revelation*, pp. 87-89. The book is an excellent introduction (and more) to reading biblical prophecy, particularly the opening chapter.

At that time "deliverers will go up on Mount Zion to govern the mountains of Esau. And the kingdom will be the Lord's" (v. 21).

This text concerns the actual destruction of a specific nation. But it describes Edom's fate in typical symbolic language common throughout the Old Testament prophets. And that language, in large part, is the vehicle for New Testament expressions of final punishment. "Edom" and "Zion" here also seem to stand as representatives of the godly and impious in general. Without claiming more than this, the passage can be instructive as we survey the Old Testament teaching on the fate of the wicked. We observe in passing that Edom's destruction, like Sodom's, left no survivors and that the last words are that the kingdom is the Lord's.

Nahum 1:2-15. Like Obadiah's oracle against Edom, Nahum's book is directed to a specific pagan people, Nineveh (Nah. 1:1). As in Psalm 50, God comes in stormy fire for judgment (vv. 3-6). He pours out His wrath like fire which no one can endure (v. 6). He pursues His enemies into darkness (v. 8). He brings their plots to an end, never to reappear (v. 9). They are consumed like dry stubble (v. 10). God cuts them down and they pass away, completely destroyed and left without descendant (vv. 12, 14, 15).

Again we get the "feel" of the prophetic judgments. God mixes metaphors freely, for He is not speaking literally. He comes in *fire* and pursues into *darkness*. No one should stop and ask how fire and darkness can coexist. The mention of "fire" calls for one emotional response; "darkness" elicits another. Both are true. God graphically describes Nineveh's plunder later in Nahum's prophecy in literal terms (Nah. 2:3-10; 3:1-3), but that language is no more fearful than this.

Note that Nineveh's judgment is pictured in terms of fire and darkness, that it consumes the people so entirely that they pass away without descendant or any hope of return.

Zephaniah 1:14-18. The "day of the Lord" is the usual prophetic expression for a time of divine judgment against a city, nation or the whole world. Then God is clearly in charge. This day stands in sharp contrast to "man's day" (the literal expression in 1 Cor. 4:3), when the wicked may occupy the throne and the righteous suffer.

Zephaniah stacks up figure upon figure as he portrays the "day of the Lord" soon to come on Jerusalem in the agency of the Babylonian armies.

> The great day of the Lord is near—near and coming quickly. Listen! The cry on the day of the Lord will be bitter, the shouting of the warrior there. That day will be a day of wrath, a day of distress and anguish, a day of trouble and ruin, a day of darkness and gloom, a day of clouds and blackness, a day of trumpet and battle cry. . . . Their blood will be poured out like dust and their entrails like filth. Neither their silver nor their gold will be able to save them on the day of the Lord's wrath. In the fire of His jealousy the whole world will be consumed, for He will make a sudden end of all who live in the earth.—vv. 14-18.

The prophet describes God's "day of judgment" (here a specific historical judgment against Jerusalem) from its victims' point of view. It is a day of wrath, distress and trouble—words Paul also uses of the final day of judgment (Rom. 2:5-9). It is a day of anguish —the best one-word description of the New Testament's "weeping and grinding of teeth." It is a day of darkness but also of consuming fire—expressions also repeated in the New Testament warnings of the End.

Zephaniah helps us see again how the Old Testament prophets, by the Spirit of God, pictured God's approaching punishment. By such passages we learn the prophetic vocabulary for divine visitations of wrath and destruction. These are emotive terms, vivid pictures, striking descriptions. They create terror and inspire awe.

We should not always assume that "the day of the Lord" refers to the eschatological end of the world. But we may be sure that it describes a visitation of divine wrath on the wicked (usually accompanied by divine mercy for true believers). We may also be sure that such passages are acquainting us with the terminology we will meet repeatedly in the New Testament when Jesus and His men warn us of the great "day of the Lord" that will bring history to its climax and settle the last account.

As we become familiar with the symbolism used by Old Testament prophets, we will also learn to look to those earlier Scriptures for the same language's meaning in the New Testament. And to that same extent we will be freed from the temptation to attach to biblical expressions literal meanings of modern derivation, meanings which have no basis in Scripture and which sometimes contradict its ordinary usage throughout.

III. Passages concerning Messianic or Eschatological Judgment

In addition to texts which state moral principles and those which illustrate temporal judgments, a number of Old Testament passages clearly speak of a Messianic or eschatological judgment. Because these texts or their contexts are so applied in the New Testament, we may read them without fear in that light ourselves. We will consider nine such passages here. Others probably could be found. But these are representative in what they say; they are not contradicted by some other texts which we have failed to disclose.

Psalm 1:3-6. This simple psalm, often memorized and loved by many, contrasts the life and end of the wicked and the righteous. The godly man is like a well-watered tree. Its leaves never wither, and it is fruitful all the year around (v. 3). The picture reminds us of the Garden of Eden in Genesis or of the Eternal City in Revelation.

In contrast to this pleasant place, the wicked are "like chaff that the wind blows away." They will not be able to stand in judgment, and their path will finally perish (vv. 4-6). The picture is one of exclusion, expulsion, disintegration and desolation. At that the psalm stops. Other passages will add details, but none will contradict what these verses say.

Psalm 2:9-12. The second psalm is clearly Messianic and is quoted frequently in the New Testament.[15] Verses 9 and 12 describe the Son's wrath against His enemies.

> You will rule them [or *break* them] with an iron scepter; You will dash them to pieces like pottery. —v. 9

> Kiss the Son, lest He be angry, and you be destroyed in your way, for His wrath can flare up in a moment. —v. 12

---

15. Matt. 3:17; 15:5; Acts 4:26; 13:33; Heb. 1:5; 5:5; 1:2; Rev. 2:26, 27; 12:5; 19:15.

The rather colorless word "perish" is further described as the result of Christ's kindled wrath, His breaking with an iron scepter. In this psalm it is compared to being shattered like earthenware. The picture is one of destruction in the ordinary sense of the word. This passage speaks of Christ's coming judgment, and it teaches us something.

Psalm 69:22-28. Because of the New Testament use of this psalm, it could also be treated as Messianic. It also fits the category of passages which deal with moral principles of divine government, and we have already discussed it there. (Since God's thoughts are greater than ours, Scripture often overlaps our categories and systematic headings. This passage is one example.)

Isaiah 11:4. This entire chapter is clearly Messianic. Paul applies the words of verse 10 to his gospel ministry among the Gentiles (Rom. 15:12). Each of the first five verses is paraphrased or echoed by New Testament writers. Verses 6-9 have been variously interpreted as describing the millennium, the gospel age, or the new heavens and earth—in each case the blessed fruit of Jesus' work of redemption. Beyond question, we hear in this passage that Spirit of Christ which informed the prophets of Jesus' suffering and glory (1 Pet. 1:9-12).

The Messiah judges justly, giving decisions for the poor of the earth. The wicked also feel His judgment, for "He will strike the earth with the rod of His mouth; with the breath of His lips He will slay the wicked" (v. 4). The language reminds us of Psalm 2. Men may scoff at Christ now, but one day He will be their judge. From His lips now flow life and peace; by them the wicked will then be slain. The picture is symbolic, but its import is clear. The passage fits the larger pattern, and it is part of the whole biblical picture.

Isaiah 33:10-24. Oppressors afflict Israel now, Isaiah says, but God has a brighter future for His people. When He "arises," the scene will change (v. 10). The wicked's efforts to protect themselves will be as disappointingly weak as one who conceives chaff and gives birth to straw. The wicked will ignite themselves by their own sins (v. 11), which will then "consume" them (v. 11). They will burn "as if to lime," blazing like "cut thornbushes" (v. 12). Here is a picture of total destruction. No metaphor could describe one more complete.

Traditionalists sometimes find everlasting conscious torment in verse 14, but three objections may be made against this interpretation.

1. The context of verses 11-12 speaks against it, picturing instead a total destruction by fire that could not possibly be more complete. The "fire" of this passage does not preserve—it consumes! That is why no wicked person can "dwell" with it.

2. The language of verse 14 probably describes the eternal holiness of God Himself, not the fire of hell. God *is* a "consuming fire" (Deut. 4:24; Heb. 12:29). Isaiah had already used this figure (Isa. 5:24, 25; 10:16-18), and He will use it again (Isa. 47:14). The fire of God's holiness always destroys whatever is not pure. As with Nadab and Abihu, the same fire which sanctifies the altar destroys the irreverent (Lev. 9:23–10:3). The "everlasting burning" of Isaiah 33:14 parallels the "consuming fire" of verse 11, and both refer best to God in His holiness.

3. Verse 14 asks a question which may be answered by the verses that follow. Just as Psalm 15 inquires who can dwell with God, then gives the answer, so this passage follows the same pattern. The answer of verses 15-16 is strikingly similar to the answer of Psalm 15. None but the person who "walks righteously and speaks what is right," who rejects extortion and bribes, who avoids evil in every form—none but this person can "dwell" on the heights. Only this one *can* dwell with the God who is a consuming fire, whose holy glory is an everlasting burning against all sin.

That the passage is eschatological is indicated by verses 17-24. Redeemed Zion will "see the King in His beauty and view a land that stretches afar" (v. 17). They will look on the eternal Jerusalem (v. 20), where none will be ill and all sins will have been forgiven (v. 24).

The "everlasting burning" of this passage does not torment perpetually. Like a blaze devouring dry thorns, it consumes the wicked. Only those walking uprightly, their sins forgiven, can dwell with such a God.

Isaiah 51:3-11. Israel may suffer in exile, but present distress only foreshadows a glorious restoration. Those who trust in God will rejoice in His salvation. Those who mock His law and reproach His people will taste and feel His wrath.

This passage is in a Messianic context. Jesus precedes it (Isa. 50:4-10) and follows it (Isa. 52:13–53:12). It looks forward to God's righteousness and salvation. Jesus has already procured these blessings, and the Holy Spirit now administers them. Their consummation will come at the End. The contrasting picture of righteous and wicked may also have some fulfillment now, but it waits till the second advent for complete actualization. We may add such passages as these to the Old Testament witness concerning the destiny of the wicked.

God will restore His people to a new Eden ringing with glad thanksgiving and songs of joy (v. 3). Even the Gentiles will share in God's righteousness and salvation (vv. 4, 5), which will last forever (vv. 6b, 8b). The wicked will have no part in this paradise. Earth's inhabitants will "die like flies" when the heavens "vanish like smoke" and the earth wears out "like a garment" (v. 6). When the righteous thrive, the wicked will perish. "For the moth will eat them up like a garment; the worm will devour them like wool" (v. 8).

This language is symbolic but true. We therefore take it seriously but not literally. God does not intend for us to picture the damned as the main course at a banquet for giant insects and their larvae. The figure is just that—a *figure*. But it stands for something. It truly describes the reality for which it stands. What is the significance of the heavens and earth vanishing like smoke or wearing out like a garment? Is it not a complete passing away so that no trace is left? What is the sense of the wicked being consumed by moths and worms like wool and other garments? Is it not total destruction, again without a trace? It is important that we recognize the symbolic nature of such passages. But it is only fair to allow the pictures to speak for themselves, to let them describe a reality which truly corresponds to the significance of the symbol. This passage can teach us something about the end of the wicked. We should let it speak in its own terms.

Isaiah 66:24. This may be the most ignored biblical passage concerning final punishment, although it gives us the specific scriptural phrase which is probably quoted most often.

Earlier in the same chapter, God contrasts the peace and comfort promised the humble (Isa. 66:2, 12-14) with the "fury" He will show His foes (v. 14). The language is figurative, typical, prophetic symbolism. God executes judgment "with fire and with His sword" (v. 16). When the visitation has ended, "many will be those slain by the Lord" (v. 16b). The wicked "meet their end together" (v. 17). The righteous and their descendants endure forever (v. 22). "All mankind" comes to worship God (v. 23)—the wicked are no more. This is the setting of the crucial verse 24. It says:

> And they will go out and look upon the dead bodies of those who rebelled against Me; their worm will not die, nor will their fire be quenched, and they will be loathsome to all mankind.

Jesus quotes these words in one of His own famous statements about final punishment (Mark 9:48), and they have formed the basis for much Christian teaching on hell ever since. It is important to look carefully, therefore, at what the verse actually says. Only then is one ready to build on it in the light of later revelation. We will consider it briefly, phrase by phrase.

The righteous "go out and look" on their enemies' corpses. Although this is clearly a symbolic picture of the future, it may well be based on an actual incident which Isaiah witnessed. In one of the greatest acts of divine deliverance since the Exodus and the Red Sea, God had answered Hezekiah's prayer and saved Jerusalem overnight from certain defeat by the Assyrians (2 Kings 18:17–19:36; Isa. 36, 37). Isaiah had strengthened Hezekiah with the Lord's encouraging message (Isa. 37:21-35). That night

> the angel of the Lord went out and put to death a hundred and eighty-five thousand men in the Assyrian camp. When the people got up the next morning—there were all the dead bodies!—Isa. 37:36.

Now Isaiah declares that the same scene will be reproduced on a vaster scale at the end of time. In the historical event of Isaiah's day (Isa. 37:36) and in his prophetic picture of the future (Isa. 66:24), the righteous contemplate with satisfaction "the dead bodies" of the wicked. They look at corpses (Hebrew: *pegerim*), not living people. They view their destruction, not their misery.[16]

Other Bible verses mention "worms" in connection with dead bodies.[17] Several kinds of flies lay eggs in the flesh of carcasses,

---

16. On God's people viewing the carcasses of their enemies with satisfaction, see also Exod. 14:30 (the prototypal event); Ps. 58:10; 91:8; Ezek. 39:9-22; Mal. 4:1-3.

17. Isa. 14:11. Job speaks thus of himself as one already dead in Job 7:5; 17:14; 21:16. The New Testament knows one case of death preceded by an attack of worms (Acts 12:23).

which hatch into larvae known as maggots. These serve a beneficial purpose in hastening decomposition. They are also a symbol of ignominy "precisely because they attack only bodies deprived of burial."[18] To the Hebrew mind, even if a man could live to be 2000 years old and have 100 children, without a proper burial he would better have been stillborn (Eccles. 6:3-6). Like Jezebel, these corpses are left unburied; they are "loathsome" to all who see them (2 Kings 9:10). Jeremiah also predicts this ultimate disgrace for God's enemies:

> At that time those slain by the Lord will be everywhere—from one end of the earth to the other. They will not be mourned or gathered up or buried, but will be like refuse lying on the ground.—Jer. 25:33.

Such discarded corpses are fit only for the worms and fire. Although death by burning was not unknown to the Old Testament,[19] that is not the picture here. To burn a corpse signified at times a thing utterly accursed or devoted to God for destruction (Josh. 7:25). It also was an act of complete contempt (Amos 2:1).[20]

Because this fire is "not quenched" or extinguished, it completely consumes what is put in it. The figure of unquenchable fire is frequent in Scripture and signifies a fire that consumes (Ezek. 20:47, 48), reduces to nothing (Amos 5:5, 6) or burns up something (Matt. 3:12).[21] Both worms and fire speak of a total and final destruction. Both terms also make this a "loathsome" scene. The righteous view it with disgust but not pity. The *final* picture is one of shame, not pain.

Traditionalist writers, as a matter of course, interpret this passage in the light of their conception of final punishment rather than forming an understanding on the basis of the passage. Jesus' use of the language is generally handled the same way. Rather than studying this passage, determining the sense of its figures and reading New Testament quotations on that foundation, commentators and theologians again and again begin with the New Testament quotations, interpret them in the light of church positions, and ignore the Isaiah text altogether.

---

18. Pétavel, *The Problem of Immortality*, p. 323.

19. "Death by burning is prescribed for two sexual offenses (Lev. 20:14; 21:9); in the story of Gen. 38:24 it is for harlotry" (Moshe Greenberg, "Crimes and Punishment," *The Interpreter's Dictionary of the Bible*, 1:741).

20. Pedersen reads later ideas into the text in his comment: "When the worms gnaw the dead body, the soul feels it" (Johannes Pedersen, *Israel: Its Life and Culture*, 1-2:180).

21. See also 1 Kings 22:17; Isa. 1:31; Jer. 4:4; 21:12; Mark 9:43, 48.

Buis does quote the verse as one of those "which hint at future retribution" but does not attempt to explain its figures. Instead, he cites Delitzsch that it speaks of "the eternal torment of the damned."[22] Braun ignores the passage entirely.[23] Isaac Watts says there would be "no punishment at all" if the text meant what it pictures, so he allegorizes the gnawing worm into "the remorse and terrible anguish of conscience which shall never be relieved," and makes the unquenchable fire "the pains and anguish which come from without."[24] Calvin regards it a mistake to say these things "related absolutely to the last judgment," although he does "not deny that they extend as far as to that judgment."[25] He does not exegete the verse at all but asserts that "the plain meaning" is

> that the wicked shall have a bad conscience as an executioner, to torment them without end . . . and finally, that they shall tremble and be agitated in a dreadful and shocking manner, as if a worm were gnawing the heart of a man, or a fire were consuming it, and yet thus consumed, he did not die.[26]

Luther also makes the worm "the bite of the conscience," an interpretation suggested also by Augustine.[27]

This allegorical interpretation, based on reading into the text something not there while passing over all that is, is very ancient, dating at least to the intertestamental apocryphal book of Judith.[28] But search as he will, one simply cannot find anything in Isaiah 66:24 about conscious suffering, much less forever. One might wish to argue the point from some other passage. But any fair use of the

---

22. Harry Buis, *The Doctrine of Eternal Punishment*, p. 13.

23. Jon E. Braun, *Whatever Happened to Hell?* pp. 130-142.

24. Isaac Watts, *The World to Come . . .* , pp. 300-301. Since Tertullian, many traditionalist authors have been concerned that the wicked not be punished too "lightly" even if that meant strengthening the plain teaching of Scripture to something more harsh.

25. John Calvin, *Commentary on the Book of the Prophet Isaiah*, 4:438.

26. Ibid., p. 439.

27. Martin Luther, *Luther's Works*, vol. 17, *Lectures on Isaiah (Chapters 40-66)*, p. 416. On Augustine's treatment of hell see Appendix A.

28. In the closing chapter of this book, following a great deliverance from the Assyrians, the heroine, Judith, leads the people in a song of victory. Clearly alluding to Isaiah 66:24, she says:

> "Woe to the nation that rises up against my race:
> The Lord Almighty will take vengeance of them in the day of judgment,
> To put fire and worms in their flesh;
> And they shall weep and feel their pain for ever."
> —Jth. 16:17.

phrases originating here must at least take account of the sense of this passage without reading into its picture extraneous ideas from a later time and place. Proper exegesis demands as much, but that is precisely what traditionalist writers have failed to do from ancient times to the present. Conditionalist authors have pointed out this deficiency time and time again, but they have customarily been ignored, their remarks dismissed without further notice.

Salmond, who defended the traditionalist view of hell, is a notable exception to that generalization. He wrote, "This is the picture at least of an absolute overthrow, an irreversible punishment overtaking the rebellious. At a later period the word [hell] was used to designate the place of future retribution."[29] Later he notes that, while the terms of Jesus' teaching are based on this passage, "it does not follow that they are limited to the use which is made of them there" and that they become "figures of a retribution of another order than any that takes effect on earth."[30]

We agree with that statement most heartily. The adjective "eternal" includes a qualitative aspect, as we have already seen, and it suggests something belonging to the Age to Come. The final punishment of the wicked will be "of another order" than that of any temporal judgment. But Scripture describes *what* it will be in terms taken from specific occasions of divine judgment within history. We ask only that any explanation of those terms at least *begin* with the scenes they first described, and then that any extension of their meaning be grounded on biblical exegesis and not traditional or dogmatic fancy.

Daniel 12:2, 3. Even scholars who tend to discount Old Testament references to the final resurrection acknowledge it in this verse.[31] The passage includes a resurrection of both good and evil,[32]

---

29. Steward D. F. Salmond, *The Christian Doctrine of Immortality*, p. 354.

30. Ibid., p. 376.

31. H. H. Rowley calls Daniel 12:2 "the only clear and universally recognized reference to resurrection in the Old Testament," according to Thomas E. Ridenhour, "Immortality and Resurrection in the Old Testament," *Dialog* 15 (Spring 1976): 107.

32. Dubarle disputes this. "It is not until the New Testament (John 5:38) that resurrection for punishment is foreseen." He suggests an alternative explanation that the wicked here are "condemned to rot away for ever in the earth, arousing the abhorrence of all flesh" (André-Marie Dubarle, "Belief in Immortality in the Old Testament and Judaism," *Immortality and Resurrection*, p. 41.

but it is not clear whether it reveals it as universal in scope. One author discusses the text in the light of its larger whole (Dan. 11:2–12:3), "whose theme is judgment," and sees the resurrection here as "a solution to the problem of the defense of the righteous in persecution."[33] Another argues that the text refers explicitly to the members of the chosen people and to them alone.[34] We do not have to pack all God's word into any one verse; further revelation makes clear what may here be obscure.

Among traditionalist writers, Buis calls Daniel 12:2 "one very clear reference to future punishment," but he makes no further comment on the passage.[35] Braun does not even mention the verse in his chapter on the Old Testament.[36]

Concerning the wicked, the text says only that of the "multitudes" who awake from the dust of the earth, with "some to everlasting life," there will be "others" who awake "to shame and everlasting contempt." The Hebrew word translated "contempt" also appears in Isaiah 66:24, where it is translated "loathsome" and describes unburied corpses. Conditionalist writer, Petavel, notes that "the sentiment of the survivors is disgust, not pity."[37] Nothing will change this sentiment; there is "everlasting contempt."

Malachi 4:1-6. These half-dozen verses stand on one side of the great period of divine silence, where they reach out expectantly to the story the Gospels resume 400 years after. Jesus Himself says John is this passage's "Elijah" (Matt. 11:14; Mark 9:11-13; Luke 1:17). Like the book of Revelation in the New, this last book of the Old Testament Scriptures (in time, not Hebrew or Greek order) contrasts the final destinies of good and evil.

The "day" of God is coming (v. 1), the "great and dreadful day of the Lord" (v. 5). For those who revere God it will bring joy. They will leap like frolicking calves as they rejoice in the healing rays of the Sun of righteousness (v. 2). This day will also bring their vindication, for they will trample down the wicked, who will be "ashes under the soles" of their feet (v. 3).

---

33. Ridenhour, "Immortality and Resurrection," p. 107.
34. Dubarle, "Belief in Immortality," p. 41.
35. Buis, *The Doctrine of Eternal Punishment*, p. 12.
36. Braun, *Whatever Happened to Hell?* pp. 130-142.
37. Pétavel, *The Problem of Immortality*, p. 323.

Arrogant evildoers will become like "stubble," and the coming day will "set them on fire." This is an all-consuming fire which will leave them "not a root or a branch" (v. 1). The expression eliminates every possibility of remnant or survivor. When God promised Judah a surviving remnant on another occasion, He used language just opposite (2 Kings 19:30; see the same figure applied to Jesus in Isa. 11:1; 53:2). It will be too late then for remedy; there is no hope of restoration or chance to escape. The godless will be "ashes under the soles" of the feet of the righteous (v. 3).

We need not literalize this prophecy or try to plan its program. These are representative symbols. But the reality they convey is in keeping with the sense of the pictures. The symbol corresponds to the fulfillment. It does not contradict it. The picture portrays the righteous rejoicing in God's salvation and the wicked gone forever. The picture does not include perpetual torment, though it does include a total consumption by destroying fire. With these sobering verses Old Testament revelation ceased. God's next prophet would cry in the desert, demanding repentance in view of the approaching fire of God (Matt. 3:7-12).

Summary

The Old Testament has very much to say about the end of the wicked. Its poetic books of Job, Psalms and Proverbs repeatedly affirm the moral principles of divine government. The wicked may thrive now and the righteous suffer, these books tell us, but that picture will not be the final one. These books reassure the godly again and again that those who trust will be vindicated, they will endure forever, they will inherit the earth. The wicked, however proud their boasts today, will one day not be found. Their place will be empty. They will vanish like a slug as it moves along. They will disappear like smoke. Men will search for them and they will not be found. Even their memory will perish. On these pillars of divine justice the world stands, and by these principles the Lord God governs His eternal kingdom.

The historical books of the Old Testament take us another step. Not only does God declare what He will do to the wicked; on many occasions He has shown us. When the first world became too wicked to exist, God destroyed it completely, wiping every living creature outside the ark from the face of the earth. That is a model of the fiery judgment awaiting the present heavens and earth. When Sodom became too sinful to continue, God rained fire and brimstone from heaven, obliterating the entire wicked population in a moment so terrible it is memorialized throughout Scripture as an example of divine judgment. From this terrible conflagration emerged not a survivor —even the ground was left scorched and barren. Only the lingering smoke remained, a grim reminder of the fate awaiting any man who attempts to quarrel with his Maker.

Cities and nations also tasted God's wrath. Edom and Judah, Babylon and Nineveh turn by turn came under His temporal judgments. Some were spared a remnant. Others were not. God described these divine visitations in terms of fire and darkness, anguish and trouble. Unquenchable fire consumed entirely until nothing was left. Again smoke ascended, the prophetic cipher for a ruin accomplished.

The inspired declarations of the prophets combine moral principle with historical fate. The details of actual destructions wrought on the earth become symbols for another divine visitation. The prophets speak to their own times, but they also stand on tiptoe and view the distant future. A day is coming, they tell us, when God will bring an end to all He has begun. That judgment will be the last.[38] Good and evil will be gathered alike to see the righteousness of the Lord they have served or spurned. Again there will be fire and storm, tempest and darkness. The slain of God will be many—corpses will lie in the street. Amidst this scene of utter contempt worms and fire will take their final toll. Nothing will remain of the wicked but ashes—the righteous will tread over them with their feet. God's kingdom will endure forever. The righteous and their children will inherit Mount Zion. Joy and singing will fill the air. All the earth will praise the Lord.

Such is the Old Testament picture of the end of the wicked.

---

38. P. T. Forsyth wrote: "For the Bible as a whole . . . history is viewed under the category of judgment (though saving judgment) and not under that of progress. . . . The course of historic events is that of a series of judgments . . . a long crescendo of judgment, ending in a crisis of all the crises, a harvest of all the harvests which had closed one age and begun a new, a grand climacteric of judgment, a last judgment, which dissipates for ever in a storm the silting up of all previous judgments, because ending a temporal world and opening an eternal" (P. T. Forsyth, *The Justification of God* [London, 1916], p. 185, quoted by Leon Morris, *The Biblical Doctrine of Judgment*, p. 60).

8

Between the Testaments

So far as the canon of Scripture is concerned, the period from Malachi to Matthew may be "the 400 silent years," but in terms of literature it was anything but quiet. Within a century after Malachi, Alexander the Great had conquered his world. He took tribute of one kind but left another of his own. The Greek language became the common tongue of civilized people, bridging communication gaps and binding together men scattered since Babel.

The Jews were widely dispersed. Large populations had settled in Egypt; others remained in Babylon and Persia; exiles spread in all directions. Those who returned to Palestine soon found themselves under foreign occupation once more. The Seleucids of Syria and the Ptolemies of Egypt competed for the mastery of this land-strip between them, relinquishing it in the end to the Romans, who installed for the New Testament period the half-breed family of Edomite Herods.

The last two centuries before Christ were troubling years for faithful Jews. Israel's faith was tried in the fire. The Syrian tyrant, Antiochus IV (175-164 B.C.),[1] one of the cruelest men in history, determined to unify his territory by enforcing Greek religion, custom and

---

1. Antiochus took the surname "Epiphanes" ("The Manifest [God]"), prompting some of his enemies to call him "Epimanes" ("The Madman"). This brief history of the period reflects N. Turner's article, "Antiochus," *The Interpreter's Dictionary of the Bible*, 1:150-151.

law. To this end he outlawed on pain of death every important practice of Jewish faith, including Sabbath observance, circumcision and
the laws concerning food. He committed the ultimate blasphemy
when he caused an altar of Zeus to be erected in the temple at Jerusalem, compelling the Jews to participate in his heathen worship.
This "abomination that makes desolate" (probably described in Daniel 11:31) had its impact but also its repercussions.

Open rebellion finally came in 167 B.C. at the little village of
Modin. A faithful priest named Mattathias, resisting an act of sacri-
lege, killed the king's representative, then fled to the countryside
with his family and an ever-enlarging band of volunteers. Mattathias
died the next year, but the guerrilla movement continued under his
son Judas, who became known as "The Hammer" (Maccabeus).
Antiochus would have exterminated the Palestinian Jews entirely,
but eastern revolts forced him to respond there instead. Judas'
courage rose with his faith (probably heralded in Hebrews 11:34); he
defeated the king's army at Emmaus and then at Beth-zur. On the
25th of Chislev, 165 B.C., Judas rededicated the temple to the worship of God and restored the daily sacrifices. This event is still
celebrated each December 25 in the Feast of Hanukkah.

Such times reveal apostates and make martyrs. They also spawned
a special type of literature known today as "apocalyptic." Parts of
Daniel in the Old Testament fit the same pattern, as does Revelation
in the New. This literature mirrored the minds of the steadfast and inspired straggling souls. Among its common traits were these: (1) a
strong sense of the otherness of God, (2) the conviction that the end
of the world is at hand, (3) a sense of man's existence in historical
time, and (4) the use of mysterious and secret revelations.[2] This
apocalyptic literature "located the believer in a minority community
and gave his life meaning by relating it to the end, soon to come,
which would reverse his present status."[3] Both Jews and Christians
produced such material until about A.D. 100.

2. William E. Beardslee, "New Testament Apocalyptic in Recent Interpretation," *Interpretation* 25, no. 4 (October 1971): 424-425.

3. Ibid., p. 424. Another scholar who has specialized in intertestamental thought reminds us of
"the fact that theological conceptions and the literature that contains them do not evolve in a
vacuum. They are the products of real people, living in concrete historical situations"
(George W. E. Nickelsburg, Jr., *Resurrection, Immortality, and Eternal Life in Intertestamental
Judaism*, p. 10).

Some of these books were included in the intertestamental Greek translation of the Hebrew Bible (though not in the final Hebrew canon) and are regarded as biblical by the Roman Catholic Church (but not by most Protestants). Generally called the "Apocrypha," these 14 or 15 books (depending on their division) are the best known of the "outside" books, but they are by no means the most important.

Of far greater interest to biblical scholars are the writings often called the "Pseudepigrapha."[4] James H. Charlesworth, a specialist in the area, lists 77 known works under this category and leaves the list open for further additions.[5] The fascination these writings hold for scholars today is seen in Charlesworth's bibliography of 1494 articles or books on the subject, all published between 1960 and 1975!

Generalizations abound concerning this intertestamental literature as a whole and regarding its teaching on final punishment. Opinions reputable scholars held as late as the 1950's have had to be modified or abandoned in the light of new discoveries. These discoveries include but are not limited to the Dead Sea Scrolls, a vast collection first found in the late 1940's and still being translated and analyzed.

It is very inviting to try to neatly box intertestamental thought, to clearly distinguish between ideas, and to label views with care. It is also impossible. The literature cannot be easily categorized—whether by its place of origin (Palestine or Diaspora), its authorship (Hellenistic Jews or those loyal to Law and tradition), or even by its precise

---

4. Literally "false writings," so called because authorship is attributed to Old Testament figures such as Moses, Baruch, Solomon, Enoch, the twelve patriarchs and others. Scholars who specialize in this genre urge against any modern connotation of fraud or deceit. "Rather than being spurious," James H. Charlesworth says, "the documents . . . are works written in honor of and inspired by Old Testament heroes. It is anachronistic and misrepresentative to suggest that there is anything innately fraudulent about the Pseudepigrapha" (James H. Charlesworth, *The Pseudepigrapha and Modern Research*, p. 25).

R. H. Charles suggests a very practical theological reason for this practice of attaching ancient names as authors of more recent works. By the third century B.C. the Law had come to be regarded as God's supreme and *final* revelation. On this view, the Law not only took the place of the pre-exilic prophets; it made any new word from God unthinkable. If anyone would gain a hearing for a new work, it must be in the name of an ancient worthy, when prophecy was still allowed to have taken place. Charles concludes: "All Jewish apocalypses, therefore, from 200 B.C. onwards were of necessity pseudonymous if they sought to exercise any real influence on the nation; for the Law was everything, belief in inspiration was dead amongst them, and their Canon was closed" (R. H. Charles, ed., *The Apocrypha and Pseudepigrapha of the Old Testament in English*, 2:viii-ix). While this was probably one factor, other scholars caution that it was not the only one.

5. Charlesworth, *The Pseudepigrapha and Modern Research*, pp. xi-xiv.

time.[6] Some of the books show clear signs of later Christian "editing" and additions. The Judaism which produced this literature also includes great diversity of thought. One who searches here for doctrinal patterns finds that the "picture is far from clear or coherent."[7] Expectations of the End were "varied and unsystematized."[8] These books present "a heterogeneous mass of ideas in constant flux."[9]

The Pseudepigrapha's influence on the New Testament has also been overstated. Charlesworth is undoubtedly correct in saying that the "often bizarre, usually rich apocalyptic traditions upon which the Pseudepigrapha almost has a monopoly were determinative for the thoughts of Dante, Bunyan, and Milton."[10] It is another matter entirely to say that "most of the ideas regarding the future life which are found in the New Testament writings had their origin in the apocalyptic writings."[11] Much of the New Testament *language* shares that background to be sure, but its crucial *ideas* regarding final punishment come from the biblical books of the Old Testament, not from these imaginative writings between the Testaments.[12]

---

6. "Not only was Palestine deeply hellenized, at least in scattered sections, but the diaspora itself contained islands of Jews loyal to Torah and traditions." Furthermore, "the geographical origin of a composition is usually the most difficult issue to resolve" (ibid., p. 24). According to Nickelsburg there was "no single Jewish orthodoxy" in intertestamental eschatology, the very idea of "a unitary Jewish view" being "a pure fiction" (Nickelsburg, *Resurrection, Immortality, and Eternal Life*, p. 180).

On diversity regarding eschatological anthropology in Palestinian Judaism, see Gunter Stemberger, *Der Leib der Auferstehung: Studien zur Anthropologie und Eschatologie des palastinischen Judentums im neutestamentlichen Zietalter (ca. 170 v. Chr.-100 n. Chr.)*, AnBib 56 (Rome: Biblical Institute, 1972). On the great diversity found in the eschatological expectations of western Diaspora Judaism, see Ulrich Fischer, *Eschatologie und Jenseitserwartung im hellenistischen Diasporajudentum*, BZNW 44 (Berlin/New York: de Gruyter, 1978). Fischer finds both wholistic and tripartite anthropologies, individualistic and cosmic hopes, and (confirming our present findings) various "final punishments" of the wicked, including total annihilation.

7. S. H. Hooke, "Life after Death: The Extra-Canonical Literature," *Expository Times*, June 1965, p. 276.

8. "Eschatology," *Dictionary of the Bible*, p. 266.

9. R. H. Charles, *A Critical History of the Doctrine of a Future Life*, p. 362. F. F. Bruce uses the intertestamental literature to illustrate the "varieties of expectation among religious Jews in the last two centuries B.C." in his "Paul on Immortality," *Scottish Journal of Theology* 24, no. 4 (November 1971): 459. The same material appears in his *Paul: Apostle of the Heart Set Free*, p. 302.

10. Charlesworth, *The Pseudepigrapha and Modern Research*, p. 25.

11. C. T. Fritsch, "Apocrypha," *The Interpreter's Dictionary of the Bible*, 1:164.

12. Writers advocating any position only confuse matters when they hastily equate similarity of language with agreement—or even worse, *origin*—of thought. A proper evangelical view of Scripture would seem to require that we give the Old Testament precedence over any extrabib-

Traditionalist writers have frequently made too much of the intertestamental literature as well. They have found certain texts which clearly describe unending conscious torment (an idea not contained in the Old Testament, as we have already seen) and, without further ado, have assigned these ideas to the language of Jesus. Shedd quotes Edersheim that the first-century Jews taught eternal punishment, and leaves it at that.[13] Pusey also argues from this single point of view, though in fairness to him we should note that he was responding to Farrar's similar overstatement in the opposite direction.[14] Buis cites the Pharisees' belief in this kind of eternal punishment, then argues from Jesus' silence that He approved of their doctrine.[15] One modern writer even quotes Philo of Alexandria as giving "the generally-held view of both the orthodox Jews and the Judeo-Christian community of that period."[16] This is roughly comparable to the situation of an archaeologist in the year A.D. 4000 uncovering a twentieth-century Christian Science reading room and proclaiming it the key to understanding Protestant beliefs of the period.

There is no question that the traditionalist understanding of hell is very ancient—or that it finds expression in the intertestamental literature of the Jews. But that literature also contains the view we

---

lical materials as the proper background for viewing and understanding the New Testament. In expressing this conviction, I acknowledge but would slightly modify the growing idea "that the proper approach to the historical Jesus is via documents and traditions contemporaneous with him" (Charlesworth, *The Pseudepigrapha and Modern Research*, p. 26).

13. William G. T. Shedd, *The Doctrine of Endless Punishment*, p. 14, note 1.

14. "The Jews believed in eternal punishment before or at the time of the Coming of our Lord, and called the place of that punishment Gehenna" (Edward Bouverie Pusey, *What Is of Faith as to Everlasting Punishment? In Reply to Dr. Farrar's Challenge in His "Eternal Hope," 1879*, p. 49). Pusey was responding to Frederic W. Farrar, who had said that "the Jews . . . never did . . . normally attach to the word Gehenna that meaning of endless torment which we attach to 'Hell'" (Frederic W. Farrar, *Eternal Hope*, p. 80). Farrar erred in citing rabbinic sources *too late* for the view of Christ's day; Pusey erred in noticing *too little* of the evidence, singling out one view to the neglect of another equally well documented.

15. Harry Buis, *The Doctrine of Eternal Punishment*, p. 24.

As we noted earlier, the Pharisees probably believed also in the pre-existence of souls, according to Josephus (*Wars* 2. 8. 14; *Antiquities* 18. 1. 3) and as perhaps reflected in John 9:2. F. F. Bruce cautions concerning Josephus' "eagerness to assimilate" his account of the Pharisees' teaching "to the Greek outlook" (Bruce, *Paul*, p. 301).

Conditionalist Edward White notes: "The points in which alone the doctrine of the Pharisees was defended both by Christ and Paul against the Sadducees, were those of the existence of spirits, and the 'resurrection of the just and unjust.'" He warns against the danger of assuming "that whatever . . . Christ did not explicitly condemn He sanctioned by His silence" and correctly observes that Jesus "taught by affirmation rather than denial" (Edward White, *Life in Christ* . . . , pp. 220-221).

16. Leslie H. Woodson, *Hell and Salvation*, p. 43.

have seen in the Old Testament that the day will come when the wicked will cease to be. Salmond, who defended the traditional doctrine, recognized this alternative of annihilation in the intertestamental writings and called attention to it in his study.[17] Strack and Billerbeck, conceded authorities in the field of later rabbinical literature, go even further. They suggest the possibility that the term "eternal punishment" in the Pseudepigrapha was itself *synonymous* with everlasting annihilation.[18] The implications of this statement, if it is correct, are staggering, literally turning upside-down a major traditionalist presupposition.

We make no claims here of being either exhaustive or final. This apocalyptic field covers a vast territory, and its literature is most complex. We will simply ask two questions, then seek to answer them. First, what views did the Jews hold concerning final punishment at the beginning of the Christian era as discerned in this apocryphal literature "outside" the canon? Second, to what extent did such views coincide with the divine revelation contained in the Old Testament?

---

17. S. D. F. Salmond concludes that "the class of literature which is the most relevant witness to the state of Jewish belief in Christ's time, shuts us up to a choice between annihilation and a penal immortality as the prevalent conception of the future of the impenitent . . . but they have no place for the idea of a universal restoration of the perverse" (Steward D. F. Salmond, *The Christian Doctrine of Immortality*, p. 359). We will note a view that the wicked will all be converted before the end. This is different from saying they will go to "hell" and later be restored— a view later expounded by Origen and others.

18. "The punishment of the godless, regardless if they were judged in the catastrophic judgment or the regular judgment, lasts forever. But the Pseudepigrapha also speaks about the destruction or the annihilation of the godless, so that one may be in doubt if to them the everlasting condemnation of the (judged) guilty simply had become synonymous with everlasting annihilation" (Hermann L. Strack and Paul Billerbeck, *Kommentar zum Neuen Testament aus Talmud und Midrasch*, 2:1096).

The German text states: "Die Bestrarung der Gottlosen, gleichviel ob sie im Katastrophengericht oder um ordentlichen Gerichtsverfahren gerichtet sind, wahrt ewig. Daneben reden die Pseudepigraphen aber auch vom Untergang oder von der Vernichtung der Gottlosen, so das man im Zweifel sein kann, ob innen die ewige Verdamnis der Gerichteten nicht vielfach gleichbedeuten gewesen ist mit deren ewiger Vernichtung."

9

The End of the Wicked in the Apocrypha

Many in the early church used the Apocrypha as "instructive and edifying," and some writers regarded these books as fully canonical. The Roman church in the West and the Orthodox communion of the East, like the Septuagint's translators, included them in the Bible. Among Protestantism's major historical bodies, the Calvinists held the Apocrypha in lowest esteem, the Anglicans in highest, and the Lutherans somewhere between. Today appreciation is growing among scholars of all persuasions for these intertestamental documents as a valuable literary link between Malachi and Matthew.

Introductory material in this chapter regarding the authors and the times and places of origin of the apocryphal books comes from appropriate articles in *The Interpreter's Dictionary of the Bible*. Such matters are highly tentative in some cases and reflect the same methods of higher criticism which date Daniel at 165 B.C., the Pastoral Epistles and 2 Peter in the second century after Christ, and call them all pseudepigraphical. Liberal scholars chuckle up their sleeves at conservatives who form views regarding the apocryphal writings on these grounds but reject such conclusions *a priori* when they come to the canonical books. We wish to be fair in this matter and claim only that the Apocrypha is intertestamental in origin and that it accurately reflects at least some views current among Jews of that period.[1]

---

1. Quotations in this chapter are from R. H. Charles' edition of *The Apocrypha and Pseudepigrapha of the Old Testament in English*, vol. 1.

Tobit

This didactic romance tells the story of a pious family from the tribe of Naphtali whom Shalmaneser took captive to Nineveh. It may date from about 200 B.C., though some Roman Catholic scholars argue for a seventh-century origin. The hero's dying words to his son Tobias detail this hopeful picture of the end time:

> All the nations which are in the whole earth, all shall turn and fear God truly, and all shall leave their idols, who err after their false error. . . . All the children of Israel that are delivered in those days, remembering God in truth, shall be gathered together and come to Jerusalem and shall dwell for ever in the land of Abraham with security, and it shall be given over to them; and they that love God in truth shall rejoice, and they that do sin and unrighteousness shall cease from all the earth.—Tob. 14:6-8.

There is no mention here of a resurrection. Righteous Israelites who are alive will inherit the promised land and rejoice forever. Sinners simply "shall cease from all the earth." Whether they are executed and consumed, as in the Old Testament, or are converted *en masse* to worship the true God is an open question, though the text suggests the latter. Conscious unending torment is nowhere in the picture.

Sirach (or Ben Sira)

Also called *Ecclesiasticus*, this book of wisdom purports to be the Greek version of a Hebrew work written by the translator's Palestinian grandfather. The Greek version probably comes from Egypt somewhere between 195-171 B.C. The author is acquainted with the ways of Hellenism, but as a loyal Jew, he is repulsed by it.

His view is that of the Old Testament. Those led astray by wine and women "will perish." "Moulder and worms will take possession" of them (Ecclus. 19:2, 3). The sinner's end will be as with fire. "Like tow wrapped together is the assembly of the ungodly, and their end is the flame of fire" (Ecclus. 21:9). Isaiah also compared the wicked's end to tow or tinder, which is no sooner ignited than it is consumed (Isa. 1:31). The only other mention of "tow" (Greek: *stippuon*) in the Old Testament observes the same fact about its combustibility (Judg.

16:9). Sirach says the wicked will so perish when their slick path slides them into "the pit of Hades" (Ecclus. 21:10).

Sirach also speaks of "the glowing fire" in which the wicked will "be devoured" and "find destruction" (Ecclus. 36:7-10). The Greek text has a "fire of wrath," and the Syriac text says "in anger and in fire." Another passage warns: "In the assembly of the wicked a fire is kindled, and in an apostate nation doth wrath burn" (Ecclus. 16:6). The following verses compare this fate to the destruction of Sodom, the extermination of the Canaanites, and an unidentified occasion on which 600,000 enemy footmen were destroyed.

The imagery of fire begins to change significance during this period. Instead of the Old Testament fire which cannot be quenched until it totally consumes, the literature begins to speak of a fire which torments its victims but does not destroy them. R. H. Charles notes signs of this transition in one passage from Sirach.

The Hebrew text of Ecclesiasticus 7:17 says "the expectation of man is *decay*," and a later rabbinic quotation repeated it as "the hope of man is the worm" (Pirqe Aboth 4. 7). But when Ben Sira translated his grandfather's words into Greek, he included an additional thought. Instead of "decay" or "the worm," he put "fire and the worm." Although the shift is discernable, Ben Sira still did not go all the way. His statement regards man in general, not specifically the wicked, and even "fire and the worm" could totally consume (as in Isa. 66:24) rather than torment forever. Still, the change seems to reflect a current opinion.

Baruch

This work, attributed to the secretary of the prophet Jeremiah, addresses the Jews in Babylon. It may date from about 150 B.C. The author urges the righteous to suffer patiently, using a figure familiar to the Old Testament. "My children, suffer patiently the wrath that is come upon you from God: for thine enemy hath persecuted thee; but shortly thou shalt see his destruction, and shall tread upon their necks" (Bar. 4:25).

A few verses later Baruch describes the coming end of Israel's enemies in terms used by Isaiah and Jeremiah and later by John in Revelation.

Miserable are the cities which thy children served:
Miserable is she that received thy sons.
For as she rejoiced at thy fall,
And was glad of thy ruin:
So shall she be grieved for her own desolation
    . . . For fire shall come upon her from the Everlasting, long
          to endure;
And she shall be inhabited of devils for a great time"
            —Bar. 4:32-35.

Jeremiah had promised that "Babylon's thick wall will be leveled
and her high gates set on fire; . . . the nations' labor is only fuel for
the flames" (Jer. 51:58). He had said God would destroy Babylon so
that "it will be desolate forever" and would "sink to rise no more"
(Jer. 51:62, 63). This is probably the meaning of Baruch's "fire long to
endure." His statement that the city would "be inhabited of devils for
a great time" likely reflects Isaiah's words that Babylon (who "will be
overthrown by God like Sodom and Gomorrah") will never again be
inhabited but will become a haunt for "desert creatures"—jackals,
owls, wild goats and hyenas (Isa. 13:19-22). Baruch uses the established language of the Old Testament prophets. Both his passages
may well have in view a temporal judgment rather than the end of
the world.

Judith

This tale of a heroic Jewish maiden who saves her people may
come from 150-125 B.C., though the date is disputed. At the end of
the story the heroine, Judith, leads Israel in a great song of victory
over their former oppressor. Her closing words warn:

"Woe to the nations that rise up against my race;
The Lord Almighty will take vengeance of them in the day of
    judgment,
To put fire and worms in their flesh;
And they shall weep and feel their pain for ever."
            —Jth. 16:17.

The fire and worms probably come from Isaiah 66:24, but now the
transition Sirach hinted at is fully brought to pass. Where Isaiah saw
the unburied corpses of God's enemies exposed to the abhorrent destruction of fire and worms, Judith introduces a completely different

idea of everlasting conscious pain. Her "fire and worms" do not destroy; they sensibly torment. They are not outside agents which consume their victim; they are internal agonies inside his flesh. The victims are not destroyed but "feel their pain forever."

This language is unmistakable. It describes the traditionalist hell. Equally unmistakable is its newness in our literature. In all the Old Testament's inspired pictures of the wicked—historical, poetic or prophetical—we have met this scene not once. We have not found this clear picture of unending conscious torment in the apocryphal material until now. Here we do.

First Maccabees

One of the more reliable sources of information concerning the stormy and eventful years it covers, this historical narrative tells the story of the Maccabean liberators and their valiant deeds. It was probably written about 110 B.C. by an author sympathetic to the Hasidic element in Judaism, which produced the Essenes and the Pharisees. In sectarian terms the book is nonpartisan, espousing the distinctive views of neither the Pharisees nor the Sadducees.

First Maccabees does not speak clearly about the eschatological end of the wicked. One passage reflects the same Old Testament outlook we have already seen, that the sinful man will meet his end in the earth. (In Daniel 12:2, revelation advances beyond this point, as by implication in a few other Old Testament texts.) The author exhorts:

> "And be not afraid of the words of a sinful man, for his glory shall be dung and worms. Today he shall be lifted up, and tomorrow he shall in no wise be found, because he is returned unto his dust, and his thought is perished."—1 Macc. 2:62-64.

Second Maccabees

Judas Maccabeus is the hero in this book, which may have been written slightly ahead of 1 Maccabees, whose saga it continues. This author goes beyond any apocryphal literature we have seen yet in clearly affirming a bodily resurrection, though it seems to be limited to the righteous. So far as the wicked are concerned, the martyr heroes here stand fast on the sovereignty and justice of God. He will punish their tormentors—of that they are sure—but, compared to much other literature, they say surprisingly little of the details.

Eleazar, a sort of Jewish Polycarp who welcomes martyrdom in his 90th year rather than renounce his God, is certain that God will punish the ungodly. He disdains threatened death, saying that "even were I for the moment to evade the punishment of men, I should not escape the hands of the Almighty in life or in death" (2 Macc. 6:26).

Chapter 7 clutches the reader's heart with its torture and death of seven brothers and their faithful mother. They encourage each other to the very last in hope of a bodily resurrection, a resurrection in which they warn their adversary he will have no part. God will be his judge, they say again and again, but their tortured final words stop with that general statement.

The second brother challenges the king with the words: "Thou cursed miscreant! Thou dost dispatch us from this life, but the King of the world shall raise us up, who have died for His laws, and revive us to life everlasting" (2 Macc. 7:9). The fourth brother similarly faces his executioner. " 'Tis meet for those who perish at men's hands to cherish hope divine that they shall be raised up by God again; but thou—thou shalt have no resurrection to life" (2 Macc. 7:14).

The fifth brother warns that God's "sovereign power will torture thee and thy seed!" (2 Macc. 7:17). The sixth brother says, "Think not thou shalt go unpunished for daring to fight against God!" (2 Macc. 7:19). The seventh draws himself up to say: "But thou, who hast devised all manner of evil against the Hebrews, thou shalt not escape the hands of God" (2 Macc. 7:31). Later he adds, "Thou shalt receive by God's judgment the just penalty of thine arrogance" (2 Macc. 7:36). Still later he says he is praying that God will make the persecutor acknowledge "in torment and plagues, that He alone is God" (2 Macc. 7:37).

This punishment may well be expected in the present life and culminate in a death from which there is no return so far as these martyrs declare. Their tormentor will have no part in the resurrection to life, and they do not seem to expect a resurrection of any other kind. If they held any views of conscious unending torment for their persecutor, the occasion of their torture and martyrdom would offer an ideal occasion to express it. But they do not, although they do warn him of God's certain vengeance.

Wisdom of Solomon

Probably written during the first century before Christ, this book was born speaking the Greek language and breathing the air of Greek philosophy. Some see here an unbiblical bodiless reward for immortal souls (Wisd. of Sol. 2:21–3:9), but the book's language about the wicked could come from the Psalms or Proverbs of the Bible. Two passages illustrate this agreement.

"But them the Lord shall laugh to scorn.
And after this they shall become a dishonored carcase,
And a reproach among the dead for ever:
Because He shall dash them speechless to the ground,
And shall shake them from the foundations,
And they shall lie utterly waste, and be in anguish,
And their memory shall perish."
—Wisd. of Sol. 4:18, 19.

"Because the hope of the ungodly is like chaff carried off by
      the wind,
And like a thin spider's web driven away by a tempest;
And like smoke which is scattered by the wind,
And passeth away as the remembrance of a guest that
      tarrieth but a day.
But the righteous live for ever,
And the Lord is their reward,
And the care for them with the Most High."
—Wisd. of Sol. 5:14, 15.

Nickelsburg notes that while the Wisdom of Solomon attributes immortality to the soul of the righteous man already, neither life nor immortality are inherent to the soul but are the result of the godly man's actions in this life. For this reason, he says, even in the Wisdom of Solomon immortality is ascribed only to the righteous, while the "wicked bring death upon themselves, death in an ultimate sense."[2]

---

2. George W. E. Nickelsburg, Jr., *Resurrection, Immortality, and Eternal Life in Intertestamental Judaism*, pp. 88, 179.

Other Apocryphal Works

The Apocrypha also includes 1 Esdras (a historical work which closely parallels Ezra-Nehemiah), 3 Maccabees (an alleged historical work of the period before 2 Maccabees but generally regarded as less reliable), and several smaller additions to canonical books (1 Baruch, Epistle of Jeremy, Prayer of Manasses, and additions to Daniel and to Esther). These vary in textual authority and religious value, and add nothing to what we have found to this point.

Summary

This body of literature called the Apocrypha, revered as canonical by Catholics, often used by the ancient church, and sadly ignored by most Protestants, stands between the divine revelation of the Old Testament and the fanciful imagination of some of the Pseudepigrapha. On the fate of the wicked this literature overwhelmingly reflects the teaching of the Old Testament. The wicked will not escape God's judgment. They will surely die. Worms will be their end. They will pass away like smoke or chaff, or burn up like tow. The righteous may hope for a resurrection and blessed life with God, but the wicked will have no part in that. Even faithful martyrs gasping final words of warning to their murderers say no more.

Judith contains the single explicit reference to conscious everlasting pain. The Greek version of Sirach changes the Hebrew in one passage to what might reflect the same view. This expectation is clearly present, but it is not the general one. On the other hand, the total, irreversible destruction of the godless was clearly anticipated by some faithful Jews as late as the first century before Christ. We will meet both views again in the Pseudepigrapha and the Dead Sea Scrolls.

10

The Pseudepigrapha and the Sinner's Doom

Although the books we call "Pseudepigrapha" stand well outside the canon of Scripture, they enjoy a popularity today among biblical scholars that has never been excelled. Some writers have exaggerated their worth, as if they were the veritable fountainhead of New Testament doctrine and eschatology. Yet even a modest estimation of these assorted writings from approximately 200 B.C.–A.D. 100 acknowledges the great contribution they make in providing historical perspective for New Testament studies.

The people of intertestamental Judaism were living, breathing, thinking folk who sometimes differed vigorously from each other on theological matters. This perfectly reasonable fact has not always come across in popular writings about the period. Today scholars stress this diversity far more than in the past, and recent works correct the common misunderstanding which supposes that "Jewish belief" was uniform, consistent or even simplistic.

On the matter of final punishment the situation has been particularly confusing. Traditionalist authors have frequently left the impression that the apocalyptic literature is filled with references to everlasting conscious torment, that this doctrine simply carried the Old Testament teaching a proper and natural step further, and that New Testament teaching should be interpreted in agreement with this

"Jewish view," which is assumed to have been both commonly and widely held.[1]

Because the literature is relatively unfamiliar to laymen, published confusion passes unnoticed and is easily multiplied by repetition. One writer says the Book of Enoch "is the great storehouse of teaching" on final punishment.[2] Another says 2 Baruch gives "the most fully developed description" of such matters.[3] Even the better articles treating intertestamental belief on the doom of sinners tend to oversimplify at times, with the author's own subconscious (and practically unavoidable) bias coloring his interpretation of difficult passages.[4] It is a good rule for any time to read with a critical eye, measuring claims against the support offered, but the advice is especially pertinent here.

The exhaustive work of Strack and Billerbeck takes notice of the wide spectrum of belief between the Testaments and during the first century after Christ, but that work is not available to English readers, and many authors have not had the benefit of its offerings.[5] The recent monograph of G. W. E. Nickelsburg, *Resurrection, Immortality, and Eternal Life in Intertestamental Judaism*, is also very helpful in this regard.[6]

This chapter will avoid bold claims and sweeping generalizations. We will simply survey a representative sampling of pseudepigraphical literature from the period 200 B.C.–A.D. 100 on the subject of final punishment.[7] Since our only purpose is to illustrate the diversity

---

1. The cautious and conservative Reformed author, Harry Buis, is a good modern example. In his *The Doctrine of Eternal Punishment* Buis notes the extravagance of certain intertestamental material but implies that eternal torment was the common Jewish view of final punishment at the time of Jesus (pp. 16-22).

2. A. Bisset, "Eternal Fire," *Dictionary of Christ and the Gospels*, 1:537.

3. S. H. Hooke, "Life after Death: The Extra-Canonical Literature," *Expository Times*, June 1965, p. 274.

4. One of the most detailed and helpful articles found in this study was J. Terence Forestell's "Christian Revelation and the Resurrection of the Wicked," *Catholic Biblical Quarterly* 19, no. 2 (April 1957): 165-189. It gives an excellent summary of intertestamental literature on this title subject, yet a thorough reading of the sources suggests several oversimplifications even here. Only one who has tried to analyze and categorize pseudepigraphal thought can properly sympathize (and tremble a little) in making such a criticism.

5. Hermann L. Strack and Paul Billerbeck, *Kommentar zum Neuen Testament aus Talmud und Midrasch*. Volume 2 contains an excursus on Sheol, Gehenna and the Garden of Eden.

6. George W. E. Nickelsburg, Jr., *Resurrection, Immortality, and Eternal Life in Intertestamental Judaism*.

7. The field of Pseudepigrapha is vast and still increasing. In this study we survey those works included in R. H. Charles' edition of *The Apocrypha and Pseudepigrapha of the Old Testament in English*, vol. 2, from which all quotations are also taken.

of opinion found among Jewish apocalyptists of the period, we will pass over fine points of debate regarding such matters as authorship, place and date of origin, or schools of thought represented.[8] We will rather summarize the data inductively, book by book, beginning with those which teach the final extinction of the wicked and moving across the spectrum to those teaching everlasting conscious torment. In each case we begin with the books generally thought to be the oldest and work forward to the early Christian decades which also saw the writing of the New Testament. In it we will ask whether these Pseudepigrapha justify a presupposition of any standardized "Jewish view" on the subject, or whether we ought to read the New Testament evidence strictly on its own terms and understand it on the basis of ordinary biblical exegesis.

The Wicked Will Totally Pass Away

The Sibylline Oracles

This is a composite work of uncertain date. Books 3-5 are generally thought to come from a Jewish author of perhaps the second century B.C. Some other parts seem much later in origin and are salted with Christian interpolations.

The Jewish core says the wicked will be totally destroyed. The author warns "Babylon" that "from the air above there shall come to thee . . . eternal perdition. And then thou shalt be as thou wast before as though thou hadst not been born" (lines 307-310). Crete, too, faces "a scourge and a dread eternal destruction," when it will be "wreathed in smoke and fire shall never leave thee but thou shalt burn" (lines 504-507). God "shall burn with fire the race of stubborn men" (line 761).

This seems to take place in a mighty conflagration which will destroy the whole earth along with all its sinners. Book 4 tells how God will carry this out.

---

8. For introductory material we have relied on James H. Charlesworth, *The Pseudepigrapha and Modern Research*, along with specific articles in *The Interpreter's Dictionary of the Bible*.

And He shall burn the whole earth, and consume the whole race of men, and . . . there shall be sooty dust. But when at last everything shall have been reduced to dust and ashes and God shall quench the giant fire, even as He kindled it, then God Himself shall fashion again the bones and ashes of men, and shall raise up mortals once more as they were before. And then the judgment shall come wherein God Himself shall give sentence, judging the world once again. And to all who have sinned with deeds of impiety a heap of earth shall cover again, and murky Tartarus and the black recesses of hell. But all who are godly shall live again on earth when God gives breath and life and grace to them, the godly.—Sib. Or. 4:76-90.

This conflagration reappears in book 5, where it involves a "battle of the stars" and results in "a new creation" (Sib. Or. 5:207-213). God will "utterly destroy" His enemies "so that dead bodies shall remain on the earth more numerous than the sand" (Sib. Or. 5:298-305).

Fragments of a Zadokite Work

Otto Betz suggests 68-63 B.C. for this work's origin, noting its kinship to certain Dead Sea Scrolls.[9] Here the wicked face God's "power and might and great fury with flames of fire . . . so that there should be no remnant, nor any to escape of them" (2:4, 5). They await "destruction" (9:12, 13) when they will be "cut off from the midst of the camp" (9:49).

Dead Sea Scrolls[10]

Few discoveries in biblical archaeology have caught the public eye like that of the documents popularly known as the Dead Sea Scrolls. The discovery in 1947 of the library and headquarters of an ancient

---

9. Charles includes this among the Pseudepigrapha, but Charlesworth does not. Betz wrote the article on this book in *The Interpreter's Dictionary of the Bible*.

10. The Dead Sea Scrolls do not properly fit under the category "Pseudepigrapha" but are included here because of their obvious overlapping with the other literature and their conspicuous bearing on the subject at hand. This historical summary is paraphrased from F. F. Bruce, "A Reappraisal of Jewish Apocalyptic Literature," *Review and Expositor* 72, no. 3 (Summer 1975): 307-310.

ascetic Jewish commune near Qumran, northwest of the Dead Sea, was heralded by daily newspapers around the world. The resultant curiosity was exploited for a while by certain sensationalists, but sober interest has outlasted all that. Today, a third of a century later, the painstaking work of deciphering, translating and analyzing continues at a slow but steady pace, the careful work of a new field of specialists in biblical studies.

The Qumran sect was evidently organized by one calling himself Teacher of Righteousness, and it functioned for about two centuries before the Roman invasion of Palestine in A.D. 66-73. These pious Jews repudiated the Hasmonean high priesthood in Jerusalem and denounced its corrupted liturgical calendar. They were the righteous remnant in their eyes, and they would be used by God to execute judgment at the rapidly-approaching End. Until then they would quietly perfect their own holiness and offer pure worship, meekly enduring whatever suffering the wicked establishment might cast their way.

These "covenanters" read their Old Testament in the light of their own movement. Isaiah's "Assyrian," Habakkuk's "Chaldean" and Daniel's "king of the North" all referred to the Romans ("Kittim") according to the Teacher of Righteousness. God had used these pagans to punish Israel's wicked priests, but God would soon punish them as well. The Qumran worshipers would become God's guerrillas in a final war against the "sons of darkness." This war would involve seven battles, and the last would be won by the direct intervention of Michael, the archangel. This victory would usher in the kingdom of God's saints and the end of the old world. The new covenant and the new age would be a reality.

Josephus' Testimony. Writers on final punishment have often cited Josephus' description of Essene belief concerning souls. According to his lengthy discussion in *Wars of the Jews* (2. 8. 11), the Essenes held the common Platonic view of immortal souls trapped during life in mortal bodies but freed at death to their natural sphere. Souls of wicked men would finally be judged and enter everlasting torment, according to Josephus' account of Essene belief. He identified this doctrine with Greek philosophy, calling it a "lure" not easily resisted by those who "once tasted their wisdom."

This evaluation must now be seriously questioned if the Qumran sectarians were indeed Essenes, as is commonly thought. The Dead

Sea Scrolls "speak plainly" of "annihilation for the wicked,"[11] as we will shortly see. "The Essene Writings From Qumran," as an important English translation terms the Dead Sea Scrolls,[12] come down squarely on the side of total extinction for sinners.

Testimony of the Scrolls. God had sent the Teacher of Righteousness "to make known to the last generations what He would do to the last generation, the congregation of traitors," according to the Damascus Document (CD 1. 11, 12). The document continues with a lengthy description of the end of sinners, comparing it to the fate of the antediluvians who perished in the Flood and of the unfaithful Israelites who fell in the wilderness. God's judgment of sinners will leave "no remnant remaining of them nor survivor" (CD 2. 6, 7). They would be "as though they had not been" (CD 2. 20).

The wicked will end in the terrible Pit of fire and darkness. The Scroll of the Rule (Manual of Discipline) tells of its horror in a formal curse against the "men of the lot of Belial."

> Be thou cursed in all the works of thy guilty ungodliness!
> May God make of thee an object of dread by the hand of the
>   Avengers of vengeance!
> May He hurl extermination after thee by the hand of all the
>   Executioners of punishment!
> Cursed be thou, without mercy, according to the darkness of
>   thy deeds!
> Be thou damned in the night of eternal fire!
>   —1QS 2. 4-8.

Such will be the fate of all who follow the Spirit of Perversity instead of the Spirit of Truth.

> And as for the Visitation of all who walk in this (Spirit),
> it consists of an abundance of blows administered by all the
>   Angels of destruction

---

11. F. F. Bruce, "Paul on Immortality," *Scottish Journal of Theology* 24, no. 4 (November 1971): 459-460. The quotation also appears in F. F. Bruce, *Paul: Apostle of the Heart Set Free*, p. 303.

G. W. E. Nickelsburg concludes that the Essenes had "a belief in, or akin to, immortality of the soul, but not resurrection" (Nickelsburg, *Resurrection, Immortality, and Eternal Life*, p. 169.

12. This is the title of a major English translation of the scrolls, from which all quotations here are taken. André Dupont-Sommer, ed., *The Essene Writings from Qumran*.

in the everlasting Pit by the furious wrath of the God of
    vengeance,
of unending dread and shame without end,
and of the disgrace of destruction by the fire of the regions of
    darkness.
And all their time from age to age
are in most sorrowful chagrin and bitterest misfortune,
in calamities of darkness till they are destroyed
with none of them surviving or escaping.
            —1QS 4. 11-14.

Some evildoers will be destroyed in the eschatological War between the Sons of Light and the Sons of Darkness. They are given no
hope of resurrection of any kind. The War Scroll instructs the men of
Qumran concerning this "final destruction for all the lot of Belial."
Wickedness will "be crushed without a remnant and without any survivor for [all the son]s of darkness" (1QM 1. 5-7). The soldiers of
Qumran are to inscribe certain war trumpets with the legend: "God
overflows all the sons of darkness: He will not withdraw His Anger
till He has destroyed them" (1QM 3. 9). God will extinguish the
enemy as He once wiped out Pharaoh. The pious conquered will become the heroic conquerors in this last great battle. This will be their
shining hour—they will "pass like a flaming torch in the straw,
devouring the wicked and returning not until the destruction of the
guilty" (1QM 11. 9-11).

Qumran commentaries on biblical books make the same point.
The explanation (*pesher*) of Psalm 37 promises that "all who rebel
against being converted from their iniquity will be cut off" (4Qp Ps
37. 1. 3, 4). "They will be wiped out and on the earth not a [wi]cked
man will be found" (4Qp Ps 1. 6-8). The wicked princes who oppressed God's people "will perish like smoke which van[ishes before
the wi]nd" (4Qp Ps 2. 8). The commentary on Habakkuk tells how
God will make an end of the Wicked Priest. "He will make him appear for judgment, and . . . He will declare him guilty and will judge
him with fire of sulphur" (1Qp Hab 10. 3-5).

Like the Psalter of the Old Testament, the Hymn Scroll of the
Qumran Community celebrates the terrors which await all the sinful
enemies. Judgment comes for some at the hands of the Sons of Light
(the warriors of Qumran). Then

The Sword of God shall hasten
and all His sons of tr[ut]h shall rouse themselves to [destroy]
    ungodliness
and all the sons of transgression shall be no more.
And . . . they shall trample (them) underfoot unto destruction
leaving no remn[ant].
            —1QH 6. 29, 30, 32.

The rest will taste God's special terrors at the end of the world. Another hymn brings that scene alive, a foretaste of the time when the earth will rumble, the mountains will crumble and dissolve, and the heat of God's wrath will turn earth's very foundations into a hellish river of molten ruin.

And the bonds of Death tightened leaving no escape,
and the torrents of Belial overflowed all the high banks
Like a fire consuming all their shores,
destroying from their channels every tree green and dry
and whipping with whirlwinds of flame
until the vanishing of all that drinks there.
It devours all the foundations of pitch
and the bases of the continent;
the foundations of the mountain are prey to fire
and the roots of flint become torrents of tar. . . .
And the eternal foundations stagger and shake
and the host of the Valiant of heaven
brandishes its whip in the world;
and it shall not end until utter destruction.
which shall be final, without anything like it.
            —1QH 3. 28-31, 35, 36.

The Psalms of Solomon

According to the common but not unanimous opinion, the Psalms of Solomon come from pre-Christian Hasidic Jews, those pious "covenanters" who begat as spiritual offspring both the Pharisees of mainstream Judaism and the ascetic Essenes of Qumran. This document likely comes from the middle of the first century B.C.

Like the Old Testament book their name suggests, these psalms anticipate a time when the wicked will vanish from the earth and never again be found. God "bringeth down the proud to eternal destruction in dishonour" (Ps. Sol. 2:35). He will "recompense the sinners for ever according to their deeds" (Ps. Sol. 2:38), which later is explained to mean their extinction. The sinner

> falleth and riseth no more. The destruction of the sinner is for ever, and he shall not be remembered, when the righteous is visited. This is the portion of sinners for ever. But they that fear the Lord shall rise to life eternal, and their life shall be in the light of the Lord, and shall come to an end no more.—Ps. Sol. 3:11-16.

Another passage says the slanderous tongue will perish in flaming fire (Ps. Sol. 12:5). Israel may hope for God's salvation forever, but sinners will "perish together at the presence of the Lord" (Ps. Sol. 12:7). When "the life of the righteous shall be forever," sinners "shall be taken away into destruction, and their memorial shall be found no more" (Ps. Sol. 13:9, 10). Their "inheritance . . . is destruction and darkness, and their iniquities shall pursue them unto Sheol beneath" (Ps. Sol. 15:11).

Sinners "shall perish for ever in the day of the Lord's judgment, when God visiteth the earth with His judgment" (Ps. Sol. 15:12). A few lines later the author repeats himself for emphasis: "sinners shall perish for ever" (Ps. Sol. 15:15).

Fourth Ezra (Fourth Esdras)

Numerous writings circulated under Ezra's name during the early Christian centuries. Charlesworth calls this one "one of the most brilliant and original of all apocryphal compositions." Scholars generally recognize an authentically Jewish core in chapters 3-14, which they believe were composed in either Hebrew or Aramaic during the final decades of the first century after Christ, probably in Palestine. Two Christian compositions written in Greek, sometimes called 5 Ezra (chs. 1, 2) and 6 Ezra (chs. 15, 16), are thought to have been added later.

Like many other works of the period, 4 Ezra has the wicked suffering immediately after their death and before the final judgment. Here that suffering consists primarily of remorse for the past and dread of the future, which are described under seven headings (4 Esd. 7:78-87). Before the end of the world there will come a series of Messianic Woes. Sinners who survive these will be converted, and all living people will hold to the truth (4 Esd. 6:25-28).

Messiah will reign in joy over His people 400 years on the earth, then He and all His subjects will die. Primeval silence will shroud the earth for seven days. Then the new age will begin, and the old order will be gone forever (4 Esd. 7:26-31). The earth will give up all its dead, and the Most High will set up His throne of judgment.

> And then shall the pit of torment appear, and over against it the place of refreshment; the furnace of Gehenna shall be manifest, and over against it the Paradise of delight.—4 Esd. 7:32, 33, 36.

When Ezra expresses sorrow that so few are finally saved, God compares them to His jewels. He rejoices over the few, He says, and continues:

> "And I will not grieve over the multitude of them that perish: for they it is who now are made like vapour, counted as smoke, are comparable unto the flame: They are fired, burn hotly, are extinguished!"
> —4 Esd. 7:61.

The Fate of the Wicked Is Stated Ambiguously

The Assumption of Moses

The date of this work is uncertain. Guesses range from the second century B.C. to the first century A.D. One passage in particular speaks of the fate of the wicked, and it is ambiguous.

> For the Most High will arise, the Eternal God alone,
> And He will appear to punish the Gentiles . . .
> And thou shalt look from on high and shalt see thy enemies
>   in Ge(henna)
> And thou shalt recognize them and rejoice,
> And thou shalt give thanks and confess thy Creator.
>   —Asmp. M. 10:7, 10.

In a footnote to the phrase "in Ge(henna)," Charles acknowledges that his text actually has *terram* for the Greek *ge* ("earth"). Rather than having the saved see their enemies "on earth," Charles makes *ge* an abbreviation for *ge(henna)*, thus amending the text to fit a view with better documentary support elsewhere in the literature. But "Gehenna" is still ambiguous since it may either consume the sinner entirely or keep him alive in torment.

Testaments of the Twelve Patriarchs

Fragments of the Testaments have been discovered among the Dead Sea Scrolls and in the synagogue geniza (storeroom for discarded scrolls) at Cairo, Egypt. Charlesworth says the material existed in recognizable form about 100 B.C. and was based on more ancient works. The present manuscripts probably include several later Christian additions and changes.

The language of the Testaments is also capable of more than one interpretation. Reuben warns women to avoid the "wiles" of head and facial adornment "because every woman who useth these wiles hath been reserved for eternal punishment" (Test. Reuben 5:5). Levi sees "fire, snow and ice made ready for the day of judgment," when God will make "retributions for vengeance on men" (Test. Levi 3:2). Those who bless God will be blessed, but everyone who curses Him "shall perish" (Test. Levi 5:6).

Unless men avoid lying and anger, they will "perish" (Test. Dan 2:1) when Messiah comes to "execute an everlasting vengeance" on Israel's enemies (Test. Dan 5:10). Besides an intermediate state of suffering after death (Test. Asher 6:5), readers are warned to escape a punishment such as fell on "Sodom, which sinned . . . and perished for ever" (Test. Asher 7:1). The context applies this statement to the Dispersion—the people are nowhere to be found in their homeland, but they are still alive and suffering somewhere else!

Benjamin closes the book with language borrowed from Daniel. "Then shall we also rise," he says, "each one over our tribe, worshipping the King of heaven. . . . Then also all men shall rise, some unto glory and some unto shame" (Test. Benjamin 10:7, 8).

Everlasting punishment and vengeance could mean that the wicked perish forever, never to return. It could also describe eternal conscious torment. The shame to which some will rise could possibly mean everlasting pain, although neither Daniel (Dan. 12:2) nor Isaiah (Isa. 66:24) picture that in the canonical precedents to this language. This book will probably continue to be a bone of contention, and both sides in the debate will likely claim it for support.

The Life of Adam and Eve

This expanded version of Genesis 1-4 probably came in a Semitic tongue from a Jewish writer of the first century before Christ. Its reference to the final doom of the wicked is also unclear.

"God will stir up for Himself a faithful people, whom He shall save for eternity, and the impious shall be punished by God their king, the men who refused to love His law. . . . Therefore the Lord shall repel from Himself the wicked, and the just shall shine like the sun, in the sight of God."—29:7-9.

Inconsistent Teaching about the Wicked's End

The Book of Jubilees

This book from the second century B.C. retells the Bible story from creation through the Exodus in the Jewish commentary form known as midrash. The opening words identify it as "the history of the division of the days of the law and of the testimony, of the events of the years, of their (year) weeks, of their Jubilees throughout all the years of the world, as the Lord spake to Moses on Mount Sinai when He went up to receive the tables of the law and of the commandment" (Bk. Jub., preface). It is generally regarded as one of the most important Pseudepigrapha. Portions of it appear among the Dead Sea Scrolls; it probably represents the same stream of Judaism which produced Essenism. The original language was likely Hebrew, although it is extant in full only in Ethiopic manuscripts. Its message about the fate of the wicked is almost totally that found throughout the Old Testament.

Again and again Jubilees stresses that the wicked will be utterly destroyed and perish from the earth. Aside from a single passage we will note, this is its exclusive word concerning the ungodly, and even there the language is capable of that interpretation. Abraham warns Isaac against following the way of sinners lest he "sin a sin unto death before the Most High God." God would then "hide His face from thee," Isaac is told, "and give thee back into the hands of the transgression, and root thee out of the land, and thy seed likewise from under heaven, and thy name and thy seed shall perish from the whole earth" (Bk. Jub. 21:22).

Later Abraham tells Jacob of the idolaters' end.

"There shall be no hope for them in the land of the living;
And there shall be no remembrance of them on the earth;
For they shall descend into Sheol,
And into the place of condemnation shall they go,
As the children of Sodom were taken away from the earth
So will all those who worship idols be taken away."

—Bk. Jub. 22:22.

When Esau wants a fatherly blessing, Isaac tells him instead that he will "sin a complete sin unto death, and thy seed shall be rooted out from under heaven" (Bk. Jub. 26:34). Isaac blesses Levi with the promise that his food will "fail not unto all the ages," while those who hate him will "be rooted out and perish" (Bk. Jub. 31:16, 17). Anyone who afflicts and curses Judah "shall be rooted out and destroyed from the earth and be accursed" (Bk. Jub. 31:20).

The sin of incest is especially heinous. For this abomination "there is no atonement for ever to atone for the man." Such a man "is to be put to death and slain, and stoned with stones, and rooted out from the midst of the people of our God. For to no man who does so in Israel is it permitted to remain alive a single day on the earth, for he is abominable and unclean" (Bk. Jub. 33:13, 14). This unforgivable sin never has atonement precisely because the man is speedily executed before the sun goes down!

While these passages all speak of total destruction, it is not clear if their penalty follows a final judgment or is to be carried out wholly in time and history. A few other texts seem to refer clearly to an eschatological judgment at the End.

God blesses Jacob with the words: "I will give to thy seed all the earth which is under heaven, and they shall judge all the nations according to their desires, and after that they shall get possession of the whole earth and inherit it for ever " (Bk. Jub. 32:19). This picture could be borrowed from numerous Old Testament passages which portray a similar scene. The wicked will be "judged" (here at the hand of Israel)—never to be mentioned again—and the righteous inherit the earth.

Jubilees specifically describes in one passage an earthly Messianic kingdom, at the end of which comes judgment. The *spirits* of the righteous rise in everlasting joy, but their bodies rest in the earth. This text says the wicked are judged, but on their final fate it leaves us in the dark.

> And all their days [the righteous] shall complete and live in peace and in joy, and there shall be no Satan [or "satan"—accuser] nor any evil destroyer; for all their days shall be days of blessing and healing. . . . And the righteous shall see and be thankful, and rejoice with joy for ever and ever, and shall see all their judgments and all their curses on their enemies. And their bones shall rest in the earth, and their spirits shall have much joy, and they shall know that it is the Lord who executes judgment, and shows mercy to hundreds and thousands and to all that love Him.—Bk. Jub. 23:29-31.

Because the Philistines mistreated Isaac, another passage curses them in view of a final day of judgment.

> And no remnant shall be left to them, nor one that shall be saved on the day of the wrath of judgment; for destruction and rooting out and expulsion from the earth is the whole seed of the Philistines (reserved), and there shall no longer be left for these Caphthorim a name or a seed on the earth. . . . And neither name nor seed shall be left to him on all the earth; for into eternal malediction shall he depart. And thus it is written and engraven concerning him on the heavenly tablets, to do unto him on the day of judgment, so that he may be rooted out of the earth.—Bk. Jub. 24:30, 32, 33.

"Eternal malediction" is their fate on "the day of the wrath of judgment." The passage specifically describes that destiny as expulsion and being rooted out of the earth, a destruction which leaves no remnant, seed or even name forever.

One passage in Jubilees could easily suggest the idea of conscious everlasting torment, although its context does not seem to require that meaning. Isaac warns Jacob and Esau of the punishment that will befall either of them who ever attacks his brother after Isaac dies. The penalty will begin in the present life. "Everyone that devises evil against his brother shall fall into his hand, and shall be rooted out of the land of the living, and his seed shall be destroyed from under the heaven." But that is not all, as the warning continues:

> "But on the day of turbulence and execration and indignation and anger, with flaming devouring fire as He burnt Sodom, so likewise will He burn his land and his city and all that is his, and he shall be

blotted out of the book of the discipline of the children of men, and not be recorded in the book of life, but in that which is appointed to destruction, and he shall depart into eternal execration: so that their condemnation may be always renewed in hate and in execration and in wrath and in torment and in indignation and in plagues and in disease for ever."—Bk. Jub. 36:9-11.

These last words sound much like the unending conscious torment of the traditional hell, clearly seen already in Judith. Two considerations, however, weigh against that interpretation here. First, if this is the author's meaning, it is the only place he reveals it in the entire book. Furthermore, it would seem to contradict what he consistently affirms whenever he otherwise mentions the subject. Second, the context itself suggests his more usual view of the wicked's destruction. The day of "turbulence and indignation and anger" is also the "day of execration." He describes it as a day of vengeance like that which came on Sodom: "with flaming fire as He burnt Sodom, so likewise will He burn his land." The sinner is not found in "the book of life" (i.e., listed among the living) but is "appointed to destruction." He departs into "eternal execration"—that is, he is cut off forever. His condemnation is "always renewed"; not being exhausted in this life, it extends into the Age to Come. Now there are plagues and disease; then there will be hate and execration, wrath and indignation and torment. We do not wish to twist the author's words to fit a particular view. The literature will amply document both expectations. We simply call attention to these details for fair consideration.

But what of the "torment" in this passage? Does not that word require everlasting *conscious pain?* The author of Jubilees sheds light on that question in another place as he tells how Simeon and Levi avenged the rape of their sister Dinah by the Shechemites.

And Simeon and Levi came unexpectedly to Shechem and executed judgment on all the men of Shechem, and slew all the men . . . and left not a single one remaining in it: they slew all *in torments* because they had dishonored their sister Dinah. . . . And the Lord delivered them into the hands of the sons of Jacob that they might exterminate them with the sword and execute judgment upon them. . . . See how the Shechemites fared and their sons: how they were delivered into the hands of two sons of Jacob, and they slew them *under tortures.*
—Bk. Jub. 30:4-6, 17.

The fate of the men of Shechem is clear. Simeon and Levi "slew" them, "executed judgment" on them, "exterminated them with the sword." What is interesting is that the author of Jubilees describes this by saying "they slew all in *torments*" and later that "they slew them under *tortures*." The punishment involved torments and tortures, but its end was extermination. Might not the same scene be in view in the ambiguous passage we have just seen? If so, Jubilees gives a single, consistent view of the end of the wicked—final extermination forever. If this interpretation is not permissible, Jubilees offers a mixed and inconsistent picture. Several times it expects sinners finally to be exterminated, though one passage threatens everlasting conscious torment.

First (Ethiopic) Enoch

Often called Ethiopic Enoch to distinguish it from 2 (Slavonic) Enoch and 3 (Hebrew) Enoch, this book is extant in its entirety only in Ethiopic, preserved because of its canonical status in the Ethiopic Church. That text is based on a Greek version, according to F. F. Bruce, who says the bulk of the work probably comes from the second century before Christ.[13]

Enoch is divided into five major parts, four of which are quoted among the Dead Sea Scrolls. This book made a deep impression on other authors of its time and thereafter. It appears in allusion or quotation in the Book of Jubilees, the Testaments of the Twelve Patriarchs, the Assumption of Moses, 2 Baruch and 4 Ezra among the Pseudepigrapha. It contains the words which Jude attributes to "Enoch," as well as many phrases scattered throughout the rest of the New Testament. Numerous church fathers quote from this Enoch, many of them by name.

Of its five sections, the one most relevant to New Testament doctrine is the "Similitudes," which speak of "*the* [rather than "a"] Son of Man." Interestingly, this is the only section not yet found among the scrolls at Qumran, which might reflect a later date! According to R. H. Charles, the doctrine of a resurrection "was made a commonplace of Jewish theology" by this book.[14]

---

13. Bruce, "Jewish Apocalyptic Literature," pp. 310-312.
14. Charles, *Apocrypha and Pseudepigrapha*, 2:185.

Although it does not strictly concern our study of final punishment, we note in passing Enoch's detailed concern with detention and torment, even before the great judgment, for both wicked angels (1 En. 19:1, 2; 21:1-10) and certain sinful men (1 En. 22:11-13; 103:5-8). At times 1 Enoch has sinners finally exterminated; at other times he has them enduring conscious pain forever.

Sinners Exterminated Forever. In some passages sinners are "driven from the face of the earth" (1 En. 38:1) and "perish" (1 En. 38:5), their life "at an end" (1 En. 38:6). It had been better for such people never to have been born (1 En. 38:2). Apostates will not be found in heaven or on earth after "the day of suffering and tribulation" (1 En. 45:1, 2). Enoch seems to teach annihilation when he quotes God as saying:

> "And I will transform the heaven and make it an eternal
> blessing and light:
> And I will cause Mine elect ones to dwell upon it:
> But the sinners and evil-doers shall not set foot thereon.
> . . . But for the sinners there is judgment impending with Me,
> So that I shall destroy them from the face of the earth."
> —1 En. 45:4-6.

Enoch warns sinners in the next chapter that "darkness shall be their dwelling, and worms shall be their bed, and they shall have no hope for rising from their beds" (1 En. 46:4). When God judges, "the unrepentant shall perish before Him" (1 En. 50:4). Sinners "shall be destroyed before the face of the Lord of Spirits, and they shall be banished from off the face of His earth, and they shall perish for ever and ever" (1 En. 53:2).

Enoch saw "the angels of punishment" as they prepared "instruments of Satan" by which God's enemies would "be destroyed" (1 En. 53:3-5). In another place the angels "execute vengeance" on those who have oppressed God's children. The enemies "shall be a spectacle for the righteous and for His elect" when God's "sword is drunk with their blood." The righteous "shall never thenceforward see the face of the sinners and unrighteous" (1 En. 62:11-13). Sinners "shall die with the sinners, and the apostate go down with the apostate" (1 En. 81:7, 8). (Charles surmises in a footnote that they "go down" to Gehenna.)

Enoch sees a parable about wicked rulers and apostate Israelites. In it 70 shepherds and their blind sheep are

> judged and found guilty and cast into this fiery abyss, and they burned. . . . And I saw those sheep burning and their bones burning.
> —1 En. 90:25-27.

Charles has rearranged the text which says that "sin shall perish in darkness for ever, and shall no more be seen from that day for ever-more" (1 En. 92:5), which he thinks speaks of the flood in the days of Noah.

A clearer passage warns:

> "And now, know ye that ye are prepared for the day of destruction: wherefore do not hope to live, ye sinners, but ye shall depart and die; for ye know of no ransom; for ye are prepared for the day of the great judgment, for the day of tribulation and great shame for your spirits."
> —1 En. 98:10.

A few verses later it said that sinners "shall have no peace but die a sudden death" (1 En. 98:16).

God uses fire to destroy the wicked. The heathen are "cast into the judgment of fire, and shall perish in wrath and in grievous judgment for ever" (1 En. 92:9). Sinners "perish in the day of unrighteousness" (1 En. 97:1), "in shame and in slaughter and in great destitution" when their spirits are "cast into the furnace of fire" (1 En. 98:3).

"Ye shall perish, and no happy life shall be yours," Enoch warns (1 En. 99:1). This will come to pass when the wicked are "trodden under foot upon the earth" (1 En. 99:2) or are "slain in Sheol" (1 En. 99:11). They will burn in "blazing flames burning worse than fire" (1 En. 100:9) and will "be utterly consumed" (1 En. 99:12). One passage describes this fiery destruction in graphic and explicit terms.

> "I will give them over into the hands of Mine elect:
> As straw in the fire so shall they burn before the face of the
>   holy:
> As lead in the water shall they sink before the face of the
>   righteous,
> And no trace of them shall any more be found.
> And on the day of their affliction there shall be rest on the
>   earth,
> And before them they shall fall and not rise again."
> —1 En. 48:8, 9.

Sinners Suffer Conscious Pain Forever. At other times 1 Enoch seems to expect the wicked to suffer forever in conscious pain. Enoch sees an "accursed valley" (Gehenna) outside Jerusalem which is described as the place of judgment for sinners. "In the last days there shall be upon them the spectacle of righteous judgment in the presence of the righteous for ever" (1 En. 27:1-3). This might mean conscious pain that lasts forever, though it could also describe a judgment of everlasting destruction in the sense of irreversible extinction.

In another place Noah sees a river of fiery molten metal with the smell of sulphur, flowing together with a valley of streams of fire. There fallen angels await judgment. There also wicked kings are punished after death as "a testimony," because "those waters will change and become a fire which burns for ever" (1 En. 67:4-13). Whether this fire will then consume sinners or only torment them we are not here told.

Finally, in what Charles calls an "independent addition" to the book, it is said that sinners "shall cry and make lamentation in a place that is a chaotic wilderness, and in the fire shall they burn; for there is no earth there." An angel describes the scene as the place where "are cast the spirits of sinners and blasphemers, and of those who work wickedness" (1 En. 108:3-6). The passage also has "their names . . . blotted out of the book of life," "their seed destroyed for ever," and "their spirits . . . slain," so its meaning is not totally clear.

Second (Syriac) Baruch

Except for a Greek fragment, this whole book is extant only in one Syriac manuscript. By general consent it is said to have been composed during the final decades of the first century after Christ, but its original language is still debated.

Some argue that this work teaches conscious torment forever. There will be a judgment according to sins and righteous deeds (2 Bar. 24:1-4) after the Messiah has an advent (back to heaven, Charles thinks) in glory (2 Bar. 30:1).

> Then all who have fallen asleep in hope of Him shall rise again. . . .
> But the souls of the wicked, when they behold all these things, shall
> then waste away the more. For they shall know that their torment has
> come and their perdition has arrived.—2 Bar. 30:2-5.

There is no question in 2 Baruch that the wicked will "depart to torment" (2 Bar. 44:12; 59:2; 64:7-10; 83:8) or that "the dwelling of . . . many shall be in the fire" (2 Bar. 44:15). The earth will give up the sinners just as it received them, that they might "suffer torment." They will see the righteous transformed into the splendor of angels; then they will "depart to be tormented" (2 Bar. 51:5, 6). Whether the torment ends in extinction or continues in conscious pain the author does not here say.

In other places, however, Baruch says clearly that "a fire shall consume their thoughts" (2 Bar. 48:39). Sinners go "to corruption," and there is no numbering of "those whom the fire devours" (2 Bar. 48:43). There will be no turning back then, no change of ways or place for prayer when the wicked come to judgment (2 Bar. 85:12). All that remains is "the sentence of corruption, the way of fire, and the path which bringeth to Gehenna" (2 Bar. 85:13). God will then "destroy those who are polluted with sins" (2 Bar. 85:15).

In one passage Baruch multiplies similies like those found in the Old Testament psalms. God's enemies will "be like a vapour" (2 Bar. 82:3), "be made like unto a drop" (v. 4), "be accounted as spittle" (v. 5). "As smoke shall they pass away" (v. 6), "as grass that withers shall they fade away" (v. 7), "as a wave that passes shall they be broken" (v. 8). They "shall pass away as a passing cloud" (v. 9).

The Wicked Will Suffer Conscious Pain Forever

Second (Slavonic) Enoch

Most scholars think this "Book of the Secrets of Enoch" was written in Greek, shortly before the destruction of the temple in A.D. 70, in either Palestine or Egypt. Like 1 (Ethiopic) Enoch, this Enoch sees angels (2 En. 7:1, 2) and men (2 En. 41:1) waiting in torment before the judgment. The wicked will "perish," and they must anticipate "the limitless judgment" (2 En. 40:12).

Enoch sees a place where

murky fire constantly flameth aloft, and a fiery river (comes) forth, and that whole place is everywhere fire, and everywhere frost and ice, thirst and shivering, while the bonds are very cruel, and the angels fearful and merciless, bearing angry weapons, merciless torture.

This, he is told, is prepared for sinners "for eternal inheritance" (2 En. 10:1-6). Every false speech (and speaker?) "will be cut with the blade of the sword of death, and thrown into the fire, and shall burn for all time" (2 En. 63:4). One wonders even here if "for all time" might describe the irremediable *effect* of the burning rather than conscious pain, especially since those thrown into the fire have already been "cut with the blade of the sword of death." This example illustrates the difficulty modern interpreters face when grappling with particular terms used by pseudepigraphical advocates of both eternal extinction and everlasting torment. The same problem arises in later literature on the subject from the New Testament onward. Unless an author is explicit in his view, his language will likely be disputed, and readers of opposing convictions will jointly claim him for support.

Fourth Maccabees

Eusebius and Jerome attributed this book to Flavius Josephus, but modern scholars regard it as the work of a Jew of Stoic leanings who had mastered both Greek thought and language. The hub of the book tells the story of the faithful mother and her seven sons, all martyred under the tyranny of Antiochus Epiphanes (see 2 Macc. 7:1-42). The author of 4 Maccabees uses their case to illustrate victory through "the supreme power of reason."

The seven sons warn their wicked torturer of "torment by fire for ever" (4 Macc. 9:9), "torments without end" (4 Macc. 10:12), and an "eternal doom" (4 Macc. 10:15). This will be "a more rapid and an eternal fire and torments which shall not leave hold on thee to all eternity" (4 Macc. 12:12). Whoever transgresses God's ordinances must also know that "a great struggle and peril of the soul awaits in eternal torment" (4 Macc. 13:15).

Summary

The Pseudepigrapha offers us a variety of Jewish expectations regarding the final end of sinners. It is absolutely clear that there is no such thing as "the Jewish view" on the matter. Neither is it proper to say that everlasting conscious torment is the primary or predominant view in this literature. This expectation appears quite clearly in a handful of passages. It is a possible interpretation in several other cases. For present purposes we will allow them all to those of that persuasion.

It is also absolutely clear that the pseudepigraphical literature thoroughly documents the older view of the sinner's total extinction as one Jewish opinion current during the period 200 B.C.–A.D. 100. This doom is frequently accomplished by fire and is usually preceded by a period of conscious anguish and suffering. In looking for a time when sinners will perish from the face of the earth and never again be found, these writers repeat the frequent testimony of the Old Testament. With the exception of one clear passage in Judith and one ambiguous text in Sirach, this is also the view of the Apocrypha.

Because of this unquestionable range of opinion, which can be so thoroughly documented, we cannot presume a single attitude among Jews of the time of Christ on this subject. We cannot read Jesus' words or those of the New Testament writers with any presuppositions supposedly based on a uniform intertestamental opinion.

We must deny categorically the common assumption that Jesus' hearers all held to everlasting torment. We must not assume that Jesus endorsed such a view simply because He nowhere explicitly denied it. We are free to examine the teaching of the New Testament at face value and to determine the meaning of its terms according to the ordinary methods of proper biblical exegesis. The literary and linguistic background for this exegesis includes the Apocrypha and Pseudepigrapha, but rising high and towering over it all we see the inspired revelation contained in the Scriptures of the Old Testament.

11

Final Punishment in the Teaching of Jesus

The ultimate support for the doctrine of the final punishment of unrepentant sinners is the teaching of Jesus Christ Himself.[1] Yet men have received Jesus' teaching in many ways, as author MacCulloch points out. "It has been taken with absolute literalness; it has been spiritualized; it has been regarded as subject to interpolation, greater or less; or its originality is admitted, but its expected fulfilment is regarded as a mistake and an illusion."[2] Some even deny that Jesus ever taught what Matthew reports, dismissing these statements as "bitter anti-Jewish sentiments" rising out of "a mutual escalation of hatred caused by a poaching of converts."[3]

Yet even the most liberal scholarly methods of Gospel criticism have to conclude that Jesus said a great deal about the terrible fate awaiting those who reject God's mercy. He spoke of exclusion from the kingdom, the severity of wrongdoing, the destruction of unrepentant sinners—and He taught that opportunity to repent was cut off at death. Try as one might, "it is impossible to eliminate sayings

---

1. It is seemly, therefore, that the present chapter should be our most lengthy one.

2. J. A. MacCulloch, "Eschatology," *Encyclopedia of Religion and Ethics*, 5:381-382. On modern approaches to Jesus' eschatological message in general, see Howard C. Kee, "The Development of Eschatology in the New Testament," *Journal of Bible and Religion* 20, no. 3 (July 1952): 187-193.

3. D. E. H. Whiteley, "Liberal Christianity in the New Testament," *Modern Churchman* 13, no. 1 (October 1969): 26.

of Jesus which give terrible warning as to the possibility of loss and exclusion."[4] Even a study of *the goodness of God* must include these facts if it is candid and true to Scripture. In his excellent book of that title, John W. Wenham notes that Jesus

> spoke often of hell. . . . In sheer number these statements are inescapable. In intensity they are fearful. We are here faced with the ultimate horror of God's universe, before which we stand aghast, longing to escape, but as in a nightmare unable to move. We cannot escape, for we know *who* said these things, we know his tenderness, we know the authority of his words and we know that this is the language (be it more or less symbolic) which *he* regarded as best fitted to describe the price of impenitence. It is Love who speaks like this, it is God himself.[5]

Knowing who this is that speaks to us, let us pray God for open eyes, ears and hearts. We will meet His words again on the last day! (John 12:48).

One might approach Jesus' teaching from several directions. In this study we will page through the Gospels in a simple discussion and summary of the data they contain. We will begin with Matthew, not so much because he is first in canonical order, but because he records more that Jesus said on this subject than any of the other Evangelists. This should not surprise us when we remember that he is writing particularly for a Jewish audience and this theme of divine judgment and final retribution had long lain close to the Hebrew heart.[6] If Mark, Luke or John supply additional detail, we will include that testimony as we proceed. Finally, we will take a look at the few relevant Gospel passages not found in Matthew, ending our inquiry with a summary and some conclusions.

---

4. A. M. Ramsey, quoted by Alan M. Fairhurst, "The Problem Posed by the Severe Sayings Attributed to Jesus in the Synoptic Gospels," *Scottish Journal of Theology* 23 (1970): 79.

5. John W. Wenham, *The Goodness of God*, pp. 20-21.

6. It is not surprising that Matthew has such an interest in final punishment. He writes for the Jews, whose knowledge of the true God led them to expect a final day of reckoning at the end of history. In the Old Testament, life on the earth has purpose and destiny in fellowship with God; it is not the cyclical view of history held by many Greeks, for instance, although it becomes that if God is removed from the picture (as Ecclesiastes makes clear). For more on this see chapter on the Old Testament.

Matthew 3:10, 12

John the Baptist picks up the thread of divine revelation where Malachi had laid it down. The last verses of the Old Testament promise that Elijah will come to prepare men for the day of the Lord. The Gospels open their door, and there to greet us is Malachi's "Elijah," who is also Isaiah's "voice in the wilderness." Nazarite by commission and priest's son by birth, he is also a prophet—but so much more! This one is Messiah's harbinger, *martys* in the sense of "witness," but authenticating his message by a *martyr* death. He is John the Baptizer, whose austere diet and rugged wardrobe only brought to mind the ancient times, underscoring the impression that after four centuries of silence Israel's sovereign God was speaking once again.

Like Habakkuk's message before him, John's word calls on men to run. He warns of fiery judgment following almost on his heels. When the Pharisees come to check him out, John compares them to desert reptiles, fleeing before a wilderness fire. John cries out of coming wrath (Matt. 3:7; Luke 3:7), a theme which continues through the New Testament.[7] Men can escape this judgment only by repentance followed by faith in the Lamb of God, to whom John first points and then takes backstage forever.

"The ax is already at the root of the trees," he announces, "and every tree that does not produce good fruit will be cut down and thrown into the fire" (Matt. 3:10). Every orchard-man recognized the figure, one so familiar Jesus would choose it for his Parable of the Fig Tree (Luke 13:6-9). Trees with bad fruit are *burned* (Matt. 7:19), as are unfruitful vines (John 15:6) and useless weeds (Matt. 13:40). In Jesus' teaching, as in John's, these figures from the land represent sinners in the end. They stand for false prophets, hypocritical hearers, sunshine soldiers or fruitless disciples. In each case they are burned up.

Jesus will "baptize you with the Holy Spirit and with fire," John says (Matt. 3:11). Luke records the same words, but Mark promises the Holy Spirit and stops, perhaps because his Christian readers in Rome would know well already a "fire" of persecution; they needed encouragement now, not warning (Mark 1:7, 8). This future baptism

---

7. Rom. 2:5, 8; 5:9; Eph. 5:6; Col. 3:6; 1 Thess. 1:10; 5:9; Rev. 6:16, 17; 11:18; 19:15. On John the Baptist and his warnings see Charles H. H. Scobie, *John the Baptist*, p. 68.

of fire is almost certainly to be understood alongside John's other references to fire; it is the fire of judgment, the judgment that would break first over the head of Jesus Himself, qualifying Him in God's program to then administer it to His enemies. Daniel had spoken of a river of fire flowing from the flaming throne of the Ancient of Days (Dan. 7:9, 10). As the Son of Man of the end-time, Jesus would be immersed in *that* river even as John baptized Him in the waters of Jordan. These two baptisms—in water and in fire—would form a great parenthesis around the Savior's earthly ministry; it must be accomplished before Jesus could baptize in the Holy Spirit.[8]

The Son of Man would suffer, the Lamb would die in silence, but this same One would come again as Judge. John proclaims that, too, as he introduces Jesus to Israel. "His winnowing fork is in His hand, and He will clear His threshing floor, gathering the wheat into His barn and burning up the chaff with unquenchable fire" (Matt. 3:12). As in the Old Testament, "unquenchable fire" represents a fire of judgment which cannot be stopped. On and on it comes, driven by the wind of God's righteous fury—burning irresistibly, crackling, flaming, consuming—until nothing is left but silence and smoke.[9] The Old Testament Scriptures give ample background for understanding this judgment-fire; like them, John sees it as "burning up" the chaff.

Matthew 5:20

"I tell you that unless your righteousness surpasses that of the Pharisees and the teachers of the law, you will certainly not enter the kingdom of heaven."

This verse may well be the key that unlocks the Sermon on the Mount. The Pharisees and scribes were old hands at seeking right standing before God's court (Rom. 9:31–10:5). The scribes would *reason* their way to acquittal. Jesus refutes their rationalizing on six counts in chapter 5 (vv. 21, 27, 31, 33, 38, 43). The Pharisees would

---

8. On the relation of Jesus' baptism to His larger ministry in the light of the entire Bible, see Everett F. Harrison, *A Short Life of Christ* (Grand Rapids: William B. Eerdmans Publishing Co., 1968), pp. 66-78.

9. See Isa. 1:31; 34:10, 11; Jer. 4:4; 7:20; 17:27; 21:12; Ezek. 20:47, 48; Amos 5:6; contrast Ps. 118:12; Heb. 11:34.

parade their way into the kingdom. In chapter 6 Jesus deflates all such pseudo-piety toward men (v. 3), God (v. 5) or even self (v. 16). Only with the righteousness God provides can anyone enter His kingdom (Matt. 6:33). Jesus offers this righteousness freely to those who come confessing need and making no claims of their own (Matt. 5:3-12; Isa. 64:6/61:10).

Not to enter the kingdom will be the fate of those who lack true righteousness. We will meet this description again.

Matthew 5:22

One point at which Jesus countered the scribes' rationalizing was God's prohibition of murder. Passing by all the hand-me-down teaching of the ancients (a common formula of scribal teaching began: "Rabbi X said that Rabbi Y said that Rabbi Z said thus-and-so"), Jesus taught as One who *had* authority (Matt. 7:29). In God's eyes, He said, anger in any degree is dangerous and culpable.

"Anyone who is angry with his brother will be subject to judgment. . . . Anyone who says to his brother, 'Raca,' is answerable to the Sanhedrin. But anyone who says, 'You fool!' will be in danger of the fire of hell."

These three figures of punishment—judgment, Sanhedrin and fire of hell—"are not ascending but rather parallel phrases, seen in the similarity of the cause of the judgment. There is little difference between being angry with one's brother, insulting him, and calling him a fool."[10] There is apparently no basis for the common explanation that Jesus here describes a succession of greater Jewish crimes with penalties correspondingly severe.[11]

This is the Savior's first specific reference to Gehenna, by now a technical term in Jewish sources for the fiery pit in which the godless will meet their final doom. "Entrance into hell indicates spiritual ruin in the starkest terms," writes William L. Lane.[12] The word would mean nothing to Gentiles—it appears only once in the New Testa-

---

10. Joseph Arthur Baird, *The Justice of God in the Teaching of Jesus*, p. 226.

11. W. D. Davies, *The Setting of the Sermon on the Mount*, pp. 235-239.

12. William L. Lane, *The Gospel According to Mark*, The New International Commentary on the New Testament, p. 349.

ment outside the Gospels, and that is in the very "Jewish" book of James. It does not appear in pagan Greek literature or even the Septuagint,[13] nor does Josephus mention it anywhere.[14] But to Jesus' hearers *gehenna* had a long history, and it was all bad.

The Greek word *gehenna* transliterated the Hebrew "Valley of (the sons of) Hinnom." Several sites have been identified, but most authorities now locate it on the west and south of Jerusalem. A "deep and yawning gorge" that never contains water, the valley descends over 600 feet from its original source. At the lower end are numerous rock tombs, indicating its possible use as a potter's field.[15]

The valley bore this name at least as early as the writing of Joshua (Josh. 15:8; 18:16), though nothing is known of its origin. It was the site of child-sacrifices to Moloch in the days of Ahaz and Manasseh (apparently in 2 Kings 16:3; 21:6). This earned it the name "Topheth," a place to be spit on or abhorred.[16] This "Topheth" may have become a gigantic pyre for burning corpses in the days of Hezekiah after God slew 185,000 Assyrian soldiers in a night and saved Jerusalem (Isa. 30:31-33; 37:36). Jeremiah predicted that it would be filled to overflowing with Israelite corpses when God judged them for their sins (Jer. 7:31-33; 19:2-13). Josephus indicates that the same valley was heaped with dead bodies of the Jews following the Roman siege of Jerusalem about A.D. 69-70.[17] In what is probably the classic Old Testament passage behind New Testament teaching on hell, Isaiah pictures the same kind of scene following the Lord's slaughter of sinners at the end of the world (Isa. 66:15, 16, 24). Josiah desecrated

---

13. H. Bietenhard, "Gehenna," *The New International Dictionary of New Testament Theology*, 2:208.

14. Joachim Jeremias, "Gehenna," *Theological Dictionary of the New Testament*, 1:658.

15. George L. Robinson, "Gehenna," *A Dictionary of Christ and the Gospels*, 1:635-636. According to *The Jewish Encyclopedia* the valley's modern name is Wadi al-Rababah ("Gehinnom," *The Jewish Encyclopedia*, vol. 5, col. 583.

16. "Hell," *The Protestant Dictionary*, p. 287. See also Louis Berkhof, *Reformed Dogmatics*, 2:344.

A. R. Fausset derives the name "Tophet" from the drums (*toph*) used to drown out the screams and cries of children being offered to Moloch (*The Englishman's Critical and Expository Bible Cyclopaedia*, p. 281). I have not seen this mentioned elsewhere.

Moloch may be Melech, the "King-god," vocalized with the vowels of *bosheth* ("shame"), perhaps the Baal (a Semitic word for "Lord") of Tyre. So says Charles Venn Pilcher, *The Hereafter in Jewish and Christian Thought, with Special Reference to the Doctrine of Resurrection*, p. 83.

17. According to Emmanuel Pétavel, *The Problem of Immortality*, p. 193. He gives reference to Josephus as: "*Wars*, vi. 8, #5; v. 12, #7."

the repugnant valley as part of his godly reform (2 Kings 23:10). Long before the time of Jesus, the Valley of Hinnom had become crusted over with connotations of whatever is "condemned, useless, corrupt and forever discarded."[18]

Between the Testaments a tendency arose in Jewish literature to relate visions of last things to names and persons from the Old Testament. Armageddon, Jerusalem and the Garden of Eden all became stylized descriptions of things to come. So did the Valley of Hinnom —*gehenna*.[19] The thought of Gehenna as a place of eschatological punishment appears in intertestamental literature shortly before 100 B.C., though the actual place is unnamed.[20] It becomes "this accursed valley" (1 En. 27:2, 3), the "station of vengeance" and "future torment" (2 Bar. 59:10, 11), the "pit of destruction" (Pirke Aboth 5:19), the "furnace of Gehenna" and "pit of torment" (4 Esd. 7:36).

The imagery becomes almost commonplace in Jewish literature of this period, but there is contradictory testimony as to exactly what happens there. We have seen a few passages in the Pseudepigrapha which specifically anticipate everlasting torment of conscious bodies and/or souls, as well as one such verse in the Apocrypha. Many other passages within the intertestamental literature also picture the wicked being punished by fire, but it is the consuming, unquenchable fire of the Old Testament which utterly destroys forever, leaving only smoke as its reminder. It is fair to say that, to those who first heard the Lord, Gehenna would convey a sense of total horror and disgust. Beyond that, however, one must speak with extreme caution.

It is commonly said that Gehenna served as Jerusalem's garbage dump, "a necessary hygienic incinerator outside the walls,"[21] though some have asked for more evidence.[22] One writer described that scene like this:

---

18. Calvin D. Linton, "The Sorrows of Hell," *Christianity Today* 16 (19 November 1971): 12.

19. T. H. Gaster, "Gehenna," *The Interpreter's Dictionary of the Bible*, 2:362.

20. Hermann L. Strack and Paul Billerbeck, *Kommentar zum Neuen Testament aus Talmud und Midrasch*, 2:1029. Hereafter "Strack and Billerbeck."

21. T. G. Dunning, "What Has Become of Heaven and Hell?" *Baptist Quarterly* 20, no. 8 (October 1964): 353.

22. A. Bisset says the statement from Kimchi comes too late (A.D. 1200) to be accepted without further evidence (A. Bisset, "Eternal Fire," *Dictionary of Christ and the Gospels*, 1:536). W. G. T. Shedd quotes Robinson that there is no evidence for a Gehenna garbage dump in Christ's day (William G. T. Shedd, *The Doctrine of Endless Punishment*, p. 43).

Here the fires burned day and night, destroying the garbage and purifying the atmosphere from the smell of rotten fish or decaying vegetation. In time of war the carcases of vanquished enemies might mingle
with the refuse, thus furnishing patriotic wiiters with a clue as to the
destiny of their own persecutors. They were destined to be destroyed
in the fires that were never quenched.[23]

If this was the case, Gehenna once more was a place of undying
worm and irresistible fire, an abhorrent place where crawling maggots and smoldering heat raced each other to consume the putrifying
fare served them each day.

In the rabbinic lore of later Judaism, Gehenna was greatly
embellished. Originally a place of punishment for Israel only, it soon
broadened to include all sinners. From about the days of the apostle
Paul, Gehenna became the rabbis' general term for the intermediate
state. Still later it became a purgatory.[24]

Some of these developments show traces of foreign influence, perhaps by the Zoroastrian eschatology of Iran. There, fire is the means
of testing at the last judgment. The mountains, which are made of
metal, melt and flow over the earth like a river. As men pass into this
molten metal, they are either purified or destroyed. In the end,
everything, including hell itself, will be purified by fire.[25]

The Greek philosopher, Heraclitus of Ephesus, also taught that
each world era ends with a great conflagration, returning everything
to the primal fire, from it producing a new world. The Stoics later included some of these ideas in their concept of the end of the world by
fire (called the *ekpyrōsis*).[26]

Later rabbinic tradition placed Gehenna in an enormous under-
ground cavern beneath the earth with the solid ground resting over it
like the lid of a kettle over boiling water. Its entrance was narrow,
somewhere in the neighborhood of Jerusalem. There Abraham sat at
its gate to see that no circumcised man entered in. Some rabbis said

---

23. J. Arthur Hoyles, "The Punishment of the Wicked after Death," *London Quarterly and Holborn Review*, April 1957, p. 118.

24. Strack and Billerbeck, 2:1032-1033; F. F. Bruce, "Paul on Immortality," *Scottish Journal of Theology* 24, no. 4 (November 1971): 459. See also idem, *Paul: Apostle of the Heart Set Free*, p. 302.

25. Scobie, *John the Baptist*, p. 68; H. Bietenhard, "Fire," *The New International Dictionary of New Testament Theology*, 1:653-654. Concerning the probable influence of Persian concepts on Pharisaic doctrine, see Bruce, *Paul*, p. 47.

26. Bietenhard, "Fire," pp. 653-654.

the setting sun reflected the glare from the fires of Gehenna or that Gehenna's heat warmed the waters of the Sea of Tiberias.[27]

The Babylonian Talmud had the worst Jewish sinners sentenced to Gehenna for 12 months. Then "their bodies are destroyed, their souls are burned, and the wind strews the ashes under the feet of the pious." All who enter Gehenna come out, with three exceptions: those who committed adultery or shamed their neighbors or vilified them. In the end, God would take the sun from its case, and it would heal the pious and punish the sinners. There would be no Gehenna in the future world.[28]

Some rabbis were sympathetic; others were harsh. One can find quotes of torment by snow, smoke, thirst and rebellious animals. Others speak of the righteous observing the torments of the damned, "tossing in their pain like the pieces of boiling meat in a cauldron." Still others, more benevolent, said light flooded even Gehenna each Sabbath, and the wicked, too, had a day of rest.[29]

On the duration of the punishment, the rabbis contradicted each other. Some believed that the pain would continue forever with or without Gehenna, while others ended punishment with the last judgment. Whether this last view allowed a future life for the wicked or looked for their total annihilation cannot be determined conclusively.[30]

One of the more romantic stories of the later rabbis had the damned in Gehenna hear worship in paradise. The sinners were so moved by its majesty that at the end of a particular blessing they all added their "amen." God overheard the "amen" and asked about its origin. Someone explained that it came from the lost in Gehenna, and God, moved with pity, commanded that they should all be released to join the worship in paradise.

However interesting all this rabbinic lore may be, it is largely irrelevant for biblical studies because it comes so late.[31] We are thrown

---

27. Pilcher, *Hereafter*, p. 89.

28. "Ge-hinnom," *The Jewish Encyclopedia*, vol. 5, cols. 581-583.

29. Strack and Billerbeck, 2:1076; Pilcher, *Hereafter*, pp. 85-86, 91.

30. J. Terence Forestell, "Christian Revelation and the Resurrection of the Wicked," *Catholic Biblical Quarterly* 19, no. 2 (April 1957): 176-177; Hedwig Wahle, "Die Lehren des rabbinischen Judentums über das Leben nach dem Tod," *Kairos: Zeitschrift fur Religionswissenschaft und Theologie* 14, no. 4 (Jahrgang 1972): 302-305, 308-309.

31. Frederick W. Farrar devotes 60 pages to Jewish eschatology in his *Eternal Hope*, concluding that "rabbinic opinion" was "generally" that souls are punished according to faults,

back instead to the intertestamental literature to determine the popular concepts of Jesus' day, and there, too, we find contradictory opinions. At the end of our search we must come again to the fullness of Jesus' teaching—His warnings, His parables, His similes—as seen against the background of the Old Testament Scriptures and as illuminated by the post-Pentecost writings of the Spirit-filled men who later "remembered" Jesus' teaching and "understood."[32]

Matthew 5:25, 26

Regardless of the precise nature of final punishment, Jesus stressed that men must use the present opportunity if they hope to avoid it. This is His primary point in these words from the Sermon on the Mount.

> "Settle matters quickly with your adversary who is taking you to court. Do it while you are still with him on the way, or he may hand you over to the judge, and the judge may hand you over to the officer, and you may be thrown into prison. I tell you the truth, you will not get out until you have paid the last penny."

This passage is used as a proof-text by men of almost every opinion. Roman Catholic theologians use it in the interest of purgatory. Others think it favors the restoration position. Others claim it for eternal torment. Luke's parallel is no clearer (Luke 12:58, 59), nor is the Parable of the Unmerciful Servant, which includes the same principle (Matt. 18:34, 35).

We commend the following conclusions of Salmond, an advocate of eternal torment. He pointed to "the helplessness of the man when once in the prison, the finality of his condition there, the hopelessness of discharging his debt." Our Lord speaks here, he goes on, "of a

with annihilation the worst punishment possible (Excursus v). S. D. F. Salmond correctly notes that Farrar's use of the rabbinic literature missed the mark because it failed to take into account the late date from which much of it came (Steward D. F. Salmond, *The Christian Doctrine of Immortality*, pp. 364, 371).

32. John 14:16-18, 25, 26; 16:8-14. 'The doctrine delivered in the Gospels appears to need, and to promise, further explanations, combinations, and developments. The character of that ministry on the whole is introductory" (Thomas Dehany Bernard, *The Progress of Doctrine in the New Testament*, p. 74). Later Bernard writes: 'Though in the teaching of Jesus all the truth might be *implied*, it was not all *opened*; therefore the Holy Ghost was to add that which had not been delivered, as well as to recall that which had been already spoken" (p. 89).

justice which is inexorable, a law of retribution which [the victim] cannot avert, a peril which cannot be stayed."[33]

Traditionalists sometimes point to the "tormentors" in the latter passage as proof of everlasting conscious pain. The verb form of the same word appears in Revelation 9:5, however, where the "torment" specifically lasts for five months. The New Testament uses the word metaphorically and literally, physically and spiritually, in time and in eternity.[34] In the Septuagint, *basanos* usually translates *asham*, "which regularly refers to God's destruction because of guilt."[35] The word itself does not determine the duration of the torment it describes. Conditionalist author, Guillebaud, scrutinizes the details of Jesus' parable and comes more to the point.

> A prisoner who never comes out of prison does not live there eternally. The slave who was delivered to the tormentors till he should pay two million pounds would not escape from them by payment, but he would assuredly die in the end: why should not the same result be at least a possibility in the application?[36]

Matthew 5:29, 30

The end of sin is so terrible that one comes out winner even if he has to discard a cherished member of his body in order to avoid it. Loss of *one* limb now is far better than *total* loss *hereafter*. "If your right eye causes you to sin," Jesus says, "gouge it out and throw it away. It is better for you to lose one part of your body than for your whole body to be thrown into hell. And if your right hand causes you to sin, cut it off and throw it away. It is better for you to lose one part of your body than for your whole body to go into hell."

Jesus uses verbs which emphasize the sense of being rejected, banished, expelled. "Throw" (*ballō*) away eye or hand, He says—as men discard worthless salt (Matt. 5:13), dead grass (Matt. 6:30) or inedible fish (Matt. 13:48). That is better far than having your *whole body* "thrown" away on the day of judgment! This word has many other uses, of course, and we do not suggest that it has any inherent

---

33. Salmond, *The Christian Doctrine of Immortality*, p. 379.

34. Johannes Schneider, "Basanos," *Theological Dictionary of the New Testament*, 1:561-563.

35. Baird, *Justice of God*, p. 232.

36. Harold E. Guillebaud, *The Righteous Judge: A Study of the Biblical Doctrine of Everlasting Punishment*, p. 21.

eschatological significance. At the same time, it is interesting to note
how frequently Matthew writes *ballō* when speaking of the doom of
the lost (Matt. 3:10; 5:25; 7:19; 13:42, 50; 18:8, 9, 30). The second
comparison in the passage also stresses the idea of banishment: better
to lose one part of the body than for the whole body to "go off away"
(*apelthē*) into hell.

Again Jesus makes Gehenna the place of final punishment. Here
He gives no graphic description of its destruction or even its duration; only this, that those who enter it go from another place, having
been discarded and expelled by God. The picture is one of total loss,
and it is entirely in keeping with the Old Testament to see that loss as
ultimately consummated in destruction by fire.

Matthew 7:13, 14

The gate through which men enter upon the way to life is narrow
and small, Jesus warns. There *is* another gate—a wide one through
which many now press—but it leads to destruction. Jesus admonishes
the disciples:

> "Enter through the narrow gate. For wide is the gate and broad is the
> road that leads to destruction, and many enter through it. But small is
> the gate and narrow the road that leads to life, and only a few find it."

Our Lord shows us the kingdom of God in the shape of a city. It is
surrounded by a wall with gates which are opened each day but
closed at night and in times of danger. Whenever the gates are closed,
one can enter only by the narrow gate—a small gate built into the
main gate—so small it can admit but one person at a time. Through
this narrow gate only those can enter whose names are properly recorded on the city's role of inhabitants (its "book of life," if you
please). This is the picture A. J. Mattill draws in a recent, careful
study of the passage. He argues convincingly that "life" here is the life
of the kingdom of heaven; that the word translated "narrow" (*thlibō*)
refers to end-time tribulations that come on God's people, and that
Jesus' primary tone is one of urgency.[37]

---

37. A. J. Mattill, Jr., "'The Way of Tribulation,'" *Journal of Biblical Literature* 98, no. 4 (December 1979): 531-546.

The emphasis here is not on the doom awaiting the many—
"destruction"—but on the necessity for haste to avoid this imminent
doom. Mattill paraphrases Jesus' warning:

> Hurry, before the eschatological storm breaks loose, to enter into the
> city of God through the narrow gate, which is wide enough to admit
> only one registered citizen at a time. For wide is the gate and broad is
> the road which is free of persecution, the comfortable way which leads
> to destruction in hell, and there are many who enter through this gate.
> Because narrow is the gate and great are the end-time tribulations and
> persecutions on the narrow way which leads to eternal life in the
> kingdom of heaven, and only a few people find it.[38]

As in the last passage we read, here, too, Jesus offers us a choice:
persecution now or destruction hereafter. To be thrown into Gehenna (Matt. 5:29, 30) is the "destruction" of this text. Or, to say it the
other direction, those thrown into hell will be destroyed.

Matthew 7:19

If Jesus warns men of impending destruction, so did the prophets
before Him. Both He and they also confronted false prophets who
lurked nearby, ready to usher the gullible through the broad gate
onto the wide road. "Watch out for false prophets," Jesus continues
(Matt. 7:15). You recognize them by their fruits. Then Jesus speaks of
their end.

> "Every tree that does not bear good fruit is cut down and thrown into
> the fire."

We have met this figure already, and we will see it again. J. Arthur
Baird examines this saying in the light of the larger context. Jesus is
giving a series of "crisis contacts" in which He compares the condition and destiny of the kingdom-man with that of the evil man (Matt.
7:13-27). He places the few/life over against the many/destruction
(vv. 13, 14). He contrasts doer/kingdom with evildoer/depart (vv.
21-23). He compares wise/not-fall to the foolish/destined-to-fall (vv.
24-27). This verse is part of a similar contrast. The good tree not cut

---

38. Ibid., p. 546.

down is compared with the bad tree destined to be cut down and thrown into the fire. Casting into the fire parallels destruction (v. 13), rejection (v. 23) and the ruin of a house (v. 27). Baird concludes: "If one carries out the logical imagery here, the fire would seem to refer to the destruction of a tree already dead," a saying similar to Luke 12:5, which we will note later.[39]

Matthew 7:23

Alongside the threatening false prophets, Jesus now places hypocrites among the people. These come forward in the judgment to say they have prophesied, exorcised demons and performed miracles in Jesus' name, and therefore should be admitted to the kingdom. Jesus does not question their accomplishments but disowns them nonetheless, saying they did not do the will of the Father (Matt. 7:21, 22). "Then I will tell them plainly," Jesus continues, "I never knew you. Away from Me, you evildoers!"

The last sentence is also found in Psalm 6:8. There David rebukes hypocrites who profess God's name but deny His power to save. The claim of those in Jesus' story to have prophesied in the name of the Lord also reminds us of similar words from the book of Jeremiah (Jer. 14:14; 27:15). There God says of certain false prophets who promised peace and an easy way, "I did not send them, though they *prophesied in the name of the Lord.*"

Regardless of their sins, the point is clear: those who do not truly know Jesus on the earth will be turned away by Him at the judgment!

Matthew 7:27

With this Parable of the Wise and Foolish Builders, Jesus concludes the Sermon on the Mount in Matthew. The foolish man builds with no foundation, and his house crumbles before the storm. "The rain came down, the streams rose, and the winds blew and beat against that house, and it fell with a great crash."

Ben Sira also contrasted the fool with a solidly-constructed house.

---

39. Baird, *Justice of God*, p. 225.

"As timber girt and fixed into the wall is not loosened by an earthquake, so a heart established on well-advised counsel will not be afraid in time of danger" (Sir. 22:16). More pertinent is Ezekiel's portrayal of God's judgment-storm which will test all men and make false prophets evident by their destruction (Ezek. 13:1-16).

> "Therefore this is what the Sovereign Lord says: In My wrath I will unleash a violent wind, and in My anger hailstones and torrents of rain will fall with destructive fury. I will tear down the wall you have covered with whitewash and will level it to the ground so that its foundation will be laid bare. When it falls, you will be destroyed in it, and you will know that I am the Lord."—Ezek. 13:13, 14.

The house lacking foundation (cf. Matt. 16:18; Heb. 11:10) has a *great fall*, if we read Matthew's Greek literally. Luke says it had a great "ruin" (*hrēgma*, Luke 6:49),[40] from a verb used of wine bottles bursting (Luke 5:37), nets ripping apart with fish (Luke 5:6), or maddened swine tearing someone to pieces with their teeth (Matt. 7:6). He also says the destruction came "immediately" ("the moment the torrent struck," NIV) and that it was great. One who has seen a house demolished by hurricane, tornado or flood can appreciate both the suddenness and the severity of such a destruction. Jesus' figure is forceful and almost universally understood.

Matthew 8:11, 12

Again Jesus stresses the element of exclusion awaiting the unrepentant. It is a surprising exclusion accompanied by great anguish and remorse. By the saying, Jesus responds to an outstanding exercise of faith from a Roman centurion who came seeking healing for a cherished servant.

> "I say to you that many will come from the east and the west, and will take their places at the feast with Abraham, Isaac and Jacob in the kingdom of heaven. But the subjects of the kingdom will be thrown outside, into the darkness, where there will be weeping and gnashing of teeth."

---

40. This word stands for *negeph* in the Septuagint, a Hebrew term used most often for a divine judgment of destruction. See Ex. 12:13; 30:12; Num. 8:19; 16:46, 47; Josh. 22:17; Isa. 8:14.

Those who come "from the east and the west" are certainly Gentiles. Both the hope and the language are straight from the Old Testament (Ps. 107:3; Isa. 49:12; 59:19; Mal. 1:11). Instead of "the subjects of the kingdom" (a Jewish concept characteristic of Matthew's Gospel), Luke has Jesus saying "you yourselves," which is who He really meant (Luke 13:28). In his larger context Luke combines what Matthew tells here and in Matthew 7:23 (Luke 13:27-29). Where Matthew has the false disciples report their miracles, Luke has them remind Jesus that they once ate with Him in the streets of their city. Table fellowship is important throughout Luke-Acts. But all reminders and claims come to nothing. The Messianic banquet is reserved for those who come when God invites—regardless of their other interests and occupations, even if they are blind and halt and lame (as the Parable of the Wedding Feast makes clear). Luke ends the episode with Jesus' statement that "there are those who are last who will be first, and first who will be last" (Luke 13:30).

Here, too, those rejected are "thrown outside" (from *ballō*, already noted, strengthened by *ek*, "out") into the darkness. The familiar "outer darkness" of the older version conveys better the extent of this "bouncing" beyond the perimeter illuminated at all by lights inside the house.

In the Old Testament, darkness was a characteristic of Sheol, but that is probably not in Jesus' mind here. Darkness also describes the judgment of the "day of the Lord" in the prophets, and that allusion likely does fit. Both Matthew and Luke have the adverb of place, "there" (*ekei*), a point the New International Version makes clearer in Matthew 8:12 with its "where." Jesus says that *there*, in that outer darkness, will be weeping and grinding of teeth. This latter expression "recurs in verbatim fashion seven times in an eschatological framework, and each time as an elaboration on the nature of final punishment."[41] We will return to that in a moment.

The Old Testament "day of the Lord" was also a day of darkness, even thick darkness. Then, too, "the cry" is bitter (Zeph. 1:14). That picture ends with "the fire of His jealousy," by which "the whole world will be consumed" (Zeph. 1:18).

---

41. Baird, *Justice of God*, p. 225.

Throughout our literature weeping is a common Hebrew symbol for fear, misery or extreme grief, often because of God's judgment on sinners. People weep, for example, when Jerusalem is destroyed (Isa. 22:12) or when they are exiled from their homeland (Bar. 4:11). James warns the rich to weep for fear of God's coming judgment (James 5:1). The prophets picture people weeping over the death or destruction of others (Isa. 16:9; Jer. 9:1; 48:32; Rev. 18:9); one entire Old Testament book—Lamentations—is devoted to this activity.

We have already considered 4 Ezra 7:80-87, a pseudepigraphal work from the first century A.D. There the damned weep seven ways during their intermediate detention before the judgment. They weep in shame and remorse for the past, and in fear and dread of the future, but most of all as they get a glimpse of the glory of God, before whom they will soon be judged. This portrayal is in keeping with the biblical references already cited. Together they appear to warrant Baird's statement that "there is little precedent for interpreting Jesus' use of 'weeping' as a symbol for the torment accompanying the actual punishment of the *eschaton*."[42]

In the passages we have seen, weeping speaks more of *terror* and *extreme loss*, not so much of actual *pain*. It is part of that "fearful expectation of judgment," and it pounds into our consciousness once more that "it is a dreadful thing to fall into the hands of the living God" (Heb. 10:27, 31).

Most often in the Bible, the grinding of teeth describes the wrath of an adversary about to kill his victim—the teeth belong to the tormentor, not the tormented (Job 16:9; Ps. 35:16; 37:12; Lam. 2:16; Acts 7:54). Psalm 112 may be the single exception.

The psalm begins, "Blessed is the man who fears the Lord" (v. 1), whom it describes in verses 2-9 (Paul borrows verse 9 in context in 2 Cor. 9:9). David assures us that "even in darkness light dawns for the upright" (v. 4). Then comes the psalm's final verse. "The wicked man will see and be vexed, he will *gnash his teeth and waste away*; the longings of the wicked will come to nothing" (v. 10). As before, the wicked man's gnashing of teeth seems to express his rage against the righteous. But even while he grinds his teeth in fury, he wastes away and comes to nothing.

---

42. Ibid., p. 229.

It is helpful to consider together the seven Gospel occurrences of
this frightful pair, "weeping and grinding of teeth." When we do, we
find that the expression

- modifies "throw into darkness outside" (Matt. 8:12; 22:13;
  25:30);

- accompanies "you yourself thrown out" (Luke 13:28);

- follows "assign him a place with the hypocrites" (Matt. 24:51);

- modifies "weed out of his kingdom" and "throw away" (Matt.
  13:41, 42);

- accompanies "separate the wicked from the righteous" (Matt.
  13:49, 50).

In each instance those consigned to "weeping and grinding of teeth"
are separated from others who are approved. Each time the expression accompanies a specific act of banishment, expulsion or rejection.
The last two passages add that those excluded and banished are
thrown into "the fiery furnace," a fact not necessary for "weeping
and grinding of teeth," as shown by all the other cases. There is no indication that God will miraculously intervene for these, as He once
did for Daniel's three friends, to keep them alive. May we not suppose, then, that this "fiery furnace" does to its victims precisely what
the enemies of Shadrach, Meshach and Abednego hoped theirs
would do to them? (Dan. 3:15-27). Unless God intervenes, where is
any hope? Certainly no other god can save from such a fate! (Dan.
3:15, 28).

In scriptural usage the expression "weeping and grinding of teeth"
seems to indicate two separate activities. The first reflects the terror
of the doomed as they begin to truly realize that God has thrown
them out as worthless and as they anticipate the execution of His
sentence. The second seems to express the bitter rage and acrimony
they feel toward God, who sentenced them, and toward the redeemed, who will forever be blessed. The common assumption that
"weeping and grinding of teeth" describes the everlasting agony of
souls in conscious torment is the interpretation of a later age, and it
lacks any clear biblical support.

In closing, we echo Paul's admonition to "consider . . . the kindness and sternness of God" (Rom. 11:22). On the first point, we

observe that every warning of weeping and grinding of teeth is addressed to someone who rejected God's offered grace. Not one is directed to men such as those of ancient Nineveh or even Sodom and Gomorrah. Whatever the anguish awaiting those who die without knowing the gospel—and Scripture nowhere extends them any hope —it certainly will not include the remorse of remembering such rejected opportunities or the terror of facing a God whose Son they have knowingly despised. On the second point, these words remind us that "the terrors and despair of the lost at the throne of judgment, as we find them portrayed in the Bible, cannot be exaggerated."[43]

Matthew 10:28

Little wonder that Jesus warned: "Do not be afraid of those who kill the body but cannot kill the soul. Rather, be afraid of the one who can destroy both soul and body in hell." This context, too, includes divine rejection and expulsion, for Jesus says He will personally disown traitorous disciples in the presence of the Father (Matt. 10:33). Only God should be ultimately feared, Jesus says, and James repeats the point in speaking of God, "who is able to save and destroy" (James 4:12).

Lest one read into Matthew's account any Platonic dualism regarding man's being, we have Luke's record of the same words: "Do not be afraid of those who kill the body and after that can do no more. But . . . fear him who, after the killing of the body, has power to throw you into hell. Yes, I tell you, fear him" (Luke 12:4, 5). This passage does not teach the immortality of every man's soul; it teaches rather that God can kill the soul as well as the body. Unless Jesus is making idle threats, the very warning implies that God will execute such a sentence on those who persistently rebel against His authority and resist every overture of mercy.[44]

---

43. Basil F. C. Atkinson, *Life and Immortality: An Examination of the Nature and Meaning of Life and Death as They Are Revealed in the Scriptures,* p. 102.

44. Cullmann writes: "We hear in Jesus' saying in Matthew 10:28 that the soul can be killed. The soul is not immortal. There must be resurrection for both [body and soul]; for since the Fall the whole man is 'sown corruptible'" (Oscar Cullmann, *Immortality of the Soul or Resurrection of the Dead?* pp. 36-37). For similar statements see earlier chapters here on immortality of the soul.

Man's own nature as a psychosomatic unity, created from nothing by the God who alone gives him life, corresponds precisely to the words of the Lord. Baird elaborates:

> This is the dimension of death, which only becomes alive when that higher potential of the soul takes on the dimension of the Kingdom. If the individual rejects this Spirit, new life does not come and he remains in the physical realm of death. . . . When the body is killed, its psychosomatic counterpart, tied to the body and possessing nothing beyond itself, must suffer the same fate. As Matthew says, *both* soul and body are destroyed in *gehenna.*"[45]

This raises a most interesting point. For if man depends wholly on God for his existence day by day, and if the wicked are banished absolutely from God's presence and are deprived of any divine blessing, the question must arise how they can continue to exist for any period of time. But there is more. Not only does Scripture say throughout that *life* in any dimension is a gift of God; it is also a matter of record that "immortality" and "incorruption" are promised as exclusively to the righteous as are "glory" and "honor" (Rom. 2:7, 10; 1 Cor. 15:42-44, 50, 54). All will be raised, but some will "rise to live" while others will "rise to be condemned" (John 5:28, 29; Dan. 12:1, 2).

On this matter traditionalist writers have for the most part been strangely silent. When they have spoken, they have often applied to the wicked descriptions of the resurrected body which Paul reserves for the righteous alone. Such an indiscriminate use of terms characterizes the writings of Athenagoras, Augustine and Chrysostom,[46] and it has been carried on by traditionalist advocates since. Calvin was aware of this problem, though he never seems to have met it head-on.[47] Luther posed the difficult question himself but refused to give it much thought.[48] It has often been observed that his chief concern was justification, not eschatology. Many modern authors, both Catholic and Protestant, seeing no biblical stepladder down from this

---

45. Baird, *Justice of God*, pp. 222-223. On the relations between body, Holy Spirit, resurrection, cosmos and the new age, see Joseph Blenkinsopp, "Theological Synthesis and Hermeneutical Conclusions," *Immortality and Resurrection*, pp. 122-125.

46. See quotations and references in Henry Constable, *Duration and Nature of Future Punishment*, p. 81; William G. T. Shedd, *Dogmatic Theology*, 3:491-492; J. N. D. Kelly, *Early Christian Doctrines*, p. 483.

47. John Calvin *Institutes* 3. 25. 9.

48. Ewald M. Plass, comp., *What Luther Says: An Anthology*, 2:628, #1922.

tightrope, simply leap into the philosophical net of the immortality of the soul.[49]

Conditionalist Henry Constable challenged the common notion that the wicked, too, will be raised incorruptible, arguing that resurrection within itself requires no essential change from a former state. Speaking of his traditionalist opponents, he wrote:

> They all tell us that a *change* will pass upon the wicked at their resurrection! We ask for proof. They cannot say that there cannot be a resurrection without a change; for, unfortunately for them, there have been resurrections where no change has taken place. All the resurrections before that of Christ were such. He was the "first fruits from the dead," *because* in the case of others raised before Him *no change from mortality* took place. They cannot say that there cannot be a resurrection followed by death; for, again, the cases of Jairus' daughter, and the widow's son, and Lazarus, would confront and confound them; for all these, after they were raised, died again. We ask them for proof that the bodies of the wicked will undergo *any change* at their resurrection.[50]

Had Constable lived a hundred years later, he would have found some scholarly support. F. F. Bruce, dean of evangelical scholars, says that it is curious though perhaps accidental "that in Paul's letters there is no clear reference to the resurrection of the wicked."[51] Murray Harris, a professor at Trinity Evangelical Divinity School near Chicago, calls it a "distinctive feature of the Christian view of resurrection" that the righteous dead are transformed as well as revived. He uses the same illustration as Constable in making his point. "To be revived is not to be resurrected: the raising of Lazarus (Jn. 11:1-44) or of the widow of Nain's son (Lk. 7:11-17) was a restoration to temporary physical life (they came to life only ultimately to die once more), not a resurrection to permanent spiritual life."[52] Harris observes that according to the New Testament there is a reanimation that leads to judgment, not to life but to the "second death" (Dan. 12:2; John 5:29; Rev. 20:4-6, 11-15). He notes that

---

49. M. E. Williams, "Soul, Human, Immortality of," *New Catholic Encyclopedia*, 12:469; Charles F. Baker, *A Dispensational Theology*, quotes Shedd with approval from his *Dogmatic Theology*, 2:652. See further examples in chapter on immortality.

50. Constable, *Future Punishment*, p. 83.

51. Bruce, "Paul on Immortality," p. 458; idem, *Paul*, p. 301.

52. Murray Harris, "Resurrection and Immortality: Eight Theses," *Themelios* 1, no. 2 (Spring 1976): 51-52.

in the Pauline Epistles resurrection seems to be depicted as a privilege reserved for the new humanity in Christ. In any event, whatever the anthropological state of the wicked dead after they have regained 'life', they are certainly not possessors of spiritual bodies, since the *sōma pneumatikon* [spiritual body] is imperishable and therefore not subject to 'the second death'.[53]

W. G. T. Shedd, a powerful advocate of everlasting conscious torment, made the same point, which he never entirely reconciled with his overall conclusion. In *The Doctrine of Endless Punishment* Shedd wrote:

> The bodies of the wicked, on the contrary, are not delivered from the power of Sheol, or the grave, by a blessed and glorious resurrection, but are still kept under its dominion by a "resurrection to shame and everlasting contempt" (Dan. 12:2). Though the wicked are raised from the dead, yet this is no triumph for them over death and the grave. Their resurrection bodies are not "celestial" and "glorified," like those of the redeemed, but are suited to the nature of their evil and malignant souls.[54]

This being the case, does it not follow that the wicked, deprived of any life from God and subjected to the destructive force of Gehenna besides, will eventually lose all vitality and truly die? May we not think of a glowing ember which, removed from the fireplace, finally loses all its fire? Or can we not compare the case to an electric heater, now unplugged from its source of power, which glows for a short period of time but finally and inevitably goes out? Robert Mounce, a contemporary conservative commentator, describes the lake of fire like this:

> It is the second death, that is, the destiny of those whose temporary resurrection results only in a return to death and its punishment. Alford writes, "As there is a second and higher life, so there is also a

---

53. Ibid., p. 52. Paul Tillich has some good words on this, when taken at face value and apart from his special meanings, when he says: "Condemnation can only mean that the creature is left to the nonbeing it has chosen. The symbol 'eternal death' is even more expressive" (Paul Tillich, *Systematic Theology* [Chicago: University of Chicago Press, 1951, 1957], 2:78, quoted by C. C. Goen [with reservations, as here!], "The Modern Discussion of Eschatology," *Review and Expositor* 57, no. 2 [April 1960]: 124).

54. Shedd, *The Doctrine of Endless Punishment*, pp. 39-41.

second and deeper death. And as after that life there is no more death ([Rev.] ch. xxi. 4), so after that death there is no more life" (pp. 735-36).[55]

Our Lord's warning is plain. Man's power to kill stops with the body and the horizons of the Present Age. The death man inflicts is not final, for God will call forth the dead from the earth and give the righteous immortality. God's ability to kill and destroy is without limit. It reaches deeper than the physical and further than the present. God can kill both body and soul, both now and hereafter.

In Matthew's account Jesus uses "kill" and "destroy" in parallel fashion, apparently making them interchangeable. Luke's Gospel is striking in another way. There Jesus says, "Fear him who, *after the killing of the body*, has power to *throw you into hell*." This is the identical sequence described in Isaiah 66. There, too, God first slays His enemies, then throws their dead bodies into the consuming fire (v. 24). Throughout Luke-Acts the beloved physician shows a thorough acquaintance with the prophet Isaiah and a special affinity for his language and concepts. Is it any surprise that Luke rather than Matthew repeats Jesus' words in a form which so closely resembles Isaiah's picture of the eschatological punishment?

Far from lessening the anxiety of sinners, this understanding of Jesus' words intensifies their dread. "Yes, I tell you," Jesus says, "*fear him!*" Here is an urgency our careless generation badly needs to learn. When morality is determined on the basis of human polls rather than divine precepts, when "right to choose" is placed ahead of "right to live," when "success" is measured according to the blessing of mammon and life's goal consists of a single long pilgrimage to its shrine, we need to hear the thunder and see the lightening and feel the force of the voice of Almighty God. This earth will crumble one day, and the universe will pass away in a cosmic conflagration. Where, then, shall these things be? Jesus' words have lost none of their

---

55. Robert H. Mounce, *The Book of Revelation*, The New International Commentary on the New Testament, p. 367. Homer Hailey gives the same quotation in his *Revelation: An Introduction and Commentary*, p. 403.

   Henry Constable wrote: "The unjust are not raised in incorruption; they are not raised in immortality. . . . For the bodies of the unjust are raised only in their old mortality. They are thus raised for punishment. Raised in their old mortality, the pains of hell will again, must again reduce them to a second death, from which there is no promise of a resurrection" (Constable, *Future Punishment*, p. 94). Is this not the plain meaning of Alford's words?

authority—or their power—when He says, "I will tell you whom to fear. Fear God, who can kill the body and cast you into hell!" Guillebaud drives home this point with power.

> But let none imagine that because eternal punishment does not mean everlasting torment, therefore it is a mild penalty which need not be dreaded. . . . No more dreadful mistake could be made than so to consider the matter. . . . Having faced death once in this world, the lost soul must face it again, under circumstances of unutterable shame and horror. God will not then be One who can be ignored or patronized, He will be known for what He is, the One who fills heaven and earth. Then the Almighty King, who had offered him salvation and would so gladly have saved him, will reject him and pronounce him only fit for destruction.
>
> The instinct, which so often makes even the suicide struggle desperately for life at the last, will surely be far more powerful as the soul faces the final disintegration of personality, the utter end, and what an awful end! How terrible the process of destruction will be will depend on the degree of each soul's guilt before God, . . . how much light has been disobeyed. But in any case what an awful thing it must be to be rejected by God as worthless, and cast upon the bonfire as rubbish to be destroyed, realizing as never before what might have been if God's salvation had been accepted. Remember those words of the Lord Jesus Christ . . . "There shall be the weeping and gnashing of teeth."[56]

Matthew 10:39

If man cannot ultimately destroy another's life, and if God can so kill a man in his totality that nothing survives, life and death alike take on new meaning in the Present Age. Jesus points to that meaning when He says, "Whoever finds his life will lose it, and whoever loses his life for My sake will find it."

The same saying which appears here, in a context of the disciples' suffering, appears again in all the Synoptics in a discussion regarding Jesus' own death (Matt. 16:21-28; Mark 8:31-9:1; Luke 9:22-27). Jesus tells the disciples that He must be killed and rise again (Matt. 16:21). They must also deny their own selves and take up the cross daily (Matt. 16:24). One must not seek to save his own life— although he will truly find it if he loses it for Jesus (Matt. 16:25).

56. Guillebaud, *Righteous Judge*, p. 45.

What is a man's advantage, Jesus asks, if he gains the whole world but loses his own life? (Matt. 16:26).

The New International Version sentimentally continues the Authorized Version's "soul" in Matthew 16:26, though it inconsistently translates the identical Greek word "life" one verse earlier. Instead of "soul," Luke simply says "himself" (*heauton*, "very self," NIV), making it absolutely clear that Jesus used *psychē* (soul) in the wholistic Hebraic sense, not in the dualistic sense of Greek philosophy (perpetuated still in much pietism and revivalism).

The context suggests that "finding one's life" and "losing one's life" should be taken at face value with the normal meanings. Jesus explains His own approaching *death* and resurrection to *life* (v. 21). He warns against attempting to save one's own *life* and promises that whoever loses his *life* for the Lord will find it in the end (v. 25). No man *in this world* willingly exchanges his *psychē* (his very self) for any amount of riches (v. 26), a principle extended in Jesus' questions to the Age to Come. Some standing in sight of Jesus would see an advent of the Son of Man before they tasted *death* (v. 28). When Jesus comes in glory with the angels to reward each person, some will *lose their life*; others will *find life*.

We do not question that "life" includes *more* than mere existence —a point made as often by conditionalist writers as by traditionalists. Nor do we deny that "life" and "death" sometimes have figurative meanings in the Scriptures. The entire flow of thought in this context, however, as well as the general use here of these words, invites us to ask two questions. First, since "life" may mean *more* than mere existence but never (to our knowledge) means *less*, on what basis can "loss of life" mean *less* than the loss of existence, even though here it obviously implies the loss of far more? Eternal "death" involves *more* than temporal "death," but surely it involves no *less*. Second, what warrant does this context provide for making "lose one's life" and "find one's life" figurative in verses 25-26 when the same thoughts are so obviously literal in all the verses both before these and after?

Matthew 11:22-24

It will be "more bearable" for Tyre and Sidon on the day of judgment than for Khorazin and Bethsaida, Jesus says. It will be "more bearable" for Sodom then than for Capernaum. Luke records essentially the same words (Luke 10:13-15). Jesus here indicates that there will be degrees of punishment at the end, based on degrees of culpability (see also Matt. 12:41, 42/Luke 11:29-32). What will be Capernaum's fate? Will she be "lifted up"? No! She will "go down to Hades." This language comes from the Old Testament prophets as they threatened first Babylon (Isa. 14:13, 15) and then Tyre (Ezek. 26:19-21). In the case of those cities the threat's temporal execution meant their disappearance, never to be found again, though others around them continued to enjoy life. Jesus here personifies cities, however, and we do not wish to make too much of these words in our study of the final punishment of individual sinners.

Matthew 12:31, 32

Once, when Jesus healed a demon-possessed man who was both blind and mute, certain Pharisees attributed His astounding power to Beelzebub, the prince of demons. In response Jesus sternly warned:

> "The blasphemy against the Spirit will not be forgiven. Anyone who speaks . . . against the Holy Spirit will not be forgiven, either in this age or in the age to come."

Where Matthew uses the apocalyptic language of the two ages, Mark compresses the same idea into an eschatological adjective. The person "will never be forgiven; he is guilty of an *eternal* sin" (Mark 3:29). Luke eliminates the language of eschatology altogether, stating simply that "he will not be forgiven" (Luke 12:10). These parallels explain each other. The "eternal sin" is not a sin committed without end, as if sinners in hell forever continue to sin and therefore forever feel the penal blows.[57] It was the specific sin of blasphemy against the

---

57. A. A. Hodge says, for example: "The instant a soul sins it is cut off from the communion and life of God. As long as it continues in that state it will continue to sin. As long as it continues to sin, it will deserve his wrath and curse. It is obvious that the sinful tempers and conduct indulged in hell will deserve and receive punishment as strictly as those previously indulged in this life" (Archibald Alexander Hodge, *Outlines of Theology*, pp. 584-585).

Augustus Hopkins Strong argues that eternal sin demands eternal punishment and that the depraved will continue to sin even in hell (A. H. Strong, *Systematic Theology*, 3:1048-1049). He creates a moral dilemma without seeming to realize it. On the one hand, he says that "habit begets fixity of character, and in the spiritual world sinful acts . . . produce a permanent state of sin, which the soul, unaided, cannot change" (p. 1049). On the other hand, he argues that

Holy Spirit, the agent of divine power in the new age by whom Jesus performed His miracles of the kingdom of heaven. This specific sin was committed at a particular point of time well within the bounds of earthly history. The "eternal" sin denies and repels the only One who can forgive, and so can never be forgiven—even in the coming age of eternity.

To say the sin is never forgiven is not the same as saying its perpetrators will always endure conscious torment for committing it.[58] It is possible in our society for a convicted murderer to be pardoned. But if he is *not* forgiven, the *form* of his punishment is beside the point. He is no more pardoned if he is executed for his crime than if he spends 100 years in prison. The traditionalist author, Salmond, said it better than we can:

> The phrase in question is an absolutely exclusive phrase. It means that neither in the present nor in the future, neither in this dispensation nor in what follows it, neither before nor after Christ's Coming, is there forgiveness for this sin. It is difficult to see how the irremediableness of the condition could be more distinctly expressed.[59]

"benevolence in God may to the end permit the existence of sin and may continue to punish the sinner . . . because [God] . . . provides for the highest possible freedom and holiness in the creature through eternity" (p. 1053). How one can reconcile these two statements or call such an arrangement "the benevolence of God" is beyond my ability to understand.

Henry Constable responded to this type of argument by pointing out that (1) Scripture never suggests any such idea as sin in hell but (2) specifically states over and over that future punishment is for deeds "done in the body" during present life in this age. "Just fancy an earthly judge sentencing a criminal to a punishment too severe for the offence committed, and then gravely justifying his sentence by the observation that *the criminal would be sure to deserve it all by his conduct in gaol* [jail]!" (Constable, *Future Punishment*, pp. 107-109; quotation on p. 109).

58. A. A. Hodge is an example of one who presents the "unpardonable sin" as evidence for everlasting conscious torment (Hodge, *Outlines of Theology*, p. 582).

59. Salmond, *The Christian Doctrine of Immortality*, p. 381. In the last century Frederic W. Farrar, archdeacon and canon of Westminster, stirred a British tempest that blew in all directions when he preached a series of sermons in Westminster Abbey (November-December 1877) on final punishment. These were published (in self-defense according to his preface) as *Eternal Hope* in 1879. When Edward Bouverie Pusey replied with his *What Is of Faith as to Everlasting Punishment? In Reply to Dr. Farrar's Challenge in His "Eternal Hope,"* 1879 in 1880, Farrar responded in 1881 with his *Mercy and Judgment: A Few Last Words on Christian Eschatology with Reference to Dr. Pusey's "What Is of Faith?"* Farrar disagreed with both traditionalists and conditionalists, arguing most of all for a "larger hope" beyond the bounds of the present life. Pusey had a kind of "larger hope" of his own, insisting that Ahab, Absalom, Herod and even Antiochus Epiphanes may have experienced death-bed repentance and be saved (Pusey, *What Is of Faith?* pp. 12-14).

A modern conservative writer who argues for the possibility of conversion in the Age to Come is Brethren scholar, Vernard Eller, *The Most Revealing Book of the Bible: Making Sense Out of Revelation*, pp. 199-201.

Matthew 13:30, 40-43

In this Parable of the Weeds the farmer tells his servants to let wheat and weeds grow together until the harvest. "At that time," the owner says, "I will tell the harvesters: First collect the weeds and tie them in bundles to be burned, then gather the wheat and bring it into my barn" (v. 30). We have already seen figures from the land which involve burning what is rejected. Here Jesus gives His own interpretation.

> "As the weeds are pulled up and burned in the fire, so it will be at the end of the age. The Son of Man will send out His angels, and they will weed out of His kingdom everything that causes sin and all who do evil. They will throw them into the fiery furnace, where there will be weeping and gnashing of teeth. Then the righteous will shine like the sun in the kingdom of their Father."—vv. 40-43.

Two witnesses tell us this picture is eschatological. Not only does Jesus specifically apply the parable to "the end of the age"; His language has that background in the Old Testament. Both Nestle's Greek text and the New American Standard Bible cross-reference the expression, "everything that causes sin and all who do evil," to Zephaniah 1:3. When one turns to that verse in the standard English translations, he will not find those words in the text, though the Revised Standard Version and New American Standard Bible give them in a marginal note and the New International Version has a note saying "Hebrew uncertain." Some manuscripts of the Greek Old Testament do have these very words in this prophetic passage which goes on to describe the terrible "day of the Lord."

Jesus' promise that "the righteous will shine like the sun" seems to come from Daniel 12:3, which follows on the heels of a major Old Testament passage regarding final punishment (examined in a previous chapter). One might think also of Malachi 4:1-3, where the "sun of righteousness arises" for the righteous while the wicked become ashes under the soles of their feet. In the present parable the workers pull the weeds up and burn them in the fire, a figure of what the angels will do to sinners at the end of the world according to Jesus' own "*as . . . so.*"

Matthew 13:48-50

This Parable of the Net closely resembles the Parable of the Weeds in its word about final punishment. The net in the story drew "all kinds of fish," and the fishermen "collected the good fish in baskets, but threw the bad away" (v. 48). Jesus explained the figure.

> "This is how it will be at the end of the age. The angels will come and separate the wicked from the righteous and throw them into the fiery furnace, where there will be weeping and gnashing of teeth."—vv. 49, 50.

The Lord's emphasis here is clearly on exclusion. Many who profess to follow Him do not really know Him at all. Today they blend in with the true disciples, but God's own time of separation is coming. Jesus makes this point in many of His sayings; it is an essential element in both the Greek (*krisis*, "crisis") and English words for judgment. In the first century or the twentieth, men who profess to believe in hell tend almost always to think of it as for someone else. Jesus draws us up short in that presumption: God's great separation will hold many surprises!

Habakkuk described the predatory Chaldeans as fishermen with an insatiable net dragging through the nations, "fish" being a symbol of utter helplessness; but that comparison adds nothing to our understanding here (Hab. 1:14-17).

Matthew 18:8, 9

The greatest in the kingdom of heaven is the person most like a little child, Jesus tells the competitive and ambitious disciples. And woe to whoever turns one of God's little ones out of the road or causes such a one to sin! Jesus repeats in essence what He had said earlier about forfeiting a member of the body in order to escape Gehenna (Matt. 5:29, 30).

> "If your hand or your foot causes you to sin, cut it off and throw it away. It is better for you to enter life maimed or crippled than to have two hands or two feet and be thrown into eternal fire [*to pyr to*

aiōnion]. And if your eye causes you to sin, gouge it out and throw it away. It is better for you to enter life with one eye than to have two eyes and be thrown into the fire of hell [*tēn geennan tou pyros*]."

Gehenna here is called the "eternal fire." In another place Jesus says the "eternal fire" was prepared for the devil and his angels (Matt. 25:41). This is paralleled by reference to the kingdom, which was "prepared since the creation of the world" (v. 34). The "fire" seems to be at least as old as creation in this language; it is clear that it will extend beyond the Present Age. It is therefore said to be "eternal," since it neither begins nor ends with the Present Age. The phrase does not say what "eternal fire" will do to those thrown into it. Jesus does say the fire, like the kingdom, was "prepared"; but whereas God designed the kingdom especially for the redeemed, the fire was made for the fallen angels (2 Pet. 2:4-9; Jude 6). God formed the human creatures for glory with Himself, a destiny wholly of grace. If man aligns himself instead with the rebel creatures of a higher and previous order, he must finally share their fate.

Where Matthew has the "eternal fire," Mark speaks simply of being "thrown/going into hell" (Mark 9:43, 45, 47). As in the matter of "eternal sin," Mark uses the straightforward language of prose rather than the terminology of apocalyptic. There is general agreement among scholars that both Evangelists record words spoken originally in Aramaic. Matthew's language may add flavor and force, but it should not be naively interpreted in a way that contradicts Mark's. Luke's account of the incident stops short of this conversation (Luke 17:1, 2).

Jesus' chief thrust concerns care for the "little ones." Calvin captures that concern in his commentary on the passage. He does not elaborate at all on final punishment but simply admonishes that "whoever . . . desires to escape that fearful punishment which Christ denounces, let him stretch out his hand to the *little ones* who are despised by the world, and let him kindly assist them in keeping the path of duty."[60]

That Jesus should talk of self-mutilation in this pastoral context is interesting in the light of Zechariah 11:17. There, too, the subject is

---

60. John Calvin, *Commentary on a Harmony of the Evangelists, Matthew, Mark, and Luke,* 2:336.

God's concern for His helpless people, and the curse on a worthless shepherd is the loss of his right arm and right eye. Verses earlier the flock pays off their worthy shepherd with 30 pieces of silver, the Mosaic price of a wounded slave (Exod. 21:32). The shepherd throws the paltry sum to the potter in the house of the Lord (Zech. 11:12, 13).

Mark also adds to Matthew's record a phrase taken from Isaiah 66:24. That passage describes hell as the place "where their worm does not die, and the fire is not quenched" (Mark 9:48; some manuscripts add the same words as vv. 44, 45). Instead of Isaiah's "their fire," Jesus says simply "the fire," showing there is no special significance to the pronoun, although "their" agrees with Matthew's statement that while the fire was "prepared" for others it will also be the fate of these.

The "worm" here is the kind that feeds on dead bodies (*skōlēx*); we have examined the figure before. There is no basis anywhere in Scripture for making the worm a metaphor for remorse, a practice now almost universal and documented as early as Origen. This is a devouring worm, and what it eats—in Isaiah's picture here quoted without amendment—is already dead.

The devouring worm is aided by a *consuming* fire. Besides the biblical references already noted to "unquenchable fire" which bear this out, we mention pagan Homer's reference to "unquenchable fire" used by the Trojans against the Grecian ships (*Iliad* 16. 123, 194; 1. 599) and ecclesiastical Eusebius' "unquenchable fire" which burns a martyr to ashes (*Eccl. Hist.* 6. 41). In His repeated use of the phrase, Jesus presupposes that God's final decision concerning each person "is irreversible and entails eternal consequences."[61] Or to borrow words written a century ago,

> The expressions of . . . "unquenchable fire," &c. may mean merely that there is to be *no deliverance,*—no revival,—no restoration,—of the condemned. "Death," simply, does not shut out the hope of being brought to life again: "eternal death" does. "Fire" may be *quenched* before it has entirely consumed what it is burning: "unquenchable fire" would seem most naturally to mean that which destroys it utterly.[62]

---

61. Lane, *The Gospel According to Mark*, p. 347.
62. Richard Whately, *A View of the Scripture Revelations concerning a Future State*, p. 183.

Mark continues with a saying he alone records: "Everyone will be salted with fire" (Mark 9:49). In the next verse Jesus admonishes, "Have salt in yourselves, and be at peace with each other." Some traditionalists have presented the cryptic epigram of verse 49 in support of everlasting conscious torment. "Fire is usually destructive," says A. H. Strong, "but this unquenchable fire will act like salt, preserving instead of destroying."[63] A. B. Bruce mentions this interpretation in *The Expositor's Greek Testament* but says he sees "no necessity to regard" it as the proper view.[64] The interpretation not only lacks scriptural precedent; it aligns verse 49 against verse 48. Given this meaning, the ambiguous salt contradicts the unquenchable fire as that term is defined by numerous other passages which are quite clear.

Conditionalist Edward White suggests another approach. "The meaning may be," he surmises, "that every such sacrifice to the avenging Justice will be, *like 'Lot's wife,'* 'salted with fire,' preserved as a monument in death of the tremendous results of rebellion against the Omnipotent."[65] While this suggestion at least builds on the biblical precedent of a notable prototype of divine punishment, it also falls short of convincing.

Traditionalist advocate, Salmond, aims still another direction for insight. He reminds us that "salt was the sign of the binding obligation of the covenant, and the covenant-relation had its terrible side to the faithless as well as its gracious side to the faithful."[66] Wrath and righteousness are both *covenant* concepts, as many modern authors have shown. But just when Salmond raises the intriguing point, he suddenly walks away and leaves us standing without showing us how to use his insight to make sense of this mysterious saying.

The interpretation with the best support is probably that given by William L. Lane. Having already shown the close relation between Mark's Gospel and the fires of persecution, he reads this passage in that light.

---

63. Strong, *Systematic Theology*, 3:1036. A. W. Pink compares this preservation as by salt to God's preserving the burning bush (Exod. 3) and keeping the bodies of the three Hebrews in the fiery furnace (Dan. 3) (Arthur W. Pink, *Eternal Punishment*, p. 27). We agree totally that God is able to so preserve the bodies of the wicked to endure eternal conscious torment. We simply see nothing in Scripture to indicate that He will, and much there to indicate that He will not.

64. A. B. Bruce, in *The Expositor's Greek Testament*, ed. W. Robertson Nicoll, vol. 1, p. 407.

65. Edward White, *Life in Christ . . .* , p. 409.

66. Salmond, *The Christian Doctrine of Immortality*, p. 377, note 1.

The thought of the sacrifice of an offending member of the body (verses 43-47) is here carried a step further: every disciple is to be a sacrifice for God (cf. Rom. 12:1). In the OT the Temple sacrifices had to be accompanied by salt (Lev. 2:13; Ezek. 43:24; cf. Ex. 30:35). The salt-sacrifice metaphor is appropriate to a situation of suffering and trial in which the principle of sacrifice cultivated with respect to the individual members of the body is now severely tested. The disciples must be seasoned with salt, like the sacrifice. This will take place through fiery trials (cf. I Peter 1:7; 4:12)."[67]

This explanation enjoys the support of its immediate context, the outlook of the book of Mark as a whole, and the background material regarding salt and sacrifices in the Old Testament. Jesus offers His disciples a choice: the *fire of persecution* now or the *fire of Gehenna* later. He speaks straight from the shoulder—He does not play games or leave us guessing. On this decision hangs our eternal destiny.

Nestle's Greek text gives two cross-references on this passage: Isaiah 66:24 and Judith 16:21. We examined the first in our look at the Old Testament, and the second when we surveyed the Apocrypha. These cross-references offer opposing pictures of the end of the wicked, so our options are clearly set forth. We choose to follow Isaiah and ignore Judith.

Matthew 21:33-44

Jesus revises Isaiah's Song of the Vineyard (Isa. 5:1-7) to drive home His own warning of God's rejection again of faithless Israel. This comes in a series of parables and confrontations during the final days of the ministry. Taken together, they bring to a boil the rage of the Pharisees and chief priests until it finally explodes in Jesus' arrest and their demand for His crucifixion (Matt. 21:45, 46).

The parable does not deal directly with the end of the world. Matthew, chapter 24, and perhaps 1 Thessalonians 2:15, 16 indicate its judgment might have come crashing down—along with the Jewish national hopes—by the hands of the Romans in A.D. 69-70. Yet temporal judgments often prefigure the great and final one, so even that interpretation leaves room for the passage in our present study. But

---

67. Lane, *The Gospel According to Mark*, p. 349.

how does it picture the judgment it threatens? "What" is the punishment regardless of its "when"?

In Matthew's account Jesus says the owner "will bring those wretches to a wretched end" (v. 41). He then changes from parabolic narrative to address His hearers directly. "Therefore I tell you that the kingdom of God will be taken away from you and given to a people who will produce its fruit" (v. 43). Mark and Luke both say the vineyard-owner will "kill those tenants" (Mark 12:9; Luke 20:16).

Matthew[68] and Luke then add Jesus' statement that "He who falls on this stone will be broken to pieces, but he on whom it falls will be crushed" (Matt. 21:44; Luke 20:18), language based on Daniel's interpretation of the great image in Nebuchadnezzar's dream (Dan. 2:34, 35, 44, 45). Along the way we might observe Daniel's comparison of the ruined and broken image to "chaff on a threshing floor in the summer" which "the wind swept . . . away without leaving a trace" (Dan. 2:35), the same figure Psalm 1 uses for the wicked's end. Daniel applies the language to human kingdoms; Jesus particularizes it to individual persons.

Whatever its relevance to the individual destiny of the wicked, we may summarize the parable's judgment like this. They lose all privileges of the kingdom; they are brought to death in a wretched end. If we may include the data from Daniel, the wind blows them away without leaving a trace. We cannot be sure if the judgment is temporal or eschatological, but it is described in these terms.

Matthew 22:13

The Parable of the Wedding Banquet also ends on a tragic note. The king discovers a guest improperly clad. The man has no excuse; he is speechless (Matt. 22:12). Now comes the punch line:

> "Then the king told the attendants, 'Tie him hand and foot, and throw him outside, into the darkness, where there will be weeping and gnashing of teeth.' For many are invited, but few are chosen."—v. 14.

Found only in Matthew, this parable serves there as a sort of epilogue to the Parable of the Great Banquet, which Luke also reports

---

68. This verse in Matthew does not appear in some Greek manuscripts or the Revised Standard Version. It is unquestioned in Luke.

(Matt. 22:1-14; Luke 14:15-24). The first-century work known as 4 Ezra provides a close parallel to Jesus' saying that "many are invited, but few are chosen." When Ezra laments the small number who are saved and the great crowds of the damned, he is told, "Many have been created, but few shall be saved" (4 Ezra 8:3).

Jesus may mean only that the generosity of God's invitation dwarfs the meagerness of man's response. Those "chosen" are *few* compared to the *many* God "invites." In the parable the spotlight is on the improperly dressed guest rather than those who never made an appearance. As it happens, the "few" are even fewer than those who come. The warning is for us who accept God's invitation, not for those who reject it.

There seems to be no historical support for the favored explanation that the Palestinian host provided his guests with a wedding garment, though the gospel application usually made is certainly true. Jeremias suggests that this is not a special festive garment at all but a freshly-washed garment still unsoiled. He cites a similar parable from a first-century rabbi which identifies the clean garment as repentance—preferably on the day before one dies. "But here," Jeremias says, "we must choose between the rabbinic answer and the Gospel's." He then directs us to Isaiah 61:10 and Revelation 22:14, where the robes are God's forgiveness and imputed righteousness.[69] The contrast between Matthew and rabbi may not be accidental. "What has not been sufficiently recognized," writes W. D. Davies, "is the extent to which . . . the period when Matthew emerged was one of the codification of Law in Judaism and of the reformulation or reformation of worship."[70]

So far as final punishment, this parable provides nothing new. We have encountered its language already—the expulsion into the outside darkness and the weeping and grinding of teeth. It does underscore that those who respond to Christ's invitation must come only in the robes woven by His perfect obedience to God and made spotless by His cleansing blood (Gal. 3:27; Rev. 7:14; cf. Zech. 3:1-8; Rev. 3:18).[71]

---

69. Joachim Jeremias, *The Parables of Jesus*, pp. 65, 188-189.

70. Davies, *Sermon on the Mount*, p. 300. He warns that his remarks concerning a possible relationship between rabbinic Judaism and Matthean Christianity are only "tentative and exploratory."

71. Revelation 19:8 has the saved dressed in "fine linen, bright and clean," which "stands for the righteous acts of the saints." This is spoken in a different form of reference from our

Matthew 24:50, 51

Jesus alternates His warnings—first to the self-righteous Pharisees, who presume from past privilege that they will inherit God's kingdom—then to His own disciples, who are beginning to recognize the Pharisees' error but stand in danger of repeating it themselves. The Lord exhorts us to watchfulness in this illustration of a reckless and profligate servant suddenly surprised when his master returns. The story ends with a warning:

> "The master of that servant will come on a day when he does not expect him and at an hour he is not aware of. He will cut him to pieces and assign him a place with the hypocrites, where there will be weeping and gnashing of teeth."

Luke omits the "weeping and gnashing of teeth" and puts "unbelievers" instead of "hypocrites." Both changes are easily explained in terms of intended audiences. Luke writes for Gentiles, and Matthew for Jews. Luke also continues quoting Jesus after Matthew stops, providing the parable's only unique contribution to our study. Jesus says:

> "That servant who knows his master's will and does not get ready or does not do what his master wants will be beaten with many blows. But the one who does not know and does things deserving punishment will be beaten with few blows. From everyone who has been given much, much will be demanded; and from the one who has been entrusted with much, much more will be asked."—Luke 12:47, 48.

These words clearly involve degrees of punishment in proportion to light spurned and opportunity neglected. Here traditionalists and conditionalists fully agree, though at times each camp has used the

---

passage in the Gospels or even Isaiah 64:6, where "all our righteous acts are like filthy [lit. "menstruous"] rags." On the paradox of grace and works in judgment see C. Leslie Mitton, "Present Justification and Final Judgment: A Discussion of the Parable of the Sheep and the Goats," *Expository Times* 68, no. 2 (November 1956): 46-50, and especially Herman N. Ridderbos, *Paul: An Outline of His Theology*, pp. 178-181. Ridderbos further recommends G. C. Berkouwer (*Faith and Justification*, pp. 103-112) and Schrenk (*Theological Dictionary of the New Testament*, 2:208). One quotation from Ridderbos: "For just as absolutely as faith is involved in justification by the grace of God and by nothing else, even so work emanates from this same faith; as faith it cannot remain empty and workless, but becomes known as faith precisely in works" (p. 180).

point as an argument against the other.[72] A close reading of the text raises another question, however, which neither side seems to have considered.

The villain in the story is cut in pieces and thrown out to the hypocrites/unbelievers. But of the other two servants, beaten with stripes few and many, the parable says no such thing. Are they of a character entirely different from the villain? If the man cut in pieces and thrown out stands for those God will finally exclude from His company and banish to hell—as common opinion holds on both sides of the controversy—of whom are the beaten servants types? Do they return to the master's good graces following their beatings? Do they represent some finally saved though punished first in a degree appropriate to their guilt? Does the free grace of God leave any place for such a scheme (many very orthodox theologians have entertained similar views through the centuries)? If so, the phrase "degrees of punishment" takes on even greater meaning. Or do we press the text too literally in even raising such a question?

Whatever the answer to those questions, no one in the story is tormented forever. One man receives a few blows; another many. The worst fellow is cut in pieces and thrown out—a terrible punishment, for sure, but still far from eternal conscious torment.

Luke takes us further yet. "I have come to bring fire on the earth," Jesus says, "and how I wish it were already kindled!" (Luke 12:49). This is the first "fire" in the passage, and it is evidently the same judgment-fire which John had before announced that Jesus would bring (Matt. 3:10-12). But the fire falls on Jesus first—in the "baptism" that awaits Him on Golgotha (Luke 12:50). We will consider that fire in some detail in the next chapter as a foretaste of the fire at the end of the world.

Matthew 25:30

In our day the "one-talent man" is often an object of pity. Jesus' parable is not so sympathetic; there he is "lazy" and "worthless." At

---

72. Traditionalists: Louis Berkhof (*Reformed Dogmatics*, 2:345); A. A. Hodge (*Outlines of Theology*, pp. 580-581); W. G. T. Shedd (*The Doctrine of Endless Punishment*, p. 131, note 1); E. B. Pusey (*What Is of Faith?* pp. 9-10). Pusey here even says that "we cannot tell how far the exposure of infants may be a sin in China . . . or cannibalism in a nation of cannibals." Conditionalists: Henry Constable (*Future Punishment*, pp. 1-2); LeRoy Edwin Froom (*The Conditionalist Faith of Our Fathers*, 1:496).

the end he loses what little capital he had, then is thrown "outside, into the darkness where there will be weeping and gnashing of teeth."

Mark summarizes the story as a lesson on vigilance but omits Matthew's ending describing the master's return (Mark 13:32-36). Luke gives the parable in detail, also without Matthew's ending, but he introduces a subplot and some new characters. Early in his story a group of citizens refuse to acknowledge the master's authority (Luke 19:14). At the end the master has them arrested and executed before his eyes (v. 27). Neither Mark nor Luke add to our picture of final punishment, though each gives his own special admonition or warning.

Matthew 25:41, 46

Perhaps the most famous of all Jesus' words concerning final punishment, the sayings in these two verses conclude the Parable of the Sheep and the Goats (Matt. 25:31-46). That parable, in turn, closes a series of crisis parables in which Jesus exhorts the disciples to keep their eyes open and their hands busy in view of His future glorious coming.[73] The three parables are our Lord's rousing end to His fifth and last discourse in Matthew's carefully-worked arrangement of material.[74] Jesus' teaching in each case climaxes with a story or saying concerning the stakes of discipleship, so that (in Matthew at least) we may say Jesus' teaching always brings us to this same point regardless of where it starts.

The Parable of the Sheep and the Goats has been interpreted many ways. Dispensationalists who agree with *The New Scofield Reference Bible* here see a judgment of individual Gentiles who are alive at Christ's second coming, based on their treatment of Jews during the great tribulation just ended.[75] Most exegetes, however, probably agree with Jeremias and Hunter that it speaks of the great judgment

---

73. They are The Ten Virgins (Matt. 25:1-13), The Talents (Matt. 25:14-30) and this one. For a lively, practical discussion of their different emphases, see Eller, *Most Revealing Book*, pp. 11-14, esp. p. 18.

74. Besides an introduction (ch. 1-4) and an epilogue (ch. 28), Matthew presents his material in five units, each consisting of a discourse by Jesus followed by a section of narrative. Each discourse stops with the same saying that Jesus had ended His teaching/parable (Matt. 7:28; 11:1; 13:53; 19:1; 26:1).

75. *The New Scofield Reference Bible.*

at the end of the world,[76] although they disagree on the identity of "the least of these brothers," whose treatment becomes the standard of judgment.[77]

J. A. T. Robinson has defended the parable's authenticity against critics; Théo Preiss has beautifully shown its poetic structure.[78] Perhaps "the most sombre and haunting" of all Christ's parables, this one has as its burden "doomsday and eternal separation."[79] The gathering of God's scattered flock is a familiar feature of the Messianic age (Isa. 40:11; Ezek. 34:11-31; John 10:1-16; 11:52). In Ezekiel 34:17 God promises to "judge . . . between rams and goats." According to Dalman, flocks in Palestine were often mixed. Shepherds separated sheep from goats each night, the goats requiring protection from the cold, the sheep preferring open air.[80] This is the setting of Jesus' story, which is incidental to the contrasting judgments.

Those on the right hand are told to "take your inheritance, the kingdom prepared for you since the creation of the world" (v. 34). Jesus' first discourse in Matthew has some receive the kingdom (Matt. 5:3), and now so does His last. In the first case they are the "poor in spirit"; here they are those who have been so generous to the needy. We think of the similar language used of the Macedonians, whose "extreme poverty welled up in rich generosity" (2 Cor. 8:1-5).

To those on the left hand the Son of Man says: "Depart from Me, you who are cursed, into the eternal fire prepared for the devil and his angels" (v. 41). Again Jesus speaks of banishment and the "eternal fire." We have examined both figures already. Here the contrast is the point. Sheep and goats alike are sent to an appropriate destiny. In each case it has been "prepared" (see discussion on Matt. 18:8, 9); in each case it is described as "eternal." That the language flows along

---

76. Jeremias, *The Parables of Jesus*, pp. 206ff; Archibald M. Hunter, *The Parables Then and Now*, pp. 115ff.

77. Davies (*Sermon on the Mount*, pp. 98-99) argues that they are Christ's disciples among the nations. Hunter and Jeremias see them as simply the needy, whether disciples or not (op. cit.). The context seems to support Davies, as does the use of "brothers" throughout Matthew; Hunter's and Jeremias' point is made in the Parable of the Good Samaritan, though without a specific judgment scene.

78. Both cited in Archibald M. Hunter, *Interpreting the Parables*; Robinson on p. 118, Preiss on pp. 88-89.

79. Hunter, *The Parables Then and Now*, p. 115.

80. G. Dalman, *Arbeit und Sitte in Palastina* (Gütersloh, 1939), 6:99; reference given by Jeremias, *The Parables of Jesus*, p. 206.

channels so parallel only highlights the split into opposite directions looming just ahead.

Cursed. The "cursed" are certainly under God's imprecation, but the word itself says nothing of what it involves. It is the common word for human curses, as opposed to blessings, both in its verb form (Ps. 62:4; Matt. 5:44; Rom. 12:14; James 3:9) and as a noun (Judg. 9:57). Sometimes it describes one who has died a horrible death or has been executed, such as a hanged corpse (Deut. 21:22, 23), Jezebel (2 Kings 9:34) or the exterminated Canaanites (Wisd. 12:11; cf. Sir. 41:9). The noun is used a few times in connection with fire. Worthless land is "cursed" and burned (Heb. 6:8); Jotham's curse is fulfilled when a tower of people are burned to death (Judg. 9:57). When Jesus cursed the fig tree, it withered and died (Mark 11:21).

Sin carries a curse throughout the Bible. It falls on the ground in the beginning (Gen. 3:17), through the law when broken (Gal. 3:10, 13), and always in connection with God's covenant (Deut. 11:26; 30:1; Mal. 2:2). In the case of the covenant it is once said to be death (Deut. 30:19), the fate that befell Jesus when He became a "curse" for us (Gal. 3:10, 13). Seductive amoral teachers will be cursed, according to 2 Peter 2:14; the context describes their fate as destruction and perishing (v. 12) or as "blackest darkness" (v. 17).

Eternal Fire. Here the curse is banishment into the eternal fire. Apparently pre-existent (prepared for the devil and his angels), it is also the fire of the Age to Come. It is difficult to avoid the qualitative force of "eternal" in this passage—though applied in the starkest contrast imaginable and though its quantitative meaning is not denied.[81] Men may fear human wrath—or covet human blessing. Compared to the issues of God's great judgment, both become mere specks on the horizon.

Bligh says the parable's flavor is that of contemporary Judaism, and he argues that "only the original twists—that which jars with the perspective of His contemporary patriots"—are unique to Jesus. He

---

81. See previous discussion of this word in chapter on the adjective "eternal." In *The Eternity of Hell Torments Considered*, the eighteenth-century English Arian, William Whiston, argued that the life of the blessed is not strictly eternal either, though longer by far than the torments of the wicked. D. P. Walker calls this "an entirely novel step" in his *The Decline of Hell: Seventeenth-Century Discussions of Eternal Torment*, p. 99.

gives other Gospel examples in which Jesus quotes His opponents' own words against them and uses their rhetoric to ridicule them. They could have agreed wholeheartedly with every detail of this parable but two—*who* goes each direction and *why*. These things alone, according to Bligh, are the points Jesus wishes to make.[82] We can appreciate his reasoning and agree that those are the chief emphases, but are happy to follow Jesus' words *all* the way.

We have already seen how the New Testament uses the adjective *aiōnios* of the *result* of processes and acts (Heb. 5:9; 6:2; 9:12). The entire Old Testament and the teaching of Jesus suggest that we understand it that way here. Whatever *aiōnios* means, one should have good cause for not translating it the same way when it appears twice in one verse. The King James translators betrayed theological bias and not linguistic expertise with their "everlasting" punishment but "eternal" life, "a purely wanton and arbitrary variation."[83]

Neither the fire nor the punishment are of this age—in origin or in quality. When the wicked have perished, it will be forever—their destruction and punishment is unending as well as qualitatively different from anything we now know. The fire is also "eternal" in this sense—just as Sodom was destroyed by "eternal fire" since its results were to last forever (Jude 7). The life is also "eternal" in quality as well as quantity. Because *both* ideas fit the case so that we cannot choose one to the exclusion of the other, and because both "eternal" and "everlasting" tend to do this very thing, we repeat without embarrassment our earlier (unoriginal) invitation for a new English adjective—perhaps a neutral transliteration such as "aionic" or "aionion."[84]

We must be careful in pressing the parallel between "eternal" life and "eternal" punishment that we do not fall into any spirit of vindictiveness or ungodly joy at the fate of the wicked. Since Augustine (see Appendix A), traditionalists have argued that unless "eternal punishment" means endless torment, we have no assurance that

---

82. P. H. Bligh, "Eternal Fire, Eternal Punishment, Eternal Life (Mt 25:41, 46)," *Expository Times* 83, no. 1 (October 1971): 9-11. Bligh cites as other examples Matt. 22:41-46; Luke 5:32; 18:11, 12; John 10:34f.

83. Farrar, *Eternal Hope*, p. 198. The New International Version corrects this inconsistency in Matthew 25 but lapses into it in 2 Thessalonians 1:9.

84. In my article, "Putting Hell in Its Place," *Christianity Today*, 6 August 1976, pp. 14-17. The suggestion has been made for centuries by men whose shoes I am unworthy to untie.

"eternal life" secures our endless joy. Many have cautioned against taking delight in the fate of the lost, a sure sign that some have done just that.

Regardless of his other weaknesses on the subject, Frederic W. Farrar needs to be heard every time that parallel is drawn. "Our sure and certain hope of everlasting happiness rests on no such miserable foundation as the disputed meaning of a Greek adjective which is used over and over again of things transitory," he began. "If we need texts on which to rest it we may find plenty" (Isa. 25:6-8; Hos. 13:14; Luke 20:36; 1 Cor. 15; 2 Tim. 1:10; 1 Pet. 1:4; 5:4; Rev. 21:4). Furthermore, he said, the meaning of this same adjective *aiōnios* may be altered by the word it modifies, even in the same verse, citing as examples Habakkuk 3:6 and Romans 16:25, 26.

But Farrar was also a great preacher, and his soberest words are directed to any who ask how they can be confident of everlasting happiness unless they know the damned will suffer without end. The whole question Farrar regarded as wicked and selfish, and his response exploded from the heart:

> I call God to witness that so far from regretting the possible loss of some billions of aeons of bliss by attaching to the word *aiōnios* a sense in which scores of times it is undeniably found, I would here, and now, and kneeling on my knees, ask Him that I might die as the beasts that perish, and for ever cease to be, rather than that my worst enemy should, for one single year, endure the hell described by Tertullian, or Minucius Felix, or Jonathan Edwards, or Dr. Pusey, or Mr. Furniss, or Mr. Moody, or Mr. Spurgeon.[85]

We do not follow Farrar's interpretation of "eternal," but we take off our hat to his unselfish spirit, which rates a place alongside Moses (Exod. 32:32) and Paul (Rom. 9:3) in charity that can only be described as like Jesus Christ, who is God over all (John 3:16; Gal. 2:20).

Punishment. The meaning of *kolasis* ("punishment") is also disputed. According to Aristotle this word points to the one who suffers, while its synonym *timōria* points to the one who inflicts. Trench repeats this distinction in his *New Testament Synonyms*, according

---

85. Farrar, *Eternal Hope*, pp. 197-202; quotation on p. 202.

to Salmond, who cautions against overstatement. Salmond cites Plutarch for nonbiblical exceptions, as well as numerous references from Hellenistic and early Christian literature.[86] *Kolasis* denotes punishment *inflicted* as well as *received*; it is at home with concepts such as wrath, justice or vengeance (Acts 4:21 has the verb). What is *kolasis* here is *timōria* in Hebrews 10:29. Synonyms by nature are agreeably interchangeable, but they reserve the right at times to stand on their own feet and have their individual say!

Moulton-Milligan[87] say that "cut short" seems to have been the original sense of the word, with "prune" or "cutting down" a derived but familiar meaning in the time of Jesus. The only other New Testament occurrence of *kolasis* (1 John 4:18) fits this definition, they say, for fear "checks development," and in that sense it has to do with punishment (NIV). Moulton-Milligan here see "the idea of 'deprivation,' and kind of *poena damni*."

The Septuagint puts *kolasis* for *mikshol*, which means a stumbling-block that leads to ruin. The word Jesus uses is applied to the Egyptian's plague (Wisd. of Sol. 11:13; 16:2, 24) but also to their death in the Red Sea (Wisd. of Sol. 19:4). It refers to punishment by death in 1 Samuel 25:31 and Ezekiel 21:15. "Punishment" may certainly include conscious pain, as in all the examples above, but it does not have to. The same word is applied to an idol of wood or stone in Wisdom of Solomon, which says that "that which was made [idol] shall be punished together with him that made it" (Wisd. of Sol. 14:10).

It is interesting to compare Jesus' statement of contrasting fates here with the one He gives in John 5:29, and both of those with Daniel's (Dan. 12:2). This is what we find:

Matthew. . . go away to eternal life . . . . . go away to eternal punishment;

John . . . . . . rise to live . . . . rise to be condemned;

Daniel. . . . . awake to everlasting life . . . awake to shame and everlasting contempt.

---

86. Salmond, *The Christian Doctrine of Immortality*, p. 386.

87. James Hope Moulton and George Milligan, *The Vocabulary of the Greek Testament Illustrated from the Papyri and Other Non-Literary Sources*, p. 352.

What is said of the righteous is in each case the same. They rise/go to everlasting (eternal) life. On the basis of the comparison, the "condemnation" of "shame and everlasting contempt" is the same as the "eternal punishment" awaiting the wicked. If we may take Isaiah 66:24 as a further inspired description of the "contempt" mentioned in Daniel, the picture clearly involves the total destruction by fire and worms of corpses the Lord has slain. It is an "everlasting" contempt because the state is irreversible. Because it is God's judgment against sin, it is not mere happenstance but an everlasting "punishment."[88]

Traditionalists sometimes object that irreversible (therefore endless) extinction is actually no "punishment" at all. Yet throughout human history men have willingly chosen the severest tortures, life imprisonment, or exile into intolerable circumstances and total isolation rather than face the final cutting off of their expected years of life. A. W. Pink argues for conscious torment, but he makes our point in explaining the reason behind the figure "second death" as a symbol of hell. "To the normal man death is the object he fears above all others," he writes. "It is that from which he naturally shrinks. It is that which he most dreads."[89] Salmond, a defender of the traditional view, agrees with this innate dread of nonexistence, even among primitive peoples.

> "The ideal of annihilation," says Plutarch, "was intolerable to the Greek mind. If they had no choice left them between entire extinction and an eternity of torment in Hades, they would have chosen the latter; almost all, men and women both, would have surrendered themselves to the teeth of Cerberus, or the buckets of the Danaidae, rather than to nonentity."[90]

T. H. Huxley is reported to have said he would prefer the traditionalist's hell to annihilation, as did Milton's Belial in *Paradise Lost*.[91]

---

88. The Bible emphasizes in many places that man's final destiny will be pronounced by the sovereign God, whether good or bad. See Ps. 62:12; Prov. 24:12; Rom. 2:6; 2 Cor. 5:10; Eph. 6:8; Col. 3:25; Rev. 2:23; 20:12; 22:11, 12.

89. Pink, *Eternal Punishment*, p. 22.

90. Salmond, *The Christian Doctrine of Immortality* pp. 608-609. Although Salmond offers the data as evidence against extinction, it seems to me to backfire in his face.

91. According to T. F. Glasson, "Human Destiny: Has Christian Teaching Changed?" *Modern Churchman* 12, no. 4 (July 1969): 294.

Constable quotes Witsius, a framer of Protestant orthodoxy, as asking: "May it not, in its measure, be reckoned an infinite punishment, should God please to doom man, who is by nature a candidate for immortality, to total annihilation, from whence he should never be suffered to return to life?" (*Covenants* 1. 5. 42).[92] Augustine made the same point in his *The City of God*. "Where a very serious crime is punished by death and the execution of the sentence takes only a minute, no laws consider that minute as the measure of the punishment, but rather the fact that the criminal is forever removed from the community of the living." (See his statement in context in Appendix A.)

On this basis we regard a 20-year prison sentence to be greater than a 10-year sentence, a 50-year sentence worse than one for 20, and life imprisonment greater than these all. Yet, as Constable pointed out,

> From the earliest records of our race *capital* punishment has been reckoned as not only the greatest but also the most lasting of all punishments; and it is only reckoned the greatest because it is the most lasting. A flogging, inflicted on a petty thief, inflicts more actual pain than decapitation or hanging inflicts upon a murderer. Why then is it greater and more lasting? Because it has deprived the sufferer of every hour of that life which but for it he would have had. *Its duration is supposed co-existent with the period of his natural life.*[93]

Indeed, "to cease to be is the final tragedy which can befall a living soul who is able to receive the gift of eternal life."[94]

We might imagine the case of two foreign ambassadors, both kidnapped by the same band of terrorists. The captors brutalize one of them for three days, then cut off one of his ears and return him to his family. They protect the other from any harm for the same three days—even treat him kindly—but shoot him dead at the last minute on a sudden whim. Which man's punishment is greater? Who suffers the greater loss?

If one protests that utter extinction is no punishment at all, he might think of a Southeast Asian village suddenly attacked by guerrillas. They cut down all inhabitants in their sleep, then burn the

---

92. Constable, *Future Punishment*, p. 13.

93. Ibid., p. 12.

94. William Strawson, *Jesus and the Future Life: A Study in the Synoptic Gospels*, p. 155.

village to the ground. Would anyone defend the murderers on the grounds that the sleeping inhabitants felt no pain, or protest that the ashes of the villages still remain?

Some insist that "annihilation" is "an extremely abstract idea, too philosophical, in fact, to find a natural place within the limits of the realistic biblical eschatology."[95] Most conditionalists have steered away from the term for that very reason, preferring such biblical verbs as "die," "destroy" or "perish." But before one objects that laws of thermodynamics do not allow anything to be truly destroyed, he will do well to consider that the same laws say nothing is truly created either. We are in a different realm from the inductive physicists. The God of the Bible is a God who calls into being things which do not exist, who gives life to the dead, and who is able to destroy both body and soul in hell! Again we hear Jesus' exhortation —"fear Him!"

Jonathan Edwards, too, concedes this point. In a chapter entitled "Concerning the Endless Punishment of Those Who Die Impenitent," Edwards—whose name is popularly (if unfairly) synonymous with preaching the horrors of eternal torment—writes approximately 15,000 words against various ideas of restoration or universal salvation. Other than a two-sentence denial of annihilation in his opening paragraph, he mentions it only one time. In a lengthy paragraph (#31) Edwards responds to the idea that the wicked will suffer penal pains according to the precise measure of divine justice, then will be exterminated.

"On this," he writes, "I would observe that there is nothing got by such a scheme; no relief from the arguments taken from Scripture, for the proper eternity of future punishment." In other words, sinners can find no comfort in this understanding of hell, for it is as properly eternal and scripturally horrible as the common view of unending conscious torment! He reaffirms the concession at the end of his paragraph. If "eternal punishment" does not consist of conscious unending torment but rather extinction forever, then it is as fully "eternal" with or without the preceding penal pains, he says. And therefore "it answers the scripture expressions as well, to suppose that they shall be annihilated immediately, without any long pains, provided the annihilation be everlasting."[96] He is arguing *ad*

---

95. Geerhardus Vos, *The Pauline Eschatology*, p. 294.

96. Jonathan Edwards, *The Works of Jonathan Edwards*, 2:515-525; quotation on p. 524.

hominem in response to those who insisted on a very, very lengthy period of pain which would be followed by extinction. He is not agreeing to the view we present. But his paragraph (which readers are urged to study for themselves) is most significant in that it raises *no scriptural objection* to eternal extinction—only that "the supposition of the length of their torments [before death] is brought in without any necessity."[97]

Isaac Watts, whose book on *The World to Come* championed the traditional understanding of hell, later raised the question in his *The Ruine and Recovery of Mankind* whether death's penalty threatened in the Garden of Eden might not include "the utter destruction of the life of the soul as well as of the body," so that God would "utterly destroy and annihilate His creatures for ever."[98] Froom repeats Avary Holmes Forbes' statement (in *The Last Enemy*, p. 69) that Charles Spurgeon also said in later life: "I have no quarrel with the Conditional Immortality doctrine."[99] Froom also relates a personal conversation with W. Graham Scroggie, widely-used devotional speaker and pastor for seven years of Spurgeon's Metropolitan Tabernacle in London, in which Scroggie gave him explicit permission to "quote me whenever and wherever you please as being a believer in Conditionalism."[100]

Contemporary evangelical author, Calvin D. Linton, says he can "strike hands in a momentary bargain" with the idea of eternal extinction if it can "be held in balance with seemingly contrary teachings" such as unquenchable fire, undying worm, and wailing and gnashing of teeth.[101] And John W. Wenham writes in *The Goodness of God* that "the possibility that the lost will eventually pass out of existence, needs much more serious attention."[102] He concludes his

---

97. Ibid., p. 524.

98. Quoted with reference by White, *Life in Christ*, p. xi; and Froom, *Conditionalist Faith*, 2:220.

99. Froom, *Conditionalist Faith*, 2:797.

100. Ibid., pp. 910-911. Froom says the meeting took place on December 22, 1957. He reports that Scroggie sat up in his sickbed, grasped Froom's hand and said, "Brother Froom, I believe that God has raised you up for this great task. I am praying for you every day. You may quote me whenever and wherever you please as being a believer in Conditionalism." Froom clearly intends to present Scroggie as holding to the final extinction of the wicked.

101. Calvin D. Linton, "The Sorrows of Hell," *Christianity Today* 16 (19 November 1971): 13.

102. Wenham, *The Goodness of God*, p. 34.

chapter on hell with a call for just such open-minded study of this alternative, saying "we shall consider ourselves under no obligation to defend the notion of unending torment, until the arguments of the conditionalists have been refuted."[103]

Conclusion. In this parable Jesus teaches an end-time judgment which divides men into two categories and sentences them to corresponding but opposite dooms. In this apocalyptic picture the wicked are banished into pre-existent, eschatological fire prepared for the satanic angels. There they will eventually be destroyed forever, both body and soul, as the divine penalty for sin. Other passages imply a period of conscious pain involving body and soul, but the "eternal punishment" itself is the capital execution, the everlasting loss of existence, the everlasting loss of the eternal life of joy and blessing in company with God and the redeemed. Jude but repeats the Master's thought here when he gives Sodom and Gomorrah as the prototype of those "who suffer the punishment of eternal fire" (Jude 7), as does Peter in saying that God "made them an example of what is going to happen to the ungodly" by "burning them to ashes" (2 Pet. 2:6).

Matthew 26:24

As Jesus' last supper with the disciples drew to a close, the Lord began to say that one of them would betray Him. The disciples protest, but Jesus insists:

> "The Son of Man will go just as it is written about Him. But woe to that man who betrays the Son of Man! It would be better for him if he had not been born."

The statement appears in Matthew 26:24 and Mark 14:21. Instead of scriptural prediction, Luke points to divine foreordination, which is really the same, and he stops short of the final sentence (Luke 22:22).

Supporters of conscious unending torment often cite this saying of Jesus as if only that fate is a condition worse than never having been born. Jesus does not say, however, that this is a fate worse than *death*, but a fate worse than *non-birth*. The language also occurs in a

---

103. Ibid., pp. 40-41.

parable in the pseudepigraphical 1 (Ethiopic) Enoch. There it is said of sinners in judgment, "It had been good for them if they had not been born" (1 En. 38:2). In the verses following, the sinners are destroyed: "the kings and the mighty perish . . . and . . . none . . . seek . . . mercy . . . for their life is at an end" (vv. 5, 6). Is it not far worse to lose a cherished possession than never to have known it? Who is happier—the man born with empty eye-sockets who never sees the sun, or the man whose sight is suddenly cut off in the middle of a busy life? Do we not regard the death of the young a special tragedy merely because of the expected years they lost?

Job, too, wishes he had never been born (Job 3). In his case the desire is prompted by severe and painful suffering. The language can therefore fit either view of final punishment, but it demands neither.

Luke 16:19-31

Once, as Jesus taught on stewardship and covetousness, the Pharisees sneered at His word. Jesus replied with an assortment of remarks, culminating in this parable. A close comparison of the parable to its immediate context reveals so many parallels that one marvels at the intricate connection. Yet many advocates of eternal conscious torment write as though the story had no context at all, as if its primary point is one found nowhere in the context. Buis says, for example, "This parable so clearly teaches the orthodox doctrine of eternal punishment that the opponents of the doctrine are hard pressed to know what to do with it."[104]

The plot of the parable, the reversal of earthly fortunes after death, was familiar in popular Palestinian stories of Jesus' time. Hugo Gressmann cites a Greek parallel from a first-century Egyptian papy-

---

104. Harry Buis, *The Doctrine of Eternal Punishment*, p. 39. After the *Christianity Today* article on hell, my friend Jon Zens, a Reformed Baptist pastor and prolific writer, protested the statement that the New Testament does not "give any particular descriptions of the torments of hell." "Why," he asked, "does he not deal seriously with Luke 16:19-31? . . . We must let this passage say *something* to us" (Jon Zens, "Do the Flames Ever Stop in Hell?" *Free Grace Broadcaster*, March-April 1978, pp. 1-2).

Norval Geldenhuys concludes, on the other hand, that Jesus "related this parable not in order to satisfy our curiosity about life after death but to emphasise vividly the tremendous seriousness of life on this side of the grave." The story is therefore "a parable and not . . . a real occurrence from which various questions in connection with the hereafter may be answered" (Norval Geldenhuys, *The Gospel of Luke*, The New International Commentary on the New Testament, pp. 427; 429, note 10; see also notes 5, 6, 7, 12).

rus, and he says there are at least seven versions of the story in Jewish literature. One of the most famous involved a poor student of the Law and a rich publican named Bar Ma'jan.[105] There are differences between these stories and Jesus', of course, and therein lies the Lord's uniqueness. But the basic plot was well-known folklore.

Froom cites a discourse of Josephus concerning Hades which paints almost precisely the same picture found in Luke. He concludes that "Jesus was clearly using a then-common tradition of the Jews to press home a moral lesson in a related field."[106] Although the Whiston edition of Josephus offers a lengthy defense of the treatise's authenticity on internal and external grounds,[107] most scholars today regard it as spurious, as conditionalists Edward White and Henry Constable both note.[108]

Traditionalists generally begin their interpretation of the parable with the word "Hades," which they ordinarily regard as the place of punishment entered by the lost at death, to be changed at the last judgment only in intensity and permanence. This understanding became prominent in the High Middle Ages (as we will outline in a later chapter), and it was mediated into Protestantism largely through the influence of John Calvin (see earlier chapters on immortality and the fathers, also Appendix B). It puts some stress on the pagan Greek background of "Hades" but fails to appreciate sufficiently the biblical usage of the term in either Old or New Testament.

---

105. These stories found by Gressmann are cited in Karel Hanhart, *The Intermediate State in the New Testament*, pp. 192-193, who also refers to Rudolph Bultmann, *Geschichte der synoptischen Tradition* [History of the synoptic tradition] (1931), pp. 212f, 221f; in Bruce R. Reichenbach, *Is Man the Phoenix?* p. 184. For a summary of the tales, Reichenbach refers also to H. M. Creed, *The Gospel According to St. Luke* (London: Macmillan & Co., 1957), pp. 208-210.

   Some protest the label "parable," arguing that since Jesus began, "There was a certain rich man," what follows must be history and not parable. This argument falls, however, in the light of other parables in Luke's Gospel which began with similar or identical statements (Luke 12:16; 13:6; 14:16; 15:11; 16:1; 18:1, 2; 18:9, 10; 19:11, 12; 20:9).

106. Froom, *Conditionalist Faith*, 1:252-256. The complete text is found in William Whiston, tr., *Josephus: Complete Works*, pp. 637-638. For all its deficiencies, William Sanford LaSor calls Whiston's edition "the *best complete English translation of Josephus*" (p. xi; italics his).

107. Whiston, *Josephus*, pp. 708-715.

108. White, *Life in Christ*, p. 183; Constable, *Future Punishment*, pp. 46-47. I was delighted when Froom pointed out what promised to be such a helpful bit of background information, then equally dismayed when White and Constable took it away. Better never to have the hope than to have it, then lose it forever!

Hades. In Greek mythology Hades was the god of the under-world, then the name of the nether world itself. Charon ferried the souls of the dead across the rivers Styx or Acheron into this abode, where the watchdog Cerberus guarded the gate so none might escape. The pagan myth contained all the elements for medieval eschatology: there was the pleasant Elysium, the gloomy and miserable Tartarus, and even the Plains of Asphodel, where ghosts could wander who were suited for neither of the above. Ruling beside the god was his queen Proserpine (or Persephne), whom he had raped from the world above.[109]

The word *hadēs* came into biblical usage when the Septuagint translators chose it to represent the Hebrew *sheol*, an Old Testament concept vastly different from the pagan Greek notions just outlined. Sheol, too, received all the dead, as we have noted in another chapter, but the Old Testament has no specific division there involving either punishment or reward. Intertestamental Judaism held at least two opinions on Hades. Those who expected a partial resurrection (of the righteous only) saw Hades as everlasting (for the wicked); those who looked for a general resurrection naturally thought of it as temporary.[110] Rabbinic opinion was so varied, and the terminology in such a state of flux, that both *hadēs* and *gehenna* are sometimes the abode of the dead, sometimes the place of final punishment, sometimes interchangeable, sometimes distinct. Modern scholars also disagree on the terms. Jeremias sees a sharp distinction between the two words in the New Testament,[111] while Hanhart argues that the New Testament usage of *hadēs* does not go beyond the Old Testament meaning of *sheol*.[112]

In all the confusion, we can best pin down something solid by looking at specific texts. Jesus' statement that Capernaum will go down to Hades (Matt. 11:23; Luke 10:15) needs no pagan background; it finds ample precedent in both Isaiah (Isa. 14:10-15) and Ezekiel (Ezek. 32:17-32). "Sheol is the great leveller."[113] The Lord's

---

109. William F. Arndt and F. Wilbur Gingrich, trs., *A Greek-English Lexicon of the New Testament and Other Early Christian Literature*, p. 16; E. Royston Pike, *Encyclopaedia of Religion and Religions*, p. 170.

110. Joachim Jeremias, "Hades," *Theological Dictionary of the New Testament*, 1:147-148.

111. Ibid.

112. Hanhart, *Intermediate State*, pp. 32, 35.

113. Strawson, *Jesus and the Future Life*, p. 138.

confidence that the "gates of Hades" will not prevail against His church (Matt. 16:18)[114] is illuminated by other Jewish literature using the same expression, usually as a synonym for death itself (Job 38:17; Isa. 38:18; cf. 3 Macc. 5:51; Wisd. of Sol. 16:13).[115]

Sheol's gates are no longer one-way, its fortress no longer is impregnable, for Jesus has come in the power of God's kingdom. He will destroy death's hold if He has to carry off the gates like Samson! In quoting Hosea 13:14, Paul substitutes "death" for "Hades/Sheol" (1 Cor. 15:55), indicating the close relationship between the two. Jesus went to "Hades" like all the dead, but unlike the rest He broke out in victory (Acts 2:27, 31). He now holds the keys to "death and Hades" (Rev. 1:18), which both will yield their dead when He comes again to judge, then will both be cast into the "lake of fire" (Rev. 20:13-15). It is in keeping with the historical nature of biblical religion that the New Testament speaks this way of Hades—not theoretically or systematically, but in terms of what has really happened in the case of Jesus Christ. We should not build a whole doctrine, therefore, on a single use of a word, even if it were elsewhere than in a parable on a different subject!

Context. The parable's interpretation must include its context.[116] And nothing in the context remotely suggests the final state of the wicked,[117] though Jesus does clearly intend to teach several other lessons. He has been preaching on covetousness and stewardship (Luke 16:1-13); the rich man's only implied sin is his totally selfish neglect of Lazarus.[118] When the Pharisees[119] sneer at Jesus' teaching,

---

114. That Jesus speaks of the church (*ekklēsia*) rather than His promise to build it is seen in His use of the feminine pronoun ("will not prevail against her"). The other fact is implied in this one.

115. The possible exception is Psalm of Solomon 16:1, 2, which associates the "gates of hades" with sinners. Even there, however, the phrase denotes death.

116. Hanhart notes several studies involving the context. Two which link the parable to all sections of the chapter are by J. D. M. Derrett, in *New Testament Studies* 7, no. 3, pp. 198ff; 7, no. 4, pp. 364ff (Hanhart, *Intermediate State*, pp. 191-192).

117. Hanhart disagrees, claiming that "most recent commentators" hold the opposite view than here stated (Harnhart, *Intermediate State*, pp. 190-191, 198).

118. Hanhart disagrees again. He argues that the rich man's distinction was not his character but his wealth. "While the sinner must seek this righteousness, the oppressed have it already" (ibid., pp. 195-197).

119. For some reason, many modern commentators pass over the context entirely and say the parable was directed to the Sadducees. I cannot set aside the biblical text on the basis of critical methodology.

He warns them against self-justification, reminding them that God knows their hearts and that what men highly value God often detests (vv. 14, 15). The rich man and Lazarus provide perfect illustrations of this truth, too, as the parable twice contrasts them alongside each other—first showing man's estimation and then showing God's (vv. 19, 25). Perhaps most important of all, the Pharisees are wasting every opportunity to hear and obey God, though they live in the most critical of times (vv. 16, 17). This is the same mistake the rich man made on earth, a mistake his brothers continue to make after he is gone.[120] It is also the *only* conclusion Jesus specifically draws in His punch line at the end of the story (v. 31). The saying about divorce in verse 18 seems totally out of place regardless of the parable's interpretation, but even that may reflect an Old Testament arrangement of material. In Deuteronomy 23-24, Moses also discusses selfishness (Deut. 23:19-25), then divorce (Deut. 24:1-5), then concern for the poor (Deut. 24:6-22).

Jeremias classes the parable with three others he calls "double-edged" (Matt. 22:1-14; 20:1-16; Luke 15:11-32). In each case Jesus begins with a story familiar to His hearers. But having gained their attention and probably their approval, He throws in an "epilogue" which contains His real message. The stress is therefore on that second point—in this case the plight of the five living brothers who are ignoring the Word of God. The parable should not be called The Rich Man and Lazarus, says Jeremias, but The Six Brothers.[121]

Hunter discerns the same emphasis, and he gives this summary of Jesus' intended message: "If a man cannot be humane with the Old Testament in his hand and Lazarus on his doorstep, nothing—neither a visitant from the other world nor a revelation of the horrors of Hell—will teach him otherwise."[122] The Pharisees prove Jesus right here, too. They already ignore Moses and the prophets; when the apostles confront them with a risen Jesus, they will ignore that message as well.

This, then, is Jesus' stated message. These are the points, raised already in His context, which He illustrates by the parable. The two-

---

120. Verses 27-29. Even if the parable intends to teach about post-mortem affairs (which the context nowhere indicates), this point alone would identify the scene as contemporary with on-going earth life.

121. Jeremias, *The Parables of Jesus*, p. 186.

122. Hunter, *Interpreting the Parables*, p. 84.

fold circumstances after death are a vehicle for the story, and they involve language familiar to Jesus' hearers—language drawn, not from the divine revelation of the Old Testament, but from intertestamental and first-century folklore. Even if that language teaches something of punishment after death, it occurs before the final judgment while others are still living on the earth, even before the gospel becomes a reality and men turn from Moses and the prophets to hear Jesus. There is no clear exegetical basis in Luke 16 for any conclusions concerning the end of the wicked.

John 3:16

This favorite verse of so many contrasts "eternal life" on the one hand with "perish" on the other. God's love in the gift of His Son guarantees true believers the first; the passage says absolutely nothing to illuminate the second. "Perish" is a common descriptive verb for the fate of the wicked throughout the Bible. Taken at face value, it agrees with all the biblical material we have seen.

John 3:36

Again "eternal life" stands as an alternative, this time to "God's wrath remain[ing]." The *realized* aspect of both is emphasized. "Already" eternal life is here for the believer; "already" God's wrath rests (and continues to rest) on one who rejects the Son of God, who is Life. The statement reminds us of Deuteronomy 29:20, where all the covenant curses not only come ("fall," NIV) on the highhanded rebel, but "rest" (NASB) on him as well. The text literally says the curses "lie down" on him, evoking an image of a beast of prey. So long as one rejects Jesus, God's wrath "remains," for nothing else can turn it away.

John 5:28, 29

We looked at this passage briefly at Matthew 25:46. Jesus says "a time is coming when all who are in their graves will hear His voice and come out—those who have done good will rise to live, and those who have done evil will rise to be condemned." The words are much like those of Daniel 12:2. "Condemnation" is a judicial verdict; it says nothing of the sentence or its execution. Again the emphasis is on the "already"—what will happen *then* is determined by men's response to Jesus *now* (vv. 21-27).

The Sadducees denied any resurrection, but it was the strong hope of the Pharisees and many in Israel.[123] Even so, F. F. Bruce warns against assuming too much uniformity in Jewish belief at the time.[124] Regardless of the popular expectation, we rest here on the word of the Son of God. Since Jesus is speaking, we must hear what He says and stop where He stops.

Summary and Conclusion

In dealing with the subject of final punishment, traditionalists have often ignored the Old Testament, oversimplified the intertestamental material, and read the New Testament in the light of that misunderstanding. They have been strong in defense of biblical authority but weak in using the Bible. Conditionalists have walked through the Old Testament, picking up nuggets, but they have shown little interest in mining deeper. Usually they look long enough to gather favorable evidence without going into more detail. A truly "biblical" view must include both Old and New Testament witnesses, noting the distinctive teaching of each as well as the areas of repetition. Ebeling offers this challenge to biblical theologians in general.

> In "biblical theology" the theologian who devotes himself specially to studying the connexion of the Old and New Testaments must give account of his understanding of the Bible as a whole, that is, above all of the theological problems that arise from the variety of the biblical witness considered in relation to its inner unity. . . . But, be it noted, this "biblical theology" would not be an independent substitute for dogmatics and would hardly correspond to the pietist ideal of a simple theology, but would be a task for historical theology of uncommon complexity.[125]

---

123. Acts 23:6; 24:20, 21; 26:6, 7; 28:20. Robert J. Kepple, "The Hope of Israel, the Resurrection of the Dead, and Jesus: A Study of Their Relationship in Acts with Particular Regard to the Understanding of Paul's Trial Defense," *Journal of the Evangelical Theological Society* 20, no. 3 (September 1977): 231-242.

124. Bruce, *Paul*, pp. 300-301.

125. Gerhard Ebeling, "The Meaning of 'Biblical Theology,'" *Journal of Theological Studies*, New Series 6, no. 2 (October 1955): 224-225.

Gerhard Hasel summarizes the relationship between Old Testament and New like this:

> The NT completes the OT's incompleteness and yet moves beyond to the final *eschaton*. From the OT to the NT and beyond there is one continuous movement in the direction of the *eschaton*, the coming of the Day of the Lord. . . . On this pilgrimage there are many stops, many initial fulfillments, but each one of them becomes a point of departure again until all promises will finally be fulfilled at the end of time.[126]

Hasel calls for a "multiplex approach" which recognizes "similarity and dissimilarity, old and new, continuity and discontinuity, etc., without in the least distorting the original historical witness and literal sense nor falling short in the larger kerygmatic intention and context to which the OT itself testifies and which the NT assumes."[127] We make no claims to have been exhaustive in this study, but we have aimed at faithfulness to these ideals so far as we have gone.

So far as Jesus' own teaching on final punishment, we have found it in every point agreeable to the Old Testament witness and limited in its major figures to teaching found there. Rather than absorbing the fanciful details of intertestamental apocalyptic, Jesus borrowed some of its language when useful to communication, but He expressed ideas found in the prophets and illustrated by Old Testament examples of divine judgment. So far as comparing Jesus' teaching on hell with that of His contemporaries, Strawson makes six observations, then draws five conclusions.[128] Our study confirms them all.

There is no suggestion that the righteous will gloat over the wicked. Jesus gives no idea that the delights of heaven are increased by contrast with the torments of hell. There is no levity in Jesus' teaching on this subject. Rather, He uses what He says about Gehenna to reinforce His appeal for personal self-discipline and obedience. Jesus never talks about the danger of hell to people other than His listeners—His teaching always warns "you," whether disciple, Pharisee or scribe. There is no dwelling on torture, no stirring up nationalist feelings against the Romans, no mention of foreigners being

---

126. Gerhard F. Hasel, *New Testament Theology: Basic Issues in the Current Debate*, p. 196.
127. Ibid., p. 198.
128. Strawson, *Jesus and the Future Life*, pp. 147-150.

consigned to hell. Contemporary Jewish literature illustrates exceptions at every point.

Strawson concludes that in His setting Jesus' teaching about hell "must be regarded as mild, without emphasis on details, and restricted in its application." It is always directed to the persons addressed. "It is no exaggeration to say that if he were to use the idea of Gehenna at all, he could scarcely have used it with less controversial or objectionable meaning." Jesus clearly spoke on the subject in all synoptic Gospels. It is "inescapable" that Jesus did teach "the reality of future condemnation."

G. C. Berkouwer, the great contemporary Reformed theologian, is very concerned that we take Christ's warnings with the utmost seriousness and always in the light of the gospel which Jesus offers.

> The proclamation of salvation is a witness of profound seriousness. The New Testament constantly presents an apparent ultimatum that is inextricably connected with this proclamation.
>
> It would be a mistake to underestimate this seriousness. The Word speaks of being cast away and rejected, of curse and judgment. The proclamation of the gospel contains a warning against unbelief, and the way of unbelief is portrayed as the way of outermost darkness and lostness and the severance of all relationships. In a variety of images and concepts, the Gospels warn against the possibility of a "definitive destruction." Such warnings are not meant to orient us to the eschaton, but continually to confront us with an admonition to open our eyes to the light and see the salvation, not to harden our hearts (cf. Heb. 3).[129]

Men often fail to appreciate the seriousness of Christ's warnings, he continues, because they do not view them under the light of the salvation Christ offers first.

> It is in the context of that gospel that the subject of the outer darkness arises. . . . All such threats are not arranged symmetrically beside the gospel, but proceed from it and can be understood only in its light. The outer darkness is contrasted to the brilliant light; the gospel's saving disturbance penetrates the religious terrain where everyone presumes to be safe and secure. . . . On the one side the gospel proclaims

---

129. G. C. Berkouwer, *The Return of Christ*, p. 413. In a 1937 Oberlin (Ohio) College S.T.M. thesis entitled "The Permanent Validity of the Idea of Hell," Joe Belcastro gives a personal testimony as one who began doubtful and resisting but ended affirming the validity of hell in preaching, though urging that it should be with hope.

the Kingdom, the wedding feast, the light, the opened door; on the opposite side darkness, desertion, the flames of the unquenchable fire (Mark 9:43, 48). The relationship of this to the gospel accentuates and illuminates the seriousness of these warnings.[130]

Failure to do this can result only in harm and in the complete distortion of the biblical perspective on final punishment. Berkouwer explains how this has often happened.

> In the course of time, the word "hell," as translation of the Greek *géenna*, was divorced from the relationships in which it is invariably found in Scripture, and came to be treated by many as a ruthless threat, an expression of extreme harshness, in which all feelings of compassion had perished. When this happened, the critical relationship in the New Testament between "Gehenna" and the invitation, love, and covenant of God was lost. . . . People speak of "heaven" and "hell" as if they were objective magnitudes like any other thing, situation, or place. Who knows how much damage is done, for example, in the life of a young child who is subjected to moralistic preaching of "hell" as the final outcome of "sin" without the light of the joy of the gospel? "Hell" can easily assume a magical, terrifying dimension that speaks only of the incalculable, all-consuming wrath of God, and says nothing of His love. . . . It is not difficult to understand why the word "hell" has come to be associated only with cruelty and hatred if it is proclaimed without regard for the preaching of the only way out.[131]

Not only does such preaching miss the mark of the biblical witness; it is finally ineffective in motivating the hearers. Berkouwer describes how that happens.

> As a result, every treatment of "hell" as an independent topic lacks genuine seriousness. It may assume the appearance of earnestness, but such seriousness is not of the biblical kind, which talks about the beauty "of the feet of those who preach good news" (Rom. 10:15). This seriousness is not something that can be analyzed on psychological or anthropological grounds, but only on the basis of the salvation proclaimed (cf. Heb. 2:3). If this is ignored, salvation and judgment become far removed from each other, and the preaching of the judgment becomes an isolated, intimidating prophecy of doom, which ultimately will fall on deaf ears. The call to faith and the warning can only go out in the light of Christ's abandonment and His encounter

---

130. Berkouwer, *The Return of Christ*, pp. 414-415.
131. Ibid., p. 416.

with the outer darkness. Thus the preaching of judgment does not relativize the depth and universality of the gospel, but confirms it according to the incontrovertible witness of the whole New Testament.[132]

This gospel which Jesus came preaching—and doing in His kingdom miracles—is the unique element He introduces into what has gone before. David knew a thousand years earlier that the wages of sin is death. What he was unable to see then was how God could save the sinner out of death and still be true to His law. Jesus stood in the room of both law and sin, and resolved the divine dilemma.

It is impossible to separate Jesus' own person from what He teaches, so we may also say that Jesus is the unique element of the New Testament. This is our own conclusion, but it is widely held by scholars representing a wide spectrum of biblical disciplines and denominational affiliation.[133] However wide the circles of Jesus' teaching, they grow concentrically smaller until finally they rest on Him. The Son of Man must be killed and rise again. This is nothing other than that He Himself finally demonstrates both God's wrath and His salvation.

The gospel, Paul would later write, already "reveals" both sides of God's judgment-verdict—His vindication (righteousness) on the one hand, His wrath on the other (Rom. 1:16-18). We can learn the same truth in the Gospels as we read Jesus' parables and watch what happens to Him. "This is one of the inevitable conclusions toward which the logic of the love, the wrath, the imperative, and the condition of God's justice has been driving us."[134] It is not a matter of a few passages here and there. It is "an essential element of the very nature of God as the tension between his love and wrath results in imperative and condition."[135]

---

132. Ibid., pp. 421-422.

133. Forestell, "Christian Revelation," pp. 180-181; Hanhart, *Intermediate State*, p. 33; Pilcher, *Hereafter*, p. 100; Max Wilcox, "On Investigating the Use of the Old Testament in the New Testament," *Text and Interpretation: Studies in the New Testament Presented to Matthew Black*, pp. 242-243. Wilcox concludes that "early Christian Bible-exegesis is part of the contemporary Jewish Bible-exegesis, distinguished from the latter first and foremost by acceptance of the resurrection and the resultant implied 'messianic' role of Jesus" (p. 243).

134. Baird, *Justice of God*, p. 234.

135. Ibid., pp. 234-235.

As John's Gospel says so often, light has invaded the darkness, and all men are put on the spot. The crisis is here now—in that sense judgment has already arrived. God is on the throne, and the Son of Man stands in the dock. Prosecutor and defender are at hand. Over Jesus' head hangs the heavy cloud of sin, but He Himself is spotless. Ultimate conflict is inescapable. When light and darkness finally come crashing together, the universe will quake with the impact. If we look quickly, we will see for a moment the end of the world. Jesus' greatest revelation comes not in His parables but in His history—at Golgotha and at the Garden Tomb. Nowhere in all the Bible will we find a clearer, more concrete picture of the victory of life—or of the reality and horror of hell.

12

Golgotha and Gehenna (Jesus' Death and the Punishment of the Lost)

The literature concerning final punishment contains a number of surprises, and one of the greatest is the scant attention given to the death of Jesus Christ. For the New Testament is quite clear that Jesus not only died but that He died because of sin and in the place of sinners. More than that, the death He died was in some true and real sense the sinner's death—the death required by sin—the death we should have died and must finally have died had Jesus not taken it upon Himself in our stead. We read statements like these: "Christ died for the ungodly"; He "died for us" (Rom. 5:6, 8). "God made Him who had no sin to be sin for us" (2 Cor. 5:21). "Christ redeemed us from the curse of the law by becoming a curse for us" (Gal. 3:13).

"Once you were alienated from God. . . . But now He has reconciled you by Christ's physical body through death" (Col. 1:21). "Christ Jesus . . . gave Himself as a ransom for all men" (1 Tim. 2:5, 6). He "gave Himself for us to redeem us from all wickedness" (Titus 2:14). Jesus "suffered death, so that by the grace of God He might taste death for everyone" (Heb. 2:9). "Christ was sacrificed once to take away the sins of many people" (Heb. 9:28). "He Himself bore our sins in His body on the tree" (1 Pet. 2:24). "Christ died for sins once for all, the righteous for the unrighteous, to bring you to God" (1 Pet. 3:18). "He is the atoning sacrifice for our sins, and not only for ours but also for the sins of the whole world" (1 John 2:2).

215

"Jesus Christ laid down His life for us" (1 John 3:16). Jesus is the One "who loves us and has freed us from our sins by His blood" (Rev. 1:5).

There is a riddle here for human logic and expectation. The Savior's death gives life, and men can only marvel at what they see (Isa. 52:15). When the Prince of Life comes, His own people put Him to death (Acts 3:15). Yet they do it in ignorance (Acts 3:17) and thereby fulfill their own prophetic Scriptures (Acts 3:18). The God of many happy surprises saves His people by His apparent tragedy and in such a way that He leaves human boasting without a single place to stand (1 Cor. 1:18-25, 31). Indeed, this "secret wisdom" of God's eternal purpose utilized the very rebellion of the rulers of this age to accomplish a work in which they would never willingly have cooperated had they understood what was transpiring (1 Cor. 2:6-8). Neither angels nor prophets could anticipate what God performed here. We know it now only by the Holy Spirit's revelation through the gospel proclamation (1 Cor. 2:10; Eph. 3:1-5; 1 Pet. 1:10-12). By that gospel light, however, the entire scene changes hues. The gory becomes the glory, and the central cross of those three on Golgotha becomes a window into God's final judgment-verdicts of acquittal and of condemnation (Rom. 1:17, 18; 3:23-26).

Eschatology Is an Aspect of Christology

Many New Testament scholars today are quick to point out how eschatology itself is essentially Christology. Jesus Himself is the key to Last Things. This is in contrast to the view which defines Last Things as a series of events having no integral relation to the life, death and resurrection of Jesus Christ. The Lutheran scholar, Berkemeyer, describes this latter view as one which believes "that God has lifted the veil so that his saints and prophets could see ahead of time when the end would come, what will happen in those last days, the series of cosmic events which will take place, what form judgment and eternal destiny will take." In this view "a careful deciphering and a logical, imaginative fitting together of the varied Bible pictures will produce the authentic answer," though its proponents "may not agree upon the way to fit the puzzle together."[1]

---

1. William C. Berkemeyer, "The Eschatological Dilemma," *Lutheran Quarterly* 7, no. 3 (August 1955): 234.

The New Testament pattern of interpretation points another direction. It explains prophecy, not by arranging isolated bits and looking to the future, but by reading it all in the light of the past, particularly that chain of events "when through the cross and resurrection Christ fought and won the decisive battle which makes the eventual victory sure."[2] The future still holds many unanswered questions, but whatever those answers may be, they all will "be controlled by and consistent with this Christ-event of the past."[3]

F. F. Bruce suggests that perhaps "we should say that the New Testament reveals the 'last thing' to be really the 'Last One,' the *Eschatos* (cf. 'the First and the Last' as a title of Jesus in Rev. 1:17, 2:8, 22:13)."[4] C. H. Dodd reminds us that "At the last frontier-post we shall encounter God in Christ."[5] The 1955 Evanston assembly of the World Council of Churches put it this way:

> We do not know what is coming to us. But we know who is coming. It is he who meets us every day and who meets us at the end—Jesus Christ our Lord.[6]

Although New Testament writers interpret the gospel by a wide variety of figures and in many different frameworks, they "unite in affirming that with Jesus the New Age has dawned, but that the consummation of that Age awaits future realization."[7] And they agree that the inauguration anticipates the consummation, or—to put it the other way—that the end will only complete and make evident what is already true in Jesus Christ. With Christ's death and resurrection, eschatology has already begun. On Pentecost Peter announced the "beginning of the End." The details of that day were "last-times" details, whether we think of the announcement that the resurrection

---

2. Ibid.

3. Ibid.

4. F. F. Bruce, "Eschatology," *London Quarterly and Holborn Review*, April 1958, p. 100.

5. C. H. Dodd, *The Coming of Christ*, p. 58, quoted by Bruce, "Eschatology," p. 100. Dodd's words quoted here are fully biblical, though in his earlier works he stressed the "already" aspect of eschatology at the expense of the "not yet." In later works he corrected this imbalance.

6. *The Evanston Report: The Second Assembly of the World Council of Churches* (New York, 1955), p. 3. We can applaud these words even while we lament the virtual abandonment of biblical evangelism in recent decades by the World Council of Churches.

7. Howard C. Kee, "The Development of Eschatology in the New Testament," *Journal of Bible and Religion* 20, no. 3 (July 1952): 193.

had begun, the outpouring of the Spirit, or the actual remission of sins. But "inauguration points on to the consummation," and "this consummation, this goal, must be as truly bound up with [Jesus'] person as the inauguration was."[8]

This perspective guided the Reformers past whirlpools of prophetic speculation and held them steady through the rapids of imaginative interpretation. Holwerda regards such a Christ-centered understanding of prophecy as a fundamental part of Calvin's heritage. For the Genevan Reformer, he says, almost all prophecies are fulfilled on a continuum rather than in a single moment of time. The reason for this is "the Christ who incorporates within Himself both Advent and Return: both the fulfillment already completed and the fulfillment that will one day be fully revealed."[9] For Calvin, a given prophecy "can contain only what as a matter of fact has happened and will happen in Christ. Thus every prophecy announcing final victory receives a twofold fulfillment in the Advent and Return of Christ."[10] We suggest that the same may be said of every prophecy announcing God's judgment and punishment of sin.

Ridderbos continues the same approach in contemporary Reformed theology. The "interdependence between the 'eschatological' and the 'christological' ground motif of Paul's preaching . . . is determinative for insight into the real nature of Paul's preaching of Christ," he writes.[11] "Paul's eschatology is not determined by any traditional eschatological schema, but by the actual acting of God in Christ."[12]

G. R. Beasley-Murray, a prominent Baptist scholar and specialist in the field of apocalyptic, makes the same point. "Christ is the agent of God in that judgment on history which leads to its goal in the kingdom of God; and alike the judgments and the kingdom are the issue of the judgment and redemption wrought in and through the life, death, and resurrection of the Son of God."[13] Jesus not only in-

---

8. Bruce, "Eschatology," p. 103.

9. David E. Holwerda, "Eschatology and History: A Look at Calvin's Eschatological Vision," *Exploring the Heritage of John Calvin*, p. 125.

10. Ibid., p. 126.

11. Herman N. Ridderbos, *Paul: An Outline of His Theology*, p. 49.

12. Ibid., p. 52.

13. G. R. Beasley-Murray, "New Testament Apocalyptic—A Christological Eschatology," *Review and Expositor* 72, no. 3 (Summer 1975): 330.

augurates the end-time events; He also concludes them. He is the Last as well as the First in eschatology as well as in God's saving purpose in general. This means that

> for Christian faith eschatology is an aspect of christology. Whether we are thinking in terms of the history of mankind, or the destiny of the individual, or the meaning of the universe, we are driven back ultimately to the significance of the incarnation and the redemption wrought by God in Christ.[14]

Pannenberg is even more explicit. He insists that the *end* of history has erupted *within* history, particularly in the resurrection of Jesus Christ. The gospel not only declares the past; it pronounces the future. Tupper summarizes Pannenberg's thought like this:

> As the pre-happening of the End of history, therefore, Jesus' history and destiny constitute the final revelation of God. While God remains active in the events of history after Christ, the prolepsis of revelation in the eschatological history of Jesus precludes any distinctively new disclosure of God which will surpass the Christ event.[15]

Jesus indeed says that "a time is coming" when all men will rise to be judged, then part company forever. But because He *is* "the Last," eschatology is subsumed under Christology, and Jesus can say in the same passage that that time "has now come" (John 5:24-29).

Calvary Reveals God's Final Judgment

The Old Testament prophets spoke of "the sufferings of Christ" and "the glories that would follow" (1 Pet. 1:11), a point Jesus Himself made more than once (Matt. 16:21; Luke 18:31-33; 24:25-27, 44-48; John 17:1-5). Yet what is this *suffering* and *glory* if not the eschatological judgment of God—seen both as divine vengeance on sin and the vindication and exaltation of righteousness? In an exhaustive study of *The Justice of God in the Teaching of Jesus*, Baird finds that Jesus personified all that He taught on this subject, so that

---

14. Ibid.

15. E. Frank Tupper, "The Revival of Apocalyptic in Biblical and Theological Studies," *Review and Expositor* 72, no. 3 (Summer 1975): 296.

Jesus Himself "was absolutely consumed by his involvement in the crisis of God." Baird explains:

> His life and message was a prism that brought the rays of God's being and nature to flaming focus in himself. He saw his own mission and person as the symbol, the agent, and the very incarnation of the judgment of God.[16]

A little later Baird suggests the "very interesting possibility" that "Jesus went to the cross as the last great acted parable of his life, wherein he portrayed in ways beyond comprehension the justice of God and his own involvement therein." In so doing, the cross became "Jesus' creative extension of Moses' great acted parable of judgment, Ebal and Gerizim."[17]

Alan Richardson comes from a different direction to arrive at the same point. Jesus "clearly regards himself as related to *orgē* [wrath] and *krisis* [judgment] as he is related to *basileia* [kingdom], *zoē* [life] or *doxa* [glory]." More than that, Richardson says, "it is Christ himself who is the actual bearer of the divine *orgē* [wrath]." The outcome is that the cross of Christ "is the visible, historical manifestation of the *orgē tou theou* [wrath of God]: it is the supreme revelation of the wrath of God against all ungodliness and unrighteousness of men (Rom. 1. 18; cf. II Cor. 5.21; Mark 15.34)."[18]

C. K. Barrett agrees. Romans 1-3 reveals the fundamental pattern of Paul's theology, Barrett writes. "Righteousness" and "wrath" are both eschatological words—words related to the effects of the last judgment. Yet the gospel proclaims that "both belong to the present" because of what has happened to Jesus of Nazareth.[19] This means "the last event has already begun, precipitated by the life, death and resurrection of Jesus, who clearly is the central figure in the whole scheme."[20] Ridderbos also acknowledges that in Christ's death "God has sat in judgment, has judged sin, and in this way he has caused his eschatological judgment to be revealed in the present time."[21] Hans

16. Joseph Arthur Baird, *The Justice of God in the Teaching of Jesus*, p. 237.

17. Ibid., p. 251.

18. Alan Richardson, *An Introduction to the Theology of the New Testament*, p. 77.

19. C. K. Barrett, "New Testament Eschatology: Part I," *Scottish Journal of Theology* 6, no. 2 (June 1953): 147.

20. Ibid., p. 150.

21. Ridderbos, *Paul*, p. 168.

Conzelmann writes that divine anger against sin has always been poured out but that the gospel shows us what it was. He continues:

> The new element since Christ is that now, through the proclamation of the gospel, man can recognize what God's judgment on sin always was. . . . Thus, wrath is made visible to me by the preaching of the gospel.[22]

These men represent a variety of theological perspectives, and they have their own differences on the fine points involved here. Yet they all agree (and we may join them while reserving the right to differ also in certain details) that the Passion of Jesus Christ revealed in a unique way God's judgment against sin, and that in a genuine way it revealed also what awaits at the end of the world for those who reject Christ now. The author of the Epistle to the Hebrews drew Jesus' experience and man's final judgment along parallel lines. "As" it is ordained to man to be judged, he wrote, "so" it happened to Christ. What is more, he continues, Christ stood in the place of the sinner in judgment, since He died for sin (Heb. 9:27, 28).

Jesus' Death Was "for Sin"

The cross of Christ was no mere example of divine judgment; it was God's judgment *par excellence*—the judgment withheld already for centuries from many to whom it was due (Rom. 3:25; Heb. 9:15, 26-28; cf. NIV footnote to Isa. 53:8). Here Jesus is utterly forsaken by God, and it is the consistent view of the Old Testament that God turns away from the one with whom He is angry. Even if Scripture never expressly states that Jesus stood under the divine wrath, all it says about His death forces us to that conclusion.[23]

Jesus Himself approached this death with "prayers and petitions," with "loud cries and tears" (Heb. 5:7). Though He moved resolutely toward it, it was as One "deeply distressed and troubled," His soul "overwhelmed with sorrow to the point of death" (Mark 14:33, 34).

---

22. Hans Conzelmann, *An Outline of the Theology of the New Testament*, p. 241. Conzelmann says precious little in this *Outline* about God's wrath, judgment or hell. His remark here has obvious validity but should not detract from the uniqueness of the cross as God's great judgment-event.

23. So states G. Stahlin, *"Orgē"* [Wrath], *Theological Dictionary of the New Testament*, 5:446.

He prayed "in anguish," and His sweat "was like drops of blood falling to the ground" (Luke 22:44). In the words of John Wenham,

> There was something so solemn about the way that he spoke of his death that the disciples were afraid to ask him what he meant. There was something so frightening about his demeanour as he strode ahead of them that they were 'filled with awe'.[24]

Oscar Cullmann is well known for his appraisal of the horror with which Jesus viewed His death, a dread Cullmann attributes to Jesus' understanding of death in general. But more is at stake here than anthropology, as Leon Morris reminds us.

> It was not death as such that He feared. It was the particular death that He was to die, that death which is 'the wages of sin' as Paul puts it (Rom. 6:23), the death in which He was at one with sinners, sharing their lot, bearing their sins, dying their death.[25]

Not only did Jesus view His own death as "a ransom" for sinners; New Testament writers likewise make that connection. For Paul in particular, notes Ridderbos, "Christ's death is determined primarily by its connection with the power and guilt of sin."[26] For Paul the young rabbi, "the fact that God allowed Jesus to hang on a tree was the decisive disproof of his Messiahship," for Jesus "was plainly cursed by God."[27] There was no mistaking this scandal of a crucified Messiah. For Paul it was "worse than a contradiction in terms; the very idea was an outrageous blasphemy."[28]

Yet this death, this death *for sin*, was why Jesus had come into this world. "What shall I say?" He had agonized on the way to Jerusalem. "Father, save Me from this hour?" His answer was quick and firm. "No, it was for this very reason I came to this hour. Father, glorify Your name!" (John 12:27, 28) For this hour, indeed, the Lamb was slain before the foundation of the world (Rev. 13:8). Like any sacrificial animal, Jesus had lain aborning on the hay. He is "Christ, our Passover Lamb" (1 Cor. 5:7), "the Lamb of God, who takes away the sin of the world" (John 1:29).

---

24. John W. Wenham, *The Goodness of God*, p. 169.
25. Leon Morris, *The Cross in the New Testament*, p. 47.
26. Ridderbos, *Paul*, p. 55.
27. Wenham, *The Goodness of God*, p. 168.
28. F. F. Bruce, *Paul: Apostle of the Heart Set Free*, p. 71.

Jesus had come to John for baptism, not descending in a cloud or even riding in a chariot, but slowly and in His turn, standing there in the line of *sinners*. If we picture the others figuratively washing their sins away in the water, we may rightly picture the sinless Jesus there taking them all on Himself.[29] He is both scapegoat and sacrifice "for atonement" and "for Azazel." When Jesus finally makes atonement by His own blood, He also removes sin as far as east is from west (Ps. 103:12). The Greek word for "forgive" used most often by the Evangelists in reporting what Jesus said has as its root two words which mean "to take away" (*aphiēmi*).

This river scene with John is one parenthesis in Jesus' saving work, for there He publicly takes on the assignment for which He left heavenly riches on behalf of poor sinners. But that baptism in water required another in blood, and Jesus could not rest in His soul until it too was accomplished (Luke 12:50). Only then could He say, "It is finished" (John 19:30), and commit His faithful life to the faithful Creator. When Jesus died, the toilsome labor of His soul was ended, and both He and the Father were satisfied (Isa. 53:11). At Jordan, Jesus had been "numbered with the transgressors"; at Golgotha He "bore the sin of many" (Isa. 53:12). Jesus Christ is He "who came by water and blood." This is the testimony God has given about His Son (1 John 5:6, 9).

The gospel story is painted against the background of the Old Testament's broad strokes. The Evangelists draw their picture of Jesus' life, death and resurrection on top of a canvas already covered by another bold word. That word is "covenant." When we look closely at the canvas, we see that this word too is adorned, like a colorful letter drawn by some medieval calligrapher, with scenes of Canaan and of Eden. Jesus was "born of a woman, born under law" (Gal. 4:4). The first statement speaks of His humanity. He is the Second Adam, the second representative Man. The latter term tells us that Jesus is a Son of the Torah—but even more. He is True Israel, the true Vine of God's planting (John 15:1). The two figures are but concentric circles picturing God's covenant, and Jesus now encompasses them both. Integral to each is the recurring pattern of covenantal stipulations, covenantal blessings and covenantal curses. As Second Adam and

---

29. G. Stahlin speaks of Jesus' baptism in Jordan as "the figure of wrathful judgment" in his article, "*Orgē*," p. 466. Meredith G. Kline discusses this concept of covenantal malediction in the light of Old Testament covenants in his *By Oath Consigned*, pp. 39-49.

True Israel, Jesus does what neither Adam nor Israel had ever been able to do. He keeps the stipulations, earns the blessings, then takes on Himself all the curses of the broken covenant.

Robert D. Brinsmead elaborates:

> In Leviticus and Deuteronomy 28-30 these curses come in handfuls. They are awful threats which may first appear out of all proportion to the sins committed. But sin, being a breach of the covenant, is an affront to the covenant God and an insult to His infinite majesty. . . . The curses included hunger and thirst (Deut. 28:48; Isa. 65:13), desolation (Isa. 5:6; Zeph. 1:15), poverty (Deut. 28:31), the scorn of passers-by (Jer. 19:8), darkness (Isa. 13:10; Amos 5:18-20), earthquake (Isa. 13:13; Amos 1:1), being "cut off" from among the people (Ex. 12:15, 19; 31:14; Lev. 7:25; Jer. 44:7-11), death by hanging on a tree (Deut. 21:23), a brass heaven (Deut. 28:23) and no help when one cries for help (Deut. 28:31; Isa. 10:3).[30]

> Christ . . . was hungry (Matt. 4:2; 21:18). He was so poor He had no place to lay His head (Matt. 8:20). On the cross He cried, "I am thirsty!" (John 19:28). He was mocked and derided (Mark 15:29-31) and deserted by His friends (Matt. 26:56, 69-75). He was hanged on a tree as a cursed man (Gal. 3:13) and "cut off" from His people (Isa. 53:8). As He hung on the cross, the heavens were as brass. He was as one who cries for help and receives none (Mark 15:34). He died as the great covenant breaker and endured the unabated fury of all the covenantal curses. The cosmic scope of the curses is portrayed in Matthew. As Christ bore the sins of the broken covenant, darkness descended over the land (Matt. 27:45), the earth shook, and the rocks split (Matt. 27:51). But by dying Jesus carried away the curses of the covenant.[31]

A man with only an Old Testament in his hand could view the scene of Good Friday and know that Jesus is "stricken by God, smitten by Him, and afflicted" (Isa. 53:4). The Law makes that plain enough. But the gospel tells us why the Sinless One is so treated. Certain patristic and medieval theologians spun great arguments from human philosophies of justice to explain and justify everlasting punishment. The New Testament does not do that. It begins with God's law, with God's covenants, with the divine wrath which accompanies such covenants. Then it takes us by the hand and leads us through the winding streets to a place clearly outside the Holy City.[32]

---

30. Robert D. Brinsmead, *Covenant*, p. 81.

31. Ibid., p. 83.

32. T. G. Dunning writes: "Hell, like Gehenna of old, is out of bounds to the Holy City. Hell's

There it shows us the ultimate penalty for sin. This time it does not take us to the rocky valley of Hinnom—the worst symbol intertestamental apocalyptists could imagine. Instead, it takes us to a stone hill in the shape of a skull. There it points us to a wooden stake to which is nailed the lifeless body of a sinless Man. Here, it says, is the greatest revelation of God's wrath against all the ungodliness and wickedness of men.

This is no impersonal transaction, as if divine wrath were a matter of mere mechanics. Nor does it partake of any sinful vindictiveness as human wrath is so prone to do. We cannot begin to comprehend, far less express, what it meant that "God the mighty Maker died for man, the creature's sin." Righteousness and peace kissed that day (Ps. 85:10). God became both "just and the justifier" (Rom. 3:26). Something happened to which, of every historical event that has ever transpired, man can alone look and receive in the empty hands of God-given faith the amazing and yet righteous grace he so desperately needs.

Markus Barth captures something of the sense of the cosmic judgment which occurred that Friday on Calvary.

> With this the proceedings before God's throne reach their most abysmal point. No wonder Jesus cries out to the Father who sent him, "My God, my God, why hast Thou forsaken me?" No wonder darkness shrouds the whole world. This is the horrible judgment of the living God. The words "anger," "curse," "sin," "cross," "crucified with him" cannot be sweetened. They cannot be relativized. They present an offense . . . that cannot be removed by any wisdom. . . . In spite of Jesus' truthfulness and love, all of God's anger reigns here. Here is hellish thirst and torment, the Godforsakenness of God's own child. . . .
>
> In the death of his Son, God does not merely make felt what it means to bear sins and die under the curse; he feels it himself. Sin and death are no longer alien to God. Now everything that has to do with

---

deepest meaning is the loss of the divine presence, the complete absence of fellowship with God and a condition of final unalterable alienation from Him" (T. G. Dunning, "What Has Become of Heaven and Hell?" *Baptist Quarterly* 20, no. 8 [October 1964]: 357). This is precisely what we see at Calvary. Jesus was cast outside Jerusalem to die, God refused to come to His aid, and Jesus was never again to be known as He once had been known in the flesh (cf. 2 Cor. 5:16, 19, 21). Jesus became a reject from the covenant society of Yahweh, a man under God's ban and curse, totally "cut off" from fellowship (life) with God and God's people.

Yet in the light of Jesus' subsequent resurrection, this exclusion from Jerusalem became a symbol of encouragement for the confused and forlorn recipients of the Epistle to the Hebrews (Heb. 13:12-14). When a city thrusts *God* out (as the resurrection showed Jerusalem had done in excluding Jesus) and it is about to crumble, absence from it is no longer so bad!

the living, obeying, hoping, achieving, doing, suffering, and dying of men has been incorporated into the relation between Father and Son. As it is manifested, it cries out to heaven. . . .

Here God openly stands against God, the Father against the Son, the benevolent, promising God addressed in prayers, against what God makes and allows in the world of facts and events. No theoretical or doctrinal theodicy is able to break in and save the day. Even the true and loving Son can only ask, "Why have you . . . ?" . . .

The earth trembles. The sun fades away. This is the horror of the judgment: God is silent. An eclipse of the living God, a victory of death over life, the end of all religion, all law and justice, all morality—it is this that comes in at 3:00 p.m. on Good Friday. A Hell, deeper and hotter than anything one might imagine . . . has opened its maw, devoured God's Son, and become all-victorious.

> The one true God has let himself,
> for me, lost man and hopeless,
> Be given unto death.

The judgment is adjourned at this time, to reconvene day after tomorrow at the crack of dawn.[33]

Jesus Died the Sinner's Own Death

Jesus not only died "for sin"; He died in the very place of sinners. He does not remain a third party, even one acting on behalf of another. He becomes man in order to be the first party, to "be made sin" (2 Cor. 5:21, KJV), to "become a curse" (Gal. 3:13). It is in His "physical body" that He reconciled us through death (Col. 1:22). He bore our sins "in His body" on the cross (1 Pet. 2:24). God gave Jesus a *body* in which to perform perfect human obedience, to "do the will of God," and having done that will, Jesus sacrificed that *body* once for all (Heb. 10:5-10). He "took up our infirmities and carried our sorrows" (Isa. 53:4). He "was pierced for our transgressions, He was crushed for our iniquities; the punishment that brought us peace was upon Him" (Isa. 53:5). "The Lord has laid on Him the iniquity of us all" (Isa. 53:6). Jesus bore His people's iniquities and their sin—He took it all on Himself, the single horrible mass viewed in general and all its specific manifestations (Isa. 53:11, 12).

---

33. Markus Barth, *Justification: Pauline Texts Interpreted in the Light of the Old and New Testaments*, pp. 47-48.

Orthodox theologians have rightly insisted on this personal identification of Jesus with the actual punishment due the sinner. Calvin
wrote:

> This is our acquittal: the guilt that held us liable for punishment has
> been transferred to the head of the Son of God [Isa. 53:12]. We must,
> above all, remember this substitution, lest we tremble and remain anx-
> ious throughout life--as if God's righteous vengeance, which the Son
> of God has taken upon himself, still hung over us.[34]

Calvin saw Jesus as the Lamb of God, "taking upon himself the
penalty that we owe" so that "he has wiped out our guilt before
God's judgment."[35] This is what Peter meant in saying that Jesus
"bare our sins in His own body." The Reformer explained that Jesus
"bore the punishment and vengeance due for our sins" so that we "see
plainly that Christ bore the penalty of sins to deliver his own people
from them."[36]

This is what it means that Christ's death was *vicarious*, insists
Berkhof: "that Christ as our substitute suffered the punishment due
to us, and in our place met all the requirements of the law."[37] Jesus
"voluntarily took our place and suffered the penalty which was due
to us and so made atonement for our sin," writes Boettner.[38]
Quistorp quotes Calvin that Jesus surrendered His soul as well as His
body to complete abandonment, suffering "the most terrible
torments of a lost and reprobate man."[39] Jesus was "suffering in his
soul the terrible torments of a condemned and forsaken man."[40]

To use the familiar language, Jesus suffered *hell* for His
people—the very hell they would have suffered had He not taken
their place. John Calvin did not hesitate to use such strong language
on the matter, as this passage from his *Institutes* makes clear.

---

34. John Calvin *Institutes* 2. 16. 5.

35. Ibid. 3. 4. 26.

36. Ibid. 3. 4. 30.

37. Louis Berkhof, *Vicarious Atonement through Christ*, p. 111.

James D. G. Dunn charges that "substitution" is too narrow and individualistic a word here,
arguing that "Jesus represents *man*, not just a man, on the cross." He suggests that "representation" includes the positive sense of "substitution" and also avoids its overexclusiveness (James
D. G. Dunn, "Paul's Understanding of the Death of Jesus," *Reconciliation and Hope: New Testament Essays on Atonement and Eschatology*, pp. 140-141.

38. Loraine Boettner, *The Person of Christ*, p. 92.

39. Heinrich Quistorp, *Calvin's Doctrine of the Last Things*, p. 77.

40. Calvin *Institutes* 2. 16. 10.

If Christ had died only a bodily death, it would have been ineffectual. No—it was expedient at the same time for him to undergo the severity of God's vengeance, to appease his wrath and satisfy his just judgment. For this reason, he must also grapple hand to hand with the armies of hell and the dread of everlasting death. . . . No wonder, then, if he is said to have descended into hell,[41] for he suffered the death that God in his wrath had inflicted upon the wicked![42]

Jesus' Death Involved Total Destruction

Here is the point to which we must finally come. If Jesus' death "reveals" God's last judgment, if His death was "for sin" and "instead of sinner," if it entailed the penalty and curse and condemnation of sin pronounced throughout the Bible, what does the cross teach us about final punishment? Here conditionalists have frequently pounded their pulpits and traditionalists have often crouched down in their pews. James D. G. Dunn, known for particular advocacy of neither view, sees total destruction as the essence of the Levitical sacrifices which foreshadowed Christ's offering.

Paul saw the death of the sacrificial animal as the death of the sinner *qua* sinner, that is, the destruction of his sin. The manner in which the sin offering dealt with sin was by its death. The sacrificial animal,

---

41. The Apostles' Creed says of Christ that "He descended into Hades," a doctrine commonly known as the *descensus ad infernos*. The first appearance of this clause is evidently in the so-called Fourth Formula of Sirmium (A.D. 359), where it was proposed by the Syriac theologian, Markus of Arethusa. Originally it was intended to mean only that Jesus truly died. Rufinus, presbyter of Aquileia, said the phrase explained an old doctrine rather than adding a new one, and for that reason the Aquileian creed omitted the clause "was crucified, dead, and buried," replacing it with the new expression *"descendit in inferna."* Most medieval and modern forms of the Apostles' Creed include the clause but also retain the original statement that Jesus "was crucified, dead, and buried."

In the Latin church of the West a related doctrine evolved of a triumphal procession of Christ through the underworld, redeeming Old Testament saints and taking them with Him in His ascension to heaven. This doctrine, known as "the harrowing of hell," became a very popular theme in medieval literature and plays. Some later developments have Christ redeeming the souls of all men from hell at His second coming.

On the *descensus* clause of the creed see Jürgen Moltmann, "Descent into Hell," *Duke Divinity School Review* 33, no. 2 (Spring 1968): 117; Martin H. Scharlemann, "He Descended into Hell," *Concordia Theological Monthly* 27, no. 2 (February 1956): 81-83; William G. T. Shedd, *The Doctrine of Endless Punishment*, p. 70. On "the harrowing of hell" see J. A. MacCulloch, *The Harrowing of Hell*, and—what was probably its original seed—the third-century *The Gospel of Nicodemus* (also known as The Acts of Pontius Pilate), especially chapters 15-19. The Gospel of Nicodemus is contained, among other places, in *The Apocryphal Books of the New Testament*.

42. Calvin *Institutes* 2. 16. 10.

> identified with the offerer in his sin, had to be destroyed in order to destroy the sin which it embodied. The sprinkling, smearing and pouring away of the sacrificial blood in the sight of God indicated that the life was wholly destroyed, and with it the sin of the sinner.[43]

This is the just doom also of sinful man, Dunn continues—utter destruction.

> Had there been a way for fallen man to overcome his fallenness . . . Christ would not have died. . . . But Christ, Man, died because there is no other way for man—any man. His death is an acknowledgement that there is no way out for fallen men except through death—no answer to sinful flesh except its destruction in death. "Man could not be helped other than through his annihilation".[44]

This is the meaning of Jesus' death, according to Dunn, as touching the consequences of sin. He takes issue with those who say Jesus' death simply "turns away" God's wrath. Jesus did not turn it away, Dunn argues. Rather, He accepted it fully on Himself, draining it to the dregs until no drop or trickle is left for any whom He saves.

> The destructive consequences of sin do not suddenly evaporate. On the contrary, they are focused in fuller intensity on the sin—that is, on fallen humanity in Jesus. In Jesus on the cross was focused not only man's sin, but the wrath which follows upon that sin. The destructive consequences of sin are such that if they were allowed to work themselves out fully in man himself they would destroy him as a spiritual being. This process of destruction is speeded up in the case of Jesus, the representative man, the *hilastērion*, and destroys him. The wrath of God destroys the sin by letting the full destructive consequences of sin work themselves out and exhaust themselves in Jesus. . . . If we have understood Paul's theology of sacrifice aright the primary thought is the *destruction* of the malignant, poisonous organism of sin. Any thought of *punishment* is secondary.[45]

---

43. Dunn, "Death of Jesus," p. 136. Dunn is no universalist, as two quotations suffice to illustrate.

On page 137 he writes: "But only those who, like the offerer of old, identify themselves with the sacrifice, may know the other half of the chiasmus, the life of Christ beyond the death of sin, the righteousness of God in Christ."

On pages 130-131 he writes of Christ: "In his risen life he represents only those who identify themselves with him, with his death (in baptism), only those who acknowledge the Risen One as Lord (2 Cor. 5:15). . . . In short, as Last Adam Jesus represents only those who experience life-giving Spirit (1 Cor. 15:45)."

44. Ibid., p. 130.

45. Ibid., p. 139.

Oscar Cullman makes the same point in his well-known discussion of immortality and resurrection. Jesus, he writes,

> can conquer death only by actually dying, by betaking Himself to the sphere of death, the destroyer of life, to the sphere of 'nothingness', of abandonment by God. . . . Whoever wants to conquer death must die; he must really cease to live—not simply live on as an immortal soul, but die in body and soul, lose life itself, the most precious good which God has given us. . . . Furthermore, if life is to issue out of so genuine a death as this, a new divine act of creation is necessary. And this act of creation calls back to life not just a part of the man, but the whole man—all that God had created and death had annihilated.[46]

The Bible exhausts the vocabulary of dying in speaking of what happened to Jesus. He *"died* for our sins" (1 Cor. 15:3). He *laid down His "life [psychē]"* (John 10:15). He was *destroyed* (Matt. 27:20, KJV) or *killed* (Acts 3:15). Jesus compared His own death to the *dissolution* of a kernel of wheat in the same passage that means *losing one's life (psychē)* rather than loving it in order to find life eternal (John 12:23-26). Jesus *"poured out His life [psychē] unto death"* and in so doing was "numbered with the transgressors" (Isa. 53:12).

In the beginning God gave man being instead of non-being, and He had warned then that sin would bring death in the place of life (Gen. 2:17). From the very first the wages of sin was *death*, and Jesus underwent the very same sentence pronounced in the primal Garden. Some may object that the original curse entailed death forever, dissolution with no hope of a resurrection, and that this did not befall Jesus. Conditionalist author, Edward White, admitted that this would be a problem—if Jesus had been only human—but he saw in Jesus' divinity the impossibility of such *permanent* destruction. White reasoned:

> If Jesus had been the Son of David only, He could not legally have risen from the dead. . . . He must have suffered everlasting destruction. His human spirit must have passed away for ever. The humanity which had been 'made under the law' must abide under that law; the representative of a guilty race could have trodden the path of life no more.

---

46. Oscar Cullmann, *Immortality of the Soul or Resurrection of the Dead? The Witness of the New Testament*, pp. 25-26.

But the Saviour was Divine. As man, identified with human nature, He died, and His death became a sin-offering; as God He could not die. As man He was 'made under the law;' as God He was above the law laid on creatures. And therefore, when the curse had taken effect upon the manhood, it was still open to the Divine Inhabitant, absorbing the Spirit into His own essence, to restore the 'destroyed Temple' from its ruins; and, taking possession of it, in virtue of His Divinity (not, legally, as a man), 'to raise it up on the third day.' He arose, therefore, as the Divine Conqueror of death . . . and was thus 'declared to be the Son of God with power, according to the Spirit of holiness, by *His resurrection* from the dead' (Rom. i. 4). He rose, not 'in the likeness of sinful flesh;' not 'under the law,' but in the character of the 'Lord from Heaven,' 'our Lord and our God' . . . having delivered us from wrath by the death of His humanity, to endow us with immortality through the life of His divinity.[47]

We naturally recoil from such a thought, that the Son of God could truly have perished—even for a moment. Yet is this not the same difficulty we face in accepting Jesus' true *kenosis* and humiliation in becoming a *man*? (Phil. 2:5-10). In the first century the Docetics tried to avoid the implications of saying that the incarnate God truly died, but the apostolic witnesses refused to yield an inch (1 John 5:6-10). Even John Calvin objected in his *Psychopannychia* that it was unthinkable that Jesus' "soul" truly died or even slept (see Appendix B). But Calvin answered his own objection in the *Institutes* as he expounded on how Christ performed the office of Redeemer in procuring our salvation.

There is no reason why Christ's weakness should alarm us. For he was not compelled by violence or necessity, but was induced purely by his love for us and by his mercy to submit to it. But all that he voluntarily suffered for us does not in the least detract from his power.[48]

We only bow the lower before such amazing grace, saying with John, "This is how we know what love is: Jesus Christ laid down His life for us" (1 John 3:16), or with Paul, that "God demonstrates His own love for us in this: While we were still sinners, Christ died for us" (Rom. 5:8).

---

47. Edward White, *Life in Christ* . . . , pp. 243-244.
48. Calvin *Institutes* 2. 16. 12.

Some protest that Christ's death was not a true pattern of the judgment awaiting sinners in hell, since Jesus was an infinite person and could absorb infinite punishment in a single moment. Finite sinners, this argument goes, will require conscious punishment in infinite duration for justice to have its way. This whole logic of "finite" and "infinite" punishment and victims is totally without biblical basis, springing instead from medieval speculation grounded in feudalistic canons of justice. The entire approach is protested today on philosophical grounds, which is proper since that was also its origin.[49] More than that, this philosophy itself leaves room for the question whether the "infinite" punishment of hell might not be defined in some terms other than conscious torment for endless time. If *death* is seen to be destruction without limitation (which the traditional view has not allowed), then is not penal death *itself* an *infinite* punishment, especially if it is an eternal death which is forever irreversible? Karl Barth speaks, for example, of Christ "suffering the eternal wrath of God," a phrase Stahlin quotes with apparent approval in his *Theological Dictionary of the New Testament* article on "wrath."[50]

Edward White considered the traditional line of thought concerning "infinite" and "finite" suffering and finally charged that it was unbiblical. Philosophy's arm is not strong enough, he insisted, to change what he regarded the natural and simplest meaning of Christ's "death."

It does not, however, appear to be anywhere stated that the indwelling of the Divinity changed the character of the curse of the law, in the case of our Lord, from everlasting misery, into literal death. It will, therefore, be sufficient to receive the simpler representation, that the 'Man Christ Jesus' endured that curse. For aught that the Scripture reveals, Jesus, as a man, might as justly have been required to endure everlasting suffering—supposing this to have been the legal curse—as that shameful, painful death which He actually underwent. If it be asserted that it was the presence of the Godhead within which dispensed with the infliction of endless pains, through the substitution of an Infinite Majesty for the infinitely extended misery of a finite being,

49. One modern review of this medieval argument that is critical of it on philosophical grounds is that of Marilyn McCord Adams, "Hell and the God of Justice," *Religious Studies* 11, no. 4 (December 1975): 433-447. Ms. Adams also does away with infinite bliss on philosophical grounds. Her article therefore reaffirms the necessity of beginning with biblical exegesis and basing all reasoning on an authoritative Word of God, a sword which cuts two directions!

50. Stahlin, "*Orgē*," p. 445.

we reply, that this is an 'afterthought of theology' which finds no place in the authoritative record.[51]

The "abnormal act" of God saving sinners belongs to the "mystery of godliness" (1 Tim. 3:16). As such, it is not explained on the basis of anything we can see in nature, find in law, discover by human reason or observe in all creation. We will try in vain to analyze and explain this "hidden wisdom" in terms of human philosophy or judicial theory—whether medieval or modern! Only the innermost mind of the Godhead fathoms all these *"why's"* and *"wherefore's."* White insisted that we must leave the matter there.

> The reason is not found in a calculation of consequences in the external world, nor in any supposed counterweight of pain or terror in a finite being, that must be placed vicariously in the lightened scale of forgiveness; but in the heights and depths of the Godhead alone; in the holiness which abhors evil; in the rectitude which intensely loves the law; in the wisdom which must demonstrate that the Salvation of Sinners is no easy process; and in the boundless grace which resolves to endure all that sin and sinners can inflict, as a demonstration of the impossibility there is, even for Omnipotence, to save by an arbitrary act, without a 'ransom' and a sacrifice.[52]

Strong writes, "Hell, as well as the Cross, indicates God's estimate of sin."[53] In the light of the words of Isaiah and John, Peter and Paul, and Jesus Himself, we suggest that his sentence should be changed. It would better read: "Hell, as *revealed* in the Cross, indicates God's estimate of sin." But the "mystery of godliness" did not end with the cross. Jesus was "vindicated by the Spirit" (1 Tim. 3:16) and "declared with power to be the Son of God by His resurrection from the dead" (Rom. 1:4). Jesus' resurrection was proof of *His* "justification" (from the Jewish charge of blasphemy) as well as of *ours* (Rom. 4:25).

Every scriptural implication is that if Jesus had not been raised, *He*—like those fallen asleep in Him—would simply have perished (1 Cor. 15:18). His resurrection reverses every such estimation of affairs, assuring us instead of the death of Death (2 Tim. 1:10; Heb.

---

51. White, *Life in Christ*, p. 241.

52. Ibid., p. 260.

53. Augustus Hopkins Strong, *Systematic Theology*, 3:1050.

2:14; Rev. 20:14). As Boettner puts it, Christ's resurrection "showed that His work had fully satisfied the demands of the law (the law which God established at the original creation, that the soul that committed sin should die), and that death therefore had no further hold on Him nor on any of those for whom He died."[54]

---

54. Boettner, *The Person of Christ*, p. 94.

13

The Wages of Sin in the Writings Of Paul

It is widely held that Jesus taught much about final punishment but that Paul said relatively little.[1] If one places all Jesus said on the subject alongside the writings of Paul, he might compare the quantities and agree with this view. But if he views the teachings of either in the larger literary context, he might wish to question the statement on both counts. Compared to the apocalyptic literature of His day and the previous two centuries, Jesus gave very *few* details on the end of the wicked. What He did say may be traced to the Old Testament Scriptures in almost every detail (the name "Gehenna" as the place of final punishment is one of very few exceptions). There is little need to look to the intertestamental literature at all to make sense of Jesus' figures and forms of speech. On the other hand, if one examines Paul's language in the light of its Old Testament background—especially dressed in its Septuagint Greek—the few key terms Paul does use flush with vivid meaning. Phrases that first appear bland and colorless begin to darken with the smoky storm of Sinai and to echo the thunderous tones of the prophets.

---

1. Buis refers to only five Pauline passages (Rom. 2:3-9, 12; 1 Cor. 3:17; 2 Cor. 5:10; 1 Thess. 5:3; 2 Thess. 1:6-9). He introduces Paul's teaching with the comment that "much less is stated about punishment in the future state than was revealed by Jesus. However," there is even in Paul's writings "a strong conviction regarding the serious alternatives which are involved" (Harry Buis, *The Doctrine of Eternal Punishment*, p. 43).

We will consider Paul's Epistles in general groups in the order they are commonly held to have been written. First we note the Thessalonian correspondence, then the major Epistles to the Galatians, the Corinthians and the Romans, and finally the so-called Prison Epistles to the Ephesians, Colossians and Philippians.[2] Words sometimes alter in meaning with the passing of time and events. Paul himself received an abundance of revelations over the years through which the Holy Spirit gradually led him into the fullness of truth he should proclaim (2 Cor. 12:1, 7; Gal. 1:11, 12; Eph. 3:3-6, 9; 1 Tim. 4:1). We do not wish to "homogenize" words that should express a rich variety of meaning; we do desire to be sensitive to any developments of doctrine as Scripture progressively unfolds.[3]

The Thessalonian Correspondence

1 Thessalonians 1:9, 10. Shortly after leaving the new believers at Thessalonica, Paul seems to have written them this letter, probably from Corinth in A.D. 50-51. He reviews their reception of his preaching, how they had "turned to God from idols to serve the living and true God, and to wait for His Son from heaven, whom He raised from the dead—Jesus, who rescues us from the coming wrath."

In these words, surely among our earliest from Paul's hand, the apostle to the Gentiles mentions four themes which characterize his preaching (as recorded in Acts) and which reappear throughout his Epistles whenever he discusses the end of the world.

1. The gospel calls men (here largely pagan idolaters) to know and serve the one, true, living God. This is none other than the Creator God of Israel, as Paul affirms in both his recorded addresses to pagan

---

2. There is no mention of final punishment in the Pastoral Epistles to Timothy and Titus, probably Paul's final canonical works. Hebrews will be treated later as non-Pauline.

3. Some prefer Clark Pinnock's phrase "cumulative revelation," by which he means to designate "the *teleological* direction of revelation with the emphasis on the building up of the total truth picture." Because revelation came "gradually in chronological progression," Pinnock says Scripture "needs to be read with regard for the place each passage occupies in the revelation process." The pinnacle of divine revelation was the appearance of Jesus Christ, who also is Himself the key to interpreting Scripture both before and after His coming (see Clark H. Pinnock, *Biblical Revelation: The Foundation of Christian Theology,* p. 214).

The same thought may be expressed by the common phrase "progressive revelation" so long as the term is kept free of humanistic evolutionary ideas.

audiences (Acts 14:15-17; 17:22-31). Paul speaks in the name of the God of his fathers. He presents the gospel as the continuation and fulfillment of the Old Testament story, not a competitor to it.

2. God has raised Jesus from the dead, so declaring Him to be His Son (Rom. 1:4).

3. Jesus has gone back to the Father in heaven, but believers are to eagerly await His promised return (1 Cor. 1:7; Phil. 3:20).

4. Jesus' return will mark the end of the present world order. God will then pour out His wrath on the unrepentant, but Jesus will save believers from that wrath.

Wrath to come was no new theme with Paul. We have already found it integral to the message of John the Baptist as he presented Jesus to Israel (Matt. 3:7; Luke 3:7). This wrath is linked to Jesus so closely that it already lies like a beast of prey over the one who rejects Him (John 3:36). More than that, Jesus drains its cup Himself on Calvary as He becomes a "curse," is "made sin," and carries away in His own body the sin of the world (Gal. 3:13; 2 Cor. 5:21; John 1:29; 1 Pet. 2:24). Already the gospel reveals this wrath of the end-time (Rom. 1:18). Jerusalem's destruction by the Romans is viewed as a partial demonstration of the same wrath against unbelieving Israel, who rejected Jesus (Luke 21:23; cf. 1 Thess. 2:16). We will examine Paul's elaboration on the eschatological wrath as we proceed.

There is a popular notion that the Old Testament reveals a God of wrath, the New Testament a God of mercy and love. Nothing could be further from the truth. In his perceptive book, *The Goodness of God*, John W. Wenham shows how the theme of divine wrath runs through the entire Bible. Rather than omitting or softening the Old Testament wrath of God, Wenham concludes that the New Testament complements it, completes it, agrees with it, highlights and quotes it, and sometimes "outdoes" it.[4] Gustav Stahlin agrees. In his article on "wrath" in Kittel's, he insists that in no sense does the New Testament regard God's wrath as "an inconsistent bit of OT religion which has been dragged in, as though reference to God's wrath be-

---

4. John W. Wenham, *The Goodness of God*, pp. 16-23. Paul speaks of God's eschatological "wrath" in Rom. 1:18; 2:8; Eph. 5:6; Col. 3:6; 1 Thess. 1:10; 5:9; He speaks of Jesus saving His people from that wrath in Phil. 1:28; 3:20; 1 Thess. 1:10.

longed only to the OT and reference to His love were confined to the NT."[5]

Still less does the New Testament picture Jesus as the spineless figure of decadent liberal imagination, indifferent to God's law and honor, the author of a painless atonement who stands ready to bypass repentance, sweep all sin under a cosmic rug, and dispense cheap grace to one and all alike. Nor does Jesus show us the unsympathetic god of a certain distorted fundamentalism, who stands over his people in spiked boots holding a whip in his hand, ready at the slightest slip to thrash them unmercifully and throw them into hell.

Jesus always shows us a God of infinite mercy but of equal holiness. His mercy is totally undeserved and absolutely free—facts which demand greater wrath when men thumb their noses at God's marvelous offer. Jesus teaches this in His parables and demonstrates it in His own substitutionary death for sinners. Mercy and wrath go together in the Bible; each highlights the other. As Stahlin observes:

> Only he who knows the greatness of wrath will be mastered by the greatness of mercy. The converse is also true: Only he who has experienced the greatness of mercy can measure how great wrath must be. For the wrath of God arises from His love and mercy. Where mercy meets with the ungodly will of man rather than faith and gratitude, with goodwill and the response of love, love becomes wrath. . . . In Christ mankind is divided into those who are freed from wrath inasmuch as they are ready to be saved by His mercy, and those who remain under wrath because they despise His mercy.[6]

The Synoptics picture Jesus throughout in three basic roles, Baird writes, "and through them all like a mighty theme runs Jesus' emphasis on the judgment of God." The result is that whenever "one brings Jesus' gospel to focus at any point, there one finds a strong revelation of the judgment of God."[7]

Whenever one comes to know the *God* of the Bible, he finds no difficulty understanding how divine judgment is "an essential, inalienable, and fundamental aspect of the outlook of faith."[8] Eternal judg-

---

5. G. Stahlin, "*Orgē*," *Theological Dictionary of the New Testament*, 5:422.

6. Ibid., p. 425.

7. Joseph Arthur Baird, *The Justice of God in the Teaching of Jesus*, p. 250.

8. The phrase belongs to Gustaf Aulén, quoted by Leon Morris, *The Biblical Doctrine of Judgment*, p. 55.

ment is a "first principle" of Christ (Heb. 6:1, 2). It is so fundamental to Christian teaching that the New Testament never feels a need to argue *for* it, though it feels perfectly free to argue *from* it.[9]

It is significant that even in the Old Testament, nouns for God's wrath are consistently linked with the covenant name Yahweh or Jehovah, an association which occurs more than 50 times. Fichtner observes that Genesis contains no term for the wrath of God, though numerous words fill that place from the Exodus and Sinai onward.[10] Paul reasons from the Old Testament, we remember, in Romans and Galatians as he relates God's wrath to God's law (Gal. 3:10) or when he insists that God is within the bounds of His own justice in condemning Jew and Gentile alike (Rom. 1-4). Ridderbos can say that "God's wrath is altogether determined by his righteousness and holiness."[11] And Karl Barth is surely beyond dispute when he writes:

> The wrath of God is to unbelief the discovery of His righteousness, for God is not mocked. The wrath of God is the righteousness of God— apart from and without Christ.[12]

We have already seen throughout the Old Testament that God's wrath against sin results in the total destruction of the sinner. The Psalms and Proverbs repeatedly speak of a time when the wicked will be no more, their place will not be found, and even their name will be forgotten. The prophets contribute a whole vocabulary of divine wrath and destruction as they tell of floods that rise, storms that destroy, swords that slay and blood that flows, moths and worms that consume, fire that devours and smoke that ascends. Poetry and prophecy alike build on God's actual acts of past judgment within history. Outstanding examples are the Flood, which destroyed a world and abolished all but eight members of its race, and the storm of fire and sulfur which utterly obliterated Sodom and Gomorrah, leaving neither a single survivor within nor a trace of the cities forever.

---

9. Morris' observation (ibid.).

10. J. Fichtner, *"Orgē," Theological Dictionary of the New Testament*, 5:396. Morris, too, observes that judgment for the Israelite was exercised in the context of the covenant, under God in community with the people. "It is no accident," he says, "that judgment is often linked with words like *chesed* [kindness] and *tsedeq* [justice, righteousness], which are integral to the whole conception of covenant" (Morris, *The Biblical Doctrine of Judgment*, p. 19).

11. Herman N. Ridderbos, *Paul: An Outline of His Theology*, p. 109.

12. Karl Barth, *The Epistle to the Romans*, p. 43. Barth is commenting on Romans 1:18.

It should not surprise us to read, therefore, that in the Old Testament "the wrath of Yahweh aims at destruction, at full extirpation."[13] Whenever God's sovereign anger breaks forth, "the existence of those concerned is at stake." And whenever his existence is at stake, "the man of the old covenant detects the wrath of his God."[14] This is why the Old Testament's metaphors and figures for judgment convey such "destructive power and irresistible force,"[15] such "annihilating might and irresistible power."[16]

Scholars are still debating whether God's wrath is the personal fury of an offended Being or the impersonal outworking of sin's inbuilt self-destruction.[17] We must agree with the first group that God's wrath is as fully personal as His mercy, that one who views a wrath apart from the personal God very easily rationalizes an impersonal "God" without wrath.[18] At the same time, since sin at its root expresses rebellion against God, who alone gives and sustains life, we fully agree with James D. G. Dunn that "the outworking of the destructive consequences of sin" is "destructive for the wholeness of man in his relationships."[19] God's wrath is not capricious, nor is it vindictive in any way that is unjust. Paul carefully pictures God's final wrath in personal terms (Rom. 2:8, 9), but he insists with equal vigor that God is both longsuffering (Rom. 9:22; 1 Thess. 2:16) and just (Rom. 3:5, 6).

---

13. Fichtner, "Orgē," *Theological Dictionary of the New Testament*, 5:400. An earlier translation by Dorothea M. Barton and P. R. Ackroyd is far more forceful. The same sentence there reads: 'The basic effect of Yahweh's wrath is intended to be annihilation, complete obliteration" (J. Fichtner, "Orgē," *Bible Key Words*, 4:33).

14. Fichtner, "Orgē," *Theological Dictionary of the New Testament*, 5:399.

15. Ibid.

16. Fichtner, "Orgē," *Bible Key Words*, p. 29. The full sentence says: 'The annihilating might of God's wrath and his irresistible power are displayed in the metaphors and pictorial phrases used for what that wrath brings about."

17. John W. Wenham gives a suggestive bibliography regarding this controversy in *The Goodness of God*, p. 187. Authors holding the personalized view include G. Stahlin, R. V. G. Tasker and Leon Morris. Authors holding the depersonalized view include C. H. Dodd, G. H. C. MacGregor, A. T. Hanson and D. E. H. Whiteley.

18. Wenham writes: "It is uncomfortable to sinful people to live continually under the all-seeing eye of the all-knowing Judge. Therefore Christians have been tempted to soft-pedal the theme of judgment. The theme of hell has been quietly omitted, and the wrath of God has been de-personalized. The wrath of God is thought of as the outworking of a deistic machine, in which God is not immediately and personally involved. But it is because wrath is personal that mercy is personal" (ibid., p. 187).

19. James D. G. Dunn, "Paul's Understanding of the Death of Jesus," *Reconciliation and Hope: New Testament Essays on Atonement and Eschatology*, p. 139. On this point Dunn refers "particularly" to S. H. Travis' unpublished doctoral dissertation entitled "Divine Retribution in the Thought of Paul" (Cambridge University, 1970).

When Paul reminds the Thessalonians that the Jesus for whom they wait will deliver them from the coming wrath, he writes as a Hebrew born of Hebrews, reared in the Old Testament Scriptures. When he later gives more details on the subject, he phrases those as well in language and symbols already established by the Jewish prophets, who spoke for the same God these pagan Thessalonians had now turned to serve. The wrath to come was not a new revelation. The Savior Jesus Christ was. The first was known by the Law. The second is the good news of the gospel.

1 Thessalonians 4:6. Gentile converts faced special temptation to sexual immorality, for they lacked the disciplinary training the Jews had received from the Law. Paul urges holiness within the church, therefore, in matters of sexual purity. Fornication is forbidden, and "the Lord will punish men for all such sins."

Literally, he writes that the "Lord is Avenger" concerning such matters. The same phrase appears in the Greek text of Psalm 94:1. Neither that passage nor this context add to the picture, stating only the fact with its implicit threat of punishment from such a God.

1 Thessalonians 5:2, 3. God will avenge in wrath on the day He has appointed (cf. Acts 17:30, 31), here called "the day of the Lord." The later prophets of the Old Testament had used this expression often for judgments that were temporal and local as well as for the final judgment that would be final and universal. They use identical language to describe the effects of such a day in either case.

Paul once contrasts God's day with "human day," the literal term translated "man's judgment" in 1 Corinthians 4:3 (KJV). Today man has his say. Tomorrow God will have His. God's present forbearance indicates merciful restraint, not ignorance or unconcern. Those who resist present mercy will discover that God has actually been "storing up" His wrath for them all the while (Rom. 2:4-6).

Paul describes this day as "the day of the Lord" (1 Cor. 5:5; cf. 2 Pet. 3:10, 12), the regular expression of the Old Testament prophets. Throughout Scripture that day brings a double issue: wrath and salvation.[20] Paul speaks therefore of "the day of God's wrath" (Rom.

---

20. For an excellent discussion of this point that is "meaty" and still understandable to the layman, see Robert D. Brinsmead's monographs, *Covenant* (pp. 41-55) and *The Pattern of Redemptive History* (pp. 135-152).

2:5) and also "the day of redemption" (Eph. 4:30), but they are the same day. Both wrath and redemption manifest God's righteousness, so this is also "the day [Christ] comes to be glorified . . . and to be marveled at" (2 Thess. 1:10). Since Jesus will be God's Savior and Destroyer, this is also "the day of Christ" (Phil. 2:16) or "the day of our Lord Jesus Christ" (1 Cor. 1:8; cf. Rev. 6:17). Peter also mentions "the day [God] visits us" (1 Pet. 2:12). This will be "the great day" (Jude 6), "the last day" (John 6:39), "the day of judgment" (1 John 4:17).

Whatever we call the day on which it occurs, the event of final judgment is most important, and it encompasses many important truths.

> It stresses man's accountability and the certainty that justice will final-ly triumph over all the wrongs which are part and parcel of life here and now. . . . This doctrine gives meaning to life. . . . The Christian view of judgment means that history moves to a goal. . . . Judgment protects the idea of the triumph of God and of good. It is unthinkable that the present conflict between good and evil should last throughout eternity. Judgment means that evil will be disposed of authoritatively, decisively, finally. Judgment means that in the end God's will will be perfectly done.[21]

The Bible insists that there will be a resurrection of the wicked as well as the good and that all men will stand before God to give account and be judged. Scripture holds no brief for those who say the wicked end with the first death (such as the so-called Jehovah's Witnesses). Rather, it repudiates their doctrine time and time again (Dan. 12:2; John 5:29; Acts 24:15; Rev. 21:8).

Paul here says that God's "day" will be unexpected (1 Thess. 5:2), sudden (v. 3) and inescapable (v. 3). In all three respects it will resemble God's previous judgments on sinners, particularly in the Flood (Matt. 24:36-44; Luke 17:26-35). Although men assure each other with words of "peace and safety," Paul insists that "destruction will come on them suddenly, as labor pains on a pregnant woman, and they will not escape" (v. 3).

The "destruction" (*olethros*) that is here "sudden" is later said to be "everlasting" (2 Thess. 1:9). Only Paul uses the word in the New Testament. The sinful man at Corinth is to be delivered over to Satan

---

21. Morris, *The Biblical Doctrine of Judgment*, p. 72.

for the "destruction" of the flesh (1 Cor. 5:5). The desire for riches may lead to "destruction" ("ruin," NIV) even now (1 Tim. 6:9). Paul uses a cognate noun for the destroyer that wiped out a generation of Israelites in the wilderness (1 Cor. 10:10). The author of Hebrews uses a verb form for the destroyer who slaughtered the firstborn throughout Egypt (Heb. 11:28). The last two passages clearly involve execution and extermination, though the meaning of the first is ambiguous and the second is metaphorical. None of them hints at conscious unending torment. The description of God's judgment in this passage brings to mind the Flood's extinction of the wicked—a judgment they were unable to escape then or to reverse forever.

1 Thessalonians 5:9. Paul's readers need not fear, however. "For God did not appoint us to suffer wrath but to receive salvation through our Lord Jesus Christ." The Epistle closes as it opened, with the alternate fates of "wrath" from God and "salvation" through Jesus. The two stand side by side as opposing destinies. Verse 10 says the righteous will "live together with Him," an outcome exactly opposite the kind of "destruction" we have already suggested.

2 Thessalonians 1:5-10. Present persecution and trials inspire hope and joy when viewed in the larger balance of God's coming judgment. The more one suffers for Jesus now, the greater he can anticipate the day when God will settle the accounts! In the same way, rest is most inviting to the person who labors the hardest now. Suffering believers may know that "God is just" and will finally even the score. Paul spells out what this means.

The Thessalonian Christians now knew "trouble"; then they will find "relief" (*anesin*, from which the trade name "Anacin"). Those who now oppress will then receive the "trouble" they have been dishing out—and far more! "Trouble" translates *thlipsis*, which literally means "pressure." The word is frequently used by New Testament writers for the kind of pressure which comes to believers caught between the "pull" of the old age (flesh and sin) and the "pull" of the new age (Spirit and righteousness). The word clearly requires conscious agony, and there will be plenty of time for that, even if it finally ends in extermination. Jesus plainly spoke of "weeping and grinding of teeth" more than once, as we have seen already. Paul does not stop with the "trouble," however, as he continues.

The King James Version says Jesus will "be revealed from heaven with His mighty angels, in flaming fire taking vengeance" (vv. 7, 8). The New International Version and Revised Standard Version place the "flaming fire" with the phrase preceding it rather than the one following. Jesus "is revealed from heaven in blazing fire with His powerful angels" (NIV) or "is revealed from heaven with His mighty angels in flaming fire" (RSV). Both meanings are possible from the Greek, and commentators are divided. Leon Morris argues for the latter primarily to preserve the unity of the three prepositional phrases. Jesus will be "revealed" (*apokalypsis*—apocalypse):

[1] from heaven
[2] in blazing fire
[3] with His powerful angels.[22]

Thus accompanied by His angels, robed in fire, descending from heaven, Jesus will then be seen as He is (see Matt. 25:31; Jude 14; Rev. 1:1, 7, 13-16). In this interpretation the "blazing fire" has to do with the glory of Jesus' person, not specifically the punishment inflicted on the wicked.

But there is another consideration. The entire passage contains several conceptual points of contact and even verbal parallels with Isaiah 66, an important Old Testament apocalyptic passage already noted, which also contrasts judgment and hope. The Thessalonians are presently excluded by their fellow citizens; so were the faithful Israelites Isaiah comforted (1 Thess. 2:14ff; Isa. 66:5). In each case the faithful hope for a day when circumstances will be reversed (2 Thess. 1:5-7; Isa. 66:6, 14), a standard characteristic of apocalyptic literature. Both passages speak of "inflicting" or "repaying" "vengeance" (2 Thess. 1:6, 8; Isa. 66:7, 15).[23] Both passages have the Lord

---

22. Leon Morris, *The First and Second Epistles to the Thessalonians*, The New International Commentary on the New Testament, p. 202.

One might question the propriety of the New International Version's translators in here reversing the order of Paul's last two prepositional phrases in the interest of their favored interpretation. The same meaning could be signified by merely adding a comma, as in the Revised Standard Version. What if their choice of meanings should prove to be the wrong one?

23. Both the Revised Standard Version and King James Version correctly translate the phrase in verse 8 as "inflicting" or "taking vengeance." There appears to be no textual basis for the New International Version's "He will punish those." Paul uses the participial phrase *didontos ekdikēsin*, and Isaiah 66:15 (LXX) had the infinitival phrase *apodounai ekdikēsin*. On the other hand, it is unfortunate that the English words "vengeance" and "revenge" have popularly taken on a tone of ungodly vindictiveness so that the New International Version's committees were somewhat limited in final options.

coming "in fire" (2 Thess. 1:7; Isa. 66:15).[24]

If we may read Paul against this background of Isaiah 66, Morris' suggestion still holds true. Indeed, he cites the verse himself to illustrate his point. But while the fire belongs to Christ's revelation in glory, may it not also be a means of His vengeance? This possiblity is clearly supported by Isaiah, is a possible interpretation of what follows in Thessalonians, and is explicitly declared in several other passages.

Not only does God come with fire in Isaiah (Isa. 66:15); He also brings down "His rebuke with flames of fire" (v. 15) and "with fire" executes judgment (v. 16). In this passage the rebuke and judgment of fire result in "many . . . slain by the Lord" (v. 16). The chapter ends with the "dead bodies" of the slain being given over to fire and worm so that they become "loathsome to all mankind." We have considered this passage at length both in the chapter on the Old Testament and with reference to the teaching of Jesus.

The same picture, drawn with the vivid symbols of prophetic apocalypticism, appears also in Revelation 19:21 and 20:9. There God's foes are destroyed respectively by sword and by fire from heaven. It may also be in view in 2 Peter 3:7, which says the present heavens and earth "are reserved for fire, being kept for the day of judgment *and destruction of ungodly men.*" It is in keeping with the biblical picture that the fire which symbolizes God's holiness destroys those who do not reverently respond to it. The same fire from heaven which lit the altar also destroyed Aaron's irreverent sons (Lev. 9:24–10:3). The God who is called "a consuming fire" (Heb. 12:29) is jealous for His glory. Those who reject the sin offering He has provided are not only left without a sacrifice for sin; they also must anticipate "fearful . . . judgment" and the "raging fire that will consume the enemies of God" (Heb. 10:26, 27). An acceptable offering or the sinner himself: those are the only options still.

We suggest that this consuming fire will be the means of the "everlasting destruction" Paul mentions in 2 Thessalonians 1:9. Commenting on this passage, Ridderbos says that "there is in this fire an indication of the inexorableness of punishment and the irretrievableness of those who fall under the judgment of God (2 Thess. 1:8), a punishment and a fate from which Christ will keep and deliver his own

---

24. Isaiah has *en phlogi pyros*, and Paul has *en pyri phlogos*. Several lesser Greek manuscripts of Thessalonians have words identical to those found in Isaiah.

(1 Thess. 1:10; 5:9; Rom. 5:9)."[25] We have met this fire of God's holiness with which no unforgiven sinner can long dwell in Isaiah 33:10-17. Here we meet it again. It consumes all that is not holy.

The wicked are here "punished" with everlasting destruction. Such destruction is the just penalty of a righteous God. The word translated "penalty" emphasizes the idea of a lawful process, "of a punishment meted out as the result of an even-handed assessment of the rights of the case."[26] It is from the same root word as "just" in verse 6 and "vengeance" ("punish," NIV) in verse 8.

It is *aiōnios* punishment in both senses we have discussed. It is "eternal" in quality since it belongs to the Age to Come. It is "everlasting" in quantity since it will never end. It is not only inescapable; having once occurred, it is also irreversible. Like "eternal judgment" (Heb. 6:2), "eternal redemption" (Heb. 9:12) and "eternal salvation" (Heb. 5:9)—all the everlasting results of actions once completed—we suggest that this "everlasting destruction" also is the unending result of an action or process of destroying, not the process or action itself. However short or long may be the time of the destroying, a point on which Scripture leaves us in awesome and mysterious silence, its result is made clear. The wicked, once destroyed, will never be seen again.

The wicked are so "punished with everlasting destruction *from the presence* of the Lord, and from the glory of His power" (2 Thess. 1:9, KJV). This reading accurately reflects the ambiguity of the original, which may be interpreted two ways. Either (a) the everlasting destruction *issues from* the presence of the Lord, or (b) it *consists of exclusion from* the presence of the Lord. The King James Version allows the first; the Revised Standard Version, New American Standard Bible and New International Version all translate to mean the second.

Pétavel, an advocate of conditionalism, argues for the first view—that the wicked are "*consumed* by the 'fire of the face' of the Lord."[27] Interestingly enough, so does Strong, an advocate of the traditional understanding of hell.[28] Thayer's lexicon also gives the pronoun this meaning, translating the passage as "destruction proceeding from the

---

25. Ridderbos, *Paul*, p. 554.
26. Morris, *Thessalonians*, p. 205.
27. Emmanuel Pétavel, *The Problem of Immortality*, p. 571.
28. Augustus Hopkins Strong, *Systematic Theology*, 3:1034.

(incensed, wrathful) countenance of the Lord."[29] Moffatt also favors this interpretation in *The Expositor's Greek Testament*, noting that the "overwhelming manifestation of the divine glory sweeps from before it . . . into endless ruin the disobedient."[30] The same prepositional phrase is used in Acts 3:19, where it clearly has the idea of source or origin. It also appears in the Greek text of Jeremiah 4:26, which speaks of cities burned with fire "from the face of the Lord" (*apo prosōpou kyriou*), evidently with the same sense of origin or cause.

Arndt and Gingrich, on the other hand, think the pronoun *apo* here means "away from the presence of,"[31] as does Morris, who contrasts this fate with that of the righteous who are forever "with the Lord" (1 Thess. 4:17).[32]

But again we ask whether we must choose either to the exclusion of the other? May we not affirm that both interpretations are true? A look at the Old Testament seems to bear out this suggestion. Paul's entire phrase, "from the presence of the Lord and from the glory of His power," appears verbatim three times in the Greek text of Isaiah 2 (vv. 10, 19, 21), a context which also discusses the Lord's exaltation and the wicked's destruction in the last days.[33] The Hebrew text uses an idiom: "from the face (presence) of the fear of the Lord." Standard English versions translate it various ways: "for fear of" (KJV), "from before the terror of" (RSV), "from dread of" (NIV). The Septuagint translators, however, transposed the Hebraism word for word into Greek, and that is the phrase Paul quotes here (only dropping the word "fear"). But what does Isaiah describe?

The prophet first warns, then predicts that men will flee to the rocks and caves for fear when God appears to judge. They flee *because of* dread of the Lord (KJV, NIV) but also *away from* His approaching terror (RSV).[34] Both meanings are included here, and both

---

29. Joseph Henry Thayer, tr., *A Greek-English Lexicon of the New Testament*, p. 59.

30. James Moffatt, "The First and Second Epistles to the Thessalonians," *The Expositor's Greek Testament*, ed. W. Robertson Nicoll, vol. 4, p. 46.

31. William F. Arndt and F. Wilbur Gingrich, trs., *A Greek-English Lexicon of the New Testament and Other Early Christian Literature*, "apo," p. 86.

32. Morris, *Thessalonians*, p. 206.

33. In each case the Septuagint of Isaiah has *apo prosōpou tou phobou kyriou kai apo tēs doxēs tēs ischyos autou*. Paul has the same words in the same order except he drops the single word *phobou*.

34. The figure probably comes from actual practice, as when Israel fled from enemies to hide

seem to fit Paul's similar description in Thessalonians. But God's appearance affects more than just men.

It is important that when God comes to punish sinners, the whole earth suffers in the consequences. God "rises to shake the earth" (Isa. 2:21). Delitzsch remarks:

> Thus the judgment would fall upon the earth without any limitation, upon men universally . . . and upon the totality of nature as interwoven in the history of man—one complete whole, in which sin, and therefore wrath, had gained the upper hand. When Jehovah rose up, *i.e.* stood up from His heavenly throne, to reveal the glory manifested in heaven, and turn its judicial fiery side towards the sinful earth, the earth would receive such a shock as would throw it into a state resembling the chaos of the beginning. We may see very clearly from Rev. vi. 15, where this description is borrowed, that the prophet is here describing the last judgment, although from a national point of view and bounded by a national horizon.[35]

The same return to primeval chaos figures in the judgment scene of Isaiah 24:1-6, 18-20 and in Jeremiah 4:23-26. In the first the earth finally "falls—never to rise again" (Isa. 24:20); its inhabitants "are burned up, and very few are left" (Isa. 24:6). In the second Jeremiah watches as the judgment transpires. It is a reversal of the creation story, as if the film of Genesis 1 were now run backward through the projector. Man disappears from the land and birds from the air (Gen. 1:25), the fruitful ground becomes a barren desert (v. 26), the mountains tremble and shake (v. 24), the lights go out of the heavens (v. 23). The earth is left "formless and empty" (v. 23), just as it once began. We are also reminded of the time of Noah, when once before the floodgates of heaven opened and the earth's foundations crumbled (Gen. 7:11; Isa. 24:18, 19); of the judgment at Golgotha, when again the earth trembled under the curse of the broken covenant (Matt. 27:51); and of similar New Testament predictions regarding the end of the world (Heb. 12:26-29; 2 Pet. 3:10-13).

The pattern takes on slightly different forms throughout the Bible, but it is the same recurring pattern. God, who created the earth and gave man life, also can take away that life and destroy the earth. Yet believers in any age may look beyond even that. For when the fire

---

in rocks, holes and caves (Judg. 6:2; 1 Sam. 13:6; 14:11). The same picture reappears in Revelation 6:15, 16.

35. Franz Delitzsch, *Biblical Commentary on the Prophecies of Isaiah*, 1:125-126.

has consumed sinners and the earth has shaken from its place, there will be new heavens and a new earth—the unshakable kingdom of God in which righteousness will dwell forever (Rom. 8:21; Heb. 12:28, 29; 2 Pet. 3:13).

Here we have come full circle. Paul tells the Thessalonians that the wicked will be punished with everlasting destruction. It will proceed from God's glorious, fiery presence. It will also remove the wicked away from His presence forever (2 Thess. 1:9).[36] The faithful will then be counted worthy of the kingdom of God for which they had once suffered (v. 5). Perfect justice will balance the books against every ungodly persecutor (vv. 6-8). The last word is that Jesus Christ will be glorified and marveled at among the believers (v. 10). This, too, was part of Isaiah's vision of God's great day.

> They raise their voices, they shout for joy;
> from the west they acclaim the Lord's majesty.
> Therefore in the east give glory to the Lord;
> exalt the name of the Lord, the God of Israel,
> in the islands of the sea.
> From the ends of the earth we hear singing:
> "Glory to the Righteous One."
>
> —Isa. 24:14-16.

This is one of Paul's most detailed descriptions of the end of the wicked, yet Morris quotes Neil's remark that its

most notable feature is the reticence of the description. What in normal apocalyptic literature would have included a lurid picture of the

---

36. The ultimate state of perfection which Paul describes in 1 Corinthians 15:27, 28 will then have arrived, the time when "God himself again fills all things with his glorious presence" (Ridderbos, *Paul*, p. 561). Yet (Ridderbos does *not* make this connection) Jesus and Paul both tell us that the wicked will be expelled from God's presence (Matt. 25:41, 46; 2 Thess. 1:9). Conditionalists have reasoned like this: (1) God's presence will fill all that is, in every place; (2) the wicked will not be in His presence; (3) therefore the wicked will no longer exist.

Donald G. Bloesch, on the other hand, believes that while God's "grace and love will finally encompass all . . . this does not mean that his grace and love will be manifest in the same way for every person." Hell, as well as heaven, he sees as a product of divine love. "Man is in hell," Bloesch writes, "not because God is absent but because he is present, and therefore man is constantly reminded of his guilt and infamy. Hell is exclusion from communion with God, but not exclusion from the presence of God. Even redemptive love is present in hell, but not in the sense that the rejected are brought to redemption; nonetheless, they are ineluctably exposed to redemption" (Donald G. Bloesch, *Essentials of Evangelical Theology*, 2:225). Such reasoning is indeed provocative—perhaps even inviting—certainly representative of a keen and dramatic literary mind (Bloesch acknowledges certain credit to C. S. Lewis, *The Great Divorce*). Still the question remains: Where is its exegetical basis in Scripture?

tortures of the damned and the bliss of the righteous, in Paul's hands becomes a restrained background of Judgment with the light focussed on the Person of Christ as Judge.[37]

If it does not share the "lurid details" of much apocalyptic literature, it nevertheless is saturated in the prophetic symbolism of the Old Testament. Certain intertestamental writers took the Old Testament language and added everlasting conscious torment. Paul takes the Old Testament language and adds *Jesus Christ*. This is a chief difference between intertestamental writers and Paul.

Nothing in the language here requires or even clearly suggests conscious unending torment. Over and over, however, Paul's words, inspired by the Holy Spirit, send us to the former Scriptures, where time and time again the outcome of sinners is made clear. They will perish, be destroyed, be burned up, be gone forever. When God rises to judge the earth, creation itself returns to chaos! How much more vulnerable is man, Isaiah asks us,

> who has but a breath in his nostrils.
> Of what account is he?
> —Isa. 2:22.

The Major Epistles

In Acts 13-14, Luke tells how Paul founded churches in Antioch, Iconium, Lystra and Derbe during his first missionary trip. These were all cities of southern Galatia, a huge Roman province stretching through the mountain and plain of what now is central Turkey. Later these churches were troubled by false teachers who insisted that salvation depended on obedience to the Mosaic Law. Paul responded with the Epistle we call Galatians. Its message is clear, though details of its origin and recipients are not.

During his second missionary journey Paul also visited Corinth, a city of ancient Greece rebuilt by the Romans (Acts 18). A cosmopolitan center of trade and travel, Corinth was perhaps best known for its licentiousness. This centered around the temple of Aphrodite with its thousands of cult prostitutes, who served in the name of the goddess of love, but unbridled behavior so characterized the city that "to

---

37. Morris, *Thessalonians*, p. 202.

Corinthianize" became a well-known expression for utter debauchery.

Paul probably wrote 1 Corinthians about A.D. 54 from Ephesus in response to reports of friction and immorality within the church (1 Cor. 1:11; 5:1) and in answer to a list of questions the church had sent him in a letter (1 Cor. 7:1; 16:17). A year or two later he likely wrote 2 Corinthians, perhaps from some Greek city in the Roman province of Macedonia. From a statement in this Epistle, it seems Paul had written another letter to Corinth between the two we have (2 Cor. 4:2) and that this is his third and hopefully last Epistle before he sees the church again in person (2 Cor. 13:10). Second Corinthians is intensely personal. Paul defends his ministry against some very malicious and carping critics. He also exhorts the church to complete their share in the great Gentile collection by which Paul would bring his own apostolic ministry to a head and demonstrate in a concrete way the unity he had preached between Jews and Gentiles in Christ.

The Epistle to the Romans must have come a year or two later, perhaps about A.D. 57. Paul seems to write from Corinth, where he is en route to Jerusalem with the collection from Gentile churches (Acts 20), and he hopes to come to Rome when that mission has been completed. Perhaps he will continue on to Spain for a much-needed rest (Rom. 15:23-29). The letter to the Romans is his introductory letter to these disciples he has never seen as well as his explanation of the gospel he preaches and its place in the perspective of God's larger plan of redemption. It has often been called Paul's gospel "manifesto."

Together, the Epistles to the Corinthians, the Galatians and the Romans make up Paul's best-known Epistles. They are "major" because of their extensive development of important themes and in view of their influence on the later Christian church. In them all, Paul touches on the final destiny of the wicked, and they exemplify his most detailed teaching during the prime of his ministry.

Galatians 1:8, 9. The gospel Paul has preached is the only message worthy of that name, he tells the Galatians. Those troubling them are actually perverting the gospel of Christ. Then comes the double warning:

> But even if we or an angel from heaven should preach a gospel other than the one we preached to you, let him be eternally condemned! As

we have already said, so now I say again: If anybody is preaching to you a gospel other than what you accepted, let him be eternally condemned!

The New International Version's "eternally condemned" is interpretive though it is probably correct. The Revised Standard Version and King James Version are more precise in their "accursed," though none of the three consistently translates the same word everywhere it appears. Paul actually wrote *anathema* (see 1 Cor. 16:22, KJV). The word literally meant something set up or laid by to be kept, as a votive offering might be hung on a temple wall after being devoted to a god. Because offerings devoted to the true God were commonly burnt in their entirety or otherwise destroyed, the word in biblical usage signifies something "accursed" or doomed to destruction.

Paul uses it this way in two other Epistles. He tells the Romans that he would sacrifice himself as one marked for destruction (*anathema*) if by that he could save his Israelite brethren (Rom. 9:3). Moses had made a similar offer to God for the people (Exod. 32:32). Neither Moses nor Paul could fill such a function since they both were sinners themselves, also in need of a substitute. The Lord Jesus did bear the full penalty given one accursed by God, though Paul warns that it is blasphemy to say Jesus Himself deserved what He received (1 Cor. 12:3). What happened to Jesus on Golgotha was the proper fate of one made *anathema*, however, though the Holy Spirit reveals through the gospel that the innocent Jesus there stood in the place of us sinners.

Death by execution was the sentence this word called for, as seen in the case of Jesus and in the Old Testament background we will shortly note. A verb form of the word appears four times in the New Testament, in each case meaning to swear an oath calling down God's *anathema* curse if one is not telling the truth (Mark 14:71; Acts 23:12, 14, 21).

The Septuagint had ordinarily used *anathema* as the Greek translation of the Hebrew *herem*, the usual term for something "devoted" to God and therefore, under ordinary circumstances, to be totally destroyed. It is used of the Canaanites whom God tells Israel to "totally destroy" and whom they do "completely destroy" (Num. 21:2, 3; words in quotation marks represent *herem*, Hebrew; or *anathema*, Greek). A New International Version footnote to this passage says the Hebrew word "refers to the irrevocable giving over of things or persons to the Lord, often by totally destroying them." The site of this destruction is called Hormah (from *herem*), which the Greek text gives as Anathema. The same name is given the town of Zephath during the time of the Judges for the very same reason (Judg. 1:17).[38] Zechariah later wishes to make it clear that glorified Jerusalem will always be inhabited, so he uses the same word, promising that it will never be *anathema* ("destroyed," Zech. 14:11, NIV).[39]

When the Canaanite spoils are "set apart for destruction," the Septuagint uses *anathema* (Deut. 7:26). The most famous incident involved Achan and Jericho. The city and all its spoils were *anathema* or "devoted to destruction," and so would be any Israelite who took from its spoils for himself (Josh. 6:17, 18; 7:12). Achan did just that and paid the precise penalty the word demanded. He was utterly destroyed—in his case stoned to death, burned with fire and covered with rocks (Josh. 7:25, 26). No Israelite would have doubted that Achan was destroyed because there were physical remains. None would chortle that Achan, after all, was not chemically "annihilated"! Nor did they think that "destruction" meant he should be fastened in a cage and tortured endlessly. They knew what it meant to be *herem/anathema*, and they carried that out.

This is the word's meaning throughout the Scriptures, including the passage we are now considering in Galatians. Because Paul refers to a punishment of the Age to Come, we need not automatically assign *anathema* a meaning it has never had before. The method of God's punishment will surely be different, but the meaning of it will be the same. If even an angel from heaven preaches a different gospel, Paul says he comes under this sentence. He is *anathema*—*herem* —devoted to utter destruction.

Galatians 5:21. The Christian is not tied up by Law, but neither is he free to live out his sinful desires. The same Spirit who liberates from legalism also legislates against fleshly license (Gal. 5:16-18). Believers must not give in to their sinful nature, and Paul regards it as obvious what kind of life that forbids (vv. 19-21). Those who "live

---

38. The word is *"anathema"* in Codex Vaticanus. Codex Alexandrinus instead has *"ex-olethreusis,"* formed from the verb Peter uses in Acts 3:23. This apparent interchangeability is especially interesting since New Testament writers use both original words in connection with the fate of the wicked.

39. Zechariah's words seem to be in view in Revelation 22:3, where John uses *katathema* ("curse"), a slightly different form of the same noun.

like this will not inherit the kingdom of God" (v. 21). Paul makes a similar statement to the Ephesians (Eph. 5:5) and to the Corinthians (1 Cor. 6:9, 10).

His words speak of exclusion rather than infliction; they describe what sinners will lose, not what they will find. Paul may well be echoing the Master in these pronouncements, for Jesus, too, spoke often of being thrown out of God's kingdom and excluded from the eternal bliss God has prepared for the saved. (See comments earlier on Matt. 5:20; 7:23; 8:11, 12; 13:40-43; 22:13; 25:31-46.) Paul here adds nothing to what Jesus had said already.

Galatians 6:8. The Epistle ends on a similar note. "The one who sows to please his sinful nature, from that nature will reap destruction; the one who sows to please the Spirit, from the Spirit will reap eternal life."

The New International Version expands Paul's "flesh" (*sarx*—not *sōma*, "body") to "sinful nature," but we are more concerned here with the consequences than with the crime. One wonders why the New International Version's translators chose "destruction" instead of "corruption" to represent *phthora*, however, especially since the latter was already familiar through the King James Version, Revised Standard Version and New American Standard Bible, and preferred by the New International Version at least once elsewhere (2 Pet. 1:4).

In ordinary Greek this word spoke of "ruin, destruction, dissolution, deterioration, corruption" according to Arndt and Gingrich.[40] Paul uses it of perishable food (Col. 2:22) and of the world which is decaying (Rom. 8:21). Peter applies it to animals destined to be killed (2 Peter 2:12, NIV "destroyed"). Arndt and Gingrich cite nonbiblical sources where the word refers to an abortion or a miscarriage; it had the same meaning in Christian literature of the second century. "You shall not murder a child by abortion" is the injunction of both Barnabas (19:5) and the Didache (2:2). "Abortion" is *phthora*, which Paul uses here.

Metaphorically, the word could be used in a moral sense as in the "depravity" of wicked men (2 Pet. 2:12). The verb (*phtheirō*) meant to "corrupt" or to "ruin" and can speak of destroying a house (1 Cor. 3:17), seducing a virgin (2 Cor. 11:3), ruining a man financially (2 Cor. 7:2), or corrupting someone's morals (1 Cor. 15:33;

---

40. Arndt and Gingrich, *Greek-English Lexicon*, *"phthora,"* p. 865.

Eph. 4:22; Rev. 19:2). We merely observe that the maiden's virginity is forever gone though she continues to live, the man's financial security is annihilated though he personally survives, the building *as a building* is destroyed even if its blocks remain, and the good character which once existed is no longer to be found.

Annihilation, in the scientific sense of a modern physicist, is not under consideration, but that in no way lessens the true "ruin," "corruption" or "destruction" of what once was but is no more. This would hardly be worth mentioning except for a frequent argument of some authors on which it has a bearing. According to many traditionalists, when these words are applied to final punishment they cannot have their normal meaning, since even such biblical figures as ashes under foot or smoke rising in the air do not signify actual, literal, material *annihilation*. Having ruled out this supposed "literal" sense of "destroy," "ruin" and "perish," this argument goes on to point out that only figurative or metaphorical meanings are left. The conclusion is then drawn that "destroy," "ruin" and "perish" must mean eternal conscious torment, not extinction. Words which on their face would seem to suggest "loss of life" are said to signify a "life of loss" instead.

Buis' expresses the common argument like this:

> The annihilationist places a great emphasis on the fact that the figure of 'fire' is used in the Bible to describe future punishment; and fire, they point out, always destroys. . . . But the fact is that when you burn something it is not annihilated, it simply changes form.[41]

Salmond insists that death, destruction, perdition and such terms do not mean what they seem when applied to future punishment, but he argues from man's immortality. If these words "are used of objects whose nature it is to cease to be," he writes, "they will have the literal sense. But if they are employed of objects whose nature is the opposite, they will have a larger meaning."[42] He might better have said that "they will have an *opposite* meaning," for that is really what he means. Immortal souls *cannot* die, perish or be destroyed, he is arguing. Therefore these words cannot have their common meaning when applied to future punishment.

---

41. Buis, *The Doctrine of Eternal Punishment*, pp. 125-126.
42. Steward D. F. Salmond, *The Christian Doctrine of Immortality*, p. 615.

Like most of the great theologians of orthodoxy, Shedd stops short of Salmond's argument, conceding that the same God who created man's body and soul can also destroy both if He so chooses. But Shedd denies that the Bible teaches God will do this:

> Both matter and mind can be annihilated by the same Being who created them from nothing. Whether he will cease to uphold any particular work of his hand, can be known only by revelation. In the material world, we see no evidence of such an intention. We are told that "the elements shall melt with fervent heat," but not that they shall be annihilated. And certainly, all that God has said in Revelation in regard to creation, redemption, and perdition, implies and teaches that he intends to uphold, and not to annihilate the human spirit; to perpetuate, and not extinguish its self-consciousness.[43]

These are three common ways traditionalist authors deal with the major words Paul uses to describe the end of the wicked. The first argues that man *cannot* really die, perish or be destroyed, because his immortal nature makes it impossible—although the words would mean just what they sound like if his nature allowed it. The second argues that God is fully capable of destroying man entirely ("immortal soul" and all), since He created him in the first place—but that the Bible doesn't say He will. The third argues that even if the Bible does speak of consuming fire, for example, fire does not technically *annihilate*—so words like "perish" or "destroy" are out of place anyway! We agree with the third position, that fire does not technically "annihilate"; with the second, that Paul's words mean what they sound like anyway; and with the first, that the Bible does use them to describe what will happen to unrepentant sinners.

We see no reason to regard biblical statements concerning ashes underfoot or smoke rising forever as literal, physical descriptions. We do believe that God uses these terms to convey to our emotions such feelings of dread, horror and finality which the actual scene will elicit. We also strongly urge that such biblical pictures come far closer to what really will take place than any of the many others which uninspired theologians have manufactured since. Human language is integrally related to human experience in the Present Age. All biblical teaching about the Age to Come must therefore be accommodative language to some extent, since it describes realities of

---

43. William G. T. Shedd, *The Doctrine of Endless Punishment*, p. 94.

an age which has none of the limitations of space and time that characterize the present creation. All the biblical language is true, though it is not intended to be analytical (a point missed by many traditionalists). We ought therefore to take it seriously though not literally (a point missed by many conditionalists).

It is most strange to object that because biblical figures of eschatological destruction do not fit our scientific view of physical annihilation, they must be emptied of their ordinary meaning altogether. Scripture uses them to say *something*; surely that "something" is not the precise *opposite* of their usual sense. A perusal of the literature indicates that Salmond hit the nail on the head: the ordinary meaning of "die," "perish," "corrupt" or "destroy" is ruled out automatically by many theologians and authors who assume the immortality of the wicked and therefore cannot allow the words their usual definitions. Yet the greatest orthodox theologians of the past two thousand years have insisted, when the chips were down, that God, who created, can also destroy. In this they have merely echoed the words of the Son of God Himself, who warned that we should fear God, who "is able to destroy both body and soul in hell." Even if the wicked should be assumed immortal, God is able to destroy them. But Scripture always attributes incorruptibility and immortality to the glorified bodies of the righteous in the Age to Come, never of "souls" apart from bodies, of the righteous now, or of the wicked at any time.

There is no good reason, therefore, not to take Paul's primary words in their most ordinary and common senses. He says the wicked will "perish," "die," be "corrupted" or be "destroyed." Those terms have very definite connotations to the most simple person. We need not suddenly become technical physicists worrying about material "annihilation." When we speak of final punishment, we are speaking of a realm which transcends the present space-time world with all its laws of energy, matter and thermodynamics.

We do not deny that all these key terms are used at times in a figurative or metaphorical sense. Yet the very fact that a word can have such an extended sense presupposes an ordinary and literal sense in the first place. Furthermore, the ordinary sense gives meaning to the figurative or extended usage, not the other way around. It is highly questionable, therefore, whether one should so casually dismiss Paul's word "corruption" or its verb form "to corrupt" when used of the sinner's doom (1 Cor. 3:17; Gal. 6:8; cf. Jude 10), especially when the only reason given is a dogmatic argument concerning the nature of hell—itself the subject under consideration.

The adjective member of this family is *phthartos*, and all agree that it means something subject to corruption or decay. It occurs six times in the New Testament, four times in Paul's writings, and twice in Peter's. In every case it is used in a specific contrast between something that passes away (perishes or decays) and something that endures.

Paul contrasts "mortal" creatures and the immortal God (Rom. 1:23), the crown that "will not last" and one that lasts forever (1 Cor. 9:25). He contrasts our present body, which is "perishable," with the glorified resurrection body, which will not be (1 Cor. 15:53, 54). Peter contrasts "perishable" silver and gold with the eternal redemptive blood of Jesus Christ (1 Pet. 1:18), or "perishable" seed with the imperishable word of God (1 Pet. 1:23).

What comfort is there in the thought of an "imperishable" God, crown or resurrection body if the "perishable" thing really lasts forever all the same? Why is it so clear that the adjective signifies things which come to an end, but the noun and the verb, used in the same eschatological connection, suddenly take on figurative and metaphorical meanings? Is this sober exegesis, or is it whistling through a graveyard rather than facing a dogmatic weakness head-on?

Paul's statement in Galatians 6:8 is also an explicit contrast between the issue of the flesh ("sinful nature," *sarx*) on the one hand and the harvest of the Spirit on the other. The first brings forth *corruption* (may we think of a miscarriage?). The second brings *eternal life*.

The most natural opposite of *life* is *death* or *non-life*. It is not *life in misery*. The fact that "eternal life" involves so much *more* than mere existence only heightens Paul's contrast involving "corruption." If ordinary *life* stands over against *death*, can the opposite of "eternal" life be any *less* drastic? By what means can "loss of life" be converted to a "life of loss"? If the "life" is of a more precious and enduring quality than any we now fully experience, that makes the *loss* of it all the more tragic, but it is more terrible precisely because it is *loss*.

Whether one translates it "corruption," "decay," "perishable" or "destroy," this word-family talks about *loss, ruin, deterioration* and *dissolution*. There is no reason to introduce the philosophical or technical scientific concept of physical annihilation; it is completely beside the point of Paul's words here. That fact, however, takes nothing away from the point he does make.

1 Corinthians 3:17. "If anyone destroys God's temple," Paul warns, "God will destroy him." The context here concerns divisions in the church, and Paul adds to his caution a word of explanation: "You [plural] are that temple." Dissensions and factions are among the obvious acts of the sinful nature which Paul has told the Galatians result in "destruction" or "corruption" (Gal. 5:20; 6:8). Now he warns the Corinthians against the same sins. The verb he writes here (*phtheirō*, "destroy") is a cognate to the noun "corruption" or "destruction" which he used in Galatians.

The unity of God's temple must be kept intact if there is truly to be a temple. A heap of broken blocks is no building, as witness the Wailing Wall in Jerusalem today. Such physical remains only increase the sense of loss felt by those who observe them. Even if the Old Testament pictures of corpses eaten by worms and fire or of rising smoke were intended to be literal, physical descriptions of the end of sinners (we do not believe they are), such material remains as ashes or smoke would not belie the threat of this passage that "God will destroy" the one who destroys His temple. As a matter of fact, we have already met Jesus' statement a number of times that God differs from men in that He is able to destroy man *totally*—a point every orthodox theologian concedes.

1 Corinthians 6:9, 10. Again Paul says that the immoral will not inherit the kingdom of God. See the discussion on Galatians 5:21.

1 Corinthians 16:22. "If anyone does not love the Lord—a curse be on him." The King James Version says "let him be anathema"; the Revised Standard Version says "let him be accursed." The word is the same one Paul used in Galatians 1:8, 9, which discussion see.

Romans 1:18. "The wrath of God is being revealed from heaven against all the godlessness and wickedness of men who suppress the truth by their wickedness," Paul declares. "Revealed" has eschatological overtones here and in the verse preceding. There Paul had said that "in the gospel a righteousness from God is revealed." Both times he uses the verb *apokalyptō*—"to uncover" or "to reveal"—from which stem comes the name "Apocalypse" (Revelation), then the

English adjective "apocalyptic" describing it and literature of the same kind. The last day will be a time for uncovering all that is now hidden. We have already noted Paul's statement that Jesus Himself will then be revealed as He is (2 Thess. 1:7; cf. 1 Cor. 4:3-5; 1 John 3:2).

The last day has not yet come, but already the gospel story of Jesus Christ's death and resurrection "reveals" its most important features. Those features are the *divine righteousness* (or verdict of acquittal) and *divine wrath*. These are the two issues of God's judgment: vindication on one hand; condemnation on the other.

As representative Man, Jesus has already passed before God's tribunal—successfully. The person who believes the gospel will enter the judgment empty-handed, pointing in that day only to the satisfactory work Jesus has accomplished apart from him and on his behalf. Since the believer already knows the standard of God's judgment (perfection), the plea he will present before the divine tribunal (Jesus Christ alone, by faith), and the estimate God places on that appeal (justification, righteousness, vindication or acquittal), the last day will not take him by surprise, and he can anticipate it now without doubt or fear.

In a similar way the gospel already uncovers God's negative verdict of judgment. But divine wrath against sin is uncovered in the very same preview that reveals divine righteousness—that is, the death and resurrection of Jesus Christ. This very "revealing" character of the gospel makes the period of time it is preached the "last days," for it declares that the act of resurrection and judgment has already begun with the Man, Jesus of Nazareth. The consummation remains, but it will be just that—the completion and fulfillment of what is already known in principle through the gospel.

The death of Jesus Christ "reveals" the divine wrath in a way no apocalyptic literature ever could, however powerful its imagination or picturesque its terms. We cannot possibly fathom all we see at Calvary, yet the scene is so important for understanding God's wrath that it demands a chapter of its own in the present study.

Romans 1:32. It is "God's righteous decree" that those who give themselves over to the depravity described in Romans 1:21-31 "deserve death." Paul will say twice again in Romans that sin leads to "death" (Rom. 6:21, 23). That was God's sentence pronounced to Adam in the Garden (Gen. 2:17). Plato would later teach the Greeks that death was a friend which separated the immortal soul from the imprisoning body. But no Hebrew prophet ever spoke in such terms, nor does any word of Scripture. Death is God's punishment for sin, and in Romans 6:23 it stands in stark contrast to eternal "life." See the further discussion on Galatians 6:8.

Romans 2:6-11. Along with the major Thessalonian passage already examined (2 Thess. 1:6-10), these verses contain Paul's most detailed teaching concerning the fate of the lost. In both places the context concerns the justice of God's judgment—as it involves suffering Christians and their persecutors (Thessalonians), and as it concerns the impenitent and the faithful (Romans). In Thessalonians God's justice gives comfort and inspires hope; in Romans it warns against carelessness and calls indifference up short. Let us consider the pertinent phrases in order.

> God "will give to each person according to what he has done." To those who by persistence in doing good seek glory, honor and immortality, He will give eternal life. But for those who are self-seeking and who reject the truth and follow evil, there will be wrath and anger. There will be trouble and distress for every human being who does evil: first for the Jew, then for the Gentile; but glory, honor and peace for everyone who does good: first for the Jew, then for the Gentile. For God does not show favoritism.

Paul first states the principle that God will recompense men individually and fairly. He echoes David, who had used the same words in view of God's strength and love (Ps. 62:12; LXX, v. 13). Solomon had repeated the words in a warning against cowardice and moral neutrality (Prov. 24:12). Both settings figure also in Paul's discussion that follows.

Some individuals persistently do the good, by this demonstrating their search for glory, honor and immortality. God will give these eternal life (v. 7), a kind of sum-word which also includes "glory, honor and immortality" (vv. 7, 10). For Paul, immortality is always God's gift to the faithful, to be awarded in the resurrection. He never views it as a quality inherent to man, nor does he ever attribute it to the wicked. This fact bears repeating since it is so often overlooked. "Eternal life" is not mere *existence*—it is the deathless life of God's glorified people, who share in Christ's own honor in the Age to Come.

Over against these (Paul uses the contrasting *men/de* construction in vv. 7, 8) are other individuals who prefer evil to truth, pleasing themselves to pleasing God. God will give them an award also, but it will consist of "wrath and anger, trouble and distress." The first pair (wrath and anger) describe the retribution from the standpoint of God's displeasure and contrast with the eternal life promised the righteous a verse earlier. The second pair (trouble and distress) describe the same punishment from the standpoint of its recipients in contrast to the bliss promised the righteous a verse later.[44]

"Wrath" is *orgē*, a word often found in passages that speak of eschatological judgment (see comments on 1 Thess. 1:10). When the synonym "anger" (*thymos*) accompanies it, it is usually to strengthen or intensify the meaning. The pair occur together of man's anger (Eph. 4:31; Col. 3:8) and of God's (Rev. 14:10; 16:19; 19:15). *Righteous* judgment does not exclude God's personal *fury* against willful and unrepentant sinners. Justice, in fact, demands it!

The pair "trouble" (*thlipsis*) and "distress" (*stenochōria*) also appear in combination elsewhere in Paul's Epistles. God's people encounter this team of opponents in the present world, he says, but they cannot separate the believer from God's love (Rom. 8:35). Such "trouble and hardship" actually mark the faithful as God's true servants (2 Cor. 6:4). Paul is one of those who are "hard pressed . . . but not crushed," and he uses these same two words in participle form to say so (2 Cor. 4:8). This last translation is suggestive for our present verse. Judgment day will find the wicked "hard pressed"—to the point of being "crushed."

Paul's readers who knew the Greek Old Testament would likely remember Zephaniah 1:14-18 as they read his words here. Time and again Paul repeats in this gospel setting the words and phrases Zephaniah had used in his classic description of the great day of the Lord. Zephaniah spoke of "the day of the Lord's wrath" (v. 18), and so did Paul (v. 5).[45] Zephaniah pictured "wrath" (*orgē*, v. 15) and "distress" (*thlipsis*, vv. 15, 17; Paul's "trouble") as well as "trouble" (v. 15, not Paul's Greek word).

If we read the prophet as a background to the apostle, Paul's description pales by comparison. Romans emphasizes God's *justice* (vv.

---

44. So also John Murray, *The Epistle to the Romans,* The New International Commentary on the New Testament, p. 66. The New International Version brings out Paul's contrast quite clearly.

45. Zephaniah used the Tetragrammaton for God's name, which was read *Adonai* and the Septuagint translated as *Kyrios*. Paul omits *kyriou* in his expression "the day of wrath." For Paul the title *Kyrios* now belongs to the exalted and glorified Jesus Christ.

5, 6, 11) and includes the wicked's punishment under that. Zephaniah's portrayal is unmixed terror as he describes the "day of wrath." He mixes metaphors freely. First the prophet says that sinners' "blood will be poured out like dust and their entrails like filth" (v. 17). Then he says God will "consume" the whole world in "the fire of His jealousy" (v. 18). Literalists could probably arrange a scenario, but Zephaniah does not. He is painting an abstract picture. Both scenes have a single meaning: God "will make a sudden end of all who live in the earth" (v. 18).

Is not Paul making the same point? Not once in this passage does he mention everlasting torment. Immortality for him is always God's gift to the saved, as are incorruption, glory, honor and eternal life. Like Jesus before him, Paul freely borrows from the Old Testament's prophetic vocabulary. Also like Jesus, he adds to the Old Testament picture—not gory details of unending tortures, as did some of his contemporaries and many of his successors, but the shining, single beam of the gospel. Illuminated most brightly in that light is the figure of Jesus Himself. *Jesus*, not lurid details of conscious torment, is the contribution the New Testament makes to the Old Testament's apocalyptic literature.

The cross has replaced the Valley of Hinnom as the best picture of God's wrath. In advance of the cross, Jesus spoke of His death in guarded terms and used the intertestamental term "Gehenna" of the fate of the wicked. After the cross, however, and the descent of the Spirit on Pentecost, no New Testament writer ever again uses that phrase of final punishment.[46] Paul, who says more on the subject by far than any of the others, points continually to Jesus' death as its clearest revelation. With the death and resurrection of Jesus, judgment day has already begun. The gospel "reveals" it to men and women everywhere. It is God's last call to repent!

Romans 2:12. God gave the Jews greater privileges than the Gentiles, and with them greater responsibilities. But God will judge righteously in both cases. "All who sin apart from the law will also perish apart from the law," Paul writes here. John Murray comments:

---

46. The Gospels were *written* after the fact, of course, but they represent themselves as giving the words Jesus had spoken previously while on the earth.

The perishing referred to can be none other than that defined in the
preceding verses as consisting in the infliction of God's wrath and indignation and the endurance of tribulation and anguish in contrast
with the glory, honour, incorruption, and peace bestowed upon the
heirs of eternal life.[47]

All would agree with Murray that Paul draws a contrast between
those who "perish" and those who receive "immortality." Perishing
therefore comes down on the side of mortality. That Paul always attributes immortality exclusively to the saved, while freely and frequently speaking of corruption, death, destruction and perishing
with regard to the wicked, strongly suggests that the wicked will be
revived[48] in a mortal and corruptible body, suffer according to God's
exact justice, then finally pass away forever in the ultimate penal extinction John calls the "second death."

Traditionalist writers so often make the point that "perish" (*apollymi*) is used of ruined wineskins (Matt. 9:17) and spoiled food (John
6:12) that casual readers tend to go away thinking the word's primary meaning must be very mild indeed. In fact, it appears 92 times in
the New Testament, 13 times in Paul's letters. Most often it refers to
actual *death*.[49] Sometimes it is contrasted with enduring, eternal
life.[50] It is the regular term for the "lost" or for those who are
"perishing."[51] Several times it describes the final state of the wicked
in the Age to Come.[52]

To those who are "perishing" the gospel has a "stench of death"—a
fact in keeping with our earlier suggestion that they will be raised
mortal, then return to corruption and final extinction in hell (2 Cor.
2:16). Peter uses this word of the fate which befell the world before
the Flood (2 Pet. 3:6). Paul (1 Cor. 10:9, 10) and Jude (Jude 5) use it
to describe Israel's destruction in the wilderness.

Jesus once draws a specific picture in which this word stands for
one possibility and the resurrection to life represents the other (John
6:39). Along the same line, Paul says that if Christ has not been

---

47. Murray, *The Epistle to the Romans*, p. 70.

48. See the discussion on Matthew 10:28 in the previous chapter.

49. Matt. 2:13; 8:25; 12:14; 16:25; 21:41; 22:7; 26:52; 27:20; John 10:10; 11:50; 18:14; Acts
5:37; 1 Cor. 10:9, 10; Jude 5, 11.

50. John 6:27; 10:28; 12:25; Heb. 1:11; 1 Pet. 1:7.

51. Matt. 10:6; 15:24; 18:11; 1 Cor. 1:18, 19; 2 Cor. 2:15; 4:3; 2 Thess. 2:10; etc.

52. Matt. 5:29, 30; 10:28; John 3:16; 17:12; 2 Pet. 3:9.

raised, then "those who have fallen asleep in Christ are *lost*" (1 Cor.
15:18; the same word). What would be the state of dead believers
without Christ's resurrection? This picture, alongside the great
Flood, Israelite corpses scattered across the desert, the "stench of
death," and the common use of this term to describe ordinary death,
all make it plain that we should think of something more than burst
wineskins or wasted food when we read it used of the doom of the
ungodly. Taken literally, these various pictures contradict each
other. Taken seriously, they paint a single picture of utter, shameful
extinction.

Romans 6:21, 23. Twice Paul says that sin leads to "death,"
which he places in opposition to "eternal life." In our present experience, life and death are opposites, and the dead no longer are
among the living. Eternal life is the opposite of eternal death. Paul
never gives us reason to suppose that eternal *death* is anything other
than what it sounds like. Rather, he strengthens the connotations by
such words as "perish," "destruction" and "corruption."

Ephesians 5:5, 6. Paul warns against immorality and the deceit-
fulness of sin in these words.

> For of this you can be sure: No immoral, impure or greedy person
> —such a man is an idolater—has any inheritance in the kingdom of
> Christ and of God. Let no one deceive you with empty words, for be-
> cause of such things God's wrath comes on those who are disobedient.

We have met both of Paul's expressions already. On exclusion
from the kingdom, see remarks on 1 Corinthians 6:9, 10. On the
wrath of God, see comments on Romans 2:8 and 1 Thessalonians
1:10.

Philippians 1:28. Like their fellow Greeks at Thessalonica, the
Philippian disciples met opposition from their neighbors. Paul encourages them with the prospect that their very persecution is a present sign of God's impending judgment—and their full salvation! Do
not be "frightened in any way by those who oppose you," he says.
"This is a sign to them that they will be destroyed, but that you will
be saved—and that by God."

"Destruction" here is *apōleias*, from *apollymi*. See the discussion
on Romans 2:12. Paul contrasts this fate of the wicked with the

reward of the righteous, who will be saved (*sōtēria*). He had done the same for the Thessalonians (1 Thess. 1:10). Jesus also pointed believers to God, who is able to "save" and to "destroy" (Matt. 10:28; cf. James 4:12).

Philippians 3:19. Some "live as enemies of the cross of Christ," Paul has just noted (v. 18). Of such he now says:

> Their destiny is destruction, their god is their stomach, and their glory is in their shame. Their mind is on earthly things.

The end ("destiny," *telos*) of such sinners is "destruction." The word is *apōleia*, the same used in Philippians 1:28, from *apollymi*, which Paul uses in Romans 2:12, discussed already. Here the apostle contrasts "destruction" with being immortalized in glory. Though they suffer now, he says, believers look forward to the coming of a Savior, the Lord Jesus (v. 20). He will then "transform our lowly bodies so that they will be like His glorious body" (v. 21). Paul discusses this change in the bodies of the saved in his great resurrection chapter (1 Cor. 15:42-54). Again we observe that, for Paul, immortality is God's resurrection boon to the righteous. The wicked will also rise to face judgment, but their "destiny is destruction." They have served their stomach (carnal appetites) as their god; it cannot give immortality but will perish itself (1 Cor. 6:13; note contrast in v. 14).

Colossians 3:6. Sins of the earthly nature may give pleasure now, but because of them "the wrath of God is coming." On the expression see previous comments (Rom. 2:8; 1 Thess. 1:10).

Paul's Language in Its Philosophical Context

In his classic conditionalist work of the nineteenth century, Henry Constable developed an argument in detail concerning the meaning of Paul's major words for the end of the wicked, based on their usage in the philosophical discussion concerning immortality both before and during the time of Paul. Edward White, Constable's contemporary and himself a noted advocate of conditional immortality,

made the same argument. As has been the case with many conditionalist arguments, this one has been completely ignored by traditionalist writers. If there is no satisfactory answer, perhaps that ought to be
stated. If there is a good answer, someone ought to bring it forward
and lay Constable's argument to rest.

Constable began by pointing out that the subject of immortality
was a topic of lively discussion in Paul's day among philosophers and
also among the common people. Paul's primary terms for the fate of
the wicked—"corrupt," "die," "destroy"—were all stock words in
this ongoing discussion. According to Constable,

> In every school the question before us was discussed in the phrases
> and language of the New Testament. In Jerusalem and Rome, at Ath-
> ens and Corinth, in Ephesus and Antioch—wherever a Christian
> preacher opened his mouth to speak to man of his future destiny—
> were Platonists, or Epicureans, or Stoics, or Alexandrians, to whom
> the question of immortality was a question of solemn thought, with
> whom the phrases in which the preacher addressed them as to their
> solemn future were familiar household words.[53]

Particularly well known was Plato's work entitled the *Phaedo*, a
dialogue written to advance the philosopher's concept of the immortality of every soul. The *Phaedo* told the story of the martyrdom of
Socrates, who, on the day he was to die, discoursed with his friends
about death and his hope beyond it. Socrates' hope was the immortality of the soul. He believed that any philosopher should not only
meet death courageously but actually welcome it, since (in his view)
death freed the immortal soul from imprisonment in the mortal body
to its former, natural state.

White says that the *Phaedo* "was as well known among the reading
population of the Macedonian and Roman empires as any tragedy of
Shakespeare is known among English readers"[54] and that it was both
well known and widely studied in Paul's day, 400 years after it was
written. The words Plato used to express his leading ideas, according
to White, "formed a fixed element of thought and speech over the
wide area where his works were studied in the numerous academies
and schools around the Mediterranean shores."[55]

---

53. Henry Constable, *Duration and Nature of Future Punishment*, pp. 42-43.

54. Edward White, *Life in Christ* . . . , p. 260.

55. Ibid.

At one point in the conversation, Socrates' friend Cebes expresses disagreement with what the philosopher is saying. Socrates held that the soul continued after death in a state preferable to the one it occupied before. Cebes was inclined to think, on the other hand, that the soul, "when it has departed from the body, *nowhere any longer exists*, but on whatever day a man dies, on that day it is destroyed (*diaphtheiretai*) and perishes (*apollyetai*); the moment it departs and goes forth from the body it is dispersed like breath or smoke, and flies abroad, and is gone, and *no longer exists anywhere*."[56] Whether Cebes was right or wrong in his opinion is not nearly so important for our study as the terminology he used to express his view. For his two most important words, by which he describes the utter annihilation of the soul, are two of the primary words Paul uses to describe the end of the wicked.

Plato argues that every soul is immortal by nature. He therefore denies that any soul can ever become extinct or pass out of existence. In what terms does Plato express this denial? Constable answers with conviction:

> *In the very terms in which the punishment of the wicked is asserted in the New Testament!* When the latter says the soul shall die, Plato says it shall not die; when the latter says it shall be destroyed, Plato says it shall not be destroyed; when the latter says it shall perish and suffer corruption, Plato says it shall not perish and is incorruptible. The phrases are the very same, only that what Plato denies of all souls alike the New Testament asserts of some of the souls of men.[57]

White makes the same observation. Both Plato and Paul use the terms "death" (*thanatos*), "destruction" (*apōleia*), "corruption" (*phthora*), "perish" (*olethros*) and "die" (*apothnēskō*)—but with this difference: Plato says none of these things will ever befall the soul, for it possesses immortality; Paul says these are the very words which best tell the destiny of those who resist God and refuse to believe in Jesus. Furthermore, White continues,

> In Plato's dialogue these words stand for *extinction of life*, for that idea only, and in the strongest possible contrast to the idea of

---

56. R. F. Weymouth, from a letter to Emmanuel Pétavel. Quoted in Pétavel's conditionalist work, *The Problem of Immortality*, pp. 493-494.

57. Constable, *Future Punishment*, p. 42.

perpetuation of being. Our argument is that in the New Testament they signify precisely the same doom,—the final and absolute *extinction of life* in the case of the wicked.[58]

On the other hand, Plato believed that some would be punished forever (or at least for a very long time after death). According to him, such reprobate souls can continue in misery because they possess "immortality," are "indestructible" and "immortal." Yet, Constable affirms,

> *Not one of these is ever used in the New Testament to describe the future condition of the lost.* Let our opponents, whether they follow Augustine or Origen, show us but one such term applied to the wicked, and we will allow that we are wrong.[59]

Others in Paul's day believed and taught universal annihilation. They held that when men died they perished completely and forever, both body and soul, and there was no future life of any kind for any person. The Epicureans represented such a view among the Greeks, and the Sadducees did among the Jews. "Now," asks Constable, "in what terms and by what language did such men set forth their views? *Simply and entirely by their application to all men alike of the very terms which the New Testament applies to the future punishment of the wicked.*"[60]

Such a mass of evidence calls for careful consideration. R. F. Weymouth, a Greek scholar and translator of the New Testament, wrote:

> My mind fails to conceive a grosser misinterpretation of language than when the five or six strongest words which the Greek tongue possesses, signifying "destroy," or "destruction," are explained to mean maintaining an everlasting but wretched existence. To translate black as white is nothing to this.[61]

---

58. White, *Life in Christ*, p. 361. White discusses the Greek words and their familiar usage in the philosophical dialogue concerning immortality on pages 362-364. Constable gives quotations from the same discourses in both Greek and English in his *Future Punishment*, pp. 42-45.

59. Constable, *Future Punishment*, p. 48.

60. Ibid., pp. 48-49.

61. As quoted by Edward White in *Life in Christ*, p. 365, from a letter. Modern examples of the practice Weymouth denounced include G. Stahlin's statement that "eschatological *apōleia* in its most terrible form is not, of course, annihilation or extinction of being; it is eternal *basanismos* [torment]" (Stahlin, "*Orgē*," *Theological Dictionary of the New Testament*,

Weymouth's challenge is daring and unequivocal. Constable and White also press their point with vigor. Is there a traditionalist answer which can meet this evidence fairly and squarely? The literature of the past does not reveal it. Can anyone stand in the gap? Are these conditionalist challengers enemy Goliaths wrongfully provoking God's people? Or are they modern Gideons sent to tear down a hollow Baal who they already know is powerless to make a response?

5:444). Another is O. Oepke's remark concerning *apōleia* ("destruction") that "What is meant here is not a simple extinction of existence, but an everlasting state of torment and death" (O. Oepke, *"Apōleia," Theological Dictionary of the New Testament,* 1:397). These are conclusions to be proved, not presuppositions from which to begin reading the Bible.

14

Final Punishment in the Rest of the New Testament

We have now briefly examined final punishment in the teaching of Jesus, as revealed in the great judgment on Calvary, and as presented in the writings of Paul. In this chapter we will summarize the evidence to be found in the rest of the New Testament.

James, Hebrews and the sermons found in Acts all speak from a "Jewish" standpoint and may present such teaching as was commonly given or received within a Palestinian Messianic community. Hebrews may be written by someone outside Palestine, and Luke of course was a Gentile; but the generalization still has merit. Peter, Jude and John also are Hebrews of Palestinian origin, but they evidently address their works to churches composed of either Gentiles or Diaspora Jews. The Epistles of 2 Peter and Jude are very much alike, and both use apocalyptic language as a vehicle for expression.

Revelation is commonly called the Apocalypse (from the Greek word meaning a "revelation") and gives its name to other literature which shares its thoroughly-characteristic style. In past years certain scholars looked largely to pagan or Gentile literature for help in deciphering Revelation's symbols. More and more today, however, they are recognizing the immense dependence this book has on the Old Testament itself.[1] Second Peter, Jude or possibly the book of Revelation were in all likelihood the last New Testament books to be written.

---

1. Numerous quotations could be given from theologians and commentators alike. We will offer some of those statements later, noting here that not only Revelation but the entire New

Hebrews

The authorship, audience, time and place of origin of Hebrews are all still in question.[2] Internal evidence suggests that this sermonic exhortation was written for Hebrew-Christian believers who at some time beyond their initial conversion and experience of the new life have second thoughts about the commitment they have made—and what they have left behind. The author constantly explains the new covenant in terms of the old one it has superseded. He uses Old Testament Scripture frequently, and he always points to Jesus Christ. In the matter of final punishment the book of Hebrews also speaks with Jesus Christ in view—in terms and pictures well familiar to any who have read the Old Testament.

Hebrews 2:2, 3. Because Jesus is so much greater than the angels in His person and in His position, His hearers are under special responsibility. Moses' law was mediated by angels (Acts 7:38; Gal. 3:19), and its violators were punished severely. "How shall we escape if we ignore such a great salvation . . . announced by the Lord?" the writer here asks. The answer is obvious—there will be no escape. This passage gives no details of that terrible and certain punishment, but it does make those two points plain.

Some have argued that this punishment "worse than death" must be everlasting conscious torment. That is a possibility—so far as the silence of this passage goes—but it is not the only possibility. Jesus' warning that God can destroy body and soul in hell reminds us that God is able to destroy *totally* and *forever*. Even the Mosaic executioners could not do that. Even capital punishment now will be as nothing compared to the horror of rising in the resurrection unto

---

Testament from Jesus onward builds on the foundation of Old Testament teaching and eschatology. This is taken for granted in most areas by biblical theologians, but it has been overlooked in most traditionalist literature when it comes to interpreting New Testament symbols and terms describing final punishment. Evangelicals who hold a high view of Scripture surely should lead the way in making this relationship clear in theory and useful in practice. Instead, they have often talked as if the Old Testament had little or nothing to offer, then have turned to the uninspired intertestamental literature to give content to New Testament language. Without doubt, that literature must be considered (and considered *carefully*—it has its own surprises!), but it ought never to hold the uppermost position over the Old Testament Word of God.

2. I have attempted a popular summary of these matters in *Our Man In Heaven: An Exposition of the Epistle to the Hebrews*, pp. 11-14.

condemnation only to perish forever in the second and final death. Yet even that is not all the punishment involved, as Hebrews itself later will make clear.

Hebrews 6:1, 2. The resurrection of the dead (*anastaseōs nekrōn*, not *ek tōn nekrōn*) is a foundational teaching of Christianity, as is the doctrine of eternal judgment. Both resurrection and judgment are eschatological events—part of the end-time agenda. Yet both have already started in the case of Jesus of Nazareth (Heb. 9:27, 28).[3] A great day of reckoning is coming when all who have lived will rise to hear God's final word of judgment on their lives. This point is so integral to true Christianity that our author here calls it "elementary."

Regardless of the precise nature of hell, there is absolutely no argument between conditionalists and traditionalists on this point.[4] Biblical orthodoxy requires a final, universal resurrection and judgment

---

3. This is one key to understanding the gospel principle of justification by faith and certainly a key to Hebrews 9:27, 28 in its larger context. The passage and theme are the subject of exposition in my little booklet, *One Life, Death and Judgment*.

4. Harold E. Guillebaud, traditionalist turned conditionalist, wrote: "We are living in days when the awful possibilities of human wickedness are being revealed as they have not been for centuries, and faith would have a hard task indeed, if it could not be sure that God will demand a full account for all the abominable cruelties and wrongs that are done on earth. And this would be impossible, if the only alternative to eternal life were a painless end to existence at the time of bodily death. The resurrection to judgment, and the infliction of penal suffering, are absolutely essential to the justice of God" (Harold E. Guillebaud, *The Righteous Judge: A Study of the Biblical Doctrine of Everlasting Punishment*, p. 65).

Henry Constable, author of the conditionalist classic, *Duration and Nature of Future Punishment*, stressed the same point, sharply distinguishing his position from that which denies that the wicked will rise to face judgment. Constable wrote: "We have no sympathy with those who deny the resurrection of the wicked. We know that there are writers who hold our view of the destruction of the ungodly, who also . . . hold that they will never rise to judgment. . . . But now, once for all, we disavow any connection or sympathy with them on this point. We think their view false, and mischievous in the extreme. . . . For ourselves, we have no doubt that the resurrection of the wicked is taught as plainly as that of the just, and that if we give up the one we may quite as well give up the other" (pp. 78-79).

In spite of such statements, traditionalist authors often lump together all who question the received understanding of final punishment. According to Frank S. Mead's *Handbook of Denominations in the United States*, the Advent Christian Church, the Church of God (General Conference) and the Primitive Advent Christian Church all hold to the view, expressed by Constable and Guillebaud, that the wicked will rise to face God in judgment and finally be exterminated in the lake of fire (following the degree of penal suffering set by divine justice). The Seventh-day Adventists hold the same view, which, because of their numbers, is generally associated with their name (pp. 20-22). The so-called Jehovah's Witnesses, on the other hand, hold that the incorrigibly wicked who have died will never be resurrected at all; their only "hell" is the grave (p. 156; see *Let God Be True*, pp. 283-291).

Donald Bloesch overlooks this important distinction and makes Seventh-day Adventists of the Jehovah's Witnesses; Jon Braun errs the other direction and implies that all but traditionalists hold the Jehovah's Witness position (Donald G. Bloesch, *Essentials of Evangelical Theology*, 2:219; Jon E. Braun, *Whatever Happened to Hell?* p. 49).

before God which issues in opposing verdicts of everlasting consequence. Such "catholic" creeds as the Apostles' Creed and the Nicene Creed go no further.

Judgment is "eternal" in quality since it belongs to the Age to Come. It is "eternal" in quantity since its *results* (though not its action) endure forever. On this point see the discussion regarding *aiōnios* and words of action in chapter 3.

Hebrews 6:8. Those who have tasted the new life in Christ are urged to go on to maturity. The author warns that apostasy is nothing short of recrucifying the Son of God (Heb. 6:4-6). If Jesus is not all He claimed to be—and therefore worthy of worship and allegiance even to death—He is neither a good man nor a person about whom one might choose to be indifferent, but rather a blasphemer to be denounced and Himself condemned. Apostasy reaffirms the judgment the Jewish scribes demanded and Pilate made official.

God blesses even farm land when it is fruitful (v. 7), and He will surely do no less for His people (vv. 9, 10). But unproductive land also serves to warn professing believers. For "land that produces thorns and thistles is worthless and is in danger of being cursed. In the end it will be burned."

Thorns and thistles are directly related to sin, as is the "curse" (Gen. 3:17, 18). Can the land here be anything other than a figure of "worthless" disciples who claim to know Christ but bear no fruit? God had used the figure before to warn His people, and there seems no reason why He is not here doing it again (Isa. 5:1ff; Matt. 21:33ff). Men do not burn a field of briars to cause pain but to destroy what is useless; and though the burnt-off land remains, those thorns and thistles are forever gone. Does this figure illustrate something directly opposite to what it pictures?

Harry Buis repeats the common view that Jehovah's Witness founder, Charles T. Russell, borrowed his doctrine of annihilation from the Seventh-day Adventists (Harry Buis, *The Doctrine of Eternal Punishment*, p. 145). Seventh-day Adventist author, LeRoy Edwin Froom, vehemently denies the association and disavows any connection with the "un-Christian positions" of Russell and his followers. He says Russell was indebted instead to the mainstream evangelical Advent Christian Church for his original thought, which he then perverted into its present form (LeRoy Edwin Froom, *The Conditionalist Faith Of Our Fathers*, 2:667). So long as the confusion of positions remains, however, Froom's historical technicality will do little to alleviate the common guilt by association. Prospects for this are not too bright since, according to Norman T. Burns, such confusion of resurrectionists and anti-resurrectionists has characterized much of the literature concerning mortalism for several centuries (Norman T. Burns, *Christian Mortalism from Tyndale to Milton*, pp. 13-14).

Hebrews 10:27-31. Christ's atonement sacrifice was offered once for all time. Those who come to God on its basis and merit may therefore come boldly, confidently and continually (Heb. 10:12-14, 19-25). But the same fact also carries a dire warning. For if someone rejects *this* offering, nowhere in the universe or in all human history is there another one God will approve and accept. Any who "deliberately keep on sinning" therefore thrust away their only hope (Heb. 10:26; cf. Num. 15:30, 31). For such people there remains "only a fearful expectation of judgment and of raging fire that will consume the enemies of God" (v. 27).

Now the author makes explicit what he hinted at earlier. Those who to the end brush off God's offers of mercy will then find only judgment—and a raging, consuming fire. A. W. Pink, a prolific Calvinist author and commentator, says this term denotes "the resistless, tormenting, destroying efficacy of God's terrible wrath, and emphasizes its dreadful fierceness."[5] We note that this fire consumes or devours God's enemies, an allusion to the fate of Nadab and Abihu, who were similarly devoured by fire from God (Lev. 10:2).[6] We met such a fire numerous places in the Old Testament as well as in the teaching of John the Baptist, Jesus and the apostle Paul.

Even before the fire there is the torture of awaiting sentence, already knowing the outcome; of being pursued with no hope of escape; of beholding the righteous Judge face to face with the full knowledge of willful rebellion and crimes. Earthly illustrations of such horror fill our literature. We remember the burdened criminal of *Crime and Punishment*, the runaway slave of *Uncle Tom's Cabin* or *Roots*, who desperately flees from bloodthirsty hounds. We think of the fugitive of Hugo's *Les Miserables*, with never a moment of rest without fear.

Who can imagine the dread the condemned murderer feels on the morning of his execution as he first wakes, then lies on his cot in anticipation like a man sunk in a silent pond, crushed beneath its stagnant weight? Or who can really describe the agony of the sentenced criminal standing blindfolded on the gallows, his heart pounding

---

5. Arthur W. Pink, *An Exposition of Hebrews*, p. 613.

6. Pink says the term "consuming fire" probably alludes to the case of Nadab and Abihu, but he then quotes J. Owen's statement that "this fire shall ever prey upon them, and never utterly consume them (ibid., p. 613). The result is an allusion which pictures the exact opposite of what it is used to illustrate!

wildly, drowning out the roll of drums which will be his final lullaby? Who can say *that* is not worse than the act of dying itself?

Yet how much worse—how infinitely worse—to face the God whose love one has knowingly spurned time and time again, to hear His judgment sentence echo across the vast and stark silence of eternity, and to see the consuming flames just ahead? We should understand this imagery symbolically and not literally, but God's symbols accurately portray the truth they express.[7]

Rebels who rejected the law of Moses "died without mercy" (v. 28). Again the author implies that a greater salvation carries greater responsibility, so those who reject it will be punished even "more severely" (v. 29). "It is a dreadful thing to fall into the hands of the living God" (v. 31).

Hebrews 10:39. Though the author warns his readers repeatedly against apostasy or unbelief, he also reassures them time and time again with expressions of confidence that they will do what is right. They are to persevere, for Habakkuk (Hab. 2:3, 4) had said that God is not pleased with shrinkers (Heb. 10:38). "But we are not of those who shrink back and are destroyed," our author writes, "but of those who believe and are saved." As we have seen other places already, "destruction" here also is opposed to being "saved." This is the same word (*apōleian*) Paul so often used.

Hebrews 12:25, 29. Again the contrast is made between old and new covenants, again in terms of accountability and ultimate punishment. "If they did not escape," the author asks, "how much less will we, if we turn away from Him who warns us from heaven?" The Epistle opened almost with such a question (Heb. 2:3), which it repeated (Heb. 10:29) and repeats again. The plain answer is that there is no escape.[8]

---

7. Traditionalists who say such a view is an "easy way out" not only pass over such Scripture passages as this one; they also fail to consider seriously the very real torment involved in the case the passage describes.

8. It is my conviction that there is no escape after this life, although such a respected Reformed author as Donald G. Bloesch feels the necessity to leave hell's door unlocked from the outside with the possibility at least that some there may be eventually restored. Bloesch says: "We do not wish to build fences around God's grace, however, and we do not preclude the possibility that some in hell might finally be translated into heaven" (Bloesch, *Essentials of Evangelical Theology*, 2:226).

We will develop the thought further in a later chapter on the subject, but it seems the traditionalist view will always carry the temptation for such "restoration" or Apocatastasis, if only

Verse 29 picks up on a thought expressed in Hebrews 10:27. There the author had spoken of "raging fire that will consume the enemies of God." Here he says "for our God is a consuming fire." We have seen already the thought that God's very holiness is a fire which consumes all that is not pure (Isa. 33:14; 2 Thess. 1:7). "As a fire consumes combustible matter cast into it, so God will destroy sinners," writes A. W. Pink.[9]

The expression "consuming fire" (*pyr katanaliskon*) occurs twice in Deuteronomy (Deut. 4:24; 9:3, LXX). Both verses have "your" God;[10] Hebrews has "our" God. Even the author takes this warning seriously. How dare we regard it less lightly than he?

James

James 1:15. Throughout his Epistle, James corrects and admonishes some who are long on words but short on work. If people today blame the devil for their sins, some known to James wanted to blame God. He corrects this error by fingering evil desire as the culprit. Desire, James says, conceives; then "it gives birth to sin; and sin, when it is full-grown, gives birth to death." Evil Desire may be enticing, and its offspring, Sin, may appear charming indeed; but when Sin matures and bears its own natural child, that child will surely be Death. What a horrible surprise—just imagine the stunned expression on the family's face as they look in the crib!

The figure is akin to Paul's when he says the one sowing to please the sinful nature will from it reap "corruption" (Gal. 6:8), a word used among other things for a miscarriage or abortion. The contrast in James is with verse 18—*God* gave *us* birth through the word of truth so we might be a firstfruit of His new creation. The new crea-

---

on the maxim that "where there's life there's hope." If hell's fire is truly irresistible ("unquenchable") and its results irreversible ("eternal") so that it is indeed a "consuming fire," there is no universalist or restorationist possibility. Then it becomes evident that "today is the day of salvation," and the gospel's offer of pardon is seen in all its urgency.

9. Pink, *An Exposition of Hebrews*, pp. 1102-1103. Pink elsewhere denies what he here states, so that in the end dogmatic theology triumphs over biblical exegesis. In their respective books advocating the traditionalist interpretation, Harry Buis and Jon Braun both completely ignore Hebrews 12:29 as well as the same picture every place it appears in Scripture.

10. Both passages in Deuteronomy refer to the Canaanites. Deuteronomy 9:3 says also that God will *exolethreuō* the Canaanites and the Israelites will *apollymi* them. Both verbs are applied to final punishment in the New Testament. The Canaanites were to be totally exterminated.

tion stands over against death; they are the two alternatives when the Present Age has passed away.

James 4:12. Our responsibility toward God's law ought to be obedience, not sitting in judgment. James both cautions and informs us when he writes:

> There is only one Lawgiver and Judge, the One who is able to save and destroy. But you—who are you to judge your neighbor?

Since God gave the law, only He has the right to call men into account regarding it. Besides, only God can bring to pass any judgment sentence—for good or for ill. The contrast here is between "save" and "destroy." Surely James is remembering the words of Jesus in Matthew 10:28, which see.[11]

James 5:1-6. "Misery" awaits the wicked rich. Corroded gold and silver will "eat your flesh like fire," James warns. Like the rich man of Luke 16:19-31, those James rebukes "have lived on earth in luxury and self-indulgence." Little did they know they were "fattening" themselves "in the day of slaughter." The well-spread banquet table appears in a different light to the man who knows he will be executed tomorrow! On the figure see Isaiah 3:11-26; Amos 4:1-3; especially Jude 10.

James 5:19, 20. Christians have a mutual responsibility to watch for the welfare of one another. "Whoever turns a sinner away from his error will save him from death and cover a multitude of sins." The New International Version has "him" for *psychē*, a common biblical usage, correcting the King James Version's "soul," which has been so long read in alien terms of Grecian dualism. "Salvation" is from "death." James nowhere hints that he really means anything else.

Four times James refers to the final outcome of sin. Twice it is "death," one time misery followed by "slaughter," once it is "destruction."

---

11. It is instructive to compare James' teaching throughout the Epistle with the words of Jesus as reported in the Gospels, particularly in Matthew's Sermon on the Mount.

Acts of the Apostles

Acts 3:23. For all its accounts of evangelism and summaries of apostolic proclamation, Acts says precious little about final punishment. Peter's warning here is the only actual statement I found on the subject in this book. The stress in the earliest preaching seems to have been on the blessings of salvation offered in the name of Jesus.

In Acts 3:22, 23, Peter paraphrases Deuteronomy 18:15, 19. Jesus is *the* Prophet of all prophets, and Moses had warned that if anyone does not listen to God's prophet, God Himself "will call him to account" ("will require it of him," KJV, RSV, NASB). Peter changes the statement to the third person and uses a different, passive verb: such a one "will be completely cut off from among his people." This word (*exolothreuō*) means "to destroy utterly, to root out" according to Arndt and Gingrich.[12] A cognate word is translated as the *destroyer* two other places (1 Cor. 10:10; Heb. 11:28).

Peter's word is the ordinary translation in the Septuagint for the Hebrew *karath*, the usual Old Testament verb for capital punishment or total extermination. It is the fate prescribed for the man who refuses circumcision (Gen. 17:14), for those who eat leaven during the Passover period (Exod. 12:15, 19), and for whoever fails to bring his offering to the Tent of Meeting in the wilderness (Lev. 17:4, 9). It is also used of God's destruction in the Flood (Gen. 9:11). The same word describes the fate of evildoers in general in the Old Testament,[13] and it is applied specifically to the Messiah, who would later suffer the fate due to sinners (Dan. 9:26).[14]

The verb appears only here in the New Testament, where it "signifies the utterness of the destruction from the people," though not necessarily more than capital punishment. "If the word has any eschatological bearing," observes *The Expositor's Greek Testament*, "it would support the theory of annihilation more easily."[15]

---

12. William F. Arndt and F. Wilbur Gingrich, trs., *A Greek-English Lexicon of the New Testament and Other Early Christian Literature*, p. 276.

13. In Psalm 37:9, 22, 28, 34, 38 and Proverbs 2:22 among others.

14. The English text also says the Suffering Servant will be "cut off" (Isa. 53:8), but that is a different Hebrew verb (*gazar*) from this.

15. "The Acts of the Apostles," *The Expositor's Greek Testament*, ed. W. Robertson Nicoll, vol. 2, p. 118.

First Peter

Peter's first Epistle can be described as a combination handbook and travel guide for Christian pilgrims who are passing through this world en route to their heavenly home. Several passages suggest a connection with the Christian initiation of water baptism. Peter is especially concerned that the new believers live holy and fruitful lives before their pagan neighbors and that they be ready to endure suffering if God calls them to that. Over and over the book mentions "suffering" and "glory," and always in that order. The emphasis is on Christian faith and life; little is said about the end of the wicked. One passage touches on that at the close of chapter 4.

1 Peter 4:17, 18. If you suffer for Christ's sake, Peter urges, do not be ashamed but praise God for the privilege (cf. Matt. 5:11, 12; Phil. 1:29).

> For it is time for judgment to begin with the family of God; and if it begins with us, what will the outcome be for those who do not obey the gospel of God? And,
>
> > "If it is hard for the righteous to be saved,
> > what will become of the ungodly and the sinner?"

Again we meet the principle that great privilege brings great responsibility. In saying that judgment is about to begin with the house of God, Peter brings an Old Testament incident to mind. In the days of Judah's captivity Ezekiel saw a vision which explained why the tragedy had occurred. He observed idolatry in the very precincts of the temple (Ezek. 8). God's glory rose from above the cherubim and prepared to desert the premises (Ezek. 9:3). All who grieved for the abominations received a mark on their foreheads for protection; all others were to be slaughtered without compassion or pity (Ezek. 9:4-6). Then came the order: "Begin at My sanctuary" (Ezek. 9:6).

The time has come again, Peter says, for judgment. Again it goes out from God's *house.*[16] Persecution proves the faith of some, the essential unbelief of others. In either case it manifests the quality of

---

16. The Greek has *oikos*, by which Peter evidently refers to God's *family*, the church. The New International Version obscures the Old Testament background, however, by interpreting the word ("family") rather than translating ("house" = "temple" in Ezekiel) it.

the profession. It also serves as a warning to the persecutors, as another Old Testament prophet of the Exile had also made clear.

Jeremiah also explains the captivity to Israel and reveals that it will be for 70 years (Jer. 25:1-11). At the end of that time God says He will utterly destroy Babylon forever, then punish all the nations of the earth (Jer. 25:12-16). If pagan kingdoms hesitate to receive this word of judgment, God points them to Israel's own fate as proof that He is in earnest. "See," He says, "I am beginning to bring disaster on the city that bears My Name, and will you indeed go unpunished?" (Jer. 25:29). If God judges His own people, how certain that He will judge their enemies!

Peter now makes the same point. If judgment "begins with us," he asks, viewing the tribulations through which believers must here pass, "what will the outcome be for those who do not obey the gospel of God?" In context, God judges His family by present afflictions, though that judgment relates to the final judgment as we have already seen. Present judgments also come at times on the wicked (throughout the Old Testament are temporal judgments; we note the destruction of Jerusalem and Rome in the New), but these are also related to the issues of the last day. This passage should be included in our study, although it adds no additional content to our understanding of final doom.

Peter's next statement shows that he views present troubles, though it may also suggest a final reckoning. He quotes a proverb to illustrate his point. "If it is hard for the righteous to be saved, what will become of the ungodly and the sinner?" This is the Septuagint translation of Proverbs 11:31. Even the godly must pass along a rough and thorny trail on their way to final salvation, and they have the gift of faith to sustain them. How will those who do not know God ever make it through life? Even in this world, the implication is, God's people are blessed in their suffering.

The Hebrew proverb was slightly different. The New International Version translates it: "If the righteous receive their due on earth, how much more the ungodly and the sinner?" In light of the teaching of both Psalms and Proverbs concerning the end of the wicked, this statement may well point to future punishment. Surely the time is coming that the wicked will be recompensed—and in such a manifest way that faith in God's justice will be thoroughly vindicated.

The entire passage begins with Old Testament concepts (from proverb and from prophet) which it gives a Christian application.

There is no basis whatsoever for the notion, sometimes expressed on the text, that those who are saved will "barely squeak into heaven." All who enter there will do so through faith in Jesus Christ and not by their own record. For that reason they will receive "a rich welcome" accompanied by "praise, glory and honor" (2 Pet. 1:11; 1 Pet. 1:7).

Second Peter

Liberal scholars dispute both the traditional date and authorship of this Epistle, but conservative scholars point to their lack of conclusive proof as well as to the care taken by the early councils to exclude unauthentic works from the canon. We accept it as from the apostle whose name it bears and as a general sequel to 1 Peter.

Peter responds to skeptics who scoff at Christ's delayed return. He reassures believers of the reliability of the apostles' eyewitness testimony and of the divine origin of Scripture. And he assures them that licentious and spurious (false) teachers will certainly come to a terrible but appropriate end. There is an obvious correspondence between 2 Peter 2 and the Epistle of Jude in actual wording as well as in thought. We will consider them separately with this in mind.

2 Peter 2:1-21. Pseudo-teachers bringing seductive heresies will finally meet condemnation (v. 3) and swift destruction (vv. 1, 3). Both "condemnation" (*krima*) and "destruction" (*apōleia*) are familiar New Testament words for the end of the lost. Jesus used the first and Paul the second. Each expresses an aspect of God's sovereignty, who alone can recall even the dead to give account and who alone can totally and eternally destroy. Neither word carries any inherent meaning of everlasting conscious torment, although that meaning has been read into "destruction" since Tertullian and Augustine.

Peter gives three great examples to illustrate the certainty of his warning. Two of them we examined at length while considering the Old Testament—namely, the Flood, which destroyed the old world (v. 5), and the destruction of Sodom and Gomorrah by fire from heaven (v. 6). Throughout the Bible we have found these two events mentioned time after time, standard and favorite prototypes of God's judgment against sin. Each case involved a total destruction with sinners exterminated and their sinful way of life annihilated forever. When evildoers obstinately refused to turn loose their wickedness, even with God's judgment beating at the door, God had no other choice: sin and sinners perished together. (This is a thought worth pondering when someone suggests that sinners in hell will continue to sin forever, so that both sin and sinners are eternal, only out of sight.)

Peter particularly displays Sodom and Gomorrah as an example of final condemnation and the end of the wicked. God condemned the twin cities, he says, "by burning them to ashes, and made them an example of what is going to happen to the ungodly" (v. 6). Other translations do not change the sense. The Revised Standard Version says that "by turning . . . to ashes He condemned them to extinction"; the King James Version says "turning . . . into ashes, condemned with an overthrow."

Peter's verb (*tephroō*) is a rare word found only here in the New Testament. Moulton-Milligan cite nonbiblical sources where the word describes an eruption of the volcano, Vesuvius, and they say the verb means either "cover with ashes" or "reduce to ashes."[17] Thayer's lexicon has "reduce to ashes," and Arndt-Gingrich suggest "cover with or reduce to ashes." *The Expositor's Greek Testament* prefers "cover up with" over "reduce to."[18] This is the same *picture* we met in Isaiah 66:24, Malachi 4:1-3, Matthew 3:10, 12 and other places in both Testaments. It portrays total destruction by fire from God, a scene strengthened by the adjectives "unquenchable" (it cannot be stopped in its destruction) and "eternal" (its effects will never be reversed). Peter's language here is so clear and forceful that traditionalist authors are simply at a loss to comment on it at all.[19]

As a third illustration of God's ability to hold the ungodly for judgment, Peter cites the fallen angels. God sent even them to "hell," where they are held in "gloomy dungeons" for judgment. These fallen angels held special fascination for certain apocalyptic writers between the Testaments; we observed several references to them in the

---

17. James Hope Moulton and George Milligan, *The Vocabulary of the Greek Testament Illustrated from the Papyri and Other Non-Literary Sources*, p. 632.

18. Joseph Henry Thayer, tr., *A Greek-English Lexicon of the New Testament*, p. 621; Arndt and Gingrich, *Greek-English Lexicon*, p. 821; R. H. Strachan, "The Second Epistle General of Peter," *The Expositor's Greek Testament*, ed. Nicoll, vol. 5, p. 135.

19. Neither Harry Buis (*The Doctrine of Eternal Punishment*) nor Jon Braun (*Whatever Happened to Hell?*) deal with this passage at all. Nor does Donald G. Bloesch in his chapter, "Heaven and Hell" (*Essentials of Evangelical Theology*, vol. 2). Even R. C. H. Lenski, whose exposition is frequently marked by concern with the most minute detail, is oddly silent at this point (R. C. H. Lenski, *The Interpretation of the Epistles of St. Peter, St. John and St. Jude*).

books attributed to Enoch. Peter appears to reflect this literature more than once, and Jude quotes from Enoch by name (Jude 14, 15). Peter probably has the fallen angels in mind when he writes of the "spirits in prison" in his first Epistle (1 Pet. 3:19, 20, 22).[20]

He literally says here that they are kept in *Tartarus*, for which most English versions strangely put "hell." The word appears only once in Scripture, here borrowed from the literature of classical Greek. In the *Odyssey* (11. 575) Homer makes Tartarus the place where the Titans were enchained for endless punishment. Both Homer and Plato also call the place Hades, which is the Septuagint's usual choice in translating the Hebrew *sheol*.[21] Whatever one might make of this passage and the angels in Tartarus, it adds nothing to our understanding of the final doom of human sinners, since (1) it concerns angels, not men, and (2) it speaks of detention before the judgment rather than punishment following.[22]

After a description of the pseudo-teachers' crimes, Peter returns to their punishment. Like brute beasts "born only to be caught and destroyed," these men too "will perish" (v. 12). Both "destroy" and "perish" translate the same word (*phthora*, see Gal. 6:8). Peter pictures brute beasts and wicked men coming to the same final end, though the men must first face God's judgment, sentence and consuming fire.

"Blackest darkness is reserved for them" (v. 17). Jude completes the simile, comparing the spurious teachers to "wandering stars, for whom blackest darkness has been reserved forever" (Jude 13). Like the comparison with Sodom and the death of brute beasts, this figure also suggests and harmonizes with the idea of final, total extinction.

The apostate's fate is worse than that of one who never knew the

---

20. This is R. T. France's conclusion, following a thorough and critical examination of the passage, in "Exegesis in Practice: Two Samples," *New Testament Interpretation: Essays on Principles and Methods*, pp. 264-281.

21. A. R. Fausset, *The Englishman's Critical and Expository Bible Cyclopaedia*, p. 281; William G. T. Shedd, *The Doctrine of Endless Punishment*, p. 42.

22. Buis describes the language of this chapter as "very forceful" but makes almost no comment on it at all (Buis, *The Doctrine of Eternal Punishment*, p. 45). Braun ignores everything in the chapter except the word "Tartarus," which he calls "extremely illuminating on the subject of the judgment of God and ensuing punishment," and on which he writes more than a page (Braun, *Whatever Happened to Hell?* pp. 151-153).

The New International Version and Revised Standard Version ("continuing their punishment") represent the Greek better than the King James Version ("to be punished") in verse 9. This idea, also found in Enoch, has to do with angels, and it can be extended to men only on the basis of more evidence than this passage gives.

way of righteousness (2 Pet. 2:20-22). We are reminded of similar comparative statements in the Epistle to the Hebrews (Heb. 2:2, 3; 10:27-31; 12:25). Traditionalists and conditionalists affirm together that there will be degrees of punishment—the first, by varying external circumstances or internal sensitivity to them; the second, by length of time in hell prior to the second death. Another interpretation of the passage sees an entirely different point: the difficulty or impossibility of reclaiming one who has rejected known truth (cf. Heb. 6:4-6; 12:16-17). It certainly does not require or even support eternal conscious torment.

2 Peter 3:6-9. Scoffers conclude that "everything goes on as it has" and mock at Christ's promised coming (v. 4). Peter reminds his readers that the same opinion was expressed by the generation which perished in the Flood and that God's judgment again will crash into man's comfortable and routine way of life. Once before, the world "was deluged and destroyed" by water at God's command. By the same word "the present heavens and earth are reserved for fire, being kept for the day of judgment and destruction of ungodly men."

The implication here is that the fire which will melt the elements will also accomplish the destruction of ungodly men. "The 'tares' are to be 'burned' on the field where they grew."[23] Whether Peter speaks of the old world being "destroyed" or the future end of ungodly men ("destruction," v. 7; "perish," v. 9), he uses the same verb (*apollymi*) or noun (*apōleia*). Both words were among Paul's most familiar terms for the end of the wicked.

Peter's alternatives of repentance or perishing (v. 9) echo a similar warning of Jesus Himself (Luke 13:3). The disciple remembers the Master's words, and the Spirit leads him into further truth than Jesus had clearly spoken on earth (John 14:26; 16:12-14).

Jude

Jude 4-7. We have noted already the great similarity between 2 Peter 2 and Jude. Spurred on by the infiltration of some "godless men, who change the grace of our God into a license for immorality and deny Jesus Christ our only Sovereign and Lord," Jude urges his

---

23. Edward White, *Life in Christ* . . . , p. 352.

readers everywhere to "contend for the faith that [God has] once for all entrusted to the saints" (vv. 3, 4). God will surely punish such men, and He is well able to guard all who abide in His love. The first fact takes away frustration; the second removes anxiety.

Like Peter, Jude points to past examples of God's righteous judgment. Unbelieving Israel was "destroyed" (*apollymi*) in the wilderness (cf. 1 Cor. 10:5-11; Heb. 3:16-19). Angels who sinned have been kept in "everlasting chains" in darkness, awaiting judgment. Sodom and Gomorrah in particular "serve as an example of those who suffer the punishment of eternal fire."

There is some question as to the nature of Sodom's "example." Lenski says these cities are an "indication or sign (not 'example,' our versions), that points like a finger to 'eternal fire.'"[24] The New International Version could be read this way, as it inserts "of those who" between Peter's "serve as an example" and "suffer . . . punishment of eternal fire." Bietenhard calls attention to one contemporary Jewish idea that the people of Sodom and Gomorrah were even then suffering fiery punishment.[25] One might read this into the Revised Standard Version's wording: "serve as an example by undergoing a punishment of eternal fire."

Neither view seems best to fit the evidence. Jude's word translated "example" (*deigma*) simply does not mean "indication or sign," as Lenski suggests, but rather (as English versions agree) "example." Moulton-Milligan find numerous references in nonbiblical Greek where the word is used of "samples of corn and produce."[26] Though the precise word appears only here in the New Testament, several other forms of it are used elsewhere. Yet *deigmatizō* (Col. 2:15), *paradeigmatizō* (Matt. 1:19; Heb. 9:9) and *hypodeigma* (John 13:15; Heb. 4:11; 8:5; 9:23; James 5:10; 2 Pet. 2:6) all speak of "examples," whether of good or bad. Nor does Jude say that Sodomites are a vague and general example of those who actually will suffer the punishment of eternal fire, but that they themselves exemplify that very punishment.

There is no biblical hint that Sodom and Gomorrah's inhabitants presently endure conscious torment; several passages, in fact, make a

---

24. Lenski, *Interpretation*, p. 625.

25. H. Bietenhard, "Fire," *The New International Dictionary of New Testament Theology*, 1:657.

26. Moulton-Milligan, *Vocabulary of the Greek Testament*, p. 137.

point of their abiding extinction.[27] One of the Jewish texts cited for
the view actually teaches the opposite, and another reflects a source
well outside mainstream Judaism.[28]

In the end, Jude says just what he seems to say, and the King James
Version may translate it most faithfully after all. The sinners of
Sodom are "set forth for an example, suffering the vengeance of eternal fire." The passage *defines* "eternal fire." It is a fire from God
which destroys sinners totally and forever. The Sodomites illustrate
it, and the ungodly had better take note of the warning. Peter says
the same thing in unequivocal language in his remark that God condemned these cities "by burning them to ashes, and made them an example of what is going to happen to the ungodly" (2 Pet. 2:6). Jude
will bring our thoughts back to Sodom's fire a little later.

Jude 13. These wicked teachers are "wandering stars, for whom
blackest darkness has been reserved forever." See the remarks on
2 Peter 2:17.

Jude 23. God is able to keep His own people from falling, Jude
says, and he urges his readers to build themselves up, pray in the
Spirit, and keep themselves in God's love (vv. 20, 21, 24). They are
also to care for one another: be tender with some; "snatch others
from the fire and save them; to others show mercy, mixed with fear
—hating even the clothing stained by corrupted flesh."

The figure of being snatched from the fire comes from Amos 4:11.
The prophet reminds a remnant: "You were like a burning stick
snatched from the fire" when God overthrew some as He once had
Sodom and Gomorrah. When total destruction and extinction came
on some, Amos says to the survivors, you were snatched from the
fire in the bare nick of time—like a stick already beginning to burn!

---

27. Old Testament allusions to Sodom's destruction include Deut. 29:23; Isa. 13:19-22; 34:10;
Jer. 49:18; 50:40; Lam. 4:6; Zeph. 2:9.

28. J. B. Mayor (*The Expositor's Greek Testament*, ed. Nicoll, vol. 5, p. 261) cites Wisdom
10:7 and a passage from Philo. The Wisdom text says of Sodom: "To whose wickedness a
smoking waste still witnesseth, and plants bearing fair fruit that cometh not to ripeness . . ."
This pictures Sodom as a desolate ruin (the view Abraham saw the morning after), not the
Sodomites in fiery torment as Mayor suggests. Philo's opinion is better documented, but he
does not represent a majority opinion within Judaism either in Palestine or among the
Diaspora.

The legend of fruit growing at Sodom's site which crumbled at a touch was still current in the
fifth century, since Augustine refers to it in book 21 of his *The City of God* (see Appendix A).

The same language reappears in Zechariah 3:2. God there says to Satan: "The Lord rebuke you! . . . Is not this man [Joshua the high priest] a burning stick snatched from the fire?" Here the "fire" was the Babylonian Exile, from which many who entered never returned. Joshua had been spared, and Satan now seeks his destruction.

Jude's statement concerning "the clothing stained by corrupted flesh" may well reflect this same passage in Zechariah. The next verses tell how Joshua stood dressed in filthy clothes before the angel. These are removed and replaced by rich garments and a clean turban. The angel tells Joshua: "See, I have taken away your sin, and I will put rich garments on you" (Zech. 3:3-5). There is an obvious connection between this symbolic incident and the New Testament teaching regarding being "clothed" with Christ and dressed in perfect righteousness to stand before God (Gal. 3:27; Eph. 4:22-24; Phil. 3:9; Rev. 3:18).

For Jude, those "snatched from the fire" are given "eternal life" (v. 21). To be sure, "life" means far *more* than mere existence, but it includes that as well; why should not its denial exclude everything "life" encompasses, existence included? Jude's picture of contrasting fates portrays no survival whatsoever for those thrown into the fire. He has said earlier that "eternal fire" (the opposite of "eternal life") is the punishment which befell Sodom and Gomorrah. It is everlasting destruction, blackest darkness forever. In this he agrees with Peter, Hebrews, James, Acts, Paul, Jesus and the entire Old Testament.

First John

John says relatively little about final punishment in his Gospel, as we noted earlier, and the same is true of his Epistles. Of the three letters, only the first touches on the subject, and it but once.

1 John 5:16, 17. "There is a sin that leads to death," John writes, "and there is sin that does not lead to death" (v. 17). Whatever the distinction, the outcomes are made clear. They are "death" and "not death." One is either dead or he is not dead. Over against death stands life. In our present experience there is no sharper contrast than life and death. God could not possibly use a clearer, more expressive word than "death," or one grasped any easier by common people of all times and places. Paul spoke of "death" as the end of sin, and he colored that word with terms like "corruption" and "destruction."

Even figurative usages depend on an actual, literal sense of words. Whenever someone uses "death" as a figure, it is because he wishes to convey the feelings conjured by our literal understanding of the term. Nowhere does Scripture indicate that it uses these words in a figurative sense when it applies them to the end of the wicked. Few things are stated more often throughout the whole Bible than that the wicked will "die," "perish," "be destroyed," pass away, be no more, and be forgotten forever.

The fact that we deal with the language of divine law and justice only strengthens the case for giving the words their most essential and ordinary meanings. Constable stresses this point at some length.

> The accepted principle of interpretation among mankind is this: "that *all language relative to law and jurisprudence*, all language descriptive of the sanctions of government, all language setting forth the penalties of crime and disobedience, *is to be accepted in its primary sense and in no other.* . . . Thus when death is announced as a penalty for crime, no controversy would for an instant be admitted as to its meaning. No lawyer, for or against the criminal, would search for dramatic or poetic secondary senses. . . . A secondary sense may be more usual and more proper *elsewhere, but not here.* Poetry and the drama, the literature of passion, imagination, and feeling, may use these terms differently; but their use is not to affect in the smallest degree *the interpretation of a law.* Here we take our stand. Here we are on sure and steady ground. The terms we have been discussing are the terms of the *Divine Law:* the jurisprudence we have been discussing is *God's jurisprudence.* The Great Governor is laying before His subjects the penalties which attach to sin. He speaks to them in the only language they can understand—their own language. He puts no new rules of interpretation upon it when He addresses them. He accepts, adopts, and uses the language of those to whom He speaks. We can then only interpret the divine penalty for sin in the sense which man has put upon all such penalties, viz. in the primary sense."[29]

The Book of Revelation

In the very nature of things, talk about final punishment involves realities which our present knowledge based on experience cannot reach. The end of the world, the visible appearance of Jesus Christ,

---

29. Constable, *Future Punishment*, p. 54.

judgment before Almighty God, the new heavens and earth on one hand and the lake of fire on the other—these all transcend any categories our finite minds have yet learned to comprehend. How can we even imagine what it means that this created order of space and time will actually come to an end? Then will come *terminus* and *telos* alike. The curtain will open then, and all humankind will enter the silent stage of a vast and starless eternity, there to carry out the final ritual which will unmask every character and make every mystery plain. But the time is not yet—though the Spirit testifies that it is at the door. And when all the words are said, we still cannot know what it will be, although the door opened for a moment in the darkness of Golgotha, and the unearthly light of the Age to Come flashed momentarily through the stone door of the Easter tomb.

Little wonder that when Scripture speaks of Last Things, it speaks in symbols, directing its message to our emotions as much and perhaps even more than to our mind. Jeremias bluntly states, "When Jesus speaks of the consummation he always uses symbols."[30] Ridderbos says the same about Paul's teaching on the final events. He writes:

> Paul's pronouncements here bear the character of flashing, prophetic warnings, which illuminate for an instant the awful seriousness of the great future, not of a doctrine that in fixed order and piece by piece indicates the component parts of the picture of the future and combines them with each other into an integral unity. This applies in particular to the punitive judgment on unbelievers and the ungodly. Paul declares the certainty of this judgment in an unmistakable way, in many respects with words that have been derived from the Old Testament preaching of judgment. He speaks of it as ruin, death, payment with an eternal destruction . . . ; wrath, indignation, tribulation, anguish. . . . But nowhere is the how, the where or the how long "treated" as a separate "subject" of Christian doctrine in the epistles of Paul that have been preserved to us.[31]

What is true of Jesus and Paul is even more obvious in the last book of the Bible. Robert H. Mounce insists that "the essential ques-

---

30. Joachim Jeremias, *The Parables of Jesus*, p. 221.

31. Herman N. Ridderbos, *Paul: An Outline of His Theology*, p. 554. C. F. D. Moule mentions Paul's discussion of "the unimaginable dimensions of the Christian verities" in connection with last things (C. F. D. Moule, *Journal of Theological Studies*, New Series 15, no. 1, p. 4, quoted by C. Leslie Mitton, "Life after Death: The After-Life in the New Testament," *Expository Times*, August 1965, p. 334).

tion" in approaching a study of Revelation is the kind of literature we are dealing with, so that an "informed sensitivity to the thought forms and vocabulary of apocalyptic is the *sine qua non* of satisfactory exegesis." Many contemporary writers have lacked that insight, Mounce charges, and as a result they have fallen into "either an indefensible literalism or a highly imaginative subjectivism."[32]

To say that Revelation uses sign language to tell its story does not detract from the seriousness of what it says. Liberals and literalists alike have misunderstood the evangelical's approach at this point according to Harry Buis. "The liberal must recognize that he fails to understand our position when he thinks we take these symbols literally," Buis writes. On the other hand, "the ultra conservative literalist must be made to understand that we have in no way abandoned the belief in eternal punishment when we advocate such a symbolical interpretation."[33]

Merely shunning literalism does not give us license to invent our own meanings for John's graphic visions, however, as Mounce has reminded us already. Even John did not invent his symbols, nor were they original with the book of Revelation. They belonged to what was almost a language of its own, drawn from an ancient tradition which had thrived already for 200 years, with biblical origins even more ancient. Beasley-Murray compares this "apocalyptic" imagery to the stereotypes of the modern political cartoon. Long usage has made certain figures familiar around the world, he says, pointing to Uncle Sam and John Bull, to the Russian Bear, the British Lion, the American Eagle and the Chinese Dragon. In a similar way, he explains, "Jewish apocalyptists had a veritable art gallery of well-known images from which to draw in their portrayals of the future."[34]

A century ago most critical scholars tried to decode Revelation on the basis of pagan mythologies, seeking parallels in the literature of

---

32. Robert H. Mounce, *The Book of Revelation,* The New International Commentary on the New Testament, p. 12. John Wenham reminds us: "Twentieth-century man does not and cannot come to the Bible with an empty mind. The very word 'hell' comes to us laden with literary and artistic associations of many centuries. Platonic philosophy clearly had a great influence on Christian thought and Greek mythology on Christian art" (John W. Wenham, *The Goodness of God,* pp. 27-28).

33. Buis, *The Doctrine of Eternal Punishment,* p. 131.

34. G. R. Beasley-Murray, "The Contribution of the Book of Revelation to the Christian Belief in Immortality," *Scottish Journal of Theology* 27, no. 1 (February 1974): 78.

Rome and Greece, of Persia and Babylon and Egypt. Seventy-five years ago they were beginning to unravel the mysteries of the Jewish literature between the Testaments, literature so like that of the Apocalypse that to describe it they coined the adjective "apocalyptic." Now that the initial excitement of discovery has somewhat passed, they are taking a closer look at that literature and are noting the differences as well as the similarities between it and the Revelation given to John.

Mounce lists some of the differences. The author of Revelation gives his own name—"John"; he speaks as one who is himself a prophet; he sees history as having both purpose and a center, with God firmly in charge of it all. Apocalyptic literature did not carry the true author's name, was often written in the name of someone else possessing more authority (pseudonymous), and perceived no meaning in history or purposeful climax based on past events.[35]

For evangelical Christians, however, the greatest difference between Revelation and intertestamental apocalyptic literature is more than format, style or even world-view. It is a matter of origin. For the Apocalypse written by John came from the Spirit of the living Lord, the same Spirit of prophecy which inspired the Old Testament penmen. And those Old Testament writings, more than any other literature of any description, are still our best guide to understanding the sometimes bizarre characters and the often puzzling events this final book of Scripture lays before our blinking eyes. Evangelical scholars in particular are beginning to emphasize the predominant place the Old Testament holds in the symbols of Revelation.

Beasley-Murray notes that John's portrayals of divine judgment "employ traditional images, above all those connected with the typology of the second exodus—hence his elaboration of the plagues of Egypt which fall on the kingdom of the new Pharaoh." Sodom's ancient fate is also reflected here. Sometimes the figures are literally inconsistent, Beasley-Murray observes, but even then "their use of the Scripture precedents for judgment is comprehensible."[36] This is only true, however, in the light of the Old Testament.

"Revelation is rooted in the Old Testament," says *Eerdman's Handbook to the Bible*. "This is where we find the clues to the mean-

---

35. Mounce, *The Book of Revelation*, pp. 23-24.
36. Beasley-Murray, "Contribution of Revelation," p. 92.

ing of the various symbols—comparing scripture with scripture."[37] William Hendriksen stresses the same point. "It must be understood," he begins, "that the book of Revelation is rooted in and is in full harmony with the rest of the sacred scriptures and must be explained on the basis of the clear teaching of the Bible everywhere."[38] Ferrell Jenkins believes that a major reason so many Christians have difficulty understanding Revelation is that "they lack an awareness of the use of the Old Testament which permeates the book." Yet it is not enough to state the fact, he points out. Mere awareness of the phenomenon does not solve the problem. Such "insight does not come without careful study and comparison of the Old Testament background parallels."[39]

As we move through the book of Revelation, we will remember first that it speaks to us in symbols. They are not given to satisfy our curiosity or to write history in advance. They grab our attention, stir our blood, arouse our fervor. They challenge us, warn us and inspire us. We will remember also that while many of the same symbols also appeared in the uninspired apocalyptic literature of the previous two centuries, their primary meaning will be learned from the prophetic literature of the Old Testament. There is a unity to divine revelation which transcends the parrotings of imaginative fiction writers, however pious and well-intentioned they might be.

We will also keep in mind the universally-accepted rule of interpretation that we should interpret obscure passages in the light of passages that are clear and not the other way around. We still will not find all the answers. We will probably not make headlines or attract a great following. But in such a course we can surely have strong confidence that we are never far off the trail. If one cannot find understanding by searching the Scriptures, praying for wisdom and keeping his eyes on Jesus, surely understanding is not to be had.

Revelation 2:16, 22, 23. Some at Pergamum followed the errors of Balaam, and others held the teaching of the "Nicolaitans." Unless these repent, Jesus warns, He will "come . . . and will fight against them with the sword of My mouth." At Thyatira, too, the false

---

37. David Alexander and Pat Alexander, eds., *Eerdmans' Handbook to the Bible*, pp. 645-646.

38. William Hendriksen, *More Than Conquerors: An Interpretation of the Book of Revelation*, p. 63.

39. Ferrell Jenkins, *The Old Testament in the Book of Revelation*, pp. 14-15.

prophetess "Jezebel" led some into idolatry and sexual immorality. Seeing no repentance, Jesus warns that He is about to "cast her on a bed of suffering," make those who commit adultery with her "suffer intensely," and "strike her children dead."

All these statements may refer to temporal judgments, perhaps of lingering or even terminal disease. Insofar as they describe final punishment, they picture a suffering that ends in death.[40]

Revelation 11:18. When the seventh trumpet sounds, John hears loud voices in heaven. They announce good news: God has triumphed gloriously over His enemies! The kingdom is the Lord's! At this the 24 heavenly elders respond, saying:

> "The time has come for judging the dead, . . .
> and for destroying those who destroy the earth."

For "destroy" John twice writes an intensive Greek verb (*diaphtheirō*) which he uses but once more. There a burning mountain is thrown into the sea, turning waters into blood, killing living creatures, and "destroying" a third of the ships in passage (Rev. 8:8, 9). Luke uses the word once for the work of moths on clothes (Luke 12:33). Paul has the same verb when he says that "outwardly we are wasting away" (2 Cor. 4:16) and as he describes the "corrupt" mind of certain men (1 Tim. 6:5). On the special justice involved in God's "destroying those who destroy the earth," compare comments on 1 Corinthians 3:17, where Paul uses a cognate verb (*phtheirō*) in a similar framework.

Surely "destruction" *involves* torment, but this passage puts the stress on the destruction and not the accompanying torture. The New Testament probably describes the pain of final punishment in greatest detail in Romans 2:8, 9, followed closely by 2 Thessalonians 1:7-10. Both these passages also end with destruction, as does the "painful" passage, Hebrews 10:26-31. God is just and He is severe, but He does not delight in even the wicked man's death and He is certainly no sadistic torturer. This is a major difference between the Bible's picture of final punishment and that found nearly everywhere else—whether from venerated churchmen or bloodthirsty pagans.

---

40. Mounce gives this explanation, noting that the expression "to 'kill with death' is a Hebraism that means 'to slay utterly' . . . or (preferably) 'to kill by pestilence.'" At the same time, he believes that such a judgment would have been viewed by those visited as also the second or final coming of Jesus (Mounce, *The Book of Revelation*, pp. 99, 105).

Revelation 14:9-11. Following the appearance of the beast from the sea and the beast from the earth, John has a brief rest from the horrors. Instead, he sees Mount Zion. There stands the Lamb, accompanied by 144,000 of His people, the earth's redeemed firstfruits in God's spiritual harvest (Rev. 14:1-5). John sees three angels who announce God's judgment in language progressively stronger. The third angel cries out with a loud voice:

> "If anyone worships the beast and his image and receives his mark on the forehead or on the hand, he, too, will drink of the wine of God's fury, which has been poured full strength into the cup of His wrath. He will be tormented with burning sulfur in the presence of the holy angels and of the Lamb. And the smoke of their torment rises for ever and ever. There is no rest day or night."

The angel's announcement includes four elements involving punishment. They are: (1) drinking the wine of God's fury poured out full strength into the cup of His wrath; (2) being tormented with burning sulfur in the sight of the angels and of the Lamb; (3) the smoke of their torment rising for ever and ever; and (4) having no rest day or night. Let us turn to the former scriptures as we ask what these pictures mean.

Wine of God's Fury. The cup of God's wrath is a well-established Old Testament symbol of divine judgment in the books of poetry (Job 21:20; Ps. 60:3; 75:8) as well as prophecy (Isa. 51:17, 22: Jer. 25:15-38; Obad. 16). The figure points to God, who mixes the drink (Ps. 75:8; Jer. 25:15-38), and also to the staggering effect the potion has on those who quaff (Ps. 60:3; Isa. 51:17, 22). Since God concocts this cup, He can adjust its potency according to His own pleasure, diluting it (as with water) or strengthening it (as with spices or perhaps even poison). To be handed the cup means being singled out for punishment from the Almighty and so entails agony, terror and fear.

Since the cup's strength reflects the degree of God's wrath, the intensity of the punishment may also vary. For God's own people it may be a stroke which sends them reeling but from which they recover (Ps. 60:3; Isa. 51:22). For His enemies it often ends in total and irreversible extinction. The prophets use language like this: "They will drink and drink and be as if they had never been" (Obad. 16). They "drink, get drunk and vomit, and fall to rise no more" (Jer. 25:27). In the end their corpses are everywhere. "They will not be mourned or gathered up or buried, but will be like refuse lying on the ground" (v. 33). They become "a ruin and an object of horror and scorn and cursing" (v. 18).

Such was the cup Jesus accepted from God's hand in Gethsemane, and to drink it unmixed He refused even the numbing wine offered by His murderers (Matt. 26:39, 42, 44; 27:34). He suffered torment of body and soul. More than that, He drained the cup of God's wrath, passively enduring the simultaneous draining of His own life into total death. Because Jesus was not pretending dead or only partially dead, His resurrection was God's ultimate triumph over Satan and signaled the coming annihilation of death itself. That could not be so had Jesus not experienced to the full everything that death involves. Because *He* accepted that cup, His people will not have to. The cup He leaves for us is a constant reminder that He has taken our place (Matt. 26:27-29).

John sees the same figure of God's cup of wrath in Revelation (Rev. 16:19; 18:6; 19:15). Here it also includes "torture and grief," but it ends in "death, mourning and famine" and in consumption by fire (Rev. 18:7-9). While Jesus "treads the winepress of the fury of the wrath of God Almighty," an angel is already calling the birds of prey to gather for God's gory supper (Rev. 19:15-18). It does not minimize the terror or pain of divine punishment that it ends in total destruction and death. Two of the other three figures found in Revelation 14:9-11 suggest that same end for those who drink God's unmixed cup there, and the third figure possibly does as well.

Burning Sulfur. In the New International Version, "burning sulfur" replaces the familiar "fire and brimstone" of older English translations. The new phrase seems easier to understand, though it probably does not "preach" as well. In the Bible the symbol derives its meaning from the annihilation of Sodom and Gomorrah, and the Old Testament uses it often to signify complete and total desolation.

At Sodom (see discussion of Genesis 19) God "rained down burning sulfur . . . out of the heavens," and the overthrow was so total that nothing remained next morning but "dense smoke rising from the land" (Gen. 19:23, 28). One of the curses of God's covenant with Israel was that their land would become "a burning waste of salt and sulfur—nothing planted, nothing sprouting, no vegetation growing on it"—so that it would "be like the destruction of Sodom and Gomorrah" (Deut. 29:23). In this passage the people are removed from the land and not actually exterminated, but the point of the figure remains. From the standpoint of the *land* they become as Sodom; where there is *burning sulfur* there are *no* people!

Bildad pictures the same fate for the wicked man on the earth. Fire and burning sulfur mark the place he once resided; his roots dry and his branches wither; his memory perishes from the earth (Job 18:15-17; cf. Ps. 11:6). For the king of Assyria, Isaiah says, God has prepared the fires of Topheth. "The breath of the Lord, like a stream of burning sulfur, sets it ablaze" (Isa. 30:33). This "burning anger" is a "consuming fire" as God "shakes the nations in the sieve of destruction" (Isa. 30:27-30). Although this picture ends in consumption by fire, it includes strokes from God's punishing rod which first strikes down and shatters (vv. 31, 32).

Edom's dust and land will also become "burning sulfur" and "blazing pitch" (Isa. 34:9) when God stretches out "the measuring line of chaos and the plumb line of desolation" (v. 11). The same picture seen in Sodom's destruction is predicted for Gog and his hordes by Ezekiel (Ezek. 38:22). This is literally inconsistent with the picture that follows, where carrion birds eat the corpses and Israel salvages the spoils, but both pictures are in perfect harmony as they sound out a message of utter extinction. Revelation 19:20, 21 has both figures and distinguishes between them, but it gives no indication of changing this basic meaning of either. (The figure also appears in Revelation 20:10 and 21:8, which we will discuss later.) Outside the book of Revelation there can be little question that burning sulfur signifies extinction, destruction, eradication, extermination and annihilation. Sometimes this is explicit; sometimes it is implied. But it is always there.

The victims in Revelation 14:9-11 suffer in the presence of the angels and the Lamb. Mounce refers to some intertestamental passages in which the righteous watch the wicked's torment with some delight, but he notes that in Revelation "there is no suggestion that the suffering of the damned takes place in the presence of martyred believers who now rejoice to see their oppressors burning in hell."[41] The Old Testament often speaks of the righteous beholding the evidence of the wicked's destruction, but it does not have them gloating

---

41. Ibid., p. 276.

over their actual pain either. (See comments on Isaiah 66:24.) God sees the whole process, however, and here the angels do as well. Actual torment is meted out according to the mixture of God's cup. Then, as the next image points out, it is forever memorialized in the smoke which remains.

Rising Smoke. By now we are seeing that the figures often overlap and that a number of Old Testament passages which mention one also mention others. Just as Sodom presents the figure of burning sulfur, so it contributed the imagery of rising smoke. When Abraham went out the next morning to look on the scene, all he saw was "dense smoke rising from the land, like smoke from a furnace" (Gen. 19:28). Nothing else remained. All was silent. The blanket of smoke spoke more eloquently than words of an annihilated city and an ungodly population who would never be seen on earth again.

Isaiah uses the same picture to describe Edom's destruction (Isa. 34:10). We have already looked at verse 9, which says that Edom's dust will become "burning sulfur" and her land "blazing pitch." Now verse 10 adds that the fire "will not be quenched night and day" and that "its smoke will rise forever." The fire here is unquenchable precisely because it is not put out until it has completely destroyed (v. 11). It consumes by night and by day. There is no relief from its burning—until it has finished its work. Then the actual burning ceases, but the smoke remains. In saying the smoke "will rise forever," the prophet evidently means what he goes on to describe in the rest of the chapter. So long as time goes on, nothing will remain at the site but the smoke of what once was Edom's proud kingdom. Again the picture of destruction by fire overlaps that of slaughter by sword (vv. 1-7). The wicked die a tormented death; the smoke reminds all onlookers that the Sovereign God has the last word. That the smoke lingers forever in the air means that the judgment's message will never become out of date.

Conditionalist writers can point out that the same word translated "torment" here is applied elsewhere (in verb form) to the tossing of an inanimate boat. Traditionalists can respond that it also describes the rich man's conscious suffering in fire in Jesus' Story of the Six Brothers (Luke 16:23, 28) or the excruciating pain of a scorpion's sting (Rev. 9:5). We agree fully with Mounce that what the angel "has proclaimed so vividly must not be undermined by euphemistic redefinition."[42] One refrains from doing that by letting the Scripture interpret itself, which is all we are asking here.

Perhaps John's later vision of the fall of Babylon best focuses on the real point at issue (Rev. 18). A voice from heaven calls on God to balance the wicked city's glory and luxury with equal measure of "torture" and grief (v. 7). This is our same word, and it clearly calls for conscious suffering. But when God answers this prayer with plagues of death, mourning and famine, He then destroys the city with a consuming fire (v. 8). Merchants and kings bewail the "torment" they see, but all they behold is the rising smoke of a destruction now completed (vv. 10, 18). The scene reminds us of Abraham looking out over the site of what had been Sodom, seeing nothing now but rising smoke. The conscious torment is past; the reality of its destruction continues; the smoke is its silent but powerful witness (cf. Rev. 19:3).

No Rest Day or Night. We may describe an action or event several ways with reference to time. We might talk of a *kind* of time. Paul worked and prayed "night and day" (1 Thess. 2:9; 3:10), but he did neither nonstop. Sometimes he prayed at nighttime, sometimes at daytime; the same may be said for his working. The Greek expresses this kind-of-time by the genitive case form.[43] Or we might speak of a *point* of time. Peter would deny Jesus in a particular night (Mark 14:30). The Greek expresses point-of-time by the locative case.[44] Or one might speak of a *duration* of time. Jesus spoke of the seed which sprouts and grows "night and day" (Mark 4:27). All day the seed is growing; all night it is growing too. The Greek expresses this duration-of-time by the accusative case.[45]

---

42. Ibid., p. 277. Mounce does not mention the Old Testament background for the smoke which goes up forever, nor does Jenkins in his *Book of Revelation*.

43. H. E. Dana and Julius R. Mantey, *A Manual Grammar of the Greek New Testament*, p. 77.
   The expression "day and night" (or "night and day") appears with this genitival construction outside Revelation in Mark 5:5; Luke 18:7; Acts 9:24; 1 Thess. 2:9; 3:10; 2 Thess. 3:8; 1 Tim. 5:5; 2 Tim. 1:3; in the Septuagint in Ps. 2:1; 32:4 (31:4, LXX); 42:3 (41:3); 55:10 (54:11); Isa. 34:10; 60:11; Jer. 9:1 (8:23); 14:17; Lam. 2:18. There appears to be no significance in the word order since John has "day and night" while Isaiah 34:10, which he seems to build on, has "night and day."

44. Ibid., p. 87. I could not find "day and night" in this dative case form. Evidently the locative point-of-time does not consistently call for such a usage.

45. Ibid., p. 93. The "day and night" expression appears with the accusative sense of duration-of-time in Mark 4:27; Luke 2:37; Acts 20:31; 26:7; Isa. 62:6 (LXX). The first and last passage seem literal; the rest appear to be hyperbole based on the literal meaning.

John here writes that these wicked people have no rest "day or night" in the genitive case, speaking of *kind* of time. They are not guaranteed rest during the day; there is no certain hope that relief will come at night. This does not say within itself that the suffering lasts all day and all night (although that may be true), but that in neither case are they immune to it. John uses the same genitival "day and night" to describe the living creatures praising (Rev. 4:8), the martyrs serving (Rev. 7:15), Satan accusing (Rev. 12:10), and the unholy trinity being tormented (Rev. 20:10). In each case the thought is the same: the action described is not by nature a daytime action, nor is it a nighttime action. It happens either and both. Guillebaud is therefore correct when he writes that these words "certainly say that there will be no break or intermission in the suffering of the followers of the Beast, *while it continues*; but in themselves they do not say that it will continue for ever."[46] The first three figures in the passage all either indicate or are agreeable to the idea that the suffering finally ends in total extinction and desolation.

The same form of "night and day" is used in Isaiah 34:10, a context noted already for its description of burning sulfur and also of rising smoke. There Edom's fire is not quenched "night and day," with the same sentence concluding, "its smoke will rise forever." Edom's fire would not be limited to a day shift or a night shift; it burned in the daytime and in the nighttime. But when it had consumed all that was there, it went out; and then its smoke ascended as a memorial to God's thorough destruction.

John describes this scene of Revelation 14:9-11 under four figures. The wine of God's fury signifies a penal judgment from the Almighty; that it is poured full strength strongly suggests a judgment culminating in absolute extinction. This extinction is preceded by some degree of conscious torment pictured as a storm of burning sulfur. That figure, too, takes us back to Sodom. There and elsewhere it results in a silent wasteland devoid of inhabitant. Scripture uses the third figure of rising smoke a number of times as well, where it indicates a continuing reminder of God's just judgment. Those so destroyed have no guarantee of relief, whether daytime or nighttime, so long as their suffering lasts.

---

46. Guillebaud, *Righteous Judge*, p. 24.

Not all commentators understand this passage as even referring to the final end of the wicked.[47] If it does, its figures must still be interpreted in the light of the Old Testament. To be sure, the New Testament may add its own new light or meaning, but such redefinition ought to be clearly justified by the text itself. It is not sufficient to take the figures out of their biblical context and explain them in the light of later dogmatic developments.

Revelation 18. In the Old Testament, Babylon had been a symbol of opposition to God's kingdom. John uses the city-name the same way. His readers would take the name as a cipher for Rome. This chapter describes the fall of Rome—of "Babylon"—of ungodly world power which vaunts itself in any age under any name. The description is borrowed almost wholly from Old Testament pictures of divine judgment against ungodly cities, whether Babylon (Isa. 21:1-10), Nineveh (Nahum) or especially Tyre (Ezek. 27).

One should not look to this chapter for a description of final punishment, therefore; but because some of the language occurs in passages which do seem to speak of that, a brief look here may be in order. This judgment against Babylon includes plagues (v. 4), torture and grief (v. 7), death, mourning and famine, and finally ends in consumption by fire (v. 8). Having been so brought to ruin (vv. 17, 19), a ruin including torment (vv. 10, 15), the smoke of the city goes up for all to see (vv. 9, 18). That the smoke goes up forever (Rev. 19:3; cf. 14:9-11) speaks of an eternal *destruction* but not everlasting *conscious torment*. It is a perpetual reminder of God's devastating judgment.[48]

Revelation 19:20; 20:10, 15; 21:8 (the Lake of Fire). Here we come to the last description in the Bible of final punishment. It is the

---

47. Homer Hailey says the picture is "in harmony with Jesus' teaching" concerning final punishment, but he does not believe Revelation describes the End until later. Hailey regards this as a judgment against imperial Rome with its emperor cult (Homer Hailey, *Revelation: An Introduction and Commentary*, p. 310).

The dispensational interpretation given by *The New Scofield Reference Bible* sees this as a picture of suffering encountered by the wicked during the great tribulation.

48. Although the chapter does not describe final punishment, its picture of destruction by fire is commonly used in Scripture for that fate. Homer Hailey sees the *significance* of the picture in Revelation 18:8 like this: 'The end comes to the great city, followed by mourning over the death and famine from the economic collapse, for 'she shall be utterly burned with fire'—totally destroyed (Rev. 17:16)" (Hailey, *Revelation*, p. 363).

fiery lake of burning sulfur, the lake of fire and brimstone. This expression does not appear anywhere else in the Bible. Even so, conditionalists and traditionalists agree that it stands for the same ultimate destiny which in the Gospels (but nowhere else in Scripture) is pictured under the name "Gehenna." The pseudepigraphical book of 1 (Ethiopic) Enoch paints a similar picture of the place where fallen angels are punished (1 En. 18:11-16; 21:7-10) as well as wicked shepherds and apostates (1 En. 90:24-27). One passage has them imprisoned forever (1 En. 21:10); another implies that they are totally burned up (1 En. 90:27).

It has been customary to say that the intertestamental literature clearly and generally taught eternal conscious torment and that Jesus and New Testament writers borrowed the language, thereby endorsing and continuing the same understanding.[49] Strack and Billerbeck, however, raise the question whether all the intertestamental material might really intend to describe total annihilation.[50] We have seen in a previous chapter that the Old Testament picture of utter extinction clearly continues alongside those passages which appear to teach everlasting conscious torment, well into the first century after Christ. We have proceeded on the assumption that the New Testament must be allowed to speak for itself and that the Old Testament Scriptures rather than the uninspired literature of apocalyptic must be its primary outside interpreter.

Daniel's dream of four beasts provides the nearest Old Testament parallel (Dan. 7:9-12). There the Ancient of Days takes His seat on a throne that flames with fire (v. 9). A river of fire flows from before Him (v. 10). The terrible fourth beast is "slain and its body destroyed and thrown into the blazing fire." This is in specific contrast to the other beasts, who are stripped of authority but allowed to live for a

---

49. Harry Buis writes: "It is an inescapable fact that Jesus, without going to the grotesque extremes to which some of the apocalyptic writers went, places the stamp of his approval upon the general Gehenna concept which had developed during the Inter-Testamental period. . . . Jesus' teaching further proves that the Inter-Testamental development of the doctrine was in reality a sound extension of the beginnings of that doctrine which are found in the Old Testament" (Buis, *The Doctrine of Eternal Punishment*, p. 42).

50. "The punishment of the godless, regardless if they were judged in the catastrophic judgment or the regular judgment, lasts forever. But the Pseudepigrapha also speaks about the destruction or the annihilation of the godless, so that one may be in doubt if to them the everlasting condemnation of the (judged) guilty simply had become synonymous with everlasting annihilation" (Hermann L. Strack and Paul Billerbeck, *Kommentar zum Neuen Testament aus Talmud und Midrasch*, 2:1096). The German text is quoted in chapter 8, note 18.

period of time (vv. 11, 12). Unless this vision of world powers under the imagery of beasts sheds light on the lake of fire in Revelation, no light is to be had from the Old Testament. If the passage in Daniel is its background, that light reveals a fiery destruction which is expressly *not* a mere stripping of authority with a survival of life. It is more helpful to compare the four occurrences of the lake of fire in the Apocalypse itself.

The Beast and the False Prophet. The beast and false prophet are the first beings thrown into the lake (Rev. 19:20). They are not actual people but representations of persecuting civil government and of corrupting false religion. Neither institution will be perpetuated forever, nor could either suffer conscious, sensible pain. In their case the lake of fire cannot indicate *that kind* of everlasting punishment. Homer Hailey does not regard the passage as a description of Christ's second coming at all but of "the victorious war against the forces that have been under discussion."[51] He understands the fact that the beast and false prophet are "thrown alive" into the lake to mean that these two personified forces of evil actively fight against Christ until the very last moment, when He brings them to total destruction. Hailey believes that the whole passage means the "Roman Empire and emperor worship backed by the imperial power were now being brought to a final and complete end, never to rise again."[52]

Hanns Lilje, who finished his commentary while imprisoned under Hitler's Gestapo, marvels that John gives no description here of any battle. "The very moment when this purpose of God is fulfilled," he writes, "the mighty power of the beast shrivels up like a collapsed balloon, as if it had never been. It has been unmasked, and its true

---

51. Hailey, *Revelation*, p. 381. Yet he understands the *figures* here to signify "defeat and destruction" (p. 382). The armies, sword and rod he sees "destroying by divine judgment, reducing to chaff, burning, and carrying away" (p. 385). In the end the birds pick the corpses so "Not a vestige of the anti-Christian forces was left; the destruction was complete" (p. 388). If the figures *signify* such annihilation and extinction of anti-Christian forces, why would they not have the same meaning when applied in other passages to the end of the ungodly?

52. Ibid., p. 388. *The New Scofield Reference Bible* makes this the fourth item on an agenda of 10 final events. Here it sees the destruction of earth's "last and most awful tyrant," whom Satan gives power to rule during the world's final days. Mounce takes a middle course between Scofield's dispensationalism and Hailey's "historical background" approach. He speaks of "the eschatological defeat of Antichrist (an event which takes place in time and brings to a close this age as we know it) but does not require that we accept in a literal fashion the specific imagery with which the event is described" (Mounce, *The Book of Revelation*, p. 349).

character revealed: it was empty, futile presumption." So far as the meaning of the lake of fire is concerned. Lilje is content to use the word "annihilated."[53] In the case of the beast and false prophet, therefore, the lake of fire stands for utter, absolute, irreversible annihilation.

Satan. In Revelation 20:7-10 John views Evil's last great assault against Good, issuing in Evil's final downfall and everlasting destruction. The picture is built on the imagery of Ezekiel 38 and 39, down to the code names "Gog" and "Magog." Satan's hordes surround the camp of God's people, but as in the days of Elijah (2 Kings 1), fire comes down from heaven and devours them. Whereas they are toasted in their tracks, Satan himself is reserved for more singular punishment. He is "thrown into the lake of burning sulfur, where the beast and the false prophet had been thrown." Together, the vision has these three—beast, false prophet and the devil—"tormented day and night for ever and ever."

The language is symbolic, and a literal interpretation is impossible. Political power and apostate religious beguilement are not persons who can be tortured in fire. Even the vision would be impossible if these forces were not personified as creatures. We can imagine Satan being kept in deathless torment, but how does one even picture that situation in the case of impersonal abstractions? On the other hand, if the lake of fire means here what it did in Revelation 19:20, it is nothing but a symbol for annihilation.[54] But if that is its meaning, how does John see the devil "tormented day and night for ever and ever?" There is no easy solution. Yet to this point no human beings are involved in the lake of fire, nor does this passage say that any of Adam's race are tormented for ever and ever.

---

53. Hanns Lilje, *The Last Book of the Bible*, p. 246.

54. Lilje writes: "Fire from heaven falls upon these hosts, and annihilates Satan and his armies. God's will has triumphed gloriously; the 'lake of fire' means no more than this" (ibid., p. 254).

Seventh-day Adventists (and others) believe that Ezekiel 28:11-19 describes the devil under the figure of the "King of Tyre." They therefore understand verses 18-19 there to prophesy Satan's final annihilation. Ellen G. White gave this interpretation in her *The Great Controversy between Christ and Satan*, pp. 672-673.

The New Scofield Reference Bible also extends Ezekiel's lament beyond the earthly king of Tyre to Satan himself, but it then explicitly denies that these verses teach Satan's cessation of being.

C. F. Keil, among others, explains the text in detail, with recourse only to the human king of Tyre, in his *Biblical Commentary on the Prophecies of Ezekiel*, 1:409-425.

Death and Hades. Earth and sky flee away as the dead assemble to be judged before the great white throne (Rev. 20:11-13). "Then death and Hades were thrown into the lake of fire" (v. 14). More than seven centuries earlier Isaiah had looked to a time when God would "destroy the shroud that enfolds all peoples, the sheet that covers all nations," when "He will swallow up death forever" (Isa. 25:7, 8). Paul had written, "The last enemy to be destroyed is death" (1 Cor. 15:26), and he had pictured the resurrection unto life when death would be "swallowed up" in victory (v. 54). This is the consummation of God's victory. Lilje notes:

> Annihilation is itself annihilated. All that remains is the majesty of life, which is God himself. He will be all in all (I Cor. 15:23, 28).[55]

As in the case of the beast and false prophet, so with death and Hades (abstractions and not persons): the lake of fire here means annihilation. In this case it can mean nothing else. Death will be no more—forever. Now John makes the identification clear. "The lake of fire is the second death."

In other such expressions throughout Revelation, John explains the first term he uses by the second one. What are the bowls of incense in Revelation 5:8? They are prayers of the saints. What is the fine linen of Revelation 19:8? It is the righteous acts of the saints. What is the reigning a thousand years with Christ in Revelation 20:5? It is the first resurrection. And what is the *lake of fire*? It is *the second death* (Rev. 20:14). On this pattern "lake of fire" is the expression to be defined; "second death" is its clearer meaning. Such a formal observation is not conclusive, but it deserves serious consideration, and it is in keeping with all that we can understand throughout the rest of the whole Bible.[56] Death itself will die. What sense does it make to say "separation will be separated"? But what a powerful thought it is that "annihilation will be annihilated"! Then it will be true that death itself has passed away (Rev. 21:4).

The Lost. Only now do we find sinners included in this dreadful fate. "If anyone's name was not found written in the book of life, he was thrown into the lake of fire" (Rev. 20:15). The next chapter repeats the fact with elaboration. Overcomers will inherit the new

---

55. Lilje, *Last Book*, p. 256.
56. Guillebaud notes this structure in *Righteous Judge*, p. 14.

heavens and new earth, but all classes of sinners "will be in the fiery lake of burning sulfur." Again John says: "This is the second death" (Rev. 21:8). Two times John tells us the wicked end in the lake of fire. Both times he identifies the lake of fire as "the second death."

Traditionalist authors always read the equation the other direction, as if it said "the second death" (which is indefinite) *is* "the lake of fire" (which is clear). In fact, however, John says that "the lake of fire" (his symbol) *is* "the second death" (a clearer reality). Because John's statement is so understandable on the face of it, writers who hold to everlasting conscious torment are very careful to contradict what it *seems* to say.

The second death "does not mean that the soul or personality lapses into non-being," writes one esteemed scholar, "but rather that it is ultimately and finally deprived of that presence of God, and fellowship with Him which is the chief end of man and the essential condition of worthwhile existence."[57] Another says "the second death" means "existence without the resurrection of life and the crown of life, the existence that is eternal loss and dying," and he quotes Philo the Jew, who speaks of a "kind of death remaining deathless and dying."[58] This kind of language is everywhere in patristic literature from about the fourth century onward, but it is nowhere found in Scripture. Rather than the wicked experiencing a "deathless death," John tells us that death itself will die and be no more.

Even the apocalyptic specialist, G. R. Beasley-Murray, says the lake of fire does not signify annihilation but "torturous existence in the society of evil in opposition to life in the society of God."[59] Robert Mounce is more in line with the text when he writes: "It is the second death, that is, the destiny of those whose temporary resurrection results only in a return to death and its punishment." Both Mounce and Hailey quote Alford, who explained:

> "As there is a second and higher life, so there is also a second and deeper death. And as after that life there is no more death (ch. xxi. 4), so after that death there is no more life" (pp. 735-36).[60]

57. Roger Nicole, "The Punishment of the Wicked," *Christianity Today,* 9 June 1958, p. 13.

58. Steward D. F. Salmond, *The Christian Doctrine of Immortality,* pp. 428-429.

59. Quoted by Mounce, *The Book of Revelation,* p. 367.

60. Ibid., p. 367; Hailey, *Revelation,* p. 403. Mounce comments: "The grim simplicity of the

In the case of the beast and false prophet (both personifications of ungodly power or perversion), and in the case of death and Hades (both abstractions treated as persons), the lake of fire clearly means annihilation and cessation of existence. In the case of impenitent sinners, nothing in the text prevents this meaning. The context twice suggests it by explaining the lake of fire as the "second death." Everything we have seen in the rest of the Bible is in keeping with this meaning.

So far as the devil is concerned, the expression itself would seem to have the same meaning, but it becomes ambiguous and somewhat questionable in light of the specific statement that he will be tormented for ever and ever. Other prophetic passages might reverse that understanding, however, if they intend to picture Satan's destiny. Furthermore, in Revelation itself John writes "torment" when describing lifeless desolation. Whatever the case with Satan, the final punishment of the wicked is a different subject.[61]

---

narrative stands in contrast with the lurid descriptions found in Jewish apocalypticism."

This is no mere slipping into oblivion, as Bernard emphasizes: "Things do not melt quietly into the peace of the kingdom of God. There is a crash of ruin, and a winepress of the wrath of Almighty God, and a lake that burns with fire and brimstone. And this judgment falls, not only on principles and powers of evil, but on nations of men; and not only on nations, but on separate persons, even on 'every one who is not found written in the book of life'" (Thomas Dehany Bernard, *The Progress of Doctrine in the New Testament*, p. 205).

61. Homer Hailey notes Jesus' parallel of "eternal punishment" and "eternal life" (Matt. 25:46), and John's parallel between service "day and night" (Rev. 7:15) and no rest "day and night" (Rev. 14:11). He then reasons: "Since the day is in heaven and the night in hell, and since the one group serves Him day and night while the other group is tormented night and day, it follows that the night endures as long as the day. But since God is the light of the eternal day, the day (and, consequently, the night) will never end. The period of this torment, 'for ever and ever,' is the same in duration as God, for He lives 'for ever and ever' (Rev. 4:9). If there shall be total annihilation of the devil and the wicked it is not revealed" (Hailey, *Revelation*, pp. 398-399).

By way of dialogue with my respected teacher, I quickly acknowledge the parallel statements of both Jesus and John, and fully agree that the "night" lasts as long as the "day." This is a telling argument against every form of universal restorationism. But if "day" equals "heaven," and "night" equals "hell," how can there be either service or torment "day *and* night"—unless the righteous serve in heaven and hell, and the wicked suffer in hell and heaven? Does not the genitival "day and night" simply stress the quality of both blessing and suffering, that neither is limited to the day or the night (as we think of it)? Does not the above reasoning expect too much of John's figures of speech?

There is no question in the present book that the wicked are destroyed *forever*—as everlastingly as the redeemed enjoy life in immortality. But the "quantitative" meaning of "eternal" does not answer the question of the *nature* of final punishment. As to the purported silence of Scripture on the extinction of the wicked, this study leads us to conclude that the Bible reveals a great deal more than has commonly been affirmed. We traditionalists have simply failed in many cases (as Hailey often put it) to "grapple with the text."

The Element of Mystery

As we come to the close of our investigation of New Testament teaching on final punishment, it is important that we end on a word of caution. All that God has spoken on this subject He has said in symbolic language.[62] He has not given a physical, scientific description of the end of the wicked. "We need to recognize anew the element of mystery in revelation," exhorts Donald G. Bloesch.[63] If that is true in general, it is especially true concerning the Last Things. Even the much-used word "eschatology" can itself "become a substitute for careful thought" so that it leads "only to ambiguities and confusions," warns I. Howard Marshall.[64] When we study the subject of this book, we are peering at "the dark side of the far hereafter,"[65] and "vagrant speculation" needs to give way to a "reverent agnosticism."[66]

Alan Richardson writes of the atonement, but his words are fully applicable to our subject as well when he observes:

> One can construct theories and offer them as solutions of problems, but one cannot theorize about the deep mystery . . . . The NT does not do so; it offers to us not theories but vivid metaphors, which can, if we will let them operate in our imagination, make real to us the . . . truth. . . . The desire to rationalize these metaphors into theories . . . has created much division and rigidity amongst Christian bodies; the curious combination of Renaissance rationalism and evangelical zeal, which has characterized much Reformed and sect-type Christianity in recent centuries, has resulted in an unfortunate kind of sophistication which believes that the only thing to do with metaphors is to turn them into theories.[67]

James Orr makes the same point.

> The conclusion I arrive at is that we have not the elements of a complete solution, and we ought not to attempt it. What visions beyond

---

62. Augustus Hopkins Strong, *Systematic Theology*, 3:1035.

63. Donald G. Bloesch, "Crisis in Biblical Authority," *Theology Today* 35, no. 4 (January 1979): 462.

64. I. Howard Marshall, "Slippery Words: Eschatology," *Expository Times*, June 1978, p. 268.

65. The title Gerald C. Studer uses for his chapter on hell in his *After Death, What?* pp. 108-130.

66. David W. Lotz, "Heaven and Hell in the Christian Tradition," *Religion in Life* 48 (Spring 1979): 90.

67. Alan Richardson, *An Introduction to the Theology of the New Testament*, pp. 222-223.

there may be, what larger hopes, what ultimate harmonies, if such there are in store, will come in God's good time; it is not for us to anticipate them, or lift the veil where God has left it down.[68]

In another place he warns against dogmatism in these matters.

It is . . . necessary to guard against dogmatisms . . . as if eternity must not, in the nature of the case, have its undisclosed mysteries of which we here in time can frame no conception. . . . Scripture . . . with its uniformly practical aim . . . does not seek to satisfy an idle curiosity. . . . Its language is bold, popular, figurative, intense; the essential idea is to be held fast, but what is said cannot be taken as a directory to all that is to transpire in the ages upon ages of an unending duration. God's methods of dealing with sin in the eternities may prove to be as much above our present thoughts as His dealings now are with men in grace. In His hands we must be content to leave it, only using such light as His immediate revelation yields.[69]

Many have failed to heed such warnings regardless of the point they wished to establish. The literature abounds in half-truths, historical inaccuracies, assertions without proof, dogmatic assumptions, presuppositional argument, circular reasoning, and examples of "eisegesis" instead of exegesis. More literalistic authors on both sides of this question have drawn their calendars with such precision that the Lord will need a stopwatch to meet their program. This applies to many traditionalists (whether fundamentalists, dispensationalists or Calvinistic scholastics), but also to certain doctrinaire conditionalists who leave no room for the mysteries of the Age to Come and an order that transcends our experience in the present space-time creation.[70]

---

68. James Orr, *The Christian View of God and the World* (1893), p. 397, quoted in *Encyclopaedia Britannica*, 8:704.

69. James Orr, "Everlasting Punishment" (IV, 1), *The International Standard Bible Encyclopaedia*, 2:2503.

70. At times Froom seems to leave nothing to the realm of mystery and transcendence in his *Conditionalist Faith*. Edward White, one of Froom's favorite conditionalist predecessors, was more cautious in this regard, as illustrated by the following warning against overzealous curiosity:

'The doctrine of the Second Death . . . is represented in the Divine Revelation amidst 'blackness, and darkness, and tempest,' like that which covered Mount Sinai at the giving of the Law; and, therefore, none can break through to gaze into the abyss whence bursts the fire that 'burns into the midst of heaven.' To venture into those scenes with a design of exploring the shadows, on which even the flashes of Divine vengeance throw no light but rather render darkness visi-

We simply cannot pinpoint the events of the last day. All that the Bible says, with the possible exception of one or two highly-figurative passages in Revelation, indicates that the wicked will perish in the consuming fire of the holiness of the coming God. At the same time, we are unable to print out a program, to visualize exactly what will happen, or to speak with the authority of one who has been there. We know only what we are told, and on this subject God has talked to us with His hand over His mouth.

Most of all, God points us to the cross of Jesus. Unless we keep that in mind, we become like the young man who approached Jesus with a pocketful of questions when he should have come on his knees asking for mercy. Under the shadow of Golgotha we remember who and what we are. Rather than speculate, we need to pray. Rather than letting our imaginations run wild, we need to repent. And when the last day does come in all its glory and all its terror, we will realize that even our repentance needs to be repented of and even our prayers need praying for. We will fall on our faces before the risen Lord, who was dead and is alive, dissolved in prayer and praise until He touches us to rise and calls us to follow Him home.

We will do well to remember that while all God's prophecies are *true* (so that what they say really comes to pass), their fulfillment is often a matter of *correspondence* rather than mechanical literalism. Ernest F. Kevan makes the point in *Revelation and the Bible*. There he reminds us that the "fulfillment of the acorn is the oak, and the fulfillment of the apple blossom is the apple."[71] Yet who possibly could have looked at the acorn or the blossom and known that in advance? We would do well also to remember how the Jews—who had so many Old Testament prophecies of the Messiah who was to come

---

ble, be far from us. A certain part of the moral effect of the prospect of judgment to come depends on its mystery" (White, *Life in Christ*, p. 345).

To insist that we leave room for an element of mystery concerning God's final disposition of evil and those who would rather share its destruction than turn loose of it is another matter than the question of how Scripture—so far as it does—reveals that end to us. On that question we must answer with those who hope for a perfect universe where God is "all in all" and evil will exist no more. Scripture does not allow us, however, to anticipate a precise timetable of events, nor does it speak to us other than in language understandable to our present experience. This is the point we wish to make.

71. Ernest F. Kevan, "The Principles of Interpretation," *Revelation and the Bible*, ed. Carl F. H. Henry, p. 298. T. G. Dunning critiques traditionalism, conditionalism and restorationism, and suggests that each view may have "a partial truth which will find its place in a synthesis beyond human comprehension" (T. G. Dunning, "What Has Become of Heaven and Hell?" *Baptist Quarterly* 20, no. 8 [October 1964]: 356).

—failed in such large part to recognize Jesus when He finally came and fulfilled those prophecies perfectly.[72] God's fulfillments, like His thoughts, are higher than man's.

---

72. Vernard Eller makes the point. "There is, of course," he writes, "the fact that some Bible prophecies *have been* fulfilled. We do not propose to go into the matter here except to observe that the nature of those prophecies was such that, *when the event itself took place*, they could be cited as confirmation that it *had been prophesied* ahead of time. However, there is no evidence . . . that the prophecies ever made it possible for anyone to make an accurate *prediction* as to just when, where, and how the event would occur. The accomplished fulfillment of some Bible prophecies provides no excuse or justification for contemporary calendarizing" (Vernard Eller, *The Most Revealing Book of the Bible: Making Sense Out of Revelation*, pp. 13-14).

Although Daniel knew from Jeremiah's prophecy *when* the Babylonian Exile would end, and Herod's scribes knew from prophecy *where* Jesus would be born, Eller's point is still valid. Peter stresses the unknown element from the standpoint of the prophets themselves (1 Pet. 1:10-12), and Paul makes the same point from the standpoint of the fulfillment (1 Cor. 2:8, 9).

15

Second-Century Statements on Final Punishment (Apostolic Fathers to Clement of Alexandria)

The writings of the earlier church fathers are not part of the Bible, but they sometimes give valuable insight into the meaning of Scripture. At the very least, the common understanding of the second-century Christians, representing a broad geographical distribution, can take us behind many church debates, divisions, and other accidents of history which all have had a part in the making of today's systematic theologies and common opinions.

The Apostolic Fathers

This is particularly true of those writers who themselves knew people who had known the apostles and for that reason are now often called "the apostolic fathers." Men such as Ignatius of Antioch, Clement of Rome, the unknown "Barnabas," the author of the handbook called the Didache (the Greek word for "Teaching" or "Instruction"), and the venerable martyr, Polycarp, provide our nearest links to the men who wrote the New Testament and who were guided in a special way by Jesus Himself and by the Comforter He sent in His stead.

Even these second-century "fathers" sometimes erred; their own testimony does not always agree; they were influenced by all the cir-

313

cumstances of their background and environment just as we are.
Still, their common understanding of biblical subjects deserves very
careful consideration in our own attempts to gain a clearer view of
the meaning of New Testament truth.

Traditionalists and conditionalists alike claim the apostolic fathers
for support. Anyone approaching the literature on final punishment
in search of dogmatic statements or "authorities" to quote in proof of
a position can find plenty—on both sides! Constable[1] and Froom[2]
claim that all the apostolic fathers support the views of conditional
immortality, that immortality is God's gift through the redemption
of Jesus, and that the saved alone will live forever while the lost will
completely pass away.

Traditionalist advocate, Salmond, objects strenuously. The doctrine of annihilation "is a doctrine of ancient date," he concedes. But
the attempt to prove it the primitive Christian teaching, he says,
"must be pronounced a failure." He dismisses conditionalist statements from the apostolic fathers as

> either incidental statements which have to be balanced by others that
> are at once more definite and more continuous; or they are popular
> statements and simple repetitions of the terms of Scripture; or they
> mean that the soul is not absolutely self-subsistent, but depends for its
> existence and its survival on God; or they have in view only the sen-
> sitive soul as distinguished from the rational soul or responsible
> spirit.[3]

Beecher was no friend to the traditional doctrine, but he, too,
believed that Constable overstated his case regarding the apostolic
fathers. Beecher allowed that "some of these witnesses do undeniably
testify as alleged, but . . . a large number do not definitely testify to
any view except the general one of future retribution, because the
subject had never been up as a controverted question, and the end at
which they were aiming did not call for it."[4]

Forestell, a modern Catholic scholar whose tradition is thoroughly

---

1. Henry Constable, *Duration and Nature of Future Punishment*, pp. 167-170. Constable
singles out Clement of Rome for examination, regarding him as typical of the apostolic fathers.
Although Constable's identification of this author with the friend of the apostle Paul (Phil. 4:3)
is now thought highly improbable, that does not detract from the value of Clement's testimony
as an early witness on this subject.

2. LeRoy Edwin Froom, *The Conditionalist Faith of Our Fathers*, 1:757-802.

3. Steward D. F. Salmond, *The Christian Doctrine of Immortality*, pp. 593-594.

4. Edward Beecher, *History of Opinions on the Scriptural Doctrine of Retribution*, p. 122.

on the side of everlasting torment, also believes the apostolic fathers' statements leave unanswered questions. He sees there "traces of a full understanding of NT revelation" (to him, the traditionalist position) but says "we can also detect the same lack of precision regarding the fate of the wicked which we discovered in Jewish and NT sources."[5]

But traditionalist "evidence" fares little better. E. B. Pusey, the Anglican High-Churchman whose *What Is of Faith as to Everlasting Punishment?* defended unending torment against the attacks of his contemporary ecclesiastic, F. W. Farrar, claims the apostolic fathers in support of the traditional doctrine. Yet a careful look at Pusey's evidence shows few statements if any which could not have been as easily made by the staunchest conditionalist. His quotations from Ignatius concern "unquenchable fire" or "eternal fire which is never extinguished," but these terms could simply mean an irresistible fire of the Age to Come which cannot be put out until it has totally destroyed. He quotes Barnabas, 2 Clement and the Pastor of Hermas concerning "grievous torments in unquenchable fire," or "punishment," or "falling into the fire and burning," but these statements all may be reconciled with annihilation so long as it is preceded by a period of conscious suffering. He even appeals to such expressions as "death," "eternal death," "condemned to death," "utterly perish" and "die for ever"—statements which but for the most delicate handling and careful interpreting seem to prove the exact opposite of the point he wishes to make.[6]

As to Salmond's complaint that the "conditionalist" statements of the fathers are but "simple repetitions of the terms of Scripture," such a case might well work for the conditionalist cause rather than against it if "simple repetitions of the terms of Scripture" support conditionalism with greater ease than they do the traditionalist position. Conditionalists such as Constable and White had objected to the traditionalist view on the very ground that its clearest expression calls for terms never used by Scripture and that it consistently denies

---

5. J. Terence Forestell, "Christian Revelation and the Resurrection of the Wicked," *Catholic Biblical Quarterly* 19, no. 2 (April 1957): 187-188. Forestell's own examination of the apostolic fathers leads him to conclude that the Didache, Polycarp, and Clement of Rome give a conditionalist witness; Ignatius is conditionalist at times and at times unclear; Barnabas and 2 Clement are less clear. His actual discussion seems to justify the conditionalist analysis of his statement that the apostolic fathers speak with "lack of precision"—namely, that Forestell finds no clear traditionalist expressions in them whatsoever.

6. Edward Bouverie Pusey, *What Is of Faith as to Everlasting Punishment? In Reply to Dr. Farrar's Challenge in His "Eternal Hope," 1879,* pp. 172-177.

what the scriptural terms seem to affirm when taken at face value and with their ordinary definitions.

Conditionalists would counter Beecher's objections by agreeing that "future retribution" is indeed the "general" and apostolic view, to which they also agree, but that the traditional doctrine goes far beyond any teaching found in Scripture. If Beecher says "the subject had never been up as a controverted question," Constable would respond that he expected as much since everyone at that time held the conditionalist view. And Forestell's "lack of precision" would be interpreted by any conditionalist to mean only that the evidence did not support the view he expected to find and was therefore, from *his* point of view, "lacking" in precision. To any who do not defend the traditionalist view, the fact that Forestell only found "traces" in the apostolic fathers of what he considered the "full understanding" would probably be more significant than the evidence he did find, for if the traditional doctrine was ever held clearly and without confusion, it should have been in the writings of the apostolic fathers.

Let us take a look for ourselves at the writings of the apostolic fathers.[7] We have no point to prove, no ax to grind, no position to defend. We will attempt rather to sift through the material as it stands and summarize as fairly as we are able the opinions it reveals. Whatever these men believed about final punishment must still be weighed in the light of the Scriptures themselves, as must all other noncanonical literature or spoken pronouncements.

The Didache. This early Christian handbook begins by warning that there are "two ways"—the way of "life" and the way of "death" (Didache 1:1; 5:1). At the end of all things, it says, "the creation of men will enter into the fire of testing and many will fall away and perish" (Didache 16:5). There is no mention of unending conscious torment. There are no indications that "perish" means continued existence, though in a state of "ruin." This is all it says on the subject.

---

7. Unless otherwise specified, all following quotations from the apostolic fathers are my translation of the Greek text edited by Karl Bihlmeyer, *Die Apostolischen Väter*. Popular English translations include *The Apostolic Fathers*, translated by J. B. Lightfoot, and a work of the same name, translated by Edgar J. Goodspeed.

An interesting and helpful summary of Christian faith and life in the first three centuries is Everett Ferguson's *Early Christians Speak: Faith and Life in the First Three Centuries*. Unfortunately, Dr. Ferguson does not include immortality or final punishment among the subjects he treats.

The Epistle of Barnabas. This "Barnabas" almost certainly is not Paul's associate known to us from Acts, though he bears the same name. The epistle does come from early in the second century, however, and it speaks several times concerning the end of sin and sinners. "The Lord will judge the world impartially," it tells us. "Each one will receive just as he has done. . . . If one is evil, the reward of evildoing is before him" (Barn. 4:12).

Behind sin is the Black One, whose road "is crooked and full of cursing. For it is a road of eternal death with punishment, and in it are things that destroy men's souls" (Barn. 20:1). Whoever chooses evil things "will perish together with his works. For this reason is resurrection; for this reason recompense" (Barn. 21:1). Finally, Barnabas writes that the day "is near in which all things will perish with the Evil One [or "evil"]" (Barn. 21:3).

Barnabas clearly teaches future judgment, retribution for both good and evil, and divine punishment for all who follow wickedness. The end of sinners includes punishment. That end is to "perish," for sin will "destroy men's souls." The result is "eternal death."

Like the Didache, Barnabas uses these scriptural terms with no explanation. Either he knows what Scripture means and intends to convey the same thing, knows what it means and uses its language to be ambiguous, or does not know what it means and uses its terminology to be safe. Taken at face value, his words suggest the final extinction of sinners after some righteous recompense that involves "suffering."

Clement of Rome. The so-called First Epistle of Clement is regarded as an authentic work of the early second century, written by a bishop of Rome to the church at Corinth. Twice it touches on the end of the wicked. Clement is appealing for unity among some factions at Corinth, a problem Paul had tackled in his correspondence to the same church. Clement appeals for self-restraint and obedience, warning that "we shall not incur ordinary injury but rather great danger if we recklessly give ourselves over to the wishes of those men who plunge into strife and discord" (1 Clem. 14:2). He follows this with the biblical quotation that "transgressors will be cut off," using the same word (*exolothreuō*) Peter did in Acts 3:23.

The so-called Second Epistle of Clement may be from another hand at a slightly later time, but it, too, is usually listed among the works of the apostolic fathers. This Clement recalls how Jesus had said that He will tell some to "go away from Me, I do not know you, from whence you are, workers of iniquity" (2 Clem. 4:5). He quotes Jesus' warning to the apostles to "fear him who, after killing you, has power to throw soul and body into gehenna of fire" (2 Clem. 5:4). Like most other writers on the subject, he quotes Isaiah's statement concerning the wicked, that "their worm will not die and their fire will not be quenched"; but where most stop at that, he continues with the prophet that "they will be a spectacle to all flesh" (2 Clem. 7:6). In view of these things, Clement warns, "nothing can deliver us from the eternal punishment if we disobey His commands" (2 Clem. 6:7).

Later he explains in more detail, borrowing from Malachi and perhaps 2 Peter.

> "But know this," he writes, "already the day of judgment is coming as a burning oven. And some of the heavens will melt, and all the earth will melt like lead over a fire, and then the secret and open works of men will be manifest."—2 Clem. 16:3.

Finally, he comments on the words he has already quoted from Isaiah 66.

> He speaks of that day of judgment, when they will see those who lived impiously among us, and perverted the commands of Jesus Christ. But the righteous . . . will be giving glory to God when they see how those who . . . denied Jesus through their words or through their works are punished with terrible torture in unquenchable fire. —2 Clem. 17:6, 7.

Clement is familiar with scriptural language describing future punishment from both the Old and New Testaments. He quotes Isaiah in unusual detail, as well as Malachi, but also refers to two and perhaps three statements of Jesus. He might reflect words from 2 Peter. His most explicit explanation of the scriptural language says the righteous will glorify God when they see how unbelievers or apostates "are punished with terrible torture in unquenchable fire."

Traditionalists will take that to mean unending conscious torment. Conditionalists will think it only affirms horrible pains from a fire which cannot be extinguished. It says nothing of the wicked being immortal or incorruptible. It does not say how long the wicked will be tortured or what the final effect of the fire will be. The language is capable of both interpretations. Taken at face value, it more easily fits the conditionalist view, particularly since there is no further explanation to the contrary. But that, too, will continue to be a matter of debate.

Ignatius of Antioch. This bishop of Antioch was convicted as a Christian by an imperial court, then was escorted by soldiers to Rome to be executed for his faith. Along the way he encouraged the bands of Christians who came out to meet and comfort him. He also wrote letters to seven churches, which have come down to us. Four of them contain references to our subject.

To the Ephesians he exhorted:

> These are the last times. . . . Let us fear the long-suffering of God that it may not be for our condemnation. For let us either fear the coming wrath, or let us love the present grace.—Ignatius to the Ephesians 11:1.

The false teacher is "filthy" and "will go into the unquenchable fire, as also will the one who listens to him" (Ignatius to the Ephesians 16:2). Both the coming wrath and unquenchable fire are prominent expressions from Scripture which Ignatius does not further explain.

He tells the Magnesians that "two things lie before us, life and death, and each person is about to go to his own place" (Ignatius to the Magnesians 5:1). Ignatius reminds the Trallians that "Jesus Christ died for us, that by believing in His death you might escape death" (Ignatius to the Trallians 2:1). The contrasting pictures of life and death occur frequently in Scripture, as we have seen. It may be significant that Ignatius speaks of Jesus' death and the sinner's final death in the same sentence, with no indication that the word has more than one meaning in both cases.

God will call all created beings into account, according to Ignatius. He warns:

> Let no one be deceived! Even the heavenly beings and the glory of the angels, and the visible and invisible rulers, unless they believe in the blood of Christ, judgment is also for them.—Ignatius to the Smyrnaeans 6:1.

Peter and Jude also spoke of angels held for judgment, and Paul warned that angels who perverted the gospel would also become accursed.

Polycarp. Perhaps the best-known of the ancient post-apostolic martyrs, faithful Polycarp has inspired millions by his steadfast testimony unto death. He knew the apostle John, and he reflected John's words as he spoke of some Christian fundamentals.

> For everyone who does not confess that Jesus Christ is come in the flesh is antichrist. And whoever does not confess the testimony of the cross is of the devil. And whoever . . . says there is neither resurrection nor judgment, this one is Satan's firstborn.—Polycarp to the Philippians 7:1.

Polycarp clearly held that the wicked would be raised and judged, a doctrine taught by both Old and New Testaments. That is as far as he goes in this work, which is indisputably authentic.

A later work, entitled The Martyrdom of Polycarp, also quotes the great man, but its value is somewhat less since its authenticity is more difficult to establish. It gives Polycarp's words of praise as he recollects martyrs who preceded him. He says "the fire of their inhuman tormentors was cold to them, for they had before their eyes escaping the eternal and never-to-be-quenched [fire]" (Martyrdom 2:3). In the arena Polycarp addresses the governor with the words:

> You threaten me with fire which burns for an hour and after a little while is quenched. For you are ignorant of that fire of the coming judgment and eternal punishment, kept for the wicked.—Martyrdom 11:2.

Polycarp clearly intends to contrast man's fire with God's fire. Since he describes God's fire both as "eternal" and also "never-to-be-quenched," he seems to denote two different aspects of it. Does he think in terms of its other-age quality (eternal) and its unendingness (unquenchable)? Does he think of its unendingness (eternal) and its irresistibility (unquenchable)? Or does he think of its other-age quality (eternal) and its irresistibility (unquenchable)? Authors will argue, but we will probably have to wait for the Age to Come to know for sure.

Whatever its precise nature or end, the fire of God's punishment will be far worse than any man can kindle, and the prospects of avoiding it inspire martyrs now to go to the stake with a heart full of joy. Polycarp knew what the Master had meant when He warned to fear God and not man. May we learn the same lesson today.

The Epistle to Diognetus. This short letter from an unknown author gives one of the most eloquent descriptions of the life-style of early Christians, and it is worth a trip to the library for that reason alone. It is addressed to a pagan ruler, and it explains and defends the ways and thoughts of those who follow Jesus. The pagan Diognetus does not understand how Christians so easily face death for their faith. The author says his reader will also learn to despise what now seems to be death

> when you fear the real death, which is reserved for those who will be condemned to the eternal fire which will punish to the end [*mechri telous*] those delivered over to it. Then you will marvel at those who for righteousness endure the temporary fire, and you will call them blessed when you understand that fire.—Diognetus 10:7, 8.

Again the contrast is between the fire men kindle and that God will inflict. The fact that the "eternal fire" will "punish to the end" seems to indicate a destroying fire that burns until all is consumed. By contrasting this with "temporary fire," the author might believe the "eternal fire" keeps burning forever after its victims are consumed. Or he might use "temporal" for fire of the Present Age and "eternal" for fire of the Age to Come. It is easy for partisans to be dogmatic but wise for researchers to be cautious!

Conclusion. The apostolic fathers speak clearly on some points and less clearly on others. They agree with Scripture and with each other that the wicked will be raised to face God in judgment. They nowhere indicate that the wicked will be immortal, and they strongly suggest in a number of places that they will not. (In an earlier chapter we noted at length the context of their statements on immortality, which some conditionalists have overlooked.)

There is a "way of life" and a "way of death." God's punishment for the wicked will be terrible, and it will involve fire. That fire is eternal and unquenchable, just as Isaiah and Jesus had said. Nowhere do the apostolic fathers indicate that it will preserve the wicked alive or that they will endure it in conscious agony forever. They affirm, on the other hand, that the wicked will "perish," be "destroyed" and "die."

The apostolic fathers confine their remarks almost entirely to the words of Scripture—a practice which leaves unanswered questions but surely no room for disputation! (Perhaps traditionalists and conditionalists today could come together on such an agreement—that both would use without qualification every term Scripture uses on the subject, and that neither would expand his description beyond the bounds of scriptural language. Like Solomon facing the case of one baby with two mothers, we might call for the sword of the Spirit, then let the response from the two sides help us judge their respective claims!)

The Old Testament was God's first written word on the subject. Some intertestamental writers found it inadequate to express their view, so they enlarged on its picture with details of unending torment. Jesus and the apostles came back to the language of the Old Testament, borrowing only the popular place-names, Gehenna and Tartarus, from intertestamental lore. The apostolic fathers seemed content with their language. Beginning with the next century, theologians and authors for 1300 years embellished the story with much language nowhere found in Scripture. The Reformers said very little on hell, confining themselves largely to the words of Scripture. Many Protestant creeds surpassed both Scripture and the Reformers with additional explanations, as has much popular preaching ever since.

The time has come for us all to return again to biblical terminology —*all* of it from Genesis to Revelation—and to stop right there. The apostolic fathers probably knew more than we do on many spiritual matters, and that is the force of their example.

Justin Martyr and Tatian

Justin Martyr (A.D. 114-165). Justin is best known for his two *Apologies* defending the Christian faith and for his *Dialogue with Trypho the Jew.* Both his *Apologies* abound with references to the punishment by fire awaiting the wicked, which Justin regularly calls "eternal punishment" or "eternal fire" (*First Apology*, chs. 12, 17, 45; *Second Apology*, chs. 1, 8, 9). Both expressions are biblical, of course, and are used by proponents of conditionalism and traditionalism alike. Justin was a philosopher before he was a Christian, and Eusebius says that he preferred to wear his philosopher's garb when he preached. Because we do not know exactly what his opponents were saying or the precise point Justin hopes to prove or dispute, it is difficult to pin down the exact meaning of what he writes. We will notice some of his important statements which traditionalists claim support eternal torment, then some of his major pronouncements used by conditionalists in defense of total destruction. Along the way, we will suggest the response each side might make to the other.

Traditionalist Justin. Traditionalists such as Pusey point particularly to three passages in Justin's *First Apology*. In chapter 18 he argues that death is not the end of man, that there will be a resurrection and immortality. Justin speaks of earlier kings who he said

> died the death common to all, which, if it issued in insensibility, would be a godsend to all the wicked. But since sensation remains to all who have ever lived, and eternal punishment is laid up [i.e., for the wicked], see that ye neglect not to be convinced.[8]

In chapter 20 he says again that "we affirm that the souls of the wicked, being endowed with sensation even after death, are punished." When Justin says the wicked will be "endowed with sensation" or that "sensation remains" for the wicked after death, traditionalists understand him to mean that the wicked will forever be conscious of pain and that the "eternal fire" will torment them always.

In chapter 28 Justin is speaking of Satan as he writes: "That he would be sent into the fire with his host, and the men who follow him, and would be punished for an endless duration, Christ foretold." Justin's most "traditionalist" statement appears in chapter 52 of his *First Apology*. There he describes the second coming of Christ and the events that will then take place.

> He shall come from heaven with glory, accompanied by His angelic host, when also He shall raise the bodies of all men who have lived, and shall clothe those of the worthy with immortality, and shall send those of the wicked, endued with wicked sensibility, into everlasting fire with the wicked devils. . . . And in what kind of sensation and punishment the wicked are to be, hear from what was said in like manner with reference to this; it is as follows: "Their worm shall not rest, and their fire shall not be quenched;" and then shall they repent, when it profits them not.

This quotation, traditionalists insist, unquestionably aligns Justin Martyr on their side of this debate.

---

8. This quotation and those following are taken from Alexander Roberts and James Donaldson, eds., *Ante-Nicene Christian Library: Translations of the Writings of the Fathers Down to A.D. 325.* Hereafter "ANCL."

Conditionalists, however, do not concede the point. When Justin speaks of sensibility for the wicked after death in chapters 18 and 20, they say, he is refuting those who say death is the end of all men. He is not denying the final, penal, eternal extinction of the wicked, nor is he affirming the nature of the punishment appointed for the wicked. He simply insists that the first death is not the end of the wicked—they will once again be given sensibility, and they will suffer the judgment to which God sentences them in the eternal fire. How long they will suffer in that fire and whether or not they can endure it forever is not in Justin's mind at all, conditionalists affirm.

When he describes that punishment in the worm-and-fire words from Isaiah 66, Justin still does not necessarily teach eternal torment, conditionalists would say. For although he adds to Isaiah's words the statement that "then shall they repent, when it profits them not" (Isaiah had viewed *corpses* lying amidst fire and worms, where no repentance would ever occur), he still does not say how long they will continue to suffer. He might only be saying that the wicked will find the fire inescapable and that they will surely be consumed by it in spite of every attempt at repentance.

Constable gives what he obviously regards as the final answer to Justin's "traditionalist" quotations. According to him, Justin held a philosophical doctrine, then common, concerning "secret fire" which renewed or regenerated whatever it consumed. According to Constable, Justin only meant that the wicked, who were dead, would "remain immortal" inasmuch as their members would be physically "renewed" by this "secret fire" which consumed and renewed together. They would therefore be a spectacle to all onlookers even though they were not alive or conscious of the burning. Yet my own perusal of Justin Martyr's major works did not uncover such a notion, which in Constable's view was not only present but clearly discernable.[9]

Conditionalist Justin. Constable and other conditionalists also have a list of "proof-texts" from Justin Martyr. We will mention and briefly note two kinds.

---

9. Constable, *Future Punishment*, pp. 174-177. Constable quotes Tertullian as saying that this "secret fire" was a common notion in his time, and suggests that it is "not unreasonable" to assume Justin also held such a view.

In a number of places Justin seems to teach that the wicked will be raised in their old mortal bodies. The righteous will be given immortality, but the wicked will not. Conditionalists see this as proof positive that Justin understood the punishment in "eternal fire" to result in the eternal extinction of the wicked, for mortal flesh could not long endure the pains and power of hell. Justin distinguishes between himself and Plato, for example, this way:

> Plato, in like manner, used to say that Rhadamanthus and Minos would punish the wicked who came before them; and we say that the same thing will be done, but at the hand of Christ, and upon the wicked in the same bodies united again to their spirits which are now to undergo everlasting punishment; and not only, as Plato said, for a period of a thousand years. —*First Apology*, ch. 8.

The *Dialogue with Trypho* abounds with such "mortalist" sentiments, say those holding the view. Justin tells how he had encountered a certain old man, evidently a Christian, as he once walked in solitude. Justin uses their conversation to express his own ideas, though some of the following statements are attributed to the old man who becomes his teacher.

The old man agrees that not all souls die, "for that were truly a piece of good fortune to the evil." Those "which have appeared worthy of God never die; but others are punished so long as God wills them to exist and to be punished." Justin agrees that only God is truly incorruptible and that all creatures can and will die.

> For those things which exist after God . . . have the nature of decay, and are such as may be blotted out and cease to exist; for God alone is unbegotten and incorruptible, and therefore He is God, but all other things after Him are created and corruptible. For this reason souls both die and are punished. —Ch. 5.

The old man continues:

> Now, that the soul lives, no one would deny. But if it lives, it lives not as being life, but as the partaker of life. . . . Now the soul partakes of life, since God wills it to live. Thus, then, it will not even partake [of life] when God does not will it to live. For to live is not its attribute, as it is God's; but as . . . the soul leaves the body, and the man exists no longer; even so, whenever the soul must cease to exist, the spirit of life is removed from it, and there is no more soul, but it goes back to the place from whence it was taken. —Ch. 6.

It is clear, conditionalists conclude, that Justin believed the soul was mortal, that it would suffer only as long as God willed, and that finally it would pass out of existence.

Conditionalists also introduce a second line of argument. In more passages than one, they say, Justin explicitly says that the wicked will finally pass away. One example is found in chapter 44 of his *First Apology*. Justin is explaining the biblical warning of destruction by sword.

> And that expression, "The sword shall devour you," does not mean that the disobedient shall be slain by the sword, but the sword of God is fire, of which they who choose to do wickedly become the fuel. Wherefore He says, "The sword shall devour you: for the mouth of the Lord hath spoken it." And if He had spoken concerning a sword that cuts and at once dispatches, He would not have said, shall *devour*.

In chapter 7 of the *Second Apology* Justin makes the same point another way.

> Wherefore God delays causing the confusion and destruction of the whole world, by which the wicked angels and demons and men shall cease to exist, because of the seed of the Christians. . . . If it were not so . . . the fire of judgment would descend and utterly destroy all things, even as formerly the flood left no one but . . . Noah. . . . For so we say that there will be the conflagration, but not as the Stoics, according to their doctrine of all things being changed into one another, which seems most degrading. . . . But since God in the beginning made the race of angels and men with free-will, they will justly suffer in eternal fire the punishment of whatever sins they have committed.

Conditionalists proudly point to Justin, therefore, as an early supporter of their view that the wicked will rise, be judged, be expelled into hell, suffer according to the measure ordained by divine justice, and finally pass away forever.

Traditionalists naturally disagree but here seem at their weakest. They might say that Justin's remarks concerning immortality only qualify his concept by giving God *inherent* immortality while man's is derived, but Justin's other declarations that the wicked will perish as in the Flood deaden the impact of that argument. Pusey says that those statements cannot mean what conditionalists make of them because of Justin's other statements which seem to teach eternal torment. He cites the same text listed just now as favoring conditional immortality, in support of the traditionalist view, in which Justin distinguishes between his teaching and Plato's. The wicked will undergo "everlasting punishment," Justin had said, contrary to Plato, who taught punishment was "for a period of a thousand years."

But conditionalists respond that Pusey misunderstands the error Justin is refuting. Plato believed there would be a thousand-year punishment *followed by transmigration of the soul* to a fresh cycle of life in a new body. Justin denies this. The wicked will suffer, he agrees, but they will undergo *everlasting punishment*. Conditionalists say this means eternal extinction.

Round and round they have gone over Justin—who, were he living to hear the question point-blank, might quell the whole storm in a single sentence. But then, we remember, so might Paul or Peter or Jesus! In the end, most nonbiblical references are of little help except for refuting the dogmatic extremes too commonly found on both sides. We need someone to explain the explainers. Better to read them quickly, then turn our attention back to Scripture.

Tatian (Died A.D. 180). Perhaps Justin Martyr's most famous pupil, Tatian lived in Mesopotamia. He was contemporary with Athenagoras of Alexandria, Theophilus of Antioch and Irenaeus of Gaul, overlapping in his final years the young lawyer and orator, Tertullian of Carthage. Although some conditionalists dispute the point, Tatian seems to have taught the immortality of the wicked as well as the righteous. With the possible exception of Justin Martyr, his teacher, he may be the first Christian writer to explicitly express that view. From the mid-second century such expressions became almost commonplace in the writings of the fathers, a noticeable change from the earlier "apostolic fathers," who repeatedly spoke of immortality and incorruption as God's gift or reward to the faithful. Tatian's faith is explained and defended in his *Address to the Greeks*.

Christians believe, he says, "that there will be a resurrection of bodies after the consummation of all things; . . . a resurrection once for all . . . for the purpose of passing judgment" (ch. 6). Tatian denied that the soul was itself immortal, but he probably was denying what the Platonists affirmed—that it possessed inherent immortality and was pre-existent. Like other Christian apologists of the first few centuries, he insisted that God had created the soul and that it could continue only at His pleasure. (Conditionalists have sometimes missed this direction of the apologists' argument, a point discussed in an earlier chapter.) Yet unless Tatian's words are misleading indeed, he believed that God would give immortality to the wicked in the resurrection, though for eternal conscious torment and not bliss. He wrote in chapter 13 of *Address to the Greeks*:

> The soul is not itself immortal, O Greeks, but mortal. Yet it is possible for it not to die. If, indeed, it knows not the truth, it dies, and is dissolved with the body, but rises again at last at the end of the world with the body, receiving death by punishment in immortality. But, again, if it acquires the knowledge of God, it dies not, although for a time it be dissolved.

In chapter 14 he says again that "as we . . . afterwards receive the immortal with enjoyment, or the painful with immortality, so the demons . . . will have hereafter the same immortality." If he means what his words seem to say, he probably also gives a new meaning to "fuel" when he later says that a certain Greek philosopher "will be delivered up in the day of consummation as fuel for the eternal fire" (ch. 17). Unlike the fuel consumed by ordinary fire and in the biblical pictures, this "fuel" will never burn up though it continues to burn forever.

Pusey's Testimony of the Martyrs

In his defense of the traditional doctrine (*What Is of Faith as to Everlasting Punishment?*), E. B. Pusey includes a chapter citing the testimony of ancient Christian martyrs.[10] Pusey is responding to F. W. Farrar's suggestion of a "larger hope" for possible salvation beyond death, which he believes tends toward universalism or restorationism. He is not specifically rebutting conditionalism or the idea that the wicked will ultimately pass out of existence, though he denies that by what he affirms. If anyone deserves our attention, Pusey reasons, surely the martyrs do! Their words reflect the most sober thoughts of men and women about to die for their faith. We agree with Pusey entirely, and made the same point earlier regarding the seven martyred brothers of 1 and 2 Maccabees.

This material is not the most reliable, however, in terms of documentation, though we do not disparage Pusey's quotations for that reason. According to F. L. Cross, the accounts of these deaths owe

---

10. Pusey, *What Is of Faith?* pp. 154-171.

their preservation in many cases from the later commemoration of these martyrs on the anniversary of their death, a day celebrated as their "birthday" (*natalitia*). Sometimes the text came from actual court records or official minutes of the martyrdom. Some give the account as told by eyewitnesses or as reconstructed from private letters. Sometimes a local community wrote the martyr's history for liturgical use years after the death, and some accounts probably are more fiction than fact. Cross gives a bibliography and other introductory material in the section, "Acts of the Martyrs," in *The Early Christian Fathers*.[11]

Even if the martyrologies are completely accurate, however, and giving full credence to the sobriety and honesty of the great Christians they honor, Pusey's evidence is disappointing to one wishing to prove the traditionalist position by this late second-century date. Felicitas and her sons speak of eternal "destruction," "peril" and "punishment," of "everlasting destruction" and everlasting fire," even of "destruction in everlasting burning." But this is nearly all biblical language and is easily explained by the conditionalist viewpoint. Polycarp talks of "perpetual torment of eternal fire," which, if "torment" means conscious torment, supports the traditionalist view. A lady named Biblias warns against the "torments of eternal Gehenna" but does not say whether the torments continue forever or end with the sinner's extinction.

Pusey cites others who speak of "a death unto perpetual ill," "real and perpetual torments," "eternal torments," "eternal death and unutterable torments without end," "eternal burnings," "real punishment and greater perpetual torments." These expressions all seem to require everlasting conscious punishment.

Still later martyrs clearly express the traditional view. There we find such expressions as "sustain deathless punishment" or "weeping and gnashing of teeth for ever and ever." These statements, which appear at first to be biblical, prove on close investigation not only to lack scriptural precedent but to add to the scriptural language words which contradict its biblical usage.

Mixed among these statements, Pusey also quotes martyrs who speak of "eternal death," "outer darkness and unextinguishable fire," "destroying for eternity," "eternal fire which can destroy body and soul," "the punishment of eternal death," God, who "slayest the soul

---

11. F. L. Cross, "Acts of the Martyrs," *The Early Christian Fathers*, pp. 192ff.

for ever and ever," "destruction and eternal fire," "that eternal fire which burneth body and soul together," those who are "to be rooted out for ever by the true God," "perpetual destruction," "perpetual death," "perpetual punishment," God, who has "power to cast both thee and thy tyrant into Gehenna," "death and everlasting destruction." These all seem to express the conditionalist viewpoint and describe final, irreversible, eternal death in hell.

Should we interpret "perpetual torment" in the light of "perpetual death"—or the other way around? Or is there another solution? Might it not be the case, and the best explanation of Pusey's citations from the martyrs, that there was already a marked difference of opinion concerning the precise destiny of the wicked by the time of these deaths and that each person simply expresses his or her own particular understanding? We know from the literature of the period that such a difference existed. Why may not the martyrs reflect the same differences in details? All agreed that the wicked must answer to God and must be punished for their sins. There is no evident hesitancy by any to speak of that punishment in terms of fire—Jesus had done the same. Nor does there seem to be any timidity about using words like "death" or "destruction"—these had been the favorite words of the apostle Paul.

Which concept became the major one varied from person to person, or place to place, but in each case that term or figure simply became the means of explaining others which seemed to express something different. That the literature shows no internal dispute on the subject seems to reflect an acceptance by this time of either view—that the wicked would suffer eternally in conscious torment or that they would suffer in punishment which culminated in eternal death. The important point is that the wicked must answer to God, who will repay their crimes with eternal punishment by what the Bible calls the fire of hell.

Athenagoras, Irenaeus, Theophilus: Mixed Views

Athenagoras (A.D. 127-190). Athenagoras was born in Athens and trained in Platonic philosophy, then became a Christian and settled at Alexandria. He explicitly denied the annihilation of the wicked and was, according to conditionalist Constable, the first *explicit* advocate of the traditionalist view. In *A Plea for the Christians* Athenagoras wrote:

> We are persuaded that when we are removed from the present life we shall live another life, better than the present one, and heavenly, not earthly . . . or, falling with the rest, a worse one and in fire; for God has not made us as sheep or beasts of burden, a mere by-work, and that we should perish and be annihilated.—Ch. 31.

The controversy is sure to continue regarding who was first to teach conscious unending torment. What may be more important for understanding the development of doctrine is the basis on which Athenagoras reached his conclusion. For it is undisputed that he based eternal torment on his presupposition of the immortality of all men. And he rested his doctrine of immortality, not on Scripture, but on philosophical reasoning.[12] "Nothing that is endowed with reason and judgment has been created, or is created, for the use of another, whether greater or less than itself," he said, "but the sake of the life and continuance of the being itself so created." And "since the cause of man's creation is seen to lie in perpetual existence, the being so created must be preserved for ever" (*Resurrection of the Dead*, chs. 12, 13, 17, 19).

Athenagoras applies Paul's description of the glorified and immortal body to all men alike, the lost as well as the saved, a view held by many traditionalists since, but one without a shred of exegetical support. Given such a view of immortality, and excluding the possibility of universal restoration, the traditional view of hell necessarily follows. Constable writes of "the marvellous power which the introduction of the Platonic dogma of the soul's immortality had upon the doctrine of punishment."[13]

Today we see the tide turning the other direction. With the growing belief that Western culture (including the church) has assimilated a dualistic view of man from the pagan speculations of Greek philosophy, alongside a rising conviction that the Bible presents quite a different view of man, the mortal creature wholly dependent on God, the doctrine of final punishment is also coming more and more

---

12. Constable makes the point in his *Future Punishment*, p. 196. It is easily illustrated by statements throughout Athenagoras' treatise on *The Resurrection of the Dead*.

13. Constable, *Future Punishment*, p. 204.

to the forefront as a subject to be reconsidered. The result is a growing dissatisfaction with the traditionalist doctrine of everlasting conscious torment; at the same time there is a resurgence of biblical study and renewed exegetical zeal. Conditionalist Froom sees the trend as natural and quite inevitable; traditionalist Buis recognizes the situation but is puzzled as to its cause.[14]

Irenaeus (A.D. 130-202). Both sides in the controversy claim Irenaeus, Bishop of Gaul. Pusey devotes five pages to his writings, quoting references to fire that is "perpetual," "everlasting" and "eternal," and people who are "forever condemned." The longest passage Pusey quotes from Irenaeus in support of the traditional view speaks of deprivation.

> Now separation from God is Death; and separation from light is darkness, and separation from God is casting away all the good things which come from Him. . . . For though God punish them not by express dispensation, yet . . . they are deprived of all good things: and the good things from God being eternal and endless, the privation of them also is, of course, eternal and endless. Just as light being perpetual, those who have blinded themselves or have been blinded by others, are in perpetuity deprived of the enjoyment of light.[15]

Conditionalists would accept all these expressions and call Irenaeus back to the witness stand for cross-examination. Does not this explanation of deprivation really support the extinction of the wicked, they would ask. For *being* itself—as well as a *blessed* life—is a good gift of God for which man is dependent. Utter deprivation of every godly blessing would therefore include the loss of existence itself, since man, being created, did not exist until God willed to give him existence. Constable, in fact, does call on Irenaeus as a witness for his position. He introduces the Bishop of Gaul with these words:

---

14. Froom, *Conditionalist Faith*, 1:1076-1078; 2:1044-1047; Harry Buis, *The Doctrine of Eternal Punishment*, p. ix.

   Buis writes: "In our generation we have witnessed an increased belief in the deity of Christ and in the authority of the Word of God. We have witnessed a trend toward orthodoxy with regard to many other cardinal doctrines. But the doctrine of eternal punishment is strongly denied by many." Evangelical Orthodox Church bishop, Jon E. Braun, attributes this to laxity and indifference in his *Whatever Happened to Hell?* But Mennonite pastor, Gerald C. Studer, suggests another possibility. "Perhaps there is a troublesome defect in the traditional view," he writes in his *After Death, What?* p. 109.

15. Pusey, *What Is of Faith?*, pp. 182-186. The quotation is from Irenaeus, *Against Heresies*, bk. 5, ch. 27 (ANCL, 9:129-130). Froom gives the same quotation as evidence that Irenaeus taught conditionalism (Froom, *Conditionalist Faith*, 1:900).

No one of the fathers recurs more perpetually to this subject than Iranaeus does. . . . Nor is there one of the fathers who gives fuller descriptions of it. He evidently brought it forward in all the terrors he supposed to belong to it as a warning to escape from it. Yet, in all his allusions to and descriptions of it, there cannot be found a parallel to numberless passages which we might quote readily from Hippolytus, Tertullian, Augustine, and others.[16]

Constable cites, as typical expressions of Irenaeus, references to sinners "who shall be burned up as were Nadab and Abihu" by fire from the Lord, souls that perish, "punished with everlasting death," those who "pass away" and "will not endure for ever," and the wicked who will be "deprived of continuance for ever and ever."[17]

Theophilus of Antioch (Died A.D. 181-188). Pusey also quotes Theophilus of Antioch, a contemporary of Irenaeus and Athenagoras, though widely separated in location. Theophilus wrote of some who will be "tormented with eternal punishments." He quoted from Paul the contrasting picture found in Romans 2:8, 9. To the "anger and wrath, tribulation and anguish," Theophilus added the expression, "and at the last everlasting fire shall possess such men."

One wonders that Pusey would call on these expressions for support. It becomes clearer when one remembers that most traditionalist advocates (including Pusey) have directed their arguments against either those who said the first death is the sinner's final end and that the wicked will not be punished after that death (the present-day Jehovah's Witness view), or against the view that some or all sentenced to hell eventually will be restored to salvation and eternal bliss. Only secondarily have traditionalist writers opposed the understanding of final retribution which holds to eternal punishment by ultimate extinction. Remarks directed that way often have seemed more a reflex action out of a sense of traditional duty. Traditionalists have never launched a full-scale investigation of the extinction/annihilation position or even a cursory review of the scriptural basis on which it claims to rest.

---

16. Constable, *Future Punishment*, p. 187.

17. Ibid., p. 188. Constable argues that Irenaeus thinks future punishment is "eternal" because "it is the loss of blessing which is eternal. It does not consist in eternally inflicting new misery, but in the eternal loss of what might have been eternally enjoyed." We note elsewhere that both Augustine and Jonathan Edwards conceded that such a situation would satisfy the expression "eternal punishment," although both strenuously insisted that everlasting conscious torment is the biblical view.

Conditionalists are not nearly so impressed by what Theophilus says (Pusey cites but does not give the reference from *Theophilus to Autolycus*, bk. 1, ch. 14) as by what he does not say. He does *not* picture the lost man saying, as Pusey quotes Ephraem doing about A.D. 370, "I go up to doom and to chastisements which have no ending; and in torment that passeth not, I abide and am tormented." Theophilus does not say, as that same fourth-century writer does, that the Bible's "unquenchable fire" is "not consuming what it devoureth, for it was not appointed to consume, but to cause suffering and agony."[18] He does *not* ask, as Pusey quotes the later Basil as asking, "With what body shall [the lost] endure those interminable and unendurable scourges, where is the quenchless fire and the worm punishing deathlessly, and the dark and horrible abyss of hell . . . where the evils have no end?"[19]

Theophilus does quote the Greek Sibyl, as evidence that even the heathen poets believed in the punishment of the wicked, in which she spoke of the wicked who "shall daily burn in flames" (*Theophilus to Autolycus*, bk. 11, ch. 36). But even if this should be construed as holding to everlasting conscious torment, it is still light-years away from the kinds of statements which become commonplace after the days of Tertullian and finally Augustine.

As the second century drew to a close, men such as Theophilus, Irenaeus and Athenagoras bear clear testimony to a mixed view on final punishment. They all agree that the doom of the lost will be final and irreversible. Irenaeus appears to clearly support final extinction, appealing to words of Scripture. Theophilus may be read as either conditionalist or traditionalist, appealing to Scripture phrases with slight explanatory additions of his own. Athenagoras denies extinction and argues clearly for eternal conscious torment on the basis

---

18. This is inherent in the traditionalist definition of "unquenchable fire," although, as we have seen, it has absolutely no support in either the Old or New Testament. For centuries much writing and preaching has allowed uninformed imagination to give content to the expression "unquenchable fire" rather than searching the Scriptures to learn its common prophetic significance.

19. The same may be said for the figure of the undying worm as is stated above of unquenchable fire. Basil's statement that the worm will be "punishing deathlessly" is pure eisegesis and reads into a biblical figure a later traditional understanding. The primary source of this worm in Scripture is Isaiah 66:24, where it consumes dead bodies rather than punishing live ones. Scripture clearly says the wicked will "die" in the "second death"; "deathlessness" (immortality) is applied to men in the Bible only in terms of the glorified bodies of the redeemed in the resurrection unto life.

Pusey's quotations in this paragraph come from *What Is of Faith?* pp. 187-215.

of the immortality of the soul, which he grounds on philosophical reasoning.

These three men, viewed in the same order, also prefigure the general development of the doctrine of final punishment from the time of the apostolic fathers until the time of Augustine. There, for practical purposes, it reached its present form and was firmly fixed as a received dogma. But one other patristic writer had an important role in the development of this doctrine, and we will consider his contribution now.

Tertullian (Born c. A.D. 160)

Tertullian was born at Carthage in north Africa to heathen parents. His father was a centurion in the Roman proconsular service, and he named his son Quintus Septimius Florens Tertullianus. Tertullian was educated in law and rhetoric and gained a mastery of Greek. As a young man he went to Rome, where he earned a reputation as a jurist. About the year 196 he accepted Christianity and returned to Carthage. There he exchanged his Roman toga for the philosopher's pallium and undertook the lifelong advocacy of what he now considered the ultimate cause. The rigorous moralistic system propagated by the Montanists appealed to Tertullian, and about A.D. 207 he joined an African branch of the sectarian movement. He died at Carthage sometime after the year 200.[20]

Tertullian was a man of extremes. "His passionate temperament knew no half-measures or hesitations," according to Bardy, a Catholic reviewer of the Latin fathers. He "had always been an enemy of the golden mean," Bardy continues, "and even in his youth his temperament had led him into the worst excesses." As Tertullian grows older, "his gloomy pessimism increases and his exaggerations pass all bounds."[21]

---

20. Cross, *The Early Christian Fathers*, pp. 135-136; Abbé Bardy, *The Christian Latin Literature of the First Six Centuries*, pp. 28-32.

21. Bardy, *Christian Latin Literature*, pp. 29-30.

F. L. Cross described the man and his influence like this.

> Of a fiery and rugged temperament, he was by nature a rebel and
> would hardly have fitted happily into any *milieu*. . . . But he was des-
> tined to exercise a remarkable influence on Western Christendom. . . .
> Besides being the first considerable Christian Latin writer, he was also
> the first great Latin thinker. His theological perception was so sharp
> and his range so wide that he created at one stroke the theological
> vocabulary of the Western Church. . . . Almost all his writing is con-
> troversial; . . . he became a master of invective. . . . His argumenta-
> tion too often resembles a display of fireworks.[22]

Tertullian accepted the immortality of the soul, the essentially
Greek idea which had long since permeated the thinking of practically all segments of the Western world. The Platonic ideas had
evolved, Stoicism had made its modifications, and Christian writers
such as Athenagoras had changed the definition of the immortal soul
to allow for its creation by God in the beginning. With the exception
of his treatise, *Against Marcion*, Tertullian's longest work was *De
Anima* [Concerning the soul]. Cross says this treatise contained "the
first extended discussion of the soul in Christian literature." In it Tertullian discourses on the nature of the soul (chs. 4-22), the origin of
the soul (chs. 23-41), and on such related topics as death, sleep,
dreams, and the resting place of the soul after death.[23]

Tertullian supported his doctrine of the immortal soul from the
creation of man. When God breathed in the breath of life, Tertullian
said, man received the immortal soul. Like Augustine and his Catholics, then Calvin and his Protestants, Tertullian did not consider it
important that the same Genesis story also calls the brute animals
"living souls" (Gen. 1:20, 21). The essential reasoning of all three
men follows the same lines, with surprisingly little development in
1300 years.

Besides philosophical arguments and his use of the creation story,
Tertullian offered empirical testimony concerning the soul and its attributes. In his assembly, he said, was "a sister, whose lot it has been
to be favoured with sundry gifts of revelation." Among the visions
she reported to the people after the sacred services were dismissed,
Tertullian tells of one in which she saw a soul.

---

22. Cross, *The Early Christian Fathers*, pp. 135-137.
23. Ibid., p. 143.

"Amongst other things," says she, "there has been shown to me a soul in bodily shape, and a spirit has been in the habit of appearing to me; not, however, a void and empty illusion, but such as would offer itself to be even grasped by the hand, soft and transparent, and of an ethereal colour, and in form resembling that of a human being in every respect." This was her vision, and for her witness there was God.[24]

To this philosophical belief in the immortality of the soul, Tertullian brought the zeal and passion of his Latin legal training and heart. Where the Greek fathers had "virtually ignored" the biblical theme of judgment (though they were clear on its certainty and on penal retribution), Gatch says the Latin mind "was deeply concerned with the processes of history and with the moral implications of action within history."[25] The Western, Latin church began about this time to be marked by a strong sense of law and order, and this "growing tendency to set forth the relations of God and man under the general categories of politics led to emphasis upon punishment in hell."[26] Since the flesh had participated in sin, it must justly share also in the penalty for sin.

Instead of showing the sovereignty of God, who finally has the last word, a sense of proper and exact justice became the dominant theme underlying the doctrine of the resurrection. This led, in turn, to the doctrine that the soul begins to be punished immediately after death. If the body were prompted to sin by the soul, it is only fair that the soul should be held somewhat more liable than the body and should therefore endure an additional measure of punishment. This reasoning, too, would receive additional impetus from Augustine, and from him its conclusions would finally pass through Calvin into the mainstream of Reformed theology.[27]

If the souls of even wicked men are immortal and destined to live forever, and if earthly sin will be punished by what the Bible calls

---

24. Tertullian, *De Anima*, ch. 9 (*ANCL*, 15:428). Tertullian's sentence continues: " . . . and the apostle most assuredly foretold that there were to be 'spiritual gifts' in the church." Earlier he had said of the sister that "all her communications are examined with the most scrupulous care, in order that their truth may be probed." One wonders how the examiners proceeded with this communication since Scripture is totally silent on the subject and Tertullian makes no mention of an inspired confirmation.

25. Milton McC. Gatch, *Death: Meaning and Mortality in Christian Thought and Contemporary Culture*, p. 65.

26. Shailer Mathews, "Future Punishment," *A Dictionary of Religion and Ethics*, p. 178.

27. See the appendixes in this book for a close examination of Augustine's book 21 of *The City of God* and also of John Calvin's treatise on the soul, entitled *Psychopannychia*.

"eternal fire," the only conclusion Tertullian could reach was that the wicked would endure conscious unending torment. When the Bible speaks of "destruction," therefore, it does not mean what it sounds like. We should think of the soul of the wicked, he says, as " 'lost,' not in the sense of destruction but of punishment, that is, in hell."[28] When Jesus warned that man can kill the body but God can destroy both body and soul, Tertullian cautioned against taking those words literally.

> If, therefore, any one shall violently suppose that the destruction of the soul and the flesh in hell amounts to a final annihilation of the two substances, and not to their penal treatment (as if they were to be consumed, not punished), let him recollect that the fire of hell is eternal— expressly announced as an everlasting penalty; and let him then admit that it is from this circumstance that this never-ending killing is more formidable than a merely human murder, which is only temporal.[29]

Conditionalists will not let such interpretations and language pass unhindered. Tertullian and others of his view, writes Constable,

> introduce a language which, to say the least of it, is absent from Scripture. When they mean to set forth beyond mistake what they hold, they tell us that the soul is immortal and cannot die, that the bodies of the wicked will be raised incorruptible and immortal, that the wicked will never die, never perish, never be consumed, never be destroyed,

---

28. Tertullian, *Resurrection of the Flesh*, ch. 34 (*ANCL*, 15:273).

Tertullian says in the next sentence that "it is not the soul which salvation will affect, since it is 'safe' already in its own nature by reason of its immortality, but rather the flesh, which, as all readily allow, is subject to destruction." He means that man's soul is indestructible ("safe") already but that Christ will also raise and "save" the flesh so that the whole man will enjoy eternal bliss in the case of the redeemed. The result will be "the restoration of the entire man, inasmuch as the Lord purposes to save that part of him which perishes [the body], whilst he will not of course lose that portion which cannot be lost [the soul]" (p. 274).

29. Ibid., ch. 35 (*ANCL*, 15:276).

Tertullian goes on to make the argument, still heard today, that if the second death were annihilation rather than everlasting conscious torment, God would have wasted His time in raising the wicked since they had perished already. Both Scripture and reason answer the argument. Scripture makes it *superfluous* by declaring more than once that the wicked *will* be raised and judged before undergoing final punishment. That is biblical truth whether Tertullian or anyone else understands God's motivation and efficiency or not. Human reason dismisses the argument as well, for every evil unpunished in this life calls out for a final reckoning and retribution based on perfect justice. Our own system of law provides medical care at great expense to prevent a murderer's death *before he stands trial* even though the court is expected to sentence him to death. Why should we suppose that God's justice should be cheated more easily? Traditionalists make the same point all the time in support of final judgment—and with good cause!

etc. To *appearance*, this language *contradicts* that of Scripture: at all events this language is *never* applied in Scripture to the wicked. What does it arise from? Surely the language of Scripture is sufficient to express the doctrine of Scripture.[30]

Here conditionalists begin to chafe beyond any point of tolerance. Throughout Scripture, they say, the inspired figures for final punishment suggest the total and utter destruction of things that perish. Yet from Tertullian to the present, the traditionalist position on hell has not only ignored the biblical illustrations but has manufactured new ones of its own—unbiblical figures which illustrate the exact opposite! This is how Constable describes his traditionalist opponents.

> He finds it said that the wicked shall be like the beasts that perish, that they shall consume like thorns; that they shall be burnt up like chaff; that they shall be reduced to ashes like a dry branch! What is his comment on these vivid emblems? He tells us that they are strong poetic figures! We see nothing to object to this, and merely ask him *of what* are they strong poetic figures? After an immensity of talk, we find him replying that they *are poetical figures representative of the very opposite to that which they teach.* The wicked perishing like beasts means that they are never to perish, and are exceedingly unlike beasts; the wicked consuming like thorns means that they will never consume at all, and will never bear the remotest resemblance to thorns which have been consumed; the wicked being burnt up like chaff means that they are never to be burnt up, and that they will never be like chaff that has been burnt up; and their being reduced to ashes like a dry branch means that they cannot by any possibility be reduced to ashes, or bear the faintest likeness to a dry branch which has been thoroughly consumed! Whether such a handling of God's Word as this is deceitful or not, let our readers and our opponents judge.[31]

If Constable's opponents have reached a judgment, they have not yet made it public. They have continued to make the same arguments and repeat the same conclusions to which Constable was objecting. They have also, almost without exception, totally ignored the enormous mound of evidence Constable and others of his persuasion

---

30. Constable, *Future Punishment*, p. 215.

31. Ibid., pp. 75-76. Constable misreads Augustine's analogies of worms that live in hot springs, flame-resistant salamanders, and volcanoes which burn but do not consume (ibid., pp. 71-72). Augustine does not say these things prove the nature of hell or even that hell is like all these things (though he believes that). Rather, he uses these illustrations which his opponents regard as authentic to show that they are inconsistent in calling his teaching unreasonable and impossible. See appendix on Augustine for more discussion.

have collected from both the Old and New Testaments, dismissing persistent questioners or critics with the fact that almost all of Christendom has held the traditionalist view for at least 1600 years. That answer has sufficed for centuries. But today, it appears, the questioners are not going home without more.

Clement of Alexandria: An Opposite Reaction Begins

If the immortality of the soul excluded ultimate extinction as the eternal destruction awaiting sinners, Tertullian's explanation of unending torment would still find a competing view. Although souls are immortal, Origen would later argue, and cannot be destroyed by the fires of hell, they may by that same fire be eventually purged of evil and finally enter heaven. Much controversy surrounds Origen and his views even today, and we will consider that in the next chapter. Here we simply introduce another, earlier writer who may have planted the seeds which Origen watered to bear the fruit of "restorationism." That writer was Clement of Alexandria, who died about A.D. 220.

If one looks under "hell" or "eternal punishment" in the index of the *Ante-Nicene Christian Library*, he will suppose Clement of Alexandria had nothing to say on the subject. A perusal of his works will uncover a few remarks on the end of the wicked, though Clement says more about punishment in this life than in the life to come. He also stresses the disciplinary, remedial and purifying purposes of punishment rather than its penal character as retribution for sin or wrong. It is difficult for the modern reader to always know what Clement is talking about—a statement that may be made as well about many of the Greek and Latin fathers.

In his *Recognitions* Clement seems to express the view held by Tertullian.[32] In chapter 28 of book 5, for example, he writes:

---

32. "Seems," because the following quotations may also be interpreted to mean extinction. Clement may use "immortality" of the soul, as some other apologists do, to mean it survives the death of the body and will therefore stand judgment. To "endure without end" may mean there is no relief of pain so long as one exists. And "to their destruction" might signify that the wicked are finally destroyed completely. In saying there will be no repentance in hell, he might expect hell to finally destroy the sinner—therefore no exit from it by repentance. On the other hand, his choice of the word "correction" in this regard opens the door for Origen's teaching of restorationism a generation later.

But if any persist in impiety till the end of life, then as soon as the soul, which is immortal, departs, it shall pay the penalty of its persistence in impiety. For even the souls of the impious are immortal, though perhaps they themselves would wish them to end with their bodies. But it is not so; for they endure without end the torments of eternal fire, and to their destruction they have not the quality of mortality. —*ANCL*, vol. 3, p. 320.

Or, again, in book 9, chapter 13:

But those who practise wickedness of purpose . . . and who take no thought for repentance—their punishment He defers to the future. For these men do not . . . deserve to end the punishment of their crimes in the present life . . . because their correction is . . . such as to demand the punishment of eternal fire in hell; and there their souls shall seek repentance, where they shall not be able to find it.—*ANCL*, vol. 3, p. 409.

Clement specifically discusses punishment in the present life in *The Miscellanies*. One wonders, though, if he would extend these principles to include punishment after death as well.

But punishment does not avail to him who has sinned, to undo his sin, but that he may sin no more, and that no one else fall into the like. Therefore the good God corrects for these three causes: First, that he who is corrected may become better than his former self; then that those who are capable of being saved by examples may be driven back, being admonished; and thirdly, that he who is injured may not be readily despised, and be apt to receive injury.—Bk. 4, ch. 24; *ANCL*, vol. 2, p. 211.

In the next book of the same work, however, Clement says that "punishments after death" and "penal retribution by fire, were pilfered from the Barbarian philosophy both by all the poetic Muses and by the Hellenic philosophy." He goes on to quote Plato's *Republic* concerning torment in the afterlife, relates it to the psalm which calls God's angels "flaming fire," and offers it all as proof that the soul is immortal or survives bodily death. Then he asks, "Did not Plato know of the rivers of fire and the depth of the earth, and Tartarus, called by the Barbarians Gehenna, . . . introducing such corrective tortures for discipline?" (bk. 5, ch. 14; *ANCL*, vol. 2, p. 275).

The "Barbarians" here are the Hebrews as viewed by Clement's Greek audience, though Clement argues that the noblest concepts of Greek philosophy were actually "pilfered" from the Hebrews (and

Scripture), who had them first. The last sentence matters most to us, where Clement refers to Gehenna or Tartarus as "corrective tortures" intended "for discipline."

Finally, in the *Stromata* Clement speaks of a spiritual or rational fire which does not burn the flesh but purifies the soul (bk. 7, ch. 6). While retaining the immortality of the soul, Clement has begun to redefine the purpose of the fire prepared for the wicked. Athenagoras and Tertullian had done the same already with the biblical figures of fire. What began in Scripture as a consuming, devouring, irreversible fire which could not be extinguished, resisted or escaped, became for Athenagoras and Tertullian a tormenting fire that never consumed or devoured but (in some writers) miraculously reconstituted what it burnt so as to extend its painful torture forever. But where Tertullian the Latin lawyer pored over tomes of justice, Clement the Alexandrian considered the rational value of discipline. Surely it is corrective, he surmised. And though he did not carry this idea through to clearly include final punishment, he set the stage for someone else to do so. As it happened, that one was none other than Clement's own pupil, Origen.

16

Is Hell Locked from the Outside?
(Origen's "Apocatastasis" and the Question of Universalism)

Origen and His Radical Suggestion

The ideas sown by Clement of Alexandria found receptive lodging in the mind of his pupil Origen, in whose speculations they germinated into the third historic understanding of final punishment. Origen was born A.D. 185 and died A.D. 250. He succeeded Clement as the great schoolmaster of Alexandria, leaving as his heritage an enormous influence on later theology as well as the particular method of allegorical interpretation which today is associated with his name. A man of great devotion, he endured both imprisonment and torture for his faith. And although he was condemned as heretical by later councils, many modern scholars of early church history regard him as the foremost Pre-Nicene father.[1]

Writers have traditionally classed Origen with the Platonists (or Neo-Platonists) as a philosopher, a grouping conditionalist authors find most accommodating to their historical outline of the doctrine of

---

1. F. L. Cross speaks of Origen's "supreme place among the Pre-Nicenes" in his *The Early Christian Fathers*, p. 134. Everett Ferguson calls Origen "the greatest scholar and most prolific author of the early church . . . a profound thinker . . . deeply spiritual and a loyal churchman" (Tim Dowley, ed., *Eerdmans' Handbook to the History of Christianity*, p. 104).

hell.[2] There is increasing awareness now that all the church fathers imbibed and responded to a living philosophy which, like all living things, was subject to change and development. This included Origen the Alexandrian, who Henry Chadwick has shown was also extensively influenced by Stoicism. F. L. Cross concludes that Origen's "debt to Platonism has been exaggerated and that it is wrong to regard him as the exponent of any one philosophical system."[3] This does not annul the conditionalist analysis, but it does warn against oversimplification.

Origen speculated that the "fire" of hell was a purifying and refining fire. Punishment would still be involved, but it would be remedial and would result in the ultimate salvation of every soul. The three major views which have been held concerning final punishment may thus be summarized by the adjectives one uses to describe hell's fire, whether *consuming* and *devouring* (conditionalist), *torturing* and *regenerative* (traditionalist), or *purifying* and *remedial* (restorationist).[4] Clement of Alexandria had hinted at final restoration from hell

---

2. Conditionalist authors, Constable and Froom, both discuss at some length Origen's "Platonic" presupposition of the immortality of the soul. Buis follows Shedd in stressing Origen's doctrine of free will, but both traditionalist writers pass lightly over his Platonism. One can generalize with some validity that Calvinistic authors tend to link opposition to the traditional doctrine of hell with Arminian free will, while critics frequently associate the traditional understanding with what they regard as extreme Calvinistic predestinarianism. Both sides probably miss the main point, however, since Pelagius seems to have outdone Augustine in his zeal for eternal torment, and at least one Arminian author, A. H. Strong, used free will as an argument for eternal torment! (Augustus Hopkins Strong, *Systematic Theology*, 3:1053).

The traditional doctrine probably owes its firm hold in Calvinistic circles to Calvin's fantastic zeal for the immortality of the soul (see Appendix B on Calvin's *Psychopannychia*), the fact that many Anabaptists preached mortalism, Luther's later silence on the subject, and Bullinger's Second Helvetic Confession—as we have traced in another chapter. There is apparently nothing inherent to either side of the Calvinist-Arminian controversy over election and free will which should predetermine or even prejudice one's understanding of the biblical teaching on final punishment. The underlying issue is not the theological one concerning divine sovereignty or free grace (or even original sin, as Edward Beecher argued in his *History of Opinions on the Scriptural Doctrine of Retribution*, pp. 312-316) but the philosophical one concerning the nature of man. Anthropology may also be discussed as a biblical issue, but it is not co-extensive with the question of soteriology.

3. Cross, *The Early Christian Fathers*, p. 134. Everett Ferguson notes, however, that "Origen tried to express the Christian faith in terms of the prevailing Platonic philosophical ideas of his time" (Dowley, *History of Christianity*, p. 104). There is no contradiction between this statement and Cross' that Origen was not "the exponent of any one philosophical system." Mark Noll of Wheaton College recently gave some specific modern examples of the subtle influence of philosophy on hermeneutics in his article,"Who Sets the Stage for Understanding Scripture?" *Christianity Today*, 23 May 1980, pp. 14-18.

4. "Restoration" as used here is but one kind of "universalism." Some other ways one might use the term "universalism" would be to describe (1) the older doctrine of liberal Protestantism which makes God too "good" to "send anyone to hell"; (2) a particular view of the atonement,

already, and Gregory of Nyssa would express and defend the position at length a century later. Origen, however, was the first Christian writer to give the concept clear form, and it bears his name and theological label ("Apocatastasis," from the Greek word meaning "restoration") to this day.

According to D. P. Walker, Origen's speculations grew out of two principles. The first was the absolute justice and goodness of an all-powerful Creator; the second was the absolute free will of every rational being.[5] Rational beings included men, but also demons, angels and even stars. Origen assumed the pre-existence of souls, who pass through an eternal series of aeons, each having its own creation and last judgment, and each ending with a great purgation which prepares the way for the next. In such a system the same soul can go up or down the ladder of rational beings, from the lowest demon to the highest angel. Origen speculated that the series of ages might end when every soul (perhaps including Satan's) would be cleansed of sin to freely unite with God. This would be the great restoration or Apocatastasis.

Whatever colors one might detect here from other philosophies, the fabric for such a system was clearly woven from assumptions that grew in Plato's garden, the immortality of every soul being the most conspicuous of them all.

Origen's defenders insist that he offered his ideas as mere specula-

---

whether (a) Arminian (General) as opposed to Calvinistic (Particular) or (b) Barthian-Reformed as opposed to classic Reformed; (3) a doctrine that all finally *will* be saved, though from hell (Origen's Apocatastasis); (4) an open door that says all *might* finally be saved, whether argued (a) theologically (as Bloesch does) or (b) exegetically (as Eller does); or (5) simply a "larger hope" beyond the grave such as Farrar sought to defend and even Luther is quoted as having allowed. Labels are very tricky anyway, and on this subject especially they should be used sparingly and only with most careful definition.

Still another usage occurs in what Neal Punt calls a "biblical universalism" (Neal Punt, *Unconditional Good News* [Grand Rapids: William B. Eerdmans Publishing Co., 1980]). Beginning with passages of Scripture which speak of salvation or the atonement in terms of "all," the "world" or "every" man, Punt argues from a Calvinistic base that all men are elect in Christ except those the Bible specifically says will be lost. If Calvinists can allow that Scripture has no divine decree of reprobation (so God has no part in men being lost), and if Arminians can allow that Christ's atonement accomplished salvation for the elect rather than merely making it a possibility (so God has all the glory in men being saved), Punt's "biblical universalism" might provide a profitable meeting place at least for further discussion. More important to our thesis, Punt recognizes the scriptural teaching that at least *some* will be finally lost.

5. D. P. Walker, *The Decline of Hell: Seventeenth-Century Discussions of Eternal Torment*, pp. 12-13. Walker notes a revival of interest in Origen during the Renaissance, when Erasmus even used Origen's exegesis of Romans 9 against Luther's doctrine of the bondage of the will. Through Erasmus, Walker says, Origen became one strand in "the liberal Arminian tradition." We have already seen the part played by Christian mortalism in the Reformation.

tions, as possibilities, and that he was wrongfully accused of pressing them as matters of settled doctrine. There is still considerable dispute regarding the attitude of the other church fathers toward Origen, as also concerning precisely what the later church councils condemned as affecting him.

When Farrar appealed to Origen in support of his "larger hope" (for the salvation of some beyond this life), Pusey denied Farrar's interpretation but defended Origen himself. According to Pusey, Origen's *De Principiis* (or *Peri Archon*), the work containing most of his "heresies," was unknown to the church until Rufinus translated it in A.D. 398. Origen had written it while still a young man, when he had just "emerged from the philosophical schools" and was not yet settled in his own opinions. At the time, Pusey says, Origen indignantly denied in a public letter the restoration of Satan as a thought which no one could accept, "not even of unsound mind." In his popular writings Origen taught the accepted beliefs on the subject, Pusey says (citing some references), and he laid down as a rule of faith that nothing should be received as truth which was "out of harmony with the ecclesiastical and apostolic tradition." Pusey repeats Jerome's quotation of Origen that these matters "are not dogmas, but only matters of enquiry put forth lest they should seem altogether unconsidered." Jerome also says that Origen expressed regret for writing such things, blaming Ambrose, who made private matters public. Throughout his restorationist speculations, Origen used such words as "suppose," "opine" and "think," Pusey said.[6]

Others could defend Origen's suggestion of a "purifying" fire on the basis that he simply overreacted in response to the pagan Celsus. Celsus had taunted that the Christian's God kindled a fire to burn all but their own kind; and Origen, intending to defend God's kindness, said the fire would have a "purifying quality" (*katharison*) and that even Peter and Paul would have to pass through it.[7] Walker states

---

6. Edward Bouverie Pusey, *What Is of Faith as to Everlasting Punishment? In Reply to Dr. Farrar's Challenge in His "Eternal Hope," 1879*, pp. 129-133. The question of how Jerome viewed Origen—and why—illustrates the intricacy and elusiveness of this historical debate. Farrar said that Jerome lauded Origen as a great and good man. Walker concedes that point but says Jerome later repudiated Origen in no uncertain terms. Beecher agrees with both but insists that Jerome "weasled" in self-defense when he denounced Origen in a desperate attempt to save his own reputation after a critic had accused him of holding Origen's views. A reader picking up either man's book alone would be impressed by the dogmatism of all these pronouncements but would have no way of knowing that others had responding explanations.

7. Origen discusses the purifying fire in many places—among them: Origen *De Principiis* 1. 6; 2. 10; Origen *Against Celsus* 4. 13; 6. 25-26. These are found in the *Ante-Nicene Christian*

that none of these opinions attempted to defend Origen's opinions, only the man himself. "It is not until the *Letter of Resolution Concerning Origen* of 1661 that one finds a defence of the opinions themselves."[8]

Traditionalists take the same paints but draw a different landscape. According to Constable, Origen knew full well what he advocated, and he did it intentionally. Constable is kindly disposed toward Origen, however, because he sees him as reacting against the doctrine of eternal conscious torment lately popularized by Origen's fellow African, Tertullian. Both men held to the philosophical dogma of the immortality of the soul and therefore had to deny that hell's fire would consume and destroy. Tertullian said it would torment forever; Origen said it would purify and restore. According to Origen (and other conditionalists), the restorationist answer was a natural and inevitable response to the traditionalist view of hell. Constable writes:

> The fearful picture of God, exhibited by Tertullian, could not be laid in its bare horrors before the mind without drawing forth some protest. The doctrine of the age upon the soul gave the shape to the protest, and Origen came forward to make it under the title of "universal restoration." . . . Origen converts hell into a vast purgatory, and sends men and devils forth from it, purified and humbled, to the feet of the Great Father. . . . It is the old story of human thought passing from one extreme to its opposite.[9]

On this view, Tertullian and Origen each held a singular truth but agreed on a common error. Constable continues:

> Each had his undoubted share of truth. . . . If Tertullian could appeal to Scripture for the overthrow of the wicked, whether men or angels, as being of an endless nature, Origen could point from the same source to a blissful coming time when all that hath breath should praise the Lord.

Library: Translations of the Writings of the Fathers Down to A.D. 325 [hereafter "ANCL"], vols. 10, 23.

8. Walker, *Decline of Hell*, p. 15.

9. Henry Constable, *Duration and Nature of Future Punishment*, p. 219. David F. Wright remarks on the extent to which both Tertullian and Origen were influenced by thought patterns of their time as follows: 'Tertullian used the language and thought-forms of law, rhetoric and Stoicism—and Montanism; Clement and Origen used the concepts of Platonism and Pythagoreanism—and Christian Gnosticism. Origen, and even Tertullian, may at times have been so heavily influenced by them as to cross the narrow frontier that separates orthodoxy from heresy" (Dowley, *History of Christianity*, p. 109).

What was there which prevented Origen from going back to the old scriptural doctrine of [the second] death as the end of sinners, which places the two scriptural truths just mentioned in harmony and not in opposition? It was the very same dogma of the immortality of the soul which had led Athenagoras and Tertullian to their endless life in hell.[10]

But if writers disagree about Origen himself, they are no closer concerning his status within ecclesiastical "orthodoxy."

The Question of Church Councils

According to *A Dictionary of Christian Biography, Literature, Sects and Doctrines*,[11] there is no evidence that the belief in restorationism "was ever definitely condemned by any council of the church." So far as Origen's personal censure, it was only by a "general sentence passed upon the leaders of Nestorianism than singled out for special and characteristic errors." Not until the Council of Constantinople (A.D. 553) does an anathema specify "somewhat cloudily" Origen's guilt as "inventing a mythology . . . and inventing changes and migrations for our souls and bodies, and impiously uttering drunken ravings as to the future life of the dead." This "ambiguous anathema" was only then pronounced, according to this source, "by a council of no authority under the weak and vicious emperor Justinian II," and it is the "only approach to a condemnation of the eschatology of Origen which the annals of church councils present." This dictionary notes that Jerome, who disagreed with Origen's view, still spoke of it "with a tolerant fairness, as though it were almost or altogether an open question."

Edward Beecher argued that in the days of Origen "the weight of learned and influential ecclesiastics was on the side of universal restoration."[12] He names in particular Chrysostom's teacher, Diodore of Tarsus, as well as Diodore's disciple, Theodore of Mop-

---

10. Constable, *Future Punishment*, p. 220. Like traditionalists then and later, Origen also applied Paul's description of the glorified and immortal resurrection body to the wicked as well as to the righteous. He reasoned from this that "even the body which rises again of those who are to be destined to everlasting fire or to severe punishments, is by the very change of the resurrection so incorruptible, that it cannot be corrupted and dissolved even by severe punishments. If, then, such be the qualities of that body which will arise from the dead, let us now see what is the meaning of the threatening of eternal fire" (Origen *De Principiis* 2. 10. 3; *ANCL*, 10:140).

11. *A Dictionary of Christian Biography, Literature, Sects and Doctrines*, 2:194.

12. Beecher, *Scriptural Doctrine of Retribution*, p. 309.

suestia.[13] Not until the sixth century, Beecher says, was the subject even considered important enough to be given "elaborate and profound discussion."[14] Then "that despotic emperor," Justinian, "assumed to declare, by his subservient council, in the name of the Church, what the Church had never debated or decided, and what, in her best days, her most eminent leaders had rejected."[15]

Farrar gave a similar interpretation. According to him,

> "none of the first four General Councils lay down any doctrine whatever concerning the everlasting misery of the wicked, or directly or indirectly give any interpretation of the Scriptural expressions which describe their condition." The question had indeed "been most vehemently disputed and discussed, yet the Church was wisely silent, and allowed various mutually irreconcilable opinions to be held by her sons without rebuke. Neither at Nicea (A.D. 325), nor at Constantinople (A.D. 381), nor at Ephesus (A.D. 431), nor at Chalcedon (A.D. 451), was any special doctrine laid down respecting the future rewards and punishments, nor were the opinions of Origen and his followers on that subject condemned, or even alluded to."[16]

Farrar says Athanasius spoke of Origen "tenderly and admiringly as 'the marvellous and indefatigable Origen,'" and he recalls that even Augustine referred to Origen's followers as "our party of pity" and admits that "not only some, but very many" held such a merciful view.[17]

Pusey is just as dogmatic in the other direction. He insists that Origen's restorationism was condemned in the East by a synod convened by Theophilus at Alexandria and at a synod held by Epiphanius at Cyprus. It was condemned in the West, he says, by Anastasius of Rome accompanied by many bishops of the West. As to the silence of the earlier great councils, Pusey points out that they were con-

---

13. Ibid., p. 121.

14. Ibid., pp. 307-308.

15. Ibid., p. 310.

16. Frederick W. Farrar, *Eternal Hope*, p. 167. These four earliest councils are called "ecumenical" (universal or general) councils, and their conclusions are considered as expressions of Christian orthodoxy by historic churchmen of every persuasion. Not until much later did an ecclesiastical council speak specifically on final punishment; therefore the controversy regarding Origen's orthodoxy. One could wholeheartedly confess the formulations of Nicaea and Chalcedon as well as the Apostles' Creed, for example, and hold to either traditionalist or conditionalist views on the nature of eternal punishment.

17. Ibid., pp. 163-164.

cerned with other specific topics and naturally did not speak on this one. Furthermore, he says, final punishment "was not a question for a General Council; for the Church was not disturbed."[18]

So goes the debate on Origen's orthodoxy and the "official" status of the discussion on final punishment. Farrar says the subject had been widely discussed from earliest times but was left open. Beecher says it was considered so unimportant as not to merit discussion. Pusey says it was not discussed because practically everyone in the fourth and fifth centuries agreed already on the traditional view. Of the three, Pusey is probably correct, with this added note: It is almost certainly the case that the subject of final punishment was never specifically treated by an acknowledged, universal council. For that reason, and to that extent, it has therefore remained an "open question" in terms of official, historic, ecclesiastical "orthodoxy."[19]

Universalism's New Face

The doctrine of universalism seems to hold a growing fascination for a number of scholars whose roots are evangelical or Reformed. Several articles and books have appeared within the last decade which begin with the traditional view of conscious everlasting torment but give it an apologetic twist.

Instead of demonstrating divine wrath and punishment, hell (in this view) manifests divine mercy and love. Traditional orthodoxy saw hell's "apartness" as penal exile; these writers turn it into a

---

18. Pusey, *What Is of Faith?* pp. 136-137.

19. John W. Wenham says that "traditional orthodoxy" had its first formulation at the Second Council of Constantinople in 553, acknowledging that there is some question about the anathemas of a council held there ten years earlier (John W. Wenham, *The Goodness of God*, p. 28).

David F. Wright comments that this "was an age of interference and even domination by the emperors, of colourful and abrasive personalities, and of bitter antagonism between leading bishoprics. . . . In theory the first appeal was to Scripture, but [many people] frequently appealed to Scripture to confirm their theology rather than to decide it" (Dowley, *History of Christianity*, p. 156). Wright details some of the ecclesiastical politics of the period on pages 156-178.

To say that the question of final punishment was left officially open by the early councils is not to say it is left open in Scripture—which is what matters. These councils were composed of mere men—often motivated by less than honorable ambitions. The whole matter of "official orthodoxy" is of greater interest to High-Churchmen such as Farrar and Pusey (nineteenth-century Anglicans) than to those in the free church tradition or Reformed churches who stand further away from Eastern or Western Catholicism. The subject is of greater concern, therefore, to Bishop Jon Braun of the Evangelical Orthodox Church than to Reformed Church pastor, Harry Buis, though both hold the traditionalist view.

hideout where sinners can escape the unbearable presence of the all-holy God. At times Christ's words, "Depart from Me," begin to sound less like a decree of banishment and more like an answer to the question, "May I be excused?"

Some of the same authors go still one step more. If hell is the product of divine love, they seem to reason, may not that love eventually reclaim at least some who initially go there? They suggest that hell might have an exit or perhaps a back door. At the very least, they ask, might not its front door be locked only on the inside? Motivation for such a presentation is easily understood in apologetic terms. Instead of making hell "the ultimate horror," this view makes it, at best, a refining purgatory and, at worst, a "painful refuge."[20]

If the picture which has emerged in our study of final punishment has any validity at all, such restoration is totally out of the question. If the wicked are to be consumed, they can never be reformed. If God kills and destroys the unrepentant in the lake of fire so that they die, corrupt and perish, any thought that they might eventually find their way to heaven must be dismissed as romantic imagination. If the fire of hell is truly "unquenchable" so that it cannot be resisted, and if its punishment of destruction is "eternal" so that it will never be re-

---

20. Dante offered this explanation as a kind of theodicy in his *The Divine Comedy*; L. A. King repeated Dante's concept in modern form in his article, "Hell, the Painful Refuge," *Eternity*, January 1979, pp. 27ff, with *no suggestion* that hell might have an exit. C. S. Lewis seems to have popularized the notion in his *The Great Divorce* (New York: Macmillan & Co., 1946), although in the introduction he said the work was intended as a fantasy with a moral and was not intended to provide either a guess or speculation about the actual facts in the case. Lewis went a step further in his "fantasy," suggesting that if hell's inhabitants actually chose to be there rather than in the presence of God, they might some day have a change of heart and go to heaven instead. Donald G. Bloesch begins at the same point and argues theologically for a possible restoration from hell in his *Essentials of Evangelical Theology*, 2:224-230. Vernard Eller reasons for the same possibility on exegetical grounds in his *The Most Revealing Book of the Bible: Making Sense Out of Revelation*, pp. 200-205. It would be most unfair to suggest that these men all say the same thing or that any of them is a "universalist" as the word is commonly used.

Both Bloesch and Eller appeal to the statement of Revelation 21:25 that the gates of the New Jerusalem are always open. Could this not simply mean there are no enemies who threaten and that it is always day? One might describe his crimeless village by saying, "We never lock our doors." He would not mean that he was expecting company but that he certainly was *not*. Eller also calls attention to the "kings of the earth" who bring their glory and honor into the city (Rev. 21:24-26). Since nothing impure enters (v. 27), he asks whether these kings might have been purified outside the city and then found entry. He is very careful to distinguish between his suggestion and "universalism" as it is usually conceived. With his qualifications the issue becomes an exegetical one regarding passages on final punishment, not a matter to be dismissed on dogmatic grounds involving sin, the atonement, divine wrath or human responsibility. Again we say that if the thesis our study supports is correct, the universalistic possibility is ruled out of the question to begin with, whether or not we can explain the open gates of the new Jerusalem.

versed, it is inconceivable that anyone sentenced to its fate could ever be found alive again once the fire has accomplished its work.

If, on the other hand, the wicked are made immortal, if hell is also a form of God's mercy, and if God forever loves even those He finally banishes from His presence, the footsteps of restorationism will always be heard just beyond the door. The traditionalist answer, which has so long charged conditionalism with being an "easy way out," has itself become the basis for restorationist speculations which conditionalism precluded from the beginning. What once touted itself as the only explanation *severe* enough to serve justice is now marching under a banner proclaiming the *mercy* of God. If Constable were around, he would surely shake his head and exclaim, "Once more Origen has reacted against Tertullian!"

This is clearly a different sort of universalism than nineteenth-century liberal theologians proposed. Because it springs from different soil (located in Reformed and evangelical yards), this restorationism is not answered by the arguments of an earlier time.

Shedd was responding to that earlier universalism of classical liberalism, for example, when he wrote:

> Universalism has a slender exegetical basis. The Biblical data are found to be unmanageable, and resort is had to human feeling and sympathy. Its advocates quote sparingly from scripture. In particular, the words of Christ relating to eschatology are left with little citation or interpretation.[21]

Such language would provide little defense indeed should one venture forth armed with it alone to do battle against the recent form of restorationism.

Berkouwer voices just such a caution. The modern face of universalism

> does not wish to deny the guilt of sin or weaken the wrath of God. But it sees sin and wrath as *temporary*, on the ground that God's wrath and punishment are aimed at the salvation of all men. In any case there is no intention of making human feelings the basis of this doctrine.[22]

---

21. William G. T. Shedd, *The Doctrine of Endless Punishment*, p. 9.
22. G. C. Berkouwer, *The Return of Christ*, p. 390.

John W. Wenham gives a similar critique. "Universalism is usually argued [today] in terms of man as a free being living for ever within the influence of God's infinitely patient love," Wenham writes. "In his selfishness and pride man may long resist God's gentle attraction, but in the end Love will win his free and full response." In a footnote Wenham cites chapters 8-9 of John A. T. Robinson's book, *In the End, God . . .* (London, 1950), which he calls "one of his most powerful pieces of writing."[23] The old forms of universalism are still around, but their power to attract died the same day as liberalism's utopian dream.

The older universalism sprang from an obviously deficient view of Christ and His atonement. The newer universalism "continues to be advocated in strongly Christological and doxological terms," Berkouwer notes, and for this very reason "it cannot be summarily dismissed."

The philosophical arguments for the traditionalist's hell are also perceived as broken reeds. Berkouwer explains like this:

> It would be inadequate, for example, to challenge universalism on the ground that eternal punishment is a self-evident consequence of the idea of retribution. This is the notion behind the argument that there is such an appalling breadth of evil in the world that it is impossible for all of it to be absorbed in a final divine remission that would cover all guilt. . . .
>
> Such a duality breaks down because God's justice is revealed precisely in the cross. Because of this, any argument against apocatastasis that requires the justice of God to be satisfied in an eternal punishment is invalid and unbiblical.[24]

Rather than scoff at appeals to Scripture, many modern universalists appear to make it the basis for their case. As the wise woman of Tekoa described a wise king as one who "devises ways so that a banished person may not remain estranged from him" (2 Sam. 14:14), so modern advocates of restorationism picture the all-powerful and all-merciful God. Any successful confrontation must take this fundamental approach and stance into account.

The present chapter makes no attempt or claim to be exhaustive. Here we simply note the phenomenon of modern universalism, ob-

---

23. Wenham, *The Goodness of God*, p. 33.
24. Berkouwer, *The Return of Christ*, pp. 392-393.

serve the essential weakness of its major "proof-texts," and summarize the critique and response of one notable Reformed theologian who is thoroughly in touch with the modern discussion.

Some "Proof-Texts" of Universalism

The universalism of old liberalism made less appeal to Scripture than the restorationism of today, no doubt in part because of its inherently lower view of revelation. Historically, however, there were four "important considerations" which "helped to bring a measure of amelioration" from the majority view of everlasting torment. According to T. F. Glasson, those considerations were (1) the "every man" statement in the prologue to John's Gospel (John 1:9), (2) Peter's statement concerning spirits in prison (1 Pet. 3:18-20), (3) the rise of the doctrine of purgatory, and (4) the idea that any man can prepare himself for saving faith on the basis of natural reason and so be saved by God's grace.[25]

If one reads the text carefully at all, however, he finds that these appeals dissolve before his eyes. John's prologue states clearly that while the Word became publicly incarnate in Jesus, many refused to accept Him when He came. The same context also makes clear that spiritual rebirth is God's work, not man's, and that only God, not natural reason, can illuminate the heart to acknowledge and receive Jesus as God's Son. The idea of purgatory has absolutely no exegetical support, and Peter's statement about "spirits in prison" probably refers to just what it says—"spirits"—not men at all. Even if it speaks of men, that passage says nothing about the situation beyond the judgment, nor does it mention a second chance or offer of salvation beyond the present life.

It is true that Scripture in several places speaks of purification or testing by fire in both the Old (Mal. 3:2) and New (1 Cor. 3:13-15; 1 Pet. 1:7) Testaments. Even so, the context sometimes concerns present afflictions; when final judgment is in view, only those are under consideration who have served God in this life.

One might also recall Paul's "universalistic" statements that God was pleased to reconcile "all things" in Christ (Col. 1:19, 20) and at

---

25. T. F. Glasson, "Human Destiny: Has Christian Teaching Changed?" *Modern Churchman* 12, no. 4 (July 1969): 284-298.

the last will be "all in all" (1 Cor. 15:26, 28). Or one may think of John's vision of the time when God makes "everything new," when there will be neither pain nor mourning, crying nor curse (Rev. 21:4, 5; 22:3). These statements, however, often appear as one side of a study in contrasts; at other times they involve the vital word "if."

Guillebaud raises another interesting question. Philippians 2:9, 10 says that every tongue will confess Jesus' sovereignty, whether in heaven, in earth, or *under the earth*. But, Guillebaud points out, when Paul says God will "sum up all things" in Christ, he includes things in heaven and earth—but makes no mention of subterranean beings (Eph. 1:9, 10). Does this mean, Guillebaud asks, that the infernal creatures will *confess* Christ but not be included in His *saving consummation*?[26]

Universalists have appealed also to certain texts in the Gospels. But after an in-depth study entitled *The Justice of God in the Teaching of Jesus*, J. Arthur Baird concludes that those texts teach no such thing. "It is therefore necessary to reaffirm what many who hold this position admit: there is no valid evidence in the Synoptics for the doctrine of universal salvation." Such a view, he says, "must find its support in more philosophic argument and in certain debated portions of Paul and John."[27]

We have spoken of John already in passing, but note one other proof-text sometimes cited from him. Revelation 5:13 describes a beautiful scene in which all creatures everywhere praise God together. But this vision precedes the book's central drama of evil's temporary triumph, then ultimate downfall.

Paul's bold claim that every knee will one day bow before Jesus (Phil. 2:9-11) is based on Isaiah 45:23 (quoted also in Rom. 14:11). Yet Isaiah's next verse says some will be incensed and ashamed; these, according to Isaiah 41:11, will finally perish and become as nothing.

But does not Romans 11 hold out a hope that all will finally come to a saving knowledge of Christ? Kümmel notes that Paul's preaching of salvation ends with a "worshipful note of praise and not with a rationally sensible answer," and that one is therefore "unable to assert that Paul could not venture to cherish such a hope in God's all-

---

26. Harold E. Guillebaud, *The Righteous Judge: A Study of the Biblical Doctrine of Everlasting Punishment*, pp. 5-6.

27. Joseph Arthur Baird, *The Justice of God in the Teaching of Jesus*, pp. 230-232.

encompassing grace." Yet Kümmel points out that the total context of Romans 9-11 includes statements in Romans 9:32 and 11:22 which contradict this view. He also reminds us that Paul "reckons with the fact that there are men who are condemned by God and lost, and he warns even the Christians not to take God's wrath and condemnation lightly (Rom. 2:5; 11:22)."[28]

So long as one views the lost as immortalized in everlasting consciousness, the picture will occasionally blur and fade, momentarily overpowered by the other biblical picture of universal harmony and praise. When all is said, the greatest answer to universalism's challenge is the scriptural teaching of the fire that *consumes*. Only when we take the second *death* with absolute seriousness are we totally free of lingering thoughts that the damned eventually will come to know the second *life*. Origen's *refining* fire could only come on the basis of Tertullian's *regenerating* fire. Both ideas are ruled out by the scriptural teaching of a *destroying* fire.

Berkouwer's Criticisms—In Two Directions

In his book, *The Return of Christ*, the great Reformed theologian, G. C. Berkouwer, devotes one chapter to the question of "Apocatastasis" or restorationism.[29] Berkouwer does not spend much time on universalism's alleged scriptural support, nor does he attempt to answer it by the "proof-text" method. Instead, he backs off a few steps from his subject, then examines it critically in the light of the gospel as a whole.

Advocates of universal restoration make the crucial mistake, Berkouwer believes, when they begin with a single doctrine or tenet of Scripture rather than with the biblical gospel in the framework of history. Universalism starts with the unconquerable love of God and reasons from there. It therefore rests on a weak foundation, Berkouwer says, because what it says about hell and salvation is divorced from the gospel itself.

---

28. Werner Georg Kümmel, *The Theology of the New Testament According to Its Major Witnesses: Jesus—Paul—John*, pp. 243-244.

29. Berkouwer, *The Return of Christ*, pp. 387-423.

Unless one stands under the shadow of the cross when he thinks on final punishment, he has little advantage over the Greek philosophers on Mars Hill even though he may include verses of Scripture in his thinking. Berkouwer contrasts the way universalism approaches the subject with the way New Testament writers do.

> Essentially universalism looks at salvation as eschaton outside the realm of proclamation. Apocatastasis—in spite of the doxological context in which it is set—becomes a conclusion that precedes the dynamics and the appeal of the proclamation and is established by it. The love of God becomes the point of departure for this reasoning; any connection with the preaching of salvation and judgment is lost. . . . In this way it becomes obvious that the doctrine of apocatastasis is a static, timeless, unkerygmatic doctrine, a form of gnostic thought over against God and His love.
> In contrast the biblical witness to the love of God always treats it in a kerygmatic context and never announces it as a "fact" that goes over the heads of those to whom it is addressed and refers to a static eschatological fact. . . . Outside of this correlative application of the seriousness of the gospel, nothing can be said about the future that would make one any the wiser. If one tries to concern himself with it objectively, he finds himself ending up in a certain coldness, able to draw conclusions, but conclusions that have lost their comforting and admonishing character.[30]

Berkouwer charges that modern universalists are reacting in part to two errors made by the rest of the church. If he is correct, some of those who oppose restoration most vehemently have actually helped to bring it about.

One great reason for universalism's development, he says, is the "intemperate and unbiblical" preaching of the church on hell which also separates it from the gospel. This happens whenever final punishment is preached as a topic of curiosity or of mere intellectual interest. This happens whenever hell is used merely for purposes of intimidation or threatening.[31] Such preaching actually detracts from

---

30. Ibid., pp. 412-413.

31. Harry Buis chides Origen for teaching eternal damnation to the masses as a deterrent to sin while privately believing in universalism. Buis calls this "an admission of the fact that the denial of eternal punishment undermines morals" (Buis, *The Doctrine of Eternal Punishment*, p. 57). We agree with this assessment. Origen, however, has not been alone in using hell as a means of intimidation. Pusey speaks of one of Tertullian's hellish descriptions "which he probably uttered to scare the heathen" (Pusey, *What Is of Faith?* p. 11). Pusey himself said that "neither the Church nor any portion of it has so laid down any doctrine in regard to [corporeal

the seriousness of the gospel, Berkouwer says. For the true serious-ness of the gospel is that it tells man indiscriminately (not only the elect) what God has done in Christ for sinners, calls for repentance and faith, and warns of the dreadful fate awaiting those who reject such a great salvation. Whenever men preach hell out of this setting —or forget that "judgment begins with the house of God"—they lose its biblical character. In the end, Berkouwer notes, such preaching generally leads to extremes, abuses and, finally, indifference.

Another error to which Berkouwer believes universalism reacts is a scholastic understanding of election which causes men to weaken the genuine offer of the gospel. The New Testament declares over and over that God is rich in grace and mercy in a measure that we cannot possibly understand or appreciate fully now. "When the Bible talks about salvation, it does so in a way that calls up the idea of a truly overflowing abundance," writes Berkouwer. "Time and again this abundance leads to doxology, to exclamations of praise."[32] Berk-ouwer considers it a point that must be admitted that the church throughout history has often failed to take these passages seriously.

Men may separate election as well as hell from the gospel—and with the same bad results. Berkouwer believes that this has happened more than once.

> The doctrine of apocatastasis, it must be admitted, has often flour-ished in reaction against the frequent failure of the church throughout history to take seriously the "universal" passages of Scripture. The depreciation of these passages has sometimes followed from a par-ticular doctrine of election that leaves no room for the universal in-vitation to salvation, on the ground that salvation could honestly and truly be offered only to the elect. . . . Obviously this extreme does as much violence to the seriousness of the proclamation as apocatastasis does.[33]

---

sufferings] as to make the acceptance of them an integral part of the doctrine itself" (p. 18), yet he comments without hesitation that "dread of hell peoples heaven; perhaps millions have been scared back from sin by the dread of it" (p. 19). Later he remarks concerning terrifying, literalistic sermons on hell: "In the early part of this century such sermons were favourite ser-mons with the poor, because they were stirred up by them to reverent and awe-stricken thoughts" (p. 263). Is Pusey more righteous than Origen if he preaches literal suffering to scare the poor while admitting to his sophisticated readers that corporeal suffering is not essential to the doctrine? Berkouwer believes that when hell is spoken of "more for its psychological effect than out of truly evangelical concern," the preaching lacks the gospel's sound and is ineffectual in the end (Berkouwer, *The Return of Christ*, p. 420).

32. Berkouwer, *The Return of Christ*, pp. 395-396.

33. Ibid., p. 408.

The Bible calls us to preach the gospel to every man without discrimination. The proclamation of salvation is not some kind of game, some cruel charade which has God saying one thing and meaning something altogether different. Berkouwer stresses the need to be faithful in preaching the gospel, leaving the unanswerable questions of election in the hands of the sovereign God.

> It is impossible that the proclamation of salvation should go out to all, but be "actually" intended not for all but only for the elect, and that the rest would be called to acts of repentance and faith that had no real and present object anyway. This would certainly be a devaluation of the word "gospel." . . . It is impossible to sum the whole thing up by telling everyone, "Honestly, whoever comes to Christ will be saved," as if the whole gospel were defined by this kind of maxim. The true preaching of the gospel does use very nearly the same words. . . .
> This is something more than the announcement of a general maxim. It is preaching in earnest, with promise and comfort and encouragement.[34]

If anyone rushes to grab his Canons of Dort, Berkouwer anticipates the move in advance. He calls the Calvinist theologian, Herman Bavinck, as witness. Bavinck made the "profound analysis," Berkouwer says, "that the authors of the Canons of Dort did not proceed in response to an 'all or not all' dilemma." Such a statement shocks about as many Calvinists as it does Arminians, so the giant Reformed theologian gives this explanation:

The issue involved at Dort, says Bavinck, was not whether God loves all men or only a few, or whether the gospel call to salvation is seriously intended for all. It was rather whether Christ's atoning work only made salvation *possible* or whether it made it *accomplished fact*. The Arminian party held the first view; the party of Dort contended for the second. Berkouwer summarizes Bavinck in these words:

> The objection to the Arminian Remonstrants was directed against their idea that the sense of "Christ's sacrifice for all" was that the *possibility* of salvation was obtained for all through Him. The objection of the Canons of Dort was to the doctrine of *potential reconciliation*, according to which human decision must lead to the realization of this possibility.[35]

---

34. Ibid., pp. 409-410.
35. Ibid., pp. 410-411.

Berkouwer quotes Bavinck concerning the gospel's call—that the call keeps its meaning even for those who reject it, because it is "the proof of God's unending love for all sinners without distinction and seals the word that He has no pleasure in the death of a sinner."[36] Berkouwer would urge those who treasure the doctrines expressed by the Canons of Dort not to minimize the seriousness of the gospel's proclamation or to abbreviate God's genuine offer in the name of a "logical" but unscriptural doctrine.

Regardless of where one begins, Berkouwer warns, problems will always arise whenever one tries to deduce answers to questions on hell apart from the proclamation of the gospel. Only at the cross of Jesus can one truly read Scripture in the light of God's judgment— whether he seeks to know of divine mercy or of divine wrath. Questions not answered there must remain unanswered in this life. Jesus did not come to satisfy our curiosity or to make us as wise as God. He came to reveal *God*—and to call men to faith and obedience. Berkouwer ends on this note:

> Over and over the question addressed to Jesus arises in the history of the church: "Lord, will those who are saved be few?" Jesus' answer seems so noncommittal, so evasive: "Strive to enter by the narrow door" (Luke 13:23f.). But this evasiveness is only apparent. This *is* the answer to *this* question. As long as we see only in a mirror, in riddles, many questions will remain unanswered. But *this* question has been answered, once for all time.[37]

---

36. Ibid., p. 411. Bloesch discusses Karl Barth's views on hell, as does Berkouwer. Both men see Barth's concern growing out of the desire to overcome the tension between the "universal" and "particular" aspects of Christ's gospel. Bloesch says: "The logic of [Barth's] theology drives him toward an ultimate universalism, though his intention is to transcend the polarity between universalism and particularism" (Bloesch, *Essentials of Evangelical Theology*, 2:224). Berkouwer denies that Barth was a universalist, however, noting that he emphatically rejected the doctrine numerous times (Berkouwer, *The Return of Christ*, p. 399).

37. Berkouwer, *The Return of Christ*, p. 423.

17

From Patristics to Protestants: The Middle Millennium

When they spoke of the wicked's end, the apostolic fathers of the second century had contented themselves with biblical words and phrases. They did not elaborate on them—or eliminate them. Conditionalists interpret the fathers and the Bible quite literally, taking both at what seems to be face value. Traditionalists believe that both Scripture and these early authors use words in a figurative and secondary way, so that "perish," "die" and "destroy" actually signify endless conscious suffering rather than extinction or annihilation.

By the beginning of the third century the writers leave no doubt. Tertullian champions everlasting conscious torment. Clement hints at universal restoration; Origen makes it a plain possibility. Both Tertullian and Origen base their views in great measure on the philosophical doctrine that all souls are immortal, though both concede that God created them and could (but will not) destroy them as well.

The Philosophical Setting

It is easy to oversimplify such complex philosophical matters and to overgeneralize when describing the thought patterns of an ancient age. Yet it is possible to go to the other extreme as well. Particular philosophical patterns *do* exert great influence during certain periods of time. One is wise to read theologians of any period with this understanding, for creative theology often borrows heavily from the prevailing philosophy, however good its intentions may be. It will help us understand the theological developments of the eventful fourth and fifth centuries, therefore, if we can get the "feel" of the philosophical climate of those years. As it happens, that is the very purpose of a scholarly work by R. A. Norris, Jr., entitled *Manhood and Christ: The Christology of Theodore of Mopsuestia*. We will only capsule a few of his most significant thoughts here.

What began as rather unified schools of Greek philosophy had later divided into a multiplicity of sects and schools. By the time of the Council of Nicea in A.D. 325, this splintered scene had itself passed away. In its place, according to Norris, there stood "a revived, eclectic Platonism" which became "*the* philosophy of the late Roman Empire." Scholars sometimes divide this movement into a period of "Middle Platonism" and a later one of "Neo-Platonism." Yet, Norris says, "there remains a fundamental unity of outlook which characterizes the whole sweep of late imperial Platonism." One of the fundamental concerns of the "prevailingly Neo-Platonic" fourth century was the nature and destiny of man. Whoever then wished to reason on that subject talked in terms of the *soul*—"its nature, its connexion with the visible world, and its ultimate destiny."[1]

Within this period of Platonic revival, many philosophers consciously tried to reconcile Aristotle's teaching with Plato's. By and large, Norris says, they believed that the two great thinkers were in basic accord. These philosophers often retained Aristotle's method of reasoning (by syllogisms), but more important was his concept of God. To Aristotle, God was transcendent and supreme, but the philosopher conceived of God primarily as "self-thinking Intellect," the "unmoved Source of cosmic motion."[2] Yet Aristotle's ideas actually rode piggyback on Neo-Platonic philosophy. Even Aristotle was interpreted in the light of Neo-Platonic presuppositions.

Stoicism also entered the picture. The apostle Paul had faced this philosophy in the first century, and at times its influence rose to practically rule the Greco-Roman world. Norris acknowledges that Stoicism was "one of the ingredients in the highly diversified movement called Middle Platonism." But where Platonism absorbed and pre-

---

1. R. A. Norris, Jr., *Manhood and Christ: A Study in the Christology of Theodore of Mopsuestia*, pp. 3-4.
2. Ibid., pp. 5-6.

served certain of Aristotle's thoughts, Stoic elements rather "hung on," like a former coat of paint, in what Norris calls "an after-effect of their former currency in the Hellenistic world and that of the early empire."[3] In either case, Norris says, "it is to the philosophy of late Platonism itself that we must turn to define the shape of the problem of man as that was conceived in the era of the great christological debates."[4]

Even at this late date, according to Norris, the doctrine of the soul is developed against the background of Plato's classical contrast between the realm of "Being" and the realm of "Becoming." Plato explained this fundamental way of viewing all reality in the *Timaeus*, which Norris calls "a virtual textbook for the philosophy of the imperial age." He summarizes Plato's thought like this:

> 'Being' is that which is 'always the same,' and . . . is the object of knowledge in the true sense: . . . 'Becoming', on the other hand, is that which is perceived by sense: the realm of change and flux, concerning which only probable opinion is possible. . . . The distinction between Being and Becoming corresponds to that between corporeal and incorporeal. . . . The two terms of this dualism may be opposed as 'divisible' and 'indivisible' existence.
>
> This terminology, which Plato employs to contrast the realm of eternal, self-identical Forms with that of changing, perishable substance, remains fundamental for every area of later Platonic speculation. [Norris says Plato expressed the same contrast in terms like these:] . . . the difference between mutability and changelessness . . . the difference between time and eternity . . . between the sensible and the intelligible, the visible and the invisible, the corporeal and the incorporeal. . . . The order of sensible . . . is coextensive with . . . the perishable and mortal. By contrast, the intelligible world is neither in space nor in time: it is . . . immortal and imperishable.[5]

For the Neo-Platonic philosopher the problem of man rose out of this framework. Where the Old and New Testament Scriptures of Jews and Christians view reality, seen or unseen, as a single universe under the personal, living, covenant-making God, Plato and his followers had two universes and no true God. Where the Bible introduces man as a creature formed from dust and enlivened by the

---

3. Ibid., pp. 6-9.
4. Ibid., p. 9.
5. Ibid., pp. 10-11.

breath of God, this human philosophy introduces man as an eternal, immortal, incorporeal and indivisible "soul" trapped for a time in a temporal, mortal, corporeal and divisible "body." So defined, man is involved in both of Plato's realms of reality. The philosopher's problem is to determine the extent and manner of each involvement.

The same tension also arose when the Neo-Platonist viewed the material world. "From the point of view of ontology or theodicy," Norris states, "matter appears as a neutral factor and body as the lowest work of a benign Providence; but where questions of ethics or *of the nature of the soul's blessedness* are at stake, *the dualistic outlook reasserts itself*, and the fundamental contrariety of Matter and Spirit is, as it were, rediscovered" (italics supplied).[6]

If Norris is correct on this point, conditionalists such as Constable and Froom stand on solid ground in charging traditional "orthodoxy" with Platonic presuppositions even if they sometimes overstate their case in terms of technicalities and philosophical niceties. If this is true, and it appears to be, it is hard to overemphasize its importance for the doctrine of final punishment. For if one begins with a dualistic view of man and presupposes the immortality of every soul (whether inherent, created or bestowed), the only evident ultimate alternatives for the wicked are unending conscious torment or eventual restoration. Since the Scriptures so clearly eliminate the second possibility, traditional orthodoxy from about the fourth century has clung tenaciously to the first. The other alternative—penal suffering culminating in total extinction—although apparently supported by both Old and New Testaments throughout and echoed on the face by the earliest church fathers—was ruled out of the question during the fourth and fifth centuries on the basis of philosophical presuppositions. Whatever criticisms one might raise concerning Froom's work, the evidence all leads to the conclusion that on this fundamental point he is absolutely correct.

Arnobius the Anti-Platonist

It is significant that Arnobius of Sicca, who is mentioned today primarily as the chief spokesman of ancient times for the view that the wicked will finally be exterminated, devoted himself most of all

---

6. Ibid., p. 17.

to a refutation of Plato's doctrine that all souls are immortal. In fact, his comments on the end of the wicked are few and far between, and they are the natural understanding of the scriptural language if it is read without the philosophical presupposition of the immortality of the soul. Perhaps the reason Arnobius stood so lonely on final punishment is because he had so little company among the fathers in totally rejecting the pagan philosophy he had left to become a Christian.

A pagan rhetorician of Sicca Veneria in Africa Proconsularis, Arnobius did not seek admission to the church until late in his life. When the bishop hesitated to admit this former adversary, Arnobius wrote his *Adversus Nationes* [Against the heathen] in an attempt to prove his sincerity. This apology dates from about A.D. 300.

The treatise is not outstanding from a literary standpoint. F. L. Cross calls it "badly constructed and verbose," with "much tedious rhetoric" and "full of contradictions." Cross notes that Arnobius shows little understanding of the Christian faith and calls attention to the fact that he makes very little use of the Scriptures.[7] Abbé Bardy points out, however, that Arnobius had not yet received baptism, had lacked any opportunity for Bible study before he wrote *Adversus Nationes*, and evidently knew nothing of the apologists who had preceded him. But this did not keep Arnobius from pouring out his heart for the faith he wished to espouse. "Was it not enough," Bardy asks, "to set forth the vanity of idols and to be impressed by the splendour of Christian life?"[8]

Arnobius' argument comes largely in book 2. In chapter 13 he shows that many Christian doctrines ridiculed by the heathen were also held by the philosophers, specifically the worship of one God and a resurrection of the dead. The philosophers also spoke of quenchless fires of punishment, Arnobius says in chapter 14. This means that man's true death does not occur at the soul's separation from the body but afterward. With this, Arnobius begins to discuss the nature of the soul and continues his discussion through chapter 53.

---

7. F. L. Cross, *The Early Christian Fathers*, p. 184. The following quotations from the Seven Books of Arnobius *Adversus Gentes* are taken from the *Ante-Nicene Christian Library: Translations of the Writings of the Fathers Down to A.D. 325*, vol. 19.

8. Abbé Bardy, *The Christian Latin Literature of the First Six Centuries*, p. 56.

The soul is neither inherently immortal nor divine, Arnobius argues, else men would be pure, holy and of a common opinion (chs. 15, 16). Men are no different from brutes in body, maintenance of life, or reproduction of the race. If the philosophers hold out man's reason as proof of an immortal soul, Arnobius replies that not all men behave rationally (ch. 17). Besides, he says, men acquire both intelligence and skill after years of living under the pressure of necessity (ch. 18). In the same way, they have to learn the arts, grammar, music, oratory and geometry. Arnobius therefore rejects Plato's theory of reminiscence—that what men consider "learning" is actually a recollection from the soul's past experiences during previous incarnations.

As a test of his theories, Plato had proposed that a boy be reared wholly apart from human society until he was grown, then be quizzed to see what he knew without being taught. Arnobius issues the same challenge to his opponents (chs. 20-24). He gives a list of topics on which the lad should be tested. The Creator will triumph, he concludes, because a man untaught will be as ignorant as a stick or stone, while even animals may be taught to learn (ch. 25).

The soul does not have a separate, incorporeal existence from the body, Arnobius says, and therefore it cannot be immortal as the pagan philosophers asserted (chs. 26-28). To say that it is immortal leads men to be immoral[9] and makes void both ethics and philosophy in general (chs. 29, 30).

Arnobius concludes that the soul is neither mortal nor immortal of itself (ch. 31), so men ought to welcome a Savior (chs. 32, 33). Christian and pagan are alike in this regard; only through God's goodness can any spirit become immortal (chs. 34-36). Arnobius argues that the soul is not divine in its nature and that its precise origin is beyond our ability to know (chs. 37-48). There is nothing wrong with such ignorance, as even Plato seemed to admit, and no harm is done by such an opinion (chs. 49-53).

---

9. Both sides in the traditionalist/conditionalist controversy have charged the other with abetting moral laxity. Constable argued that "the very transcendent terrors" of the traditionalist hell "defeat the object of threatened penalty; for few, if any, believe in it *for themselves.*" Romanists avoid it, he said, by thinking of purgatory; skeptics use it as an excuse to dismiss God from their thoughts; even the pious who confess it think secretly that God will surely not impose it on them (Henry Constable, *Duration and Nature of Future Punishment,* pp. 162-164). Harry Buis, on the other hand, charged that annihilationism "undermines morality just as universalism does," arguing that even if the "highly ethical scholars who propound such doctrines are not led into immorality by them . . . their less moral listeners find it easier to sin because of them" (Harry Buis, *The Doctrine of Eternal Punishment,* p. 126).

For man to claim an immortal nature within himself is to reveal the greatest vanity and pride, Arnobius says. For "if men either knew themselves thoroughly, or had the slightest knowledge of God, they would never claim as their own a divine and immortal nature." Nor, "carried away by pride and arrogance, would they believe themselves to be deities of the first rank, and fellows of the highest in his exaltation" (bk. 2, ch. 19).

Arnobius echoed Paul, if perhaps unknowingly, that only God possesses immortality. "None but the Almighty God can preserve souls," he wrote, "nor is there any one besides who can give them length of days, and grant to them also a spirit which shall never die, except he who alone is immortal and everlasting, and restricted by no limit of time" (bk. 1, ch. 62).

Having denounced man's claim to immortality as gross hubris, and having answered the Platonists' arguments to his own satisfaction, Arnobius warns them concerning the death which only God can inflict and of which their pride stands them in danger.

> Do you dare to laugh at us when we speak of hell, and fires which cannot be quenched, into which we have learned that souls are cast by their foes and enemies? What, does not your Plato also, in the book which he wrote on the immortality of the soul, name the rivers Acheron, Styx, Cocytus, and Pyriphlegethon, and assert that in them souls are rolled along, engulfed, and burned up? But though a man of no little wisdom, and of accurate judgment and discernment, he essays a problem which cannot be solved. . . .
>
> And yet his opinion is not very far from the truth. For although the gentle and kindly disposed man thought it inhuman cruelty to condemn souls to death, he yet not unreasonably supposed that they are cast into rivers blazing with masses of flame, and loathsome from their foul abysses. For they are cast in, and being annihilated, pass away vainly in everlasting destruction.

This is true death, Arnobius continues, not man's physical death.

> And . . . this is man's real death, this which leaves nothing behind. For that which is seen by the eyes is a separation of soul from body,[10] not the last end—annihilation: this, I say, is man's real death, when souls which know not God shall be consumed in long-protracted torment with raging fire, into which certain fiercely cruel beings shall cast

---

10. Arnobius here uses (and seemingly accepts) the language of the philosophy he is denying. The definition of death as "separation of soul from body" is straight from Plato's *Phaedo* and the dying conversation of Socrates with his friends. There Socrates asks Simmias concerning

them, who were unknown before Christ, and brought to light only by
his wisdom.—Bk. 2, ch. 14.

The pagans have made themselves too wise in their assertions concerning man's immortality, Arnobius charges. Only God is capable
of such wisdom, and they are in danger of His ultimate punishment,
which is the total death of body and soul alike.

> Leave these things to God, and allow him to know what it is, where-
> fore, or whence; whether it must have been or not; whether something
> always existed, or whether it was produced at the first; whether it
> should be annihilated or preserved, consumed, destroyed, or restored
> in fresh vigour. Your reason is not permitted to involve you in such
> questions, and to be bruised to no purpose about things so much out
> of reach. Your interests are in jeopardy,—the salvation, I mean, of
> your souls; and unless you give yourselves to seek to know the Su-
> preme God, a cruel death awaits you when freed from the bonds of
> body, not bringing sudden annihilation,[11] but destroying by the bit-
> terness of its grievous and long-protracted punishment.—Bk. 2,
> ch. 61.

In this treatise against pagan philosophy, Arnobius does not begin
with the subject of final punishment, nor does he seem particularly
concerned to prove or even to make his point about it. His great ambition is to refute the Platonic system as a whole—and particularly its
arguments and claims concerning man's immortal soul. Having rejected that philosophical dogma, Arnobius seems to move almost un-

---

death: "Is it anything else than the separation of the soul from the body? and is not this to die,
for the body to be apart by itself separated from the soul, and for the soul to subsist apart by
itself separated from the body? Is death anything else than this?" And Simmias responds, "No,
but this." This philosophical view of man as a pre-existent, eternal soul embodied in human
form differs radically from the biblical doctrine of man as God's "earthy" creature into whom
God has breathed the breath of life so that man "became a living soul" (Gen. 2:7).

However, even if one holds that man possesses (rather than *is*) a "soul," and even if he holds
that it is "immortal" so that it consciously survives the death of the mortal body, he still is not
required to hold to eternal conscious torment. For if God created the soul in the first place, the
same God can also destroy it so that it utterly ceases to exist. The notable church fathers all
made this point, as did Calvin and modern orthodox apologists such as Edward John Carnell.
See further discussion in chapter 5, " 'The Soul Is Immortal, But . . . ' (The Philosophers versus
the Fathers)."

11. Arnobius is not denying ultimate annihilation. He is saying it will not come suddenly but,
rather, as the next sentence continues, by the process of "grievous and long-protracted punishment." This allows for great degrees of punishment according to the exact measure of divine
decree. Most conditionalists hold that eternal punishment will be preceded by varying degrees
of conscious punishment but that it properly consists of the final, ultimate, irreversible extinction in the unquenchable and consuming fire of hell.

consciously to his understanding and statements about the punishment awaiting the wicked. If God is the only source of life, and if one does not assume the soul's immortality as a governing principle, the final extinction of the wicked seems as natural as night following day.

It is an irony of theology that a modern student who searches out Arnobius' *Adversus Nationes* to see how it advocated the extinction of the wicked should discover upon reading it that Arnobius began at the same point to which even evangelical scholars now are moving more and more. The mainstream of traditional orthodoxy has long flowed in the riverbeds dug by Platonic philosophy. Arnobius rejected the riverbed, and the stream of tradition passed him by. Today's theological engineers may once again turn the river's course so that it finally waters the land he homesteaded so long ago.

A View Hardens into Orthodoxy

Though history would prove that the die was already cast in favor of conscious eternal torment, some prominent fathers of the fourth and fifth centuries nevertheless followed Origen in expecting an ultimate restoration of the wicked even from hell. Traditionalists and restorationists alike held to the immortality of the soul; Arnobius had few supporters or successors in his total repudiation of that point.

Gregory of Nyssa reasoned that the soul, having a natural affinity to God, must ultimately return to God. Any suffering it encounters first is educational, purgatorial and remedial. Farrar later gave a prominent place to the writings of this father "as proving the permissibility" of a larger hope for the wicked beyond the grave. He calls Gregory "a great and persecuted champion of the Nicene faith" whose "orthodoxy was so unimpeachable that he was one of the most prominent figures at the Council of Constantinople."[12] Gregory of Nazianzus also wondered whether unending torment was worthy of God. J. N. D. Kelly gives references for the views of both these fathers in his well-known book, *Early Christian Doctrines*.[13]

---

12. Frederic W. Farrar, *Eternal Hope*, p. 160.
13. J. N. D. Kelly, *Early Christian Doctrines*, p. 483.

Whether or not the opinion of the two Gregorys was "permissible" in their own time, there is no question about its status from about a century later. The "consuming" fire and the "refining" fire both gave way to the tormenting fire Tertullian had described. Much biblical language would find no place in the accepted discussions of final punishment during the next thousand years. More and more, orators and authors alike waxed eloquent in terminology found nowhere in the Bible. Some stressed literal, corporeal pain; many did not. But there was no question as to the everlasting conscious torment of the wicked as this understanding came to be the received orthodoxy of the medieval church.

Ambrose and Victor. Ambrose (died 397) and Victor of Antioch both interpreted hell's fire and worm as spiritual or psychological torment. Pusey quotes Ambrose that the "fire is that which the sadness over transgressions generates, because the sins pierce with compunction the mind and sense of the irrational soul of the guilty, and eat out the, as it were, bowels of conscience; which sins are generated like worms out of each, as it were from the body of the sinner." Ambrose explained the gnashing of teeth in a similar manner.[14] Victor of Antioch made the worm "an impure and wicked conscience, seeing that this pricks and gnaws the sinful soul, conscious of no good, with the stings of an useless regret, like a devouring worm." Some, he said, think the quenchless fire is "a polluted and wicked conscience" which, "like raging fire, ever feeds upon their inmost self."[15]

Chrysostom. Others, such as Chrysostom of Constantinople (died 407), pressed the literal language with more vigor. He preached on "the sea of the bottomless pit, where the punishment is not accompanied with insensibility, where there is no suffocation to end all, but in ever-lengthened torture, in burning, in strangling, they are consumed." He urged his audience to consider "how great a misery it must be to be for ever burning, and to be in darkness, and to utter unnumbered groanings, and to gnash the teeth, and not even to be heard." He talked about "the venomous worm." He warned of a fate worse than Job's, whose corruption had an end. But "to be ever burning and never consumed, and to be ever being wasted by the worm,

---

14. Quoted by Edward Bouverie Pusey, *What Is of Faith as to Everlasting Punishment? In Reply to Dr. Farrar's Challenge in His "Eternal Hope," 1879*, p. 20.

15. Ibid., pp. 268-269.

is corruption incorruptible." And "some such torment as this," Chrysostom declared, "shall the soul undergo then, when the worms surround and devour it, not for two years, nor for three, nor for ten, nor for ten thousand, but for years without end; for 'their worm,' He saith, 'dieth not.'"[16]

Such language, at the very least, is patently unscriptural on its face. It introduces a "venomous worm" found nowhere in the Bible, changes the fire that consumes to a fire that never consumes, and creates the contradictory spectacle of "corruption incorruptible." To its credit—and scriptural advantage at least over restorationism— Chrysostom's description did make final punishment unending and eternal. But by applying to the wicked the immortality and incorruptibility which Scripture applies to the righteous, Chrysostom and all others who followed Tertullian were forced to deny the apparent meaning of most biblical language on the subject and to invent in its place a self-contradictory terminology which neither the Old nor New Testament Scriptures ever use even once. If Chrysostom helped make such preaching popular, the great Augustine would make it permanent.

Augustine of Hippo. Born November 13, 354 to a pagan father and Christian mother, Augustine enjoyed the advantages of education in rhetoric, philosophy and law, and also the short-lived pleasures of sin. For nine years he belonged to the sect of the Manichaeans, but grew restless and increasingly dissatisfied. He turned to the books of the Neo-Platonists in 385, through whose eyes he learned to perceive the existence of the spiritual world and solved to his own satisfaction the philosophical problem of evil. One spring day in the year 387, Augustine was baptized by Ambrose in the basilica of Milan. Immediately he started for Africa with his devout mother and a company of friends. His beloved mother died en route, and Augustine settled for three years at Tagaste in a kind of monastic life. In 391 he made his way to Hippo and became a priest the year following. In 396 he succeeded Bishop Valerius, serving in that office until he died on August 28, 430.

Deeply conscious of his own sinfulness, Augustine was also compassionate of the faults of others. He was overwhelmed as he realized

---

16. *Ibid.*, pp. 264-265.

the total moral inability of man and also the unutterable power of divine grace. His character as well as his genius provided the power which stamped his influence indelibly on Western Christianity.[17]

Augustine did not primarily view the individual in isolation. Instead, he saw two great commonwealths or communities—the City of This World and the City of God. This focus has a judicial element, but it is not so exaggerated as we find in Tertullian, for example. Augustine is not gleeful about the fate of the lost, nor does he show a spirit of vindictiveness. Yet he does not hesitate to argue that since hell is sin's proper punishment, it is itself a "good" thing and not evil. This was how he answered the charge that unending torment made evil (as well as good) eternal—a doctrine he strongly opposed in his dualistic Manichaean adversaries.[18]

Augustine allowed that some scriptural terms describing final punishment might be understood metaphorically and that the pain suffered would vary in its severity in proportion to the sinner's guilt— infants who died unbaptized suffering least of all—but he insisted that all men would live forever, even those in hell. He warned against the false confidence of some who placed security in the fact that they were once baptized or belonged to the church and received its sacraments. He reasoned at some length against those who taught restorationism. Yet he allowed that certain sinners, Christians at heart but entangled in earthly loves, would be cleansed by a purgatorial fire and finally be saved.[19] Gregory the Great, a pope at the end of the sixth century, was a great mediator of Augustine's theology. Gregory is often considered the originator of the Western church's doctrine of purgatory.[20]

Augustine discusses this subject throughout book 21 of his *The City of God*. Because of Augustine's important position in the history of Western theology, we have examined that discussion at some

---

17. Bardy, *Christian Latin Literature*, pp. 130-135.

18. John W. Wenham, *The Goodness of God*, p. 30. Norman L. Geisler repeats Augustine's argument that hell is actually a philosophical "good" in his *Philosophy of Religion*, p. 374. Although conditionalists and restorationists stand at opposite poles and could not be further apart, they often agree in charging traditionalists with the eternity of evil and thus with unbiblical dualism.

19. Kelly gives references in his *Early Christian Doctrines*, pp. 484-485.

20. Milton McC. Gatch, *Death: Meaning and Mortality in Christian Thought and Contemporary Culture*, p. 73.

length in Appendix A at the end of this book. It is enough here to say that he presupposed the immortality of the soul, then read the biblical passages on the assumption that no sinner can ever truly die, perish or be destroyed in a literal sense. Since Scripture ruled out universal restoration, Augustine had to teach conscious eternal torment. By the fifth century, Kelly says, Augustine's views already were "everywhere paramount."[21] Supported by his endorsement, the common view quickly moved from the status of popular opinion to become unquestioned orthodoxy.

Augustine's role in the development of Christian thought was so crucial, says Gatch, "that no survey can do justice to his achievement."[22] His influence extended to medieval scholasticism, to Calvin and Reformed Protestantism, and to Tridentine Roman Catholicism alike. "The teaching of the Western church from [his time] offers hardly any exception to the reproduction of Augustine's leading lines of thought."[23] Although some of his ideas have been "tacitly dropped," Pusey writes, Augustine "has, more than any other, formed the mind of our Western Christendom."[24] Regarding the traditionalist interpretation of final punishment, Harry Buis acknowledges, Augustine's "advocacy of this position tended to cause it to become the accepted doctrine of the church for the centuries that followed."[25]

It would be difficult indeed to overstate Augustine's influence on Western theology. Yet he himself once urged:

> Do not follow my writings as Holy Scripture. When you find in Holy Scripture anything you did not believe before, believe it without doubt; but in my writings, you should hold nothing for certain.[26]

We show only respect for Augustine's true greatness by heeding this humble advice.

---

21. Kelly, *Early Christian Doctrines*, p. 484.

22. Gatch, *Death*, p. 70.

23. *A Dictionary of Christian Biography, Literature, Sects and Doctrines*, 2:197.

24. Pusey, *What Is of Faith?* pp. 172-173.

25. Buis, *The Doctrine of Eternal Punishment*, p. 61.

26. Augustine, "Preface to the Treatise on the Trinity," quoted by James Montgomery Boice, *Does Inerrancy Matter?* (Oakland: International Council on Biblical Inerrancy, 1979), p. 22.

The Middle Ages

With the decline of Rome, Europe's intellectual center gradually moved northwest, away from the ancient Mediterranean basin to the newer Germanic kingdoms. Although historical surveys of thought often omit the six or seven centuries from Augustine to Anselm and Aquinas, Gatch insists that the period be paid its due. These centuries are not noted for original thought, he says, but for "a passion to collect, preserve, and transmit the teaching of the Fathers."[27] They were followed, however, by the High Middle Ages, and Gatch does see there a turning point in Christian thinking concerning death and its meaning. In this period, he says, "the soul's immortality and its adventures after the separation of body and soul came to occupy the center of attention at the expense of the heroic picture of resurrection."[28]

Along with this emphasis on the individual, there came what Gatch calls "a new sense of tenderness," seen in theology in the cult of the Virgin Mary and in literature by the courtly romance. The general resurrection and cosmic judgment remained, but attention turned to the individual judgment believed to occur at the hour of each person's death. Logic became the theologian's basic tool, writes Gatch, and the final measure for determining authority as well.[29] The two best-known theologians of the era also clearly illustrate these developments. They are Anselm (died 1117) and Thomas Aquinas (died 1274).

Anselm (Died 1117). Like Tertullian so many years earlier, Anselm argued for unending torment on the basis of philosophy and law. In his *Cur Deus Homo* (bk. 1) and also his *Proslogion* (chs. 8-11), this philosopher-theologian set forth his traditional case. He did not attempt to exegete Scripture but, rather, defended the view he had received. Where Tertullian thought in terms of Latin law and justice, Anselm reasoned within the framework of medieval feudal society.

In that structure, punishment was determined not only by the offense committed but also by the relative worthiness of the offended

---

27. Gatch, *Death*, p. 79.
28. Ibid., p. 94.
29. Ibid., pp. 94-95.

party. The same act which the king might commit with impunity could bring a lesser noble a reprimand or even a sentence in jail. Committed by a serf, it might well mean instant death. Since God is worthy of infinite honor, Anselm reasoned, crime against Him (sin) deserves infinite punishment. But since man is a finite being, the only way he can pay an infinite penalty is to suffer for an infinite period of time. Therefore sinners must endure conscious torment forever.

It is immediately evident that Anselm does not base his strongest appeal on scriptural evidence. He neither explains the many passages which seem to teach that sinners will become extinct, nor does he interpret the more popular phrases such as "unquenchable fire," "the worm that dies not," or "fire and brimstone" in the light of their common biblical usage. He reasons from philosophy—and some modern philosophers argue that even that is fallacious.[30]

Thomas Aquinas (Died 1274). As it had been nearly a millennium earlier, the problem of the soul was again debated hotly in the thirteenth century. Thomas Aquinas built on an Aristotelian base. The idea of the soul's existence apart from the body concerned him less than it did others who reasoned from the more Platonic tradition. I. C. Brady, writing in the *New Catholic Encyclopedia*, expresses the opinion that Thomas greatly improved on the philosophical proofs for the soul's immortality, arguing as he did from its supposed spirituality and substantiality. Man's "intellectual operations" prove the soul is a spiritual subsistent being, reasoned Aquinas, so that it is subject to no corruptibility.[31]

Aquinas argued that the resurrection is necessary because of "the natural desire of man to tend to happiness," Gatch says. In the same way, ultimate punishment requires the reunion of soul and body. Whether good or bad, in this thinking, man will be "immortal, animal, and incorruptible."[32] As a follower of Aristotle, Aquinas also

---

30. Marilyn McCord Adams, "Hell and the God of Justice," *Religious Studies* 2, no. 4 (December 1975): 433-447. Ms. Adams also reasons away eternal bliss. Her article reaffirms the futility of seeking answers from philosophy which can be had only from divine revelation, whether the philosopher be Augustine or Arnobius, Aquinas or Ms. Adams. Our views must rest on biblical exegesis if they are to have the solid support of an authoritative word. Like each new weapon in the modern arms race, it seems every philosopher's argument eventually encounters the argument of another philosopher which is even mightier.

31. I. C. Brady, "Immortality of Human Soul," *New Catholic Encyclopedia*, 13:465.

32. Gatch, *Death*, p. 99. Like traditionalists before and since, Aquinas had to posit not only

viewed the soul as the "form" of the body and as incomplete without it. For this reason, too, the resurrection was a philosophical necessity, and in this he differed from the Platonists. Even though Aquinas believed that the resurrection and final judgment were needed as salvation's consummation and history's goal, in his understanding these central events of biblical eschatology lost their place of emphasis to the individual soul and its destiny immediately after death.[33]

Since the soul "had priority in the fault or merit" during its sojourn in the body, Aquinas also thought it proper that it should "have priority also in being punished or rewarded." He therefore concluded that a double retribution begins at the point of death for what man has done in life. The righteous then begin to see God; the wicked begin to suffer torment. Because even the righteous are tainted by sin's impurity, their souls must first be purged. "This is made by punishments," said Aquinas. "And this is the reason we hold that there is a purgatory."[34]

In his *Summa Contra Gentiles* Aquinas defended the justice of eternal torment by five arguments. In one he argued that to *will* a thing is as bad as to actually *do* it. A man who rejected his ultimate end for the sake of a temporal good, when he might have enjoyed his proper end throughout eternity, shows he *preferred* temporal good even through eternity. God is therefore just, Aquinas reasoned, to punish that man in the same way as if he had *sinned* eternally—with eternal punishment. Since pleasure is increased by contrast with its opposite, Aquinas reasoned that the damned would suffer forever in the plain sight of the redeemed.[35] As with the arguments of Anselm, so Aquinas' philosophical arguments also are disputed today totally apart from their scriptural merits.[36] Still, his influence on Western theology is undisputed, especially within Roman Catholicism. Some of his arguments have floated for more than seven centuries down tradition's silent stream, well into modern Protestant thought.

---

immortal souls but also incorruptible and deathless bodies for the damned. New Testament writers apply these adjectives only to God or to the glorified resurrection bodies of the righteous, never to the damned, to man's soul, or to any man in the present life.

33. Ibid., p. 99.

34. Ibid., pp. 97-98.

35. Wenham quotes from Aquinas' *Summa Theologica* (part 3, English Dominican trans., 1922, p. 107) in *The Goodness of God*, p. 31.

36. Adams, "God of Justice."

Anselm and Aquinas typify the main current of Western thought in the official medieval church. It was a theology cast in the mold of philosophy; tradition rather than exegesis filled in its details. As time passed, the tradition hardened and the distance from Scripture increased. The Bible's view of Last Things was largely lost, though such outstanding events as the resurrection, final judgment, and heaven and hell remained like some honored pieces of furniture preserved for posterity from a house that no longer existed. One writer gave this contrast: "If primitive Christian eschatology was futurist in its orientation and at once personal, social and cosmic in its scope, the traditional eschatology of the classical period was on the whole presentist in orientation and individualistic in scope."[37]

Events of the sixteenth century would shake the traditional system to its roots, and it would never again be the same. But almost of necessity the embattled Reformers would take first things first. And to them that would mean such pressing concerns as justification and the church. "First things" would not include Last Things.

The Sixteenth-Century Reformers

"Augustine," writes H. Quistorp, "as the father of Western mediaeval theology, is also the real founder of the eschatology of the medieval church, in which that of Calvin is in many respects rooted."[38] Luther and Calvin alike gave the greatest attention to those doctrines which they felt most threatened by contemporary Catholicism, specifically the authority of the Scriptures and justification by faith. Other doctrines which lay outside these bounds were not points of special controversy and did not receive the Reformers' careful, specific attention. Most elements of eschatology came in this latter category.

Martin Luther. The possible exception to this was the doctrine of purgatory, which figured prominently in Luther's controversies in particular. At first Luther accepted purgatory, though he vigorously

---

37. David W. Lotz, "Heaven and Hell in the Christian Tradition," *Religion in Life* 48 (Spring 1979): 81.

38. Heinrich Quistorp, *Calvin's Doctrine of the Last Things*, p. 193, note 1.

protested the doctrine's horrendous abuses associated, for example, with the sale of indulgences.[39] Later he rejected it as an article of faith. Finally he realized that purgatory had no scriptural foundation and abandoned the idea altogether.[40] "Purgatory is not to be admitted," he would finally say, "because it obscures the merits and grace of Christ."[41] It is important to note that Luther did not reject purgatory because of a thorough exegetical study of Last Things but, rather, because he found it in conflict with the evangelical doctrine of justification.

Luther often used the word "hell" metaphorically. According to Hans Schwartz, Luther could speak of man experiencing hell when he meant to describe the "experience of God's judgment, the despair concerning election, and the realization of being abandoned by God or of being far away from him."[42] In this, Luther spoke from his own experience. He had confronted the terror of facing God's judgment himself, and this is the way he described it:

> I myself "knew a man" [II Cor. 12:2] who claimed that he had often suffered these punishments. . . . Yet they were so great and so much like hell that no tongue could adequately express them, no pen could describe them, and one who had not himself experienced them could not believe them. And so great were they that, if they had been sustained or had lasted for half an hour, even for one tenth of an hour, he would have perished completely and all of his bones would have been reduced to ashes. . . . All that remains is the stark-naked desire for help and a terrible groaning, but it does not know where to turn for help. In this instance the person is stretched out with Christ so that all his bones may be counted, and every corner of the soul is filled with the greatest bitterness, dread, trembling, and sorrow in such a manner that all these last forever.[43]

---

39. In a March 1521 response in German to Leo X's papal bull condemning 41 theses from Luther's writings, the Reformer wrote: "The existence of a purgatory I have never denied. I still hold that it exists, as I have written and admitted many times, though I have found no way of proving it incontrovertibly from Scripture or reason. . . . I myself have come to the conclusion that there is a purgatory, but I cannot force anybody else to come to the same result" (Martin Luther, "Defense and Explanation of All the Articles," *Luther's Works*, 32:95).

40. Hans Schwartz, "Luther's Understanding of Heaven and Hell," *Interpreting Luther's Legacy*, p. 91.

41. Martin Luther, *Tischreden III*. 3695 (Weimar: Ausgabe, 1914), quoted by Gatch, *Death*,, p. 113.

42. Schwartz, "Heaven and Hell," p. 88.

43. *AE*, 31, 129, *Explanations of the Ninety-Five Theses; WA*, I, 557, 558, *Resolutiones*, 1518. Quoted in *Verdict* 2, no. 4 (August 1979): 25.

Luther understood that pictures are often necessary if man is to perceive God's realities. Schwartz concludes that "we can generalize with Luther that all spatial categories regarding the terms heaven and hell are only means of intuition which we have to use to express what is meant by these terms, or else we have to remain silent."[44] This does not mean Luther thought the wicked could expect a less fearful end than the Bible's pictures describe, but rather the opposite. No matter how horrible that hell might be pictured, Luther believed it would actually be more horrible than anyone might still imagine.

Though hell signifies man's being in and under God's wrath, Luther believed the final state would be fundamentally different from any such state now, "because the future hell will be a certain place where all the damned will be gathered and placed under the eternal wrath of God." That will be the *evident* separation between believers and unbelievers. But since the last judgment means the total end of our present world and the arrival of a new, imperishable order, even this cannot conflict with any space-time world-view.[45]

Luther knew that most hell-language was pictorial in character and did not intend to give literal, physical descriptions. Yet this very fact required him to use the pictures when talking about hell. The most excruciating torments, Luther said, will be spiritual and not physical. "The torment of hell is fear, terror, horror, fleeing, and despairing."[46] The damned will constantly "suffer pain, and constantly they will be a fiery oven." But the fiery oven means bearing God's appearance, which will endure forever. Luther's larger statement went like this:

> The fiery oven is ignited merely by the unbearable appearance of God and endures eternally. For the Day of Judgment will last for a moment only but will stand throughout eternity and will thereafter never come to an end.[47] Constantly the damned will be judged, constantly they will suffer pain, and constantly they will be a fiery oven, that is, they will be tortured within by supreme distress and tribulation. Not as though the ungodly see God and His appearance as the godly will see

---

44. Schwartz, "Heaven and Hell," p. 94.

45. Ibid., pp. 88-89.

46. Ewald M. Plass, comp., *What Luther Says: An Anthology*, 2:626, #1916.

47. Luther here refers to the fact that though judgment "will last for a moment only," its results "will stand throughout eternity." This is the same understanding we have of "eternal punishment" and "eternal destruction"—the action involved will occur and end, but its results will last forever. So also with Christ's "eternal redemption" and "eternal salvation."

Him; but they will feel the power of His presence, which they will not
be able to bear and yet will be forced to bear.[48]

Luther expressed the same point in terms of outer darkness, wailing and gnashing of teeth, and burning forever without a drop of
water to refresh.[49]

Luther clearly believed that the wicked would suffer conscious torment forever, although he understood most of the biblical language
to describe spiritual suffering rather than physical. He did not examine the conditionalist language of Scripture nor interpret the New
Testament language on final punishment in the light of its Old Testament background. On this subject, as on others, he was more a
preacher than a teacher, more a debater than a systematic theologian. He began with the medieval understanding of Last Things,
purged purgatory in the light of justification by faith, and purified
the ordinary language of the gross literalism with which it was often
used. It is no harsh criticism to say that this is as far as he went. We
respect his memory and devotion to Scripture best by attempting to
continue on from the place he stopped, seeking an even purer understanding of the infallible Word of God.

John Calvin. Like Luther, Calvin also wanted to avoid popular
extremes on Last Things. Quistorp notes that in Calvin's treatment of
eschatological subjects he "expressed himself somewhat sketchily;
only in one instance does he make an exception—in regard to the
doctrine of the immortality of the discarnate soul in the interval between death and the Last Judgment."[50] Compared to his discussion of
the eternal salvation of the elect, Calvin's descriptions of the final
doom of the godless "are only brief in comparison."[51] The Reformer
would "leave it to the foolish curiosity of others to brood over the exact nature of [hell] fire," he once wrote. "It suffices me to maintain
what Paul also in this connexion insists on, viz. that Christ will be a
severe recompenser of the godless." The only specific point Calvin
wished to make was that, "like the glory promised to believers, the
fire will last eternally."[52]

---

48. Plass, *What Luther Says*, 2:627, #1919.

49. Ibid., #1920, #1921.

50. Quistorp, *Calvin's Doctrine*, p. 55.

51. Ibid., p. 191.

52. Ibid., pp. 187-188. Calvin's comments are on Matthew 25:41 and 2 Thessalonians 1:7.

Like Luther, Calvin regarded the eternal torment itself as primarily (but not exclusively) spiritual. God's majesty and endless wrath will deprive the godless torment itself of all peace and itself torture them forever, Calvin believed. "Thus these unhappy consciences find no peace but are painfully caught up in terrible whirlwinds, they feel how the angry God tortures them, they are pierced and mangled by death-dealing arrows, cower in terror before the thunderbolt of God and are crushed by the pressure of His hand so that it would be easier to be swallowed up by some abyss or gulf rather than endure for a moment such terrors."[53] Throughout his commentaries on the Gospels, Calvin stressed the symbolic nature of Christ's language on hell, as also in the *Institutes*.[54]

Buis wished that all who followed Calvin "in his orthodoxy had followed him in his sanity of interpretation, particularly in recognizing the metaphorical nature of the language used in the Bible in describing eternal punishment." If that had been the case, he surmised, "there would have been a much less reactionary denial of the doctrine."[55] We wish that all who share Calvin's devotion to the authority of the Scripture would let the Bible itself interpret what it says about the end of the wicked rather than interpreting it in the light of an imaginary "standard Jewish view" of the first century or a philosophical presupposition (which is explicitly denied but subconsciously held) that souls are imperishable even in the Lord God's consuming fire of the Age to Come. Our concern in this study is not a reactionary one against the traditionalist view but an exegetical one based on what the Scriptures appear to actually teach repeatedly, consistently, and as emphatically as human language is able to express.

Calvin was an exegete, but he did not build his case for final punishment on an exegetical basis. Even though he could write in the *Institutes* that God's wrath "is a raging fire devouring and engulfing everything it touches,"[56] his philosophical presupposition of man's immortal soul prevented him from taking such language seriously in the matter of final punishment. Like Luther, Calvin largely began with the Augustinian theology. He constantly sought to correct the

---

53. Ibid., p. 189, quoting John Calvin *Institutes* 3. 25. 12.

54. Calvin *Institutes* 3. 25. 12

55. Buis, *The Doctrine of Eternal Punishment*, p. 80.

56. Calvin *Institutes*, 3. 25. 12.

received doctrines in the light of Jesus Christ and the gospel of justification by faith. But he did not shine the light of the cross and the
empty tomb on his doctrine of man or of the sinner's final end. He
did not interpret the popular traditionalist proof-texts in the light of
their prophetic background; like other traditionalists, he largely ignored the conditionalist passages altogether.

Calvin's first theological treatise was a work entitled *Psychopannychia*, and it was a vehement attack on the doctrine (which he
ascribed to the detestable Anabaptists) that man's "soul" either died
with the body or slept until the day of judgment. Because the hated
Anabaptists were associated with this doctrine, Calvin's opposition
to it increased all the more. And even though Luther and Tyndale
had both expressed the same mortalist views as the Anabaptists, the
intense opposition of Calvin and Bullinger to the doctrine led the
other leaders to drop the subject rather than to chance dividing the
whole Reformation over what seemed to be a minor point.

We examine Calvin's *Psychopannychia* at length in Appendix B.
Like the patristic writers before him, Calvin conceded that since God
had created man's soul, He could also destroy it entirely if He
wished. Yet Calvin's philosophical mind was programmed in terms
of the immortality of the soul, and this predisposition always prevented his considering the total annihilation of sinners as a serious
possibility. It would not be fair to say that Calvin was a Platonist—
he denied man's *inherent* immortality, he affirmed that the soul had
been *created*, and he insisted that God *could* destroy it if He wished.
His doctrine of the immortality of the soul was, rather, a hindrance
which prevented Calvin from following ordinary biblical exegesis
through to a logical end. Through his primary influence Protestantism included the traditional view of final punishment. "In the work
of Luther and even more clearly in Calvin's *Institutes*, the basic shape
of expectations for man after death remained that propounded by
scholastic theology in the thirteenth century."[57]

Later Protestant theology repeated in devotionals and hymns the
ascetic piety of the Middle Ages, which turned attention from living
to dying, made the last judgment largely a private affair, and viewed
both heaven and hell in strongly individualistic terms.[58] Eschatology

---

57. Gatch, *Death*, pp. 133-134.
58. Lotz, "Heaven and Hell," p. 87.

thus became spiritualized in a way Quistorp calls "acute and ruinous." Calvin's standpoint became typical for Lutheran as well as Reformed Protestants.[59] As Augustine had fixed the tradition for later Catholicism, so Calvin sealed it with the Protestant stamp of approval 1100 years later. The understanding of Tertullian and Augustine, of Chrysostom and Anselm and Aquinas, of Calvin and Bullinger, would receive official status in many Protestant creeds.[60] Opposition from "outsiders" such as many Anabaptists (and later Adventist groups), or from heretical groups such as the Socinians (and later Jehovah's Witnesses),[61] would only harden the established churches in the received interpretation and would effectively prevent any full-scale exegetical study of the subject in the same open-minded manner other important subjects might receive.

Yet Calvin and Luther, like Augustine and even the apostle Paul, urged that men follow them only as they followed Christ. Not one of the great Reformers would discourage the most careful scrutiny of whatever they taught in the light of Jesus Christ and the sacred Scriptures of both Testaments. Quistorp puts the challenge plainly:

---

59. Quistorp, *Calvin's Doctrine*, p. 193.

60. Harry Buis (*The Doctrine of Eternal Punishment*, p. 82) and Jon E. Braun (*Whatever Happened to Hell?* pp. 112-114) both quote from these and later confessional statements. Several of these confine themselves to biblical terminology. Others go beyond the language of Scripture in explicit declarations that the wicked will "burn forever" (Second Helvetic Confession, 1566—one of the earlier and probably the most influential of all Protestant confessions) or be "tormented without end" (Augsburg Confession, 1530), or that the wicked, like the righteous, will be "immortal" (Belgic Confession of Faith, 1561). Such affirmations also go beyond such generally-acknowledged statements of faith as the Apostles' Creed (Christ "shall come to judge the quick and the dead," and there will be a "resurrection of the body") and the Nicene Creed (Christ will "judge the living and the dead," and there will be a "resurrection of the dead").

Though contained in later creeds, the explicitly traditionalist statements are found nowhere in the Bible, and they fail the test, proposed by Vincent of Lerins in the fifth century, that the church should hold what has been believed "everywhere and always and by all." The conditionalist position, on the other hand, can be expressed by verbatim quotations of many passages of Scripture throughout the entire Bible, and it is in complete accord with the ancient and universal creeds.

61. Both the Anabaptist and Socinian labels seem to have covered a wide diversity of opinion on final punishment—and the two groups were of course far from each other in their essential particulars. Opinions in either case apparently ranged from a denial that the wicked would be raised to the regular conditionalist view which affirms the resurrection of both good and evil but believes that the wicked will finally (and literally) be destroyed and perish in the second death. Today the first view is represented by the Jehovah's Witnesses. Now, as then, it is vehemently denied by traditionalists and conditionalists alike. The second view is held today by the relatively small Advent Christian Church and the much larger Seventh-day Adventist denomination, as well as by a scattering of individuals in many other mainstream, evangelical bodies.

If we would understand [Calvin] rightly we must not be afraid constantly to test his teaching by the norm of all Christian teaching which he restored to a place of honour—the Bible itself. We shall have to examine critically his special eschatology by its degree of correspondence with Scripture.[62]

This has been done to some extent within evangelical Protestantism by a few smaller bodies and quite a number of scattered individuals. But for those who compose the great mainstream it is still one unfinished task. Perhaps the present state of world crisis, the increasing sense of the urgency of mission, the deterioration of denominational, sectarian and traditional loyalties, and the mighty renewal of interest in the authority of Scripture and the objectivity of revelation will come together to make this challenge one from which we can no longer hide or step aside. Let the finest scholars do their best possible work—using every tool at their disposal—under the reverent conviction that the Bible is the very Word of the living God! There is no good reason to refuse.

---

62. Quistorp, *Calvin's Doctrine*, p. 54.

18

The Common View Questioned: Some Dissenters since the Reformation

Just as Tertullian's view of hell as conscious unending torment came, after Augustine's day and through his influence, to be the fixed orthodoxy of the Roman Catholic Church, so the same view, through Calvin and Luther—but especially the creed writers, Bullinger and Melanchthon—attained an early and secure place in Protestant doctrine as well. Some topics which had been hotly debated among the Reformers of the sixteenth century became off limits for discussion among respectable, "orthodox" Protestants within the hundred years thereafter. The proliferation of creeds and Confessions provided rallying points for the fledgling and often-persecuted Protestants, but the same documents also served to "fix" their "orthodoxy." Only when the newly-established churches had so solidified their views to the point of confessional statements could any reaction come to such "official" doctrines.

There had been an almost unbroken chain of conditionalist thought from the earliest days of the Reformation, as Froom documents and we have already briefly noted. Some, but not all those who affirmed man's creaturely mortality, also positively taught the final extinction of the wicked. So long as the question remained open for discussion, such conditionalist views were not seen as "challenges," for as yet there was no official Protestant orthodoxy to be challenged. With the formation and declaration of official statements, however, the minority position came to be viewed in a different light. What had been merely an unpopular view now became "unorthodox" at best—and "heterodox" heresy at worst.

We must read D. P. Walker in this perspective when he writes that "it is not until the mid 17th century that one finds explicit attacks on the orthodox doctrine of hell."[1] If one takes that statement to mean that until A.D. 1600 all had agreed that the wicked would become immortal and suffer conscious pain forever, he would either misread Walker's statement or (if that is what Walker intended to say, as may well be the case) his conclusion would fly in the face of much evidence which can be copiously and unquestionably documented from before the time of Christ. In terms of the official position on the subject within most of the early, established[2] Protestant churches, however, Walker's statement is a clear and fair summary of the case. By the same token, it was not until the mid-seventeenth century that Protestant orthodoxy had become so settled as to present a common and popular face.

The Seventeenth Century

Although one reading Froom's massive *The Conditionalist Faith of Our Fathers* might easily miss the fact, many whom he quotes as opposing the doctrine of the innate immortality of the soul do *not* state that they also oppose the common understanding of hell as conscious unending torment. And while the relation between these two doctrines is so strong that many of the most influential molders of uninspired Christian thought have felt forced to hold the second one because they assumed the first, that conclusion was not really necessary.

From patristic times to the present, great theologians who have held the traditionalist view of final punishment have insisted that man's immortality is derived (from his creation by God) rather than inherent (as if his soul were eternal and pre-existent). They have

---

1. D. P. Walker, *The Decline of Hell: Seventeenth-Century Discussions of Eternal Torment*, p. 4.

2. By "established" we intend to exempt the Anabaptists, for example, many of whom denied both the immortality of the soul and conscious unending torment. Not all the Reformation churches explicitly included the traditionalist view in their confessions, as we have seen already. Both the Roman and Eastern churches did, though neither of them was "Protestant."

made clear their conviction that God, who created man in the beginning, can bring him to nothing in the end if it should so please the Almighty to do it. On the other hand, though no examples come to mind, one could theoretically hold to man's natural mortality in all his totality, yet believe that God would give the wicked immortality in the resurrection as well as the righteous but consign them to everlasting torment rather than everlasting glory and joy.[3] Even with this qualification, however, Froom has documented many persons, both notable and ordinary, from the earliest Reformation stirrings who clearly held to one or both of these conditionalist views.

John Milton. One of these was John Milton (1608-1674). An Anglican of Puritan leanings, Milton later became an independent. Best known for his poetic *Paradise Lost*, Milton expressed his mortalist views in that work and also through his prose. In *Paradise Lost*, for example, Milton wrote:

> . . . It was but breath
> Of life that sinned; what dies but what had life
> And sin? The body properly had neither.
> All of me then shall die: let this appease
> The doubt, since human reach no further knows.[4]

His prose works contain the same thought. "What could be more just," Milton inquired, "than that he who had sinned in his whole person, should die in his whole person?" And "it is evident," he continued, "that the saints and believers of old, the patriarchs, prophets and apostles, without exception, held this doctrine."[5] In another place Milton concluded: "It may be inferred, unless we had rather take the heathen writers for our teachers respecting the nature of the soul, that man is a living being, intrinsically and properly one and individual not compounded or separable, not—according to the com-

---

3. The fact that this possibility is so uncommonly realized, if ever at all, suggests once again that the traditionalist view ultimately springs from an assumption that every soul is immortal and must live forever. Although traditionalists formally concede that God is able to kill and annihilate even the soul if He so desires, they interpret all the Scripture passages which seem to say that exactly as if they had declared it unthinkable and impossible. The philosophic view of immortal souls (Platonic or otherwise) may be officially denied yet still wield a determining influence on one's subconscious interpretation of Scripture.

4. John Milton, *Paradise Lost*, bk. 10, 11. 789-793, quoted by LeRoy Edwin Froom, *The Conditionalist Faith of Our Fathers*, 2:156.

5. Quoted by Froom, *Conditionalist Faith*, 2:154.

mon opinion—made up and formed of two distinct and separate na-
tures as of soul and body; but that the whole man is soul, and the
soul man."[6]

Traditionalist authors sometimes quote *Paradise Lost* to illustrate
Milton's imaginative description of hell's severity, noting that he
wrote as a poet and not a systematic theologian.[7] This very use of
Milton is itself an outstanding practical illustration of the fact that
the terrors of the lake of fire are lessened not one whit by mortalist
convictions regarding man's natural state in the present life. Milton
based his convictions on Scripture, of which he was a diligent and
earnest student, and "his religious views underwent a continual process of revision over a period of years."[8] He was neither the first man
nor the last to change his mind when confronted with additional evidence, and the drift of his thought seems to have been toward a consistent conditionalism.

John Locke. An influential philosopher and ardent advocate of
unhampered thought, John Locke rejected ecclesiastic authority as a
sufficient ground for religious conviction. Since his great philosophical work, *An Essay concerning Human Understanding*, attacked
Platonism's fundamental approach to knowledge, it is not surprising
that Locke should finally differ from basic Platonic conclusions as
well, particularly the innate immortality of the soul. In his last work,
On the Reasonableness of Christianity (1695), Locke applied his mortalist views to the subject of final punishment. "By death, some men
understand endless torments in hell fire," he remarked, "but it seems
a strange way understanding a law which requires the plainest and
directest of words, that by death should be meant eternal life in
misery."[9] Locke was an outspoken defender of the divine origin of
Scripture, which he once said had "God for its author, salvation for
its end, and truth without any mixture of error for its matter."[10] He
was also convinced that the Bible taught the wicked will finally
become extinct and be no more.

---

6. Ibid., p. 153.

7. Harry Buis, *The Doctrine of Eternal Punishment*, pp. 84-85; Jon E. Braun, *Whatever Happened to Hell?* pp. 18, 72-73.

8. Arthur Sewell, *A Study in Milton's Christian Doctrine*, p. 1.

9. John Locke, *On The Reasonableness of Christianity*, quoted by Froom, *Conditionalist
Faith*, 2:190.

10. Quoted by Froom, *Conditionalist Faith*, 2:188.

Samuel Richardson. The year 1658 saw the publication of a work bearing the imposing title: *Of the Torments of Hell: The Foundations Thereof Discover'd, Search'd, Shaken and Remov'd, with Many Infallible Proofs That There Is Not to Be a Punishment after This Life for Any to Endure That Shall Never End.* The author was Samuel Richardson, pastor of London's first Particular (Calvinist) Baptist church, established in 1633. A signatory to three editions of the confession of faith of London's seven Particular Baptist churches, Richardson presented both negative and positive arguments for the conditionalist position he espoused.[11] Twenty years later John Brandon responded to Richardson's treatise with his own work entitled *Everlasting Fire No Fancy: Being an Answer to a Late Pestilent Pamphlet; Entitled The Foundations of Hell-Torments Shaken and Removed.* Another answer came in 1720 from John Lewis. We do not agree with the wording of Richardson's title inasmuch as the consuming fire of hell *will* constitute an everlasting destruction "that shall never end," but his work shows that the traditional doctrine's critics were found also in the mainstream of respectable Protestant churches.

General Baptist Confession.[12] Shortly after Richardson published his conditionalist work, some 41 General (Arminian) Baptist "elders, deacons and brethren" met at London in 1660 and presented Charles II with *A Brief Confession or Declaration of Faith.* It represented the beliefs, they said, of more than 20,000 others besides themselves. While clearly affirming the resurrection of the wicked as well as the righteous in Article 21, the next Article affirmed that their final end will be utter extinction. The original document italicized the statement of Article 22 that *"The triumphing of the wicked is short, and the joy of the Hypocrite but for a moment; though his Excellency mount up to the Heavens, and his head reach unto the clouds, yet shall hee perish for ever, like his own dung; they which have seen him, shall say, where is hee?"* The Confession also affirmed the Holy Scriptures as the rule of faith and practice, and set forth ordinary Baptistic distinctives as "the apostolical way."

---

11. Ibid., pp. 183-185.
12. Ibid., pp. 141-142. Italics in original.

The Heretical Socinians. Besides these conditionalists who espoused a high view of Scripture, the full divinity of Jesus Christ, and the resurrection of the wicked unto condemnation, the traditional doctrine of hell had other critics who were no asset to any honorable cause. Chief among these were the Socinians, probably best remembered today for their denial that the Son is consubstantial with the Father. The group originated from the work of Fausto Socinius, whose name became its tag. Walker says that no adversaries can quote any published writings of Socinius denying either the resurrection of the wicked or eternal torment, but that they can produce passages in which he implies such denials.[13]

The Socinians flourished in Poland in the late sixteenth and early seventeenth centuries. About 1640 they were dispersed throughout Europe. The later *Compendiolum Socioanismi* (1598) gives evidence that at least some Socinians believed in the annihilation of the wicked, perhaps denying also that the wicked would even be raised. In 1654 Jonas Slichting, a chief Socinian apologist, denied the latter charge, saying that they believed in a resurrection "of the unjust for the torments of eternal fire." Two years later their adversary, Cocceius, refused Slichting's denial, terming "dishonest" his use of the expression "eternal fire" to describe a fire that totally consumes rather than perpetually torments the wicked.[14] Walker himself regards the Socinian use of the biblical terms "eternal fire" or "unquenchable fire" as "deliberately ambiguous,"[15] although one might point out that the apostolic fathers contented themselves with such scriptural language also, and their meaning is also disputed today.

Because the Socinians, like today's Jehovah's Witnesses, denied Christ's deity and (at least some of them) the resurrection of the wicked as well as the traditionalist doctrine of everlasting conscious tor-

---

13. Walker, *Decline of Hell*, pp. 73-92.

14. Many traditionalist authors persist in the same objection against conditionalists today. Yet we have seen that the language was permitted by no less defenders of the majority view than Augustine of Hippo and Jonathan Edwards, that Strack and Billerbeck say this might be its meaning throughout the Pseudepigrapha, and that a close look at the Scriptures points to the very same definition of the terms which Cocceius refused.

15. Walker, *Decline of Hell*, p. 82. On the same page, Walker quotes one of their writers who says: "I notice that, whenever this subject arises, they have kept close to scriptural terms; and thus hardly anything could be objected against them which could not also be objected against Scripture." But does this not speak *for* the conditionalist view—that it can be so easily expressed in scriptural language and that its advocates can be content to quote the words of the Bible without further elaboration to express their view?

ment, their heretical reputation smeared the latter view with the same undesirable scent as the first two opinions. Just as Calvin weighted the scales of public opinion against Christian mortalism by unfairly ascribing its source to the despised Anabaptists of the sixteenth century, so orthodox Protestants of the seventeenth century hesitated to attack the received doctrine of final punishment lest they be associated in the public mind with the heretical Socinians.[16] The similar association today between the Jehovah's Witnesses and the denial of unending conscious torment still continues to stifle a careful, unbiased study of final punishment among most evangelicals. It is no surprise, therefore, to read Walker's statement that only "the slightly crazy chiliasts" preached against the traditional doctrine in the seventeenth century, while the "sane ones either spoke not at all, or anonymously, or post-humously, or dishonestly."[17]

The Eighteenth Century

Probably very few centuries are truly dull, and certainly no two are exactly alike, but it is easy to look back from our vantage point today and suppose that the eighteenth century was one of history's most eventful—in thought as well as action. Revolution swept France in Europe and the British colonies in America. If kings protested that they ruled by divine right, their claims were drowned out by the voices and clamor of the people. Many who prided themselves as intellectuals dismissed organized religion as one of several authoritarian structures for which there was no place in a modern and enlightened age. Feeding the flames of rational and political revolution was the positive conviction that utopia was just around the bend. Almighty Reason would be its god, and one could almost say the

---

16. Ibid., pp. 8-9.

17. Ibid., pp. 262-263. The chiliasts received "courage to speak out precisely because of their delusions," Walker says. "They had the certainty of direct inspiration from God; since they were living in the Last Days, they could risk the collapse of a society which was soon in any case to give way to a totally new one."

Some of the Anabaptists whose mortalist views Calvin attacked in his *Psychopannychia* also seem to have claimed special revelations. It is interesting to note, however, that Tertullian, one of the earliest explicit advocates of the *traditionalist* doctrine, reasoned from the presupposition of immortal souls, for which he offered as evidence the testimony of an ecstatic Montanist sister who said she had seen a soul, then proceeded to describe it in detail.

Tower of Babel would be its symbol. Dogma and tradition alike were lined up to be measured by the rule of reason. Science would replace superstition, and any dogma that could not stand the test would be tossed out the door.

Interestingly enough, in this expectant climate the doctrine of man's inherent immortality found a warm welcome among rationalists and traditional Christians alike. But controversy hovered over the doctrine of hell, which, as Rowell notes, "apart from anything else, was so grossly offensive to the optimism characteristic of eighteenth-century natural religion."[18] Many popular attacks on the traditional doctrine of hell sprang from its seeming incompatibility with human hope rather than from concern for actual Bible teaching. This often moved the struggle from the field of Scripture to that of reason; by doing so it helped create an apparent choice between the two sources of authority and falsely aligned the traditionalist and conditionalist positions on hell with those two alternatives. As a result, many Bible believers were hardened in their traditionalist view of hell, and a calm study of the subject became even more unlikely than it already was.

Isaac Watts. But not all who questioned the received doctrine did so in the name of Reason. The famous hymn writer, Isaac Watts (1674-1748), who had defended the traditionalist view of final punishment in his younger life,[19] in later years wrote *The Ruine and Recovery of Mankind*, in which he raised serious questions concerning some popular assumptions of that position. More than one conditionalist author has pointed with pleasure at the pious Watts' comment that

> There is not one Place of Scripture that occurs to me, where the word *Death*, as it was first threatned in the Law of Innocency, necessarily signifies a certain miserable Immortality of the Soul, either to *Adam*, the actual Sinner, or to his Posterity. . . . That the resurrection of the body to a state of misery is threatned in the Bible for the punishment

---

18. Geoffrey Rowell, *Hell and the Victorians: A Study of the Nineteenth-Century Theological Controversies concerning Eternal Punishment and the Future Life*, pp. 28-29.

19. In 1818 Isaac Watts published his *The World to Come* . . . , in which he argued for a separate state of souls following death and the traditional understanding of hell along with "a plain answer to all the most plausible Objections."

of Adam's first sin is what I cannot prove, nor do I know in what text of Scripture to find it.[20]

Arthur Paul Davis, a biographer and scholar of Watts, describes him as "by nature charitable" and "intelligent enough to grow." This means his "views changed as opponents convinced him, and he confessed his convictions and stated his doubts with equal honesty." Because Watts held to Scripture as his authoritative source, he would not blindly accept even ecclesiastical tradition without comparing it for himself with the Bible. "With reason and scripture as his pilots," says Davis, "he was from his youth to his grave an open-minded and undogmatic searcher after religious truth."[21]

Robert Hall. A prominent English Baptist preacher of Bristol, Hall (1764-1831) was known in his day for his clear style, which he left for posterity in six volumes of his *Works*. Although not a conditionalist himself, Hall allowed room for the view under the umbrella of sound Christian faith. He wrote:

> I would only add that in my humble opinion the doctrine of the eternal duration of future misery, metaphysically considered, is not an essential article of faith, nor is the belief of it ever proposed as a term of salvation; that if we really flee from the wrath to come, by truly repenting of our sins, and laying hold of the mercy of God through Christ by a lively faith, our salvation is perfectly secure, whichever hypothesis we embrace on this most mysterious subject. The evidence accompanying the popular interpretation [of the doctrine of eternal suffering] is by no means to be compared to that which establishes our common Christianity: and therefore the fate of the Christian religion is not to be considered as implicated in the belief or disbelief of the popular doctrine.[22]

English Arians. Among the more influential questioners of the traditional doctrine of hell in eighteenth-century England were John Locke, Isaac Newton, Samuel Clarke and William Whiston. These all

---

20. Isaac Watts, *The Ruine and Recovery of Mankind* . . . , pp. 228, 230, quoted by Froom, *Conditionalist Faith*, 2:220. The first part of this quotation clearly opens the conditionalist door, but the latter part may regard the federal theology which makes Adam's posterity suffer for the original sin rather than eternal torment as such.

21. Arthur Paul Davis, *Isaac Watts: His Life and Works*, p. 103.

22. Robert Hall, *Works*, 5:529, quoted in Froom, *Conditionalist Faith*, 2:259.

knew each other, according to D. P. Walker, and all were Arians.[23] Only Whiston defended his beliefs openly, publishing in 1740 *The Eternity of Hell Torments Considered*. Some have simply lumped these English Arians with the Socinians of earlier times and dismissed them both together. Such a response is most unfair, as Walker goes on to show.

Wrong as it was, these men's Arianism grew out of an attempt to restore primitive Christian doctrine. It was not the result of an effort, such as the Socinians had made, to make the Scriptures fit a humanistic, rationalistic mold.[24] To the same end of recovering ancient Christianity, Whiston in 1715 started A Society for Promoting Primitive Christianity, an organization which still publishes works today as the Society for the Promotion of Christian Knowledge (S.P.C.K.). His rejection of the traditional doctrine of hell, says Walker, was "based almost solely on scriptural and early patristic authority."[25] Whiston indicated this even in the subtitle he chose: *A Collection of Texts of Scripture, and Testimonies of the First Three Centuries, Relating to Them*. We are not so concerned with Whiston's specific arguments or views as with the fact that he approached his study with the desire to represent the pure teaching of Scripture and the earliest church. Matthew Horber responded to Whiston's book with his own, *An Enquiry into the Scripture-Doctrine concerning the Duration of Future Punishment* (1744), as had William Dodwell in his *The Eternity of Future Punishment Asserted and Vindicated—In Answer to Mr. Whiston's Late Treatise on That Subject: In Two Sermons* (1743).

Others. Froom details numerous other eighteenth-century figures who rejected or opposed the traditionalist views on final punishment in both Britain and in America. Many reasons have been offered against the doctrine of conscious unending torment, ranging from appeals to Scripture to arguments from reason or simply intuition or

---

23. Walker, *Decline of Hell*, p. 93.

24. Ibid., p. 16. Walker says Whiston "believed that his theology would be generally accepted if he could persuade people to read the Scriptures in the light of primitive Christian literature" (p. 97).

25. Ibid., p. 97. Walker notes that the Reformation had denied the Catholic claim to infallibility but then went no further back on some subjects than Augustine. Sooner or later, he observes, some who rejected the medieval tradition were bound to question the validity of doctrines not found in the earliest Christian literature.

feeling. In this study we are concerned only with the first category, regarding any other basis as inadequate for a sound evangelical approach.

We have no sympathy with those who argue against what they believe God has said or who elevate reason over revelation or who choose to walk by feeling when it goes against the direction of faith. The conclusions presented here rest on detailed exegesis of the Bible teaching prayerfully considered according to accepted rules of interpretation consistent with the highest view of Scripture. Our question finally is: *What does Scripture actually teach?* That is really the only question that matters. That is where the discussion of this subject should take place and all conclusions be reached. The Bible is God's Word written, and whatever it actually teaches must be the only authoritative source and measure of our faith.

The Nineteenth Century

If revolution marked the eighteenth century, grand visions of progress sparked the life of the one which followed. Darwin declared man to be the noble result of a natural selection which always rewarded the fittest. Marx applied dialectical philosophy to economics and envisioned the utopian state. In Germany a different breed of biblical critics were saying the Scriptures themselves came by a long process of man's reaching upward. In America and Great Britain sophisticated liberals and hard-working millennialists anticipated the imminent arrival of God's kingdom. One group saw the path lined with trophies of man's religious endeavor; the other looked for God's cataclysmic intervention in the nick of man's wicked time—but both dreamed dreams of love and peace and joy.

Churches that had been established on strict Reformed principles were abandoning classic doctrines as out of step with the spirit of the day. Liberal preachers welcomed the new directions, conservative clergymen lamented them, and a great general populace who did not know where they were headed found comfortable pews to sit in and watch the ride. In it all, writes Geoffrey Rowell, the "flames of hell illuminated vividly the tensions of an age in which men felt that old certainties were being eroded by new knowledge, and in which an optimistic faith in progress co-existed uneasily with forebodings of the consequences of increasingly rapid social change."[26]

It was an age of theological debate. Few subjects figured more prominently overall than final punishment and the related doctrine of the immortality of the soul. By the time Harvard University Divinity School professor, Ezra Abbot, published *The Literature of the Doctrine of a Future Life* in 1880, an annotated bibliography of books on these subjects, he could list no fewer than 4977 titles.[27] More often than not, the subject was discussed on other than an exegetical basis. Changing penal theories in society made many uneasy about a view of hell that seemed wholly based on retribution; others who had discovered a personal aspect of Christianity reacted against a background which sometimes made hell the final point of a mechanical process. The debate raged especially during the half century 1830-1880.[28]

Traditionalists had argued for Christ's divinity on the ground that only such a One could offer the infinite sacrifice needed to satisfy justice in the case of sin against the infinite God. Arians and Socinians reasoned in the opposite direction. Denying Christ's deity, they consistently dismissed the need for an infinite atonement, then the threat of infinite punishment—which traditionalists said required everlasting conscious torment for finite men.[29]

To raise questions about the accepted view of hell in such a climate easily became tantamount to denying the deity of Jesus, as well as to being placed by the public mind in company with heretical Arians and Socinians. Unending conscious torment must be accepted, traditional advocates began to say, simply because God reveals it. They did not back this claim with a thorough presentation of scriptural teaching or a critical weighing of their own presuppositions and arguments. They simply affirmed it—again and again—until most people on both sides came to accept that it was so. But there were exceptions—inside mainstream evangelicalism as well as without.

---

26. Rowell, *Hell and the Victorians*, p. vii. Common arguments raised by liberal preachers of the day reflect the same spirit of the age. The first two arguments listed in *The Religious Encyclopaedia* (published in 1883) are that hell is said to be unjust and that it is said to conflict with God's infinite goodness (Francis L. Patton, "Future Punishment," *The Religious Encyclopaedia; or Dictionary of Biblical, Historical, Doctrinal, and Practical Theology*, 3:1972-1973).

27. Ezra Abbot, "The Literature of the Doctrine of a Future Life," appendix to *The Destiny of the Soul: A Critical History of the Doctrine of a Future Life*, by William R. Alger.

28. Rowell, *Hell and the Victorians*, p. 17.

29. Ibid., p. 30.

Advent Christian Church.[30] The year 1860 saw the formation of the Advent Christian Church, a Sunday-observing, mainstream evangelical body which grew out of the same mid-century millennial expectancy that also spawned a dozen other American church bodies. From the first, however, the Advent Christian group taught that the dead are unconscious until the resurrection and that the wicked will ultimately become extinct in hell and be no more. They based these views on arguments from Scripture and regarded them as the biblical replacement to the philosophical doctrine of the immortality of the soul, which they rejected. Today the group includes over 30,000 members in more than 400 local churches. It observes baptism by immersion and the Lord's Supper, engages in mission work of various kinds, and operates Aurora College (Aurora, Illinois) and Berkshire Christian College (Lenox, Massachusetts).

Church of God (General Conference).[31] The outgrowth of several local groups of kindred spirit, this church traces its American beginnings to the early nineteenth century, though its present General Conference was formed in Waterloo, Iowa in 1921. It holds the Bible as the supreme source of teaching, stresses Christ's premillennial return, and practices baptism by immersion for the remission of sins. It also believes in man's mortality and teaches the total destruction of the wicked in the second death. The group operates Oregon Bible College (Oregon, Illinois) and has some 7500 members in 121 churches.

Seventh-day Adventist Church.[32] Also rising from the intrachurch advent movement of the mid-nineteenth century was the group which crystallized into the Seventh-day Adventist Church. Its pioneer, William Miller, had "disclaimed" support or sympathy with the conditionalism espoused by certain other advent-minded associates in 1844, and a conference in Albany, New York the following year was boycotted by several conditionalists who were still stinging from the rebuff. By the time the Seventh-day Adventists organized

---

30. Frank S. Mead, *Handbook of Denominations in the United States*, pp. 21-22.

31. Ibid., pp. 22-23.

32. Ibid., pp. 19-21. Froom gives a detailed look at conditionalism in the "Adventist" movement at large (including but not limited to the Seventh-day observers) in *Conditionalist Faith*, 2:646-650, 668-701.

under that name in 1860, however, its leaders were solidly conditionalist in persuasion, and its three million members around the world today espouse a detailed and literalistic premillennial eschatology that ends for the wicked in death by actual fire.

Although out of the mainstream because of their Sabbath-keeping as well as common but unofficial standards of diet and health, the church claims to base all its teaching on the authority of Scripture. A former exclusivism has given way in recent years to a more open attitude toward others as Seventh-day Adventists seem to be blending less conspicuously into the evangelical world at large.[33]

LeRoy Edwin Froom, a Seventh-day Adventist popular author, has produced *The Conditionalist Faith of Our Fathers*,[34] a massive, two-volume work which is undoubtedly the most thorough historical, biographical and bibliographical survey of conditionalism ever published. Froom advances the literalistic end-time views held by Seventh-day Adventists, but students on any side of the subject need to read his work for the historical perspective it provides. He destroys many popular misconceptions about conditionalism, even though his book leaves a few of its own.

Jehovah's Witnesses.[35] First known as Russellites, Millennial Dawnists or International Bible Students, this group was incorporated in 1884 by its "general organizer," Charles Taze Russell. It claims to be the only religious organization with God's sanction, and its 1,658,990 members actively distribute its literature around the world. The Witnesses deny the deity of Jesus, making Him an incarnate angel. They also deny that the willfully wicked will ever rise from their graves, which they equate with "hell." They are totally at

---

33. Seventh-day Adventists are extending a hand they formerly kept close to their body, for instance, in sending complimentary subscriptions of their official, semi-professional magazine, *Ministry*, to clergymen of all faiths across America. A cautious taking of that hand is seen, for example, in Seventh-day Adventist theologian, Gerhard F. Hasel, addressing the thirtieth annual meeting of the Evangelical Theological Society in December 1978. Neither "side" gave or implied any endorsement of the other by these courtesies, but they do signify a change from the time when others listed Seventh-day Adventists alongside the cults.

34. Froom, *Conditionalist Faith*, 2 vols. (1965). This work came eight years after Harry Buis' traditionalist book and all others, which were still earlier. Jon Braun does not acknowledge its existence in his *Whatever Happened to Hell?* (1979), though John W. Wenham refers to it as a "vast work . . . of well-organized, lucid exposition" in his *The Goodness of God* (1974), p. 40. Regardless of their persuasion on the topic or their final judgment on the book, future authors dealing with final punishment ought at least to be aware of Froom's work and its general contents.

35. Mead, *Handbook of Denominations*, pp. 153-157.

odds with the idea, set forth here as scriptural, that the wicked will be raised to face God in judgment, then perish forever in the "second death" or hell.

Just as the Socinians of the seventeenth century and the Arians of the eighteenth were an embarrassment to all other opponents of the traditionalist views, so the Jehovah's Witnesses have often served as an excuse to avoid study of the subject today. Froom goes to some lengths to disassociate their denial of the traditional doctrine from his own Seventh-day Adventist movement and views.[36] Most conditionalists through the years have been careful to point out the total difference between the heretical, resurrection-denying doctrine now held by this organization and what conditionalists see as the biblical view of a post-judgment fire which totally consumes the wicked with unquenchable persistence and eternal results. Jehovah's Witnesses, as a matter of fact, are as opposed to the *conditionalist* view of hell as they are to universalism. The only point of similarity between any of the three is a rejection of the traditionalist understanding.

British Controversy. Controversy over final punishment raged in England and through Europe as well as in America. F. D. Maurice[37] of King's College in London expressed a "larger hope" in *Theological Essays* in 1853. He denied that the Greek adjective translated "eternal" (*aiōnios*) had any temporal sense at all, being entirely qualitative in meaning. For these views he was dismissed from his post at the college.

In 1860 a former Oxford professor by the name of H. B. Wilson[38] published *Essays and Reviews*, expressing hope for the salvation of all men, especially of infants. He was tried in Anglican church court, which rendered an adverse judgment against him in 1862. Two years later the higher Judicial Committee of the Privy Council reversed that decision, and the case was "dismissed without costs" to Wilson. The whole affair was surrounded by great popular controversy, and critics of the decision charged that hell had been "dismissed without

---

36. Froom, *Conditionalist Faith*, 2:663-667.

37. See the special issue of *Anglican Theological Review* 54, no. 4 (October 1972), esp. Don Cupitt, "The Language of Eschatology: F. D. Maurice's Treatment of Heaven and Hell," pp. 305-317.

38. T. F. Glasson outlines several nineteenth-century critics and their views in his article, "Human Destiny: Has Christian Teaching Changed?" *Modern Churchman* 12, no. 4 (July 1969): 284-298. Froom discusses the Wilson case in *Conditionalist Faith*, 2:394-395.

costs." Although the Church of England's official Articles originally included a traditionalist statement probably aimed at the Anabaptists, it was dropped when the Forty-Two Articles were later reduced to Thirty-Nine. Anglicanism therefore has no official position on eschatology, and its members have ranged in opinion from Pusey's ecclesiastic traditionalism to John A. T. Robinson's universalism. Many notable Anglicans, evangelical as well as otherwise, have occupied conditionalist ground in the past as well as today.

In 1877, Canon F. W. Farrar[39] preached a series of sermons in Westminster Abbey against what he considered the popular opinions on final punishment. After these were taken down in shorthand and then published, without Farrar's knowledge and against his will, in what he said were careless and inaccurate editions, he published the sermons himself "in reluctant self-defense against utter misstatements." Farrar called the book *Eternal Hope* (1879). The next year E. B. Pusey responded to Farrar with his *What Is of Faith as to Everlasting Punishment?* Farrar replied to Pusey with *Mercy and Judgment* in 1881. Although Farrar denied the literalistic, traditionalist view of hell, he also rejected both universalism and the conditionalist interpretation. His primary interest seems to have been to relax dogmatism and leave room for possible repentance beyond the grave.

Pusey, a High-Churchman with leanings toward Rome, was much concerned with the "Faith" of ecclesiastic tradition, less with scriptural exegesis. Farrar had cited many rabbinic sources as evidence that the "Jewish view" included a larger hope beyond the grave; Pusey countered with other material which nullified much of Farrar's proof. Their controversy largely concerned the possibility of salvation after the present life, and statements of both men should be read in this light. Farrar was not advancing conditionalism, and Pusey was not particularly opposing it.

Some years earlier the Baptist scholar and *Expositor* editor, Samuel Cox, argued for universalism in his *Salvator Mundi* (1877). A few years later the Methodist, Dr. Agar Beet, questioned the traditionalist view in *The Last Things* (1879), though he concluded that the Bible itself is ambiguous regarding the final destiny of the lost.

---

39. Frederick W. Farrar lived from 1831-1903 and wrote widely on biblical times. His books include a study of the Bible, books on the early churches, and a well-known life of Christ. Edward Bouverie Pusey lived from 1800-1882, taught Hebrew at Oxford, and was a leader in the Oxford movement, which urged a greater appreciation of the values of Catholic tradition and a more open posture toward Rome.

Notable Conditionalists. The nineteenth century saw a revival of conditionalism that swept across national, linguistic and denominational lines. We merely mention a few of the more notable authors. Richard Whately, Anglican archbishop of Dublin, published in 1829 his *A View of the Scripture Revelations concerning a Future State.* He was a thoroughgoing conditionalist.

Congregationalist minister, Edward White,[40] published his conditionalist convictions in 1846 under the title, *Life in Christ.* The work cost him his pulpit, so he moved to London and began anew in a deserted meeting place he was able to acquire. In the new, independent Hawley Road Chapel, White exercised an influential career of preaching, lecturing and writing. In the process he so regained the respect and esteem of his erstwhile Congregational brethren that in 1887 they elected him chairman of the Congregational Union of England and Wales.

Probably the best-known conditionalist work today from the period is Henry Constable's[41] *Duration and Nature of Future Punishment* (1868). An Anglican priest, Constable later served as prebendary or canon of Desertmore. His book went through at least six printings and exercised an influence worldwide.

Another outstanding conditionalist was Joseph B. Rotherham, who made a translation of the New Testament. In a letter published in the conditionalist *Christian World* of June 19, 1874, Rotherham said that he was "constrained to disbelieve the theological dogma of man's natural and unconditional immortality" and that, as a result, he was "free to accept the everlasting punishment of the incorrigible as their everlasting destruction."[42]

Emmanuel Pétavel-Olliff was a leading conditionalist on the Continent. Following the pastorate of a Swiss Church of London from 1863-1866, Pétavel returned to Neuchatel in Switzerland. There he published a defense of conditionalism titled in the English translation, *The Problem of Immortality* (1891). A man of his times, Pétavel regarded conditionalism as "the meeting-point . . . of biblical Christianity, rationalist Christianity, Kantism, and evangelical transformism." He was an evolutionist and later expressed the opinion that the

---

40. For a biographical sketch and brief history of White's work, see Froom, *Conditionalist Faith,* 2:322-336.

41. On Henry Constable see ibid., pp. 337-354.

42. Ibid., p. 435.

stress should be put on philosophy rather than Scripture "owing to the changed attitudes to the Bible."[43] Evangelicals will learn little of substance from Pétavel, therefore, if their interest is to determine the teaching of the authoritative Word of God.

These men were in company with many others who shared their conditionalist understanding. They held conferences, started papers, and engaged series of lectures. They differed among themselves on some points, as also traditionalists did and do. Some, like White and Constable, appealed primarily to the Scriptures; others, like Pétavel, leaned heavily on philosophy. Largely, however, the established churches simply looked the other way. In spite of much conditionalist activity and not a little heated controversy, therefore, the nineteenth century left affairs largely as it had found them. Traditionalists generally ignored the conditionalist arguments, and conditionalists lacked a recognized forum for careful and thorough dialogue with those who simply denounced their views.

The Twentieth Century

Here, as in the rest of these historical chapters, we make no pretense at being exhaustive. Instead, we simply hope to point to some major trends, prominent men and recognized movements or denominations which have a special relation to the ongoing controversy regarding final punishment.

Critics of the traditional doctrine from *outside* the evangelical mainstream interest us for two reasons. First, their arguments and conclusions are generally different from those we here propose, and we wish to make that difference very clear. Second, their opposition to traditional orthodoxy, often on ground that was blatantly unscriptural and even antiscriptural, has often acted as a catalyst to controversy, sometimes provoking evangelicals to close their eyes and ears, clutch their inherited views even more tenaciously, and develop a sensitive trigger finger in the direction of anything that sounds the slightest bit different from what they are used to hearing.

Critics *inside* mainstream, historic orthodoxy especially catch our eye since they serve as clear demonstrations that the views set forth

---

43. Quoted by Rowell, *Hell and the Victorians,* pp. 210-211.

here are neither new nor at odds with the highest possible commitment to the inspiration and authority of Scripture. That fact is especially significant in America after nearly 70 years of reaction and counter-reaction to the fundamentalist-modernist controversy which has had such an impact on religious life and thought.

The Fundamentalist-Modernist Controversy.[44] According to the guiding principle of nineteenth-century science, every phenomenon represents some universal and impersonal law of cause and effect. Philosophy also considered the thought of any supernatural interruption of the natural order to be completely absurd. Evolutionary concepts provided the explanations for both philosophy and science.

Religious "liberalism" interpreted Christianity in the same light. At its heart was dependence on subjective intuition, experience, or feeling for authority rather than the objective standard of the Holy Scriptures as the true Word of God. In the words of J. I. Packer, liberalism "reduced grace to nature, divine revelation to human reflection, faith in Christ to following His example, and receiving new life to turning over a new leaf; it turned supernatural Christianity into one more form of natural religion, a thin mixture of morals and mysticism."[45] Orthodox Christians, of course, were appalled by liberalism's philosophy and tenets, and they opposed both with a zeal that was both vigorous and proper.

The term "modernism" was a twentieth-century name for this earlier stream of thought. As a label, it seems to have come from an encyclical by Pope Pius X of September 8, 1907, entitled *Pascendi*, in which he described and stigmatized the trend as a "synthesis of all heresies." Although properly a Catholic term for liberalism at that point, the tag "modernism" (and "modernist") soon passed into Protestant polemics as well, where it worked its way into the "fundamentalist" thesaurus and still does active duty today, if not always with the same precision. In America, "modernism" shared a bed with the "social gospel" as its disciples began both to do and to teach. By the

---

44. I have relied heavily in this section on J. I. Packer's *"Fundamentalism" and the Word of God*, pp. 24-40; topical articles in *Baker's Dictionary of Theology*; and articles in the *Encyclopaedia of Religion*.

45. Packer, *"Fundamentalism,"* p. 27.

years of the early twentieth century the stage was set in the United States for a battle royal.

"Fundamentalism" was born and christened in the year 1909, when it made a literary debut in the first of twelve volumes entitled *The Fundamentals: A Testimony to the Truth*. These books were devoted to the exposition and defense of evangelical faith, and they were sponsored by two wealthy California laymen who distributed them without cost to over three million church leaders and students around the world. Authors represented all major branches of historic Protestantism, including such men as James Orr, B. B. Warfield, Sir Robert Anderson, H. C. G. Moule, W. H. Griffith-Thomas, R. A. Torrey, Dyson Hague, A. T. Pierson and G. Campbell Morgan. The "fundamentals" of faith they defended regarded the Bible (its inspiration and authority), Jesus Christ (His deity, virgin conception, miracles, substitutionary atoning death, bodily resurrection and personal return), and such topics as the reality of sin, the necessity for personal regeneration by the Holy Spirit, the power of prayer, and the obligation to evangelize.

In 1910 the General Assembly of the Northern Presbyterian Church issued a list of five specific items which it termed "the fundamentals of faith and of evangelical Christianity." These included the inspiration and infallibility of Scripture, the deity of Jesus Christ, His virgin birth and supernatural miracles, His substitutionary death for sins, and His physical resurrection and personal return. Later "fundamentalist" organizations adopted the General Assembly's list, by and large, and today it serves a still broader range of evangelical institutions as well. In May of 1919 a conference convened in Philadelphia, resulting in a group called The World's Christian Fundamentals Association. The organization required its members to confess nine points of doctrine. The ninth point went slightly beyond some earlier lists, specifying the resurrection and final disposition of all men to either eternal blessedness or eternal woe.

The "liberals," meanwhile, continued to advance their own brand of "Christianity," which is often summarized as "the fatherhood of God and the brotherhood of man." God is pure benevolence, they affirmed—certainly too good to consign anyone to the traditional hell. Every man has a divine spark; Jesus is the perfect teacher and example who brings man to his full potential. Since all men are God's children by nature, neither Jesus nor Christianity are uniquely super-natural. These were the doctrines which elicited *The Fundamentals* and which bound their evangelical opponents into an amorphous group that became known as "fundamentalists." The Baptists and Presbyterians were most affected by the controversy, followed close-ly by the Methodists and Disciples of Christ. Truly, the "fundamen-tals" of Christianity were at stake, and emotions rightfully ran high. There are older preachers today who still remember the trauma of this fight they beheld or survived forty and fifty years ago.

Anything remotely associated with the "modernists" was under-standably tainted for orthodox folk. "Modernists" denied that anyone would burn forever in conscious torment; *ergo*, anyone who even looked askance at the traditionalist hell came under immediate suspicion as a latent or closet "modernist."

It was not uncommon—and is not today in modern fundamentalist circles—to find popular, grass-roots lists of doctrines or questions in-tended for use in identifying persons suspected of "modernism." Such lists almost always include adherence to the doctrine of everlasting conscious torment, and often they specify literal fire. Ivory-tower evangelicals may scoff at the notion, but they need not drive far off the campuses to find this kind of "orthodoxy" very much alive and well.

Such reactionary theology is easily understood, and we are wholly sympathetic with its *intentions*. At the same time, it has greatly hindered the exercise of the anti-tradition principle of Protestantism and (far more important) the biblical injunction to "test all things" and "hold fast what is good." Because of this situation, most Amer-ican evangelicals have shied away from the subject of final punish-ment as if it were a snake, neither entering the study themselves nor allowing others to enter. That is certainly not the only reason for lack of study, but it must be included if the whole picture is to be seen.

Even non-evangelicals in Britain, on the other hand, were never taken with the methods of German criticism or the dogmas of the older Liberals in quite the same manner as their American cousins. Whether this was due to an inherent English conservatism, to Ameri-can softness for anything novel, or to the "defusing" effect of a British state church which itself found room to harbor all manner of theological creatures and birds, we cannot now be sure.

Whatever the cause, British evangelicals did not feel the same "modernist" pressure that threatened American orthodoxy, and consequently "fundamentalism" was never a British phenomenon either. American evangelicals sometimes find it difficult to remember this difference in backgrounds when British brethren approach questions with an obviously different perspective. British evangelicals, in turn, keep reminding Americans that it is indeed a fact.[46] Partly for this reason, perhaps, and partly because of Anglicanism's official openness on the question, British evangelicals inside and outside the state church have been somewhat less hesitant than those in America to consider the case for final extinction of the wicked.

In his book, *The Goodness of God*,[47] John W. Wenham mentions and briefly describes the works of two British authors, both firmly committed to the inspiration and final authority of Scripture, who set forth in this century the conditionalist conclusions to which they were drawn.

Harold Ernest Guillebaud. Born in 1888, Guillebaud served for a time as Anglican rector of St. Michael's, Bath, then went to Africa under the auspices of the Church Missionary Society in 1925. He returned to England from 1933-1936, then went again to Ruanda to take up his work of translation. There he became archdeacon in 1940. He translated much of the Bible, the Prayer Book, a hymnal, and Bunyan's classic, *Pilgrim's Progress*. Later he returned to Cambridge, where he served for four years as curate of St. Paul's. During that time he wrote several books, including a popular work on the atonement entitled *Why the Cross?* In it he took for granted the traditional view of hell.

A few years later Guillebaud was asked by the Inter-Varsity Fellowship to write a book on some moral difficulties of the Bible, including a final chapter on the doctrine of everlasting punishment. When he came to that chapter, he found himself unable to answer the question to his own satisfaction, so the chapter was omitted from the book (*The Moral Difficulties of the Bible*, 1941).

Guillebaud then began an intensive personal study of the subject, which resulted in another book, entitled *The Righteous Judge*, setting forth the conditionalist views to which his own study had led. Be-

---

46. Ibid., pp. 24, 29; cf. F. F. Bruce, *Answers to Questions*, pp. 206-207.
47. Wenham, *The Goodness of God*, p. 40.

cause no publisher would take the book, it had to sit on the shelf for many years. Finally, in 1964 it was published privately after the author's own death.[48] Guillebaud believed that every soul survives bodily death but that the wicked will finally perish, both body and soul, in the second death.

Following a foreword, introduction, and note on definitions, Guillebaud treated his subject under two major headings in 13 chapters. The first eight chapters asked and answered the question, "What does the Bible teach?" Chapters 9-13 answered objections commonly raised against the position Guillebaud set forth. On the first page of his introduction Guillebaud stated that his book was "written in the firm conviction that any valid doctrine of future punishment must rest upon the Word of God at every point," and that was his appeal throughout all 13 chapters which followed.

Basil F. C. Atkinson. Born in 1895, Atkinson completed his education at Magdalene College, Cambridge, serving as Under Librarian of the University Library from 1925-1960. He became renowned in evangelical circles (including the Cambridge Inter-Collegiate Christian Union) as a leader of devotional Bible readings aimed at deepening and strengthening the spiritual life of those who attended. The author of numerous books, Dr. Atkinson's works include such titles as *The Greek Language, Is the Bible True? Valiant in Fight, The War with Satan*, and *The Christian's Use of the Old Testament* as well as a commentary covering Genesis to Numbers in *The Pocket Commentary of the Bible*.

Atkinson also wrote a book entitled *Life and Immortality*, which he subtitled *An Examination of the Nature and Meaning of Life and Death As They Are Revealed in the Scriptures*. His appeal throughout is to the authority of Scripture and that alone. He holds a unitary view of man which sees death as a period of unconsciousness, a universal resurrection and judgment, everlasting life for believers, and "complete extinction and destruction out of the creation of God" for all "unrepentant sinners, the devil, evil angels, sin and death and evil of all kinds." Atkinson discusses his subject under four chapter topics which concern the nature of man, rest and darkness, resurrection and

48. Guillebaud's book is distributed by Rector B. L. Bateson, Holton Rectory, Wincanton, Somerset, U.K., as also is the book by Atkinson, discussed next.

glory, and the doom of the lost. It is a scholarly book which makes an extensive analysis of the biblical terms and which Wenham calls "the fruit of a lifetime of study" and "a remarkable piece of sustained argument." Like Guillebaud's book, Atkinson's was published privately.

The Return to a Biblical Anthropology. Around the world in recent years, the conviction has been increasing that traditional orthodoxy needs to launch an "anti-pollution" effort aimed at filtering out pagan ideas of Greek philosophy which early Christian apologists took for granted and which passed largely unnoticed through the centuries to the present day. Chief among these "Grecian" remnants said to contradict biblical teaching is the idea that man's "soul" is an entity separable from his body which can remain conscious even when the body is dead, and that it possesses (unlike the body) some quality which makes it indestructible.

Beginning with the story of creation, it is said, the entire Bible presents a different picture of man. There he is a single, wholistic being, though he may be viewed and spoken of from various points of view. He is totally *creature* and therefore inherently mortal and entirely dependent on his Creator for everything, including existence itself.

When faced with this apparent discrepancy, the ancient Christian writers actually sidestepped the issue. The soul is not *naturally* immortal, they said, or pre-existent as the Platonists declared. Its immortality is *derived*—the result of God's creative work. If *God* wishes to destroy it, they continued, He is both free and able to do so. But as soon as the subject turned to other matters, most of the fathers forgot their original distinction. When they discussed final punishment, they unconsciously assumed the Grecian view that souls are indestructible and everlasting. And on that presupposition they had to interpret all the biblical statements about the end of sinners to mean something other than extinction. Since Scripture so clearly ruled out universal restoration, everlasting torment was their only viable alternative. (Origen could develop restorationism because of his method of interpreting Scripture, which allowed for a deeper, "spiritual" meaning even if that meaning contradicted the obvious, literal sense.)

After Augustine this doctrine became almost unquestioned for a thousand years. John Calvin, who learned so much from the great theologian of Hippo, passionately defended the soul's immortality in his earliest theological work; and through his friend, Heinrich Bullinger, this presupposition and its corollary of eternal torment found its way into the major confessions of the Reformation churches.

Today evangelical scholars as well as others are drawing up short. We discussed this revolution in chapter four and will not repeat it here. We only recall such men as Reichenbach and Thielicke (Lutherans), Hoekema and Bloesch (Calvinists), and F. F. Bruce (Brethren), who have insisted time and time again that there is nothing inherently immortal about the soul, that man has no indestructible quality which guarantees his survival, that he has no death-proof substance which insures that he will live forever. These men all stress that the Scriptures urge us to place our hope in God—for the future as well as the present, for deliverance from death as well as from calamity now. The resurrection at Christ's return is our hope, not some supposed immortality inherent in our own weak and sinful selves.

The late Edward John Carnell, orthodox apologist and original faculty member at Fuller Theological Seminary, could conclude that "man neither deserves immortality nor is worthy of it" and that God "who gave life can also recall it either to damnation, blessedness, or annihilation."[49] And contemporary New Testament scholar, Murray Harris of Trinity Evangelical Divinity School, can summarize a study of biblical immortality by saying that man "is not immortal because he possesses or is a soul. He becomes immortal because God raises him from the dead."[50]

The question, therefore, is not whether man will exist forever on his *own* (Christian theologians have always denied that). It is not whether God, who created man, *can* also bring him to total extinction (that is also conceded by all). Neither is it whether God is able to make even the wicked immortal *if* He so chooses (which no one denies). The question is whether or not Scripture teaches that God *will* make the wicked immortal (along with the righteous) in the resurrection for everlasting life in pain rather than everlasting life in bliss, or whether immortality in the Age to Come is a boon promised only the righteous on the basis of Christ's redemption and victory over sin and death.

---

49. Edward John Carnell, *An Introduction to Christian Apologetics*, pp. 344-345.

50. Murray Harris, "Resurrection and Immortality: Eight Theses," *Themelios* 1, no. 2 (Spring 1976): 53.

Reduced to those terms, there is no longer any controversy. For no one, not even the greatest traditionalist, has ever presented a clear and convincing case in the affirmative to that question. In increasing numbers, on the other hand, evangelical theologians and commentators are becoming boldly explicit in pointing out biblical data which point the opposite direction—even though they generally do not carry through with the implications that has for final punishment and even though they sometimes inconsistently affirm eternal torment in practically the same breath. It is hard to escape the uneasiness that often pervades such discussions, and it is practically impossible not to come away feeling one has been on a logical merry-go-round.

Unending conscious torment was first read into biblical language on the presupposition that man's soul could never be destroyed, although that was verbally denied from the beginning. Under pressure, the ancient traditionalists began to apply descriptions of the glorified and incorruptible body to the wicked as well as the redeemed. Now that the presupposition is being recognized as alien to the Scriptures and is rapidly being discarded on that basis, the traditional interpretation of Scripture which it bore so long ago still continues. Most evangelicals, still somewhat shellshocked from the discovery of pagan parasites in what they thought was healthy thinking, have simply lacked the strength, nerve or will to follow through on the information they have assimilated already.

Perhaps a happy result of the present study will be to give those who love the Word of God the inspiration to engage this subject of final punishment head-on, with the strengthened anticipation that Scripture itself actually does allow for such conclusions as presented here and that they need therefore no longer fear to look the matter straight in the eye.

19

Traditionalism's Problem of Pain

One might suppose it a fairly simple matter to read traditional orthodoxy's major works, reduce its statements to a straightforward definition, then set down in a clear and understandable fashion the arguments on which the doctrine of eternal torment actually rests. Instead, the person who walks through the library doors and starts pulling the cards under "Punishment, Final" quickly identifies with Lewis Carroll's unsuspecting lass, Alice in Wonderland, who cheerily followed the white rabbit down his hole into a world where things really were not what they seemed.

"Orthodoxy" is a relative term, used in a historical sense, and the orthodoxy of traditionalism proves to cover a very large spectrum indeed. At one end are High-Church ecclesiastics such as the nineteenth century's aged Pusey, who found strength beyond his years to hold up the orthodox standard as he understood it. Yet Pusey is widely quoted today by many who would be shocked out of their chairs if a contemporary preacher suggested some of the points he stated with great firmness. At the other end of the spectrum are conservative fundamentalists whose literalistic grasp of the traditional doctrine puts belief in "real fire" on all but the same level of importance with the deity of Jesus, eyeing one who questions the first point with a suspicion normally reserved for deniers of the second.

Somewhere between the two is a range of Reformed orthodoxy. Although this brand has been accused and kicked around by critics for centuries as personifying the rankest form of fatalistic extremes (a characterization most undeserved except in rare and isolated cases), it actually includes those who think Jonathan Edwards should be the measure of preaching today—and also those who cower in embarrassment at his name.

One finally concludes that there is no such thing as a uniform, standardized, detailed traditionalist orthodoxy. About all one can count on from traditionalist authors is that they believe the wicked will remain alive forever, in sensible punishment of some description, so that neither they nor it will ever pass away. Traditionalists disagree among themselves on how the wicked will be able to exist forever when totally cut off from God, the extent of their number, the case of unevangelized pagans or deceased infants, the degree and nature of the punishment, and even the matter of possible salvation beyond the present life.

At the end of the nineteenth century, Farrar criticized "the common opinions respecting Hell," which he summarized in four parts: (1) "The physical torments, the material agonies of eternal punishment"; (2) "the supposition of its necessarily endless duration for all who incur it"; (3) "the opinion that it is thus incurred by the vast mass of mankind"; and (4) "that it is a doom passed irreversibly at the moment of death on all who die in a state of sin."[1]

In defense of the "orthodox" position, Pusey responded that one need not think of hell in terms of physical pains or torment other than that which comes from being deprived of all good, and that, besides, the number of those lost will probably be relatively few. He can speak for himself:

> Of these [common opinions as stated by Farrar], the third has no solid foundation whatever; it exists, probably, only in the rigid Calvinistic school, in which Dr. Farrar was educated, and from which his present opinions are a reaction. . . . The fourth is probably a misconception. . . . The first is a point, not declared to be essential to the belief in Hell.[2]

Pusey therefore insisted only on Farrar's second point: "the supposition of its necessarily endless duration for all who incur it." Even that

---

1. Frederic W. Farrar, *Eternal Hope*, quoted by Edward Bouverie Pusey, *What Is of Faith as to Everlasting Punishment? In Reply to Dr. Farrar's Challenge in His "Eternal Hope,"* 1879, pp. 5-6.

2. Pusey, *What Is of Faith?*, pp. 6-7.

he later weakened considerably by allowing for a bare minimum of pain, caused perhaps only by the deprivation of all good rather than infliction by an external source. Pusey's "orthodoxy" therefore reduces to this single point: endless conscious existence for a relatively small number of the damned, who will be cut off from all association with God and suffer to whatever extent that fact might require.

Although Pusey felt that "perhaps millions have been scared back from sin" by the dread and fear of hell (conceding in another place that the poor in particular were susceptible to being motivated by such preaching), he finally stated regarding physical sufferings that "it may suffice to say, that neither the Church nor any portion of it has so laid down any doctrine in regard to them, as to make the acceptance of them an integral part of the doctrine itself."[3] The nature of suffering, Pusey said, is simply not a matter of faith.

> As to 'pains of sense,' the Church has no where laid down as a matter of faith, the material character of the worm and the fire, or that they denote more than the gnawing of remorse. Although then it would be very rash to lay down dogmatically, that the 'fire' is *not* to be understood literally, as it has been understood almost universally by Christians, yet no one has a right to urge those representations, from which the imagination so shrinks as a ground for refusing to believe in hell, since he is left free not to believe them.[4]

If Spurgeon or others can scare the poor by preaching hellfire, Pusey seems to say, more power to them—perhaps a certain class of people are motivated best by fear. But if a more intellectual chap begins to question the Christian faith on such a basis, why, it is really not a matter of faith anyway, even though such pain "has been understood almost universally by Christians" as being physical and very real! Is such reasoning truly fair? And what, we may ask, has become of the great argument which rests so much on what has been "universally" believed for so long? The subject is far too serious to play such games with the emotions of common people, and neither Jesus nor His apostles ever did.

Some other traditionalists agree with Pusey that physical pain is not necessary for an orthodox view. A. H. Strong freely concedes

---

3. Ibid., p. 18.
4. Ibid., p. 23.

1. that future punishment does not necessarily consist of physical torments,—it may be wholly internal and spiritual; 2. that the pain and suffering of the future are not necessarily due to positive inflictions of God,—they may result entirely from the soul's sense of loss, and from the accusations of conscience; and [*even*] 3. that eternal punishment does not necessarily involve endless successions of suffering, —as God's eternity is not mere endlessness so we may not be forever subject to the law of time.[5]

Across the Calvinistic fence, Berkhof says it "is impossible to determine precisely what will constitute the eternal punishment of the wicked, and it behooves us to speak very cautiously on the subject," though he goes on to say it will include both "positive pains and sufferings in body and soul" as well as such "subjective punishments as pangs of conscience, anguish, despair, weeping and gnashing of teeth."[6]

In spite of such protests from Pusey and Strong, it is safe to say with another writer that, for much popular traditionalist preaching and writing, the fire of hell "is almost invariably understood as a real, material, inextinguishable fire, ceaselessly tormenting the damned."[7] Most would agree with Shedd that the "figures of the 'fire,' and the 'worm' are intended to denote conscious pain."[8] And if the nature of "everlasting destruction" is to be perpetual conscious torment, if Scripture uses "fire" and "worm" to signify the most horrible pain, and if God has revealed this doctrine to scare millions into heaven, then no one who believes the Bible has any right to object. Nor should theologians try to vindicate God's justice in the matter or preachers seek to alleviate the pain.

Furthermore, as Constable pointed out, there is no practical value in discussing whether such pain is to be figurative or literal—if the biblical language is meant to convey thoughts of everlasting conscious pain in the first place. Constable explained:

> If there be a literal fire consuming, and a literal worm gnawing, we know the exact pain produced: if the fire and the worm be figurative,

5. Augustus Hopkins Strong, *Systematic Theology*, 3:1035.

6. Louis Berkhof, *Reformed Dogmatics*, 2:345.

7. David W. Lotz, "Heaven and Hell in the Christian Tradition," *Religion in Life* 48 (Spring 1979): 85.

8. William G. T. Shedd, *The Doctrine of Endless Punishment*, p. 89.

they are figurative of a pain and suffering such in intensity as would be produced by the literal agents. Nothing then is really gained by rejecting the literal view . . . or by changing the *bodily pains . . . into suffering and anguish of the mind*. If the descriptions of Scripture are figures, they are at the same time *true figures*: if they are not to be understood literally, they must yet be understood as giving us the *truest and best ideas possible of the real anguish and misery of hell*. On no hypothesis can we understand hell as other than a scene where pain and anguish, mental or bodily, or both, of the most intense and terrible nature, are endured by all who have any existence there. Hell cannot by any artful handling of words, by any skilful manipulation of phrases, be toned down into a place other than of the most fearful kind. . . . The real question is, not whether they are literal or figurative, but whether the pains they point to and pourtray are pains to be endured for ever; or are pains which sooner or later produce a destruction of the sentient being from which there is no recovery.[9]

If "the plain meaning of Scripture, after all, is the old doctrine of the ecclesiastical symbols,"[10] as traditionalists maintain, there is no use trying to avoid the fact or evade the questions of those who might be troubled by it. We should still preach the pains of hell with clarity and power—not only to the poor (who have more to worry about already than other people), but also to the rich. We should hold the line at that point, not seek to make the doctrine less offensive through either alleviating circumstances or sophisticated rationalizing. If God's Word teaches that hell will be the scene of unending conscious torment of the damned, then that is that—and that is all there should be to the matter. If that *be* the case, hell is no merciful provision which demonstrates God's unending love, but a terrible and unimaginable place of pain and horror which exhausts His wrath. If the traditionalist view is correct, most of its modern advocates probably owe an apology to men like Wesley, Spurgeon and Jonathan Edwards.

The fundamental issue is not "physical" versus "spiritual" or "literal" versus "figurative." The basic controversy to be resolved is whether Scripture intends by its language to describe unending sensible suffering, as traditionalists maintain, or suffering which finally ends in total and inescapable extinction from which there will be no

---

9. Henry Constable, *Duration and Nature of Future Punishment*, pp. 100-101.

10. Francis L. Patton, "Future Punishment," *The Religious Encyclopaedia; or Dictionary of Biblical, Historical, Doctrinal, and Practical Theology*, p. 1974.

hope of return forever. Which is everlasting—the punish-*ing* or the punish-*ment*? The Bible explicitly affirms the latter and points to it throughout. It nowhere states the former, and New Testament language can be given that sense only by ignoring its ordinary usage throughout the Old Testament.

Some traditionalists have taken this bull by the horns and held fast. They believed that hell was intended to frighten people away from sin and that the Bible describes unending pain for that purpose. There is no use in belaboring this point. If such persons are correct in their understanding, what they did was the right thing to do. If Scripture truly teaches eternal torment, we should make no apologies for it. Still, when so many traditionalists work so hard to minimize the gross horror of the doctrine they profess, we might gain some degree of perspective if we hear two or three exponents of traditional orthodoxy from an earlier age.

"Rev. J. Furniss" minced no words, for example, in his traditionalist (though Catholic) tract "for children and young persons" which he called *The Sight of Hell*, as can be seen by the following excerpt.

> See on the middle of that red-hot floor stands a girl: she looks about sixteen years old. Her feet are bare. Listen; she speaks. "I have been standing on this red-hot floor for years! Look at my burnt and bleeding feet! Let me go off this burning floor for one moment!" The fifth dungeon is the red-hot oven. The little child is in the red-hot oven. Hear how it screams to come out; see how it turns and twists itself about in the fire. It beats its head against the roof of the oven. It stamps its little feet on the floor. *God was very good* to this little child. Very likely God saw it would get worse and worse, and would never repent, and so it would have to be punished *more* severely in hell. So God in His mercy called it out of the world in early childhood.[11]

Or hear Protestant Spurgeon, who probably embarrassed Pusey as much as he horrified Farrar.

> When thou diest thy soul will be tormented alone—that will be a hell for it—but at the day of judgement thy body will join thy soul, and

---

11. J. Furniss, *The Sight of Hell* (London and Dublin: Duffy), quoted by Edward White from a Mr. Lecky's *History of European Morals* in White's *Life in Christ . . .* , p. 60. This is a rather round-about quotation, admittedly, but the reader is asked to keep in mind its illustrative purpose rather than to establish a crucial or disputed point.

then thou wilt have twin hells, body and soul shall be together, each brimfull of pain, thy soul sweating in its inmost pore drops of blood and thy body from head to foot suffused with agony; conscience, judgement, memory, all tortured. . . . Thine heart beating high with fever, thy pulse rattling at an enormous rate in agony, thy limbs cracking like the martyrs in the fire and yet unburnt, thyself put in a vessel of hot oil, pained yet coming out undestroyed, all thy veins becoming a road for the hot feet of pain to travel on, every nerve a string on which the devil shall ever play his diabolical tune. . . . Fictions, sir! Again I say they are no fictions, but solid, stern truth. If God be true, and this Bible be true, what I have said is the truth, and you will find it one day to be so.[12]

Or again:

Only conceive that poor wretch in the flames, who is saying, "O for one drop of water to cool my parched tongue!" See how his tongue hangs from between his blistered lips! How it excoriates and burns the roof of his mouth as if it were a firebrand! Behold him crying for a drop of water. I will not picture the scene. Suffice it for me to close up by saying, that the hell of hells will be to thee, poor sinner, the thought that it is to be for ever. Thou wilt look up there on the throne of God,—and on it shall be written, "For ever!" When the damned jingle the burning irons of their torments, they shall say, "For ever!" When they howl, echo cries, "For ever!"

> "For ever" is written on their racks,
> "For ever" on their chains;
> "For ever" burneth in the fire,
> "For ever" ever reigns.[13]

So that non-Calvinists do not feel left out, and lest they unduly credit the Reformed side of the house with such courageous and straightforward preaching, we cite one example also from John Wesley, who wrote:

There is no business, but one uninterrupted scene of horror, to which they must be all attention. They have no interval of inattention or

---

12. Charles H. Spurgeon, Sermon No. 66, *New Park Street Pulpit*, 2:105, quoted by Emmanuel Pétavel, *The Problem of Immortality*, p. 266. Pétavel says that Spurgeon later changed his language and would probably not use this same language in his later years. Pétavel refers to an article entitled "The Christian Hell," *Nineteenth Century*, 1891, p. 712. Spurgeon scholars might wish to clarify this point.

13. From a sermon preached in 1855. Quoted by White, *Life in Christ*, p. 59.

stupidity; they are all eye, all ear, all sense. Every instant of their duration, it may be said of their whole frame that they are

> "—trembling alive all o'er,
> and smart and agonize at every pore."[14]

Perhaps the name most often associated today with severe preaching on hell is that of Jonathan Edwards. Some more recent traditionalists have found his sermons "appalling,"[15] and others have felt a need to apologize for his excesses while explaining that he really intended to be understood figuratively.[16] Others, however, quote him without apology—emboldened by their conviction that the traditionalist position is the true teaching of Scripture and must, on that authority, be declared clearly and without compromise. A. W. Pink is in this group, and he quotes with approval Edwards' description of the soul as it finally sinks terribly into the "second death" of endless torment:

> *So it will be with the soul in Hell*; it will have no strength or power to deliver itself; and its torment and horror will be so great, so mighty, so vastly disproportioned to its strength, that having no strength in the least to support itself, although it be infinitely contrary to the nature and inclination of the soul utterly to sink; yet it will sink, it will utterly and totally sink, without the least degree of remaining comfort, or strength, or courage, or hope. And though it will never be annihilated, its being and perception will never be abolished: yet such will be the infinite depth of gloominess that it will sink into, that it will be in a state of death, eternal death. . . .
>
> To help your conception, imagine yourself to be cast into a fiery oven, all of a glowing heat, or into the midst of a blowing brick-kiln, or of a great furnace, where your pain would be as much greater than that occasioned by accidentally touching a coal of fire, as the heat is greater. Imagine also that your body were to lie there for a quarter of an hour, full of fire, as full within and without as a bright coal of fire, all the while full of quick sense; what horror would you feel at the entrance of such a furnace! And how long would that quarter of an hour seem to you! . . . And how much greater would be the effect, if you knew you must endure it for a whole year, and how vastly greater

---

14. John Wesley, Sermon 78, quoted by Constable, *Future Punishment*, p. 99.

15. James Orr's term in his *The Progress of Dogma* (Grand Rapids: William B. Eerdmans Publishing Co., 1952), p. 347, quoted with apparent approval by Harry Buis, *The Doctrine of Eternal Punishment*, p. 91.

16. Strong says this in his *Systematic Theology*, 3:1035; Buis also quotes Strong with approval in *The Doctrine of Eternal Punishment*, pp. 91-92.

still, if you knew you must endure it for a thousand years! O then, how would your heart sink, if you thought, if you knew, that you must bear it forever and ever! . . . That after millions of millions of ages, your torment would be no nearer to an end, than ever it was; and that you never, never should be delivered! But your torment in Hell will be immeasurably greater than this illustration represents. How then will the heart of a poor creature sink under it! How utterly inexpressible and inconceivable must the sinking of the soul be in such a case.[17]

Rather than make apologies for such vivid and earthy descriptions of unending torment, traditionalists ought to emulate them all the more. If the wicked are to be made immortal for the purpose of enduring everlasting torture in agony, writers like Pink and preachers like Spurgeon do them an inestimable favor by making that very, very plain. Since eternal torment apparently cannot be stated clearly in scriptural language anyway, why fault the eloquence of those who strain their imaginations to get the point across? Indeed (if we may put tongue in cheek), why limit one's description to Christian writers at all when the eschatology of numerous pagan religions provides descriptions of torture which make Jonathan Edwards sound like a skeptic? If the whole point is to scare the poor and the little children, why not give them a fright they will never forget?

For those afraid of beasts, the doctrines of India and Iran might be helpful. Both have frightful watchdogs who guard the path the dead must trek or a bridge over which they must pass into the world beyond.[18] For conjuring thoughts of actual pain, one could borrow imagery from certain Chinese Buddhists. There devils in human form pull out slanderers' tongues with red-hot wires, pour molten lead down liars' throats, and grind, pound, press and screw the damned with every torture device invented by depraved mankind.[19]

If one wishes to repulse his hearers, he might use certain Hindu writings which present "worlds of nauseating disgusts, of loathsome agonies, of intolerable terrors." There some are hanged by their

---

17. Arthur W. Pink, *Eternal Punishment*, pp. 29-30.

18. G. Widengren, "Life after Death: Eschatological Ideas in Indian and Iranian Religion," *Expository Times*, September 1965, pp. 364-367. On pagan ideas of hell in general, see A. Mac-Culloch, "Eschatology," *Encyclopaedia of Religion and Ethics*, 5:373-376.

19. William Rounseville Alger, *The Destiny of the Soul: A Critical History of the Doctrine of a Future Life*, 1:109. Alger says this description is based on 24 paintings of hell from Buddhist temples as reported in *Asiatic Journal* for 1840.

tongues to be eaten or whipped by fiery and poisonous snakes; others must swallow bowls of gore, hair and corruption which are refilled as soon as they are emptied; others are packed tightly in red-hot chests and laid in furnaces forever.[20] The traditions of Islam also abound in vivid and copious descriptions of torment designed to chill the blood and tingle the ears. Unbelievers are burned until their skins are gone, then are given new skins so the process can be repeated. They are forced to drink scalding water or to hang over hot furnaces while their flesh is cut off with scissors of fire and their brains boil inside their heads.[21]

Of course, all such descriptions spring from man's imagination, and not a single one of them is ever mentioned in the Scriptures—unless one enlarges in homily, perhaps, on the "weeping and gnashing of teeth"! But why should that fact matter if the Bible truly teaches everlasting torment, yet in such a strange and round-about manner that conscious torment itself must be expressed by language never found in the Word of God? Is there any difference in principle? Are we free to assign traditionalist meanings to "eternal fire" or "eternal punishment," to the "worm that dies not" or the "fire that is not quenched," without regard to the usage of these expressions in all the prophetic literature of the Old Testament? Why may we not do the same with the "weeping and gnashing of teeth"?

Many traditionalist authors are aware of this problem and have decried language they regard as excessive. We laud their intention and encourage them to go even further in eliminating unscriptural terminology. Many pious and devout preachers have tried to confine their description of hell to language they can read in Scripture, but not finding anything explicitly traditionalist and having thought themselves bound to reject final extinction, they have grown weary of their no-man's land and sought to avoid the subject altogether. Yet this, too, was unsettling to their hearts and minds, for they knew that Scripture gives stern and fearful warnings concerning the fate of rebels and those who reject God's mercy.

Small wonder that medieval traditionalists invented a purgatory for themselves and all their friends! Or that Newman suggested that the damned would be unable to think of the past or future, relieving

---

20. Alger, *Destiny of the Soul*, 2:510.
21. Ibid., 1:204.

them of the terror of the *thought* of such endless torture.[22] Or that Farrar and even Luther[23] left room for repentance beyond the grave. Or that prominent evangelical theologians have insisted that the number of the lost will actually be very few.[24] It is no surprise that Origen tried to turn all hell into a painful classroom from which its inhabitants would finally be graduated to heaven. Or that Karl Barth wished to leave open a universalistic possibility, however rare. Or that Bloesch and others have converted hell into a merciful hide-out, painful to be sure, but less painful still than the presence of the all-holy God.

The plain fact is, however, that the Holy Scriptures do not speak a single time in such language as we have read from Furniss and Spurgeon, Wesley and Edwards. To be certain, Old and New Testaments alike warn of fiery judgment that is inescapable in its action ("unquenchable") and irreversible in its results ("eternal"). Jesus even borrows the intertestamental term *Gehenna*, but He talks about it as a place where God finally destroys both body and soul. Scripture talks about a "consuming" fire which "burns up" the chaff, the tares and the unfruitful trees. Paul warns of "death," "destruction," "corruption" and "perishing." John pictures a fiery lake which clearly *annihilates* death, the beast and the false prophet, and he gives no other description of its effect on sinners.

We do not retreat from the language of Furniss and Spurgeon and Edwards because it is harsh or out of step with a modern and sophisticated age. We reject it as *unbiblical*, the expression of a theological

---

22. So says J. Arthur Hoyles, "The Punishment of the Wicked after Death," *London Quarterly and Holborn Review*, April 1957, p. 119.

23. T. F. Glasson quotes from a letter in which Luther wrote: "God forbid that I should limit the time of acquiring faith to the present life! In the depths of the divine mercy there may be opportunity to win it in the future" (T. F. Glasson, "Human Destiny: Has Christian Teaching Changed?" *Modern Churchman* 12, no. 4 [July 1969]: 287).

24. W. G. T. Shedd wrote of hell: "It is only a spot in the universe of God. Compared with heaven, hell is narrow and limited. . . . Hell is only a corner of the universe. . . . The Bible teaches that there will always be some sin, and some death, in the universe. Some angels and men will forever be the enemies of God. But their number, compared with that of unfallen angels and redeemed men, is small" (Shedd, *The Doctrine of Endless Punishment*, p. 159). Shedd goes on to quote Hopkins, who compared the saved to the lost in terms of "many thousands to one."

John W. Wenham quotes Hodge as saying, "We have reason to believe . . . that the number of the finally lost in comparison with the whole number of the saved will be very inconsiderable," and also Warfield, who remarked about the "relatively insignificant body" who will be lost (John W. Wenham, *The Goodness of God*, p. 32).

dogma whose history we can trace back through the centuries to its first explicit pronouncement among Christians more than a hundred years after Jesus. It did not originate in an exegesis of Scripture, and it ignores most of what the Bible says about the end of the wicked. It presupposes a view of man borrowed from pagan philosophy and never once stated in the Word of God. Traditionalists cannot express their view unequivocally in language found anywhere in Scripture, and it flatly contradicts what the Bible repeatedly appears to actually say. Traditionalism's "problem" is not that it is unsympathetic but that it is unscriptural. Scripture—not sympathy—must be its only cure.

20

Focusing on the Issue

One who dives into the pool of literature on final punishment soon discovers that its waters are confused and troubled indeed. Underneath are currents which often contradict each other, tugging first one way and then another until the diver wonders if he will ever again see daylight or be able to gulp the morning air. The discovery shocks him all the more because the surface appeared so smooth and warning signs were nowhere posted which hinted at the true condition beneath the mirrored calm.

False Issues and Irrelevant Distinctions

We wish to close this study, therefore, by pointing out some of the unanswered questions, sidetracks and false issues that at times have impeded, detoured or even tripped us up as we made our own faltering way through the still unfinished roads of yet virgin woods. Such journeyman notations might serve to make the next traveler's trip a little easier and more fruitful than it would have been otherwise.

Hell's size and location are beside the point, a curious interest of rabbinic theorists and medieval speculators to which neither side of the torment/extinction discussion today usually gives the first thought. One will also discuss the case of infants and unevangelized adults on the basis of theological presuppositions which lie outside the present scope. The relative number of the lost is also beyond our

423

sphere of interest now, though most fundamentalists would likely be surprised to hear how mainstream traditionalist theologians have responded to that point. Whether there is any opportunity for repentance after death (the "larger hope," as it has been called) seems clearly negative to us, but it is not germane to the final issue, either, so long as one ends the possibility somewhere short of the gates of hell itself. Whether one views the pains of hell as spiritual or physical, or a combination of the two, is also beside the real point of this study. We are not concerned with the character of the pain but its duration. The same may be said for degrees of punishment, a point on which traditionalists and conditionalists already agree, though they differ in how they express it.

The issue between eternal extinction and eternal conscious torment cannot be decided along Calvinist-Arminian lines. Critics of the traditional orthodoxy have tried to pin the problem of hell on Reformed fatalism or exclusiveness for a long time—but without a shred of reasonable, historical or scriptural evidence. Although some claim that free will demands the eternal possibility of exit from hell, at least one Arminian traditionalist used free will to prove eternal torment. There is no reason why Calvinists or Arminians (Reformed or Wesleyan, if one prefers) *must* occupy either traditionalist or conditionalist ground, based on their classic distinctions. Though very few doctrinaire Calvinists have been conditionalists, the reasons are historical rather than dogmatic, and they concern inherited medieval tradition and Reformation politics rather than anything distinctly Protestant.

Even the matter of man's nature does not clinch the issue. Those who hold to a separable and conscious "soul" which survives bodily death freely admit the fact that God is well able to destroy both body and soul in hell if He so desires. Those who hold that man is a single being and that the body/soul distinction is functional rather than substantial do not question that God could grant immortality to the wicked as easily as to the righteous—again, if He so desired. Some conditionalists have believed in a conscious "soul" which survives physical death; others have held that the "soul" dies with the body; and still others that it sleeps.

Even less is the issue one of cowardice, liberalism or wishful thinking. Those kinds of charges add pepper to a sermon, but they are unbecoming, uninformed and unfair to most conditionalists. Traditionalist writers frequently equate their own position with respect for the Bible. Considering some of their critics the past 400 years, one can understand why. But that time is past so far as this book (and many leading conditionalists of the past) is concerned. To evangelical traditionalists (God bless them all!) we simply say: "We are on the same side of the authority issue; now let's get down to business!" (God bless a number of conditionalist authors, too, who said the same thing but never got any response.)

The Real Issue

The real issue between traditionalists and conditionalists is nothing other than this: Does Scripture teach that the wicked will be made immortal for the purpose of suffering endless pain; or does it teach that the wicked, following whatever degree and duration of pain God may justly inflict, will finally and truly die, perish and become extinct for ever and ever? One great man and eloquent writer still living said it very well, although he intended to speak for eternal torment. Hell means the loss of everything good, he pointed out. Yet those expelled to that fate have turned their backs on God and rejected all His offers of good. They have persistently said, in effect:

> "Not thy will O God, but mine be done. Not thy love, not thy purposes for me, not thy realm (the great universe itself), not thy thoughts, not thy wisdom, not (above all) thy laws, not (in short) thy life and presence and light—but *me*." Satan first shouted this defiance, and he found that, lacking the power of creation and being rather entirely derivative and created, he could only reject, he could not replace. The rebel against God does not create a new environment, he merely occupies the condition resulting from his rejection of God's environment. When one turns out the light, he does not create darkness; he merely enters its realm where no light is.[1]

The author of those well-put words believed that hell is "an existence of loss." Based on the first verses of the Bible and the doctrine of creation, we ask why it should not rather be a "loss of existence." If nothing besides the one, triune God existed until He made it, and if even His creatures exist only by His pleasure and grace, what other ground of existence can there possibly be? If even those supernatural-

---

1. Calvin D. Linton, "The Sorrows of Hell," *Christianity Today* 16 (19 November 1971): 13.

ly redeemed through Jesus' atonement can hope to live beyond the grave only on the basis of their relationship to the Father's purpose, the Son's possession and the Spirit's power, by what reasoning can one be expected to exist even a single second (much less forever) if God finally pulls His plug and forever leaves the scene?

The traditionalist answer has often been to quote Paul's description of the immortal and incorruptible body awaiting the redeemed, as if it also stood ready (in a rather fiendish way) for the wicked as well. Yet none has been willing to say the damned will have a "glorified" body, though Paul uses that term alongside the adjectives "immortal" and "incorruptible." Today traditionalist authors themselves point out the proper application of such Scriptures, noting that they have been misused in the past. In doing so, they break new ground for a fresh, scriptural doctrine of final punishment.

Traditional Arguments Summarized

Traditionalism's arguments much resemble the basement or attic of an old family homestead in which the inhabitants were addicted to saving and averse to throwing anything away. Much of the literature is repetitive; few really new arguments have been advanced since Aquinas. Not every traditional writer would make all the points which follow, but one reading even four or five traditionalist books would probably come upon most of them at least once.

Philosophy. Some have defended eternal torment philosophically. To sin against God is to offend an infinite Person, the argument goes, and such a sin requires an infinite penalty. Since man is finite, he can make infinite payment only by suffering for an infinite period of time. Anselm formed the argument in a context of feudalistic society and law, and it is not used much anymore. Some philosophers think they see holes in the reasoning; at best it is not based on Scripture. A presupposition of man's immortality lies behind the scene in most cases, and it has sometimes been argued explicitly. We have noted repeatedly, however, that the greatest traditionalist theologians of all times have admitted that the soul possesses no inherent eternality or indestructibility. Traditionalism must stand on something else.

Intuition. A sense of moral rightness has also been advanced as evidence of eternal torment. Aside from the fact that the doctrine has repelled countless others on what they thought was the same basis, that is the wrong starting point anyway. If the Genesis story of the first sin teaches anything, it teaches that our sense of moral rightness is a deceitful and inadequate guide and that, rather, we must always listen to the voice of God. Traditionalists have exploded the "moral rightness" argument well themselves when answering liberal opponents of past centuries. What is sauce for the goose is sauce for the gander.

Tradition. Almost without exception, traditionalist authors point to the popularity of their view through so many centuries. Some more ecclesiastic-minded ones have practically made that their main point. Needless to say, any Protestant, much less an evangelical one, owes more than that to his founding principle of authority and his claim to follow *Scripture alone*. As a matter of fact, such early statements as the Apostles' Creed and the Nicene Creed stop short of this subject, and none of the recognized universal (ecumenical or catholic) councils of the first five centuries made any pronouncement on it at all. There has always been a conditionalist stream in church history, and there is something to be said for the idea that the purest water might have been found somewhere outside the main medieval channel! The greatest uninspired makers and transmitters of tradition all urged us to measure what they said by the Scriptures and, given a choice, to take the latter. We do the universal, historic church no disservice and them no disrespect by following that godly advice.

Uniform Jewish View. Because it has been repeated so often, most people take it for granted that the intertestamental period saw the development of such a uniform and recognized doctrine of final punishment that we can read the New Testament with this "Jewish view" firmly in mind. Since Jesus and the apostles evidently failed to denounce this accepted view head-on, the argument goes, they obviously gave it their endorsement.

We have seen from the Apocrypha and Pseudepigrapha, however, that there was no such common understanding but, rather, the same two views between which we now are asked to choose. Strack and Billerbeck tell us that even the passages which speak of eternal perdition or eternal punishment might have been meant to convey ever-lasting extinction. Jesus borrowed the name "Gehenna" from His uninspired predecessors, but what He said about it reminds us of the Old Testament and sounds exactly like total destruction. Jesus said not one word about unending conscious torment—or the indestructibility of the wicked.

Biblical Words and Figures. Traditionalists read passages which mention "eternal" or "unquenchable" fire, smoke that ascends or a worm that does not die, and say they all describe unending conscious torment. In the course of this study we have had occasion to examine these expressions in some detail, usually in both Testaments.

"Eternal fire" is certainly not a temporary punishment which holds any promise of restoration, but it fits very well the idea of everlasting extinction such as befell the cities of Sodom and Gomorrah, as Genesis describes, the rest of the Old Testament reminds, Jesus warns and Jude plainly says. The phrase argues against restorationism but not against conditionalism.

"Unquenchable fire" is usually taken to mean perpetual pain, and it might mean that—if we had no Old Testament prophets to explain the language. There it clearly signifies a divine judgment which cannot be stopped or slowed down until its destruction is complete.

"Fire and worm" in the Bible come from Isaiah 66, where they are twin elements of destruction, feeding on dead and discarded corpses of God's enemies. The scene elicits disgust but not pity. The application of these words to physical and mental pain is a later invention with no biblical support whatsoever.

"Weeping and gnashing of teeth" are never specifically related in Scripture to any *duration* of suffering, as Hoekema also acknowledges. Rather, they suggest (as he says and we agree) "the bitterness of remorse and hopeless self-condemnation"[2] and (we add) the intensity of rage against God and divine justice by those who are finally its helpless but still defiant victims. These verbs do speak of conscious suffering which precedes final destruction; the wicked do not happily and quietly fade away. The related expression "outer darkness" speaks of expulsion and separation, but it gives not a clue of eternal conscious torment.

---

2. Anthony A. Hoekema, *The Bible and the Future*, p. 268.

Traditionalists usually make much of Jesus' statement which places the same adjective "eternal" (*aiōnios*) on both the "life" and the "punishment" of the Age to Come. And well they might, for Jesus indeed said it, and all He said is true. Conditionalists also make the same point, and here they stand beside traditionalists since both oppose the doctrine of restorationism. The question is not whether punishment is *eternal* but whether that eternal punishment *consists* of conscious pain or irreversible extinction. Based on Scripture's own use of the similar terms "eternal judgment," "eternal redemption" and "eternal salvation," we believe it not only a fair and ordinary use of words, but the most proper one, to see "eternal" modifying the result and not the process of the action in this case too.

Jesus speaks of some on whom God's wrath "remains." That certainly seems to exclude restoration, but utter destruction is far from a sign of forgiveness or renewed love. Traditionalists, not conditionalists, are continually haunted by the specter of universalism. Nor have any conditionalists we have read tried to make hell an actual provision of divine mercy and grace. Scripture tells us that God has *two* sides. There is goodness, and there is severity. They meet in the divine holiness and justice—concretely, historically and explicitly at the cross—not in some homogenized hell created by man. God is love, but He is also a *consuming fire*. Only final extinction allows that fact its full force.

We grant to traditionalists the fact that words like "perish," "destroy," "die" and "corrupt" all have metaphorical usages at times. We point out, however, that figurative meanings are possible only because of primary meanings. We also remember the accepted principle of interpretation which calls for primary meanings of words in straightforward, nonallegorical prose unless there is some reason to regard the language otherwise. Scripture never indicates that it intends less by these words than their ordinary meanings would suggest when it applies them to the final fate of the wicked. Traditionalists offer analogies of wrecked cars and burst wineskins. We have tried to examine these verbs and their cognates in the full light of the New Testament, the Septuagint, and the first-century literature of nonbiblical Greek. The gauntlet here faces the other direction: conditionalists take the words at face value regarding final punishment; traditionalists need to show cause for explaining them all away.

John speaks of "smoke ascending forever," and traditionalists have sometimes used that expression for support. The Old Testament again points the other way, however, for it uses the picture more than once to signify the silent testimony of a completed destruction. The "lake of fire" clearly *annihilates* death and Hades; there is no good reason to suppose it eternally preserves the lost from among mankind. The one passage that speaks of torment "for ever and ever" does not refer to people but to the devil, beast and false prophet. The Old Testament background to that passage describes extinction, and two of the three victims in the verse are impersonal abstractions incapable of conscious or sensible pain. All this, plus the highly symbolic context of the statement, should give us long pause before interpreting this one verse in a way that goes against all the teaching of the rest of the Bible.

Finality. Traditionalists speak of hell's *finality*—and so do we. They have jousted for centuries with universalists and restorationists of various stripes. In the bustle of battle they have simply failed to take a long, hard look at this other possibility. Consequently, they have not fully realized that it actually stands *with* them, *against* every idea that makes hell's punishment anything less than final and eternal. In all the understandable confusion, they have thrown out the baby with the bath.

Objections against Final Extinction

Not Forever. The present study reveals that beneath most objections to final extinction, one can usually find misinformation or misunderstanding. Some say everlasting extinction would not be "forever," but Augustine and Jonathan Edwards both conceded that it would. The *duration* of final punishment is clear; the question concerns its *nature*. We measure capital punishment, for example, by its permanency, not by the time required for its execution.

In the same way, the permanence of the second death is not minimized by the duration of conscious suffering which precedes it. A young man about to be removed from earthly life in the electric chair does not chortle that his pain will last but a split second. His sentence has nothing to do with the pain. This same reality, recognized by courts and criminals throughout the earth, also answers the objection that eternal extinction is really no *punishment*. For all agree that instant death before a firing squad is rightly regarded a far greater penalty than even a lifetime in prison. Furthermore, the evidence of Scripture indicates that extinction will be preceded (perhaps even brought about by) a period of conscious suffering which corresponds precisely to the sentence of divine justice. God is severe, but He is not a sadist. Though pagan literature abounds in description of hellish pain, the Word of God does not.

Not Possible. Some have objected that "annihilation" is physically impossible, that even when something is burned its smoke and ashes remain. We rejoin that no martyr approaching the stake ever took comfort by such a thought as that. Scripture does not address us in terms of Newtonian physics but of life and death; we have intentionally spoken of "extinction" rather than "annihilation" most of the time to avoid this cavil. The events of the Age to Come are not subject to physicists' inductive generalizations drawn from experience now. In addition, the same law of thermodynamics which says that nothing is destroyed also says nothing is created. God is greater than either part of the statement, and He is fully able to destroy both body and soul in hell. Rather than mock Him on that basis, unbelievers had best learn to fear!

A Dangerous View. Through the years some have protested that this view of final punishment endangers the faith. Constable responded very well to that objection a hundred years ago when he asked *what* it imperils.

> Does it imperil *our faith in God?* What attribute of His is attacked? His love! Is it the part of love to inflict eternal pain if it can be helped? His mercy! Is it the part of mercy never to be satisfied with the misery of others? His holiness! Is it essential to holiness to keep evil for ever in existence? His justice! Can justice only be satisfied with everlasting agonies? No; we do not endanger faith. We strengthen it, by allying it once more with the divine principles of mercy, equity, and justice. It is the Augustinian theory which endangers faith, and has made shipwreck of faith in the case of multitudes, by representing God as a Being of boundless injustice, caprise, and cruelty.[3]

We do not argue *for* our view on this basis; we merely urge that such a criticism fails to make it invalid.

---

3. Henry Constable, *Duration and Nature of Future Punishment,* p. 166.

Not Noble. It is said that extinction contradicts the "great value" of each individual. Is that value better appreciated by preserving man alive forever in unspeakable torment? This is essentially a humanistic argument which is most at home in a nineteenth-century case for universalism. The Bible presents man's worth in terms of his relationship with God, not as something inherent in himself (he is a clay creature). Traditionalists, on the other hand, also feel free to speak of man's sense of "total worthlessness" in hell, so this argument cuts both ways.

Not Moral. Someone objects that eternal extinction removes the fear of hell and encourages sin. Conditionalists point to the results of the traditionalist view. Augustine fled from it by inventing purgatory, Origen by formulating restorationism. Skeptics make fun of the idea or use it as an excuse to charge God with injustice. Even those who say they believe the doctrine usually think it is for someone else, so protecting themselves from the shock value it supposedly has.

Our age desperately needs to learn the fear of the Almighty, and that is one reason for the proper preaching of hell. We have attempted to stress this biblical emphasis throughout the present study. We all have rejected God's voice in nature and in conscience already. Those who reject His final word of mercy in Jesus Christ are warned in the most awesome terms. Nothing remains for such a one, Scripture says, but a fearful anticipation of judgment—and fiery indignation which will devour every adversary! One of the greatest benefits to come by recovering the scriptural teaching on hell will be to loose preachers' tongues to make very clear this alternative to salvation in the power of the Holy Spirit and in the wholesome and truthful language of the Word of God.

The pragmatic argument of results can settle the issue neither way since it begins with man's response rather than with God's revelation. The only question that should concern us is the one which asks what the Bible teaches. If it teaches eternal torment, man's reaction will not lessen that one whit. If it teaches eternal extinction, no objection of practicality can make that less true. Such objections are unworthy of evangelicals who profess to derive final authority from the Word of God.

Not Reasonable. Others object that it seems an uncalled-for act of severity to raise the wicked for judgment, only to destroy them eternally. Conditionalists scratch their heads that advocates of eternal torment should raise the question of severity. It is clear from Scripture that God will indeed raise the wicked from death (Jehovah's Witnesses and all others who deny it are simply *wrong!*)— and for no reason other than to deal with them according to deeds they committed in the body. Even human feelings of moral necessity agree to this (though by themselves they prove nothing), for many evils evidently go unpunished in the present life.

Finally, however, the traditionalist's own answer to those questioning the *justice* of his view must suffice. God, not man, is the judge of the world, and He will do what is right. Again the question reverts to one of exegesis. What does Scripture say that God *will* do? When we look there, we find it stated in dozens of ways that the wages of sin is *death*.

Not Vindictive. The objection is raised to final extinction that such punishment becomes a matter of grace as well as justice, that this view is rooted in a false conception that sees hell as a form or manifestation of benevolence instead of vindication and wrath. Yet no conditionalist discovered in this study ever argued such a thing— although more than one traditionalist has! It is the advocate of eternal torment, not of final extinction, who reasons that divine grace reaches to hell as well as to heaven, and that hell's very existence is a sign of God's mercy to those who cannot stand to be in His immediate presence. One might wish to raise this question, but it is the traditionalist's problem, not the conditionalist's.

Life Is More Than Existence. Advocates of eternal torment frequently make a great deal of the fact that eternal *life* means far more than "mere existence." The implication is that "mere existence" is included in the second *death*. Surely the *non sequitur* is obvious. A king may announce that he will come on a certain day and give abundant life to his supporters but death to his enemies. "Abundant" life would mean more than "mere existence" in that case, but death would still *be* death. An enemy would be foolish indeed to demand that the king spare his life on the basis of such an argument as this.

A Concluding Word

What traditionalist authors have never done is to take up the numerous passages in support of final extinction, then show where conditionalists have either misused the text, ignored the context, eliminated crucial information, or added data not found in the Word of God itself. They have themselves, on the other hand, ignored the rich teaching of the Old Testament, falsely presumed a uniform inter-testamental view, and interpreted the New Testament pictures and language on the basis of later philosophical tradition and ecclesiastical dogma rather than ordinary, accepted methods of scriptural exegesis.

Our case rests on a detailed examination of many passages of Scripture. They are considered in context according to regular rules of hermeneutics, using, for the most part, tools either written by or generally accepted by evangelical traditionalists. In the first place, therefore, objections ought not to be philosophical, dogmatic or pragmatic, but exegetical. Many objections raised to everlasting extinction have started at the wrong end of things and have frequently missed or avoided the real issue altogether. This is a new day the Lord has made. Its fresh opportunity should not be abused in the same way again.

We do not wish to commit ourselves to a literalistic view regarding the end of the wicked. To say that they finally corrupt, are destroyed, die and perish is not to say that there will be physical fire. The future age will be qualitatively different from the present world of space and time, and we must allow it room for its own surprises. Here we differ with many previous conditionalists who have been as literalistic as any of their traditionalist counterparts. What we have found, beyond any question, is that the Old and New Testaments alike, in a multiplicity of ways, terms, figures, pictures, expressions and examples, declare time and time again that the wicked finally will pass away and be no more, that righteousness will then fill the universe, and that God will then forever be all in all. Not one time in all of Scripture does God say that any human being will be made immortal for the purpose of suffering conscious everlasting torment.

Final punishment is not the gospel. It belongs alongside the gospel, however, as the divine threat to the sinful unbelief which rejects God's overwhelming and undeserved mercy in Jesus Christ. It is not the most important doctrine of Scripture by any means, but it is certainly not unimportant. In that light we can agree with the point of the nineteenth-century writer who said concerning the traditional doctrine of hell:

> It must be loyally proclaimed or else denounced. If believed, it should be preached from the house-tops; if not believed, it should be opposed to the very end. If this dogma be false, it is a calumny against God and a stumbling-block in the way of humanity. All the resources of apologetics would not suffice to counter-balance its baneful effects.[4]

Eternal torment is either true or it is not. God's Word gives the only authoritative answer. We wish to humbly receive whatever it says— on this or any subject—then faithfully proclaim it as befits God's stewards.

All of us are children of tradition to a great extent. J. I. Packer stated it well in his book on *"Fundamentalism" and the Word of God*. Packer wrote:

> We do not start our Christian lives by working out our faith for ourselves; it is mediated to us by Christian tradition, in the form of sermons, books and established patterns of church life and fellowship. We read our Bibles in the light of what we have learned from these sources; we approach Scripture with minds already formed by the mass of accepted opinions and viewpoints with which we have come into contact, in both the Church and the world. . . . It is easy to be unaware that it has happened; it is hard even to begin to realize how profoundly tradition in this sense has moulded us. But we are forbidden to become enslaved to human tradition, either secular or Christian, whether it be 'catholic' tradition, or 'critical' tradition, or 'ecumenical' tradition, or even 'evangelical' tradition. We may never assume the complete rightness of our own established ways of thought and practice and excuse ourselves the duty of testing and reforming them by Scripture.[5]

We do not reject the traditionalist doctrine, therefore, on moral, philosophical, intuitive, judicial or emotional grounds, nor are we much concerned with the arguments of any who do. The only question that matters here is the teaching of Scripture. Does the Word of God teach the eternal conscious torment of the lost? Our modest study fails to show that it does.

---

4. Emmanuel Pétavel, *The Problem of Immortality*, p. 267.

5. J. I. Packer, *"Fundamentalism" and the Word of God*, pp. 69-70.

We were reared on the traditionalist view—we accepted it because it was said to rest on the Bible. This closer investigation of the Scriptures indicates that we were mistaken in that assumption. A careful look discovers that both Old and New Testaments teach instead a resurrection of the wicked for the purpose of divine judgment, the fearful anticipation of a consuming fire, irrevocable expulsion from God's presence into a place where there will be weeping and grinding of teeth, such conscious suffering as the divine justice individually requires—and, finally, the total, everlasting extinction of the wicked with no hope of resurrection, restoration or recovery. Now we stand on that, on the authority of the Word of God.

We have changed once and do not mind changing again, but we were evidently wrong once through lack of careful study and do not wish to repeat the same mistake. Mere assertions and denunciations will not refute the evidence presented in this book, nor will a recital of ecclesiastical tradition.

This case rests finally on Scripture. Only Scripture can prove it wrong.

Appendix A: Augustine's Discussion of Final Punishment

A Critique of Book 21 of "The City of God"

Located in *The Fathers of the Church: A New Translation*, tr. Gerald G. Walsh and Daniel J. Honan (New York: Fathers of the Church, 1954), pp. 339-413.

In book 21 of *The City of God* Augustine answers pagan critics who scoff at his preaching of the Last Things. Although he touches on the resurrection and the last judgment, his main concern is final punishment. Augustine has taught unequivocally (as did several fathers before him) that the resurrected wicked will be immortalized in order to suffer conscious pains forever. Although he speaks of final punishment in other places, this is his most extended discussion, and it is representative of his content and method of teaching in general. We will consider his remarks under three heads: (1) Augustine's opponents and their authority; (2) Augustine's view of man and immortality; (3) Augustine's use of Scripture. In each case we will summarize his material, then make our own comments about what he has said.

Augustine's Opponents and Their Authority

Because "it seems harder to believe that the bodies of the damned are to remain in endless torment than to believe that the bodies of the saints are to continue without pain in everlasting felicity," Augustine first sets himself to prove "the possibility of eternal pain." Once this is established, it also "will greatly help to show how relatively easy it is to believe in the utterly unperturbed immortality of the bodies of the saints" (Ch. 1, p. 339. References to chapters indicate Augustine's divisions; page numbers are to *The Fathers of the Church* cited above.). He clarifies his aim in chapter 2. "It is not easy to find a proof," he says, "that will convince unbelievers of the possibility of human bodies remaining not merely active, alive, and uncorrupted after death, but also of continuing forever in the torments of fire" (p. 340). Augustine builds his case carefully.

First, he points out, there are many wonders in nature which the pagans themselves cannot explain. In chapters 2-7 Augustine enumerates several of the more fantastic. It is reported, he says, that certain animals live in fire and never burn, that certain worms live in springs too hot for man to endure (p. 340). Volcanoes in Sicily have always burned, but the mountains remain intact (p. 345). And what of straw, which keeps snow cold but fruits warm? Or fire, which blackens logs but brightens stones? (pp. 345, 346). Then there is the diamond, "so marvelously hard that neither iron nor fire can crack it. Only goat's blood, so they say, is potent enough for that" (p. 347).

There is a salt in Sicily which flows like water when thrown on a fire but crackles as if burning when pitched into water (p. 349). A well in another place issues water by day too cold to drink but by night too hot to touch (p. 350). Another well is said to have water which puts out a burning taper but lights it again after it has been extinguished (p. 350). And in the land of Sodom there are fabled apples which grow to maturity but crumble like dust and disappear into smoke when touched by man (p. 350). Besides these things are the well-known marvels of charcoal (p. 346), lime (p. 346), and the lodestone or magnet (p. 348).

It is important to note that Augustine himself does not personally believe all these wonders. "I would not want anyone to be rash enough to believe all the wonders I have mentioned," he says. "I am not myself completely convinced, except where I have had personal experience and where verification is easy for anyone" (p. 357). He names these things only to show that man's reason is no less baffled by many marvels of nature than it is by the mysteries of faith (p. 352).

The same skeptics who accept these tales charge Christians with insincerity for speaking incredible things about the life to come. Augustine insists this is not fair. "The skeptics . . . charge us with insincerity when we say that there have been (and will be) divine miracles which we cannot parallel in their personal experience. So long, at least, as they are convinced that there are natural wonders which are humanly inexplicable, they have no right to argue that this or that fact never has occurred or ever will occur, merely because no rational explanation can be given" (p. 349). If they accept things in the natural realm which are greater than reason, "why should God be unable to raise bodies from the dead and allow the bodies of the damned to suffer in eternal fire, seeing that He made a universe filled with uncounted miracles?" (p. 355). The critics' own skepticism witnesses against them. For the very "God who is to do the things which seem impossible is the . . . same God who made the promise . . . that incredible things would be accepted as credible by incredulous people" (p. 358).

Comment. Augustine is simply making an argument *ad hominem*, turning the logic of his opponents around on them. He does not believe all these wonders he cites. But he argues quite successfully that the pagans have no right to object to his doctrine that the wicked will be immortalized to burn forever on the mere grounds that they cannot understand or explain such a phenomenon. We must give him the point entirely. In matters relating to God, human reason cannot be the criterion for acceptance or rejection. Augustine has not attempted to prove his doctrine from Scripture so far, only to take away a rational objection made by his humanistic opponents. Since that is his stated purpose in this section, he should not be criticized for doing no more. Nor should we think he bases his doctrine on the "marvels" he cites from nature and reject it for that reason. He does not name these things as proof of his doctrine but as an answer to a particular objection of his opponents.

Augustine's View of Man and Immortality

Augustine's critics have also objected "that no body that can suffer pain can escape death" (p. 341). Augustine seeks to answer this by showing that pain and life can coexist forever. Here he is forced to revert to the Platonic mentality. Scripture had not dealt with such an objection since Scripture is not cast in terms of philosophy, but the philosophers had. So Augustine becomes the philosopher.

He points to physical death to make his argument clear. "The reason why a soul succumbs to pain and leaves the body is that, in this life, the link between our bodily members and the principle of their life is so weak that this link cannot stand the strain of any force that brings about very great or excessive pain. But in the world to come, the soul and body will be so united that a bond between them can be broken neither by the power of pain nor by the passing of time" (p. 342).

Man will have a different kind of flesh then as well, he says, and "there will be a different kind of death from the death of the body" (p. 342). Once "the soul is without God," he explains, "it will be incapable of escaping the pains of the body. The first kind of death drives an unwilling soul out of the body; the second death holds an unwilling soul in the body. What is common to both deaths is that it is the soul that must reluctantly suffer what the body inflicts" (p. 342).

Augustine refers to this "different flesh" again in chapter 8. Skeptics say "it is simply not in the nature of human flesh to remain unconsumed in fire" (p. 358). But they must speak of human flesh as they have known it in their own experience. And, Augustine points out, that is not even now the same kind of human flesh man once had. "For, this very human flesh . . . by its nature before the fall . . . could never suffer death," but since the fall it has "been so constituted that . . . as things now are, it must suffer death." It is permissible to argue, therefore, "that in the resurrection it will once more be differently constituted from what it is now" (p. 358).

Augustine the philosopher speaks from the viewpoint of Plato, who took for granted the maxim that "all souls are immortal." Augustine accepts Plato's axiom with the common Christian qualifications that souls had a beginning because God created them and that they were not so inherently immortal that God could not destroy them. He states this presupposition twice in chapter 3.

First he charges that the pagans overlook the fact that man has a reality higher than the body.

> That reality is the soul, without whose presence there would be neither life nor movement in the body. What is more, it is a reality that is susceptible of pain and not susceptible of death. Here, in fact, we have the reality which, conscious as it is of pain, is immortal. And it is this capacity for immortality (already, as we know, inherent in everybody's soul) which, in the world to come, will be present in the bodies of the damned. —Pages 342, 343.

If then, there is any genuine argument connecting pain and death . . . this argument would apply, if at all, to the death of the soul, since it is to the soul rather than to the body that pain pertains. But the fact is that the soul which more truly feels pain than the body, cannot die. What follows is that there is no basis whatever for arguing that . . . because bodies in the future life are to be in pain, we therefore must believe that even in the future life they will die.—Page 343.

Comment. Augustine's dialogue with his critics here comes strictly under "philosophy" and not under "Scripture." He does not pretend otherwise but attempts to meet and better his adversaries on their own ground. For his valiant efforts to do this we may give him (and other apologists before and since) due appreciation and honest respect.

Yet it is equally clear from Augustine's answer concerning pain and the body that he reasons from the Platonic presupposition of the immortality of the soul. He explicitly states this assumption twice. In the end, he makes this presupposition a fundamental basis for rejecting what otherwise sounds convincing—that the soul, being in pain, would finally succumb and die. Augustine assumes the immortality of the soul, so he is forced to reject that conclusion. He must conclude instead that souls entering into final punishment will never die.

Here Augustine, like Calvin after him, is inconsistent. When speaking of man before God, he insists that man's immortality is derived from and dependent on the grace of God. But when speaking of final punishment, he argues from the immortality of the soul as if that were a fixed point not subject to criticism or dispute. Immortality of the soul is for him, as it is for Calvin, a kind of secondary influence. He does not begin with it, but in the matter of final punishment it always crops up, diverting him from his original view of man under God to a course based instead on Platonic theory. His conscious anthropology attempted to be biblical. His unconscious anthropology was not, and it finally determined his exegesis.

We also observe that Augustine's language regarding immortality differs from Scripture's in at least three important points. Augustine attributes immortality (1) to souls (2) of the wicked (3) by creation. Scripture speaks of man's immortality (1) only in terms of the righteous, never the wicked; (2) always of an immortal *body*, never an immortal soul; and (3) as belonging to the consummation of Christ's redemptive work at the end, not something inherent in any part of man's present being. One may wish to argue for the immortalization of the wicked as well as the righteous in the resurrection, but he will have to do so on some basis other than scriptural revelation.

Augustine was a fallible human, however important his position in the history of the church, and here he is simply not biblical. It is a mark of his influence that his very reasoning has persisted for more than 15 centuries since his death. This is all the more notable since many who champion his position most devotedly are not consciously familiar with Augustine or his writings, far less with those of Plato. And it is a mark of Augustine's true greatness that in other places he urges us always to test what he says by the Word of God and to choose the teaching of Scripture over anything he might say or write.

Augustine's Use of Scripture

A fair critique of Augustine's use of Scripture will recognize two unique qualities of this work. This book in *The City of God* is (1) primarily *polemic* and not didactic, and Augustine's discussion is (2) more *philosophical* than scriptural. It is not enough to note that he speaks philosophically, then charge him with being unscriptural. Philosophers are not bound to use Scripture. Augustine is not attempting to teach the Scriptures as much as to meet his opponents. Since they raise philosophical objections to what he has previously taught, it is understandable that he should reason for page upon page with no reference to Scripture.

It is fair, however, *when* he uses Scripture, to look carefully at *how* he uses Scripture. We might observe, for example, that in this first section of Augustine's book which we have summarized, he offers nothing that could be called exegesis. He makes no reference to the Old Testament statements about the destiny of the wicked. He shows no awareness of the way Scripture commonly uses such prophetic symbolism as "unquenchable fire," the "undying worm," or the "smoke that ascends forever." He simply uses these phrases— by now familiar stock in the Christian vocabulary—as they have come to be used and interpreted in the light of the Platonic "immortality of the soul." We can illustrate *what* he says Scripture teaches, therefore, but we will search here in vain for any exegetical basis *for* that teaching. He addresses unbelievers in the name of the church. What he says is held without question to be also the teaching of Scripture.

Augustine begins chapter 9, for example, with this statement: "One thing that will happen, and most certainly happen, is what God, through His Prophet, said concerning the punishment of hell being eternal: 'Their worm shall not die, and their fire shall not be quenched'" (p. 363, quoting Isa. 66:24). Later he quotes Jesus' words of warning from Mark 9:42-48 about forfeiting hand, foot or eye in order to escape "the unquenchable fire, where the worm dies not and the fire is not quenched." No one could dare disagree with Augustine's observation that "that repetition and that emphatic warning, coming from divine lips, are enough to make any man tremble" (p. 364). He can cite Scripture for his denial "that bodies in hell will be such that they will be unaffected by the pains inflicted by fire" (p. 366), for Jesus speaks of penal suffering as well. Augustine is not sure whether the "worm" is literal or a figurative torment of the soul, though he prefers to say that both fire and worm apply to the body alike (p. 365). The fire, however, "will be material and it will torment" the bodies of damned men as well as demon-spirits who are either in or out of a body (p. 368).

Augustine believes that Scripture teaches gradations of suffering for the wicked, in keeping with divine justice. The eternal fire "will undoubtedly affect people differently according to their deserts and the pain will be made slight or serious either by varying the degree of intensity of the fire itself, according to the guilt of the sufferers, or by varying the sensitivity of the sinners to a hell that is the same for all" (pp. 377, 378).

Augustine's lack of exegesis in the first section is all the more striking by contrast with the second. Almost the entire last half of the book is devoted to refuting assorted views of those who hold out hope for restoration, remission or escape for those thrown into hell. There Augustine uses many passages in context as he examines the texts advanced by his adversaries.

Augustine believes in purgatorial suffering in the present life and after death. But all purging will be over when one enters the eternal fire (p. 377). This is "not a matter of feel, but of fact," he says. He examines the Lord's words of sentence, "Depart from me, accursed ones, into the everlasting fire which was prepared for the devil and his angels." He argues from the Apocalypse with its "pool of fire and brimstone." Here his appeal is clear. "It is Scripture, infallible Scripture, which declares that God has not spared them" (pp. 386, 387). He analyzes Christ's words in Matthew 25, where the Lord speaks in

"clear but contrasting declarations" of the righteous and the wicked
(p. 389). There is no hint anywhere, he says, of future mercy after
death, of escape from hell, of restoration from damnation, or of the
wicked overpowering their final sentence through either human
might or divine grace. Rather, there are clear and unequivocal statements from the mouth of even Jesus Himself which speak of irreversible and everlasting doom.

It is sometimes argued that this irrevocable doom cannot be eternal
extinction because such execution would not be "eternal
punishment." One would search the literature in vain for a better
refutation of this objection than he finds in chapter 11 of *The City of
God.* Augustine is speaking against "some who think it unjust that
anyone should be condemned to eternal punishment for sins, however great, committed during a period of time that was relatively
short" (p. 368). This contention contradicts the civil code of every
judicial system, he says. Other than the possible use of precise
retaliation (an eye for an eye; a tooth for a tooth), Augustine points
out, legal punishment is almost never so proportioned to the crime
"that the length of the punishment equals the time spent in
perpetrating the crime" (p. 368). Take the case of kissing another
man's wife, he suggests, and suppose the legal punishment is scourg-
ing. "The offender who took only a moment for the injury done is
rightly scourged for an incomparably longer time; however short his
pleasure, he suffers a protracted pain" (p. 369).

Then Augustine turns to capital punishment as his greatest illustration. He is showing the rightfulness of an eternal punishment for sins
committed during a short period of time. He understands "eternal
punishment" to be conscious everlasting torment. But his words
could well be used by one arguing the case for eternal extinction
—divine "capital punishment." At the very least, Augustine refutes
the argument that eternal extinction could not qualify as "eternal
punishment." These are his words:

> Where a very serious crime is punished by death and the execution of
> the sentence takes only a minute, no laws consider that minute as the
> measure of the punishment, but rather the fact that the criminal is
> forever removed from the community of the living. And, in fact, this
> removal of men from mortal society by the penalty of the first death is
> the nearest parallel we have to the removal of men from the immortal
> communion of saints by the penalty of the second death. For, just as
> the laws of temporal society make no provision for recalling a man to

that society, once he is dead in body, so the justice of the eternal communion makes no provision for recalling a man to eternal life, once he has been condemned to the death of his soul.—Pages 369, 370.

Comment. When Augustine refutes the arguments advanced for a restoration from hell, he reasons on the basis of scriptural exegesis. He shows himself well able to let Scripture speak on its own terms and in each context to make its message clear. He convinces with the authority of a truly biblical theologian in opposing the possiblity of escape from hell and in affirming that its doors open only in one direction—admitting to its terrible domain the wretched doomed who will never return or leave it forever.

The skill with which he so uses Scripture in the latter half of this book contrasts sharply with his practical non-use of Scripture in the first part. Although he wears a philosopher's hat there, his appeals to Scripture are circuitous. He assumes what he would prove and quotes biblical phrases with his own interpretation. Throughout the work he shows clear evidence from Scripture that final punishment will be *final*—irremediable and irreversible. But not once does he even attempt to show that the scriptural language requires perpetual conscious torment rather than an irreversible punishment of everlasting destruction resulting in total extinction. He does not exegete the texts to obtain his interpretation. He passes over the Old Testament language completely, with the barest exception of a passing reference. He makes no reference to the prophetic background of Jesus' symbolic language. He does not mention that the words used by Paul—terms like "death," "destruction" and "perish"—have any true significance or bearing on the subject, or that they had a long and rather common usage in philosophical discussions when Paul wrote them. Although he is a philosopher himself, he makes no mention of Plato's use of this vocabulary, specifically when speaking of the soul!

Augustine never mentions the possibility of the extinction of the wicked in hell. One interpretation for this is that he knew no one who suggested that possibility. Yet Froom shows that the view had advocates long before Augustine and even during his century. It seems at least as likely (and probably far more so) that Augustine simply has nothing to say *against* the view.

Augustine does state one presupposition, however, which prevents his considering the case for the extermination of the wicked in hell. That is the philosophical doctrine of the immortality of the soul.

Even though he differs from his Platonic opponents when discussing immortality, he slides into their frame of mind when discussing eternal punishment. In spite of his disclaimers at other times, here Augustine clings to the immortality of every soul, and this excludes the possibility of annihilation.

Augustine's philosophy erects a barricade to his exegesis. In this he sets the pace for the Western church, which for the most part has followed his thinking to this day. The sixteenth century brought Protestantism's new beginning to a crossroads on the matter. Tyndale, Luther and the Anabaptists leaned another direction. But the influence of Calvin would tilt the Reformation decisively, steering it also in Augustine's path. So it would remain until the twentieth century.

Appendix B: John Calvin's "Psychopannychia"

Subtitled: *Or a Refutation of the Error Entertained by Some Unskilful Persons Who Ignorantly Imagine That in the Interval Between Death and the Judgment the Soul Sleeps, Together with an Explanation of the Condition and Life of the Soul after This Present Life.*

Located in John Calvin, *Tracts and Treatises in Defense of the Reformed Faith*, tr. Henry Beveridge (Grand Rapids: William B. Eerdmans Publishing Co., 1958), vol. 3.

Historical Introduction

Other than a treatise on Seneca's *De Clementia*, *Psychopannychia* is Calvin's first known work and is his first theological writing. He composed it in 1534 in Orleans, France, and carried it to Basel, Switzerland, where he added a second preface. Publication was delayed, however, until 1542. The occasion of *Psychopannychia* was the progress made by certain Anabaptists whose entry into France was hindering Calvin's own reformation. He published another work against the Anabaptists in 1544, entitled *A Short Instruction Guarding the Faithful against the Errors of the Common Sect of the Anabaptists*. Because of the intensity of Calvin's dislike of the Anabaptists, one can only wonder how much his views on the soul might have differed—or at least have been subject to modification—had they not been his principal opponents on the subject. In keeping with the custom of his day, Calvin was unrestrained in describing the wickedness of his adversaries and what he held to be their heterodox views.

Calvin's first preface (Orleans, 1534) begins by speaking of "that absurd dogma" which he is about to attack. It is "their insanity," "the evil, which makes far too much progress" and which is "eating in like a cancer." He has heard but "murmurs and hoarse sounds" of it so far, but he notes that while it "lay smouldering for some ages," it "has lately begun to send forth sparks, being stirred up by some dregs of Anabaptists" who, "spread abroad far and wide, have kindled torches" (pp. 414, 415).

In his later preface from Basel in 1536, Calvin confesses that in the heat of argument he has used "some rather severe and harsh expressions" which might "give offence to delicate ears." For the sake of "some good men," he says, whose error is due to "excessive credulity or ignorance of Scripture" rather than perversity or maliciousness, he adds this explanatory second preface. Such people (who, though unnamed, certainly would have included Luther and many Lutherans) are to understand that whenever Calvin uses "some freedom of speech," he means them no offense but is always "referring to the nefarious herd of Anabaptists, from whose fountain this noxious stream did . . . first flow, and against whom," he emphasizes, "nothing I have said equals their deserts" (p. 416). The treatise closes with a warning regarding the Anabaptist source of the embattled doctrine. Calvin's final words are: "I again desire all my readers, if I shall have any, to remember that the Catabaptists (whom, as embodying all kinds of abominations, it is sufficient to have named) are the authors of this famous dogma. Well may we suspect anything that proceeds from such a forge—a forge which has already fabricated, and is daily fabricating, so many monsters" (p. 490).

The Point of Issue

And what is this "absurd dogma," this "insanity," this "evil like a cancer," this Catabaptist monster now noxiously spewed forth? Calvin states his proposition very clearly.

Our controversy, then, relates to THE HUMAN SOUL. Some, while admitting it to have a real existence, imagine that it sleeps in a state of insensibility from Death to The Judgment-day, when it will awake from its sleep; while others will sooner admit anything than its real existence, maintaining that it is merely a vital power . . . and being unable to exist without body, perishes along with the body, and vanishes away and becomes evanescent till the period when the whole man shall be raised again. We, on the other hand, maintain both that it is a substance, and after the death of the body truly lives, being endued both with sense and understanding. Both these points we undertake to prove by clear passages of Scripture.—Pages 419, 420.

Calvin sets himself to prove two things regarding the human soul: (1) that it "is a substance"; (2) that it continues to live after the body dies, possessing both "sense and understanding." His opponents affirm, on the other hand, (1) that the soul is merely a "vital power" which has no existence apart from the body, or (2) that it has specific identity separate from the body but that it dies with the body, having no continuing sense or understanding. Temporal death, they say, affects the whole man in his entirety so that no part of him is immune to it or continues to live. Calvin's title, *Psychopannychia*, states the doctrine he is affirming and comes from the Greek noun for "soul" and a verb which means "to be awake the whole night through." Calvin affirms that of the soul, and denies that it truly "sleeps."[1]

Calvin's stated authority is Scripture. He appeals to his readers to seek only the Lord's wisdom in determining truth on the subject. In the second preface he urges: "Let us shew ourselves to be such disciples as our Lord wishes to have—poor, empty, and void of self-wisdom; eager to learn but knowing nothing, and even wishing to know nothing but what He has taught; shunning everything of foreign growth as the deadliest poison" (p. 418). No true evangelical could ask for more, and few could express it as beautifully or humbly! Whether or not Calvin meets this high standard himself, we must credit him with pure motives and the noblest intentions. No one is spiritually qualified to take issue with anything he says who cannot profess the same aspirations.

Calvin reissues this appeal to measure all things by the Word of God as he opens the formal argument.

Here let human wisdom give place; for though it thinks much about the soul it perceives no certainty with regard to it. Here, too, let Philosophers give place, since on almost all subjects their regular practice is to put neither end nor measure to their dissensions, while on this subject in particular they quarrel, so that you will scarcely find two of them agreed on any single point! Plato, in some passages, talks nobly of the faculties of the soul, and Aristotle, in discoursing of it, has sur-

---

1. John Calvin touches on the same matter in his *Institutes* 3. 25. 6.

passed all in acuteness.[2] But what the soul is, and whence it is, it is vain to ask at them, or indeed at the whole body of Sages, though they certainly thought more purely and wisely on the subject than some amongst ourselves, who boast that they are the disciples of Christ. — Page 420.

Again we applaud Calvin's ambition that human wisdom should give place to divine revelation. But like all of us, the Reformer was a man of his age, and it is becoming more and more widely recognized that even the greatest men of his age failed to practice all they preached about the authority of Scripture, particularly in the matter of eschatology.[3] The medieval tradition they inherited was very strong. Stamped with the approval of the great Augustine and hallowed by centuries, traditional teaching on the soul was also the authoritative doctrine of the Roman Church.[4] For all Calvin's intention to shun everything "of foreign growth," even Reformed scholars are questioning his success here. Increasingly, the suspicion is being voiced that the potion Calvin so innocently quaffed (and bottled for

---

2. Froom quotes this sentence, without regard to its setting, to implicate Calvin with Platonism. In context, Calvin is actually disparaging philosophy as a reliable source of information on the soul, although whether he lives up to his intentions is quite another question. See LeRoy Edwin Froom, *The Conditionalist Faith of Our Fathers,* 2:122.

3. Quistorp says that "Augustine, as the father of Western mediaeval theology, is also the real founder of the eschatology of the medieval church, in which that of Calvin is in many respects rooted" (Heinrich Quistorp, *Calvin's Doctrine of the Last Things,* p. 193, note 1). Another writer says that in the eschatology of both Luther and Calvin "the basic shape of expectations for man after death remained that propounded by scholastic theology in the thirteenth century" (Milton McC. Gatch, *Death: Meaning and Mortality in Christian Thought and Contemporary Culture,* p. 134). James P. Martin makes the same criticisms in his *The Last Judgment in Protestant Theology from Orthodoxy to Ritschl,* pp. 2-5.

4. The Fifth Lateran Council (1512-1517), among other things, condemned the doctrine that the intellectual soul is mortal or is only one in all men (*A Catholic Dictionary,* p. 282). Luther sarcastically responded that the council's decrees "are, indeed, most appropriate to the papal church, for they make it possible for them to hold fast to human dreams and the doctrines of devils while they trample upon and destroy faith and the teaching of Christ" (Martin Luther, *Luther's Works,* 32:77-78). Burns gives this quote with the comment that while it does not prove that Luther regarded the continuing consciousness of the soul after death "to be a false conclusion of unreliable philosophy," the statement "does suggest that he thought that in this matter Christians were bound not by philosophy or conciliar decree" (Norman T. Burns, *Christian Mortalism from Tyndale to Milton,* pp. 28-29).

Pétavel says that this condemnation of the soul's mortality (making its immortality "official" doctrine) "in the chronological order of official dogmas is immediately before the immaculate conception of the Virgin and Papal infallibility" (Emmanuel Pétavel, *The Problem of Immortality,* p. 255). This statement is obviously prejudicial in purpose. The doctrine of Mary's immaculate conception was officially declared in 1854 by Pope Pius IX in the bull, *Ineffabilis Deus;* the Pope's infallibility became official dogma at the Vatican Council of 1870. The Fifth Lateran Council did define papal authority as over all councils. See *A Catholic Dictionary,* pp. 246, 253, 282.

his children) was actually pressed from the grapes of Plato and Aristotle, slightly distilled and gently flavored by the apologists, then passed down the table by the scholastics who received it from them. Calvin's success at filtering foreign philosophy may be questioned even on grounds of his quotation above. And at least once in the heart of his argument, Calvin's mind seems suddenly to switch tracks, so that a point which begins in Philippians ends (without saying so, perhaps without realizing it) in the *Phaedo*! Calvin writes:

> The body which decays, weighs down the soul, and confining it within an earthly habitation, greatly limits its perceptions. If the body is the prison of the soul, if the earthly habitation is a kind of fetters, what is the state of the soul when set free from this prison, when loosed from these fetters? Is it not restored to itself, and as it were made complete, so that we may truly say, that all which it gains is so much lost to the body? . . . For then the soul, having shaken off all kinds of pollution, is truly spiritual, so that it consents to the will of God, and is no longer subjected to the tyranny of the flesh; thus dwelling in tranquility, with all its thoughts fixed on God. —Pages 443, 444.

The hands are the hands of Calvin, but the voice is that of Plato. If Homer nodded and we all err, surely Calvin, too, might have slipped! Let us look now, though, at the argument of *Psychopannychia* and see how Calvin accomplishes the goals he so forcefully proposes in his beginning.

The Argument Itself

Calvin's first proposition is that the soul is itself a substance separable from the body. Scripture uses "soul" and "spirit" in various ways, Calvin notes, and he enumerates many of them. He does not make any clear distinction between "soul" and "spirit" here but uses the two terms almost interchangeably throughout the discussion (pp. 420-422).

As he often did, Calvin turns to man's creation in the image of God (Gen. 1:26). The *image* cannot be in the flesh, he says; therefore it is found in the "soul" or "spirit" which God breathed into man from His own being. The soul, Calvin concludes, is therefore a substance separate from the flesh or body. "Let that which has sprung of earth be resolved to earth," he offers. "But the soul of man is not of the earth. It was made by the mouth of the Lord, i.e., by his secret power" (p. 423). While Calvin's point could claim a formidable chain of authorities from early times—a point he happily notes—it enjoys far less favor today, even among Reformed theologians—who thereby break away from their illustrious forefather. Few biblical scholars today would wish to argue that the "soul," as a substance separate from the body, was intended by the "image of God" in Genesis or was transmitted to man's body by the breath of God.

Calvin next appeals to scattered phrases such as "the salvation of the soul" or Peter's remark that he must "put off" his "tabernacle" (pp. 425-427). The soul must be a separate substance, Calvin infers, if it can be saved; the real person of Peter must have been his soul if he could speak of "putting off" his body.

Finally, Calvin claims the support of history as he quotes from Polycarp, Milito of Sardis, and Tertullian. The soul's separate identity was well known in antiquity, Calvin says, "and so much did this belief prevail in a better age, that Tertullian places it among the common and primary conceptions of the mind which are commonly apprehended by nature" (p. 427). The immortality of the soul was also a fundamental doctrine of the "natural religion" championed by deists of the eighteenth century and liberals of the nineteenth. Its position in "natural religion" has aroused more suspicion than support among biblical scholars in the twentieth century, however. These include both Calvinists and Catholics, whose houses have chiefly nurtured the doctrine through the centuries.[5]

Calvin defines his second proposition like this:

> THAT THE SOUL, AFTER THE DEATH OF THE BODY, STILL SURVIVES, ENDUED WITH SENSE AND INTELLECT. And it is a mistake to suppose that I am here affirming anything else than THE IMMORTALITY OF THE SOUL.
> —Page 427.

As evidence for the soul's immortality, Calvin turns first to the various texts of Scripture commonly used by those making his point. These include Psalm 31:5, Matthew 10:28, Luke 23:46, John 2:19, John 19:30 and Acts 7:59. He then comments on Christ's preaching to the spirits in prison (1 Pet. 3:19; 4:6) and a few texts from the Apocrypha. Next he treats the rich man and Lazarus. Here there is controversy, he acknowledges, but advises his opponents to "consult

---

5. See quotations and references in chapter 4, note 24.

common sense, if they have any, and they will easily perceive the nature and force of the parable" (p. 432).

Having argued his two propositions at some length, Calvin turns to the common expression "sleep" or "rest," by which Scripture so often describes death. Calvin does not question this picture's frequency in Scripture. Rather, he objects to his opponents' literal interpretation. Most of all, he argues that it does not refer to the "soul," which—as his title indicates—he insists remains "awake" through the long night of death, and not only awake but "endued with sense and intellect." Two quotations illustrate and summarize this discussion.

> *First*, we give the name of "rest" to that which our opponents call "sleep." . . . *Secondly*, by "rest" we understand, not sloth, or lethargy, or anything like the drowsiness of ebriety which they attribute to the soul; but tranquility of conscience and security, which always accompanies faith, but is never complete in all its parts till after death. —Page 432.

> How often does the Spirit make mention of this *peace* in Scripture, and use the figure of "sleeping" and "resting" so familiarly, that the use of no figure is more frequent!—Page 434.

Yet Calvin insists that this is *not sleep*. Here he reaches a high point in his intended use of Scripture. Whether or not one agrees with Calvin's thesis, he must admire the Reformer's respect for the Bible and for the central position Jesus occupies as Calvin reads it. Calvin grounds his argument in the person and work of Jesus in at least two ways.

First, he argues, the divine person of Jesus could not die in the sense Calvin's opponents use the term. For

> though as God he had life in himself, yet when he assumed human nature, he received from the Father the gift of having life in himself in that nature also. These things give us the fullest assurance that Christ could not be extinguished by death, even in respect of his human nature; and that although he was truly and naturally delivered to the death which we all undergo, he, however, always retained the gift of the Father. True! death was a separation of soul and body. But the soul never lost its life. Having been commended to the Father it could not but be safe.—Page 437.

This argument rests on Calvin's first proposition that "the soul of man" is an entity having separable existence from the body. If one grants that premise, he will be moved to consider the weight of this second one. If one questions or denies that this is the biblical meaning of man's "soul," this argument will also be less impressive. Even if one grants the first supposition, he still might wish to question whether a total death including the soul contradicts any biblical teaching about Jesus' divine nature. He might wish to argue that a complete death magnifies the willing humiliation and condescension Jesus underwent on behalf of sinners.[6]

In his second Christological argument, Calvin appeals to the union between the believer and his Lord as a basis for his definition of the "sleep" of death. The believer's life is hid with Christ in God, Calvin notes. Christ is also said to live in the believer (Gal. 2:20; Col. 3:3).

> What remains for our opponents but to cry with open mouth that Christ sleeps in sleeping souls? For if Christ lives in them he also dies in them. If, therefore, the life of Christ is ours, let him who insists that our life is ended by death, pull Christ down from the right hand of the Father and consign him to the second death. If he can die, our death is certain; if he has no end of life, neither can our souls ingrafted in him be ended by any death!—Page 440.

Jesus' promise in John 5:24 speaks to the same point, Calvin says. "If an entrance has been given into eternal life, why do they interrupt it by death?" (p. 440). "Christ is our clothing, and our armour is that which the Apostle puts upon us" (p. 442).

But does not Calvin here forget, in one important respect, the great principle of *sola fide*—"faith alone"? No one can quarrel with Calvin that the believer's union with Christ is important to New Testament writers. But New Testament writers place the greater emphasis on the *resurrection*, not on the *intermediate state*. Union with Christ is important, most of all, because it means that *as surely as He is risen, so will be His people!* His resurrection, already accomplished, is the guarantee of their own. If they truly die in *soul and body*, that does not detract at all from Christ's position in heaven or from His power to raise them in the end. Rather, Paul affirms that if Christ Himself has not been raised, then believers who have "fallen asleep" in Christ have *perished!* (1 Cor. 15:18.) In spite of his diligent concern for

---

6. Calvin himself made this point regarding Christ's dread of death and other such "infirmities," saying: "But all that he voluntarily suffered for us does not in the least detract from his power" (Calvin *Institutes* 2. 16. 12).

redemption's great culmination at Christ's second coming, Calvin frequently turned his gaze from that *eschaton* to the nearer "intermediate state," a fact his friendliest critics have noted more than once.[7]

Calvin also uses allegory to define his definition of "sleep." Jesus makes Jonah's experience a type of his own, Calvin remarks. "But Jonah cried unto the Lord from the belly of the fish, and was heard. That belly is death. He therefore had his soul safe in death, and by means of it could cry unto the Lord" (p. 438). Isaac also becomes a type of Christ. "And why is it that Isaac does not die, but just because Christ has given immortality to that which is peculiar to man—I mean the soul? But the ram, the irrational animal which is given up to death in his stead, is the body. In the binding of Isaac is represented the soul, which shewed only a semblance of dying in the death of Christ" (p. 438).

Calvin also argues from Romans 14:8, 9, which states that Christ is Lord over the dead. "There can only be rule over persons who exist, the exercise of government necessarily implying the existence of subjects," he says (p. 445). The souls of the martyrs under the altar (Rev. 6:10, 11) and the thief on the cross (Luke 23:43) also show that the souls of the dead do not die but merely "rest" in blissful hope and confidence in the Lord's tender care.[8]

His argument ended, Calvin states his conclusion.

> The faith thus sustained by all prophecies, evangelical truth, and Christ himself, let us hold fast—the faith that our spirit is the image of God, like whom it lives, understands, and is eternal. As long as it is in the body it exerts its own powers; but when it quits this prison-house it returns to God, whose presence it meanwhile enjoys while it rests in the hope of a blessed Resurrection. . . . On the other hand, the spirit of the reprobate, while it waits for the dreadful judgment, is tortured by that anticipation. . . . To inquire beyond this is to plunge into the abyss of the Divine mysteries. It is enough to have learned what the Spirit, our best Teacher, deemed it sufficient to have taught.—Pages 449, 450.

Allegories which Scripture does not draw may admirably illustrate one's meaning, but they poorly prove it. In his allegory of Isaac,

---

7. See quotations and references in chapter 5, notes 28-30.

8. Froom discusses the thief on the cross at length, from a mortalist position, in *Conditionalist Faith*, 1:270-285.

Calvin is much nearer Philo of Alexandria than he is Saul of Tarsus —in content as well as style. No one can doubt that Christ is Lord over the dead—but they are still "the *dead*," contrasted in the same scriptural sentence with "the *living*." The biblical hope promises a genuine resurrection at the hands of God, who gives life to the dead. Plato's hope dims by comparison, promising only that one part of man survives the death of his other part by slipping under the door to safety at the last minute. This is especially important in the case of Jesus. To suggest that His soul "showed only a semblance of dying" seems at least to court the error of those ancient Docetists, who skirted the true death of the Son of God by also entering a plea of "appearances."

Calvin stands squarely in the tradition of Augustine, and nowhere more than in his view of man, death and immortality. Although the intermediate state is not our primary concern in the present work, the conception of the immortality of the soul which often underlies it *does* influence one's understanding of biblical texts on final punishment. Because Calvin's strong advocacy of soul-immortality was so influential on Protestant orthodoxy in its views on hell as well as concerning the intermediate state, we are justified in taking a close look at his *Psychopannychia*.

Opposing Arguments Rebutted

In the final section of *Psychopannychia* Calvin sets out to answer five positive arguments his Anabaptist foes have advanced. Besides their obvious relevance to his whole discussion, Calvin's remarks here stand as an informative measure of the changes which have overtaken the Reformed tradition since his day. First we note Calvin's statement of the Anabaptist arguments, then his major lines of rebuttal.

First Argument:

They insist, *first*, that God did not infuse into man any other soul than that which is common to him with the brutes; for Scripture ascribes the name "living soul" to all alike . . . (Gen. 1:21; 7:15).

Calvin begins with a concession but makes his own distinction. "I admit that a *living soul* is repeatedly attributed to the brutes, because they, too, have their own life," he says, "but they live after one way, man after another. Man has a living soul by which he knows and understands; they have a living soul which gives their body sense and motion. Seeing, then, that the soul of man possesses reason, intellect and will—qualities which are not annexed to the body—it is not wonderful that it subsists without the body, and does not perish like the brutes, which have nothing more than their bodily sense" (pp. 450, 451). Calvin then quotes Tertullian and Augustine for additional weight to his point.

Little can be said here except that Calvin consistently thinks and speaks of the soul and its attributes in terms refined by and inherited from pagan philosophy. In this he has been far surpassed by Calvinist scholars today who begin with the Old Testament view of man as God's wholistic creation. *Like* the brutes, he is a "living soul"; *unlike* them, he stands before God in a moral relationship and bears His image.[9]

Second Argument:

Their *second* Objection is That the Soul, though endowed with immortality, lapsed into sin, and thereby sunk and destroyed its immortality. This was the appointed punishment for sin . . . " (citing Gen. 2:17; Ezek. 18:4; Rom. 6:23; p. 453).

Calvin draws an analogy with Satan. Were the same "wages of sin" not paid to the devil as well as to man? he asks. And "yet his death was not such as to prevent him from being always awake, going about seeking whom he may devour, and working in the children of disobedience" (p. 453). Furthermore, will there "be any end to that death" in Satan's case? Certainly not! he answers, proving that the

---

9. Long-held ideas often change slowly even when newer information is accepted. J. O. Buswell, Jr., venerable author of one of my seminary textbooks (*A Systematic Theology of the Christian Religion*), notes that the "image of God" is primarily *moral*, that the word "soul" is generally *relational*, that "spirit" is *functional*, and that "neither the phrase 'breath of life' nor 'living soul,' distinguishes man from the animals"—then adds that "man is created in the image of God and is destined to live forever, whereas the beasts are not created in the image of God, and there is no reason to suppose that they have any kind of immortality" (James Oliver Buswell, Jr., *A Systematic Theology of the Christian Religion*, p. 242). Many writers on the larger spectrum regard this as an unnecessary inconsistency especially common within the Calvinistic heritage.

wicked too, "although dead . . . shall still feel eternal fire and the worm which dieth not" (p. 453).

More important for Calvin, the sinner's banishment to dust applies only to his body, not to his soul, which had a different origin.

> When God pronounces this sentence against man as a sinner, "Dust thou art, and to dust shalt thou return," does he say more than that that which has been taken from the earth shall return to the earth? Whither then does the soul go? . . . We have heard that that which is of the earth is to be returned to the earth. Why do we plunge the spirit of man under the earth? He says not that man will return to the earth, but that he who is dust will return to dust. But dust is that which was formed out of clay. It returns to dust, but not the spirit, which God derived from another quarter, and gave to man.—Pages 453, 454.

As further proof, Calvin offers the words of Job 10:9—"remember how thou hast made me of clay, and will reduce me to dust." This, he declares, "is said of the body." In verse 12 Job speaks of his "life" and "spirit" which God has given and preserved. "That life, then," Calvin distinguishes, "was not to return to dust."

If man's *first* death affects only the body, of what does that second death consist, which indisputably concerns also the soul? Here "death" does not really mean *death*, Calvin argues, as advocates of the traditional view of hell have done before and since. For the body, *death* means returning to its source in the dust. For the soul, *death* is something else entirely.

> THE DEATH OF THE SOUL is very different. It is the judgment of God, the weight of which the wretched soul cannot bear without being wholly confounded, crushed, and desperate, as both the Scriptures teach us, and experience has taught those whom God has once smitten with his terrors.—Page 454.

> As the sublime majesty of God cannot be expressed in words, so neither can his dreadful anger on those on whom he inflicts it be expressed. They see the power of the Almighty actually present; to escape it, they would plunge themselves into a thousand abysses; but escape they cannot. Who does not confess that this is very death?—Page 454.

> Would you know what the death of the soul is? It is to be without God—to be abandoned by God, and left to itself: for if God is its life, it loses its life when it loses the presence of God. . . . [It] is blind . . . is deaf . . . is lame . . . unable to support itself. . . . In short, it performs no one function of life.—Pages 454, 455.

How the soul, so cut off from God and all His benefits, performing "no one function of life," can continue to *exist* is an obvious question. Calvin follows Augustine in his answer: Because the soul is *immortal!* Here Plato "talks nobly," Calvin had said earlier. But did the soul have a beginning? Indeed—it was created out of the breath of God. Here Calvin and Augustine disagree with the Platonists. And must the soul continue forever? Not if God wills to destroy it; for, being its Creator, He is able to do so. But will He *will* to do so? No, answer Calvin and his patristic predecessors. For Scripture speaks of the "undying worm" and the "unquenchable fire."

The Platonic dogma of the immortality of the soul is *not* the final solution for Calvin and Augustine in one sense, for they both say the soul had a beginning and that God could destroy it in the future. Yet both minds are so programmed in the philosophical patterns of their times that the immortality of the soul always colors their thinking. It determines their interpretation of Scripture (the "undying worm" and "unquenchable fire"). Finally—even if indirectly—it leaves its distinctive (though inconsistent) mark on their anthropology and their eschatology.

Calvin closes his answer to the objection that the wages of sin is *death* by looking at the respective works of Adam and Jesus. 'The whole controversy turns on a comparison between Adam and Christ," he says. 'They must necessarily concede to the apostle not only that everything which had fallen in Adam is renewed in Christ, but inasmuch as the power of grace was stronger than that of sin, so much has Christ been more powerful in restoring than Adam in destroying" (p. 456).

Some of Calvin's opponents have argued that man, if he had not fallen, would have been immortal. Calvin sees Christ's work as restoring the immortality once lost. For "sin is absorbed by grace . . . and hence we conclude that the elect now are such as Adam was before his sin; and as he was created inexterminable, so now have those become who have been renewed by Christ to a better nature" (p. 457).

Calvin does not regard the fact that this argument gains immortality only for the elect (a point on which conditionalist writers raise a high banner). He quotes Paul that "death has been swallowed up in victory" (1 Cor. 15:54) but does not note that the first part of the same sentence tells *when* that saying will be fulfilled—namely, at the resurrection-transformation of the righteous. Paul stresses a *sequence* in man's glorification which Calvin here misses altogether. Man is first *mortal*, in the image of Adam; only at the end will he be given *immortality*, in the image of the heavenly Christ. Calvin has much company as he misses this point, including most church fathers from his time to the third century and most traditionalist writers from his time since. To their credit, many of Calvin's staunchest descendants today are surpassing their noble ancestor in this particular exegetical insight.

Third Argument:

Their *third* Argument, is, That those who have died are in many places said to SLEEP.—Page 457.

Calvin does not dispute the frequency of this expression in Scripture; he has already said there is none more frequent (p. 434). But "nothing so mean and abject" can be imagined in regard to Christ's soul, which also truly slept, he declares (p. 458). And as for the wicked man's "sleeping" soul, "it cannot have a worse executioner to torment it than an evil conscience. How can there be sleep amid such anguish?" (p. 458). No, Calvin assures his readers, "All these things were said of a dead body, 'sleeping,' being used as equivalent to lying or being stretched out, as sleepers do when stretched on the ground." Even the ancient pagans prove as much, he says, who name their burial grounds "cemeteries" (Greek: *koimētērion*—"sleeping place"). Since they described in "many monstrous fictions" the affections and feelings of the dead," it is evident that they understood the *body* to "sleep" in the cemetery, not the soul. Having proved to his own satisfaction "that nowhere in Scripture is the term sleep applied to the soul, when it is used to designate death," Calvin moves to answer a fourth Anabaptist argument.

Fourth Argument:

The *fourth* Argument which they urge against us, as their most powerful battering ram, is the passage in which Solomon thus writes in his Ecclesiastes, (Eccles. iii. 18-21,) "I said in my heart of the children of men that God would prove them to shew that they were like the brutes. As man dies, so do they also die. In like manner all things breathe, and man has no more than a beast of burden. All things are subject to vanity, and hasten to one place. Of earth have they been made, and to earth do they equally return. Who knows whether the spirit of the sons of Adam ascends upwards, and the spirit of beasts descends downwards?"—Pages 459, 460.

Solomon himself expels such reasoning, Calvin declares, by terming it all "vanity." With the eyes of flesh this is only "the mind of man, this his reason, this his intellect!" (p. 460). Solomon therefore adds the phrase, "Who knows whether the spirit of the sons of Adam ascends upwards?" By this Solomon tells us, Calvin says, that "human nature . . . comprehends nothing distinctly or clearly by studying, meditating and reasoning" (p. 460). But what "exceeds the capacity and little measure of the human mind, the wisdom of God explains, assuring us that the spirit of the sons of Adam ascends upwards." And on that, Calvin puts his sword back into its sheath and takes a breath before he takes it out a final time to attack his opponents' fifth argument.

Fifth Argument:

Their *fifth* Argument they thunder forth with so much noise, that it might arouse the sleeping out of the deepest sleep. They place their greatest hope of victory in it, and, when they would gloss over matters to their neophytes, place most dependence upon it as a means of shaking their faith and overcoming their good sense. There is one judgment, they say, which will render to all their reward—to the pious, glory—to the impious, hell-fire. No blessedness or misery is fixed before that day.—Page 462.

Calvin does not deny that the judgment leads into the peak of perfection. "It is admitted by all," he says, "that perfection of blessedness or glory nowhere exists except in perfect union with God" (p. 463). But that will be the *perfection* of man's blessedness, not its *beginning*, according to Calvin. "For . . . it does not follow that there is no kingdom because there is not a perfect one; on the contrary, we maintain that that which has been already begun is then to be perfected" (p. 464). Indeed, Calvin stresses, "God in himself cannot reign otherwise than he reigned from the beginning. Of his majesty there cannot be increase or diminution. But it is called 'His kingdom,' because it will be manifested to all" (p. 464).

Paul in Colossians 3:4 "indeed attributes to us a hidden life with Christ our Head beside God; he delays the glory to the day of the glory of Christ, who, as the Head of the Church, will bring his members with him" (p. 465). If Christ lives in our spirit, how can the soul (which Calvin freely interchanges with the spirit) die, even when the body does? "For it were absurd to say we perish, while our life is living!" (p. 466).

Again Calvin strengthens his argument with quotations from the fathers. "The same things have been handed down to us by tradition, from those who have cautiously and reverently handled the mysteries of God" (p. 468). So he cites Tertullian, Irenaeus and Chrysostom (p. 468), Augustine and Bernard (p. 469). The creed also, Calvin notes, confesses the resurrection—"not of the soul, but of the body." And he insists that there is no room here "for the cavil, that by 'body' is meant the whole man. We admit that it sometimes has this signification, but we cannot admit it here, where significant and simple expressions are used, in accommodation to the illiterate" (p. 470).[10]

Last of all, Calvin brings together a broad array of texts his opponents have offered which together declare that man cut off from God is as nothing, passes away, is not, cannot be found, and other such expressions. Calvin dismisses some of these as poetic or the expressions of emotional intensity. Largely, however, he says they are simply "irrelevant," for the language is metaphorical and symbolic. He concludes:

> The expression "not to be," is equivalent to *being estranged from God*. For if He is the only being who truly is, those truly are not who are not in him; because they are perpetually cast down and discarded from his presence. Then . . . they are not said to be *absolutely dead*, but dead only with reference to men. For they are no longer with men, nor in the presence of men, but only with God. Thus (to explain in one word)

---

10. Calvin made the same point in the *Institutes* 3. 25. 6. The statement in the creed originally "sought to call a halt to any abstraction of the resurrection from the total concrete reality of man's existence as created by God. In its best sense it meant that when man is raised . . . nothing of the totality of his created existence is left out by a process of abstraction" (Lynn Boliek, *The Resurrection of the Flesh: A Study of a Confessional Phrase*, p. 141).

Many Reformed scholars now differ with Calvin on this point. Anthony A. Hoekema notes the biblical emphasis on resurrection of the body and says there "is here no hint of the immortality of the soul" (Anthony Hoekema, *The Bible and the Future*, p. 88). Herman Ridderbos says "it is of paramount importance that 'body' in this context, too, does not denote the material 'part' of man, to be distinguished from the 'soul' or the 'spirit,' in the sense of the Greek dichotomy, but rather man's whole mode of existence, before as well as after the resurrection" (Herman N. Ridderbos, *Paul: An Outline of His Theology*, p. 549). Such testimony could be multiplied even more from non-Calvinist scholars.

"not to be" is *not to be visibly existing*, as expressed in the passage of
Jeremiah . . . "Rachel weeping for her children . . . for they are not"
(Jer. xxxi. 15; Matt. ii. 18.)—Pages 486, 487.

In the equation "*a* equals *b*," it is equally true that "*b* equals *a*." We
can therefore take Calvin's explanation that *not to be* is equivalent to
being estranged from God and turn it the other direction. Then *being
estranged from God* is equivalent to *not to be*. Because of Calvin's
belief in the immortality of the soul—which at times he limits to its
consciousness after the death of the body but at other times carries
over beyond the resurrection—he can state the equation the first
direction but not the second. If we come at the matter without this
presupposition of the soul's immortality, beginning instead with
Genesis 1-2, we may ask why the second form of the equation is not
the truly biblical one. For if nothing existed besides the triune God
until God created it, and if nothing can continue to exist without
God's constant provision of being, Calvin's own formula would seem
to demand the end of the sinner's existence in hell. How, we might
ask, could one "perpetually cast down and discarded from [God's]
presence," ultimately and irrevocably "estranged from God," possibly *continue* to exist—even for a moment, far less *forever*? Because
of his philosophical predisposition, Calvin cannot consider this question. But we can—and we must if we are to deal fairly and thoroughly with the material at hand.

Conclusion

Throughout the *Psychopannychia* Calvin never refers to Luther by
name, although Luther more than once expressed views which cor-
responded to those of Calvin's opponents. Far more important to
Calvin than Luther's position was the fact that this was the position
of the Anabaptists, the "nefarious herd" whose name as author of a
dogma was sufficient evidence for its condemnation. The Anabaptist
threat fired Calvin's emotions; his philosophical tradition molded his
mind.

Neither Calvin nor his theological forebears were fully comfortable with the doctrine of the soul's immortality, nor did they ever
state it with great consistency. When speaking of man before God,
Calvin and the church fathers defended the exclusive immortality of

God. Even man's soul had a beginning, and it could perish before the wrath of God, who created it. But when they spoke of final punishment, Calvin and his patristic ancestors took on a different color. The soul is immortal, they argued. That means it can never die. And that, in turn, determined the interpretation they put on the "unquenchable fire" and the "undying worm," phrases they finally explained in light of their philosophy and not of biblical usage and ordinary exegesis. The Platonic doctrine of immortal souls was not a consistently held conviction, therefore, for Calvin (or the fathers). It was more a shadowy ghost. Like some apparition of the nether world, it disappeared whenever they looked for it in the light, only to haunt them again when they expected it least.

Calvin was a man of his age, and his age was the sixteenth century. The immortality of the soul undergirded the structure of ecclesiastical thought. Like a stained-glass window in the cathedral, it had filtered the church's sunlight for 1100 years. And like the bones of a favored saint, the Platonic frame of mind it represented had been officially unquestioned and popularly hallowed most of that time. On this point Calvin bridged the gap between the tradition of Rome and the fresh planting of the Reformation. Tyndale and Luther were not of his mind, but for personal and historical reasons their influence was not determinative.

Calvin, more than any one man, put the Protestant stamp of approval on the traditional understanding of souls and of hell. The power of his influence may be seen in the history of theology since. It would please the Reformer to know that his heirs would cling to the immortality of every soul—evil as well as good—longer and with greater affection than their Lutheran, Baptist and Anglican evangelical brethren. In the light of this history before the great Reformer and also since, Calvin's *Psychopannychia* still deserves our attention.

Selective Bibliography

1. Primary Texts

Bettenson, Henry, ed. *Documents of the Christian Church.* 9th printing. New York: Oxford University Press, 1961.

Bihlmeyer, Karl, ed. *Die Apostolischen Väter.* 2nd ed. Tubingen: J. C. B. Mohr (Paul Siebeck), 1956.

Charles, R. H., ed. *The Apocrypha and Pseudepigrapha of the Old Testament in English.* 2 vols. Oxford: Clarendon Press, 1913.

Dupont-Sommer, André, ed. *The Essene Writings from Qumran.* Translated by G. Vermes from the 2nd rev. ed. of *Les Ecrits esseniens decouverts pres de la mer Morte.* Cleveland and New York: World Publishing Co., 1962.

Goodspeed, Edgar J., trans. *The Apostolic Fathers: An American Translation.* New York: Harper & Brothers, Publishers, 1950.

Holy Bible, The.

King James Version.

New American Standard Bible. La Habra, Calif.: Foundation Press Publications, 1971.

New International Version. Grand Rapids: Zondervan Bible Publishers, 1978.

The New Scofield Reference Bible. New York: Oxford University Press, 1967.

Revised Standard Version. New York: Thomas Nelson & Sons, 1952.

Nestle, Eberhard, ed. *Novum Testamentum Graece.* 24th ed. New York: American Bible Society, 1960.

"Nicodemus, The Gospel of." *The Apocryphal Books of the New Testament.* Philadelphia: David McKay, Publisher, 1901.

Pritchard, James B., ed. *Ancient Near Eastern Texts Relating to the Old Testament*. 3rd ed. Princeton, N.J.: Princeton University Press, 1969.

Rahlfs, Alfred, ed. *Septuaginta*. 7th ed. Stuttgart: Wurttembergische Bibelanstalt, 1966.

Roberts, Alexander, and Donaldson, James, eds. *Ante-Nicene Christian Library: Translations of the Writings of the Fathers Down to A.D. 325*. Edinburgh: T. & T. Clark, 1867–. Reprint. Grand Rapids: William B. Eerdmans Publishing Co., 1950.

Whiston, William, trans. *Josephus: Complete Works*. Reprint. Grand Rapids: Kregel Publications, 1969.

2. Dictionaries and Encyclopedias

Baker's Dictionary of Theology. Everett F. Harrison, editor-in-chief. Grand Rapids: Baker Book House, 1960.

Bible Key Words, vol. 4. "Law," "Wrath." Translated by Dorothea M. Barton and P. R. Ackroyd from Gerhard Kittel's *Theologisches Worterbuch zum Neuen Testament*. New York: Harper & Row, 1962.

Catholic Dictionary, A. Edited by Donald Attwater. 2nd ed. New York: Macmillan Co., 1957.

Dictionary of Christ and the Gospels, A. Edited by James Hastings. 2 vols. New York: Charles Scribner's Sons, 1906.

Dictionary of Christian Biography, Literature, Sects and Doctrines, A. Being a continuation of *The Dictionary of the Bible*, edited by William Smith and Henry Wace. London: John Murray, 1880.

Dictionary of Religion and Ethics, A. Edited by Shailer Mathews and Gerald Birney Smith. London: Waverley Book Co., 1921.

Dictionary of the Bible. Edited by James Hastings. 2nd ed., revised by F. C. Grant and H. H. Rowley. Edinburgh: T. & T. Clark, 1963.

Encyclopaedia Biblica. Edited by T. K. Cheyne and J. Sutherland Black. London: Adam & Charles Black, 1901.

Encyclopaedia of Religion. Edited by Vergilius Ferm. New York: Philosophical Library, 1945.

Encyclopaedia of Religion and Ethics. Edited by James Hastings. New York: Charles Scribner's Sons, 1912.

Encyclopaedia of Religion and Religions. E. Royston Pike. London: George Allen & Unwin, 1951.

Englishman's Critical and Expository Bible Cyclopaedia, The. Compiled and written by A. R. Fausset. London: Hodder & Stoughton, 1878.

International Standard Bible Encyclopaedia, The. Chicago: Howard-Severance Co., 1937.

Interpreter's Dictionary of the Bible, The. New York and Nashville: Abingdon Press, 1962.

Jewish Encyclopedia, The. Isidore Singer, projector and managing editor. New York: Funk & Wagnalls Co., 1925.

New Bible Dictionary, The. Edited by J. D. Douglas. Reprint. Grand Rapids: William B. Eerdmans Publishing Co., 1974.

New Catholic Encyclopedia. Washington, D.C.: Catholic University of America, 1967.

New International Dictionary of New Testament Theology, The. Edited by Colin Brown. Translated from *Theologisches Begriffslexikon zum Neuen Testament.* Grand Rapids: Zondervan Corp., 1975.

New Schaff-Herzog Encyclopedia of Religious Knowledge, The. Edited by Samuel Macauley Jackson. New York and London: Funk & Wagnalls, 1911.

Protestant Dictionary, The. Edited by Charles Sydney Carter and G. E. Alison Weeks. London: Harrison Trust, 1933.

Religious Encyclopaedia, The; or Dictionary of Biblical, Historical, Doctrinal, and Practical Theology. Based on the *Real-Encyklopadie* of Herzog, Plitt and Hauck. Edited by Philip Schaff. 3rd ed. New York: Funk & Wagnalls, 1891.

Theological Dictionary of the New Testament. Edited by Gerhard Kittel and Gerhard Friedrich. Translated by G. W. Bromiley from *Theologisches Worterbuch zum Neuen Testament.* Grand Rapids: William B. Eerdmans Publishing Co., 1964–.

Zondervan Pictoral Bible Dictionary, The. Edited by Merrill C. Tenney. Grand Rapids: Zondervan Publishing House, 1963.

3. *Commentaries*

Barth, Karl. *The Epistle to the Romans.* Translated by Edwyn C. Hoskyns from the 6th German ed. London: Oxford University Press, 1933.

Calvin, John. *Commentary on a Harmony of the Evangelists, Matthew, Mark, and Luke,* vol. 2. Translated from the Latin and collated with the French version by William Pringle. Reprint. Grand Rapids: William B. Eerdmans Publishing Co., 1957.

———. *Commentary on the Book of the Prophet Isaiah,* vol. 4. Reprint. Grand Rapids: William B. Eerdmans Publishing Co., 1948.

Delitzsch, Franz. *Biblical Commentary on the Prophecies of Isaiah*, vol. 1. Grand Rapids: William B. Eerdmans Publishing Co., 1965.

————. *Commentary on the Epistle to the Hebrews*. Translated by Thomas L. Kingsbury. Grand Rapids: William B. Eerdmans Publishing Co., 1952.

Eller, Vernard. *The Most Revealing Book of the Bible: Making Sense Out of Revelation*. Grand Rapids: William B. Eerdmans Publishing Co., 1974.

Fudge, Edward. *Our Man in Heaven: An Exposition of the Epistle to the Hebrews*. Grand Rapids: Baker Book House, 1974.

Hailey, Homer. *A Commentary on the Minor Prophets.* Grand Rapids: Baker Book House, 1972.

————. *Revelation: An Introduction and Commentary*. Baker Book House, 1979.

Hendriksen, William. *The Gospel According to John*. Grand Rapids: Baker Book House, 1967.

————. *More Than Conquerors: An Interpretation of the Book of Revelation*. Grand Rapids: Baker Book House, 1960.

Hunter, Archibald M. *The Gospel According to St. Paul*. Philadelphia: Westminster Press, 1966.

Keil, C. F. *Biblical Commentary on the Prophecies of Ezekiel*, vol. 1. Grand Rapids: William B. Eerdmans Publishing Co., n.d.

Keil, C. F., and Delitzsch, Franz. *Biblical Commentary on the Old Testament*. Reprint. Grand Rapids: William B. Eerdmans Publishing Co., n.d.

Lenski, R. C. H. *The Interpretation of the Epistles of St. Peter, St. John and St. Jude*. Columbus, Ohio: Wartburg Press, 1945.

Lilje, Hanns. *The Last Book of the Bible*. Translated by Olive Wyon from the German. Philadelphia: Muhlenberg Press, 1957.

Luther, Martin. *Luther's Works*. Vol. 17, *Lectures on Isaiah (Chapters 40-66)*. Edited by Hilton C. Oswald. St. Louis: Concordia Publishing House, 1972.

New International Commentary on the New Testament, The. F. F. Bruce, general editor. Grand Rapids: William B. Eerdmans Publishing Co.

The Book of Revelation. Robert H. Mounce. 1977.

The Epistle of Paul to the Churches of Galatia. Herman N. Ridderbos. 1953.

The Epistle to the Romans. John Murray. 1959.

The First and Second Epistles to the Thessalonians. Leon Morris. 1959.

The Gospel According to Mark. William L. Lane. 1974.

The Gospel of Luke. Norval Geldenhuys. 1951.

Nicoll, W. Robertson, ed. *The Expositor's Greek Testament*. Grand Rapids: William B. Eerdmans Publishing Co., 1961.

Pink, Arthur W. *An Exposition of Hebrews*. Grand Rapids: Baker Book House, 1954.

Strack, Hermann L., and Billerbeck, Paul. *Kommentar zum Neuen Testament aus Talmud und Midrasch*. Munchen: C. H. Beck'sche Verlagsbuchhandlung, Oskar Beck, 1928. Excursus in volume 2 on Sheol, Gehenna and the Garden of Eden.

4. *Journals and Periodicals*

Adams, Marilyn McCord. "Hell and the God of Justice." *Religious Studies* 2, no. 4 (December 1975): 433-447.

Badham, Paul. "Recent Thinking on Christian Beliefs: The Future Life." *Expository Times*, April 1977, pp. 197-202.

Barbour, R. S. "Gethsemane in the Tradition of the Passion." *New Testament Studies* 16, no. 3 (April 1970): 231-251.

Barrett, C. K. "New Testament Eschatology: Part I," *Scottish Journal of Theology* 6, no. 2 (June 1953): 136-155.

————. "New Testament Eschatology: Part II—The Gospels." *Scottish Journal of Theology* 6, no. 3 (September 1953): 225-243.

Beardslee, William E. "New Testament Apocalyptic in Recent Interpretation." *Interpretation* 25, no. 4 (October 1971): 419-435.

Beasley-Murray, G. R. "The Contribution of the Book of Revelation to the Christian Belief in Immortality." *Scottish Journal of Theology* 27, no. 1 (February 1974): 76-93.

————. "New Testament Apocalyptic—A Christological Eschatology." *Review and Expositor* 72, no. 3 (Summer 1975): 317-330.

Berkemeyer, William C. "The Eschatological Dilemma." *Lutheran Quarterly* 7, no. 3 (August 1955): 233-239.

Bligh, P. H. "Eternal Fire, Eternal Punishment, Eternal Life (Mt 25:41, 46)." *Expository Times* 83, no. 1 (October 1971): 9-11.

Bloesch, Donald G. "Crisis in Biblical Authority." *Theology Today* 35, no. 4 (January 1979): 455-462.

Brandon, S. G. F. "Life after Death: The After-Life in Ancient Egyptian Faith and Practice." *Expository Times*, April 1965, pp. 217-220.

Brinsmead, Robert D. "Man," parts 1-3. *Verdict*, August, September, December 1978.

Bruce, F. F. "Eschatology." *London Quarterly and Holborn Review*, April 1958, pp. 99-103.

———. "Paul on Immortality." *Scottish Journal of Theology* 24, no. 4 (November 1971): 457-472.

———. "A Reappraisal of Jewish Apocalyptic Literature." *Review and Expositor* 72, no. 3 (Summer 1975): 305-315.

Bultmann, Rudolph. "History and Eschatology in the New Testament." *New Testament Studies* 1, no. 1 (September 1954): 5-16.

Burns, John Barclay. "The Mythology of Death in the Old Testament." *Scottish Journal of Theology*, no. 3 (August 1973): 327-340.

Cupitt, Don. "The Language of Eschatology: F. D. Maurice's Treatment of Heaven and Hell." *Anglican Theological Review* 54, no. 4 (October 1972): 305-317.

Davies, J. G. "Factors Leading to the Emergence of Belief in the Resurrection of the Flesh." *Journal of Theological Studies* 23 (1972): 448-455.

Dockx, Pére S. "Man's Eschatological Condition." *Scottish Journal of Theology* 27, no. 1 (February 1974): 20-34.

Dunning, T. G. "What Has Become of Heaven and Hell?" *Baptist Quarterly* 20, no. 8 (October 1964): 352-361.

Ebeling, Gerhard. "The Meaning of 'Biblical Theology.'" *Journal of Theological Studies*, New Series 6, no. 2 (October 1955): 210-225.

Fairhurst, Alan M. "The Problem Posed by the Severe Sayings Attributed to Jesus in the Synoptic Gospels." *Scottish Journal of Theology* 23 (1970): 77-91.

Forestell, J. Terence. "Christian Revelation and the Resurrection of the Wicked." *Catholic Biblical Quarterly* 19, no. 2 (April 1957): 165-189.

Fudge, Edward. "The Eschatology of Ignatius of Antioch: Christocentric and Historical." *Journal of the Evangelical Theological Society* 15, no. 4 (Fall 1972): 231-237.

———. "Putting Hell in Its Place." *Christianity Today*, 6 August 1976, pp. 14-17.

Glasson, T. F. "Human Destiny: Has Christian Teaching Changed?" *Modern Churchman* 12, no. 4 (July 1969): 284-298.

Goen, C. C. "The Modern Discussion of Eschatology." *Review and Expositor* 57, no. 2 (April 1960): 107-125.

Gundry, D. W. "The Ghost in the Machine and the Body of the Resurrection." *Scottish Journal of Theology* 18, no. 2 (June 1965): 164-169.

Hamilton, Neill Q. "The Last Things in the Last Decade: The Significance of Recent Study in the Field of Eschatology." *Interpretation* 14, no. 2 (April 1960): 131-142.

Harris, Murray. "Resurrection and Immortality: Eight Theses." *Themelios* 1, no. 2 (Spring 1976): 50-55.

Heinitz, Kenneth. "Eschatology in the Teaching of Jesus." *Concordia Theological Monthly* 41, no. 8 (September 1970): 451-461.

Heller, James J. "The Resurrection of Man." *Theology Today* 15, no. 2 (July 1958): 217-229.

Herhold, Robert M. "Kübler-Ross and Life after Death." *Christian Century*, 14 April 1976, pp. 363-364.

Hodgson, Leonard. "Life after Death: The Philosophers Plato and Kant." *Expository Times*, January 1965, pp. 107-109.

Hofmann, Hans. "Immortality or Life." *Theology Today* 15, no. 2 (July 1958): 230-245.

Hooke, S. H. "Life after Death: Israel and the After-Life." *Expository Times*, May 1965, pp. 236-239.

————. "Life after Death: The Extra-Canonical Literature." *Expository Times*, June 1965, pp. 273-276.

Hoyles, J. Arthur. "The Punishment of the Wicked after Death." *London Quarterly and Holborn Review*, April 1957, pp. 118-123.

Inbody, Tyron. "Process Theology and Personal Survival." *Iliff Review* 31, no. 2 (Spring 1974): 31-42.

Jeremias, Joachim. " 'Flesh and Blood Cannot Inherit the Kingdom of God' (I Cor. xv. 50)." *New Testament Studies* 2, no. 3 (February 1956): 151-159.

Kee, Howard C. "The Development of Eschatology in the New Testament." *Journal of Bible and Religion* 20, no. 3 (July 1952): 187-193.

Kepple, Robert J. "The Hope of Israel, the Resurrection of the Dead, and Jesus: A Study of Their Relationship in Acts with Particular Regard to the Understanding of Paul's Trial Defense." *Journal of the Evangelical Theological Society* 20, no. 3 (September 1977): 231-242.

King, L. A. "Hell, the Painful Refuge." *Eternity*, January 1979, pp. 27-29, 39.

Knight, G. A. F. "Eschatology in the Old Testament." *Scottish Journal of Theology* 4, no. 4 (December 1951): 355-362.

Linton, Calvin D. "The Sorrows of Hell." *Christianity Today* 16 (19 November 1971): 12-14.

Logan, Norman A. "The Old Testament and a Future Life." *Scottish Journal of Theology* 6, no. 2 (June 1953): 165-172.

Lotz, David W. "Heaven and Hell in the Christian Tradition." *Religion in Life* 48 (Spring 1979).

Macquarrie, John. "Death and Eternal Life." *Expository Times* 89 (November 1977): 46-48.

Marshall, I. Howard. "Slippery Words: Eschatology." *Expository Times*, June 1978, pp. 264-269.

Martin, W. B. J. "Life after Death: The Poets—Victorian and Modern." *Expository Times*, February 1965, pp. 140-143.

Mattill, A. J., Jr. "'The Way of Tribulation.'" *Journal of Biblical Literature* 98, no. 4 (December 1979): 531-546.

Mitton, C. Leslie. "Life after Death: The After-Life in the New Testament." *Expository Times*, August 1965, pp. 332-337.

———. "Present Justification and Final Judgment: A Discussion of the Parable of the Sheep and the Goats." *Expository Times* 68, no. 2 (November 1956): 46-50.

Moltmann, Jürgen. "Descent into Hell." *Duke Divinity School Review* 33, no. 2 (Spring 1968): 115-119.

Motyer, J. A. "The Final State: Heaven and Hell" ("Basic Christian Doctrines: 43"). *Christianity Today*, 28 September 1962, pp. 30-31.

Müller, Gotthold. "Ungeheuerliche Ontologie: Erwagungen zur christlichen Lehre uber Holle und Allversohnung." *Evangelische Theologie*, no. 3 (1974): 256-275.

Nicole, Roger. "The Punishment of the Wicked." *Christianity Today*, 9 June 1958, pp. 13-15.

Noll, Mark. "Who Sets the Stage for Understanding Scripture?" *Christianity Today*, 23 May 1980, pp. 14-18.

O'Laughlin, Michael. "Scripture and Tradition." *Again* 2, no. 3 (July-September 1979): 14-15.

Peel, Malcolm L. "Gnostic Eschatology and the New Testament." *Novum Testamentum* 12, no. 2 (April 1970): 141-165.

Rex, H. H. "Immortality of the Soul, or Resurrection of the Dead, or What?" *Reformed Theological Review* 17, no. 3 (October 1958): 73-82.

Ridenhour, Thomas E. "Immortality and Resurrection in the Old Testament." *Dialog* 15 (Spring 1976): 104-109.

Roberts, J. W. "Some Observations on the Meaning of 'Eternal Life' in the Gospel of John." *Restoration Quarterly* 7, no. 4 (Fourth Quarter, 1963): 186-193.

Scharlemann, Martin H. "He Descended into Hell." *Concordia Theological Monthly* 27, no. 2 (February 1956): 81-94.

Scharlemann, Robert P. "Afterlife and the Eternal as a Question." *Dialog* 15, no. 2 (Spring 1976): 118-122.

Scott, J. Julius. "Some Problems in Hermeneutics for Contemporary Evangelicals." *Journal of the Evangelical Theological Society* 22, no. 1 (March 1979): 67-78.

Selwyn, E. G. "Image, Fact and Faith." *New Testament Studies* 1, no. 4 (May 1955): 235-247.

Shutt, R. J. H. "The New Testament Doctrine of the Hereafter: Universalism or Conditional Immortality." *Expository Times* 67, no. 5 (February 1956): 131-135.

Smith, Gary V. "Structure and Purpose in Genesis 1-11." *Journal of the Evangelical Theological Society* 20, no. 4 (December 1977): 307-320.

Snaith, Norman. "Justice and Immortality." *Scottish Journal of Theology* 17, no. 3 (September 1964): 309-324.

Strawson, William. "Life after Death: The Future Life in Contemporary Theology." *Expository Times*, October 1965, pp. 9-13.

Suchocki, Marjorie. "The Question of Immortality." *Journal of Religion* 57, no. 3 (July 1977): 288-306.

Sutherland, Stewart R. "What Happens after Death?" *Scottish Journal of Theology* 22, no. 4 (December 1969): 404-418.

Taylor, Vincent. "Life after Death: The Modern Situation." *Expository Times* 76, no. 3 (December 1964): 76-78.

Thomson, J. G. S. "Death and Immortality" ("Basic Christian Doctrines: 40"). *Christianity Today*, 3 August 1962, pp. 18-19.

Tupper, E. Frank. "The Revival of Apocalyptic in Biblical and Theological Studies." *Review and Expositor* 72, no. 3 (Summer 1975): 279-304.

Vawter, Bruce. "Intimations of Immortality and the Old Testament." *Journal of Biblical Literature* 91, no. 2 (June 1972): 158-171.

Wahle, Hedwig. "Die Lehren des rabbinischen Judentums über das Leben nach dem Tod." *Kairos: Zeitschrift fur Religionswissenschaft und Theologie* 14, no. 4 (Jahrgang 1972): 291-309.

Whiteley, D. E. H. "Liberal Christianity in the New Testament." *Modern Churchman* 13, no. 1 (October 1969): 16-27.

Widengren, G. "Life after Death: Eschatological Ideas in Indian and Iranian Religion." *Expository Times*, September 1965, pp. 364-367.

Wilken, Robert L. "The Immortality of the Soul and Christian Hope." *Dialog* 15, no. 2 (Spring 1976): 110-117.

Wolfson, Harry A. "Notes on Patristic Philosophy." *Harvard Theological Review* 57, no. 2 (April 1964): 119-132.

Zens, Jon. "Do the Flames Ever Stop in Hell?" *Free Grace Broadcaster*, March-April 1978, pp. 1-8.

5. Books Directly Related to the Subject

Abbot, Ezra. "The Literature of the Doctrine of a Future Life." Appendix to *The Destiny of the Soul: A Critical History of the Doctrine of a Future Life*, by William R. Alger. 10th ed. Boston: Roberts Brothers, 1880. Reprint. New York: Greenwood Press, Publishers, 1968.

Abbott, Lyman, ed. *That Unknown Country*. Springfield, Mass.: C. A. Nichols & Co., Publishers, 1891.

Alger, William Rounseville. *The Destiny of the Soul: A Critical History of the Doctrine of a Future Life*. 2 vols. 10th ed. Boston: Roberts Brothers, 1880. Reprint. New York: Greenwood Press, Publishers, 1968.

Atkinson, Basil F. C. *Life and Immortality: An Examination of the Nature and Meaning of Life and Death as They Are Revealed in the Scriptures*. Taunton, Great Britain: Phoenix Press (E. Goodman & Son), n.d.

Badham, Paul. *Christian Beliefs about Life after Death*. London: Macmillan Press, 1976.

Baird, Joseph Arthur. *The Justice of God in the Teaching of Jesus*. London: SCM Press, 1963.

Beecher, Edward. *History of Opinions on the Scriptural Doctrine of Retribution*. New York: D. Appleton & Co., 1878.

Belcastro, Joe. "The Permanent Validity of the Idea of Hell." S.T.M. thesis, Oberlin (Ohio) College, 1937.

Berkouwer, G. C. *The Return of Christ*. Translated by James Van Oosterom from the Dutch *De Wederkomst van Christus*. Grand Rapids: William B. Eerdmans Publishing Co., 1972. See especially chapter, "Apocatastasis?" pp. 387-423.

Blenkinsopp, Joseph. "Theological Synthesis and Hermeneutical Conclusions." *Immortality and Resurrection.* Edited by Pierre Benoit and Roland Murphy. London: Herder & Herder, 1970.

Boatman, Russell E. *Beyond Death: What the Bible Says about the Hereafter.* Author (2245 N. Elizabeth, Florissant, Mo. 63033), 1980.

Braun, Jon E. *Whatever Happened to Hell?* Nashville: Thomas Nelson Publishers, 1979.

Buis, Harry. *The Doctrine of Eternal Punishment.* Philadelphia: Presbyterian & Reformed Publishing Co., 1957.

Burns, Norman T. *Christian Mortalism from Tyndale to Milton.* Cambridge, Mass.: Harvard University Press, 1972.

Charles, R. H. *A Critical History of the Doctrine of a Future Life.* 2nd ed. London: Adam & Charles Black, 1913.

Constable, Henry. *Duration and Nature of Future Punishment.* 6th ed. London: Edward Hobbs, 1886.

Cullmann, Oscar. *Immortality of the Soul or Resurrection of the Dead? The Witness of the New Testament.* London: Epworth Press, 1958.

Dubarle, André-Marie. "Belief in Immortality in the Old Testament and Judaism." *Immortality and Resurrection.* Edited by Pierre Benoit and Roland Murphy. London: Herder & Herder, 1970.

Dunn, James D. G. "Paul's Understanding of the Death of Jesus." Chapter 8 in *Reconciliation and Hope: New Testament Essays on Atonement and Eschatology,* presented to L. L. Morris on his 60th birthday. Edited by Robert Banks. Grand Rapids: William B. Eerdmans Publishing Co., 1974, pp. 125-141.

Edwards, Jonathan. *The Works of Jonathan Edwards.* Revised by Edward Hickman. 2 vols. Carlisle, Penn.: Banner of Truth Trust. See especially "Concerning the Endless Punishment of Those Who Die Impenitent," vol. 2, pp. 515-525.

Farrar, Frederick W. *Eternal Hope.* London and New York: Macmillan & Co., 1879. Five sermons preached in Westminster Abbey, November-December, 1877.

————. *Mercy and Judgment: A Few Last Words on Christian Eschatology with Reference to Dr. Pusey's "What Is of Faith?"* London: Macmillan & Co., 1881.

Froom, LeRoy Edwin. *The Conditionalist Faith of Our Fathers.* 2 vols. Washington, D.C.: Review & Herald Publishing Assn., 1965.

Gatch, Milton McC. *Death: Meaning and Mortality in Christian Thought and Contemporary Culture.* New York: Seabury Press, 1969.

Guillebaud, Harold E. *The Righteous Judge: A Study of the Biblical Doctrine of Everlasting Punishment*. Taunton, Great Britain: Phoenix Press, n.d.

Hanhart, Karel. *The Intermediate State in the New Testament*. Doctoral dissertation at the University of Amsterdam. Franeker: T. Wever, September 1966.

Harris, Murray J. "Paul's View of Death." *New Dimensions in New Testament Study*. Edited by Richard N. Longenecker and Merrill C. Tenney. Grand Rapids: Zondervan Publishing House, 1974, pp. 317-328.

Hick, John. *Death and Eternal Life*. London: Collins, 1976.

Hoekema, Anthony A. *The Bible and the Future*. Grand Rapids: William B. Eerdmans Publishing Co., 1979. See especially chapter 8, "Immortality," pp. 86-91; and chapter 19, "Eternal Punishment," pp. 265-273.

Holwerda, David E. "Eschatology and History: A Look at Calvin's Eschatological Vision." *Exploring the Heritage of John Calvin*. Edited by David E. Holwerda. Grand Rapids: Baker Book House, 1976, pp. 110-139.

Kennedy, H. A. A. *St. Paul's Conceptions of the Last Things*. 2nd ed. London: Hodder & Stoughton, 1904.

Ladd, George Eldon. *The Pattern of New Testament Truth*. Grand Rapids: William B. Eerdmans Publishing Co., 1968. See especially chapter, "The Background of the Pattern," for a contrast between what Ladd calls the "Greek" and the "Hebrew" views of man.

MacCulloch, J. A. *The Harrowing of Hell*. Edinburgh: T. & T. Clark, 1930.

Martin, James P. *The Last Judgment in Protestant Theology from Orthodoxy to Ritschl*. Grand Rapids: William B. Eerdmans Publishing Co., 1963.

Martin-Achard, Robert. *From Death to Life: A Study of the Development of the Doctrine of the Resurrection in the Old Testament*. Edinburgh and London: Oliver & Boyd, 1960.

Morris, Leon. *The Biblical Doctrine of Judgment*. London: Tyndale Press, 1960.

———. *The Cross in the New Testament*. Grand Rapids: William B. Eerdmans Publishing Co., 1965.

Nickelsburg, George W. E., Jr. *Resurrection, Immortality, and Eternal Life in Intertestamental Judaism*. Harvard Theological Studies, no. 26. Cambridge, Mass.: Harvard University Press, 1972.

Norris, R. A., Jr. *Manhood and Christ: A Study in the Christology of Theodore of Mopsuestia*. London: Oxford University Press, 1963.

Pelikan, Jaroslav. *The Shape of Death: Life, Death, and Immortality in the Early Fathers*. New York: Abingdon Press, 1961.

Pétavel, Emmanuel. *The Problem of Immortality*. Translated by Frederick Ash Freer from the French. London: Elliot Stock, 1892.

Pilcher, Charles Venn. *The Hereafter in Jewish and Christian Thought, with Special Reference to the Doctrine of Resurrection*. Moorhouse Lectures, 1938. London: Society for Promoting Christian Knowledge, 1940.

Pink, Arthur W. *Eternal Punishment*. Swengel, Pa.: Reiner Publications, n.d.

Pusey, Edward Bouverie. *What Is of Faith as to Everlasting Punishment? In Reply to Dr. Farrar's Challenge in His "Eternal Hope," 1879*. Oxford: James Parker & Co., 1880.

Quistorp, Heinrich. *Calvin's Doctrine of the Last Things*. Translated by Harold Knight. London: Lutterworth Press, 1955.

Reichenbach, Bruce R. *Is Man the Phoenix?* Christian University Press (subsidiary of Christian College Consortium and William B. Eerdmans Publishing Co.), 1978.

Ridderbos, Herman N. *Paul: An Outline of His Theology*. Translated by John Richard DeWitt from the Dutch. Grand Rapids: William B. Eerdmans Publishing Co., 1975.

Robinson, H. Wheeler. *The Christian Doctrine of Man*. Edinburgh: T. & T. Clark, 1911.

Rowell, Geoffrey. *Hell and the Victorians: A Study of the Nineteenth-Century Theological Controversies concerning Eternal Punishment and the Future Life*. Oxford: Clarendon Press, 1974.

Salmond, Steward D. F. *The Christian Doctrine of Immortality*. Edinburgh: T. & T. Clark, 1895.

Schwartz, Hans. "Luther's Understanding of Heaven and Hell." *Interpreting Luther's Legacy*. Edited by F. W. Meuser and S. D. Schneider. Minneapolis: Augsburg Publishing House, 1969, pp. 83-94.

Shedd, William G. T. *The Doctrine of Endless Punishment*. New York: Charles Scribner's Sons, 1886.

Strauss, Lehman. *Life after Death: What the Bible Really Teaches*. Abridged from *We Live Forever*, 1947. Westchester, Ill.: Good News Publishers, 1979.

Strawson, William. *Jesus and the Future Life: A Study in the Synoptic Gospels*. Philadelphia: Westminster Press (London: Epworth Press), 1959.

Studer, Gerald C. *After Death, What?* Scottdale, Pa.: Herald Press, 1976.

Swete, Henry Barclay. *The Life of the World to Come.* New York: Macmillan Co. (London: Society for Promoting Christian Knowledge), 1917.

Thielicke, Helmut. *Death and Life.* Translated by Edward H. Schroeder from *Tod und Leben: Studien zur Christlichen Anthropologie* (Tubingen, 1946). Philadelphia: Fortress Press, 1970.

Torrance, T. F. *Calvin's Doctrine of Man.* London: Lutterworth Press, 1949.

————. *Space, Time and Resurrection.* Grand Rapids: William B. Eerdmans Publishing Co., 1976.

The Truth about Hell. Anonymous. East Rutherford, N.J.: Dawn Bible Students Assn., n.d.

Vos, Geerhardus. *The Pauline Eschatology.* Reprint. Grand Rapids: William B. Eerdmans Publishing Co., 1961.

Walker, D. P. *The Decline of Hell: Seventeenth-Century Discussions of Eternal Torment.* Chicago: University of Chicago Press, 1964.

Watts, Isaac. *The Ruine and Recovery of Mankind . . .* London: James Brackstone, 1742.

————. *The World to Come; or Discourses on the Joys or Sorrows of Departed Souls at Death, and the Glory or Terror of the Resurrection; to Which Is Affixed an Essay towards the Proof of a Separate State of Souls after Death: Wherein, after Some Proof of the Happiness of Heaven and a Preparation for It, There Follows, a Rational and Scriptural Account of the Punishments in Hell, and a Proof of Their Eternal Duration, with a Plain Answer to All the Most Plausible Objections.* Leeds: Davies & Booth, 1918.

Wenham, John W. *The Goodness of God.* Downer's Grove, Ill.: Inter-Varsity Press, 1974. See especially chapter 2, "Hell," pp. 27-41.

Westcott, Brooke Foss. *The Gospel of the Resurrection: Thoughts on Its Relation to Reason and History.* 4th ed. London: Macmillan & Co., 1879.

Whateley, Richard. *A View of the Scripture Revelations concerning a Future State.* 4th ed. Philadelphia: Smith, English & Co., 1873.

White, Edward. *Life in Christ: A Study of the Scripture Doctrine on the Nature of Man, the Object of the Divine Incarnation, and the Conditions of Human Immortality.* 3rd ed. London: Elliot Stock, 1878.

White, Ellen G. *The Great Controversy between Christ and Satan.* Reprint. Mountain View, Calif.: Pacific Press Publishing Assn., 1950.

Wolff, Hans Walter. *Anthropology of the Old Testament*. Translated by Margaret Kohl from *Anthropologie des Alten Testaments* (Munich, 1973). Philadelphia: Fortress Press, 1974.

Wolfson, Harry A. "Immortality and Resurrection in the Philosophy of the Church Fathers." *Immortality and Resurrection*. Edited by Krister Stendahl. New York: Macmillan Co., 1965, pp. 54-96. Reprint from Wolfson's *Religious Philosophy: A Group of Essays*, 1961, first published in *Harvard Divinity School Bulletin* 22 (1956-1957): 5-40.

Woodson, Leslie H. *Hell and Salvation*. Old Tappan, N.J.: Fleming H. Revell Co., 1973.

6. Books Indirectly Related to the Subject

Alexander, David, and Alexander, Pat, eds. *Eerdmans' Handbook to the Bible*. Grand Rapids: William B. Eerdmans Publishing Co., 1973.

Arndt, William F., and Gingrich, F. Wilbur, trs. *A Greek-English Lexicon of the New Testament and Other Early Christian Literature*. Translated and adapted from Walter Bauer's *Griechisch-Deutsches Worterbuch zu den Schriften des Neuen Testaments und der ubrigen urchristlichen Literatur*, 4th revised and augmented ed., 1952. Chicago: University of Chicago Press, 1957.

Baker, Charles F. *A Dispensational Theology*. Grand Rapids: Grace Bible College Publications, 1971.

Bardy, Abbé. *The Christian Latin Literature of the First Six Centuries*. Translated by Mary Reginald. St. Louis: B. Herder Book Co., 1930.

Barth, Markus. *Justification: Pauline Texts Interpreted in the Light of the Old and New Testaments*. Translated by A. M. Woodruff III. Grand Rapids: William B. Eerdmans Publishing Co., 1971.

Beasley-Murray, G. R. *Christ Is Alive!* London: Lutterworth Press, 1947.

Berkhof, Louis. *Principles of Biblical Interpretation*. Grand Rapids: Baker Book House, 1950.

————. *Reformed Dogmatics*, vol. 2. Grand Rapids: William B. Eerdmans Publishing Co., 1932.

————. *Vicarious Atonement through Christ*. Grand Rapids: William B. Eerdmans Publishing Co., 1936.

Bernard, Thomas Dehany. *The Progress of Doctrine in the New Testament*. New York: American Tract Society, 1907.

Bloesch, Donald G. *Essentials of Evangelical Theology*, vol. 2. San Francisco: Harper & Row, 1979.

Boettner, Loraine. *The Person of Christ*. Grand Rapids: William B. Eerdmans Publishing Co., 1943.

Boliek, Lynn. *The Resurrection of the Flesh: A Study of a Confessional Phrase*. Grand Rapids: William B. Eerdmans Publishing Co., 1962.

Brinsmead, Robert D. *Covenant*. Fallbrook, Calif.: Verdict Publications, 1979.

———. *The Pattern of Redemptive History*. Fallbrook, Calif.: Verdict Publications, 1979.

Bruce, F. F. *Answers to Questions*. Grand Rapids: Zondervan Publishing Co., 1973.

———. *Paul: Apostle of the Heart Set Free*. Grand Rapids: William B. Eerdmans Publishing Co., 1977.

Buswell, James Oliver, Jr. *A Systematic Theology of the Christian Religion*. 1-vol. ed., 3rd printing. Grand Rapids: Zondervan Publishing House, 1969.

Calvin, John. *Institutes of the Christian Religion*. Edited by John T. McNeill. Translated by Ford Lewis Battles. The Library of Christian Classics, vols. 20, 21. Philadelphia: Westminster Press, 1960.

Carnell, Edward John. *An Introduction to Christian Apologetics*. Grand Rapids: William B. Eerdmans Publishing Co., 1948.

Charlesworth, James H. *The Pseudepigrapha and Modern Research*. Septuagint and Cognate Studies, no. 7. Missoula, Mont.: Scholars Press, 1976.

Conzelmann, Hans. *An Outline of the Theology of the New Testament*. Translated by John Bowden from the 2nd ed. of *Grundriss der Theologie des Neuen Testaments* (Munich, 1968). New York: Harper & Row, Publishers, 1969.

Cross, F. L. *The Early Christian Fathers*. London: Gerald Duckworth & Co., 1960.

Dana, H. E., and Mantey, Julius R. *A Manual Grammar of the Greek New Testament*. 25th printing. New York: Macmillan Co., 1960.

Davies, W. D. *The Setting of the Sermon on the Mount*. London: Cambridge University Press, 1963.

Davis, Arthur Paul. *Isaac Watts: His Life and Works*. London: Independent Press, 1943.

Dowley, Tim, ed. *Eerdmans' Handbook to the History of Christianity*. Grand Rapids: William B. Eerdmans Publishing Co., 1977.

Dupont-Sommer, André. *The Dead Sea Scrolls*. Translated by E. Margaret Rowley. Oxford: Basil Blackwell, 1952.

Ferguson, Everett. *Early Christians Speak: Faith and Life in the First Three Centuries*. Austin, Tex.: Sweet Publishing Co., 1971.

France, R. T. "Exegesis in Practice: Two Samples." *New Testament Interpretation: Essays on Principles and Methods*. Edited by I. Howard Marshall. Grand Rapids: William B. Eerdmans Publishing Co., 1978.

Fudge, Edward. *One Life, Death and Judgment*. Athens, Ala.: Edward Fudge—Publishing, 1978.

Geisler, Norman L. *Philosophy of Religion*. Grand Rapids: Zondervan Publishing House, 1974.

Hasel, Gerhard F. *New Testament Theology: Basic Issues in the Current Debate*. Grand Rapids: William B. Eerdmans Publishing Co., 1978.

Henry, Carl F. H., ed. *Revelation and the Bible*. Grand Rapids: Baker Book House, 1958.

Hodge, Archibald Alexander. *Outlines of Theology*. Rewritten and enlarged. Grand Rapids: William B. Eerdmans Publishing Co., 1957.

Hodge, Charles. *Systematic Theology*, vol. 3. New York: Charles Scribner's & Co., 1884.

Hunter, Archibald M. *Interpreting the Parables*. London: SCM Press, 1960.

———. *The Parables Then and Now*. Philadelphia: Westminster Press, 1971.

Jenkins, Ferrell. *The Old Testament in the Book of Revelation*. Marion, Ind.: Cogdill Foundation Publications (paper, Baker Book House), 1972.

Jeremias, Joachim. *The Parables of Jesus*. Translated by S. H. Hook from the 6th ed. of *Die Gleichnisse Jesu*, 1962. London: SCM Press, 1963.

Kelly, J. N. D. *Early Christian Doctrines*. 5th ed. London: Adam & Charles Black, 1977.

Kevan, Ernest F. "The Principles of Interpretation." Chapter 18 in *Revelation and the Bible: Contemporary Evangelical Thought*. Edited by Carl F. H. Henry. Grand Rapids: Baker Book House, 1958.

Kline, Meredith G. *By Oath Consigned*. Grand Rapids: William B. Eerdmans Publishing Co., 1968.

Kümmel, Werner Georg. *The Theology of the New Testament According to Its Major Witnesses: Jesus—Paul—John*. Translated from *Die Theologie des Neuen Testaments* (Gottingen: Vandenhoeck & Ruprecht). Nashville: Abingdon Press, 1973.

Let God Be True. Anonymous. Brooklyn, N.Y.: Watchtower Bible & Tract Society, 1946.

Luther, Martin. *Luther's Works.* Edited by Jaroslav Pelikan (vols. 1-30) and Helmut T. Lehmann (vols. 31-55). American ed. St. Louis: Concordia Publishing House; Philadelphia: Muhlenberg Press, 1955-1975.

Mead, Frank S. *Handbook of Denominations in the United States.* 6th ed. Nashville: Abingdon Press, 1975.

Moulton, James Hope, and Milligan, George. *The Vocabulary of the Greek Testament Illustrated from the Papyri and Other Non-Literary Sources.* London: Hodder & Stoughton, 1963.

Orr, James. *The Resurrection of Jesus.* Grand Rapids: Zondervan Publishing House, 1965.

Packer, J. I. *"Fundamentalism" and the Word of God.* Grand Rapids: William B. Eerdmans Publishing Co., 1958.

Pedersen, Johannes. *Israel: Its Life and Culture.* 2 vols. London: Oxford University Press, 1926.

Pinnock, Clark H. *Biblical Revelation: The Foundation of Christian Theology.* Chicago: Moody Press, 1971.

————. *"Prospects for Systematic Theology." Toward a Theology for the Future.* Edited by David F. Wells and Clark H. Pinnock. Carol Stream, Ill.: Creation House, 1971.

Plass, Ewald M., comp. *What Luther Says: An Anthology*, vol. 2. St. Louis: Concordia Publishing House, 1959.

Richardson, Alan. *An Introduction to the Theology of the New Testament.* New York: Harper & Row, 1958.

Scobie, Charles H. H. *John the Baptist.* Philadelphia: Fortress Press (London: SCM Press), 1964. See pages 66-73 on "fire" in relation to divine judgment.

Sewell, Arthur. *A Study in Milton's Christian Doctrine.* London: Oxford University Press, 1939.

Shedd, William G. T. *The Doctrine of Endless Punishment.* New York: Charles Scribner's Sons, 1886.

————. *Dogmatic Theology*, vol. 3—Supplement. New York: Charles Scribner's Sons, 1894.

Strong, Augustus Hopkins. *Systematic Theology*, vol. 3. Philadelphia: Judson Press, 1909.

Thayer, Joseph Henry, tr. *A Greek-English Lexicon of the New Testament.* Grimm's Wilke's *Clavis Novi Testamenti* translated, revised and enlarged. Grand Rapids: Zondervan Publishing House, 1963.

Webber, Robert E. *Common Roots: A Call to Evangelical Maturity*. Grand Rapids: Zondervan Publishing House, 1978.

Wilcox, Max. "On Investigating the Use of the Old Testament in the New Testament." *Text and Interpretation: Studies in the New Testament Presented to Matthew Black*. Edited by Ernest Best and R. McL. Wilson. Cambridge: Cambridge University Press, 1979, pp. 231-243.

Yarnold, E. J., and Chadwick, Henry. *Truth and Authority: A Commentary on the Agreed Statement of the Anglican-Roman Catholic International Commission "Authority in the Church," Venice 1976*. London: Society for Promoting Christian Knowledge and Catholic Truth Society, 1977.

Zerwick, Maximilian. *Biblical Greek*. Rome: Scripta Pontificii Instituti Biblici, 1963.

Index of Scriptures

New Testament